PRINCIPLES OF
SAMARITAN HALACHAH

STUDIES IN JUDAISM IN LATE ANTIQUITY

EDITED BY

JACOB NEUSNER

VOLUME THIRTY-EIGHT

IAIN RUAIRIDH MAC MHANAINN BÓID

PRINCIPLES OF SAMARITAN HALACHAH

TUTA SUB AEGIDE PALLAS · EJB ·

PRINCIPLES OF SAMARITAN HALACHAH

BY

IAIN RUAIRIDH MAC MHANAINN BÓID

E. J. BRILL
LEIDEN • NEW YORK • KØBENHAVN • KÖLN
1989

Library of Congress Cataloging-in-Publication Data

Bóid, Iain Ruairidh Mac Mhanainn.
Principles of Samaritan halachah.

(Studies in Judaism in late antiquity,
ISSN 0169-961X; v. 38)
Bibliography: p.
Includes indexes.
1. Purity, Ritual—Samaritans. 2. Law,
Samaritan. I. Title. II. Series.
BM982.B65 1988 296.1'8 88-29316
ISBN 90-04-07479-1

ISSN 0169-961x
ISBN 90 04 07479 1

CONTENTS

Foreword IX
Abbreviations XI
Conventions XIII

Introduction

I. The Purpose of this Work 3
II. The Present State of Knowledge 5
III. The Method and Presentation. 16
IV. The Samaritan Texts Used 21
V. The Manuscripts 26
1. Preamble 26
2. Manuscripts of the Ṭubâkh 26
3. Manuscripts of the Kâfi 32
4. Manuscripts of the Khilâf 37
5. Manuscripts of the Farâ'iḍ 42
6. Manuscripts of the Kâshif al-Ghayâhib on Leviticus . . . 43
7. Manuscripts of the Iʿtiqâdât 44
8. The Manuscript of the Sharḥ Sûrat al-Irbot 45
9. The Manuscript of the Collected Fatâwâ of Yaʿqûb bin Hârûn 46
10. Manuscripts of Abu 'l-Fatḥ's History 46
11. Manuscripts of the Arabic Translation of the Torah . . . 47
12. The Manuscripts of the Catechism 47
13. The Manuscripts of the Answers to Gaster's Questionnaires 47
VI. The Method of Editing the Texts 48
VII. The Language of the Texts. 50

Critical Edition of the Halachic Treatises

Editorial Symbols and Conventions 54
Text 1: Kitâb aṭ-Ṭubâkh 55
Text 2: Kitâb al-Kâfi 67
Ch. XI 67
Ch. III (extract) 74
Ch. XIII (extract). 77
Ch. XII 80
Text 3: Kitâb al-Khilâf 86
Ch. VI 86

Additional passage from an appendix to ch. VI 106
Text 4: Kitâb al-Farâ'iḍ, ch. LIV 108
Text 5: Kashif al-Ghayâhib on Leviticus 113
On Lv XV 113
On Lv XII 121
Text 6: Kitâb al-I'tiqâdât, ch. VI. 124
Text 7: Sharḥ Sûrat al-Irbot (extract) 132
Text 8: Marginal Notes (from the mss.) 133
I The First Marginal Note on the Ṭubâkh 133
II The Second Marginal Note on the Ṭubâkh 134
III The First Marginal Note on the Kâfi 134
IV The Second Marginal Note on the Kâfi 135
V The Third Marginal Note on the Kâfi 135
VI The Fourth Marginal Note on the Kâfi 136
VII The First Marginal Note on the Khilâf 137
VIII The Second Marginal Note on the Khilâf 137

Translation and Commentary

Abbreviations and Conventions 140
Text 1: The Book of Insight 141
Text 2: Kitâb al-Kâfi 147
Ch. XI 147
Ch. III (extract) 151
Ch. XIII (extract) 153
Ch. XII 154
Text 3: The Book of Differences 158
Ch. VI 158
Additional passage from an appendix to ch. VI 170
Text 4: The Book of Commandments, ch. LIV 172
Text 5: Kâshif al-Ghayâhib on Leviticus 178
On Lv XV 178
On Lv XII 185
Text 6: The Book of Principles, ch. VI 187
Text 7: Extract from the Sharḥ Sûrat al-Irbot 193
Text 8: Marginal Notes in the Mss. 194
I Note I on the Book of Insight 194
II Note II on the Book of Insight 194
III Note I on the Kâfi 195
IV Note II on the Kâfi 195
V Note III on the Kâfi 196
VI Note IV on the Kâfi 196

VII Note I on the Book of Differences 197
VIII Note II on the Book of Differences. 197
Commentary 198

Conclusions

I. Summary of the Details and Principles of the Halachot 285
1. Preamble 285
2. The Intrinsic Uncleanness of Women 285
3. The Intrinsic Uncleanness of Men 301
4. Sexual Intercourse and Emission of Semen 303
5. The Uncleanness of Gentiles 304
6. Susceptibility to Uncleanness. 305
7. The Transmission of Uncleanness 305
8. The Stages of Cleansing 306
II. Observations and Theoretical Considerations 308
1. Preamble 308
2. Variation within the Samaritan Halachic System 309
3. The Relationship between Samaritan and Jewish Halachah . 317
4. Summary 327
5. Historical Excursus 328
6. The Halachic Texts 342
(a) The Relationship of the Texts to Each Other 342
(b) Authority 344
(c) Expected Readership and Purpose of the Texts 345

Bibliography 348
Indexes 357

FOREWORD

Most of all this book was written for the Samaritans, to restore to them a bit of what has been made inaccessible by their oppressed and precarious condition in the fourth captivity, the captivity of Edom; and regardless of how it is received by others, I will be well content if the Samaritans find profit in it.

Prof. Alan Crown, Head of the Dept. of Semitic Studies at Sydney University, gave me the benefit of his advice throughout the composition of this book, and it was only due to his encouragement that it was finished.

I have had valuable advice from Dr. Michael Carter, formerly of the Dept. of Semitic Studies at Sydney University and now at Columbia University; the late Dr. James Fraser, of the Dept. of Middle Eastern Studies at Melbourne University; and Dr. Heinz Pohl, of the Seminar für Semitistik und Arabistik of the Freie Universität Berlin.

The late Rabbi S.D. Sassoon graciously gave me complete access to the manuscripts in the Sassoon Collection.

It would be invidious to single out individual librarians that have helped me; but an exception must be made for Mrs. Susan Winter Young, formerly Special Collections Librarian at the Jewish Theological Seminary of America (in the United States), who went to considerable effort to locate and identify the Samaritan and Karaite mss. in the library, which are not catalogued (or even listed in full), and are mostly not labelled properly. Statements to the effect that the library never owned certain mss., which I have had given to me at various times since her departure, tend to mean only that the library has lost a ms. and no-one has noticed, because there was never a proper record.
(See below, pp. 40-41).

Finally, and most important of all, I must thank my former wife, Carmen Alfonso Boyd, whose keen mind and superlative critical ability were a constant help. She was a constant source of encouragement through a period that was very difficult for both of us. She also deserves full credit for the work she put into typing the various drafts of a difficult manuscript. It must be recognised that this book would not have been written without her patience, support, and hard work.

ABBREVIATIONS

The specialised abbreviations used in the Commentary and in the notes to the Conclusions will be found on p. 140, which should be consulted. We give here the abbreviations of the names of the books of the Torah in English and Arabic, as used throughout this work.

Gn Ex Lv Nu Dt

(Reading from right to left) تك خر اح تع تث

CONVENTIONS

We give here a few pieces of information that are relevant to the whole of this work and which are collected here so as to make them more easily accessible.

All the halachah obtained from the study of the sources is set out in the *Summary of Halachot* in the first part of the Conclusions. As this is set out in detail and in a systematic order, it is a subject index; and as complete references to the halachic sources are given in the notes to this section, it is an index to these sources. See also p. 285.

The name of the founder of one major group of Dositheans has been given as Sakta (i.e. سكته) throughout. This is the reading of all mss. of Abu 'l-Fatḥ except Ms. C, and is the form in Chronicle Adler and the two chronicles described below on pp. 46-47. Ms. C of Abu 'l-Fatḥ has سليه. No ms. of Abu 'l-Fatḥ seen by me has the form شليه given by Vilmar in his edition. As Ms. C is not particularly reliable, I have had no hesitation in following the unanimous testimony of the other text-witnesses.

The Hebrew and Aramaic are transcribed according to Ben-Ḥayyim's system. For technical reasons the form *sh* was used instead of *š*. Stress has not been marked.

Quotations of the Torah have been translated literally into English. Most of the existing English translations were unsuitable because they are not precise enough in their rendering of the halachah. In a halachic context, this deficiency would make such translations useless or misleading. Hirsch's translation was found to be a good model, which has been used with profit. I have not copied Hirsch's translation directly, first because greater precision was needed, and second, and more importantly, because the translation had to be neutral as far as possible, so as to make it clear how, in cases of disagreement, Samaritans, Karaites, and Rabbanites could all support their opinion from the text of Scripture. When it was not possible to be neutral, I had to give a translation that reflected the Samaritan understanding of the passage.

It is to be noticed that often, and particularly in editing the Kâshif al-Ghayâhib, I have translated from an Arabic translation given in the original text, and these Arabic translations are themselves not always entirely literal or neutral.

References to the Kâfi are always to chapter XI if the chapter is not specified. References to the Khilâf are always to chapter XV if the chapter is not specified.

All references to the Rabbanite halachah are to the Mishneh Torah, unless otherwise stated. Thus Mikva'ot I:1 means Mishneh Torah, Mikva'ot I:1. References to other sources will take the form Mishnah Mikva'ot I:1, Tosefta Mikva'ot I:1, and so on.

For technical reasons there are a few instances of minor divergence between the line-numbering of the Arabic text and the English translation. In such cases, the numbering in the translation has been used when making references in the Commentary and Conclusions. There are a very small number of instances of minor discrepancy between the division of the lines in the critical apparatus and the corresponding divisions in the text. These discrepancies are a result of the history of the printing of the text and were beyond the author's control.

INTRODUCTION

I. THE PURPOSE OF THIS WORK

It was the intention in preparing this work to set out and explain the whole of the Samaritan halachah on a certain subject, including the theory underlying the details of practice, the variation in both theory and practice between different Samaritan sects and groups, and the interrelationship of the halachot within that area as seen by the Samaritans themselves, along with a complete and systematic comparison of the halachah with the various traditions of the Jewish halachach. This is one of the first studies to treat a substantial or major area of halachah fully and comprehensively, although there have been partial studies of certain areas and thorough studies of certain separate details; and it is the most thorough comparative and theoretical study of any area of the Samaritan halachah ever attempted. To obtain the information, the whole of the extant Samaritan texts treating the subject had to be edited. Most of the texts have not been edited before, and no part of then has been edited critically.

The subject investigated is contamination of women by normal and abnormal vaginal bleeding, or by childbirth and the bleeding that accompanies it and follows it, contamination of men by normal seminal emissions and abnormal emissions from the penis, and the contamination of both men and women by sexual intercourse. All these are different varieties of uncleanness caused by a discharge from the person concerned (except in the case of the uncleanness of a woman from sexual intercourse), so that the uncleanness is intrinsic, not acquired by contact with some unclean thing or some other unclean person. The Samaritans themselves see this as the common factor, as we see from the heading of ch. XI of the Kâfi, and other passages listed in the Commentary at that place. There is one other kind of intrinsic uncleanness affecting people, the ࠌࠑࠓࠏࠕ. This topic has been treated very competently by Naphtali Cohn and P. R. Weis,[1] and as the halachot of the ࠌࠑࠓࠏࠕ differ from those of the subject under discussion, being either peculiar to it or similar to the halachot applying to a corpse,[2] and as there is no discharge from the person concerned, its treatment is not relevant to the present purpose.

It will be seen that the topics treated form part of a single subject, and that this subject can be distinguished naturally and easily from other subjects in the halachah, both according to logic and according to Samaritan tradition, so the subject is suitable as a unit for study on its own.

---

[1] Their work is discussed below.

[2] Both the corpse and the ࠌࠑࠓࠅࠏ can contaminate people and utensils by the mechanism called in the Jewish system אהילה.

There are three important benefits of taking the whole of a well-defined area of halachah and treating it exhaustively. The first is that the details become mutually illuminating. The second is that it becomes possible to make general statements about the halachah and its relation to the Jewish systems. It is not very profitable to compare individual points or small sections of the halachah because it is not always clear what the theoretical reasons for the differences could be. The third is that it is only by taking a whole subject that general theoretical conclusions about the theory and transmission of halachah can be reached. With due care, the conclusions can help in reaching an understanding of the theory and principles of the Samaritan system as a whole. In short, the detailed, point by point study of one set of halachot leads to general conclusions about that area of the halachah and the halachic system in general, and as the title of this work suggests, it becomes possible to draw conclusions about the theories and principles, but yet conclusions based on integration of facts and leading from them surely and inevitably, with very little speculation being needed. The path from the detailed to the general is the only possible one in this field at the present state of knowledge, and we have to follow the path where it leads, not where we think it ought to go.

The reasons for choosing this particular subject were the following:

1. The subject is still important at the present time, and we have reliable information about the modern practice.

2. It is treated in all the Samaritan halachic treatises, so the extent of variation in earlier times can be established.

3. It is one in which there are numerous divergencies between different Samaritan groups, so that the comparison gives a good sample.

4. It is treated relatively extensively in Scripture, in Leviticus XV and XII, and it is possible to see the way in which some details are supported from exegesis of Scripture, others from traditions, and others from logical deduction from other details already known from the first two sources.

5. It is one on which the various Jewish sects have always been divided, and as we have detailed information about the divergent Jewish opinions, the information obtained here about the various Samaritan opinions on the subject can be applied in future comparative studies of the sectarian differentiation within Judaism.

The need for a study of this kind will become clear if the present state of knowledge of the Samaritan halachah of this and other subjects is described.

II. THE PRESENT STATE OF KNOWLEDGE

Some details of the Samaritan halachah have been known to outsiders from the time of the Tanna'im onwards. In modern times some details of practice, some general principles, and some specific interpretations of Biblical verses are known, but only two areas of the halachah are known in any degree of completeness.[3]

To the extent that the Samaritan halachah is now known to outsiders, it is as the result of the study of the halachic treatises, which means that this knowledge depends directly on the thoroughness and accuracy of the studies of the treatises that have been made. The most important studies will be described, after which the intended contribution of this particular work in the process of elucidating the halachah will become clear.[4]

It is probably best to start with the work of Raphael Kirchheim. Kirchheim used all the fragments of Arabic texts that had been translated into European languages up to his time, as well as the Hebrew and Arabic texts that were available. His two works on the Samaritans, *Karme Shomron* and the edition of Massechet Kutim with a critical commentary, both published in 1851, contain nearly all the halachic information available from published Samaritan sources in his time. In addition he used the information on Samaritan halachah in the Jewish sources and made its significance apparent. His commentary on *Massechet Kutim* not only clarified the statements in the text edited, it also showed the connection with statements in other Jewish sources and in the process clarified these other sources as well. It is true that the corpus of halachah that can be gleaned from Kirchheim's works is not very extensive, but this is only because so much of the information on the Samaritan halachah in the Jewish sources is enigmatic, and will remain so till the knowledge of the Samaritan halachah is regained by systematic study of Samaritan sources.

Similar comments apply to Abraham Geiger, but with the difference that Geiger's work was not limited to the use of published material, and that he was able to use new Arabic sources. Ms. B of the Kashif al-Ghayâhib has a note to the effect that it was borrowed by him from September 1859 to June 1860, and the use of this book shows itself constantly in his writings. He also

---

[3] These two areas are the ࠇࠔࠁࠅࠍ and inheritance. The details of the studies on these subjects are given below. This is not to minimize the contribution made by such scholars as Geiger in elucidating certain important aspects of certain areas.

[4] Comparative studies of the Samaritan and Jewish halachah are not mentioned here unless they contribute to the understanding of the Samaritan halachah itself.

Bibliographical details of all the works mentioned in this section can be taken from the bibliography, and there is no need to repeat them here.

seems to have consulted the manuscripts of the Kâfi and Khilâf in the German libraries in his time. His contributions to the study of the Samaritan halachah are not limited to the relatively few articles of his on the subject: his major work *Hamikra Vetargumav* (originally published in German) gives information on the Samaritan halachah in passing in numerous places where it is needed to illustrate the argument.

Like Kirchheim, Geiger knew the material on the Samaritan halachah in the Jewish sources, and used it effectively, but like him, was hampered because so many of the statements are unintelligible without a general knowledge of the Samaritan halachah, a knowledge that no-one could have had in his time except for the Samaritans themselves, and that no-one except the Samaritans has now.

The monograph *Fragmenta Commentarii ad Pentateuchum Samaritano-Arabici Sex*, published by Abraham Drabkin in 1875, was the first systematic study of a Samaritan halachic treatise. The author was disadvantaged by only having fragments of the text being studied, the Khilâf, and was not always able to place the details of halachah established by study of the fragments in their place in the system of each area of the halachah. Nevertheless, the work is extremely valuable, since the author was obviously expert in the Rabbanite halachah and competent in the use of the Karaite sources, and was able to establish the meaning and implications of the texts to a degree unexpected in view of the technical difficulties and the lack of previous studies. The Latin translation seems to be accurate throughout. One might disagree with some of his comments about the essential nature of the Samaritan halachah in general, but the work has permanent value, and it is regrettable that it has been ignored by later authors.[5]

The doctoral thesis *Samaritanische Traditionen* published in 1888 by Leopold Wreschner was the first study of an extensive Samaritan halachic text. It consists of a very short introduction on the history of the Samaritan halachah, and the writings of Munajjâ bin Ṣadaqah and the Khilâf in particular, followed by a study of the content of each of the chapters and major sections in part II of the Khilâf. (Wreschner did not have access to mss. of part I of the Khilâf).[6] A few particularly important passages of the Arabic are reproduced, and of these, a few are translated as well. The only ms. available was Ms. Oriental Quarto 523 of the State Library (at that time the Royal Library) of Prussia, the ms. referred to as B_1 in my edition; he also used the fragment published by Drabkin.[7]

---

[5] The best proof of this last point is the fact that it is consistently quoted with the wrong information, indicating that the title-page has not been seen, much less the text.

[6] See Wreschner's introduction, p. XXI.

[7] Wreschner's introduction, pp. XXI-XXII.

It will be seen that because so little of the text of the Khilâf is quoted, either in the original or in translation, the reader has no way of telling if the content of each chapter of the Khilâf and the details and principles of halachah in it are understood by Wreschner. The reader's suspicions are aroused by his assumption that divergencies between Samaritan and Jewish halachah are due to heathen influence on the Samaritans, who are supposed to be the descendants of heathens who took over the religion of Israel but did not fully abandon their original religion. This assumption colours the whole of the first section of his introduction. The weakness in the argument is that the so-called heathen practices are nothing of the kind, but are genuine Israelite halachah, as will be shown. Wreschner has misunderstood the texts in numerous places, has failed to recognise agreement between Jewish and Samaritan halachah, and has not grasped the rationale behind what he gives as his main example, cleansing by fire.

On pp. 37-38 Wreschner draws comparisons between Samaritan halachah and Indian and Persian religious customs. His examples are: (1) the avoidance of intercourse with women during the forty or eighty days after childbirth, (2) the avoidance of contact with menstruating women, and (3) the cleansing of ground by fire; all of which he claims are practices not to be found in Judaism. This is quite wrong. The Karaites agree with the Samaritans on the avoidance of intercourse with women during the forty or eighty days after giving birth, and some Rabbanite communities used to avoid intercourse during this period as a *minhag*.[8] All Rabbanites agree that intercourse is not allowed during the first week or fortnight. The Mishnah itself mentions special dwellings used by Jewish women when menstruating, although there is no mention of such dwellings in later texts.[9] The avoidance of contact with menstruating women is attested in Jewish pietistic movements, as described by Büchler in his *Types of Jewish-Palestinian Piety*,[10] or as described in the *derech erets* literature, or the *Baraita Deniddah*,[11] and can be observed in modern times among some of the ultra-orthodox. On the other hand, regarding the cleansing of ground with fire, see the note on the Kâfi, ch. XII, 10, in the Commentary, and see also notes 234 and 235 to the Conclusions, where it is shown that the rationale of the practice is compatible with Judaism, even though the practice itself is not attested in Judaism.

Despite these weaknesses, we must recognise that Wreschner was disad-

---

[8] See below, Conclusions, note 201.

[9] Mishnah Niddah VII:4. Notice the variant of Tosefta Niddah VI:15.

[10] This is a major theme of the book.

[11] The Baraita Deniddah goes far beyond even Samaritan practice in its rigour in this respect.

vantaged by the shortage of previous studies,[12] and that his work still has considerable value provided it is used with discretion.

The publication by Naphtali Cohn in 1898 of his *Vorschriften betreffend die Zarâath nach dem Kitâb al-Kâfi*, on the section on the subject of ࠑࠓࠏࠕ in the Kâfi, was the first of its kind. For the first time, the whole section on a particular area of halachah was published, and equally importantly, a detailed and comprehensive exposition of the halachot on one subject became available. Cohn's understanding of the difficult text edited by him is faultless. He used the Jewish halachah on the subject expertly and was obviously at home in the Talmudic literature.

The short article *Abū'l-Ḥasan Al-Ṣūrī's Discourse on the Rules of Leprosy*, by P. R. Weis, on the subject of ࠑࠓࠏࠕ, published in 1950, gives some information in the Ṭubâkh that is not found in the Kâfi or is formulated differently there, and adds to the comparison of the Jewish and Samaritan halachah made by Cohn.

In 1902 Meier Klumel published his *Mischpâtîm*, an extract from his doctoral thesis, giving the text of the Kâshif al-Ghayâhib on Exodus XXI:1-XXII:15. The publication of the text was useful, because it made another section of the Kâshif al-Ghayâhib available, but unfortunately there are no notes on the halachah.

In 1904 Siegmund Hanover published his doctoral thesis *Das Festgesetz der Samaritaner*, an edition and translation of the Kâshif al-Ghayâhib on Lv XXIII, with notes and introduction. The notes on the halachah are perspicacious, but could have been more extensive and detailed.

In 1957 Dorreya M. ʿAbd al-ʿAl submitted a doctoral thesis entitled *A Comparative Study of the Unedited Work of Abu 'l-Ḥasan al Ṣūrī and Yūsuf ibn Salamah* at the University of Leeds, under the supervision of Dr. John Bowman. Part of the thesis consists of an edition and translation of selected chapters of the Ṭubâkh and Kâfi, with a comparison of the Rabbanite and Samaritan halachah in the areas covered by the chapters edited. The edition of the chapters of the Tubâkh is based entirely on Ms. M_1, and the edition of the chapters of the Kâfi entirely on Ms. W.

It was my original intention to use ʿAbd al-ʿAl's work as a major source, since the chapters of the Ṭubâkh and Kâfi translated and commented on by her include some of those treated in the present work. When the work was examined, however, it was found to be so inaccurate and misleading, in both the translations and the exposition of the halachah, as to be worse than useless.

---

[12] It seems that Wreschner has not realised that the cleansing of utensils by fire is normal everyday Jewish practice, and has missed the point because of this. Halachic studies by non-Jews are almost inevitably unprofitable.

We will give some examples to justify this assessment.

First, let us consider the translation.[13]

It is noticeable that the translation is not only inaccurate, but can be seen to be inaccurate at first sight, because it contains statements that are obvious nonsense, or reduce the author's arguments to meaningless verbiage.

On pp. 400-401, we find the following translation of a part of the chapter of the Ṭubâkh on animals that can be eaten:

> 'As to the creatures that swim, they are divided into two classes, some of which are absolutely permitted for use (as food) but some of which are prohibited. The kind which is permissible is that which has scales on its body and feather [sic] covering all his [sic] body'.

If we quote ʿAbd al-ʿAl's own edition of the Arabic text (p. 623) we see what has happened. The Arabic of the critical phrase says:

... ما كان له فلوس على جسمه وريش فايض على جسمه

This means: '... which has scales over its body and pectoral fins projecting from its body'.

It is surprising enough that the translator could have written such nonsense, but what is more surprising is that she did not realise that the translation simply had to be wrong. Notice, too, that immediately after this the Hebrew terms for fins and scales are used by the author of the Ṭubâkh.

Another example, from p. 420, in the translation of the chapter of the Ṭubâkh on the kinds of bleeding, corresponding to 18-20 in my edition:

> '... and she should count from the second day she becomes clean, seven whole days for purification during which no blood appears. Then on that day she with whom remains the blood four days become [sic] clean; and whatever exceeds that, whether for many days or a few, then she is clean she should also count from the second day of her being clean, seven days for purification, during which she does not see any blood'.

What is this supposed to mean?

From the same chapter, p. 421, corresponding to 26-29 in my edition:

> 'This puts an end to those who say that by "the many days" He meant forty-nine days only; He does not count "the days" that exceed that according to the saying of the Honoured Book; "many days" exceed that. He indicates by this the time from the period lord Joseph (peace upon him) until the sending of the Apostle (For him be the best prayer, and on him be the most perfect peace), which is a period lasting forty-nine days (sic.)'.

The word 'sic' in the above quotation is ʿAbd al-ʿAl's.

From the same chapter, p. 426, corresponding to 66-69 in my edition, treating *dam al-ishtibâh*:

[13] The inaccuracy, indeed meaninglessness, of the translation has been noticed by Lowy, p. 402, in regard to one passage. I once asked Prof. Bowman how it was possible to accept a translation that was so obviously impossible as to speak of fish with feathers. His answer was that the translation seemed all right, and that Samaritan authors wrote strange things.

'As to the seventh section, it is the (blood of) doubt, and the counting of the period of its impurity begins from the day on which it occurs; she (i.e. the woman) [sic] remains impure for a week and becomes clean on the seventh day before the sunset, because the sign of purity is the clarity and cleanness of the urine, thus if its (i.e. the urine's) clarity is changed even by a little, it must be impure ...'

The logical thread of the author's argument is lost; and besides, there is no mention whatever of urine in the Arabic.

From the section on the *zâb*, p. 248, corresponding to 86 in my edition:

'... thick food, such as pomegranate blossoms ...'

From ch. XI of the Kâfi, pp. 517-518, corresponding to 73-77 in my edition:

'The fifth category is that which is called "the blood of purification." And it is with married women the sign of childbirth. In the case of (the birth of) the male, if it (i.e. the impurity) is present until the thirty-third day, she can be sure that the blood will not return if she washes with water at that time; and the same applies with (the birth of) the female on the sixty-sixth day (thereafter). If it occurs before that, it is right, but if it occurs after it (that date) it is not regular, although there are some women who do not see it at all, as in the case of "the menstruation".'

The Arabic does not say this.

One more example, to illustrate the lack of critical sense. The example is taken from p. 396, from the translation of the chapter of the Ṭubâkh on the animals that can be eaten:

'As to the beast that goes on its paws among all the beasts that go on all fours, it is also prohibited... And whosoever draws near after they are dead becomes defiled, and should get rid of the defilement by washing and cleaning with plenty of water until the evening...'

The sense conveyed by this is that the person should have to keep on washing uninterruptedly till sunset, i.e. for hours on end. The Arabic of the critical section, on p. 7a of the ms., reads:

ومن دنا بهم بعد موتهم تطما ويلزمه الخلاص بالغسل والحميم بالماء والطما الى الغروب.

An accurate translation conveys a different meaning. The text says: 'Anyone that touches them after they are dead is made unclean, and has to remove the contaminant by washing [ghasl], then bathe [ḥamîm] in water, and is unclean till sunset'. The washing is to remove any contaminating substance, and the bathing is to achieve cleanness in the halachic sense, and cleanness comes at sunset. How was ʿAbd al-ʿAl's translation arrived at? The word طما has not been recognised, in a text where it is the most basic and frequent technical term!

A final example, from p. 165, from the description of the contents of the Kâfi:

'In Yūsuf ibn Salamah's work the topic is dealt with in three chapters; viz: the eleventh, twelfth, and thirteenth. The eleventh has as title: A section on the fundamental impurity that occurs to men and women, and to water creatures.'

The reader might like to have a look at the title of ch. XI of the Kâfi and the first words of the first line of text after the title to try to see where ʿAbd al-ʿAl found a reference to 'water creatures'. The exercise will be very instructive.[14]

We will now give some examples of major errors in the exposition and analysis of the halachah by ʿAbd al-ʿAl.

On pp. 200-201:

> 'The uncleanness resulting from childbirth is considered by the Samaritans to be of four kinds, to wit: that which results from giving birth to a male; that which results from giving birth to a female; that which they (i.e. the Samaritans) call "the blood of purification", and which differs in the case of the birth of a male from that of a female; and finally that which they call "the blood of doubt." ...
>
> We note that the Jews do not mention the two latter kinds of blood refereed [sic] to by the Samaritans, viz: the blood of purification and the blood of doubt ...'

The facts are that the 'blood of doubt' (i.e. *dam al-ishtibâh*) has nothing to do with childbirth, a fact which ʿAbd al-ʿAl herself makes clear on p. 168 and p. 173; that the Karaites agree with the Samaritans on the questions of 'blood of purification' and 'blood of doubt'; and that the Rabbanites recognise דם ספק, but treat it differently. (See below, Commentary, T 67 N, for the details).

On pp. 168-169, in reference to the seven kinds of bleeding listed in the Kâfi:

> 'Getting rid of the impurity caused by any kind of the above mentioned discharges, requires bathing with water (after the disappearance of the discharge) and remaining in a state of uncleanness for seven days, except in the case of giving birth to a female, where the period of purification is doubled (i.e. two weeks).'

This is quite wrong. Purification from the *då̄bå* bleeding can be attained the same day; purification from ࠃࠌ ࠈࠄࠓࠄ can be attained on the very day on which the bleeding finishes; the uncleanness due to bleeding of childbirth is not fully overcome till forty or eighty days after delivery, although it becomes less serious after seven days or fourteen days; and there is quite a difference between the seven complete days required for purification of a woman in the state of *zå̄bå* and the one part of a day followed by six complete days required for the *niddå*.

This work has only obfuscated the study of the Samaritan halachah.

---

[14] Strangely, though, in the body of the translation the passage is correctly understood. One wonders what the reason for the discrepancy might be. Has another hand been at work in the introduction? There are other inconsistencies in apparent knowledge throughout.

In 1970 Sergio Noja published an abridged translation of the Kâfi into Italian (A strange choice of language). Noja's translation is generally accurate. It does, however, suffer from the defect that because the format of the series in which it was published limited the number of pages, it had to be abridged. Noja explains that the principle followed was to translate the main part of each section and leave out digressions and details. For this reason, I have felt obliged to re-translate the chapters of the Kâfi edited by me.

There is another reason for re-translating these chapters. Noja's understanding of the meaning of these particular chapters is not always the same as mine.

In spite of these disagreements, it must be acknowledged that I have used Noja's work with profit.

In 1974 Heinz Pohl edited the *Kitâb al-Mîrâth* of Abu Isḥâq Ibrâhîm. Seven manuscripts were used.[15]

Pohl's edition is the first of its kind in several respects. It is the first complete edition of a Samaritan halachic text; the first edition of a Samaritan halachic text, or any Samaritan text in Arabic, to be based on all the known mss. (or nearly all); the first in which the problem of deriving the author's intention from the corruptions of the mss. is faced and solved; the first to fully use the Karaite literature for clarification of a Samaritan text; the first satisfactory translation of a substantial Samaritan halachic text; and the first competent study of the range of Karaite opinions in a given area of halachah in relation to the Samaritan halachah.

The Kitâb al-Mîrâth is not always representative of the Samaritan law of inheritance. However, Pohl edits, translates, and comments on all the other short texts on the same subject in the mss. of the Kitâb al-Mîrâth, which between them explain the main differences between the Kitâb al-Mîrâth and the standard halachah.

I have used Pohl's edition with profit as a model to some extent.

The monograph on the Dositheans, by S. J. Isser, published in 1976, includes a translation of the passages relating to the Dositheans in Abu 'l-Fatḥ. These passages include quite a lot of information on the Dosithean halachah.[16]

It has to be said that Isser's treatment of the halachic material does not add substantially to the understanding of it, due to certain deficiencies. First,

---

[15] The author used all the mss. known to him. He was apparently not aware of the existence of Semitic Ms. 380 in Columbia University Library, or Ms. 91 (= Samaritan Ms. 9) in the library of Dropsie College. This is no fault of the author's. The Samaritan mss. of libraries throughout the world are on the whole not adequately catalogued and sometimes not catalogued at all.

[16] The passages are reproduced in full by Isser in an appendix. It should be noted that although the passages have been reproduced from Vilmar's edition, some errors have occurred where the division in Isser's book is different to Vilmar's, and the apparatus has been misread at the point of division.

the translation and comments are entirely based on the body of the text in Vilmar's edition, whereas the correct readings (or at least the ones that are slightly less corrupted) are often in the apparatus instead. Isser explains in his preface that as he did not know enough Arabic to make his own translation, he commissioned one, which was done by Lee Scanlon. As it happens, the translation is pretty accurate, but Isser himself had no direct control over the choice between the variant readings. The second deficiency is that Isser leaves most of the pieces of halachic information given by Abu 'l-Fatḥ unexplained. There is a desultory commentary, but very few clear or definite interpretations. It is true that some of the statements of the source are obscure, but there are numerous instances of statements that (in the opinion of the present author) could have been explained, but are not even discussed. Isser was not aware of the existence of the unabridged recension of Abu 'l-Fatḥ's material to be found in the manuscripts.[17] The third deficiency is that there are instances of erroneous conclusions being drawn as a result of what seems to be inadequate understanding or knowledge of the standard Jewish sources, and the Jewish halachah, even on questions of basic halachic concepts and the practical use of the sources.

We will give a few instances to substantiate this last point.

On p. 86 Isser gives an interpretation of Mishnah Niddah IV:1 and Tosefta Niddah V:1. The words והן יושבות על כל דם (this is the reading of the best text-witnesses) probably do not mean what Isser takes them to mean (see below, T 15 N). This in itself is not a serious criticism, since in this respect he is simply following the standard commentators. What is serious is that in the last sentence on the page he interprets the gloss in the Tosefta יום שהיא טהורה בו סופרת בתוך שבעה in a way that has nothing to do with the text and is in fact the standard interpretation of the phrase והן יושבות על כל דם from the Mishnah and Tosefta quoted above. The speculations on the meaning of the passage in note 127 are unnecessary. The speculations of note 129 do not need refutation: see below, Kh 200-201 TN, on the technical terminology, which is self-explanatory if the unanimous Jewish halachah of the זבה is known. The practice described is exactly the same as the modern Rabbanite one (not mentioned by Isser) of treating נדה as זבה.

On p. 99 there is a discussion of the apparent emendation of the text of the Torah by the Dositheans. Isser says that Ibn Ezra identifies the Hebrew אזוב with the Arabic صعتر, which is the exact opposite of the truth: Ibn Ezra rejects this identification.[18] Neither does Isser realize that the traditional identification of אזוב is marjoram,[19] not thyme. The Arabic صعتر or زعتر can

[17] See below, pp. 46-47. Isser's note on p. 74 shows that he knew of the existence of one of these chronicles, but not its halachic content.

[18] See Ibn Ezra on Ex XII:22 and Lv XIV:4.

[19] See Rashi or Hirsch on Ex XII:22.

mean either thyme or marjoram, but in a halachic context is marjoram. The comments on p. 89 about the overshadowing of graves show that the author did not know the technical meaning of the term. A gloss on p. 74, line 13, shows that the author thinks the Samaritans pronounce the Tetragrammaton.

On p. 88, note 130, we find the following surprising speculation:

> 'Was this the case also with eggs, i.e. did the Rabbanites deem edible eggs found inside ritually slaughtered fowl, while perhaps not those inside fowl otherwise killed?'

Why speculate? The Rabbanite halachah is no mystery. In the course of the speculation, a passage from Qirqisâni on a separate subject is brought in for comparison, so that a false identification between Karaite and non-Dosithean Samaritan halachah is made.[20]

In the whole study, the Karaite halachah, which should have been the major tool in elucidating Abu 'l-Fatḥ's halachic statements, is applied to only two of these statements. No untranslated Karaite source is used. (No untranslated Hebrew book is used seriously at all).

For all these reasons, Isser's general conclusions about the nature of the Dosithean halachah are suspect, or at least unproven. Statements about the relationship between the Dosithean halachah and the Jewish halachah can only be made after all the items of halachic information given by Abu 'l-Fatḥ, or at least a fair number of these items, have been examined, explained, and compared with both the Rabbanite and the Karaite systems, point by point. The proportion of Abu 'l-Fatḥ's statements that Isser attempts to explain is too low for his general assessments to be relied on.

In 1977 S. Lowy published his *Principles of Samaritan Bible Exegesis*. This book is a useful contribution to the theory of the subject chosen for study, provided it is used with care,[21] and to some extent has a connection with the study of the halachah.

---

[20] There are other indications of lack of familiarity with the halachah and its sources. Isser is unable to quote his source on p. 163 in full or to identify it. The futile discussion about movement on the Sabbath on p. 26 would have been unnecessary if Origen's term *diēgēsis* had been explained in the light of the halachic concept of רשויות; and a parallel with Karaite halachah would have been illuminating here, as in so many other places.

It is true that some of the points on which I have criticised Isser's handling of the halachah are minor ones, but this is only because the Jewish halachah has been used by him in so few cases, and because so few of Abu 'l-Fatḥ's halachic statements have been treated by him, that there are very few major halachic points made available for any assessment of his handling of them.

[21] The book could profitably have included quotations from the sources to illustrate numerous statements that the reader is asked to accept on authority. The author has an unfortunate tendency to exaggerate the importance of Biblical exegesis in fixing the halachah, to make statements unsupported by evidence, and to speculate instead of letting the sources speak for themselves.

There are signs of carelessness throughout. To take a basic example, there are numerous errors in the designations of the mss. on pp. 516-517.

(a) B.M. Or. 1159 is not Samaritan and is not the Memar Marqah.

Let us now summarise the present state of knowledge. Most of the details and principles of the halachot of ࠇࠓࠏࠕ and inheritance are known (although parts of certain texts treating these subjects remain to be edited, and doubtless when this is done more details will be learnt), and some of the details of other areas of the halachah are known. However, no thorough study of the range of variation in the Samaritan halachah in one particular area has been made, neither has there been any systematic comparison of any extensive area of halachah with the Jewish systems, and so far no one has attempted a comprehensive comparative and systematic study of the principles and theory on which the details of the halachah according to the various Samaritan schools depend. Very few halachic texts have been edited, satisfactorily translated, or commented on.

It will now be clear why this work was undertaken, and what the need is that it is intended to satisfy. It will also be clear why the word "principles" was used in the title, even though the focus of the work is on one particular area of halachah. The principles established within the limits of that area can be expected to bear a relationship to the principles of other areas of the halachah, and to be a specialisation of the principles of the Samaritan halachah in general (which is itself, just like the Jewish halachah, a manifestation of the common Israelite halachah). A demonstration of the accuracy of these expectations, with specific examples, is given in the Conclusions.

(b) The Samaritan mss. in the John Rylands Library should not have been designated by the numbers they had when in Gaster's collection and in his possession. It is a very long while since the catalogue of these mss. with the new numbering was published.

(c) Ms. Gaster 1981 is not the Khilâf.

(d) B.M. Or. 881 is not Samaritan. In any case the first word of the title should be Sayr (or Sair), not Sir, which does not exist.

(e) B.M. Or. 1154 is not Samaritan.

This might be the best place to mention that soon after I had started writing this book Lowy wrote to me advising me to desist. This was not in reply to any letter of mine to him. I had never heard of him at that time. The reasons given for this advice were (a) that he had consulted mss. in Britain, and in Jerusalem; (b) that his forthcoming book on Samaritan Biblical exegesis (the book under discussion here) would cover all that could be said about the principles of the halachah; and (c) that one other person in Israel was preparing articles on the Samaritan halachah or had already published articles.

I did not take Lowy's advice. Reason (a) still puzzles me. What is to stop anyone else using the same mss. (and plenty more in other places as well as these)? Reason (b) implies that all the principles of the halachah depend on Biblical exegesis, an exaggerated claim. It also depends on the assumption that Lowy has said all there is to say about the whole Samaritan halachah. It took Maimonides a lifetime to do that for the Rabbanite halachah, and he had the help of the works of earlier authors, but the groundwork on the Samaritan halachah is not yet finished. I am sure Lowy will not be offended if I suggest he is not the superior of Maimonides. Anyway, reason (b) is contradicted by reason (c). Reason (c) assumes that the whole subject can be exhausted in a few articles, which is obviously impossible.

III. THE METHOD AND PRESENTATION

The following study takes the form of a critical edition of the relevant texts based on all the manuscripts known to me (except for manuscripts to which I was not given access and a few manuscripts of the most recent text edited, the Book of Principles); a translation of each text; and a detailed, critical, and systematic commentary on each text; all of which is followed by a concluding summary of the information obtained from a close reading of the texts edited or deduced in the Commentary, re-organized in subject order; a systematic comparison with all known Jewish traditions; and some concluding general comments on the Samaritan halachic system and the written and oral Torah.

It might be as well to explain why it was that so much attention was given to the edition of the texts, when the purpose of the work was to analyse the material provided by them; and why it was that the texts have been translated, when it might have been assumed that the reader could use the original Arabic. As to the first point, the answer is that it was impossible to get an adequate or even intelligible text without using all the manuscripts. It is true that it would be quite possible in some cases to produce a minor edition leaving out some of the manuscripts; but the only way to tell which manuscripts can safely be left out is to first produce a full edition of the text and work out the textual type of each manuscript and the inter-relationship of the text-forms.[22] As to the second point, it was not my intention at first to make a translation, thinking that any obscurities in the Arabic could be explained in the Commentary, and the reader could manage to read the rest of the Arabic without help: but when the existing translations were examined, it was found that they so often departed from the plain meaning of the Arabic (examples are given above) that perhaps it might not be so plain after all.

On reflection, the reason why a translation is necessary and why the editor is obliged to give one becomes clear: it is to be assumed that the editor, because of long and close study of the text and systematic detailed comparison of the other relevant Jewish and Samaritan texts, will have an advantage over the reader, no matter how learned, who is approaching the texts for the first time. These texts are only self-explanatory to one who has acquired the knowledge assumed by the authors of them. The Samaritan authors assume that the reader is an educated Samaritan, and write accordingly. This is not

[22] It remains true that the text of the older works is so precarious that it is very hard to establish a text that can be followed with confidence without using nearly all the manuscripts. I do not think it would be possible to edit the Kâfi or Ṭubâkh satisfactorily using less than ten or a dozen manuscripts. See, for example, T 115-116 N.

to claim any prior training in the Samaritan halachah on the part of the editor: it is simply that the editor must necessarily have acquired some knowledge of the Samaritan halachah of the subject under discussion in the process of preparing the edition and Commentary. It would not have been possible to make a satisfactory translation without the preliminary work on the Commentary. The Commentary, in turn, is based on a study of all the available subsidiary evidence, in addition to the text under discussion. Instead of editing the sections on various subjects in one treatise or two treatises, as has been done in the past, and drawing general conclusions from these passages, I have edited the section on one subject in every treatise known to me, along with clarifications in other sections of a given treatise of points treated inadequately in the main section on that subject in that treatise. The treatises illuminate each other: what is obscure in one or more of them, eventually becomes clear in another, and what is obscure in all of them becomes clear when the different texts are compared. Moreover, the data obtained from one text can be extrapolated to illuminate the others. The use of the Rabbanite and Karaite halachah was found to be specially valuable. As the Samaritan, Karaite, and Rabbanite systems have more points of agreement than disagreement, and are three variations on one system, I was able to use the Rabbanite and Karaite systems as sources of background information when analysing the various Samaritan texts. Besides this, it frequently happens that a given text illuminates itself, that is to say, an earlier section gives information needed to understand a later one, and an earlier obscurity is explained by a comment in passing later on in the text. The interpretation of each text was revised as often as necessary to remove internal contradictions, and establish the consistent meanings of technical terms, as well as to insure that the interpretation was not forced at any point. The understanding of the texts obtained in this way is quite different to the impression gained on the first reading or even on repeated readings, no matter how expert the reader might be.

It is intended that as a result of the use of all these sources, the translation will be a form of commentary in itself.

There is another, purely practical, reason for translating the sources. If all the sources on the one subject are translated on the same principles, with the technical terms consistently rendered throughout, it is then easier to see the agreements and disagreements of the sources. In addition, the reader can more conveniently examine the validity of the editor's assessment of each instance of agreement or disagreement.

The translation is intended to replace its predecessors with a more consistent, homogeneous, and accurate text. This is not to deny that some errors may remain, but it is intended that they will be less than in the earlier translations. It is to be noted that some doubtful points of translation, including some that at first sight may appear suspect, are treated and justified in the appropriate places in the Commentary.

The sources of information for the Commentary are five: (1) the text being interpreted; (2) the other Samaritan texts edited here; (3) passages in other Samaritan texts where a point is clarified in passing; (4) the Jewish halachah; and (5) occasional explicit statements about Samaritan halachah in Jewish, Moslem, or Christian sources. The information given in the Commentary is of eight kinds: (1) philological comments needed to justify the choice of reading or to clarify the text; (2) the explanation of obscurities in the exposition; (3) necessary background information; (4) a systematic statement of individual halachot; (5) an explanation of the theory and principles on which the halachot depend; (6) an explanation of the points of disagreement with other Samaritan groups mentioned by the author, in both practice and theory; (7) points of disagreement in practice and theory with the other Samaritan texts edited here; and (8) a comparison with the Rabbanite and Karaite halachah, whenever a comparison would help in understanding the Samaritan position.

The principles followed in using the Jewish halachah need some special comment. In the Commentary, comparison with the Jewish halachah has the practical purpose of clarifying obscurities in the Samaritan texts and helping in the understanding of the theory and principles assumed by the Samaritans. *A detail of Jewish halachah will not help unless its place in a particular Jewish system is understood.* Now, there are only two Jewish systems that are fully understood: the Rabbanite one and the Karaite one (in its various forms). We know isolated details of the Sadducean system, or the system of the Book of Jubilees, or the Qumran system, or the Falasha system, but we do not know these systems as systems: we do not even know many of the details of each one. In this context, there is no point in saying that the Falashas agree in a certain practice with the Samaritans if we do not know why the Falasha theory of the particular area of halachah leads to this particular practice. Comparison with the details of practice of all these Jewish groups is worth doing for its own sake, but it is irrelevant to the purpose of trying to understand the Samaritan halachic system as a system in the first place. Because of this, I have only used the Rabbanite halachic system and the Karaite halachic system for clarification of the Samaritan halachah, leaving out of consideration all the other varieties of Jewish halachah. For the same reason these two systems themselves have only been used in instances when they are needed, if the text is obscure or the implications of a statement need development. There is no comparison with the Jewish systems for its own sake, but only as it is needed to understand the Samaritan system.

All this only applies to the Commentary, and in the Conclusions a full comparison is made between the Samaritan halachah and all known varieties of Jewish halachah, point by point, and all the Jewish traditions are used to the extent that they are known.

In both the Commentary and Conclusions, references to the Rabbanite system are to the Mishneh Torah, where both the details and the theory are set out systematically. Other sources are not quoted because there is no need. The only differences from one code to another will be on fine details of *minhag*, which are not relevant. It was found that all relevant differences in *minhag*, such as the practice in some Rabbanite communities of avoiding intercourse during the whole of the forty or eighty days after childbirth instead of only during the first week or fortnight, are given in the Mishneh Torah. If the reader needs to consult the halachic sources, i.e. the Mishnah, Tosefta, Gemara Yerushalmi, Gemara Bavli, the halachic midrashim, Baraitot, and teshuvot, the source references to these will be found in the appropriate place in the notes in the editions of the Mishneh Torah. A convenient assembly of all the original Rabbanite sources is to be found in the *Torah Shelemah* on Leviticus XII and XV, and it is a simple matter to turn from the Samaritan text, where the verse underlying the point of halachah under discussion will be quoted, to the same verse in the *Torah Shelemah*, where all the relevant original sources will be found quoted in full.

References to the Karaite system are to the *Adderet Eliyahu*, *Gan ʿEden*, and *Keter Torah*, which between them give, as well as the authors' own opinions, the whole range of Karaite opinions on a given detail, with the theoretical justification of each opinion. I have compared the *Kitâb al-Anwâr wa-'l-Marâqib*, and have only found one instance of information not to be found in the other texts, which is quoted in the appropriate place in the Commentary.[23] I have read through the relevant chapters in a manuscript of the *Murshid* and have not found any necessary information not given in the three sources used. The *Eshkol Hakkofer* was read and the few details found there but not in the other sources are quoted in the Conclusions in the appropriate place.[24]

The Conclusions are in two parts: the first part, the Summary of Halachot, is concerned with the details of the halachot of the subjects investigated, and the principles underlying them, and the second part, the Observations, is concerned with the theory and principles of the Samaritan system as a whole.

The Summary of Halachot is a systematic setting-out of the details of the Samaritan halachah of the subjects studied, arranged strictly in subject order. The information is dispersed through the texts edited and the Commentary with numerous partial repetitions, clarifications of one passage by another, and digressions, and it would be very hard for the reader to derive the piece of

---

[23] On Far 2-3.

[24] Conclusions, note 234.

information required directly from the text or Commentary, because it would not be obvious where the information lay. As well as providing a systematic exposition, the summary sets out the whole range of variation in the sources on any given point, and it can be seen exactly to what extent the Samaritan halachah is uniform or not, and the process of standardisation becomes apparent.

At all times the theory and principles on which the details of halachot depend have been set out, if the information is available.

It is to be understood that there is no attempt to prove any statements made in this section, since the proof will already have been given in the Commentary in the appropriate place.

This section can be used as a subject-index to the texts edited and to the Commentary, if desired.

In the Observations certain salient general features of the Samaritan halachic system apparent from the study of the texts edited are drawn to the reader's attention. In some cases it was only possible with the present state of knowledge to point out a question that deserves further investigation in a monograph on its own; in other cases the evidence obtained from the texts studied in this work, supplemented by information already available, was enough to come to new conclusions or to confirm from another direction conclusions reached by preceding researchers. The discussion is based on the solid details derived in the commentary and presented in the Summary of Halachot: there is more synthesis than speculation. Theories have to be based on solid data. There has been no attempt to discuss matters that are not clarified in some way by the texts studied here, as this would be outside the scope of this work.

It is hoped that the discussions of theoretical matters in this section will be of help to scholars working on either the Samaritan halachic system, or the various Jewish halachic systems. Some suggestions for further research in the future are included.

IV. THE SAMARITAN TEXTS USED

All Samaritan texts that give any information about the subject under investigation were studied and edited. The texts are:[25]

From the Ṭubâkh, the chapter on the kinds of vaginal bleeding, and the chapter on the *zåb* and emission of semen.

From the Kâfi, chapter XI, on the kinds of vaginal bleeding, and on the *zåb* and emission of semen; an extract from ch. III, on the different degrees of contamination; an extract from ch. XIII, which answers a specific question about the contamination of a baby by the blood of childbirth and its contaminating effect on other people, but in the process gives detailed information about the uncleanness of a woman who has given birth which is not found elsewhere; and ch. XII, on the requirements for purification of people, artefacts, and ground, where further details of the effect of the various discharges is given. In addition, extracts from other chapters are quoted in the commentary where appropriate.

From the Khilâf, ch. VI of Part II, on the various kinds of vaginal bleeding. Two appendixes to ch. VI, one on the contaminating effect of leather from unclean animals and related subjects, and one on the mechanism of transmission of contamination from the source to people or artefacts are not included, as they did not bear on the subject; but an extract from the second appendix, treating the contaminating effect of a *zåb*, *niddå*, or *z̊åbå* on a bed, was edited, under the title of an *Additional Passage from the Khilâf*, because in the process it gives information on the Samaritan understanding of מדרס.

From the Farâ'iḍ, the chapter on the various kinds of vaginal bleeding, which is probably ch. LIV. In addition, reference is made to ch. CV, on the Red Heifer, in the commentary where appropriate.

From the Kâshif, the commentaries on ch. XV and ch. XII of Leviticus.

From the Iʿtiqâdât, ch. VI, on the kinds of vaginal bleeding.

From the Sharḥ Sûrat al-Irbot, a short extract which in passing clarifies the relationship between the halachot of the *zåb*, *niddå*, and *z̊åbå*.

All the marginal notes in all the manuscripts in the sections edited.

---

[25] See below for the details of the name, date, and other information on each text used. Notice that a series of questions in ch. XIII of the Kâfi, treating the details of contamination by objects, have not been included, because the focus of these questions is the physical mechanism of transmission, not the uncleanness as such, and this needs a separate study. This principle has been used throughout.

A *fatwa* by Yaʿqûb bin Hârûn is quoted, translated, and commented on in the commentary on Kf ch. XI, 31-32.

The information on the Dosithean halachah in Abu 'l-Fatḥ's history, as far as it is connected with the area of halachah with which we are concerned here, is quoted, translated, and commented on in the appropriate places in the commentary.

The Catechism composed by Khiḍr bin Isḥâq is referred to in the commentary where appropriate, as are Gaster's questionnaires.

The two Arabic versions of the Torah, and the Targum, were found to be too literal to give much help in understanding the halachah.

We will now give the necessary information on the authorship and date of each of these works, and some other relevant information, so as to make possible an evaluation of the information given by each.

Neither the title of the work, nor the full name of the author, nor the date of composition, are mentioned in the preface to the Kitâb aṭ-Ṭubâkh. The author's name is given in the preliminary eulogium by the scribes as Abu 'l-Ḥasan aṣ-Ṣûri, who is known as the author of several other works. His full name does not seem to be known. Samaritan tradition puts the date of composition between 1030 and 1040 C.E., and this date seems to be confirmed by circumstantial evidence.[26] We know the title of the work only by Samaritan tradition, which unanimously calls it Kitâb aṭ-Ṭubâkh (or Ṭabâkh). I am greatly indebted to Dr. Heinz Pohl for directing my attention to the existence of the word *ṭubâkh* or *ṭabâkh*, meaning 'insight' or 'deep understanding' etc., which is well-attested in Arabic literature and the Arabic lexicographical tradition (see Lane's dictionary). Now that Pohl has pointed this out, we can dispose of all the futile speculation, by both the modern Samaritans and outsiders, on what the connection with cooking might be. It is very likely that the title 'Kitâb at-Ṭubâkh' is a shortened form of some longer title, just as the titles 'Kitâb al-Kâfi' or 'Kitâb al-Khilâf' or 'Kitâb Masâ'il al-Khilâf' or 'Kâshif al-Ghayâhib' are shortened forms of longer titles.

The Kitâb al-Kâfi was written by Muhadhdhib ad-Dîn Yûsuf bin Salâmah bin Yûsuf al-ʿAskari in 433 A.H. = 1042 C.E. The full title of the work is Kitâb al-Kâfi li-man Kân bi-'l-Maʿrifah li-Kitâb Allâh Muwâfi.[27]

The Kitâb al-Khilâf was written in the middle of the twelfth century by Shams al-Ḥukamâ' Abu 'l-Faraj Munajjâ bin Ṣadaqah bin Ghurûb. The full

---

[26] Weis, *Abu'l-Ḥasan al-Ṣuri's Discourse on the Calendar*, 5-6; Gaster, *The Samaritan Literature*, 3.

[27] The information is given in the preface to the book.

title of the work is Kitâb al-Buḥûth wa-Masâ'il al-Khilâf fî-mâ bayn Millatay al-Yahûd wa-'s-Sâmirah.[28]

The Kitâb al-Farâ'iḍ was written by Nafîs ad-Dîn Abu 'l-Faraj ibn al-Kaththâr. The date of composition is not known exactly. It is known from statements in the Sharḥ Am Baqqūti (ࠏࠌ ࠁࠒࠒࠅࠕࠉ) that he was an adult in 1293 C.E., and that the Sharḥ Am Baqqūti was written during the term of office of the high Priest Fīnās bin Yūsəf, who held the position from 1308 to 1363 C.E.[29] It seems reasonable to suppose that the much more ambitious Kitâb al-Farâ'iḍ would have been written after the Sharḥ Am Baqqūti, particularly as the former seems to depend on the latter. The author must then have been born no later than 1270 C.E. If the Sharḥ Am Baqqūti was written between 1308 and 1350 (when the author would have been at least eighty) then it seems reasonable to put the date of the Kitâb al-Farâ'iḍ between 1315 and 1355 C.E., with the most probable date being between 1320 and 1345.

The first part of the Kâshif al-Ghayâhib, up till Genesis XLVI:28, was written by Musallam bin Marjân ad-Danafi, at the end of the 17th century C.E. The commentary was revised and completed by Ghazâl bin Abi 's-Surûr and Ibrâhîm bin Yaʿqûb ad-Danafi and perhaps others as well over the course of the eighteenth century.[30] The section on Exodus was written by Ghazâl, who completed his work in 1168 A.H. (= 1754 C.E.).[31] It seems that the sections on Leviticus and Numbers were written by Ibrâhîm bin Yaʿqûb, who was active up till at least 1782.[32] As the commentary was never extended to cover Deuteronomy, it is quite possible that the sections on Leviticus and Numbers were completed only shortly before the end of the author's activity. With the editing of the section on Leviticus XV, the date can be narrowed down further, since in lines 55-56 a reference is made to an event in 1160 A.H. (= 1746 C.E.), and the implication seems to be that it was at least a few years in the past. It seems, then, that the commentary on Leviticus and Numbers was written between 1750 and 1785, with a date towards the end of the period being the most likely.

The full name of the work is Kâshif al-Ghayâhib ʿan Asrâr al-Mawâhib.

There are two recensions of the Iʿtiqâdât, one by Yaʿqûb bin Hârûn and

[28] Wreschner, pp. XVII-XXII of the introduction.

[29] Halkin, *Taryag Mitsvot*, 93; Ben Ḥayyim, vol. I, 48-49.

[30] Gaster, *The Samaritan Literature*, 13.

[31] Gaster, *The Samaritan Literature*, 13. On the authorship and date of the commentary on Exodus, see the colophon to British Library Additional Ms. 19657, which is the autograph of this text.

[32] The date is taken from the index of copyists in vol. II of Robertson's catalogue of the John Rylands mss. Robertson, in his article *Ibrahim Al-ʿAyyah*, p. 342, is unable to give any more precise a dating.

the other by khiḍr bin Isḥâq.[33] The mss. copied by Yaʿqûb bin Hârûn or his descendants consistently give one recension and the ones written by Nâji bin Khiḍr or his descendants consistently give the other. (I do not know of any mss. written by Khiḍr himself). According to a preface in Ms. B, but not to be found in any other ms. seen by me, a scholar from Oxford visiting Nablus in 1312 A.H. or 3532 of the Entry (= 1894 C.E.) commissioned the composition of the work from the author, Yaʿqûb bin Hârûn. In fact, however, it was in existence before that time, since Ms. O was copied by Yaʿqûb bin Hârûn in 1892 C.E. A prefatory note by Yaʿqûb bin Hârûn in Ms. O says that the book was written in response to questions from European scholars. The date of composition is not mentioned. The same prefatory note is reproduced by the scribes of the Cornell ms. and Ms. J. A note by the scribe, Nâji bin Khiḍr, in Ms. P, says that his father, Khiḍr bin Isḥâq, composed the book (or perhaps started to compose it) in 1310 A.H. (= 1892 C.E.) so as to make reliable information available to European scholars and so as to have a work on hand which could be copied as needed, rather than having to compose answers to individual questions on each occasion, since the queries were becoming too numerous to handle. A note by Nâji bin Khidr in Ms. L says that the work was composed so as to make reliable information available in response to numerous questions, and that his father was asked to compose the book by the High Priest Yaʿqûb bin Hârûn. The date of composition is not mentioned. A note in Samaritan Ms. 181 of the John Rylands library says that the work was composed by Khiḍr in response to numerous requests for information. The date of composition is not mentioned. The note in Sassoon Ms. 382 is similar in content.

The work seems to have been untitled originally, which would account for the variations in the form of the title in the mss. The situation is as follows: Ms. O, Ms. B, and JRUL Sam. Mss. 249A, 181, 179, 182, 183, and 249 are untitled. Ms. J is untitled, but has a title on what seems from the photograph to be a slip of paper tucked inside the cover, which could be taken from the title given by the Samaritans at the time of acquisition, reading Kitâb ʿAwâʾid as-Sâmirah. Ms. P is untitled in the photographs. The catalogue gives the title as Ṭuḳûs ad-Dîn. It is possible that a fly-leaf bearing this title has been left out in the photographing, since Ms. L, written by the same scribe, bears the title Kitâb aṭ-Ṭuqûsât wa-Imân as-Sâmirah fi-ʾl-Iʿtiqâdât. Sassoon Mss. 382

[33] The fact that there are two recensions can be seen by examining the text of the mss., and the text published here is long enough to show this. Authorship is claimed by Yaʿqûb bin Hârûn on his own account, and by Nâji bin Khiḍr on behalf of his father, as will be shown below. Gaster (*Samaritan Eschatology*, p. 68) quotes a Samaritan tradition that the original author was Ibrâhîm bin Yaʿqûb (on whom, see above). Nevertheless, the text as it stands in the known mss. seems to be the result of thorough revision, even if the original work was composed earlier. There do not seem to be any mss. older than the late nineteenth century.

and 721 both bear the title Kitâb aṭ-Ṭuqûsât in the catalogue, but it is not clear whether this is the full title found in the mss. or not. The Cornell ms. bears the title Dalîl ash-Sharʿ wa-'n-Naql wa-'l-ʿAql (bi-Tarâtîb Manẓûmah kamâ yâti in sha 'Llâh) at the start, and the title Dalîl ash-Shàrʿ wa-'n-Naql wa-'l ʿAql (kamâ hûwa jâri ʿalayh al-ḥâl wa-'Llâh aʿlam) at the end of the preface. Samaritan Ms. 30 of the Seminar für Semitistik und Arabistik of the Freie Universität Berlin bears the title Kitâb al-Khulf.

The only titles likely to originate with the authors would be ones that appear in the mss. written by Yaʿqûb bin Hârûn or Nâji bin Khiḍr. As it happens, the ms. written by Yaʿqûb bin Hârûn does not bear any title. I have taken the title of Ms. L to be the full form of the title used by Nâji bin Khiḍr. In shorter form it could be quoted as Kitâb aṭ-Ṭuqûsât or Kitâb al-Iʿtiqâdât. I have chosen the latter as being more expressive of the spirit of the work.

Nowhere in any of the mss. that I have seen and nowhere in the descriptions of the mss. in the catalogues is there any trace of the supposed title Hilluch used by Gaster and others following him. I am informed by Dr. Crown that the term occurs in the correspondence to Gaster, but apparently as a description rather than a title.[34]

The Sharḥ Sûrat al-Irbot (ࠀࠓࠁࠅࠕ) was composed, according to explicit statements in the mss., by Khiḍr bin Ishâq. The date of composition is not known (except of course that it was in the late nineteenth century).

The Catechism, called Kitâb Su'âlât wa-Jawâbhum Taʿlîm al-Awlâd in the Paris ms., and Kitâb al-Madâris in the Dropsie ms., was written, according to the explicit statement of the mss., by Khiḍr bin Isḥâq. The same remarks on the dating apply as in the case of the work just mentioned.

The answers to Gaster's questionnaires are sufficiently described by Robertson in his catalogue of the Rylands mss.

Abu 'l-Fath's history was completed, according to the explicit statement of the author in his preface, in 756 A.H. (= 1355 C.E.).

For the details of the recensions of the Arabic translation of the Torah, see the item by Shehadeh in the Bibliography.

---

[34] Robertson uses the title consistently in his catalogue, but nowhere, apparently, is it to be found in the mss., except in Gaster's own handwriting. The Gaster mss. are all untitled.

V. THE MANUSCRIPTS

1. PREAMBLE

I have not seen the originals of any of the manuscripts used, and will therefore refrain from trying to add to the description given in the catalogues, except in the cases where necessary information is omitted in the catalogues or the manuscript is uncatalogued. On the other hand, enough information about each manuscript will be given to enable the reader to use the critical apparatus and understand the reasons for establishing the text on the basis of certain manuscripts; and the inter-relationship of the textual types represented by the various manuscripts will be indicated to the extent that it can be worked out.

2. MANUSCRIPTS OF THE ṬUBÂKH

a) *Manuscripts Used*

(i) Ms. O

This is Ms. Huntington 24 of the Bodleian Library at Oxford.

The ms. is undated. The scribe is Mufarrij bin Yaʿqûb. The addition of a list of the forms of the majuscule and minuscule forms of the letters of the Hebrew alphabet at the end of the ms. indicates that the ms. was written specifically to be sold to an outsider. It was probably commissioned by Huntington's agent in Damascus, which puts the date of copying between 1670 and 1680,[35] a date which according to Dr. Crown agrees with the evidence of the script. This ms. often stands against all the rest. It has affinities with P_1M_1 and L, but does not represent the same textual type. The circumstances of the copying of this ms., and its unique text, make it very likely that it was copied from a much older manuscript from the geniza of the Samaritan synagogue at Damascus.[36] This ms. is the one used as the textual base, partly because of its own age and the presumed age of its exemplar, but more importantly because it is the only one that is accurate enough for the purpose. Erroneous itacisms and slips of the pen have been corrected from P_1 or the consensus of the mss. as a whole.

There is some tendency in this ms. to write Hebrew technical terms in

[35] On Huntington's acquisition of mss., see Fraser, *Documents from a Samaritan Genizah.*

[36] The question of the origin of the exemplars of some of the mss. acquired at this time for Huntington and other Europeans forms the main subject of the article by Fraser quoted in the previous note. See also Montgomery, pp. 6-7.

Arabic letters, which seems to be a mark of antiquity in Samaritan mss. (or in this case, in the exemplar of the ms.). The same tendency is found in the oldest mss. of the Kâfi and Khilâf.

(ii) Ms. P_1

This is Arabic Ms. 4521 of the Bibliothèque Nationale in Paris, written by Marjân bin Ibrâhîm bin Ismâʿîl ad-Danafi in 1153 A.H. (= 1740 C.E.). I am indebted to Dr. Fraser for drawing my attention to its existence.

This ms. is very close to being identical with M_1. Some of the original omissions and the corrections between the lines and in the margin are the same in both mss., which means that they were not only both copied from the same exemplar, but were both revised from a second exemplar. The first exemplar could not have been a text of the type of Ms. O, since this ms. is almost free of omissions.

When P_1 and M_1 disagree with each other, P_1 tends to be the one with the correct reading. In fact, P_1 is the only ms. aside from O that was considered as a possible collating base. When P_1 differs from M_1, it tends to agree with L, a ms. that is generally reliable. I have occasionally followed P_1, or P_1M_1L, against O.

(iii) Ms. M_1

This is the first part of Samaritan Ms. 9 (or IX) of the John Rylands University Library of Manchester, the copying of which was started in 1103 A.H. (= 1692 C.E.) by Ibrâhîm bin Murjân bin Ismâʿîl ad-Danafi, continued by Ibrâhîm bin Ismâʿîl ad-Danafi, and completed by Musallam bin Marjân bin Ibrâhîm bin Ismâʿîl ad-Danafi and his brother ʿAbdullâh in 1123 A.H. (= 1711 C.E.). The section edited here was written by the first scribe.

(iv) Ms. L

This is Ms. Oriental 12257 of the British Library in London, written in 1256 A.H. (= 1840 C.E.) by ʿImrân bin Salâmah bin Ghazâl (up to p. 79) and Yaʿqûb bin Hârûn bin Salâmah bin Ghazâl bin Isḥâq al-Kâhin al-Lâwi (p. 80 onwards). The text edited here is taken from the part of the ms. written by the first scribe.

Two other works are bound up with this text. For the details, see Shunnar.

The ms. is very accurate. Its textual type is hard to classify, as it sometimes agrees with O, sometimes with P_1M_1, and sometimes with the later mss.

(v) Ms. M_2

This is Ms. Samaritan 171 of the John Rylands University Library at Manchester, written in 1300 A.H. (= 1882 C.E.) by Murjân bin Asʿad bin Ismâʿîl bin Ibrâhîm bin Ismâʿîl ad-Danafi.

The text of the ms. tends to agree with P_1M_1. When it differs, it tends to agree with the consensus of the later mss. It has a special affinity with Ms. P_3.

(vi) Ms. P_3

This is Samaritan Ms. 36 of the Bibliothèque Nationale in Paris, written in 1320 A.H. (= 1902 C.E.) by Ḥilmi bin Yaʿqûb Shalabi.

This ms. belongs to the same family as Ms. M_2, although there are some instances of divergence between the two.

(vii) Ms. C_2

This is Ms. 22 of the Frere Collection in the library of Girton College at Cambridge, written in 1322 A.H. (= 1904 C.E.) by Ibrâhîm bin Yûsuf bin Yûsuf (sic) bin Salâm (sic) ad-Danafi.

The text has affinities with Ms. L on the one hand, and Ms. K on the other hand.

(viii) Ms. P_2

This is Samaritan Ms. 35 of the Bibliothèque Nationale in Paris, written in 1321 A.H. (= 1903 C.E.) by the High Priest Yaʿqûb bin Hârûn. I am indebted to Dr. Fraser for giving me a copy of his list of mss. in this library, from which I knew of the existence of P_2 and P_3.

This ms. is of particular importance, as the colophon informs us that the scribe attempted to remove the disturbing number of textual corruptions by comparing several reliable and old mss. A reasonable guess would be that he used the ancient ms. in the High Priest's Library, ms. N 123 in Shunnar's list, dated 800 A.H. (= 1397/98 C.E.), but there is no telling which other mss. were used. The base text seems to have been of the general type of Mss. P_1M_1, which has been collated against a text of the type of Ms. L. There are no certain instances of the influence of a text of the type of Ms. O. There are numerous instances of readings diverging from all the earlier mss. collated.

(ix) Ms. C_1

This is Ms. 13 of the Frere Collection in the library of Girton College at Cambridge, written in 1326 A.H. (= 1908 C.E.) by Abu 'l-Ḥasan bin Yaʿqûb bin Hârûn bin Salâmah the Priest.

The text is very similar to the consensus of Mss. P_1M_1L, but shows the influence of a text of the type of Ms. P_2 where P_2 disagrees with P_1M_1L. There are numerous readings not attested in any of the earlier mss. collated by me. There are also numerous obvious scribal errors, which is probably to be expected, as it is almost certain that the ms. was copied specifically for sale. (On the circumstances of the acquisition of the Frere mss., see the Biographical Notice in Loewe's catalogue of the collection).

(x) Ms. N

This is Ms. Adler 1363, in the library of the Jewish Theological Seminary in New York. There is no colophon and no information about the date of copying or the scribe. The absence of the colophon indicates that the ms. was written specifically for sale, probably somewhere in the period from 1902 to 1908 when so many of the modern mss. were written, and quite possibly in 1908 when Adler was acquiring Samaritan mss.

The text agrees with Ms. M_2 on the whole, but there are instances of the influence of texts of the type of Ms. L, or Ms. P_2, or Mss. C_2KS. There are numerous unique readings, and some conflate readings.

(xi) Ms. K

This ms. has no colophon, and bears no information about the date of copying or the scribe. It was formerly owned by Paul Kahle, and so perhaps was bought by him in 1908, when he was in Nablus and was advising Miss Frere on the purchase of mss., and at the same time buying mss. for himself. (These circumstances are alluded to in numerous places in the descriptions of the individual mss. in the catalogue of the Frere Collection, and are mentioned in the introduction to the catalogue and in the biographical note). The ms. is now in private hands. I am not at liberty to explain how I got a photocopy of the ms.

The text has affinities with L, with P_1M_1, and with C_2NS. When the text departs from the consensus of the older mss., it tends to agree with Ms. C_2. There are numerous unique readings, most of which seem to be secondary.

(xii) Ms. D

This is Samaritan Ms. 43 in the Library of Dropsie College, written in 1301 A.H. (= 1884 C.E.) by Salâmah bin ʿImrân bin Salâmah bin Ghazâl bin Isḥâq bin Ibrâhîm bin Ishâq bin Ṣadaqah bin Yûsuf bin Ghazâl bin Yûsuf bin Ghazâl bin Yûsuf bin Ibrâhîm bin ʿAbd Allâh bin Salâmah ak-Kūʾən al-Labi. This ms. belongs to the same family as Ms. K, but with less secondary readings.

(xiii) Ms. S

This is Ms. 386 of the Sassoon Collection, written in 1329 A.H. (= 1911 C.E.) by ʿIzzat bin Ismâʿîl bin Isrâʾîl bin Ismâʿîl bin Ibrâhîm ad-Danafi.

The textual affinities are with Ms. K, Ms. N, and Ms. C_1.

(xiv) Ms. G (and H)

This is Samaritan Ms. 174 of the John Rylands University Library at Manchester, written in the year 3562 of the Entry (= 1924 C.E.) by ࠀࠁ ࠇࠎࠃࠄ ࠁࠍ ࠉࠏࠒࠁ ࠁࠍ ࠀࠄࠓࠍ ࠄࠊࠄࠍ.

The text of this ms. differs from all the others, apparently due to secondary recension. The nearest affinities of the exemplar before revision seem to have been with the consensus of the modern mss. (which might have been expected) and in particular with Ms. C_1, Ms. K, and Ms. S.

In this ms., all technical Hebrew terms are translated into Arabic. The whole text is written in Hebrew letters.

There is a Hebrew text in parallel columns with the Arabic. The Hebrew and the Arabic do not always agree, and the Hebrew has been collated and its readings noted in the apparatus, to the extent that the text can be re-translated into Arabic with confidence. The forms of the Hebrew technical terminology, translated into Arabic in the Arabic text, have been preserved in the Hebrew text, and are collated in full.

The Arabic text is given the symbol G, and the Hebrew text the symbol H.

(xv) Ms. F

This is Ms. Samaritan 31 in the library of the Seminar für Semitistik und Arabistik in the Freie Universität Berlin, written in 1376 A.H. (= 1957 C.E.) by Yûsuf bin Abi 'l-Ḥasan bin Yaʿqûb bin Hârûn bin Salâmah bin Ghazâl. It is a text of the same Hebrew translation as in Ms. H.

The two forms of the Hebrew translation, i.e. H and F, are nearly, but not quite identical, and it seems that the Hebrew text in F has had some superficial revision against an Arabic text.

(xvi)

The readings of an expanded quotation of T 114-117 in a marginal note in some mss. of the Kâfi are recorded in the apparatus under the designation حاشيه. See pp. 135-136.

b) *Manuscripts Not Used*

(i) Semitic Ms. 393 in the library of Columbia University in New York

Repeated attemps to get a microfilm of this ms. were unsuccessful. The library staff inform me that the ms. has been lost, but as the information given in the various replies is conflicting, and the title of the ms. is quoted along with reference nos. that belong to other mss., it is impossible to tell what the real situation is. Whether or not it is lost, it is unobtainable. This ms. was once borrowed by Prof. A. S. Halkin (see the references to Halkin's remarks quoted on pp. 40-41).

(ii) Ms. Adler 1362

I am informed by the Special Collections Librarian of the Jewish Theological Seminary that this ms. was not amongst the bulk of the Adler Collection acquired by the Seminary. The ms. has been lost.

(iii) Mss. 123 and 152 (according to Shunnar's list) in the library of the High Priest

It was not possible to get microfilms of these mss.

(iv) Samaritan Ms. 175 of the John Rylands Library

This is a ms. of the Hebrew translation. The form of the translation was found to agree exactly with the Hebrew column of Ms. G.

(v) Ms. M_3

This is Samaritan Ms. 173 of the John Rylands Library. The first chapters, including the chapter edited here, are missing.

(vi)

So that it will not seem to have been forgotten, it should be pointed out that Samaritan Ms. 172 of the John Rylands Library is not the Ṭubâkh, as the catalogue has it, but the Kitâb al-Farâ'iḍ. I am indebted to Heinz Pohl for drawing my attention to this.

(vii)

Sassoon Ms. 726 was examined and was found not to be a commentary on the Ṭubâkh, as the catalogue has it.

c) *The Inter-Relationship of the Text-Forms*

The mss. do not form clearly-defined families, but they can be classified to some extent, provided it is understood that in any given instance the grouping need not be the typical one.

The mss. can be divided as follows:

O
P_1M_1
L
M_2P_3
P_2
C_2C_1KDS
N
GHF

The major division is between Ms. O and all the rest. After this, there is a tendency for OP_1M_1, or OP_1M_1L, to stand together against all the rest. Of the rest, there is a tendency for GHF to form a distinct secondary recension as opposed to $M_2P_3P_2C_2C_1KS$. Ms. P_2 and Ms. N both have a mixed text and will often agree with one ms. family or another. All the modern mss. show the influence of a text of the type of P_1M_1, and of the type of L, but on the other hand, agree sporadically with O against P_1M_1 and L.

3. Manuscripts of the Kâfi

a) *Manuscripts Used*

(i) Ms. J

This is Ms. Samaritan Octavo 7 of the Jewish National and University Library in Jerusalem.

The ms. consists of two substantial sections of text from one or two old mss. bound up with each other, and with the missing sections of text copied by the restorer, Nâji bin Khiḍr bin Isḥâq bin Salâmah bin Ghazâl the Priest, in 1320 A.H. (= 1902 C.E.).

The sections of text have been given the following symbols:

J(a) refers to one of the fragments.

J(b) refers to the other fragment.

J(c) refers to the sections replaced by the restorer.

The sections are placed in the ms. as follows:

The frontispiece, and pages 1-19, from the start of ch. 1 to part-way through ch. III: J(c).

Pages 20-35, as far as part-way through ch. IV: J(b).

Pages 60-173 (except for the top half of p. 80 and the top third of p. 81, a few words at the top of pp. 82, 83, and 92, and the whole of pp. 234-135): J(a).

The missing words on pp. 82, 83, and 92, and the whole of pp. 134-135: J(c).

Pages 174-196: J(c).

The chapters and sections of the Kâfi edited here are taken from the fragments as follows:

Ch. XI is taken from J(a).

Ch. III is taken from J(b).

Ch. XIII is taken from J(a).

Ch. XII is taken from J(a). In the section numbered 17-26 in this edition, corresponding to the top of p. 82 of the ms., part of the text is from J(a) and part from J(c), the source of all readings being indicated in the apparatus. In the section 36 (from the word *mâ* onwards) — 38 (corresponding to the top of p. 83 of the ms.) the text of the ms. is J(c). In the section 39-41 (up to the word *bi-qawluh*) the text is mainly J(c), with some isolated words from J(a), the source of all words being indicated in the apparatus.

According to Dr. Crown, both J(a) and J(b) were written in Nablus in about 1436 or 1437. The scribe of J(a) is Åb'råm bin Yē'ūsha (who also wrote Ms. Sassoon 726).

The Textual Type of the Fragments

J(a) belongs to the same family as Ms. D. These two consistently stand against all the other mss. in preserving the correct text. Of the two, J(a) is slightly more accurate than D. The edition of chs. XI, XIII, and XII is based on J(a), with obvious scribal errors corrected according to D.

J(b) is clearly superior to any of the other mss. in ch. III. Ms. D is not extant in ch. III, so it is not easy to establish the textual affinities of J(b) in this chapter, but certainly the relationship of J(b) to the younger mss. is the same as the relationship of J(a) to the younger mss.

I am inclined to think that J(a) and J(b) are two sections of one ms., which was originally written by two different scribes. This would explain the apparent identity of the textual type of both fragments, and the apparent coincidence of the restorer finding two sections of text of identical date.

J(c) belongs with the inferior group of the modern mss., which will be defined later.

(ii) Ms. D

This is a substantial fragment of 58 leaves in the library of the Deutsche Morgenländische Gesellschaft in Leipzig, no. 129 in Wehr's catalogue. It extends from about half-way through ch. IV to about three-quarters of the way through ch. XIII, finishing what would have been about five or six lines before the start of the extract from ch. XIII edited here.

This ms. belongs to the same textual family as Ms. J. Dr. Crown dates it between 1470 and 1476. The script is typical of a scribe trained in Nablus, but there are signs of Egyptian influence, which could indicate that the scribe worked in Egypt.

Ms. D, like the oldest mss. of the Ṭubâkh and Khilâf, tends to write Hebrew technical terms in Arabic letters.

(iii) Ms. S_1

This is Ms. 716 of the Sassoon Collection, written in 748 A.H. (= 1347 C.E.) by Abu 's-Surûr bin Yûsuf bin Abi 's-Surûr bin Abi Saʿd the Physician of Ashkelon. (The cataloguer of the Sassoon mss. has not noticed that there is a colophon). The ms. is written in Hebrew letters. It was pieced together and re-bound in 1247 A.H. (= 1832 C.E.) by ʿImrân bin Salâmah, who seems to be responsible for some corrections which have been noted as S^3 in the apparatus to this edition. This ms., in spite of its age, is not particularly reliable, although it is certainly more reliable than the modern mss. When neither J(a)(b) nor D had an acceptable reading, the reading of S_1 was taken if it was a possible one.

(iv) Ms. N

This is Ms. 15 of the Sulzberger Collection in the library of the Jewish Theological Seminary in New York.

This is a copy of Ms. S_1, made by Aba 'l-Ḥasan bin Yaʿqûb bin Hârûn bin

Salâmah bin Ghazâl the Priest in 1322 A.H. (= 1904 C.E.). Like the original, it is written in Hebrew letters.

In spite of the scribe's use of Ms. S_1 as his basic text, he departs from it in numerous instances. When he does this, he tends to use either a reading of the type of J(a)(b) D or one in agreement with the more reliable modern mss. On the whole, his judgment is very good, and readings in Ms. N that disagree with Ms. S_1 deserve careful consideration. When N disagrees with S_1, it tends to agree with W.

(v) Ms. L_1

This is Additional Ms. 19656 of the British Library, written in 1201 A.H. (= 1786 C.E.) by Yûsuf bin Salâmah bin Surûr bin Yûsuf bin Surûr bin Isḥâq aṣ-Ṣabâḥi.

The text seems to be mixed, sometimes agreeing with JD, sometimes with S_1, and sometimes with the less reliable modern mss. There are numerous errors.

(vi) Ms. B

This is Ms. Oriental Quarto 965 of the State Library of Prussia (at present in the care of the Sitzungsberichte Preussischer Kulturbesitz in West Berlin), written in 1318 A.H. (= 1900 C.E.) by Abu 'l-Ḥasan bin Yaʿqûb bin Hârûn bin Salâmah bin Ghazâl bin Isḥâq the Priest.

Of all the modern mss., this is one of the most reliable. It is the equal of Ms. S_1, and far better than Ms. L_1. It is noticeable that it tends to agree with Mss. J(a)(b)D against the rest in important instances, although in most instances it tends to agree with the consensus of the modern mss. Its nearest affinities are with Ms. W and Mss. L_2S_2.

(vii) Ms. W

This is a ms. formerly in the possession of the late P. R. Weis, lecturer in the University of Manchester, written by Nimr bin Salâmah bin Ismâʿîl bin Ṣadaqah in 1320 A.H. (= 1902 C.E.). The present whereabouts of the ms. are unknown. I am not at liberty to name the source from which I got the photocopy.

The text of this ms. is very hard to classify. It clearly belongs with Mss. CL_3AF_1, but agrees with Mss. J(a)(b)D and Ms. S_1 in numerous instances, and often goes its own way. On the whole, whichever group of mss. it agrees with, its reading is correct or at least possible, and it seems that its text is the result of skilful collation. This impression is confirmed by the numerous alterations of readings in the handwriting of the original scribe. This ms. is close to being the equal of Ms. B in reliability, and is essential for any critical edition of the text.

Ms. W tends to agree with N when N disagrees with S_1.

(viii) Ms. C

This is Ms. 12 of the Frere Collection in the library of Girton College at Cambridge, written in 1322 A.H. (= 1904 C.E.) by the High Priest Yâʿqûb bin Hârûn bin Salâmah.

The same comments made on the text of Ms. B apply to this ms. as well. On the whole, it has less of a tendency to agree with J(a)(b)D and more of a tendency to agree with the modern mss. Its nearest affinities are with Ms. W and Ms. L_3.

(ix) Ms. L_2

This is Oriental Ms. 10813 of the British Library. There is no colophon and no information about the scribe or date of copying. The handwriting seems to belong to Nâji bin Khiḍr.

This ms. needs to be used with care, as it represents a distinctive recension (along with S_2) and the readings of this ms., or this ms. and S_2, are unlikely to be original unless confirmed by other mss.

(x) Ms. S_2

This is Ms. 385 of the Sassoon Collection, written in 1322 A.H. (= 1904 C.E.) by Barhûm bin Yûsuf Salâmah.

See the comments on L_2.

(xi) Ms. P

This is Samaritan Ms. 6 in the Library of Dropsie College, written in 1305 A.H. (= 1888 C.E.) by Salâmah bin ʿImrân bin Salâmah bin Ghazâl ak-Kūʾən al-Labi.

This ms. belongs to an otherwise unattested textual group. It is generally accurate and is an important text-witness.

(xii) Ms. L_3

This is Oriental Ms. 10876 of the British Library, written in 1324 A.H. (= 1906 C.E.) by Abu ʾl-Ḥasan bin Yaʿqûb bin Hârûn bin Salâmah bin Ghazâl bin Isḥâq the Priest. The ms. is written in Hebrew letters.

This ms. belongs to a distinctive recension to which belong L_3AF_1, and with which W and C and GF_2 often agree. The readings of this recension are unlikely to be original unless confirmed by mss. representing other text-forms.

(xiii) Ms. A

This is Ms. G 99 Sup. of the Ambrosian Library in Milan, written in 1962 C.E. by Yûsuf bin Abi ʾl-Ḥasan bin Yaʿqûb bin Hârûn the Priest.

This ms., along with F_1, represents a sub-group within the group represented by L_3AF_1, and sometimes W or C or GF_2. This sub-group has a distinctly inferior text and its distinctive readings are generally to be treated with suspicion. There is, however, one important exception: very often AF_1 disagree with the other mss. just mentioned and have a correct reading otherwise only attested by J(a)D or J(b)D, and they have some value because of this if used with care, particularly in passages where J(a) or J(b) or D have perished. It seems that some sporadic collation has been made with much older mss.

Both A and F_1 have numerous scribal errors.

(xiv) Ms. F_1

This is Samaritan Ms. 33 in the library of the Seminar für Semististik und Arabistik in the Freie Universität Berlin, written in 1382 A.H. (= 1963 C.E.) by Yûsuf bin Abi 'l-Ḥasan bin Yaʿqûb.

On the text, see the comments on Ms. A. Although the two mss. are written by the same scribe and are representatives of the same sub-group, F_1 is superior to A.

(xv) Ms. G

This is Samaritan Ms. 155 in the John Rylands University Library of Manchester, written in 1326 H or 1908 C.E. by ࠀࠁࠉࠔࠏ ࠁࠍ. It is the autograph of the Hebrew translation (see the catalogue entry).

The text seems to have undergone some recension in the process of translation. The Arabic original seems to have been a ms. of the type of W or L_2S_2 or L_3AF_1; probably mss. of several types were consulted. On the whole, although it tends to agree with the secondary recensions, its text is almost free of errors, and it has a tendency to agree with J(a)D or J(b)D against the rest of the mss. in important instances. It is an important text-witness.

(xvi) Ms. F_2

This is Samaritan Ms. 32 in the library of the Seminar für Semitistik und Arabistik in the Freie Universität Berlin, written in 1958 by Yûsuf bin Abi 'l-Ḥasan bin Yaʿqûb. It is a ms. of the Hebrew translation.

Ms. F_2 does not always agree with Ms. G, partly because the rendering of the Arabic has been improved in spots, partly because sporadic revision seems to have been made against other Arabic texts.

b) *Manuscripts Not Used*

(i) Ms. Adler 1595

Inquiries to the library of the Jewish Theological Seminary were not successful. It is clear from the replies that the staff are unable to locate the ms., but it is not clear whether this is because the library never acquired the ms. in the first place, or because the Samaritan mss. are not identified and labelled.

(ii) Mss. 140 and 147 (according to Shunnar's list) in the library of the High Priest

It was not possible to get microfilms of these mss.

(iii) Samaritan Ms. 156 of the John Rylands Library

This is a ms. of the Hebrew translation. The library staff inform me that they were unable to make a legible photograph of the ms., which is extensively damaged by water.

(iv) Ms. Firkovich Samaritan IV:1 in the Leningrad Public Library

It has so far not been possible to get a photocopy of this. It is a single leaf, according to Vilsker (private communication). I will comment on it in a future study.

c) *The Inter-Relationship of the Text-Forms*

The mss. can be classified into the following groups:

J(a)(b)D
$S_1N(L_1)$
W
B
$C(L_1)$
L_2S_2
P
$J(c)L_3AF_1$
GF_2

Ms. B, Ms. C, Ms. L_1, Ms. W, and Ms. P, have a mixed text. Ms. N often agrees with BCW or L_3AF_1. Mss. BCW have affinities with each other.

The mss. can be classified into major groups as follows:

J(a)(b)D
$S_1N(L_1)$
$BCW(N)(L_1)(P)$
$L_2S_2(P)$
$(N)J(c)L_3AF_1GF_2$

It is to be noticed that L_1NP will not fall neatly into these groupings.

4. Manuscripts of the Khilâf

a) *Manuscripts Used*

(i) Ms. S_1

This is Ms. 717 of the Sassoon Library. The colophon has not survived.

The ms. was pieced together, restored, and re-bound in 1254 A.H. (= 1838 C.E.) by ʿImrân bin Salâmah bin Ghazâl the Priest.

The ms. was written by two different scribes. (This fact is not mentioned in the catalogue). Dr. Crown dates the scripts to about 1664. The first scribe is Mufarrij bin Yaʿqûb (who also wrote part of Rylands Ms. Sam. 27). Pages 1-25 (nearly to the end of Ch. IV) are by the first scribe. Pages 26-29 (near the start of ch. V) are by the second scribe. Pages 30-37 (about a sixth of the way through ch. V) are by the first scribe. Pages 38-205 (about two-thirds of the way through ch. VII) are by the second scribe, except for pages 138 (at the start of ch. VII) to 149 (about a tenth of the way through ch. VII) which were written by the restorer. Pages 206-209 are by the restorer. Pages 210-215 are by the first scribe. Pages 216-219 are by the second scribe. Pages 220-225 are by the first scribe. Page 226, the last page of the text of the Khilâf, is by the restorer.

The section edited here was written by the second scribe.

The ms. has a strong tendency to write Hebrew technical terms in Arabic letters, a mark of antiquity found in the oldest mss. of the Ṭubâkh and Kâfi.

The dots of letters are left out by the second scribe whenever they would not be needed by a fluent reader. In most cases this does not cause any problem, but in a few cases when a word could have been read in two different ways I have had to list the exact form as it appears in the ms. in the apparatus so as not to give the impression that the scribe necessarily intended one particular reading.

This ms. tends to stand against all the rest, though it is sometimes supported by Ms. B_1. It was the only ms. accurate enough to use as the collating base for the edition. Errors have usually been corrected against B_1S_2 or B_2L. I have occasionally departed from S_1 when it stood against the other reliable mss. and its reading was not superior to theirs, or seemed to be secondary.

(ii) Ms. B_1

This is Ms. Oriental Quarto 523 of the State Library of Prussia, at present in the care of the Sitzungsberichte Preussischer Kulturbesitz in West Berlin, written in 1868 C.E. or 1285 A.H. The name of the scribe is not mentioned. The handwriting is the same as in Ms. B of the Kâshif.

The dating according to the Christian calendar, as well as the Moslem one, and the omission of the name of the scribe, indicates that the ms. was commissioned, presumably by Petermann on behalf of the library.

The text of the ms. is very good. It agrees to some extent with Ms. S_1 and to some extent with Mss. B_2L, but its nearest relative is Ms. S_2.

(iii) Ms. S_2

This is Ms. 377 of the Sassoon Collection. My copy of the ms. is incomplete, so I am not able to say whether there is a colophon. None is mentioned in the catalogue. The handwriting belongs to Yaʿqûb bin Hârûn.

The text of this ms. has affinities with Ms. B_1, to a lesser extent with B_2L, and to a lesser extent still with S_1. Mss. B_1 and S_2 have a text intermediate between S_1 and B_2L, although they do not necessarily agree with each other in any particular instance.

(iv) Ms. D

This is Samaritan Ms. 12 in the Library of Dropsie College, written in 1324 A.H. (= 1906 C.E.) by Nuʿmân bin Yûsuf bin ʿAbd al-Laṭîf bin Ismâʿîl bin Ibrâhîm as-Sarâwi ad-Danafi. It belongs in the same group as Ms. S_2, though there are some instances of agreement with B_1 against S_2.

(v) Ms. B_2

This is Ms. Oriental Quarto 964 of the State Library of Prussia, at present in the care of the Sitzungsberichte Preussischer Kulturbesitz, in West Berlin, written in 1312 A.H. (= 1894 C.E.) by Nâji bin Khiḍr bin Isḥâq the Priest.

This ms. and Ms. L are the most reliable after $S_1B_1S_2$, and there are numerous instances in which B_2L have preserved the correct reading where it has been corrupted in $S_1B_1S_2$.

(vi) Ms. L

This is Oriental Ms. 10863 of the British Library in London, written in 1327 A.H. (= 1909 C.E.) by Nâji bin Khiḍr bin Isḥâq bin Salâmah bin Ghazâl the Priest.

This ms. was written by the same scribe as Ms. B_2, and has a very similar text. Nevertheless, the two mss. are not identical, and although Ms. L is superior to Ms. B_2 on the whole, there are instances where the reverse is the case.

(vii) The Quotations of the Khilâf in the Iʿtiqâdât

These are marked with the symbol P. The text has affinities partly with B_1S_2, and partly with JU, occasionally agrees with B_2L, and often goes its own way. The readings of this text have not been recorded where it paraphrases its source. Its readings are not to be inferred from silence.

(viii) Ms. J

This is the second part of Ms. Samaritan Octavo 5 of the Jewish National and University Library in Jerusalem, written in 1321 A.H. (= 1903 C.E.) by Jamîl bin Murjân bin Salâmah bin Murjân al-Yûsufi. The contents of the ms. are wrongly described in the library's handlist.

In general, this ms. and its relative, Ms. U, represent a text that has undergone some recension, and which is definitely less accurate than the consensus of Mss. $S_1B_1S_2$ or Mss. B_2L. Nevertheless, there are a few instances in which Mss. JU are the only ones to preserve an intelligible text.

(ix) Ms. U

This is Ms. O. Nova 520 of Uppsala University Library, written in 1326 A.H. (= 1908 C.E.) by Munîr ʿAbd Allâh.

This ms. belongs to the same recension as Ms. J. It is very clearly and carefully written in a handwriting full of character. There are numerous scribal errors, possibly due to the use of an exemplar that was hard to read, but these are easily corrected from Ms. J. The ms. is particularly valuable for its extensive marginal notes on ch. VII, not to be found in any other ms. seen by me.

(x) Ms. C

This is Ms. 14 of the Frere Collection in the library of Girton College at Cambridge, written in 1324 A.H. (= 1906 C.E.) by the High Priest Yaʿqûb bin Hârûn bin Salâmah bin Ghazâl.

This ms., along with Ms. G, represents a secondary recension. Nevertheless, there are a few instances where CG, or JUCG, preserve the correct reading against the other manuscripts.

(xi) Ms. G (and H)

This is Samaritan Ms. 150 of the John Rylands University Library of Manchester, written 3570 of the Entry (= 1932 C.E.) by [illegible] i.e. Abu ʾl-Ḥasan bin Yaʿqûb bin Hârûn. The ms. is in double columns, Arabic original and Hebrew translation, both written in Hebrew letters.

The text belongs to the same recension as Ms. C, although it is less accurate.

Hebrew technical terms have been translated into Arabic in the Arabic text, but are preserved in their original form in the Hebrew text. Both forms are given in the apparatus, with the forms in the Hebrew text marked with the symbol H.

(xii) Ms. Adler 1360

See below.

b) *Manuscripts Not Used*

(i) Ms. Adler 1360

I am informed by the Special Collections Librarian of the Jewish Theological Seminary that this ms. was not amongst the bulk of the Adler Collection acquired by the Seminary. This does not seem to be possible, since A. S. Halkin was able to borrow a ms. of the Khilâf from the Seminary

Library (see *The Relation of the Samaritans to Saadia Gaon*, p. 272, and *Samaritan Polemics against the Jews*, pp. 14-15). At some stage the Library has lost any record that it ever had this ms. Halkin quotes some extracts from this ms. in the first-mentioned article, and these have been quoted in full in the note on Kh 77-110 in the Commentary. On the textual type of this ms., see below. The readings of this ms. are marked as N in the Apparatus.

(ii) Mss. 137, 146, and 160 (according to Shunnar's list) in the library of the High Priest

It was not possible to get microfilms of these.

(iii) Samaritan Ms. 147 of the John Rylands Library

The form of the Hebrew translation in this ms. was found to be the same as in Ms. G.

(iv) Samaritan Mss. 148, 149, 151 of the John Rylands Library

These are mss. of the Hebrew translation. The library staff inform me that they were unable to make legible photographs of the mss., which are extensively damaged by water.

(v)

The fragments edited by Drabkin do not include any part of ch. VI.

(vi)

The fragment of the Khilâf that makes up the first part of Ms. Samaritan d.4 of the Bodleian Library does not correspond to any part of ch. VI.

c) *The Inter-Relationship of the Text-Forms*

The major division is between $S_1B_1S_2DB_2L$, on the one hand, and JUCG on the other hand, with P agreeing sometimes with one group and sometimes with the other. The ms. lost or forgotten by the Jewish Theological Seminary seems, as far as can be judged by the extracts quoted by Halkin, to be closely related to Mss. S_2D. According to the catalogue of the Adler mss., Ms. Adler 1360 was copied in 1320 A.H. (= 1902 C.E.), and if this ms. is the one that was lent by the J.T.S., it would therefore have been copied at about the same time as Mss. S_2D.

A more detailed division of the mss. is as follows:

S_1
B_1S_2DN
B_2L
P
JU
CG

Mss. B_1S_2D have affinities with both S_1 and B_2L. The quotations in P have affinities with both $B_1S_2B_2L$ and JU.

d) *Manuscripts of Part I of the Khilâf*

It might be convenient to list here the known mss. of Part I of the Khilâf, as their existence does not seem to be widely known.

Ms. Sassoon 784

Ms. Sassoon 718

British Library Oriental Ms. 12279

Library of the High Priest, Ms. 159

Samaritan Ms. 157 of the John Rylands Library. (The text is left unidentified in the catalogue, but examination shows it to be a Hebrew translation of the chapter on circumcision in Part I of the Khilâf).

5. The Manuscripts of the Farâ'iḍ

a) Ms. S

This is Ms. 719 of the Sassoon Collection in Jerusalem. The ms. is incomplete at the start and the end, and the colophon has not survived. The ms. has been written by two different scribes, with the changeover occurring at p. 29, part-way through ch. LXXIV. Dr. Crown dates the script of both sections in the mid fifteenth century, and identifies the second scribe as Å̊bīsha bin Fīnās bin Å̊bīsha bin Fīnās.

Only this ms. has the fragment of ch. LIV edited here.

The ms. has been made hard to read by staining and fading. For some reason the writing is faint in the top right-hand corner of the right-hand pages and the top left-hand corner of the left-hand pages, which I suspect is the effect of inadequate lighting at the top corners of each exposure.

Aside from this, the ms. is not very accurate. It is clearly and carefully written, with vocalization and syllable markers, but has numerous readings that are plainly nonsense. (Actually, it resembles the ms. of Abu 'l-Fatḥ called C by Vilmar in this respect). When the text is examined more closely, numerous other errors, which could not be called nonsense in themselves, but certainly make nonsense of the author's meaning, become apparent. As well as this, in the section of text edited here there is an omission by homoioteleuton.

It would not have been possible to establish a correct text of this chapter if the corresponding sections of the Ṭubâkh, Kâfi, and Khilâf had not been edited first, and even then it would not have been possible to restore the text completely without reference to the Karaite halachic handbooks.

b) Ms. M

This is Samaritan Ms. 172 of the John Rylands University Library of Manchester, written in 1343 A.H. (= 1924 C.E.) by Abu 'l-Ḥasan bin Yaʿqûb bin Hârûn the Priest. The catalogue identifies this ms. wrongly, and I am indebted to Dr. Heinz Pohl for drawing my attention to it.

The text of this ms. starts at a point corresponding to p. 11 of Ms. S, with the start of ch. LV, so it was not possible to use it for the text edited here. I have used it for other sections referred to in various places in the Commentary, mainly ch. CV (numbered ch. XXVIII in this ms.), as a check on Ms. S.

6. Manuscripts of the Kâshif al-Ghayâhib on Leviticus

a) *Manuscripts Used*

(i) Ms. B

This is Ms. Petermann 1:4 of the State Library of Prussia, at present in the care of the Sitzungsberichte Preussischer Kulturbesitz in West Berlin. The ms. is in three volumes, and covers Genesis, Exodus, Leviticus, and Numbers. Genesis is catalogued with the symbol 1:4a, Exodus the symbol 1:4b, and Leviticus and Numbers, in a single volume, 1:4c. A note at the end of the volume containing Genesis gives the date of completion of copying of that volume as 1854 C.E., and Exodus, Leviticus, and Numbers were presumably finished the same year or the next year. There is no information on the scribe. The handwriting is the same as in Ms. B_1 of the Khilâf.

The text is very accurate. This ms. is used as the basis of the edition, with scribal errors corrected against Mss. US. In a few cases the reading of Mss. US has been used when it was more intelligible or gave more detailed information.

(ii) Ms. U

This is Ms. O. Nova 517 of Uppsala University Library. The catalogue gives the name of the scribe as ʿImrân bin Isḥâq, but does not give any date. There is no indication of the name of the scribe in the print used by me, but the last page could be missing. The librarian informs me that the Samaritan mss. were acquired in 1922, from the estate of the late Professor Sven Linder. Ms. O. Nova 519 was written by the same scribe in 1915, and it seems reasonable to assume that O. Nova 517 was written at the same time.

This ms. belongs to the same recension as Ms. S. Mss. US represent a different recension to Ms. B, not often differing in the amount of information given, but very often differing in the wording.

(iii) Ms. S

This is Ms. 375 of the Sassoon Collection. My copy of the ms. is incomplete, so I am not able to say whether there is a colophon. None is mentioned in the catalogue. The handwriting belongs to Ya'qûb bin Hârûn.

The text belongs to the same recension as Ms. U.

7. Manuscripts of the I'tiqâdât

a) *Manuscripts Used*

(i) Ms. O

This is Ms. Arabic d. 43 of the Bodleian Library at Oxford, written in 1892 C.E. by Yå:qob bin Å̊rron the Priest. I am indebted to Dr. Fraser for drawing my attention to its existence.

This is the oldest ms. known to me, and has been chosen as the base text so as to make it easier to see the changes of wording from one manuscript to another. It should be remembered that as all the mss. were written down by the authors of the two recensions, or were copied from mss. written by them, all of them are accurate, however much they might differ from each other.

(ii) Ms. B

This is Ms. 14 of the Barton Collection in Boston University Library, written by Shafîq son of the High Priest Ya'qûb bin Hârûn. No date is given.

This ms. belongs to the same recension as Ms. O.

(iii) Ms. J

This is Ms. Samaritan Octavo 32 of the Jewish National and University Library in Jerusalem, written by Ya'qûb bin Shafîq the Priest (i.e. the son of the scribe of Ms. B and the grandson of the scribe of Ms. O). No date is given.

This ms. has a text derived from the text-type of Mss. OB, but with considerable re-wording. There is no change in the content or the information given.

(iv) Ms. P

This is Ms. Oriental Quarto 962 of the State Library of Prussia, at present in the care of the Sitzungsberichte Preussischer Kulturbesitz in West Berlin. There is no colophon. The handwriting belongs to Nâji bin Khiḍr, the son of the author of this recension.

This ms. belongs to the same recension as Ms. L. Both of these mss. represent the recension prepared by Khidr bin Isḥâq. There are considerable differences of wording between this recension and the one prepared by Yå:qob bin Årron, but no differences in the content or information given.

(v) Ms. L

This is Oriental Ms. 12250 of the British Library, written in 1326 A.H. (= 1909 C.E.) by Nâji bin Fīnās bin Isḥâq bin Salâmah bin Ghazâl the Priest (who is, of course, Nâji bin Khiḍr).

This ms. belongs to the same recension as Ms. P.

b) *Manuscripts Not Used*

Most of the mss. listed below were examined and it was found that no purpose would be served by entering their readings in the apparatus, as the variants were trivial ones and did not affect the meaning, and all the mss. belonged to one or other of the recensions represented by the mss. collated.

(i)

Ms. A19 in Cornell University Library.

(ii)

Samaritan Ms. 30 in the library of the Seminar für Semitistik und Arabistik in the Freie Universität Berlin.

(iii)

Samaritan Mss. 249A, 181, 179, 182, 183, 249 in the John Rylands University Library of Manchester.

(iv)

Sassoon Mss. 382 and 721. (I have not seen these two).

(v)

Dropsie College, Samaritan Ms. 13.

8. The Manuscript of the Sharḥ Sûrat al-Irbot

The ms. used was Ms. Sulzberger 18 in the library of the Jewish Theological Seminary in New York, written by Nâji bin Khiḍr. The last leaf, bearing the second part of the colophon and the date, has perished.

As the ms. is clearly written and its text was free of errors, there was no need to use any other mss. The following other mss. known to me are listed here for the reader's information:

(a) Samaritan Ms. 250 of the John Rylands Library

(b) Oriental Ms. 12293 of the British Library.

9. The Manuscript of the Collected Fatâwa of Ya'qûb bin Hârûn

The ms. used was Ms. Samaritan Octavo 6 of the Jewish National and University Library, written by the author in 1326 A.H. (= 1909 C.E.). The only other ms. known to me is Samaritan Ms. 14 in the Library of Dropsie College.

10. Manuscripts of Abu 'l-Fatḥ's History

I have re-collated all the mss. used by Vilmar for his edition, in the sections treating the Dosithean halachah, and have collated another eight mss. as well. As the mss. were only collated so as to check the reliability of Vilmar's text, there is no need to list them here. In the extracts used, it was found that there were very few significant variants not recorded by Vilmar, though there were numerous significant variants not recorded by Vilmar in other parts of the reports on the Dositheans in this text.[37]

I have consulted mss. of two other recensions of Abu 'l-Fatḥ. They are:

(a) Ms. 7 of the Barton Collection in Boston University Library
(b) Oriental Ms. 7927 of the British Library (located by Dr. Fraser)
(c) Ms. 4934 in the Semitic Museum of Harvard University
(d) Ms. Sulzberger 14 in the library of the Jewish Theological Seminar in New York
(e) Ms. Oriental Quarto 963 in the State Library of Prussia
(f) Ms. Samaritan 37 in the Seminar für Semitistik und Arabistik in the Freie Universität Berlin
(g) Ms. 18 of the Frere Collection in Girton College at Cambridge
(h) Ms. 86 (= Samaritan Ms. 5) in the Library of Dropsie College
(i) Ms. Samaritan Octavo 10 in the Jewish National and University Library.

Mss. (a) (b) (c) (d) (e) (f) (g) (h) represent a superior and unabridged form of the text of the History of Abu '-Fatḥ.

Ms. (i) represents a historical work in Hebrew derived in part from the unabridged recension of Abu 'l-Fatḥ.

As it happens, in the places in the Commentary where the opinions of the Dositheans are discussed, these two recensions do not add anything essential, and the intention of Abu 'l-Fatḥ is clear enough from the abridged recension published by Vilmar, so there was no need to complicate the discussion by referring to the other two chronicles.[38] It should be noted, however, that it is

---

[37] All substantial variants that affect the sense have been given in each case, including those not recorded by Vilmar. See also above, p. xiii.

[38] If circumstances permit, it is my intention to edit the material relating to the Dositheans in Abu 'l-Fatḥ and the other chronicles mentioned above, with a commentary on their halachah and ideas, and a study of the relationship between the various Dosithean sects and groups.

only by chance that this is the case, and any adequate analysis of other aspects of the Dosithean halachah must make use of the unabridged text.

11. Manuscripts of the Arabic Translation of the Torah

There are at least two recensions of the Arabic translation of the Torah, an earlier one related to Saadya's version, and a later one.[39] The printed editions give the later recension. For the earlier recension, I have used the following mss.:
(a) British Library Oriental Ms. 1450, written in 1759.
(b) British Library Oriental Ms. 10754, written before 1382.

12. Manuscripts of the Catechism

The ms. used was Samaritan Ms. 37 of the Bibliothèque Nationale in Paris. As the ms. is clearly written and free of errors, there was no need to use any other.

The only other mss. of this work known to me are Samaritan Ms. 325 of the John Rylands Library (a Hebrew translation) and Samaritan Ms. 15 in the Library of Dropsie College.

13. Manuscripts of the Answers to Gaster's Questionnaires

These are:
(a) Ms. Samaritan 317 of the John Rylands Library.
(b) Ms. Samaritan 318 of the same library.

---

[39] See Shehadeh's study for details of the recensions.

VI. THE METHOD OF EDITING THE TEXTS

In editing each text, the basic manuscript is followed as far as possible. If the basic manuscript is corrupt or inferior, the reading of the oldest or most reliable other mss. is used. All the readings of all the manuscripts are made available, and if the editor has made the wrong choice, the reader has all the information and can make an independent decision, and if the editor is right, the reasons for the choice will be clear.

The spelling of the basic ms. is followed. Variants of spelling, such as راة for رات, or جرا for جرى, or البتا for البته, or هو for هوا, are not recorded, except in the very few cases when the distribution of the forms of the spelling is related to the distribution of substantial variants. Alterations of the plural masculine case endings -ûn and -în are recorded. The addition or omission of a final *alif* as a case-marker is not recorded, unless special circumstances make it necessary. The presence or absence of *hamzah* is not recorded. It should be mentioned that the mss. hardly ever use *hamzah*, and for this reason it has not been used much in the edition. It seems that the glottal stop had been lost between vowels in most environments, as in modern Arabic. In the very few instances where there is a *hamzah* in a ms. and its presence is related to other variants, or is otherwise important, it is recorded.

All the mss. are unvocalised, with the single exception of the ms. of the Farâ'iḍ. In the case of this particular text, the vocalisation has been entered in the edition in a few cases of possible ambiguity or difficulty.

The readings of the Hebrew translations are recorded if the Arabic readings behind them can be determined. Readings of the Hebrew translations are not to be assumed from silence.

Very few emendations have been made. Those that have been made are mostly minor, and are justified in the Commentary. I believe they commend themselves by their appropriateness in the context, and by the clear signs of textual derangement in the mss. in each case.

Here is a list of the passages where an emendation is made:

Ṭubâkh: 59; 86.

Kâfi: Ch. III, 34; ch. XII, 27.

Khilâf: 8 (but see Ms. S_1); 25; 251; Additional Passage 16 (but only one ms. is extant here).

Farâ'iḍ: There are special problems in editing a text on the basis of one ms. See the Commentary, where all emendations are listed.

Kâshif: Ch. XV, 33; 40; 57; 77; ch. XII, 11; 27.

I'tiqâdât: No emendations.

Shorter pieces: No emendations in the usual sense, but see M.N. III:5.

Abbreviations of words in Biblical quotations have been replaced by the full form of the word, except when there might be some doubt about the exact form of the word intended or when there was some connection with readings mentioned in the apparatus, in which case the necessary information has been recorded in the apparatus.

The exception to this is the Kitâb al-Farâ'iḍ, in which case full details of abbreviations have been given in every instance.

VII. THE LANGUAGE OF THE TEXTS

The older texts are written in normal literary Arabic of their period, such as a Moslem author might have used for a historical, geographical, legal, or theological treatise, or such as is used in government papers of the period. Lest it be thought that the language is more modern than would be expected of a Moslem of the same period, it should be pointed out that the printed editions of Moslem texts of this period tend to classicise the language of the mss. The mss. of such texts are less classicising than a modern newspaper, and neither the Koran nor modern literary style should be taken as a standard of literary Arabic in the Mediaeval period. In particular, government documents of the period tend to be written in a form of language intermediate between classical and the contemporary language of the period. There is nothing distinctively Samaritan about the language of the Samaritan texts edited. The later texts edited are written in a form of literary Arabic typical of documents of the Turkish period, as might have been expected.[40]

The following items could be added to the Arabic dictionaries:

حلال in the sense of orifice of the penis or the penis itself, Kâfi ch. XI, 5. The word is recorded in Dozy's dictionary, but the additional instance deserves recording.

اجرى in the sense of better-integrated or fitting in better, applied to an argument or decision, Kâfi ch. XI, 72; Khilâf 231; 233; 237; and other places listed in the note on the Kâfi. The word is not recorded in the dictionaries at all.

الباء, a word of unknown meaning, in the Kâshif, ch. XV, 60 and 64. It is possible that the mss. are corrupt at this point.

The verb طا (sometimes طمى), meaning 'to become unclean', future يطا (sometimes يطمي), the derived nouns طا (sometimes طمي) and طاوه, and the derived adjective طمي, which occur constantly throughout the texts edited, are not recorded by the dictionaries.

معلوله . On the technical meaning of this word, as a contaminated object, see the Additional Passage from the Khilâf, 1 N.

The list of exegetical terms in Kh 127-128 deserves recording, as the dictionaries do not record these in their technical sense.

The occasional replacement of ض by د, and ط by ت, characteristic of

[40] Turkisms in the spelling of the mss. of the Khilâf have been noticed by Wreschner, introduction, p. xxx. Although these forms of spelling are not original in the older texts, they are original in the later ones.

some forms of Lebanese-Syrian-Palestinian pronunciation, has not been recorded. I have not found any examples of the replacement of ظ by ز.[41]

The forms انواع and افواه, infinitives of stem IV of hollow verbs, but in the form of the infinitives of strong verbs (Kf ch. III, 24; Kh 29) deserve recording. Notice that both of these forms are instances of denominatives.

There is one very important difference between the vocabulary of the Samaritan texts edited here and the vocabulary of Jewish texts in Arabic from the same periods, and that is that whereas the Jewish authors tend to use Hebrew technical terms, both words and phrases, very liberally, the Samaritans restrict this use to a few unstranslatable terms, and otherwise endeavour to find Arabic equivalents for Hebrew terms. This tendency is so pervasive and consistent that anyone familiar with the Jewish literature in Arabic will immediately be struck by the difference on opening the texts edited here at any passage at random. Of course, a part of the Arabic vocabulary was already available, in the form of Moslem technical terms, which could then be re-used in a new context. Thus we find that شريعه consistently renders [Samaritan], that امام consistently renders [Samaritan], that فرايض renders [Samaritan], that علما renders [Samaritan], that متجنب renders [Samaritan] (see p. 152), that نجاسه renders [Samaritan], and so on. In other cases an ordinary Arabic word becomes a technical term, as المقدس for [Samaritan], حيض for [Samaritan], ذوب for [Samaritan], مسمد for the Aramaic [Samaritan] (see p. 243), ناطر for the Aramaic [Samaritan] (p. 243), محتمل for some term corresponding to the Jewish term אסמכתא (see p. 253), and so on. Some of these meanings are specialised enough to deserve recording in the dictionaries.

In view of this very definite tendency to use native terminology whenever possible, I suggest that the use of the terms طا, طاوه and so on, mentioned above, is to be seen as the use of a rare or specialised Arabic term, rather than the introduction of a Hebrew or Aramaic set of words into Arabic (although of course it is possible that the words had earlier been borrowed by Arabic-speaking Moslems or Christians from Syriac).

[41] See Wreschner, introduction, p. xxx. Notice the form ظبط in line 71 of the Book of Principles.

CRITICAL EDITION OF THE HALACHIC TREATISES

EDITORIAL SYMBOLS

- [marks the end of the lemma.
- \+ marks an addition after the lemma in the ms.
- → marks an addition before the lemma in the ms.
- < marks the omission of the lemma in the ms.
- ∩ means that all the words from just after the first occurrence of the lemma, up to and including the second occurrence, have been omitted by homoioteleuton in the ms.
- ∩ < means that the lemma has been omitted by homoioteleuton in the ms.
- [ ] These mark a restoration of a word or part of a word that is illegible in the ms.
- < > In the Farâ'iḍ, this marks an emendation of the single ms. If these brackets are empty, it means that the editor has deleted a word from the manuscript. The details of all such emendations or restorations are given in the Commentary. (The reason for the difference in the symbol for the Farâ'iḍ as opposed to the other texts is that very often several emendations or restorations occurred near each other, and it was essential to show where each one started and ended).
- ° ° ° ° In the Farâ'iḍ, circles over letters mean that they are only partly legible.
- [......] In the Farâ'iḍ, this marks a completely illegible word or phrase, which could not be restored exactly from the context.
- † † In all texts except the Farâ'iḍ, daggers mark an emendation against all the mss.
- ■ marks an illegible letter which could not be restored.
- × marks a scribal error or impossible reading.
- * A raised asterisk denotes the original reading of the ms. Thus: B^{*}.
- ^{2} A raised figure 2 denotes an emendation apparently made by the original scribe. Thus: B^{2}.
- ^{3} A raised figure 3 denotes an emendation apparently made by a later scribe. Thus: B^{3}.
- ^{txt} The body of the text of the ms. Thus: B^{txt}.
- ^{mg} The margin of the ms. Thus: B^{mg}.
- (السَّاير) This term refers to the consensus of the Arabic mss. as opposed to the reading of other mss. listed separately. (This expression is frequently used in indicating the agreement of some of the Arabic mss. with the Hebrew translation. Note that the readings of the Hebrew translation are never to be assumed from silence, because the style of the translation often makes retroversion uncertain).
- ( ) These enclose the editor's comments.
- ; The semi-colon separates the different variants to one lemma.
- [[ ]] These mark what the editor considers to be an interpolation.

CONVENTIONS

Variants on phrases or whole lines are noted before variants on words within such phrases or lines. Variants on groups of lines (mostly omissions by homoioteleuton) are noted before variants on phrases or whole lines within such a group of lines.

The punctuation and paragraphing are the editor's.

The line-division is the editor's.

The few vowel-symbols used in the edition of the Farâ'iḍ are in the original (see p. 48).

All lists of ms. sigla are to be read from right to left.

TEXT 1

[كتاب الطباخ]

الكلام في انواع الدما التي توجب النجاسات وبيان احكامها

الدما ينقسم الى سبعة اقسام دم ࠍࠃࠄ ودم [Samaritan] ودم [Samaritan] ودم [Samaritan] وهو قسمان قسم يختص بالذكر وقسم يختص بالانثى ودم [Samaritan] ودم الاشتباه. كل واحد من هذه الدما له حكم مخالف الاخر.

بيان ذلك

دم [Samaritan] الاول منها وهو الذي يحضر عقيب الطهر بادرة الطما. وحكمه سبعة ايام حسب قوله [Samaritan] [Samaritan] [Samaritan] [Samaritan] [Samaritan] [Samaritan] [Samaritan]

---

١ الدما] [Samaritan] FHG التي توجب النجاسات] [Samaritan] FHG التي] الذي P_2 احكامها] احكام × P_3M_2 ؛ [Samaritan] FHG

٢ الدما] الدم $FHGP_2$ الى] > G اقسام] + [Samaritan] G دم [$DC_1C_2M_1O$ [Samaritan] ; $SKM_2^2P_3P_2L_2$ > NM_2*L*P_1 [Samaritan] [Samaritan] G ودم [Samaritan] ودم] > M_2 ودم [Samaritan] [$NC_2P_3M_2$ ∩ ودم] [Samaritan] SKM_2P_2 ودم] > ∩ P_1* [Samaritan] [$NC_2P_3M_2M_1P_1^2O$ [Samaritan] ؛ G [Samaritan] $FHKDC_1P_2L$ ودم [$SDC_1C_2LM_1P_1O$ [Samaritan] $KNM_2P_3P_2$ [Samaritan] [Samaritan] G ؛ [Samaritan] M_1 ؛ [Samaritan] C_2 ؛ [Samaritan] O ودم [$KC_1C_2LM_1P_1O$ [Samaritan] $SNP_3P_2M_2$ [Samaritan] [Samaritan] G

٣ قسمان] > × C_1 قسم يختص بالذكد وقسم] > × C_2 يختص (اول)] [Samaritan] G بذكر C_1 يختص (ثاني)] [Samaritan] G ودم [$DC_1C_2M_1P_1O$ [Samaritan] $SKNM_2P_3P_2L$ كل] وكل $FHGSC_1P_2L$

٣-٤ واحد من هذه الدما] [Samaritan] FHG

٤ هذه] هذا P_2

٦ دم [Samaritan] الاول منها] [Samaritan] [Samaritan] FHG دم [$DNC_2M_1P_1O$ [Samaritan] $SKC_1P_3M_2P_2L$ هو $NP_3M_2P_1$ الطما] [Samaritan] قوله] + تعالى K

٧-٨ (كل الايه بحروف عربيه) O [Samaritan] G

٧ [Samaritan] > ∩ SC_1 [Samaritan] [Samaritan] LP_1

ࠁࠁࠔࠓࠄ ࠔࠁࠏࠕ ࠉࠌࠉࠌ ࠕࠄࠉࠄ ࠁࠍࠃࠕࠄ وتمامه (اح ١٥ : ١٩). والذي يدل على انه الذي يحضر عقيب الطهر قوله تعالى ࠅࠀࠀࠔࠄ ࠀࠔࠓ ࠉࠔࠊࠁ ࠀࠉࠔࠄ ࠀࠕࠄ ࠅࠕࠄࠉࠄ ࠁࠍࠃࠕࠄ ࠏࠋࠉࠅ ࠉࠈࠌࠀ ࠔࠁࠏࠕ ࠉࠌࠉࠌ (ايه ٢٤). وكلما يخالطه من الالات ولاجسام يلزمه سبعة ايام.

القسم الثاني وهو دم ࠃࠁࠄ وهو الذي يحضر ثاني ࠄࠍࠃࠄ وفي مدة الاسبوع. حكمه واحد يخلص الانسان منه في يوم دنوه به. دليل ذلك ما تعتمد عليه الامه ان السباغه اذا فارقت الدم ونقيت منه في اليوم السابع من الاسبوع الاول قبل غيبة الشمس طهرت. وهذا هو الموجود في نقل الامه مجمعون عليه لا يوجد فيهم من يرى خلافه.

القسم الثالث وهو المسمى ࠆࠁࠄ ࠌࠓࠁ وبيانه اذا بقى الدم مع الامراه لم تنقا منه وغياب الشمس ليلة الثامن ونقيت مبه في اليوم الثامن او التاسع او العاشر يجب ان يهمل الايام الزايده عن اليوم السابع التي كان فيها حضور الدما وتعد ثاني يوم النقا سبعة ايام كمل

١٠-٨ ࠔࠁࠏࠕ ࠉࠌࠉࠌ ∩ C_1

٨ ࠁࠍࠃࠕࠄ (كل الساير) FH] < SNP_3M_2L وتمامه < G الذي P_1

٩ يدل] + عنه K انه الذي يحضر عقيب الطهر] ذلك ايضا $FHGSNP_2L$ تعالى (كل الساير) FH] < SLK

١٠-٩ (الايه بحروف عربيه) O ࠅࠀࠍ ࠀࠍࠈࠉࠇࠀࠏࠀ ࠌࠍࠈࠉࠇࠏ ࠁࠓࠂࠋࠄࠀ ࠔࠏࠄࠀ ࠅࠕࠀࠄࠓ ࠀࠋࠄࠌࠌࠄ ࠏࠋࠉࠄ ࠆࠓࠍࠌ ࠔࠁࠏࠄ ࠀࠉࠀࠌ G

٩ ࠅࠀࠀࠔࠄ ࠀࠔࠓ $[SDKC_1C_2P_3M_2L^*M_1P_1O$ ࠅࠀࠌ ࠔࠊࠁ $FHGP_2L^2$

١٠ ࠀࠉࠔࠄ] < × P_1 ࠀࠕࠄ $[FHGNC_1C_2P_3M_2P_2L^2P_1^*O$ + ࠔࠊࠁࠕ ࠆࠓࠏ $SDKL^*P_1^2$ ࠅࠕࠄࠉࠄ] ࠕࠄࠉࠄ K^2

١١ يلزم C_2

١٢ دم] ࠃࠌ KC_1L ࠃࠁࠄ $[M_2M_1^2P_1O$ ࠃࠍࠉࠁࠄ G ؛ ࠃࠅࠄ $FHSDKNC_1C_2P_3P_2L^2$ ؛ ࠃࠄࠅࠄ L^* ؛ ࠆࠁࠄ × M_1^* ࠄࠍࠃࠄ] ࠔࠍ ࠀࠋࠄࠉࠑ G ؛ < S في $KDNP_3P_1$

١٣ ويخلص P_3 دليل ذلك] ࠀࠋࠃࠋࠉࠋ ࠏࠋࠉ ࠃࠋࠊ FHG ما تعتمد] ࠌࠀ ࠕࠐࠏࠋࠄ ࠀࠋࠀࠌࠄ ࠅࠀࠏࠕࠌࠃࠀ FHG تعتمد] يعتمد KD ؛ يعمد C_2 السباغه] ࠀࠋࠀࠌࠓࠀࠄ FHG ؛ السابغه C_1M_1 ؛ الساعده × C_2

١٤-١٣ اذا فارقت] ࠀࠍ ࠏࠃࠌࠕ FHG اذا < × C_1

١٤ ونقيت] وبقيت × C_1 من الاسبوع < K غيب C_1

١٥ وهذه SC_1 مجمعون $[SNC_2M_2LM_1P_1O$ مجموعون (مجموعين K) $KDC_1P_3P_2$ ؛ ࠅࠌࠂࠌࠅࠏࠅࠍ FHG يوجد] يجد $KDC_1P_3P_2$ فيهم] منهم P_3M_2 الثالث] ࠀࠋࠕࠀࠍ × HG ࠆࠁࠄ (الساير) FH] ࠀࠋࠊࠍࠉࠁ G ؛ ࠆࠅࠄ S منه] منها C_1

١٧ وغياب] وغابت K ؛ وغابة D ؛ وغايته × C_2 ؛ ࠅࠏࠓࠅࠁ FHG الشمس] < FHG الثامن ∩ $NP_3M_2P_2L^2$ منه (الساير) FH] < S والتاسع $GP_3P_2P_1$ والعاشر $GP_3P_2P_1$ تهمل FHM_1 ؛ يمهل × D

١٨ الايام (الساير) FH] ࠄࠃࠄ ࠀࠋࠀࠉࠀࠌ G عن] على N السابع (الساير) FH] < L^2 الذي P_1 فيها حضور الدما (الساير) FH] حضور الدما فيها S ؛ ࠐࠉࠄ ࠇࠑࠅࠓ ࠀࠋࠃࠌ G ثاني يوم $[SDKNC_1C_2P_2LP_1O$ من ثاني يوم $M_2^*M_1$ ؛ من يوم $P_3M_2^2$ ؛ ࠐࠉ ࠀࠋࠉࠅࠌ ࠀࠋࠕࠀࠍࠉ FHG

نقا لا يظهر فيها دم وتطهر في ذلك اليوم. ايضا يلزم من يستمر الدم معها اربعة ايام وما زاد عنها ايام كثيره او قليله يله يلزمها ايضا من يوم تخلص تعد من ثاني يوم النقا سبعة ايام نقا لا ترى شيا من الدم. دليل ذلك قوله تعالى [Samaritan] وتمامه الى قوله [Samaritan] (ايات ٢٥,٢٨) فساوى تعالى بين الحال التي تزيد عن الاسبوع الاول وبين ايام كثيره بقوله بعد [Samaritan] فبطل بذلك قول من يقول ان هيميم يريد بها تسعه واربعين يوما لا ياخذ هيميم فقط ازيد من ذلك بقول الكتاب العزيز [Samaritan]

---

١٩ النقا] [Samaritan] FHG نقا لا] نقلاً × SC_1 فيه N ايضا] [Samaritan] FHG ؛ < L^* يلزم] + [Samaritan] G الدم معها (الساير) FH] معها الدم C_1L ؛ عليها الدم GS

٢٠ [Samaritan] G من] في SC_1L ؛ < K تخلص] [Samaritan] G ثاني] [Samaritan] G النقا] [Samaritan] G ؛ < $P_3M_2P_1$ نقا لا] نقلا × SC_1 ترى] ترى فيهم L ؛ يرى فيهم S ؛ يرى فيها C_1

٢١ من الدم] في اله × C_1 دليل ذلك] [Samaritan] G بقوله C_1

٢١-٢٢ [Samaritan] G

٢١ [Samaritan] < × P_1

٢٢ [Samaritan] < P_3M_2 [Samaritan] × H ؛ [Samaritan] × C_1

٢٣ [Samaritan] $DKM_1{}^*P_1O$ [Samaritan] × C_2 ؛ [Samaritan] S ؛ [Samaritan] NP_3M_2 ؛ [Samaritan] $FHGC_1P_2LM_1^2$ وتمامه] وفتمامه × C_1 ؛ فتمامه L ؛ < GSC_2

٢٣-٢٤ [Samaritan] G

٢٣ [Samaritan] [Samaritan] × N

٢٤ بين] بينها × P_3

٢٥ التي] الذي GP_3M_2 ؛ < × C_2 تزيد $SKC_1C_2M_1P_1O$] تزيد $GDNP_3M_2P_2L$ الاول (الساير FH) < K [Samaritan] ([Samaritan] × D)] [Samaritan] G ؛ [Samaritan] × C_2 ؛ [Samaritan] M_2 ؛ [Samaritan] × P_3

٢٥-٢٦ [Samaritan] .... هيميم < × $NM_1{}^*P_1{}^*$

٢٦ [Samaritan] $SDKC_1C_2LM_1^2P_1^2O$ < $GP_3M_2P_2$ بذلك $GSDC_1C_2LP_1^2O$] ذلك K ؛ < $FHGP_3P_2M_2M_1^2$ قول من يقول] من قول × C_1 قول (الساير FH] < SC_1 ان < × C_2 هيميم $SC_1L^*M_1^2O$] [Samaritan] C_2 ؛ هيميم [Samaritan] × L^2 ؛ [Samaritan] × $DKP_3M_2P_2P_1^2$ ؛ [Samaritan] × G ؛ [Samaritan] × FH يريد] يزيد × M_1^2O بها] [Samaritan] × G ؛ < L^*

٢٧ يوما $FHGO$] + فقط × $SDKC_1C_2P_3M_2P_2L^2M_1^2$ ؛ (لا يثبت مكان لفظة فقط) $NL^*M_1{}^*P_1$ لا ياخذ هيميم] [Samaritan] FHG ؛ < × $NL^*M_1{}^*P_1$ لا] الا × C_2 هيميم M_1^2O] [Samaritan] $SKC_1C_2P_3M_2P_2L$ فقط O] < × $FHGSDKC_1C_2P_3M_2P_2L^2M_1^2$ ؛ (لا يثبت مكان لفظة فقط) $NL^*M_1ßP_1$ ازيد (الساير FH] < × N

ࠁࠉࠌࠉࠌ ࠄࠓࠁࠉࠌ (خر ٦ : ٢٣) يريد بذلك من نوبة السيد يوسف عليه السلام الى بعثة الرسول عليه السلام وقدره تفيد تسعه واربعين يوما. وهذان القسمان وما يزيد عنها وحكمها حكم الحال الزايد عن الاسبوع الاول الذي هو ࠏࠕ ࠍࠃࠕࠄ.

وهذا ايضا يخالف طايفة اليهود القرايين لان عندهم ان ࠄࠍࠃࠄ هو الدم الاول وما يجري في ثاني حال فهو ࠆࠁ وهذا مخالف من وجهين. الاول قوله تعالى ࠁࠋࠀ ࠏࠕ ࠍࠃࠕࠄ يريد به ما زاد عن زمان ࠍࠃࠕࠄ كثير او قليل ࠅࠏࠕ ࠍࠃࠕࠄ سبعة ايام لقوله تعالى ࠔࠁࠏࠕ ࠉࠌࠉࠌ ࠕࠄࠉࠄ ࠁࠍࠃࠕࠄ (ايه ١٩). فجعل ان طمها الاسبوع الاول حكم ࠋࠋࠍࠃࠄ لا ࠋࠋࠆࠁࠄ ولا ࠋࠋࠃࠁࠄ في الاسبوع الاول حكم ولا عقله. والوجه الثاني ان ࠅࠏࠕ في العبراني تفيد محتملات عده كل واحد منها

٢٧-٢٨ بقول .... بذلك ∩ M_1*

٢٧ بقول الكتاب العزيز] ࠔࠉࠄ الكتاب ࠀࠋࠌࠒࠃࠎ ࠒࠀࠋ FHG بقول] يقول NP_2 ࠅࠔࠀࠍ ࠊࠉ ࠕࠋࠔ ࠀࠋࠀࠉࠀࠔ ࠀࠋࠔࠀࠉࠃࠄ G ؛ (الايه في حروف عربيه) M_1 ࠁࠉࠌࠉࠌ > × $P_3M_2P_2P_1$*

٢٨ نوبة] توبة × C_1 ؛ نبوة × K عليه السلام ∩ $P_3M_2M_1$*P_1*

٢٩ الرسول] + ࠎࠉࠃࠍࠀ ࠌࠅࠎࠉ FHG عليه السلام [$SDNC_1C_2LM_1^2P_1^2O$ ࠏࠋࠉࠄ ࠀࠋࠑࠋࠀࠕ ࠅࠀࠋࠎࠋࠀࠌ FHG ؛ عليه افضل الصلاه واتم السلام K ؛ صلوات الله عليه P_2 وقدره تفيد] وقد تقبد × C_1 وقدره] ࠅࠒࠃࠓࠄ FHG تفيد [$GDKC_1C_2LM_1P_1$ تقيد × SO ؛ > $FHNP_3M_2P_2$ وهذان] وهذه × C_1 وما] ما × L عنها] منها P_1O

٣٠ وحكمها] وحكمها × $SDKC_2$ الذي (الساير FH] > K ࠏࠕ ࠍࠃࠕࠄ FH] ࠅࠃࠕ ࠁࠏࠃࠕࠄࠀ G ؛ ࠏࠕ ࠄࠍࠃࠄ $NP_2P_3M_2M_1P_1$* ؛ ࠏࠕ ࠍࠃࠕࠄ (ࠄࠍࠃࠄ P_1^2) هو الدم $C_2SDKC_1LP_1^2O$

٣١ ايضا (الساير FH] > S* القرايين] والقرايين × $DC_1C_2P_3$ ؛ والقرابين × SC_1 لان (الساير FH] > L* ان > FHG

٣٢ وما يجي في ثاني حال] ࠅࠀࠋࠉࠉ ࠉࠕࠉࠅ ࠁࠏࠃࠄ FHG في > K فهو] ࠄࠅࠀ G ࠆࠁ (الساير FH] ࠆࠁࠉࠀ G ؛ دم ࠆࠁ P_3 تعالى (الساير FH] > K

٣٣-٣٤ ࠊࠉ ࠕࠆࠅࠁ ࠅࠃࠕ ࠁࠏࠃࠕࠄࠀ G

٣٣ ࠍࠃࠕࠄ] ࠄࠉࠉࠅࠀ G ؛ ࠄࠍࠃࠄ L كثير او قليل (الساير FH] قليلا كثيرا S ࠅࠏࠕ ࠍࠃࠕࠄ] ࠅࠔࠀࠍ ࠀࠋࠄࠉࠉ G ࠅࠏࠕ] و (الحرف العربي) ࠏࠕ M_1 ࠍࠃࠕࠄ (ثاني)] ࠄࠍࠃࠄ P_3M_1

٣٤ تعالى (الساير FH] > K ࠆࠁࠏࠄ ࠀࠉࠌࠀࠔ ࠀࠅࠔࠍ ࠊࠉ ࠁࠏࠃࠕࠄࠀ G يميم M_1 بندته O ان > FHG

٣٥ ࠋࠋࠍࠃࠄ (FHSC₁LM₁O ࠋࠋࠄࠉࠉ G ؛ ࠋࠋࠍࠃࠕࠄ $NP_3M_2P_1$* ؛ ࠋࠋࠍࠕࠄ × P_2 ؛ ࠋࠍࠃࠕࠄ $DKC_2P_3P_1^2$ ࠋࠋࠆࠁࠄ [SC_1LM_1O ࠋࠋࠀࠉࠁ G ؛ ࠋࠆࠁࠄ ࠋࠋࠃࠁࠄ [SC_1LM_1O ࠋࠃࠅࠄ $DKC_2P_1^2$ ؛ ࠀࠋࠅ × SC_1 $DKNC_2P_3M_2P_2P_1$ ࠋࠋࠍࠃࠕࠄ × $NP_3M_2P_1$* ؛ ࠋࠋࠍࠃࠄ × P_2 ؛ ࠋࠍࠃࠄ × F ؛ ࠋࠆࠁࠄ × H ؛ ࠋࠋࠀࠉࠁ G

٣٦ الثاني] + من الوجوه FHG ان ࠅࠏࠕ [$SDKC_1C_2LP_1^2O$ > $FHGNP_3M_2P_2M_1P_1$* تفيد] وتفيد M_1 ؛ + ࠀࠋࠔࠏࠍࠉ G منها ∩ P_2

يفيد مده طويله واسعه. منها ما قيل فيها حكايه عن الست ࠃࠓࠊ ࠍࠔࠉࠌ وما اظهره العبد في بابها بقوله ࠋࠏࠕ ࠏࠓࠁ ࠋࠏࠕ ࠑࠀࠕ ࠄࠔࠀࠁࠅࠕ (تك ٢٤ : ١١) وقوله عن السيد يعقوب حكايه عن ما فعله الله معه من قوله ࠅࠉࠀࠊࠋ ࠂࠌ ࠀࠊࠅࠋ

٤٠ ࠊࠎࠐࠍࠅ وتمامه (تك ٣١ : ١٥) وفيما حكاه الرسول عليه السلام بتشريف ࠔࠁࠈ ࠋࠅࠉ في الوقت المشار اليه بقوله ࠁࠏࠕ ࠄࠄࠅࠀ ࠄࠁࠃࠉࠋ ࠉࠄࠅࠄ ࠀࠕ ࠔࠁࠈ ࠄࠋࠅࠉ (تث ١٠ : ٨). وكل قسم من هذه الاقسام يفيد مده واسعه والمده الذي يحضر فيها الدم الاول المسما ࠍࠃࠄ ࠃࠅࠕࠄ حال ضيق اقل قليل من قسمة الزمان وهو جزو لا ينقسم مثله كالجزو الذي لا يتجزا من الجواهر.

٤٥ والقسم الرابع دم الولاده. وهو ينقسم قسمين. الذي يظهر عند ولادة الذكر وحكمه سبعة ايام بقوله تعالى ࠅࠈࠌࠀࠄ ࠔࠁࠏࠕ ࠉࠌࠉࠌ ࠊࠉࠌࠉ ࠍࠃࠕ ࠃࠅࠕࠄ ࠕࠈࠌࠀ (اح ١٢ : ٢) والدم الذي في ايام ࠈࠄࠓࠄ المسما ࠃࠌࠉ ࠈࠄࠓࠄ لقوله تعالى ࠕࠔࠁ ࠁࠃࠌࠉ ࠈࠄࠓࠄ ࠉࠌࠉࠌ (هناك). القسم الخامس الدم الذي

---

٣٧ مده طويله] ࠌࠃࠄ ࠈࠅࠉࠋࠄ FHG فيها فيه S ࠃࠓࠊ] DKC$_2$M$_2$M$_1$P$_1$O ربقه
SNP$_3$C$_1$P$_2$L ؛ ࠌࠍࠄࠀ ࠃࠓࠊ FHG اظهر P$_1$

٣٨ بابها] حكايتها DKC$_2$ ؛ ࠁࠀࠁࠄࠀ FHG بقوله (الساير) [FH < C$_2$ ࠋࠏࠕ ࠏࠓࠁ
ࠋࠏࠕ ࠑࠀࠕ ࠄࠔࠀࠁࠅࠕ G ࠋࠏࠕ (ثاني)] ࠋࠏࠕ × SN وقوله (الساير) [FH
+ تعالى KC$_2$

٣٩ يعقوب] ࠉࠏࠒࠅࠁ C$_1$ ؛ يعقوب (الساير) [FH + عليه السلام K الله (الساير) [FH < M$_1$ معه
(الساير) [FH له C$_1$ ࠀࠊࠋ ࠍࠃࠄ ࠀࠋࠋࠄ ࠋࠅ G

٤٠ ࠊࠎࠐࠍࠅ] + ࠅࠉࠀࠊࠋ K وتمامه] < FHGP$_3$ فيها P$_1$ السلام (الساير) [FH افضل
السلام واتم السلام K

٤٠-٤١ سبط لاوي GP$_2$

٤١ ࠔࠁࠈ G

٤١-٤٢ ࠔࠁࠈ ࠋࠅࠉ ࠁࠏࠕ ࠄࠄࠅࠀ ࠄࠁࠃࠉࠋ ࠉࠄࠅࠄ ࠀࠕ G

٤٢ ࠄࠋࠅࠉ] + ࠅࠊࠋ ࠒࠎࠌ ࠌࠍ ࠄࠀࠋࠀࠒࠎࠀࠌ K هذا M$_1$P$_1$ يفيد] + ࠌࠃࠄ G

٤٣ التي تحضر SC$_1$ ࠀࠋࠃࠌ G ࠃࠅࠕࠄ] ࠃࠅࠕࠄ FH ؛ ࠀࠋࠌࠎࠌࠀ G ؛ ࠃࠅࠕࠄ S
جزو] جزوه C$_1$ ؛ جزوا SP$_2$ لا (الساير) [FH ولا S

٤٤ كالجزوه C$_1$ لا] < × SC$_1$

٤٥ ࠅࠈࠌࠀࠄ G وحكمه (الساير) [FH حكمه C$_2$

٤٦ تعالى (الساير) [FH < C$_1$

٤٦-٤٧ ࠅࠈࠌࠀࠄ ࠔࠁࠏࠕ ࠉࠌࠉࠌ ࠊࠉࠌࠉ ࠍࠃࠕ ࠃࠅࠕࠄ ࠕࠈࠌࠀ G

٤٦ ࠅࠈࠌࠀࠄ NM$_2$P$_1$ ࠕࠈࠌࠀ × N ࠃࠅࠕࠄ × N الذي] ࠀࠋࠃࠉ FHG

٤٧ ࠈࠄࠓࠄ] هنده M$_1$ ؛ ࠀࠋࠈࠄࠓࠄ G ؛ ࠈࠄࠓࠄ M$_1$

٤٨ تعالى (الساير) [FH < SDKC$_2$L ࠅࠔࠋࠔࠉࠌ ࠉࠅࠌ ࠅࠔࠋࠔࠕ ࠉࠌࠉࠌ G
ࠀࠋࠒࠎࠌ × N القسم] والقسم DKC$_2$ ؛ < M$_2$

يجي مع ولادة الانثى وحكمه اسبوعين لقوله تعالى ࠅࠀࠌ ࠍࠒࠁࠄ ࠕࠋࠃ ࠅࠈࠌࠀࠄ ࠔࠁࠅࠏࠉࠌ ࠊࠍࠃࠕࠄ (ايه ٥). والدم الذي يجي في مدة الاسبوعين الزايد عن دم الولاده حكمه حكم ࠄࠍࠃࠄ فمن خالطه ودنا به لزمه يقيم سبعة ايام لقوله ࠊࠍࠃࠕࠄ.

القسم السادس المسما ࠃࠌࠉ ࠈࠄࠓࠄ وهو ينقسم قسمين. القسم الاول الذي يحضر للمراه في مدة النقا بالثلاثه وثلاثون يوما حسب قوله ࠅࠔࠋࠔࠉࠌ ࠉࠅࠌ ࠅࠔࠋࠔࠕ ࠉࠌࠉࠌ ࠕࠔࠁ ࠁࠃࠌࠉ ࠈࠄࠓࠄ (ايه ٤). وحكمه من دنا به وخالطه من الاجسام والالات يحصل في ثاني حال لانها اذا تفارقه وتنقا منه في يوم كمال الثلاثه وثلاثون يوما تطهر. واما الدم الذي يحضر في سته وستين يوما الزايد عن الاسبوعين الذي يتعلق بالانثى فهو جاري مجرى ما يحضر في الثلاثه وثلاثون يوما فمن دنا به من الاجسام والالات يخلص في ثاني حال دنوه به† لان † الامراه اذا خلصت منه في السته وستين يوما تطهر.

واما ان حضر منها بعد هذه المده لم تطهر لقوله تعالى ࠁࠊࠋ ࠒࠃࠔ ࠋࠀ ࠕࠂࠏ ࠅࠀࠋ ࠄࠌࠒࠃࠔ ࠋࠀ ࠕࠁࠅࠀ ࠏࠃ ࠌࠋࠀࠕ ࠉࠌࠉ ࠈࠄࠓࠄ (ايه ٤). فحكمه اذا رات الامراه دم بعد كمال المده المعينه حكم ࠄࠆࠁࠄ يلزم عنه سبعة ايام نقا لان

٤٩-٥٠ ࠅࠀࠍ ࠀࠍࠕࠉ ࠕࠋࠃ ࠕࠍࠂࠎ ࠀࠎࠁࠅࠏࠉࠍ ࠊࠏࠀࠃࠕࠄࠀ G

٥٠ ࠈࠌࠀࠄ N ࠊࠍࠃࠕࠄ والدم] < × $NM_2M_1P_1$ الاسبوعين] الاسبوع × C_1

٥١ دم] < FHG ࠄࠍࠃࠄ] ࠀࠋࠏࠀࠃ G يقيم (الساير FH] تقيم C_2 ؛ < C_1M_2 لقواه] + تعالى $FHGP_2$

٥٢ ࠊࠍࠃࠕࠄ] ࠊࠏࠀࠃࠕࠄࠀ G

٥٣ القسم (الساير FH] والقسم DKC_2 السادس (الساير FH] الخامس × M_1* ࠃࠌࠉ ࠈࠄࠓࠄ] ࠃࠌ ࠈࠄࠓࠄࠀ G قسمين] ࠋࠒࠎࠌࠉࠍ G ؛ الى قسمين S

٥٤ مدة النقا] ࠀࠉࠀࠌ ࠀࠋࠍࠒࠀࠅࠄ FHG النقا] النفاس DKC_2 بالثلاثه [$C_2P_3LP_1O$ الثلاثه $GDKNC_1M_2P_2M_1$ ؛ بثلاثه S وثلاثون] وثلاثين GM_2P_2 ؛ والثلاثون S

٥٤-٥٥ ࠅࠕࠋࠕࠉࠍ ࠉࠅࠌ ࠅࠕࠋࠕࠄ ࠀࠉࠀࠌ ࠕࠒࠏࠃ ࠐࠉ ࠃࠌ ࠈࠄࠀࠓࠕࠄࠀ G

٥٤ ࠔࠋࠔࠉࠌ S

٥٥ ࠅࠀࠉࠌ FHG ࠉࠔࠁࠉ FHG وخالطه] < FHG

٥٦ يحصل (الساير FH] يخلص × D^2K اذا [$GDKC_1P_2LM_1P_1O$ < × $FHSNC_2P_3M_2$ وثلاثون] والثلاثون S

٥٧ الذي] < × C_2 الذي يتعلق] ࠀࠋࠌࠕࠏࠋࠒ HG ࠄࠅࠀ G

٥٨ ما يحضر] < × K والثلاثون C_1 يخلص] خلص D

٥٩ ࠄࠀࠋࠄ G دنو N به] < HGM_2P_2 لان] لكن (كل المخطوطات FH اذا] < × N*

٥٩-٦٠ تطهر .... تطهر] $FHGNP_3M_2P_2$ ∩ $SDKC_1C_2M_1P_1O$

٦٠ لقوله تعالى] < FH

٦٢ فحكمه [DKC_2O < × $FHGSC_1LP_1^2$ ؛ (لا يثبت مكان اللفظه) $NP_3M_2P_2M_1P_1$* اذا .... المعينه [$FHGDSC_1C_2LP_1^2O$ < ∩ $NP_3M_2P_2M_1P_1$* اذا [$DC_2P_1^2O$ واذا $FHGSC_1L$ رات] ارادت

حكم الزياده عن تلك المدتين كحكم ما زاد عن [illegible] وايامها لانه تعالى قد مثل هاتين المدتين [illegible] وايامها بقوله في الذكر [illegible] [illegible] [illegible] (ايه ٢) وقوله في الانثى [illegible] [illegible] (ايه ٥) وكلما يزيد عن [illegible] وعن ايام [illegible] فحكمه سبعة ايام نقا.

واما السابع فهو الشبهه فيلزم ايام الشبهه. ويكون العدد من يوم حضور الدم وتقيم به اسبوعا وتطهر اذا نقيت في اليوم السابع قبل غيبة الشمس. لان الطهر علامته الصفا ونقا البراه فاذا مالت عن الصفا الى اقل قليل لزم الطما. لان مثله مثل الما الصافي اذا خالطه يسير من الالوان مثل الزعفران وغيره فيتغير لونه بمقدار ما يمازجه من الالوان ويكون قوته وكثرته بمقدار ما يمازجه. وكذلك علامة الطهر اذا مالت الى الغبره والزرقه والخضره والصفره والبلغميه كان علامة طما لان علامة البراه في الطهر الصفا والنقا لا يقادره شي من الاشيا.

فهذه هي الالوان في الشبهه قد بان لك حكمها.

واما حكم المنضجع مع كل امراه يكون عليها حكم من هذه الاقسام المذكوره التي

الامراه] + [illegible] FHG   دم (الساير) FH] < P_1 المده (الساير) FH] < P_1 × S
المعينه O] + فحكمه × DKC_2L ؛ + فحكم $SC_1P_1^2$ ؛ + [illegible] × G ؛ (لا يثبت مكان لفظة فحكمه ومثلها) $NP_3M_2P_2M_1P_1$* [illegible] FHG

٦٣ [illegible]] هنده M_1 ؛ [illegible] G

٦٣-٦٤ وايامها ∩ P_1

٦٣ قد مثل] امثل C_1 ؛ [illegible] FHG

٦٤ [illegible] [$FHP_2LM_1P_1$ بهنده O ؛ [illegible] N ؛ [illegible] $SDC_1P_3M_2$ لقوله × C_1L
في الذكر] < × SC_1 [illegible] G   [illegible]] [illegible]
في] < × P_1 SL

٦٥ [illegible]] [illegible] G   [illegible] (اول)] [illegible] G   وعن $SNC_2P_3M_1O$] او عن $DKC_1M_2P_2LP_1$ ؛ [illegible] G   [illegible] (ثاني)] [illegible] G   [illegible] G

٦٧ واما] + الدم $FHGSCP_2P_1$ فهو] + دم FHGDK   الشبهه (اول)] الاشتباه DK   فيلزم] فلزم P_1 ؛ ويلزم C_1 ايام (الساير) FH] < $NM_2M_1P_1$ ويقيم × K   به $SNP_3P_2M_1O$] < $DKC_1C_2M_2LP_1$

٦٨ اسبوعا] اسبوعان × N   غيبة] غياب S ؛ غيابت C_1 ؛ [illegible] G   علامته] [illegible] × FHG

٦٩ عن] < × S   لزمه P_1 يسير] بشير × C_2

٧٠ فيتغير] فيغير GP_2P_1 ما] < × S

٧١ الغبره] الغيره × SC_1 والزقه والخضره والصفره] [illegible] والاصفر [illegible] G
والزرقه] < H   والصفره والخضره M_1

٧٢ طما (الساير) FH] الطما SC_1L يقادره C_1LO] يغادره × $FHGDKSM_1P_1$ ؛ يفادره (او يغادره) × M_2P_2 ؛ يفادره × NC_2

٧٣ [illegible] G   هي] < N   في (الساير) FH] + دم DKC_2 الشبهه] الاشتباه KC_2 قد] < G

٧٤ حكمها $SP_3M_2M_1P_1O$] احكامها (حكامها × L) $DKNC_1C_2P_2L$ الاقسام] الاحكام * M_1 الذي M_1

توجب احكام الطهاوات ࠔࠊࠁࠕ ࠆࠓࠏ يلزم كلاهما القتل لقوله تعالى ࠅࠀࠉࠔ ࠀࠔࠓ ࠉࠔࠊࠁ ࠀࠕ ࠀࠔࠄ ࠃࠅࠄ ࠅࠂࠋࠄ ࠀࠕ ࠏࠓࠅࠕࠄ ࠀࠕ ࠌࠒࠅࠓࠄ ࠄࠏࠓࠅࠄ ࠅࠄࠉࠀ ࠂࠋࠕࠄ ࠀࠕ ࠌࠒࠅࠓ ࠃࠌࠉࠄ ࠅࠍࠊࠓࠕࠅ ࠔࠍࠉࠄࠌ ࠌࠒࠓࠁ ࠏࠌࠌ (اح ٢٠ : ١٨).

الكلام في ࠄࠆࠅࠁ وبيان اقسامه وتعيين منازل احكام الطهاوات فيه مما يتعلق بالذكور من الناس.

فصل

يعرض للذكور من الناس من جنس ࠄࠆࠅࠁ ما ليس هوا ࠆࠅࠁ مثل ࠒࠓࠉ ࠋࠉࠋࠄ ࠔࠊࠁࠕ ࠆࠓࠏ وما يعرض عند اطلاق البول من قبل ومن بعد مثل اللزوجه ومثل تغير الما شبه المقه وحدة الصابون او مثل الخيط الممتد ومثل ما يلحق بعض الناس من فكر او اثار شهوه او حمو مزاج او عن حركه عنيفه او حمل اثقال او غدا غليظ مثل

---

٧٥ احكام (الساير) [FH احكامها P_2 ؛ > × M_1 ࠔࠊࠁࠕ ࠆࠓࠏ] [Samaritan] G كلاهما] كلامها × L بقوله N تعالى (الساير) [FH > C_1P_2

٧٥-٧٨ [Samaritan] (اقرا [Samaritan]) G

٧٦ [Samaritan] × C_1 [Samaritan] N [Samaritan] × P_1 [Samaritan] > M_2

٧٨ [Samaritan] × S ؛ [Samaritan] × K ؛ [Samaritan] × C_1 [Samaritan] (الساير) [FH + تم N

٧٩ ࠄࠆࠅࠁ] [Samaritan] G ؛ [Samaritan] P_2M_2 اقسامه] اقامة × S تعيين × C_2

٨٠ في الذكور K من الناس ∩ DKC_2

٨٢ يعرض] تعرض P_1 ؛ بغرض × $P_3M_2M_1$ الذكور $P_3M_2M_1P_1$ ࠄࠆࠅࠁ] [Samaritan] G ؛ [Samaritan] P_3M_2 وما × DKC_2 ࠆࠅࠁ] [Samaritan] G

٨٢-٨٣ [Samaritan] G

٨٣ [Samaritan] FHDKP₂ ؛ [Samaritan] × S اطلاق] + [Samaritan] G من قبل (الساير) [FH > × O ومن > × C_1 مثل (الساير) [FH] من N اللزوجه] الزوجه × P_3M_2 ؛ لزوجه $GDKC_2$

٨٤ تغير الما] [Samaritan] FHG تغير] تغيير NP_3 الما شبه] الماشبه × S [Samaritan] G وحدة (وحدث (D)] محده × N او مثل] ومثل $FHSC_2M_2$ ما] [Samaritan] G بعض] > DK × من] > FHG

٨٥ فكره N او (اول)] + من P_3M_2 او .... عنيفه] > ∩ P_3 عن] [Samaritan] G عنيفه] عتيقه × N ؛ [Samaritan] × FHG اثقال] [Samaritan] G ؛ > M_2

† الجلبان † والقلقاس والعدش ولحم البقر والغنم والماعز والالبان والاجبان والاسماك. وكلما يعرض للانسان من جنس [illegible] من جملة هذه الاقسام فهو يجري مجرى [illegible] [illegible] ومثل [illegible] حكمه الحميم بالما والخلاص منه يوم حدوثه.

والذي يلزم فيه العدد سبعة ايام نقا قسمان. وهو ان يكون يحدث رطوبه لازمه يدر من راس القضيب ويكون حضوره من غير سبب من الاسباب المقدم ذكرها وهو المقال فيه [illegible] (اح ١٥ : ٣). والقسم الثاني يبرز من راس القضيب شي غليظ له قوام يتجمد ويصير كالفلس على راس القضيب يختمه وهو المقال فيه [illegible] (هناك). فهذان القسمان متى حضر احدهما لانسان يوم واستدام ثاني يوم يجب العزله منه طول مدة مقامه مع من يراه ويحضر له الى ان ينقا منه. فاذا نقى منه يعد له من ثاني يوم يرى النقا سبعة ايام نقا لا يرى فيها شي منه لا يسير ولا كثير حسب قوله تعالى في فصل [illegible]

---

٨٦ الجلبان] الجلنان × $FSDKNC_1C_2P_3LP_1O$ ؛ الجلنار × M_1 ؛ الحلنا × P_2 ؛ الجنان × M_2 ؛ [illegible] HG × والقلقاس] والقلقاز N والعدس (السابر) FH] > P_1 والغنم] [illegible] G الماعز × DO والاجبان] والاجبات × C_1 والاسماك] والاسمال × C_1

٨٧ مجرى] + ذلك × S [illegible] G

٨٧-٨٨ [illegible] ومثل [illegible]] [illegible] G

٨٨ ومثل] قر × C_1 وحكمه C_1 منه] > P_3P_1 يوم GNP_2LO] في يوم $SDKC_1C_2P_3M_2M_1P_1$

٨٩ فيه] > K قسمان] [illegible] FHG يكون] > GK يدر (السابر) FH] يرد × DKC_2

٩٠ فيها × K

٩١ [illegible]] [illegible] جسمه [illegible] G [illegible] $DKNC_1C_2P_3M_2L^*M_1P_1O$ [illegible] $FHGSP^2L_2$

٩١-٩٢ راس القضيب ∩ G

٩٢ يتجمد] متجمد $SDKC_2L$ ؛ يجمد M_2 ويصيره × M_1 ويختمه SNM_2P_1

٩٢ ٩٣ [illegible] G

٩٣ فهذان] فهذه × NP_1 [illegible] FHG

٩٤ العزله] العزل له × O مقامها × C_1

٩٤-٩٥ منه (اول) .... النقا] > ∩ DKC_2

٩٥ نقى] انقى C_1 يعد] + من × S من ثاني يوم] [illegible] FHG فيها] فيهم GSC_1L منه] منهم × S

٩٦ تعالى (السابر) FH] > S [illegible] ؛ × N [illegible] FH ؛ > P_1

ࠈࠌࠀ ࠄࠅࠀ وتمامه الى قوله ࠓࠓ ࠁࠔࠓࠅ ࠌࠆࠅࠁࠅ ࠀࠅ ࠄࠇࠕࠌ ࠁࠔࠓࠅ ࠌࠆࠅࠁࠅ ࠈࠌࠀ ࠄࠅࠀ (ايه ٣).

ويلزم فى مدة طماه ان يبعد عن مساكن الاطهار الى ظاهر المدينه الى المواضع المنقطعه الذي ليس لا حد فيها تصرف لقوله تعالى ࠅࠉࠔࠋࠇࠅ ࠌࠍ ࠄࠌࠇࠍࠄ ࠊࠋ ࠑࠓࠅࠏ ࠅࠊࠋ ࠆࠁ ࠅࠊࠋ ࠈࠌࠀ ࠋࠍࠐࠔ ࠌࠆࠊࠓ ࠅࠏࠃ ࠍࠒࠁࠄ (تع ٥ : ٢-٣).

ومن دنا بفراشه او بشي من الالات التي يجلس عليه او المكان الذي يكون مقيما فيه او بالحيوان الذي يركب عليه من دنا منه من ساير الاطهار ويطها ويخلص من طماه بالغسل والحميم حسب قوله ࠅࠊࠋ ࠄࠍࠂࠏ ࠁࠊࠋ ࠄࠊࠋࠉ ࠀࠔࠓ ࠉࠔࠊࠁ ࠄࠆࠁ ࠏࠋࠉࠅ ࠉࠈࠌࠀ (انظر ايه ٥، وايات ٤-٦، ٩-١٠).

واذا تفل على موضع طاهر او اله طاهره يجب غسلها وحميمها بالما لقوله تعالى

٩٦-٩٧ [illegible] G

٩٧ الى] + عند K

٩٧-٩٨ [illegible] G

٩٧ ࠓࠓ] ࠓࠁ × C_1

٩٨ ࠌࠆࠅࠁࠅ] ࠀࠕ ࠆࠅࠁࠅ $SNC_2M_2^3$ ࠈࠌࠀ ࠄࠅࠀ] ࠈࠌࠀ ࠄࠉࠀ $DKC_2P_3M_2M_1P_1O$ ؛ ࠈࠌࠀࠕࠅ ࠄࠉࠀ N؛ (L ࠄࠉ) $FHGSC_1P_2L$

٩٩ في .... الى] < × N ويلزمه D طما × SC_1 ان] < G مساكن] مساكره × C_1P_3 ظاهر المدينه] [illegible] G الموضع × C_1

١٠٠ لا حد] لا احد P_1؛ لا × D^*؛ حد لا × C_2 تصرف] تعرف × C_1P_3 تعالى (الساير FH] < C_1

١٠١-١٠٢ [illegible] G

١٠١ [illegible] (O + [illegible] (D [illegible]) [illegible] ([illegible]) × M_1P_1 [illegible] [illegible] ([illegible] C_1L؛ [illegible] NP_3M_2؛ [illegible] P_2) $FHGSDKNC_1C_2P_3M_2P_2LM_1P_1$

١٠٣ ومن دنا] [illegible] G دنا] + ايضا P_3M_2 بفراسه او] < × F وبشي P_1 من] [illegible] × G عليه] عليها $GSKC_1P_2L$ او المكان] والمكان C_1؛ + او $DKNC_2P_3M_2M_1P_1O$

١٠٤ بالحيوان] $SDKNC_1C_2LO$ الحيوان $GP_3M_2P_2M_1P_1$ عليه .... الاطهار] < × F من دنا] [illegible] G ويطها] يطها SC_1P_2L؛ [illegible] G يخلص × DK

١٠٥ والحميم] + بالماء GSC_1P_2L قوله $DNC_2P_3M_2M_1P_1O$] + تعالى $FHGSKC_1P_2L$

١٠٦-١٠٧ [illegible] في اي [illegible] G ࠄࠆࠁ ࠏࠋࠉࠅ] ࠏࠋࠉࠅ ࠄࠆࠁ FHDK

١٠٧ تفل] $FHGDKC_2M_2L$ تقل × M_1؛ ثقل × P_1O؛ نقل × SC_1P_3؛ انتقل × P_2 وحميمها (الساير FH] < M_1P_1 غسلها وحميمها] عليها وحملها × P_2 وحميمها (وحمها GNL؛ او حمها S_1C_1)] < $P_3M_2M_1P_1$ تعالى (الساير FH] < O

ࠅࠊࠉ ࠉࠓࠒ ࠄࠆࠁ ࠁࠈࠄࠅࠓ ࠅࠊࠁࠎ ࠁࠂࠃࠉࠅ ࠅࠓࠇࠑ ࠁࠌࠉࠌ ࠅࠈࠌࠀ ࠏࠃ ࠄࠏࠓࠁ (يه ٨).

فاذا مس الذايب بيده شيا من الالات الطاهره وهي لثقه حكم الطما يغسلها بالما وتطما الى الغروب. واراد تعالى بذكر اليد اللثقه ليفرق بين حكم ࠄࠆࠁ وبين حكم ࠄࠍࠃࠄ لان ࠄࠍࠃࠄ اذا خالطها شيا من الاجسام والالات لزمها سبعة ايام ولما كان ࠄࠆࠁ اخف طما من ࠄࠍࠃࠄ بين تعالى حكم مخالطه وهو الغسل والخلاص بالما من الطما في ذلك اليوم وقت الغروب. اذ لو لم بين ذلك بهذا الفصل لوجب من طريق القياس على ࠄࠍࠃࠄ ان يطما من يخالطها اي عين ࠄࠆࠁ سبعة ايام لانه قال عنها ان صاحبها يعد سبعة ايام نقا ولا يطهر الى ان يكمل له سبعة ايام وهذا هو المراد بذكر ࠄࠆࠁ لان جسمه اذا دنا بشي من الالات الطاهره لزمه الطما من غير لثق.

واذا عرض له في مبدا الامر يوم واحد ونتي منه في ذلك اليوم لا يلزمه عنه عزله ولا

١٠٨-١٠٩ [Samaritan script] G

١٠٨ ࠅࠓࠇࠑ ࠁࠌࠉࠌ] < P_3

١١٠ حكم الطما يغسلها بالما وتطما] [Samaritan script] × FHG الطما] > × C_1 الطما يغسلها] > × N يغسلها $SP_3M_2M_1$] تغسلها P_1؛ بغسلها DKC_1P_2CLO ويطما P_2P_1

١١١ واراد] وازاد × C_1؛ واذا × S؛ + الله K اللثقه] الثقه × O ليفرق] للفرق O؛ [Samaritan script] G؛ ليعرف × DK ࠄࠆࠁ] [Samaritan script] G حكم (ثاني) (الساير) FH] < SC_1 ࠄࠍࠃࠄ] [Samaritan script] G

١١٢ ࠄࠍࠃࠄ] هنده P_3O؛ [Samaritan script] G؛ هذه N؛ هتيك M_2 خالطها O] خالطت (خالطة $SDNP_1$) خالطته $FHGSDKNC_1P_3M_2P_2LM_1P_1$ × C_2

١١٣ مخالطه O] ما يخالطه (الساير) والخلاص بالما $DKNC_2P_3M_2M_1P_1O$] بالما والخلاص $FHGC_1P_2L$ الطما] [Samaritan script] G

١١٤ ذلك اليوم وقت الغروب $DKNC_2P_3M_2M_1P_1O$] غروب ذلك اليوم وقت الغروب S؛ ذلك اليوم P_2؛ [Samaritan script] FHG؛ غروب هذا اليوم C_1L لم] > × S بهذا] بهذه $NP_3M_2P_1$؛ في هذا K لوجب] [Samaritan script] G؛ يوجب S على] عن K

١١٥ ࠄࠍࠃࠄ] هنده NP_3؛ [Samaritan script] G؛ هتيك M_2 يطما] [Samaritan script] G من يخالطها اي عين] من خالط عين (الحاشيه) من يخالطها $GSNP_3M_2LP_1$ من يخالطه C_1P_2؛ من مخالطها × DC_2M_1O؛ مخالطها K اي عين $GSNC_1P_2L$] عين عن × $P_3M_1P_1O$؛ اعني عن × DKC_2؛ عين × M_2 ࠄࠆࠁ] هزب N؛ [Samaritan script] G

١١٦ سبعة ايام] ∩ (الحاشيه) سبعة ايام .... يعد $FGSC_1P_2L$] ان يطما ويعد × $P_3M_2M_1P_1O$؛ ان يطما × DKC_2؛ ان يطما لانه قال عنها ان صاحبها يعد × N نقا ... سبعة ايام $FSDKNC_2P_3M_2LM_1P_1O$] ∩ GC_1P_2 ايام DKC_2SL (الحاشيه)] + نقا $FGNC_1P_3M_2P_2M_1P_1O$ هذا (الحاشيه) المراد] والمرد × C_2 بذكر $SDKC_1M_3P_2C_2M_2LO$] بذكره (الحلشيه)؛ + يد (ايد M_1P_1) × $FHGNP_3M_1P_1$

١١٧ الالات الطاهره (الساير) FH] الاله الطاهره (الحاشيه)؛ الالات N لزمه ... لثق] غير لثق لزمه الطما واذا عرض له ان يلمس شي من الاله الطهاره كذلك لزمه الطما ويطهر ليومه (الحاشيه) يلزمه (الساير) FH] يلزم C_2P_2

يلزمه عزله الا ان يدوم في اليوم الثاني لان دوامه يدل على مرض قد حدث في المثانه فيجب
١٢ مداواته.

واكبر دواه الاعتزال ليتحسر الانسان على نقسه بانقطاعه. ويلزم نفسه الحميه والامتناع من الغديه الداره والانقطاع لله وافتقاد الاحوال. فحينيذ يخلص الانسان وعند خلاصه يعرف قدر النعيم عليه.

والسلام

---

١١٩ يلزمه (السايز) FH] يلزم C_2 العزله D مرض] مرق × C_1 في المثانه] بالمثانه P_3 ؛ [Samaritan script] G

١٢٠ مداواته] مداوتها C_1 ؛ دواها *M_2 ؛ دوائه P_3 ؛ دواء M_2

١٢١ دواه] دواها × C_1 ويلزم نفسه الحميه والامتناع] [Samaritan script] G الحميه والامتناع] الامتناع FH

١٢٢ من الغديه الداره] [Samaritan script] FHG الغديه C_1 الداره] < × N وافتقاد الاحوال] والافتقاد والاحوال × P_1 يخلص] < × C_2

١٢٣ النعمه D

١٢٤ والسلام (السايز) FH] السلام KC_1 ؛ والسلامه C_2

TEXT 2

[كتاب الكافي]

[باب ١١]

باب فيما يعرض من الطموات الجوهريه للرجال والنسا

اما ما يعرض للرجال

فمنه اسم يسمى ࠄࠁ وهو ما يعرض عند اطلاق البول من قبل ومن بعد مثل اللزوجه او شي يماثل حدة الصابون او الصابون او شي يشبه ريال البقر ممتد كالخيط. ومنه قسم يكون يحصل عن اثر مجامعه ومنه ما يحصل عن الحلال من بروده. ومنه ما يعرض عن استعمال مواكيل غليظه موجبه لذلك. ومنه ما يعرض عن داعي شهوه غالبه. وكلما يعرض من هذه الاقسام المذكوره يلزم منه ما يلزم من ࠃࠓࠌ ࠋࠌࠋࠀ ࠀࠔࠀࠉࠁ وهو الحميم بالما والعقله الى الغروب.

١ (حروف عبرانيه) P   باب $PBNS_1DJ$] الباب الحادي عشر $F_2GF_1AL_3L_2S_2CWL_1$ للرجال والنسا (السابر) F_2G] الى الرجال والنسا F_1AW ؛ للنسا وللرجال L_1
٢ للرجال (السابر) F_2G] للرجل A
٣ בשל × L_3 اسم $F_2GF_1AL_3PL_2S_2CWL_1NS_1$] قسم BDJ   مثل (السابر) F_2G] من A ؛ > B   اللزوجه] الزوجه × L_3L_1 ؛ للزوجه × A
٤ حدة] رغوه (غره × F_1) F_1A ؛ > F_2G او الصابون $W^*BS_1^*J$] > $F_2GF_1S_2L_1ND$ ؛ + نفسه $AL_3PL_2W^2S_1^3$ ريال $PS_2L_2L_1N_1S_1$] ريالة F_1AL_3CWB ؛ (ريال او ريالة) F_2G ؛ غيال × DJ   الممتد B   كالخيط DJ] كالخيوط (بالخيوط L_3) (السابر) F_2G
٥ يكون] > J   يحصل] > × D^* ؛ يعرض D^2 الحلال D] الخلال × F_2GF_1PAJ ؛ انحلال × $L_3L_2S_2CWBL_1NS_1$
٦ مواكيل] ماكل S_2 ؛ طعام F_1 موجبه لذلك] > F_2GS_2 وغالبه × D
٧ المذكوره] + المتقدمه D   يلزم (اول)] ويلزم L_1 ࠀࠔࠀࠉࠁ L_3CBDJ] ࠀࠔࠀࠉࠌࠁ $PL_2L_1NS_1$ ؛ ࠀࠔࠀࠉࠁ ࠄࠓࠃ F_1A ؛ ࠀࠔࠉࠁࠍ ࠄࠓࠃ W ؛ > P_2GS_2
١٦-٧ ࠀࠔࠀࠉࠌࠁ] ∩ F_1
٨ والعقله الى الغروب] > A

فصل

قال الشيخ. اذا عرض لانسان افتراق او احتراق في راس القضيب عند اطلاق البول فان كان اعتبر عند اطلاقه ولم يجد عارض يوجب ذلك فلا يلزمه نجس وكذلك عند انتهى البول لا يلزمه نجس الا ان يكون سبب اخر من الاقسام المتقدمه اذ الاحتراق والافتراق قد يعرض احدهما عن عجله او عن حبس تقدم. وانما اذا عرض لزوجه قبل او بعد او امتداد ذلك هو الموجب للطما. وان تبع البول نقط ولا يكون فيه احد علايم الطما لا يلزمه الطما. وانما يلزم منه ان يحرم فيما يقع عليه من القماش اذا فرض الصلاوه.

واما [Samaritan] [Samaritan] [Samaritan] فانهما في الطما منزله واحده ويلزمهما [Samaritan].

فصل فيما هو غليظ الحكم ويلزم منه العدد ويجب فيه النقا سبعة ايام

وهو رطوبه لزجه مستمره عند اطلاق البول في كل دفعه ويبقى منه بقيه من رطوبه ويبس ويبقى منه قشر رقيق فيوجب ختم راس القضيب فيعسر البول في المره الثانيه. فيلزم صاحبه الاعتزال مدة وجود ذلك. وهذا اسمه ࠄࠇࠕࠉࠌ ࠁࠔࠓࠅ (اح ١٥ : ٣) وعكسه عقيب اطلاق البول وهو المسمى ࠓࠓ ࠁࠔࠓࠅ (هناك). فمن حيث يعرض ذلك على

---

١٠ الى انسان L_2S_2 او احتراق (الساير) F_2G] واحتراق AL_1 عند (الساير) F_2G] عن L_2S_2

١١ فان كان اعتبر] فاعتبر A عند] عن × P يجد] يوجد S_2J يوجب] يجب J فلا] لا J يلزمه] يلزم A ؛ يلزم له P

١١-١٢ نجس] ∩ L_3

١٢ انتهى] + اطلاق F_1ACW اذ] او × B

١٣ تعرض × J [Samaritan] × N_1 عن (اول) D] على J ؛ من (الساير) او بعد (الساير) F_2G] وبعد J او امتداد (الساير) F_2G] وامتداد D

١٣-١٤ بعد .... احد] < × L_3

١٤ هو] هي S_2N_1 الطما J نقط (الساير) F_2G] نقطه J يكون] < S_2 الطما (ثاني) DJ] طما (الساير)

١٥ يلزم منه ان يحرم] يحرم عليه J يلزم] يلزمه L_1 يقع (الساير) F_2G] [Samaritan] L_3 عليه] < × الصلاوه DJ] الصلاه (الساير) J

١٦ [Samaritan] CBJ] [Samaritan] PL_1NS_1D ؛ [Samaritan] × S_2 ؛ [Samaritan] L_2 ؛ [Samaritan] [Samaritan] W ؛ [Samaritan] [Samaritan] وهو الحميم بالما × A منهما D] منها × (الساير)

١٧ [Samaritan] AW

١٨ فيه النقا] فيه J ؛ النقا فيه A

١٩ [Samaritan] × C لزجه] + ولزوجه D ؛ + لزوجه × L_2

٢٠ ويبس] وليس × B منه DJ] منها (الساير)؛ عنها A ختم] < × J فيعسر] [Samaritan] × L_3

٢١ صاحبه الاعتزال] < × L_1 الاعتزال S_1DJ] الانعزال (الاعزال × P) (الساير)

٢٢ عقيب] < × DJ

الرجل يجب عليه العزل والانقطاع عن مواضع الاطهار حسب قوله [Samaritan] وتمامه في اجناس الطموات.

ومن دنا به او بشي من الاته او كسواته او فراشها لزمه الغسل والصبوغ منه حسب قوله [Samaritan] (انظر اح ١٥ : ٥ وايضا ايات ٤-٦).

وان تفل [Samaritan] على موضع طاهر او اله طاهره تطما حسب قوله [Samaritan] (ايه ٨). والبا في [Samaritan] يفيد اعني على الطاهر من كل اله ويتلثق منه. اله جديده من ملبوس او ملبوس ينجس ويجب ان يطهر بالما على الوجه المامور به المعتمد عليه المنقول شرعا.

مساله

فان قيل ما الفايده في قوله [Samaritan] وتمامه (ايه ١١). فالجواب هذا عايد الى العضو الذي يبرز منه ما يوجب النجاسه. وايضا ان [Samaritan] اذا لمس [Samaritan] (ايات ١ – ٢) الذي

---

٢٣ عليه] < × J العزله F_1A عن] من P موضع J الاطهار] الطهاره F_2GF_1 قوله] + تعالى $F_2GF_1AL_2S_2W$ $[L_3PCBL_1NS_1DJ$

٢٤ [Samaritan] DJ] + [Samaritan] (الساير) F_2G

٢٥ ومن .... الغسل] < × L_3 الاته او كسواته (كسوته A) او فراشه (الساير) F_2G] من الاثياب او الفراش F_1 والصبوغ] < F_2

٢٦ (حروف عربيه) D [Samaritan] F_2

٢٨ تفل] نقل × ABL_1S_1*؛ نفل × F_1 [Samaritan] الذاب] J على موضع طاهر او اله طاهره] < × L_2S_2 او] + على A [Samaritan] × F_1PCB قوله] + تعالى S_2W [Samaritan] F_2AL_1

٢٩ [Samaritan] B

٣٠ والبا في [Samaritan]] والبا في [Samaritan] F_2G؛ والباقي [Samaritan] × C_1؛ $AL_3L_2S_2PCWBNL_1S_1$ × [Samaritan]؛ والباقي [Samaritan] (طهور D) × DJ يفيد] [Samaritan] × F_1C؛ < × A؛ + على × D

٣٠-٣١ ويتلثق .... ملبوس (ثاني)] [Samaritan] (= من نحاس وحديد وملبوس) × F_2G

٣٠ ويتلثق] ويلتثق L_3C؛ يلثق A؛ يثق × F_1؛ ويتعلق × D منه BL_1S_1*DJ] به $F_1L_3W^2NS_1^2$؛ باي × W*PL_2S_2

٣١ او ملبوس $L_2PWL_1S_1DJ$] < × $F_1AL_3S_2CBN$ ينجس DJ] تنجس $L_3PL_2CWBL_1NS_1$؛ نجس × F_1A؛ < × F_2GS_2 ويجب ان (الساير) F_2G] ويطهر ان F_1؛ يطاهر $S_2L_2L_1NS_1$ يطهر] يتطهر P

٣٤-٣٥ (حروف عربيه) D [Samaritan] × L_2

٣٥ فتمامه L_2 فالجواب DJ] الجواب (الساير) يبرز منه ما يوجب] تبرز منه J

٣٦ ان] + من × S_2L_2 [Samaritan] (هطا D) DJ] يطا ([Samaritan] APS_2L_2B) × (الساير) F_2G الذي DJ] او الذي (والذي × P) × (الساير) F_2G

يخرج منه ما يوجب الطما فاي شي لمسه من جميع الاشيا قبل شطف يده بالما يلزمه النجس. وهذا هو الفرق بينه وبين من عليه حكم [illegible] ويحصل من ذلك ايضا معرفة الفرق بينه وبين ࠄࠍࠃࠄ اذ الخلاص لمن لمسه هذا يكون بالحميم والغروب والخلاص لمن لمسه ࠄࠍࠃࠄ لا يكون الا بعد سبعة ايام.

وكل صاحب مرض من هولاى يلزمه الافتراد والانقطاع والطلب بالخلاص ليحل مما قد صار اليه.

فصل فيما يعرض من الطموات الجوهريه للنسا

وهي سبعة اقسام.

اولها ࠄࠍࠃࠄ وهي اول شي يعرض للمراه وهو الذي يلزمها منه سبعة ايام لا مما يتبعه.

قال الشيخ

ان اقسام الدما سبعه.

فاولها ࠄࠍࠃࠄ دليل ذلك قوله تعالى ࠅࠀࠌ ࠔࠊࠁ ࠉࠔࠊࠁ ࠀࠉࠔ ࠀࠕࠄ ࠅࠕࠄࠉ ࠍࠃࠕࠄ ࠏࠋࠉࠅ ࠅࠈࠌࠀ ࠔࠁࠏࠕ ࠉࠌࠉࠌ (اح ١٥ : ٢٤) اذ الرجل لم يجامع المراه الا وهي طاهره وذلك ان مجامعة الامراه وعليها حكم

---

٣٧ ما DJ] مما × (الساير) F_2G ؛ من × A فاي DJ] × واي (الساير)؛ باي × F_1 شطف (الساير) F_2G] غسل A بالما (الساير) F_2G] > A يلزمه النجس (الساير) F_2G] يلزم النجس منه F_1AL_3C

٣٨ حكم] > × B قري ليله D وتحصل D ايضا من ذلك F_2GW ايضا (الساير) F_2G] > J هنده D

٣٩ لمسه] لمس $F_2GS_2L_2L_1$ بالحميم] بالحكم × B والغروب BL_1S_1*DJ] والعقله للغروب × (الساير) لمسه] لمس P

٤٠ لا يكون] + له خلاص × A بعد] > × W*L_1

٤١ من .... ليحل] يخلص × A الافتراد] الافتراق L_1 بالخلاص JD] باخلاص (الساير) ليحل J] ليخلص (الساير) يلزمه] يلزم P وهي] وهو $S_2L_2NS_1$ اقسام] انواع P

٤٤-٤٥ سبعة] ∩ L_1 ،

٤٥ وهي] وهو P يلزمها $F_2PS_2BNS_1DJ$] يلزمه GL_2WL_1 ؛ يلزم F_1AL_3C منه (الساير) F_2G] > W ؛ + الاجتناب F_1

٤٨ ان] من × A الدم $F_2GF_1S_2$ سبعه $F_2GWBL_1S_1$*DJ] + منازل $F_1AL_3PS_2L_2CNS_1^2$

٤٩ اولها F_2GAL_3C ࠄࠍࠃࠄ DJ] هو ࠄࠍࠃࠄ (الساير)

٥١ ان] > F_1A عليها L_3C

عقلة النجاسه قد حرمه الله تعالى على اسراييل بقوله ࠅࠀࠉࠔ ࠀࠔࠓ ࠉࠔࠊࠁ ࠀࠕ ࠀࠔࠄ ࠃࠅࠄ ࠅࠂࠋࠄ وتمامه الى قوله ࠅࠍࠊࠓࠕࠅ ࠔࠍࠉࠄࠌ (اح ٢٠ : ١٨). فلم يقربها الا وهي طاهره وانما كانت في اواخر مسافة الطهر فيعرض وقت المجامعه حصول الطمث. فسماه الله تعالى ࠍࠃࠄ وقال فيه ما تقدم وهو ࠅࠕࠄࠉࠄ ࠍࠃࠕࠄ ࠈࠌࠀࠄ.

القسم الثاني من اقسام الدما ࠃࠌ ࠃࠅࠄ وهو الذي يجي بعد ࠄࠍࠃࠄ ثم يستمر مدة الاسبوع. والقياس على ان في النسا من تراه وفيهن من لا تراه وايضا فيهن من ينقطع عنها في النهار بعينه وفيهن من يستمر ثاني يوم وثالث يوم والى انتهى الاسبوع. وفيهن من يفاودها فيستمر الى غد الاسبوع فتلتزم به القيام في حكم الطما اسبوعا ثانيا. ثم يروح عليها من اصل المسافه الذي عرفتها لنفسها.

القسم الثالث ࠃࠌ ࠆࠁࠄ وهو الذي يحصل فيه تعكيس الامراه بعد الاسبوعين. ومدة وجوده تهمل العدد وحكم الخلاص منه ان يفاردها ويعدم ثم تعد منه نقا سبعة ايام. وهو الذي ورد فيه قوله تعالى ࠁࠋࠀ ࠏࠕ ࠍࠃࠕࠄ ووصفه ࠃࠌࠄ ࠉࠌࠉࠌ ࠓࠁࠉࠌ

---

٥٢ قد] ࠒࠃ × N   تعالى] > NS1*   على (الساير) G] + ال F2F1AL3W   لقوله A
[ࠅࠀࠉࠔ] ࠅࠀࠔࠓ × S2

٥٣ ࠄࠅࠄࠄ F2F1   فتمامه L2   قوله] + تعالى A

٥٢ ٥٣ (حروف عربته) D

٥٣ [ࠔࠋࠇࠄ] + ࠔࠌࠃ ࠁࠀࠓࠌ J

٥٤ انما F1L1   كانت] اذا كانت F1AL3CW   اواخر] اخر L1   الطمث (ࠄࠈࠌࠀࠄ N ؛ الطاة B)
[F2GPS2L2L1NS1DJ الطما F1AL3WCB   فسماه] فسما × A

٥٥ الله [PS2S1²DJ > (الساير)   نده D   فقال A   وهو [S2L2BL1NS1DJ وهي
F2GF1AL3CW ࠅࠕࠄࠉࠄ L2

٥٦ القسم الثاني DJ] المنزله الثانيه (الساير)   الدما (الساير) F2G] الطما F1ACW   ࠃࠌ ࠃࠅࠄ] دم دوه D ؛
دم ࠃࠅࠄ PL2 ؛ ࠃࠅࠄ BS1*   بعد] + ࠃࠌ F2GA

٥٧ والقياس] والنفاس × L1S1*   على] + ذلك F2GL2S2

٥٧-٥٨ من ... وفيهن] > ∩ A

٥٧ وفيهن] فيهن B

٥٨ وفيهن] ∩ W*BL1S1*   يستمر DJ] + الى (الساير)   والى DJ] الى (الساير)

٥٩ يفاودها DJ] يفادرها × F1P2L1 ؛ يفاردها × F2GA ؛ يغادرها × L3S2WCBNS1   ويستمر NJ   غد]
غدا L1 ؛ عند × F1A   فيلزم D] فتلزم J ؛ فتلزم PL2S2BL1NS1 ؛ فيلزمها L3WC ؛ يلزمها F1A
القيام D] ؛ المقام (الساير)   حكم (الساير) F2G] > J   واسبوعا B   يروح] يزول F1 ؛ تمر A

٦٠ اصل] > F1A   التي J   عرفتها F1ADJ] قد عرفتها L3PS2L2CWBL1NS1   لنفسها] الى نفسها
× A ؛ + اسبوعا B

٦١ القسم الثالث DJ] المنزله الثالثه (الساير)   دمّ زبّه D   يحصل (الساير) F2G] > J   فيه] في ×
B   الاسبوعين] ࠄࠔࠁࠏࠅࠕ F2G

٦٢ تهمل] فهما × J   العدد] العده L3   منه نقا] من نقاه L2L1 ؛ ࠔࠋ ࠍࠒࠉࠌ × N

٦٣ الذي] + قد A   بلا عت ندته D   بيميم ربيم D

(ايه ٢٥). فكل يوم ليس لها فيه عدد هو [Samaritan] موجود لها وانما سماه تعالى [Samaritan] من حيث ان [Samaritan] المخصوص بصفته سريع الانقطاع ولزوم الاسبوع منه لسرعة زواله فان استمر فلا يكون [Samaritan] بل يبقى [Samaritan] بخلاف [Samaritan] الذي يحصل منه من عارضه لوقته وليس يحصل منه عقله الا الى الغروب.

القسم الرابع هو [Samaritan] وهو ينقسم قسمان ولها حكمان. احدهما الوارد مع ولادة الذكر والاخر مع الانثى. وحكمه في الذكر سبعة ايام وفي الانثى تتضاعف المده. وسبب تضاعفه غلظ الدم وكدورته وكثرته عن دم الذكر. وصفته وقياسه كثوب غمس في خابية الصباغ ولم يحصل الغرض منه في لونه الا بعودة غمسه في الخابيه فيتضاعف في اللون. والاجره من وجه اخر ان الانثى محل التكليف في ذلك واحكامه.

القسم السادس وهو المسمى [Samaritan] وهو الذي قد يكون علايم النسا في نفاسهن. اما في الذكر فاذا حضر في الثالث والثلاثين كان لها كالامان على الصبوغ في وقته من غير تعكيس وكذلك في الانثى في السادس والستين فان ورد قبل ذلك وكان ايراده صحيح وان ورد بعده فكان خلاف المراد.

وان كان فيهن من لا تراه كره كما في [Samaritan] فيجيها اولا ثم ينقطع عنها لوقته فلا ترى غيره بل تستمر خالصه نقيه.

٦٤ فكل] وكل P ليس] > J × لها (اول) (الساير) F_2G] > A نده D لها (ثاني) (الساير) F_2G] > L_1 وانما سماه] واسماه J زب D
٦٥ هنده D بسرعته F_1AL_3 زواله] انقطاعه وزواله F_1AL_3C
٦٦ نده D زبه D [Samaritan] (هدوه) D) $F_2GF_1AL_3L_2S_2C^2DJ$] [Samaritan] $WC^*BL_1NS_1$ يحصل DJ] يخلص (الساير) منه] + نجس D
٦٧ الا] > × P
٦٨ القسم الرابع DJ] المنزله الرابعه (الساير) هو WJ] وهو (الساير) [Samaritan] (دمٓ D) F_1APS_2BDJ] دم L_2WCL_1 مع ولادة] عن ولاده مع ولادة L_3A
٦٩ والاخر] والثاني S_2 مع] + ولادة S_2 الانثى] ∩ AL_3CN تتضاعف] تضاعف S_2 ؛ لتضاعف A
٧٠ تضاعفه] يتضاعف L_1 ؛ تضاعفها CB ؛ تضاعف المده F_1 غلظ الدم وكدورته وكثرته (الساير) F_2G] كثره الدم وكدورته J
٧١ الصباغ .... الخابيه] > ∩ F_2G ولم DJ] فلم (الساير) فيتضاعف] فتتضاعف × L_1 ؛ فتضاعف × B
٧٢ من L_1] ومن × (الساير) ان] > B
٧٣ القسم السادس DJ] المنزله الخامسه × (الساير) F_2G
٧٤ والثلاثين] وثلاثين AS_1D ؛ والثاني × F_2GL_2 الصبوغ] الطهور (الطهر F_1) والصبوغ F_2GF_1A
٧٥ تعكيس APL_2DJ] تعكس (الساير) في (اول)] > P الانثى] الثاني × F_2GL_2 والستين] وستين B فان] كان × L_2S_2 وكان DJ] فكان $APL_2S_2BL_1NS_1$ ؛ كان F_1L_3CW
٧٦ فكان] كان F_1W خلاف] ورد خلاف D
٧٧ لا تراه] الاتراه × L_1 كره] مره $L_3S_2L_2N$ فتجيها D ثم ينقطع] فينقطع F_1
٧٨ ترى] يرى A

القسم السابع وهو دم الاشتباه. وهو تغير يحصل فى اللون اما الى الغبره او الى الزرقه او الى الصفره فيحصل منه الاشتباه ويجب اهمال الامراه مدة وجوده اذ الطهر لا يكون الا مع وجود الصفا وما كان غير صافي فهو غير طاهر. ومثاله الما الصافي الذي ان خالطه شي بان به عرضه.

فصل في احكام لمس اعيان الطموات

فمن لمس عين ࠄࠍࠃࠄ يلزمه الطما ࠔࠁࠏࠕ ࠉࠌࠉࠌ (١٥ : ٢٤). ومن لمس عين ࠄࠆࠁࠄ فيحصل لوقته. الدليل على ذلك ان الامراه الذي عادتها ان تطهر لسبعة ايام اذا فارقت الدم الذي هو ࠄࠆࠁ قبل غياب الشمس باقل قليل طهرت وخالطت الاطهار وخلصت. من لمس عين ࠄࠆࠁࠄ فلا يلزمه اسبوعا.

وكل واحد من الانواع المذكوره مما ذكر له مده فيلزم من لمس عينه عدد كالمده اللازمه لصاحبه.

ويحرم فيه وقوع المجامعه في كل واحد من هذه الاقسام لغلظ الحكم.

---

٧٩ القسم السابع [DJ المنزله السادسه × (السابر) F₂G ࠔࠆ PS₂ تغير [S₂DJ تغيير (السابر) الغبره] الغيره × F₁ ؛ العرره × L₁ او (اول) [DJ واما (السابر)

٧٩–٨٠ او الى] والى L₁

٨٠ اذ الطهر [L₃PBNS₁ اذا الطهر × F₁AS₂L₂WCL₁ ؛ اذا تطهر × DJ

٨١ الصفا وما كان غير] > ∩ N ان] اذا B ؛ > L₁S₁* خالطه [PL₂DJ خالطته (السابر)

٨٢ غرضه × BL₃

٨٣ فصل [DJ المنزله السابعه × (السابر) F₂G احكام] > D* اعيان [DJ > (السابر) F₂G

٨٤ هنده D ࠔࠁࠏࠕ ࠉࠌࠉࠌ (شبعت يميم D) [S₂L₂NS₁DJ سبعة ايام F₁AL₃WCBL₁

٨٥ ࠄࠆࠁࠄ (هدّوة D) [F₂GF₁AL₃S₂L₂²BL₁DJ ࠄࠃࠁࠄ WCNS₁ ؛ ࠄࠁࠍࠄ × L₂* فيحصل [D* فيخلص × (السابر) F₂G تطهر] يطهر × D لسبعة] بسبعة L₂ ؛ السبعة × L₁

٨٦ ࠄࠆࠁ [F₂GF₁L₃S₂BL₁J ࠄࠃࠁ WCN₁S₁ ؛ ࠆࠁ ࠄࠆࠁ A ؛ تدّة × D غياب] غيبة D

٨٧ من [L₂DJ ومن (السابر) F₂G ࠄࠆࠁࠄ [J ࠄࠃࠌࠄ (هزبه D) × (السابر) F₂G

٨٨ مما] ما × J ؛ فما × F₁AB له] > A عينه] عين عينه × L₂*L₁ عدد] عده S₂ اللازم × D

٩٠ واحده AL₂ الحكم] + والله اعلم WC ؛ + والله اعلم بكل شي A ؛ + والله اعلم بالحق والحكم B

[كتاب الكافي]

[فصل من الباب الثالث]

فصل

الطهاره بالما من انواع [Samaritan]

وهو قسمان قسم من ذات الانسان متعلق به وقسم لدنوه بغيره. فاما القسم المتعلق به فهو مثل الطما الذي هو جوهري الذات. واما الدنو بغيره فهو مثل [Samaritan] [Samaritan] [Samaritan] [Samaritan] وما شابه ذلك وما قيس على كل صفه بصفتها.

فصل منازل الطهاره

وهي ثلاث اقسام [Samaritan] [Samaritan] [Samaritan] فمن منازل الطما ما يلزم صاحبه الثلاثه ومنه ما يلزم قسمان منها ومنه ما يلزم قسم واحد. وهو صاحب [Samaritan] [Samaritan] [Samaritan] يلزمه فرض [Samaritan] فقط لكل واحد منها. دليل ذلك قوله تعالى في [Samaritan] [Samaritan] [Samaritan] [Samaritan] [Samaritan] [Samaritan] [Samaritan] [Samaritan] [Samaritan] [Samaritan] [Samaritan] [Samaritan] الى قوله [Samaritan] [Samaritan] [Samaritan] [Samaritan] [Samaritan]

---

٢ الطهر J بالما] من الما J [Samaritan]] الطموات W ؛ الطميات F_1 ؛ النجاسات A

٣ لدنوه بغيره] الدنوه (الدنو A) بغيره × F_1A ؛ لدنوه بغير × L_3C بغيره] من غيره S_2

٤ [Samaritan] × F_1A التي F_1A جوهري] جوهي × L_3C الذات] الدان × W بغيره] × يفيده × F_1 [Samaritan] (الساير) F_2G] [Samaritan] F_1AC

٤–٥ [Samaritan] [Samaritan]] [Samaritan] [Samaritan] F_2GA

٥ [Samaritan] (الساير) F_2G] [Samaritan] W ؛ [Samaritan] × F_1 كل] < × A

٧ ثلاث WL_1J] ثلاثه (او ثلاثة) (الساير) اقسام (الساير) F_2G] اسامي L_3CN [Samaritan] [Samaritan] (الساير) F_2G] [Samaritan] [Samaritan] L_3C [Samaritan] × A

٨ ومنه] ومنها F_1L_3C يلزم] يلزمه F_1AL_3C منها] < P ومنه] ومنها L_3CJ ما] < × A يلزم $F_1APS_2L_2WBL_1{}^*J$] يلزمه $L_3CL_1^2NS_1$ واحد] منها A

٩ [Samaritan] $PS_2L_2L_1S_1$] [Samaritan] W ؛ [Samaritan] [Samaritan] $F_2GF_1AL_3C$ ؛ [Samaritan] [Samaritan] BN ؛ [Samaritan] J يلزمه] يلزم F_1 ؛ ويلزم منه A [Samaritan] ([Samaritan] L_1) $PS_2L_2L_1S_1J$] [Samaritan] L_3WCBN ذلك] < × L_2

١٠ في [Samaritan] [Samaritan]] < P* [Samaritan]] + واما × L_1

١١ قوله $PS_2L_2WS_1J$] + تعالى F_2GL_1 ؛ + [Samaritan] [Samaritan] [Samaritan] [Samaritan] [Samaritan] F_1AL_3CBN [Samaritan] × L_2

[Samaritan] (تث ٢٣ : ١١–١٢). واما [Samaritan] قال فيه الباري تعالى [Samaritan] (اح ١٥ : ١٢). هذا الذي يلزم فيه حكم [Samaritan].

وينضاف اليه سنن متعمله لم يذكرها الشرع الشريف صرحا لكنه اشار الى بعضها بما يذكر في مكانه. فمن ذلك انه اذا اطلق البول الرقيق وعرض له افتراق عند مبدا اطلاقه فان كان تقدم له افتقاد راس القضيب ولم يرى فيه قبل اطلاقه ما اوجب ذلك فيجب ان يفتقده عند انفصال اطلاق البول فان وجد لزوجه او شي يمتد مثل لعاب البقر فلزمه يتطهر [Samaritan] فقط. وان لم يجد لا اولا ولا اخرا مع وجود الافتراق فلا يلزمه اثبات حكم العرض عليه لان الافتراق يحصل كثيرا من تزاحم الما في خروجه وكذلك الاحتراق لا يلزم منه التطهير الا مع وجود علامه مما ذكر.

قال

فان كان صاحب [Samaritan] المسماه جنابه ومعنى هذا الاسم انه اذا عرضت يتجنب صاحبها مخالطة الاطهار.

---

١٢ [Samaritan] [$S_2L_2WBL_1S_1$ [Samaritan] $F_2GF_1AL_3PCNJ$ واما] + قوله عن [Samaritan] F_2GA ؛ [Samaritan] CN ؛ $F_2GF_1L_3$ وقال L_1

١٢-١٣ فيه الباري تعالى J] الله فيه $L_3PS_2L_2BNS_1$ ؛ الله فيها WC ؛ الله عنه F_1 ؛ فيه A

١٣ [Samaritan] F_1AL_3C

١٤ يلزم] يلزمه L_1 ؛ > A   حكم J] > (الساير)   [Samaritan]] الرحيصه L_1 ؛ [Samaritan] AW ؛ [Samaritan] F_2G

١٥ ويضاف A   سنن] سنين × L_2 متعمله J] مفعوله $GAPS_2L_2WBL_1NS_1$ ؛ مفعوله له × L_3C ؛ معقوله × F_1 الشريف J] > (الساير) F_2G صرحا J] صراحا $L_3PCWL_1NS_1$ ؛ صريحا F_1AB

١٦ اطلق] اعرض F_1 الرقيق $F_2GPS_2L_2WL_1$] الزقيق × J ؛ العقيق × L_3CBNS_1 وعرض] يعرض × J   مبدا] ابتدا $CBNS_1$

١٧ ولم] لم A ؛ وله × F_1 اوجب] وجب × L_1

١٨ يفتقده J] يفتقد (الساير)   اطلاق البول J] الاطلاق $F_2GL_3PS_2L_2CBL_1NS_1$ ؛ البول F_1AW^2 ؛ > × W*   فان وجد] [Samaritan] × N   فان] فاذا L_3C فلزمه $PS_2L_2WBL_1NS_1J$] فيلزمه $F_1L_3^2C$ ؛ [Samaritan] L_3* ؛ لزمه A   يتطهر $PS_2L_2WL_1S_1J$] يطهر ABN ؛ التطهر F_1C ؛ [Samaritan] L_3

١٩ [Samaritan]] [Samaritan] F_2G ؛ [Samaritan] C ؛ [Samaritan] A ؛ [Samaritan] × F_1 يجد (الساير) F_2G] + له BN ؛ يوجد له L_3C لا اوله ولا اخر L_1 يلزمه] يلزم L_2

٢٠ العرض $PS_2L_2WL_1S_1J$] الغرض × L_3C ؛ الفرض × F_1ABN يحصل .... الاحتراق] > ∩ J   تحصل × S_2L_2 تزحم B   الاحتراق] الافتراق A

٢١ التطهر B

٢٣ عرضت $F_1PS_2L_1NS_1J$] عرضته L_3L_2WCB ؛ عرضه × A

٢٤ يتجنب] بتجنب × F_1 ؛ تجنب × L_3C مخالطة] مخالطته (مخالتطه × B) CB

قال

فان لمس احد فينجس منه وان لمس اللامس اقواما ينجسوا منه الى انفصال الثالث والرابع اذا لمسه الثالث لم يلزم الرابع منه ملزم.

قال

وذلك لان الطها قسمان كما قلنا جوهري وغير جوهري فالجوهري لو لمس ما لمس لزمه النجس وانما قلنا ان انفصاله من الثالث بعدم الجوهريه فيه لا يلزم التسلسل. فان قال قايلا ان الثاني كالثالث لم لا وقع الانفصال الا من الثالث الجواب ان الثالث اصل في انفصال امور من حال الى حال شرعا ونقلا سنه وحكم. من ذلك انه لما خلق الله الدنيا مستبحره ذكر الاستبحار وذكر الثالث بانفصاله عن الصفه الاولى. ولما ذكر ࠅࠋࠓࠒࠉࠏ † بالانواع الاصلي † كملت له الاضاة في الثالث وانفصال الظلام الاعظم. وعلى ذلك قاسو الناس اعتمادات اعتمدوها كما اعتمد ࠔࠌࠏࠅࠍ ࠅࠋࠅࠉ في ࠔࠊࠌ لما قال ࠅࠉࠄࠉ ࠁࠉࠅࠌ ࠄࠔࠋࠉࠔࠉ ࠁࠄࠉࠅࠕࠌ ࠊࠀࠁࠉࠌ (تك ٣٤ : ٢٥). ومثله ذكر الثالث في قصة فرعون ࠅࠉࠄࠉ ࠁࠉࠅࠌ ࠄࠔࠋࠉࠔࠉ ࠉࠅࠌ ࠄࠅࠋࠃࠕ ࠀࠕ ࠐࠓࠏࠄ (تك ٤٠ : ٢٠). وامثال ذلك كثير.

---

٢٦ اللامس] > × F_1 — يتنجسوا A — الثالث] ࠕࠅࠋࠕࠋࠅࠕ × N

٢٧ لم] لا F_1AL_3CBN — ملزم $[PS_2L_2W^*NS_1J$ ما لزم الثالث F_1AL_3C ؛ ما يلزم × B ؛ ملزم الثالث W^2

٢٨ وقال F_1L_3C

٢٩ الطها] ࠋࠈࠌࠅ × F_1

٢٩-٣٠ قلنا] ∩ L_2

٢٩ وغير جوهري] > × L_1 — لمس (اول)] + قدر A — لمس لزمه النجس] لزم لمسه نجسه × W ؛ يلمس نجسه × A — لزمه] ما لزم منه × F_1

٣٠ النجاسه F_1 — بعدم] بعدهم × L_3^2C ؛ ࠁࠏࠃࠌ × L_3^* ؛ بعد × A — الجوهريه] الجوهري × F_1A — لا] ما F_1 — فان $[F_1APS_2L_2WL_1S_1J$ وان L_3CBN

٣١ لم لا $[P^2S_2L_2L_1S_1J$ كما × F_1 ؛ لا × W ؛ لم × GAL_3P^*CNB — وقع] اوقع × L_3C ؛ نوقع × A — في] من × B

٣٢ من حال] منحال × WL_1 — ونقلا J] وعقلا (السابر) F_2G — ولما] + ان W — ࠅࠋࠓࠒࠉࠏ $[L_3P^*CJ$ ࠅࠋࠅࠓࠒࠉࠏ $S_2L_2L_1NS_1$ ؛ ࠋࠓࠒࠉࠏ × A ؛ ࠅࠋࠒࠓࠉࠏ × F_1 ؛ الارقي × B ؛ ࠅࠋࠄࠓࠒࠉࠏ P^2 ؛ ࠄࠓࠒࠉࠏ W

٣٤ بالانواع الاصلي] بالأنواع الاصله × J ؛ بلا انواع للاضات × NS_1 ؛ بلا انوار (بلانوار × L_2) للاضاة × $F_1L_3PS_2L_2CWBL_1$ ؛ بلا انذار للاضاة × A — كملت له] كلب × F_1 — الظلم L_2

٣٥ الناس] > F_1AL_3C — سمعان ولاوي F_1L_3C

٣٦ ࠊࠀࠁࠉࠌ $[F_1AS_2^*L_2CL_1NS_1$ ࠊࠀࠅࠁࠉࠌ ؛ P ࠊࠅࠀࠁࠉࠌ ؛ J ࠊࠅࠁࠉࠌ GS_2^2WB — ومثله] ومثال × A ؛ وما له × F_1 — ثالث × F_1

فصل

المنزله الثانيه وهي [Samaritan] اذا عرض لصاحب [Samaritan] [Samaritan] شي اتصل باقمشتهما من نجاستها لزمه [Samaritan] [Samaritan] كذلك ما الزم به المتطهر من [Samaritan] [Samaritan] [Samaritan].

واما [Samaritan] [Samaritan] وهو المسما ناطر فيلزمه الاقسام الثلاثه. وكذلك [Samaritan] واتباعه. ويذكر في باب الطهاوات على مراتبها.

[كتاب الكافي]

[فصل من الباب الثالث عشر]

قال الشيخ

اذا عرض على مولود عارض من ذاته او من خارج ولم يمكن غسله وتطهيره قبل الختانه فهل يلزم القادم عليه ليختنه عدد اسبوعا ام لا.

الجواب

قيل في ذلك وجهين.

احدهما انه لا يلزمه عدد اسبوعا. دليل ذلك ما يعتمدوه في بعض البلاد من ختن

---

٤١ [Samaritan] [Samaritan] $F_2GF_1L_3$ ؛ [Samaritan] J باقمشتها $[F_2GL_3PS_2L_2CNS_1$ كاقشتها × F_1B ؛ قشمتها × A ؛ باقشمها × J ؛ باقشتهم WL_1 نجاستها] نجاستها F_1B [Samaritan] [J [Samaritan] (الساير) [Samaritan] (الساير) $[F_2G$ [Samaritan] $PS_2L_2WL_1$

٤٢ كذلك J] وكذلك (الساير) F_2G الزم] لزم L_1 [Samaritan] × B [Samaritan] او ACL_1 ؛ او من F_1

٤٣ ناطر ([Samaritan] P)] ناظر BN فيلزم × F_1

٤٤ واتباعه $[PWLS_1J$ واتباعها (الساير) F_2G في باب] < × F_1 مراتبها (الساير) $[F_2G$ + انشا الله تعالى S_2 ؛ + انشا الله تعالى اذا من وساعد الى الوصول P

١ قال $[F_2GL_3WL_1DJ$ فصل قال $F_1APS_2L_2CBNS_1$

٢ مولود] المولود PB ؛ ملود × A او من] ومن × D يمكن (الساير) $[F_2G$ يكن L_3 وتطهيره $[BL_1S_1{}^*DJ$ + بالما (الساير) F_2G

٣ ليختنه $[F_2GPS_2L_2S_1^3DJ$ ليختنه لنجسه × L_3CN ؛ النجسه ليختنه × W ؛ لنجسه × $BL_1S_1{}^*$ ؛ < × F_1A عدد (الساير) $[F_2G$ < W^* اسبوعا (الساير) $[F_2G$ + من قدومه عليه ليختنه F_1A

٥ قيل في] يقال عن A

٦ احدهما] الاول A يلزمه] يلزم F_1AW^* اسبوعا (الساير) $[F_2G$ + على القادم عليه ليختنه F_1 يعتمدوه [DJ يعتمد (الساير) ختن (الساير) $[F_2G$ تطهير A

المولود وهو طاهر. فمن حيث جاز طهر المولود في وقته عند الغسل فلا يلزم من لمسه قبل الغسل اسبوعا لا الختان ولا غيره.

والوجه الثاني انه يلزم الختان اسبوعا. قال صاحب هذا الراى انه لا يجوز تطهير المولود الا بعد عدد اسبوعا بعد الغسل وذلك لوروده مع الدم فلا يفصله العدد الا بعد الغسل ولو استمر مهما استمر مثاله ان الانسان اذا كان ناطر وطهر المنزله الاوله واقام مهما اقام بلا ࠌࠉࠍࠃࠄ فاي يوم عبرت عليه كان ثالث اول مره وسابع اخر مره فكان عدم عبور ࠀࠋࠌࠉࠍࠃࠄ عليه سببا لسقوط الايام. ومما يعتمدوه النسا الاسرايليات انه اذا حضرت ࠄࠍࠃࠄ في اخر نهاره وليس يحصل للامراه غسل قبل غيبة الشمس واغتسلت فيضيع عليها ذلك اليوم ولا يحسب. اذ لو حققته قبل غيبة الشمس وافضلت بالما المنزله الاوله لكان ذلك اليوم داخل في العدد. كذلك المولود من حيث لا غسل بالما وقد كان مقامه داخلا في الدم ثم خرج صحبته. فلا طهر له بغير ذلك ومسحه بالخرق لا يفيد طهرا ولا ينفصل المنزله الاوله الا بالما.

---

٧ طهر] الطهر × D* المولود DJ] الولد (الساير)

٨ ٩ يلزم] ∩ S_2

٨ الختان] الختانه × D

٩ انه] < F_1AW

٩-١٠ اسبوعا] ∩ L_1*

٩ المولود] الولد $L_2L_1^2$ الا] < × P

١٠ عدد] < F_2GS_2 وبعد A

١١ مهما استمر مثاله] على هذه الحاله F_1 مثاله DJ] مثال ذلك (الساير) ناطر (ࠍࠀࠈࠓ F_1AP) [F_1AL_3WCDJ ناظر $S_2L_2BL_1NS_1$ وطهر DJ] فطهر (الساير) واقام] وقام × L_1 مهما اقام] منهم × F_1

١٢ ࠌࠉࠍࠃࠄ [PWL_1J مى نده D ؛ ࠌࠉ ࠍࠃࠄ (الساير) ثالث DJ] الثالث (الساير) F_2G وسابع J] او سابع WL_1S_1*D ؛ او السابع $F_2GF_1APS_2L_2L_3CBNS_1^2$ اخر مره] اخره × L_3C ؛ اخرهم F_1A فكان DJ] وكان (الساير) عدم] × عند J

١٣ ࠀࠋࠌࠉࠍࠃࠄ] ࠀࠋࠌࠉ ࠍࠃࠄ A ؛ المى نده D لسقوط DJ] في سقوط (الساير) ومما] وما D يعتمدوه (يعتمده W) [L_3WCL_1DJ يعتنو (يعتنوا S_2L_2) $F_2GPS_2L_2BNS_1$ الاسراييليه F_2GAD اذا DJ] ان (الساير) F_2G

١٤ حضرت] حدثت F_1AL_3C ࠄࠍࠃࠄ (الساير) F_2G] < D نهار P وليس J] ولم (الساير) غيبة] غياب B الشمس (الساير) F_2G] قرص الشمس F_1AL_3 واغتسلت DJ] + بعد (الساير) F_2G

١٥ يضيع W اليوم] النهار F_1 حققته D] حفته × J ؛ لحقته × (الساير) ؛ لحقة × F_1 وافضلت (الساير) F_2G] واتصلت × WL_1J في الما A

١٦ داخل (الساير) F_2G] حسب لها وداخل F_1AL_3C وكذلك L_1 لا] لم L_3C غسل] يغسل B

ويبقى بعد الاغتسال تحت حكم العدد لما برز اولا. مما يقوي ذلك ما يعتمدوه النسوان في يدهن اليسرى التي يغسلوا بها مكان الدم وقت الاغتسال فانها تبقى بعد الغسل بالما تحت العدد دون باقي الاعضا.

قال

فان كان قد تقدم على الولد غسل في ثاني يوم ولادته او ثالثه فهل يجزي التطهير ام لا.

الجواب

ان اغتسال الولد في اي يوم حصل يجزي له ويبقى تحت العدد من وقت ذلك. بل قد يتفق لبعض النسوان ان تحصل ولادتها في الحمام فيحصل بزوال العرض بلوغ الغرض.

قال

فان غسل الولد بالما من فوق وركيه ونازل الى كعابه والعضو المطلوب ثم لمسه الختان

---

١٧ صحبته] صتحبه × W ذلك DJ] غسل (الساير) F_2G بالخرق] بالخرقه PW ؛ بالحزف × B ؛ [illegible] × L_3 يفيد D] يفيده (الساير)

١٨ ينفصل DJ] تنفصل (الساير) F_2G

١٩ العدد J] العده (الساير) مما D] ومما (الساير) يعتمدوه S_2DJ] يعتمدونه (الساير) ؛ يعتمدون A النسوان] النساء F_1A

٢٠ يدهن] [illegible] L_3 ؛ يدهم F_1S_2 الذي F_1AL_3C يغسلوا (الساير) F_2G] ينظفون F_1 الاغتسال] الغسل F_1 الاغتسال DJ] + بالما (الساير) F_2G فانها] بانها F_1AL_3WC

٢١ العدد DJ] العده (الساير) الاعضا] [illegible] × S_1

٢٣ على الولد D] للولد (الساير) ولادته او ثالثه (الساير) F_2G] من ميلاده او يوم الثالث B ولادته] ولاده $PS_2L_2NS_1$ او ثالثه] او ثالث يوم L_3C ؛ وثالث يوم F_1A يجزي] يجرى × L_2L_1 ؛ + له P التطهير DJ] له (به F_2GB) طهرا (طهر S_2L_2) (الساير) F_2G

٢٥ اعتسال الولد D] اطاغتسال (الغشل F_1A) للولد (الساير) يحصل يجرى × L_2 العدد DJ] العده (الساير) قد] < D

٢٧ يتفق تبقى × B لبعض النسوان] لبعض النساء F_1 ؛ بعض النسوان A ؛ للنسوان S_2 ؛ النسوان L_2 تحصل J] يحصل (الساير) ؛ تصادف F_1 ولادتها] ولادها $PS_2L_2BNS_1$ العرض] الغرض × L_3W*L_1 ؛ الفرض × B بلوغ DJ] حصول (في حصول A ؛ حصل P) (الساير)

٢٧ قال DJ] + الشيخ (الساير) F_2G

٢٨ وركيه] الوركه F_1 ؛ ركبه × F_2GJ ؛ ركبته × D الى] < D كعابه] كعبيه S_2 ؛ كعبه F_1 المطلوبه F_1A

بعد ذلك فلا يلزمه عدد اسبوعا. واما القابله التي تلقى الولد من الملة فقد نقل انها تبقى مدة ايام تسمى اوثر لا تاكل بيدها ولا تلمس بها قوت النفس.

[كتاب الكافي]

[الباب الثاني عشر]

باب في اجناس الطموات وشروطها واحكامها

قال الشيخ
تنقسم في طهرها الى اربعة اقسام.

فمنها ما يطهر بالما ومنها ما يطهر بالنار ومنها ما يقبل الطهر بحكمه بالما والنار ومنها ما لا يطهر لا بالما ولا بالنار. وقد نبه الشارع تعالى على ذلك بقوله ࠊࠋ ࠃࠁࠓ ࠀࠔࠓ ࠉࠁࠅࠀ ࠁࠀࠔ ࠕࠏࠁࠉࠓࠅ ࠁࠀࠔ الى قوله ࠅࠊࠋ ࠀࠔࠓ ࠋࠀ ࠉࠁࠅࠀ ࠁࠀࠔ ࠕࠏࠁࠉࠓࠅ ࠁࠌࠉࠌ (تع ٣١ : ٢٣).

اما ما يقبل الطهر بالما دون النار فمثل ࠊࠋࠉ ࠏࠑ وانواعه التي تقبل الطهر وذلك بعد ان يعتمد فيه ࠕࠔࠈࠉࠐࠕ كقوله تعالى ࠅࠊࠋ ࠊࠋࠉ ࠏࠑ ࠉࠔࠈࠐ ࠁࠌࠉࠌ

٢٩ يلزمه] يلزم $F_1AS_2L_3C$ عدد (الساير) F_2G] < *WD التى DJ] الذي (الساير)؛ ان F_1A
تلقى (تلقا PL_2BNS_1)]؛ تلقت × F_1L_3C؛ تلت × A؛ تقبل W الولد] + اذا كانت F_1AL_3
تبقى] < × D WCN^3
٢٩-٣٠ فقد .... تسمى] فيحكم عليها [illegible] سبعة ايام كوامل وتسمى A مدة ايام] مده D
٣٠ اوثر $L_3PL_2BNS_1DJ$] [illegible] C؛ الاوتر WL_3؛ ايام الاوتر S_2؛ ايام [illegible] F_1A؛ [illegible]
ولا تلمس] وتلمس × B بها] لها × F_1 لنفس F_1 F_2G
١ باب PNDJ] ١٢ باب S_1؛ الباب الثاني عشر $F_1AL_3S_2L_2WCL_1$؛ باب ثاني عثر B؛ [illegible]
F_2G في] > S_1 واحكامها $F_2GS_2L_2BS_1DJ$] + عده ١٢ N؛ + وفيه فصل فيما لا يطهر لا بما (بالما L_1) ولا بنار (بالنار L_1) $F_1AL_3WCL_1$
٣ تنقسم J] الطموات تنقسم (الساير) F_2G ما] لا × A الطهر] > × A بحكم × A وبالنار D
D
٥ يطهر F_2GDJ] + البته (الساير) يطهر .... بالما] > × A نبه] قال A الشارع (الساير) F_2G]
الشرع A
٨ ما] > × B فمثل] ومثل × D؛ مثل × J الذي F_1A تقبل L_1DJ] يقبل (الساير)
٩ ان] > J ࠕࠔࠈࠉࠐࠕ] × J كقوله D] لقوله (الساير) (حروف عربيه) D

(اح ١٥ : ١٢). وهو خليه الى حين يزول منه ما يمكن زواله مما قد اكتسبه باستعماله. ثم بعد ذلك يعتمد فيه ࠈࠁࠉࠋࠄ لما غلظ حكمه ࠅࠓࠇࠑ لما كان خفيف الحكم في ترتيب النجاسات. وذلك سنةً ونقلاً. وكذلك كل مستعمل من انواع الرصاص والنحاس الذي اذا دخل النار هلك. فكان طهره بالما اسلم فهوا اولى بعد حصول ࠄࠔࠈࠉࠐࠄ وكذلك انواع الملابس الذهبيه الذي يفسد صيغها عند اجتماعها بالنار. وكذلك قال ࠀࠊ ࠀࠕ ࠄࠆࠄࠁ ࠅࠀࠕ ࠄࠊࠎࠐ الى قوله ࠊࠋ ࠃࠁࠓ ࠀࠔࠓ ࠉࠁࠅࠀ ࠁࠀࠔ ࠕࠏࠁࠉࠓࠅ ࠁࠀࠔ ࠅࠈࠄࠓ ࠅࠊࠋ ࠀࠔࠓ ࠋࠀ ࠉࠁࠅࠀ ࠁࠀࠔ ࠕࠏࠁࠉࠓࠅ ࠁࠌࠉࠌ (تع ٣١ : ٢٢-٢٣). فما كان اذا عارضته النار لا تفسده واراد الانسان يطهره بها جاز له ذلك. والما فهو اقبل للتطهير لجميع الاجناس لان من انواع المصاغه ما اذا قابل النار يفسد وما امر الله تعالى بذلك ولقد كفى في قوله ࠊࠋ ࠃࠁࠓ ࠀࠔࠓ ࠉࠁࠅࠀ ليريد لكل صفه ما قبلته بالتطهير.

والعقل في تدبر ذلك قايما مقام الشرع.

---

١٠ خليه DJ] حكمه (حكم L_3) × (الساير) F_2G حين J] ان (الساير) يمكن] يمكنه A

١١ طبيله D لما غلظ حكمه] حكم × F_1 لما] لمن × A ࠅࠓࠇࠑ J] ࠅࠓࠇࠑࠄ F_2GP^*؛ ࠅࠓࠇࠉࠑ L_2؛ ࠅࠓࠇࠉࠑࠄ $S_2L_3WCBL_1NS_1$؛ ورحيصه D؛ ࠄࠓࠇࠉࠑࠄ A

١٢ النجاسه P سنةً ونقلاً DJ] سنه ونقل (الساير) كل DJ] ما كان (الساير) F_2G انواع J] اجناس (الساير)

١٣ طهره (الساير) F_2G] طهرها $PS_2L_2NS_1$ هشطيفه D

١٤ الذهبيه] ࠀࠋࠃࠄࠁࠉࠄ × NS_1؛ ࠀࠋࠆࠄࠁࠉࠄ × L_3؛ < × F_2GS_2 الذي L_1DJ] التي (الساير) يفسد F_1AWL_1] تفسد $L_3PS_2L_2CBNS_1D^2$؛ نفسد J؛ < D^* صيغها F_1AWL_1J] صغتها × (الساير)

١٤-١٦ (حروف عربيه) D

١٥ ࠄࠊࠎࠐ] + ࠅࠀࠕ ࠄࠍࠇࠔࠕ F_1A

١٥-١٦ ࠉࠁࠅࠀ ࠁࠀࠔ] ∩ $S_2L_2S_1^*$ ࠉࠁࠅࠀ .... ࠀࠔࠓ] < S_1^3

١٧ عارضته PS_2WCBNS_1] عارضة × $F_2GF_1AL_2J$؛ عارضه × L_1D تفسده $F_2GL_3L_2BNS_1D$] تفسد × S_2؛ يفسده × $CL_1J(c)$؛ يفسد × F_1AW واراد] واباد × J(c) يطهره (الساير) F_2G] بطهره PS_2WNS_1

١٨ بها F_2GD] بما × BL_1؛ ايما × $AL_3PS_2L_2WCNS_1^3$؛ الما × J(c)؛ ࠌࠌࠀ × S_1^*؛ اذا × F_1 فهو] < F_1AL_1؛ ذلك] جايز P اقبل] اقيل × L_1 للتطهير] التطهير J(c)؛ لتطهير S_2؛ ࠋࠋࠈࠄࠓ L_3 بجميع $F_1AJ(c)$ الاجناس] الانواع × S_2B

١٩ المصاغه] المصاغ F_1AWC؛ ࠀࠋࠌࠑࠀࠂࠏ × L_3 يفسد] الا بعد × L_1 وما] واما × J(c) كني $F_1AL_3WCL_1DJ(c)$] اكفى (اكفا B) $PS_2L_2BNS_1$ في قوله] بقوله F_1؛ قوله L_1

٢٠ ليريد $WBNS_1^2DJ(c)$] ࠁࠉࠓࠉࠃ × S_1^*؛ فيريد $F_1APS_2L_2L_1$؛ فيبر × L_3C لكل] كل J(c) صفه ما] صفتها × J(c) ࠒࠀࠁࠋࠕࠄ × NS_1 بالتطهير] بالنظير × B في] فيه × $F_1AWJ(c)$

٢١ تدبير P قايما] قياما × B؛ فاتما × DJ(c)

فصل فيما يقبل الطهر بالنار

فمن ذلك ارض نجسه اما من ࠌࠕ او من ࠍࠃࠄ او لحقها رطوبه ممن عليه عقلة نجاسه اما من ما او فضلة طعام يقع منه على تلك الارض وينطف. فتطهر ذلك المكان يكون بالنار. ان كان موضع ندّه بصفة حمكه المنقول المفهوم دفعه واحده. وان كان ميت كان له منزله اوله في اليوم الاول دفعه واحده واليوم الثالث دفعه قبل نضح مينده عليه † واليوم السابع دفعه قبل نضح مينده عليه † ودفعه بعد نضحه لتعبر النار على المكان دفعه ثانيه. وهذا شرع مفهوم من اقسام ࠉࠋࠄࠃࠕ معرفه عنمن باشر وعنمن نظر.

واي ارض جلس عليها صاحب عقله ولا يلحقها شي من رطوبه لا يلزم الارض الا ان يلحقها شي من طما الجالس عليها بصفة نجاسته.

فموضع ࠁࠉࠕ ࠌࠕ فطهره على منازله بالنار. وموضع تلد فيه الامراه يطهر بالنار ويخلص لوقته اذا لم يكن فيه حكم ࠌࠕ.

---

٢٣ من P ࠌࠕ [$PCBL_1NS_1DJ(c)$ مت S_2 ؛ ميت $F_1AL_3L_2W$ او] اذا × L_1 ؛ اما L_3 من (ثابي) [D + ࠌࠃ × $ACBL_1$ ؛ + ࠌࠃ × L_3NS_1 ؛ + دم × $S_2L_2WJ(c)$ ؛ ࠌࠃࠌ × F_2G ࠍࠃࠄ (نده D)] ࠄࠍࠃࠄ $S_2L_2BNS_1$ عقلة] > $J(c)$

٢٤ او] + من F_1AB تقع × $J(c)$ منه] عنه C تلك] ذلك A وينطف [F_1ABD او ينطف × $L_3S_2L_2CNS_1$ ؛ او نطف (ࠉࠄ ࠁࠁࠓࠄࠕ) × F_2G ؛ وينضف $J(c)$ ؛ ينطف × L_1 فتطهر [$L_3{*}D$ فطهر × $J(c)$ ؛ فيطهر × F_1AWL_1 ؛ فتطهير $L_3^2PS_2L_2CBNS_1$ ذلك المكان ذلك المكان × $J(c)$

٢٥ ويكون × F_1AWL_1 بالنار] بالنور × B كان] كل × F_1AW ندّه [$DJ(a)$ ࠍࠃࠄ (السابر) بصفة [D فصفة $J(c)$ ؛ فبصفة (السابر) حكمه [PS_2BNS_1 حكم (السابر) والمفهوم F_1AW

٢٦ ٢ دفعه واحده] ∩ $BL_1J(c)$

٢٥ وان] → واليوم الثالث دفعه × $J(a)$ وان [$F_1AWDJ(a)$ فان × $L_3PS_2L_2CNS_1$

٢٦ كان [D + مكان $F_1AL_3PS_2L_2CWBL_1NS_1J(a)$ منزله] > × ${S_1}^*$ في اليوم] واليوم × ${D}^*$ دفعه] > ${P}^*$ مينده [$J(a)$ مى نده D ؛ في نده × A ؛ ࠌࠉࠍࠃࠄ PS_2L_1 ؛ ࠌࠉ ࠍࠃࠄ F_1L_2WCB ؛ ࠌࠉࠍࠃࠄ L_3NS_1

٢٧ ٢ دفعه قبل نضح مينده عليه] ∩ (في كل المخطوطات)

٢٧ لتعبر [D بتعبر $J(a)$ ؛ بغير × (السابر) على المكان] > $W{*}L_1J(a)$ دفعه (ثاني)] + واحده $W{*}L_1$

٢٨ وهذا] وهذه A شرع] اشرع D مفهوم [$F_1AL_3WCL_1DJ(a)$ يفهم $PS_2L_2BNS_1$ اخذ [BN احد × $PS_2L_2S_1D$ ؛ جملة × $F_1AL_3WCL_1J(a)$ الاقسام × D ࠉࠋࠄࠃࠕ [$DJ(a)$ ࠉࠋࠄࠃ × L_1 ؛ الحق × $F_1APS_2L_2WCB$ ؛ ࠉࠋࠄࠃ × L_3NS_1 معرفه [$F_1AWL_1DJ(a)$ معرفته × $L_3PS_2L_2CBNS_1$ باشر وعنمن] > $W{*}L_1J(a)$ باشر] ناشر × D

٢٩ ولا] لا L_3C

٣٠ ش من] > A الارض [$F_1AL_3WCL_1DJ(a)$ + ملزم $PS_2L_2BNS_1$ يلحقها [$PS_2L_2BNS_1DJ(a)$ لحقها $F_1AL_3WCL_1$ شي] > L_2NS_1 نجاسته [$L_3L_2WCL_1DJ(a)$ نجاسه × $F_2GF_1APS_2BNS_1$

٣١ ࠁࠉࠕ ࠌࠕ] ࠁࠉࠕࠌࠕ مت D ؛ نجاسة الميت F_1AL_3CW طهره P منازله [$L_3PS_2L_2CBNS_1$ منزله × $F_2GGF_1AWL_1DJ(a)$ بالنار] ∩ C

٣٢ ࠌࠕ] مث D ؛ ميت F_1A ؛ الميت WCL_1

فان نقط من دم الولاده وحفر وزال زوالا كليا طهر فان اعتمد فيه بعد ذلك التطهير بالنار فهو اولى.

وكذلك كل شي يكون ثقيل يعجز عن حمله وكبير الحجم لا يوجد مكان يصبغه فيكون طهره بالنار. ونحن نعتمد ذلك ويقاس عليه ما هذه صفته. ويكون المجال في ذلك والعقل يدبره ويحكم فيه.

فصل فيما لا يطهر لا بالما ولا بالنار

فمن ذلك قلفة القلب المقول فيها ࠅࠌࠋࠕࠌ ࠀࠕ ࠏࠓࠋࠕ ࠋࠁࠁࠊࠌ (تث ١٠ : ١٦). فلا يطهر لا بالما ولا بالنار فان ذلك الخبث في الانسان. وايضا نظر العين فيما لا يحل لها نظره لان الشارع تعالى نهي عنه بقوله ࠅࠋࠀ ࠕࠕࠅࠓࠅ ࠀࠇࠓࠉ ࠋࠁࠁࠊࠌ ࠅࠀࠇࠓࠉ ࠏࠉࠍࠉࠊࠌ (تع ١٥ : ٣٩). واخرجه مخرج الفعل وان لم يكن وطى فقال ࠀࠔࠓ ࠀࠕࠌ ࠆࠍࠉࠌ (هناك) فجعل النظر الحاصل عنه اثره مقام الفعل. وايضا زواج الفروج المحرمه لا تطهر لا بالما ولا بالنار. وكذلك وجود القلفه فيمن لم يكن

---

٣٣ فان] ∩ L_3 من] منه × C ؛ A <   دم] الدم × A فان] فمن × B التطهر × A

٣٥ وكذلك] + يكون L_3C كل] < × L_1 يكون] < L_1 عن] من L_3 الحجم $F_1APWL_1S_1DJ(a)$] الجرم $L_3S_2L_2CBN$ لا $F_1AS_2WL_1DJ(a)$] ولا $L_3PL_2CBNS_1$ مكان $L_1DJ(a)$] + من الما (الساير)   يكون F_1AW

٣٦ طهره] طهر × S_2L_2 نعتمد] فنعتمد $S_2L_2BL_1$ هذه] هذا $L_3CNJ(c)$ المجال] المحال × F_1 والعقل D] العقل $AJ(c)$ ؛ للعقل (الساير) F_2G ؛ للفعل × L_1 ؛ (لا تمكن قرايته) L_3*

٣٧ يدبره] تدبره $J(c)$

٣٨ فصل] الباب الثالث عشر $F_2GS_2L_2$ ؛ ࠁࠀࠁ P فيما لا يطهر] < × A فيما] ࠁࠌࠀ L_3 لا (ثاني)] الا × $J(c)$

٣٩ (حروف عربيه) D

٤٠ في النار F_1 فان ذلك $J(a)$] وكذلك × (الساير) F_2G الخبث] الحسب × B ؛ الجنايه × A ؛ النجس × P الانسان] النار × L_3N*   وايضا (الساير) F_2G] ࠀࠉࠑࠀ L_3 عين S_2

٤١ فيما D] الى ما (الساير) $J(c)$ لا] < × $L_3BJ(c)$ نظر $J(c)$ الشارع تعالى (الساير) F_2G] الشارع AS_2W ؛ الشرع F_1 نهي] نص F_2GL_2 بقوله] + تعالى L_3C

٤١-٤٢ (حروف عربيه) D

٤١ ࠋࠀ F_1

٤٢-٤٣ واخرجه ... فقال] < × CN_1*

٤٢ واخرجه $DJ(a)$] واخرجها (الساير)   لم] < × F_1 وطي] ࠅࠀࠇࠓࠉ L_3 ؛ وطن × F_1

٤٣ فقال] نقال × F_1 ࠆࠍࠉࠌ] ࠋࠌ؛ × $J(a)$ النظر (الساير) F_2G] الناظر F_1A عنه (الساير) F_2G] < A اثر F_1 اثره $DJ(a)$] + قايم (القايم C) (الساير)

٤٤ زواج] الزواج × L_1 تطهر $DJ(a)$] يطهر × (الساير)   القلف F_1A

قطعها لا يطهر البته كما قال ابا عوض في ࠔࠓࠄࠊࠀ ࠄࠄࠀ قال ࠄࠔࠀ ࠓࠁࠀ ࠅࠋ ࠔࠓࠔࠄ ࠋࠀ وكذلك كلام الفحشا. ولبس الفرا من جلود الحيوان المحرمه وجلود الحيوان المباح المذبوح بغير الملة او مذبوح بيد اهل الملة وعرض عليه نجس وهو طري قبل ان يكفى فيه ما يدبغه فلا يطهر البته. وكذلك ࠀࠔࠏࠒࠊࠄࠉ وهو الذي يكون من اجماع ࠀࠄࠔࠓ ࠀࠕࠁࠔࠍࠄࠔ فلا يطهر البته. فهذه اصول ويقاس عليها ما هوا مشابه لها.

وذلك مثل طعام غير الملي اذا اكله انسان من الملة فلا يطهر منه لا بالما ولا بالنار. فهذه الاقسام حرمت على اسرايل.

[كما هوا في DJ(a)]

ويحرم عليهم الصنايع المهنيه ما تذكر اصوله ليقاس عليه ما ماثله. وذلك مثل الدباغه والصباغه وامثالها.

ويحرم عليهم ايضا سكن المواضع القذره العديمة التطهر وقليلة الما وسكن الخاواطي والخمامير واماكن الفسق.

فان كل هولاي يدخلون في اسم ࠁࠔࠅ ولا منهم طهر البته ولا ينقى كل واحد منهم جمله.

وايضا من جامع امراه عليها عقلة نجاسه ثم استحموا فلا يحصل لهم بذلك طهر البته.

---

٤٥ لا .... عوض] > × B   قال] + الشيخ PS_2L_2 ابا] ابو F_1A ࠔࠓࠄࠊࠀ] ࠅࠔࠓࠄࠊࠀ
L_2 ؛ مدينة × B

٤٦ ࠋࠀ] > × *B ؛ + اعني البحر الكبير ليس مطهرا له B   الفحشه L_2S_2 ولبس] ࠀࠋࠄࠆ ×
L_3 الفرا] الغرا (ࠅࠋࠏࠓࠄ L_3) × L_3B المحرمه AWD] المحرم (الساير) J(a)

٤٧ بيد .... بيد] بيد اهل الملة او مذبوح بيد اخر من × A   بغير D²J(a)] بيد غير $F_1AS_2L_2WBNS_1D$* ؛ بيد غير اهل L_3PCL_1 الملة (اول)] > S_2 الملة] ∩ BDJ(a)

٤٨ يكفى (يلفى J) DJ(a)] يلقى × (الساير) ؛ يبقى × A   يدبغه] يدفعه × D   في البته A   يكون من اجماع J(a)] يكون من (الساير) F_2G ؛ يكون فيه D

٤٩ هصمر J(a)   ࠀࠕࠁࠔتيم D   في البته F_1A فهذه DJ(a)] وهذه (الساير)   ويقاس F_1ADJ] وينقاس (الساير) ؛ ينقاس P

٥٠ وذلك] وكذلك × B   مثل F_1DJ] فمثل $L_3PL_2CWBL_1NS_1$ ؛ مثال S_2 ؛ من A   الملي DJ] الملة BL_1S_1* ؛ اهل الملة $F_1AL_3PS_2L_2WCNS_1^3$ فلا] لا S_2 منه] > S_2 بالما .... بالنار] بما .... بنار L_3C وهذه S_2

٥١ على] + ال F_1AW

٥٢ ويحرم J(a)] وتحرم D   المهنيه J(a)] المهينه × D   يذكر D] تذكر J(a)

٥٤ المواضع D] الاماكن J(a)   التطهر J] الطهر × D

٥٦ هولاي J(a)] + لا × D   طها D

[كما هوا في ساير المخطوطات]

وما يحرم من الصنايع على كل اسرييلي من اصول لها نذكر ليقاس عليها ما هوا مثلها من الصنايع المهنيه مثل الدباغه والصباغه وامثال ذلك.

ويحرم عليهم سكن اراضي لا يحل لهم سكنها من اثارات قذره عديمة التطهر وقليلة الما. ومثل سكن اماكن الخواطي والخمامير واماكن الفسق.

فان كل هاولاي يدخلوا في حكم طما ولا يجوز الحميم منها ولا التطهير منها الا بانفا كل صنف مما ذكر لكل قاصد طهر ويدعي انه من اهل الملة الاسراييليه لينفى عنه اعراض لا تطهر لا بالما ولا بالنار.

ومن جامع امراه عليها عقلة نجاسه لا تطهير لها بالما البته.

---

٥٩ اسراييلي] اسراييل L_2 من .... المهنيه] < × S_2 من] < × W^* اصول لها] اصولها F_1 لها نذكر] نذكرها C نذكر] تذكر F_1L_3W ليقاس] بقياس × B

٦٠ الصنايع] الصُنع F_1 المهنيه S_1*[PL_2CBN$] المهني × A ؛ المهينه × $L_3WL_1N^2$ الدباغ S_2L_2N والصباغه] والصباغ L_3C ؛ والصناعه × F_1 ذلك] + من الصنايع المهينه × S_2

٦١ اثارات قذره S_1[L_3PS_2L_2CBN$] الاماكن F_1AWL_1 العديمة WL_1 التطهر $J(c)$[APNS_1$] التطهير $F_1L_3S_2L_2WCBL_1$ وقليلة] وقليه × L_1 ؛ قليل B

٦٢ سكن] < S_2W^* والخمامير] < A

٦٣ هاولاى] + لا × B [illegible] F_1APS_2 التطهر P منها (الساير) G[F_2$] < F_1 بانفا] بنفي AS_2 كل] < S_2

٦٤ صنف] صفه S_2L_2 مما] كما × A

٦٦ ومن جامع] واضطجمع مع × F_1 ومن (الساير) G[F_2$] من S_2L_2 امراه] (الساير) G[F_2$] زوجته A عليها] وعليها F_1 لها S_1[F_2GL_3PCWBL_1N$] لهم F_1A ؛ لها × S_2L_2 في البته A

TEXT 3

[كتاب الخلاف]

المقاله السادسه

قد عزمنا الان على ذكر ما يتعلق بشريعة ࠄࠍࠃࠄ ࠅࠄࠆࠁࠄ ࠅࠄࠉࠋࠉࠃࠄ من الاحكام. وذكر احكام الدما المختلفه باختلاف اوصافها. وان كان جنسها واحد وتميز ما يبرز منه من احد الاعضا عن غيره باحكام تخصه. فان كان ظهوره وبروزه على طريق من جاري العاده سمي بعرف الشرع ࠃࠌ ࠍࠃࠄ وان تكرر حدوثه على وجوه تباين بها جاري العاده ويخرج عن حدوده كان ࠃࠌ ࠆࠁࠄ وله احكام تخصه. (كما ࠋࠆࠁ ايضا اذا تكرر حدوث ذوبه وزاد في قدره وكميته وكذلك في كيفيته من نحو ان يكون ࠓࠓ او ࠄࠇࠅࠌ (اح ١٥ : ٣) لزج او جاف † قحل †. فانه بهذه الوجوه يتميز من ࠁࠏࠋ ࠄࠃࠉ). واما دما الوالده فتعين بحسب طبيعة المولود ان كان ذكرا او انثى فبتغير صفات المولود في الجنس يتغير احكام الدم. ثم ما يحدث قبل الولاده وفي حال الولاده ومن بعد

---

٢ قد عزمنا الان على ذكر ما] S_1 فيما (السابر) ࠄࠍࠃࠄ] ࠉࠋࠍࠃࠄ G ࠅࠄࠆࠁࠄ] ࠅࠉࠋࠃࠅࠄ × G؛ ࠄࠍࠃࠄ ࠅࠄࠃࠅࠄ × C ࠄࠆࠁࠄ ࠅࠄࠉࠋࠉࠃࠄ] ࠉࠋࠃࠉࠉࠁࠄ G ࠅࠉࠋࠅࠉࠋࠃࠄ

٣ من الاحكام] DLS_2S_1 > (السابر) ذكر DS_2 كان] > GC

٤ الاحكام D كان] > GDS_2

٥ بعرف] ࠏࠍ ࠏࠓࠐ G ࠍࠃࠄ] ࠉࠋࠍࠃࠄ G يباين D بها] ࠐࠉࠄࠉ G

٦ يخرج D ࠆࠁࠄ] زبه S_1؛ ࠆࠉࠉࠁࠄ G وله] ولها UJ ࠋࠆࠁ] ࠋࠆࠉࠉࠁ G ايضا] > C اذا] اذ UJ

٧ حدوثة LB_2DB_1 في] > L كذلك D كيفيته $CLDS_2B_1S_1$] كيفيه × $GCUJB_2$ ࠉࠅ S_2

٨ جاف B_1] حاف S_1؛ حاف × LB_2DS_2؛ صاف × GCUJ قحل] فحل S_1؛ محل × $GCUJLB_2DS_2B_1$ بهذه] بهذا J؛ ࠐࠉ ࠄࠃࠄ G

٨ ٩ ࠁࠏࠋ ࠄࠃࠉ] ࠉࠉࠅࠄࠁ ࠉࠋࠄࠃࠉ G

٩ الوالده] ࠉࠋࠅࠋࠉࠃࠄ G فتعين LB_2D] فيتعين × $GCJS_2B_1$؛ فسفتن × S_1؛ فتيعن × U طبيعة] طبعة L فبتغير] فيتغير × S_2B_1 صفات] صافات × U

١٠ يتغير] ࠉࠉࠏࠉࠃ G؛ بتغير × S_2B_1؛ تغير D ما × J في × S_2 الولاده] الوالده × D من × S_2

الولاده فالاحكام تتعدد وتتغاير بحسب مراتب حدوثه في الزمان مقرون بالحادث. والكلام في ࠃࠌ ࠈࠌࠀࠄ ومعناه عندنا والحكم الذي يلزمه. ومعناه ايضا عندهم وما يلزمه من الحكم على حسب اعتقادهم في تفسير هذه اللفظه ومعناها.

ونبدي اولا ࠃࠌ ࠈࠄࠓࠄ وحقيقته.

فنقول ان الشارع تعالى تحكم وحكمه مقبول في هذه الدما باحكام يقتضي مراعاة مقصوده. وما تقضيه حكمته فيها مشقه زايده وتلك المشقه هي التكليف من غير ان تكون هذه الاحكام لازمه عن اجناس هذا الدم وجوبا لا يجوز ان يرد التكليف فيها بخلاف ذلك وانما يزيد عنه ولا ينقص منه كالاحكام في العقليه التي يلزم فيها الحكم عن انفس الافعال والاعيان كالصدق والكذب والعدل والجور والحكمه والسغه ولزوم الاتقان وحسن النظام والعبث والسكر والكفران. فان هذه الافعال يلزم عنها الحكم وجوبا من حسن او قبيح لا يجوز ان يرد فيها التكليف بخلاف ذلك. وكذلك الاعيان كالجمل والخنزير والارنب الى ساير ما وصفه بانه ࠈࠌࠀ ࠅࠔࠒࠑ لا يجوز ان يرد التكلبف فيه بخلاف ما ورد لانها نجسة العين والذات ولا تحتمل الا حكما واحدا ولا يجوز دعوى جواز النسخ فيها وامثالها وتجويز تغير احكامها وتبدلها حتى تكون نجسة العين اليوم وفى زمان غد تكون طاهرة العين تصلح للقربان بل الحكم لها ابدا لا تزول عنها اوصافها † ولا تقلب † ولا تتغير في وقت اخر.

١١ فالاحكام] فلاحكام × CJ تتعدد] تتعد × S_1 وتتغير × GB_2DS_2 في] وفي B_2

١٢ دم B_2 ࠈࠌࠀࠄ G ومعناها J يلزمه] يلزم B_2 ؛ + ࠅࠌࠌࠌࠅ G من] في U

١٣ الحكم] الاحكام × U هذه] هذا GB_2 ࠈࠄࠓࠄ] ࠈࠄࠓࠄࠅ G

١٤ ونبدي] $UB_2S_2B_1S_1$ ونبتدي CJL ؛ (ونبدي او ونبتدي) H ؛ فنبتدي D ؛ ࠅࠌࠈࠄࠓࠄࠅ G في ࠃࠌ

١٥ فنقول (الساير) H] ࠁࠀࠓࠅࠁ G هذه] هذا C الدما] الدم × G يقتضي] ࠌࠒࠈࠓࠌ

G تقضيه [ULB_2S_2 تقتضيه $GCJDB_1S_1$

١٧ هذا] هذه LB_2S_1* الدم] الدما × S_1* ولا B_2

١٨ منه] < G في] < S_1 فيها] < DS_2 عن] ࠌࠍࠅ G ؛ < × B_2 انفس] نفس C

١٩ والعدل] < GCB_2 ولزوم] ولزم × S_2 وحسن] والعدل × B_2

٢٠ والعبث] والبعث × B_1 يلزم عنها] ࠌࠒࠌ ࠅࠌࠍࠅ × G

٢١ الاعيان] < × U

٢٢ ࠈࠌࠀ ࠅࠔࠒࠑ] طما وشقص S_1 ؛ ࠈࠌࠀ ࠅࠔࠒࠑ G ࠅࠔࠒࠑ] ࠅࠔࠒࠑ × C

٢٣ تحتمل] يحتمل J ولا يجوز] < × C ولا [ULB_2DS_2 فلا × GJB_1S_1

٢٤ وتجوز S_2 تغيير × C وتبدلها [$LB_2DS_2B_1S_1$ وتبديلها × GCUJ واليوم × J

٢٥ ولا تقلب ولا تتغير] ولا تقبل ولا تتغير × LB_2 ؛ ولا تبدل ولا تقبل × B_1 ؛ ولا تقبل × GCUJ ؛ ولا سدل ولا ستقل × S_1 ؛ ولا تبدل ولا تتغير S_2 ؛ ولا تتبدل ولا تتغير D وقت] وفي × L

واما احكام الدما المذكوره فليسة كذلك اذ ليس لها من نفس ذواتها واعيانها ان يكون لها هذه الاحكام وجنس الدم ليس له في نفسه ان يكون نجسا. الا ترى انه يخرج بالاسهال وبافواه العروق [illegible] وبالرعاف وبالفصد ولا يكون له حكم نجس. فالمرجوع في احكامه العايده الى اختلاف اوصافه الا لحكم الشارع بما تحكم به. وبالتاييد الوارد فيها وفي غيرها مما هو من جنسها يزول توهم النسخ وجوازه لان الرسول قد اخبرنا ان المصلحه بشريعته دايمه اعتقادا وفعلا.

وانما قدمت هذه المقدمه لان اليهود عندهم ان احكام الدما عايده الى جنس الدم وما له من الوصف ويوصفون فيها الوانا يجب عن بعضها الطا وعن بعضها الطهر وان معرفة الدم الطاهر في الدما المنبعثه من الفرج والدم النجس لا يعرفه كل احدا بل له علما يعرفون اختلاف اوصافه وما منه نجس منجس وما منه طاهر. ويرجعون في صحة ذلك الى قوله تعالى ࠊࠉ ࠉࠐࠋࠀ ࠌࠌࠊ ࠃࠁࠓ ࠋࠌࠔࠐࠈ ࠁࠉࠍ ࠃࠌ ࠋࠃࠌ (تث ١٧ : ٨).
وهذا منهم غلط لان الشارع انما كلف خلقه الالتزام باحكام الدم المنبعث عن الفرج وتغاير

٢٧ المذكور × B_2 فليسة (فليست S_1)] فليس U تكون U الا] لا × B_2 انه] انه با × B_2 ؛ بان × L ؛ ان × DS_2
٢٨ يخرج] (خالي) B_2 ؛ الجرح × DS_2 ؛ يحرح × L
٢٩ بالاسهال] لاسهال × L ؛ بالابتهال × S_2 [illegible]] وبالبتوليم S_1 ؛ [illegible] G وبالرعاف] وبالرعارف × J وبالفصد $CLDS_2B_1S_1$] وبالقصد × $GUJB_2$
٣٠ فالمرجوع] في المرجوع × U له] + حكم DS_2 احكامها × B_2* الى اختلاف] لاختلاف C اوصافها × LB_2 الا LB_2S_2D] الى × $GCUJB_1S_1$ لحكم LB_2*DS_2] يحكم × S_1 ؛ تحكم × B_2^2 ؛ الحكم × $GCUJB_1$ الشارع LDS_2S_1] الشرعى × $GCUJB_1$ ؛ > B_2 بما تحكم به] > × B_2 تحكم LDS_2] بحكم S_1 ؛ يحكم × $GUJB_1$ ؛ يحكمه × C
٣١ وبالتاييد LDB_2S_1] وبالتايد S_2 ؛ بالتاييد × $GCUJB_1$ مما] ما × LS_2 توهم] يوهم × U ؛ بوهم × GC النسخ] النجس × C* الرسول S_1] + سلام عليه B_2 ؛ + سلام الله عليه $GCUJLDS_2B_1$
٣٢ اعتقادا $LB_2DS_2B_1S_1$] اعتادا GCUJ
٣٣ قدمت] قدمته × S_2 عندهم LB_2DS_2] يعتقدون $GCJB_1S_1$ ؛ يقتضون U
٣٤ ويوصفون LB_2DS_2] ويصفون $GCUJB_1S_1$ الطا LB_2DS_2] النجس $GCUJB_1S_1$ وعن بعضها] ومن بعضها B_2 ؛ وبعضها L معرفته × D
٣٥ في LB_2DS_2] من $GCUJB_1S_1$ كل] > × D احدا (احدٍ D) $LB_2DS_2B_1S_1$] + اي كاين من كان GCUJ
٣٦ صحة] > UJ الى] > × U
٣٧ [illegible] G
٣٨ الشارع] + تعالى UJ

احكامه لتغاير اوصافه فحيث الخارج منه من هذا العضو يلزم عنه نجس مطلقا وباختلاف اوصاف حدوثه يلزم عنه احكام متغايره.

اول ذلك قول الشارع تعالى ذكره ࠅࠀࠔࠄ ࠊࠉ ࠕࠄࠉࠄ ࠆࠁࠄ ࠃࠌ ࠉࠄࠉࠄ ࠆࠁࠄ ࠁࠁࠔࠓࠄ ومعناه وامراه ان تصير ذايبه ويكون ذوابها من دم يبرز من فرجها فسبعة ايام تبقى في عقلة الدم النده (اح ١٥ : ١٩). وهذا اشاره الى من يجيها الدم على العاده في استفراغه. ومعنى ࠍࠃࠕࠄ بطريق اللغه هو النفى والابعاد والتفرد والوحده نظير قوله ࠍࠏ ࠅࠍࠃ يعني مضطرب وفريد ومعناها شرعا الابعاد عن الاطهار. وسمي نفس الدم بذلك لانه سبب النعّدّه. وصار بعرف الشرع لا يعقل من اللفظ الا الدم الاول الذي يلزم عنه ࠄࠍࠏࠃࠄ.

والزمان المعلوم الذي يبرز منها في باقي الاسبوع يسمى ࠃࠌ ࠃࠅࠄ.

وحقيقة ࠄࠃࠅࠄ في اللغه هو المرض ومن الذوبان ايضا من ࠌࠃࠉࠁࠅࠕ ࠍࠐࠔ (اح ٢٦ : ١٦) الا ان ࠌࠃࠉࠁࠅࠕ ࠍࠐࠔ من لغة دوّبيّب هو الذوبان وليس في لغتها واو بل موضعه با. الا انه في الشرع قد اطلق على من يبرز منها دم من فرجها لقوله تعالى

---

٣٩ هذا] هذه GCLB$_2$DS$_2$ UJB$_1$S$_1$ عنه] منه GC ؛ > D النجس GC مطلقا] مطلق LB$_2$DS$_2$ GCUJB$_1$S$_1$

٣٩-٤٠ عنه] ∩ H نجس .... متغايره] > × G

٤١ ذكره] > D ࠔࠁࠏࠕ ࠉࠌࠉࠌ ࠕࠄࠉࠄ ࠁࠍࠃࠕࠄ ࠅࠊࠋ ࠄࠍࠂࠏ ࠁࠄ ࠉࠈࠌࠀ ࠏࠃ ࠄࠏࠓࠁ G

٤٢ ومعناه] اعني S$_2$ ؛ اي D وامراه .... فرجها] > G وامراه] اي امراه C ان] اذ B$_2$S$_2$ ؛ > C ذوبها D

٤٣ الدم النده] ࠃࠌ ࠍࠃࠕࠄ LB$_2$D ؛ دم ࠍࠃࠕࠄ S$_2$S$_1$ ؛ ࠃࠌ ࠍࠃࠕࠄ B$_1$ ؛ دم ࠍࠃࠄ CJ ؛ ࠃࠌ ࠍࠃࠄ U ؛ ࠃࠌ ࠍࠃࠄ H ؛ ࠃࠌ ࠁࠏࠃࠕࠄ G وهذا] وهذه JLB$_2$DS$_2$B$_1$S$_1$ GCU اشاره] اشار B$_1$ الى من لمس C الى] > × L

٤٤ في استفراغه] وفي استفراغه LDS$_1$ ؛ واستفراغه × B$_2$ ؛ في استفراقه × B$_1$ (استقراقه × J) × GCUJS$_2$ ࠁࠌ ࠃࠌࠃࠁ G وهو D والبعاد × D

٤٥ والوحده] والواحده GCLDS$_2$S$_1$ × UB$_2$B$_1$ ؛ واحده × J ࠍࠏ ࠅࠍࠃ] ࠍࠏࠉࠍࠉࠌ ࠅࠍࠃࠉࠍࠄ G مضطرب] مطرود LB$_2$DB$_1$S$_1$ GCUJS$_2$ عن] على × J

٤٦ لانه] + ࠄࠄ G النعده] ࠌࠍࠏࠃࠕࠄ S$_1$ ؛ ࠌࠍࠃࠕࠄ CULB$_2$S$_2$B$_1$ GJD بعرف] يعرف × H*GJ يعقل] يفعل × ULB$_2$DS$_2$B$_1$S$_1$ GCJ

٤٧ الاول] الاولى GC ؛ > × J ࠄࠍࠏࠃࠄ] ࠄࠍࠃࠄ JD

٤٨ والذي × B$_1$S$_2$ تسمى × J ࠃࠅࠄ] ࠃࠅࠅࠄ CUJ

٤٩ ومن] وهو × U ايضا من ࠌࠃࠉࠁࠅࠕ] > × U من] ࠃࠌ × B$_1$ ࠌࠃࠉࠁࠅࠕ ࠍࠐࠔ] ࠅࠌࠃࠉࠁࠕ ࠍࠐࠔࠌ G

٥٠ ࠌࠃࠉࠁࠅࠕ ࠍࠐࠔ] ࠅࠌࠃࠉࠁࠕ ࠍࠐࠔࠌ G لغة] + ࠌࠃࠉࠁࠅࠕ ࠍࠐࠔ من لغة × U دوبيب] ࠃࠅࠁࠉࠁ LB$_2$S$_1$ GCUJDS$_2$B$_1$ هو] وهو (السابر) LB$_2$D

٥١ واو] دوا × B بالا انه] بالاوانه × B$_1$ با] ࠁ S$_1$ ؛ با ࠁ LB$_2$ ؛ يا × GCUJ ؛ ࠁ DS$_2$ منها] > C

ࠅࠀࠉࠔ ࠀࠔࠓ ࠉࠔࠊࠁ ࠀࠕ ࠀࠔࠄ ࠃࠅࠄ (اح ٢٠ : ١٨) وهويعم كل من هي في هذه الحاله ولا يختص ࠁࠀࠋࠍࠃࠄ وحدها من دون ࠄࠆࠁࠄ ࠅࠄࠉࠋࠃࠄ. الا ان مشهور استعماله مما يخص ࠄࠍࠃࠄ كقوله تعالى ࠊࠉࠌࠉ ࠍࠃࠕ ࠃࠅࠕࠄ ࠕࠈࠌࠀ (اح ١٢ : ٢). وقوله ࠅࠈࠌࠀࠄ ࠔࠁࠅࠏࠉࠌ ࠊࠍࠃࠕࠄ (ايه ٥). ࠅࠉࠌࠉ ࠍࠃࠕ ࠃࠅࠕࠄ هي السبعة الايام المشروعه اللازمه بتحكمه تعالى عن ࠍࠃࠕ ࠃࠅࠕࠄ ࠅࠍࠃࠕ ࠃࠅࠕࠄ يرجع به الى الدم الاول لان جميع ࠃࠌ ࠃࠅࠕࠄ لا يلزم من شي منه سبعة ايام الا الحادث الاول وهو ࠍࠃࠕ ࠃࠅࠕࠄ لان عنه وجب ابعادها ونفيها المشتق منه ࠄࠍࠃࠄ وقد صار هذا الاسم بالعرف اسم للدم الاول من ࠃࠌ ࠃࠅࠕࠄ.

وقوله ࠔࠁࠅࠏࠉࠌ ࠊࠍࠃࠕࠄ يريد به المضعفه ويعني اسبوعين محدودين كل واحد منها لا يزيد عن سبعه.

واذا تكرر حدوث ࠍࠃࠕ ࠃࠅࠕࠄ وجات في اليوم الاول والثامن فلا يزيد عن ان يكون

---

٥٢ ࠅࠀࠉ ࠀࠍࠎࠀࠍ ࠉࠑࠈࠂࠏ ࠌࠏ ࠀࠌࠓࠀࠄ ࠇࠀࠉࠑࠄ G

٥٣ الحاله $LB_2DS_2B_1S_1$] العاده GCUJ ࠁࠀࠋࠍࠃࠄ DB_1] ࠁࠀࠋࠍࠃࠏ L ؛ ࠀࠋࠍࠃࠏ B_2 ؛ ࠁࠄࠍࠃࠄ $GCUJS_2S_1$ دون] < × L* ࠄࠆࠁࠄ] ࠀࠋࠇࠀࠉࠑࠄ G ࠅࠄࠉࠋࠃࠄ LB_2] ࠅࠄࠉࠋࠉࠃࠄ $HCUJDS_2B_1S_1$ ؛ ࠅࠀࠋࠅࠀࠋࠃࠄ G

٥٤ مشهور] المشهور S_2 ؛ شهور × B_1 مما] بما S_2 ࠄࠍࠃࠄ] ࠄࠍࠃࠏ B_2 كقوله] لقوله × LD ؛ ࠇࠎࠁ ࠒࠅࠋࠄ G تعالى] < GLD ࠅࠀࠉࠀࠌ ࠋࠍࠂࠀࠎࠕࠄࠀ ࠁࠄࠀ ࠕࠍࠂࠎ G ࠃࠅࠕࠄ $GS_2DB_1S_1$] ࠃࠄࠅࠕࠄ UJ ؛ ࠃࠄࠅࠕ CLB_2

٥٥ ࠅࠕࠍࠂࠎ ࠀࠎࠁࠅࠏࠉࠍ ࠇࠎࠁ ࠋࠍࠂࠀࠎࠕࠄࠀ G ࠔࠁࠅࠏࠉࠌ] ࠔࠁࠏࠕࠉࠌ × J

٥٦ ࠅࠉࠌࠉ] ࠊࠉࠌࠉ × U ؛ ࠅࠉࠅࠌ × GC ࠍࠃࠕ ࠃࠅࠕࠄ] ࠋࠍࠂࠀࠎࠄ ࠃࠅࠁࠄࠀ G

٥٦-٥٧ ࠃࠅࠕࠄ] ∩ C

٥٦ الايام] ايام GLD تعالى] < G عن] ࠏࠋࠉ GL

٥٦-٥٧ ࠍࠃࠕ ࠃࠅࠕࠄ] ࠋࠍࠂࠀࠎࠄ ࠃࠅࠁࠄࠀ G

٥٧ ࠅࠍࠃࠕ ࠃࠅࠕࠄ] ࠅࠋࠍࠂࠀࠎࠄ ࠃࠅࠁࠄࠀ G ؛ ࠅࠍࠃࠕ ࠃࠁࠕࠄ S_1^2 ؛ < × B_1S_1* الاول] + هي السبعة ايام المشهوره اللازمه بتحكمه على ࠍࠃࠕ ࠃࠅࠕࠄ × C ࠃࠌ] دم C ࠃࠅࠕࠄ] ࠃࠄࠅࠕࠄ C ؛ ࠃࠄࠅࠕ B_2 ؛ ࠃࠅࠁࠄࠀ G

٥٧-٥٨ لا .... منه] من لمس منه شي لزمه × S_2 ؛ من لمس شي منه × D

٥٨ من شي] < × B_1 من] + يكسف × B_2 ࠍࠃࠕ ࠃࠅࠕࠄ] ࠋࠍࠂࠀࠎࠄ ࠃࠅࠁࠄࠀ G ࠍࠃࠕ] ࠃࠕ × B_2

٥٩ منه] + ࠊࠋࠌࠄ G ؛ من × DS_2 بالعرف] ࠁࠀࠋࠕࠏࠓࠉࠐ × G

٥٩-٦٠ ࠃࠌ ࠃࠅࠕࠄ $CUJS_2B_1$] دم دوته S_1 ؛ ࠃࠌ ࠃࠅࠁࠄࠀ G ؛ ࠃࠌ (دم B_2D) ࠍࠃࠕࠄ × LB_2D

٦١ ࠔࠁࠅࠏࠉࠌ ࠊࠍࠃࠕࠄ] ࠀࠎࠁࠅࠏࠉࠍ ࠊࠍࠂࠀࠎࠕࠄࠀ G المضعفه] الضعفه JLD ويعني] ومعنى × GC ؛ يعني DS_2

٦٣ عن] ࠏࠋࠉ G ان] < × DS_2

ࠍࠃࠕࠄ ولا تعلق ࠋࠈࠌࠀࠅࠕ بتكررها مهما كان المنبعث معتادا لا يخرج عن العاده بخلاف راي عانان.

فالدم الاول يلزم عنه سبعة ايام تبعد وتنني من الاطهار وقد صار هذا الاسم يوضع على الدم الاول عرفا لما كان هو الموجب دون الذي يجيها في اليوم الثاني والثالث. ولو كان الذي يجيها في خلال الاسبوع متحلل لايامه يوجب سبعه لكان الاصل المقرر الذي جعله الشارع قاعده للقياس منفسدا ومنحرما فلا يلزم عن الاول سبعه ابدا الا اذا لم يجيها في جملة الاسبوع خلا ذلك الاول فقط وهذا لا يطرد. وقد وجدنا ذلك الاصل مطردا اذ كان الشارع تعالى قد نص عليه بالقياس لقوله ࠔࠁࠏࠕ ࠉࠌࠉࠌ ࠊࠉࠌࠉ ࠍࠃࠕ ࠃࠅࠕࠄ ࠕࠈࠌࠀ (اح ١٢ : ٢). وكذلك ࠅࠈࠌࠀࠄ ࠔࠁࠏࠉࠌ ࠊࠍࠃࠕࠄ (ايه ٥). فالدم الاول اذا ابدا يلزم عنه سبعة ايام ويوكد ذلك قوله تعالى ࠅࠀࠌ ࠔࠊࠁ ࠉࠔࠊࠁ ࠀࠉࠔ ࠀࠕࠄ ࠅࠕࠄࠉ ࠍࠃࠕࠄ ࠏࠋࠉࠅ ࠅࠈࠌࠀ ࠔࠁࠏࠕ ࠉࠌࠉࠌ (اح ١٥ : ٢٤). وهو الدم المسمى ࠍࠃࠄ ࠅࠍࠃࠕࠄ بعرف الشرع كما ذكرنا.

وقد خالف الفيومي هذا وتكلف في اثبات ما غلب في ظنه من الحكم ادله ركيكه هي الشبهه الفاسده اولى من ان يكون ادله وامارات. فزعم ان هذا الخطاب مقول في حق من اتطا زوجته في زمان ࠍࠃࠕࠄ وهو عالم بانها ࠍࠃࠄ. وهو على مذهبنا مقول في حق من

---

٦٤ تعلق] يتعلق × B_2 ࠋࠈࠌࠀࠅࠕ] ࠋࠋࠈࠌࠀࠅࠕࠄ G معتادا] مقادا × S_2

٦٥ راي عانان] رايات عانات × LB_2 ؛ زاياة (خالي) × D

٦٦ تبعد $GCDS_2B_1S_1$] تعد × LB_2 ؛ < × UJ من] عن C هذا] < GC

٦٧ الاول] < GC

٦٨ اليوم] يوم × LB_2 والثالث] ࠅࠄࠔࠋࠉࠔࠉ ࠄࠔࠋࠉࠔࠉ G الذي] < × B_2 لايامه] لايام D ؛ الاباحه × B_2 جعله] جعل × B_2

٦٩ منفسدا ومنحرما] (خالي) D ومتحرما B_2 عن] من J

٧٠ اذ $GCDS_2B_1S_1$] اذا × $UJLB_2$

٧٢-٧١ ࠅࠔࠁࠏࠕ ࠉࠌࠉࠌ ࠊࠉࠌࠉ ࠍࠃࠕ ࠃࠅࠕࠄ ࠕࠈࠌࠀ G ࠉࠌࠉࠌ] < × UB_2 ؛ ࠊࠉࠌࠉ] < D

٧٣ ࠅࠈࠌࠀࠄ ࠔࠁࠏࠉࠌ ࠊࠍࠃࠕࠄ G

٧٤ فالدم الاول] فالاول D

٧٥-٧٤ ࠅࠀࠌ ࠔࠊࠁ ࠉࠔࠊࠁ ࠀࠉࠔ ࠀࠕࠄ ࠅࠕࠄࠉ ࠍࠃࠕࠄ ࠏࠋࠉࠅ ࠅࠈࠌࠀ ࠔࠁࠏࠕ ࠉࠌࠉࠌ G

٧٥ وهو $DS_2B_1S_1$] وهذا $GCUJLB_2$ وندته S_1 بعرف] يعرف × J

٧٦ ذكرنا LB_2DS_1] ذكرناه $GCUJS_2B_1$ من] في LB_2D ادله] اوله × S_2 ركيكه] كيكه × S_2 هي] هو B_2 ؛ وهي S_1

٧٧ الشبهه] الشبه DS_2 ؛ بالسببه × S_1 ؛ اشبه × S_2 ان] < D او امارات DB_1

انضجع مع زوجته اما بمجرد نوم او وطى على انه بمطلق النوم ومجرده اولى مع علمه انها
٨٠ طاهره في مبدا الامر واوله ثم طرى عليها حدوث الدم في اثنا حال. ونفى عنه حكم القتل
واوجب عليه ان يطها سبعة ايام كالتي ينبعث منها ذلك الدم. فمقدمة هذا الفعل على راي
الفيومي محظوره وعلى راينا جايزه لانه نام معها وانضجع على اعتقاد طهر فحدث الدم في
اثنا فعله فتنجسا جميعا. وجعله الشارع مع حكم نظايره واشتباه نجاستهم من طريق الجايز
لا من طريق المحظور كقوله تعالى ולאיש אשר ישכב עם טמאה
٨٥ (اح ١٥ : ٣٣). واذا كان هذا انما جات نجاسته عن مقدمه جايزه لا محظوره. وكان نطق
الخطاب محتملا لمجرد النوم ومحتملا للوطى معا وكانت المقدمه جايزه على الوجهين.
فان ما اعتمده الفيومي باطل من وحهين.

احدهما انه جعل محل المحتمل صريحا. ولو كان صريحا لما افتقر في التعيين الى قرينه.
ونظير ذلك قوله تعالى ואשה אשר ישכב איש אתה שכבת
٩٠ זרע ורחצו במים (ايه ١٨). فلو كان مجرد אלשכיבה صريحا في
الوطى لما احتاج في القرينه وهو قوله שכבת זרע فهو بجهله جعل المحتمل صريحا.
وغلط ايضا في قوله تعالى ותהיה נדתה עליו (ايه ٢٤). حكم

---

٧٩ بمطلق] بطلق U   علمه] > × GC
٨٠ حال] حاله PLB_2D
٨١ ان] انه C   ان يطها] [illegible] G   انبعث S_1 فمقدمة (الساير P] فمقدم D ؛ فتقدم B_2
٨٢ محظورا × B_2 وعلى] على × B_2DS_2
٨٣ فتنجسا (الساير P] [illegible] G   نظايره] يظاير له × S_1
٨٣ ٨٤ من طريق] ∩ LB_2D
٨٤ كقوله (الساير P] لقوله LS_1 [illegible] G
٨٥-٨٦ جايزه] ∩ D
٨٥ جايزه] وجايز × L
٨٦ معا (الساير P] > U   المتقدمه (الساير P] [illegible] G
٨٨ فان (الساير P] > U   انه جعل محل المحتمل PB_2] انه جعل المحتمل S_1 ؛ جعل انه محل المحتمل × L ؛ انه محل المحتمل × $GCUJNDS_2B_1$ صريحا] ∩ S_1*   كان] + ليسه × GC   في] > N   التعيين] التعين × S_2NDB_1
٨٩ قوله تعالى > N   تعالى (الساير P] > B_2
٨٩-٩٠ [illegible] G
٩٠ ولو PC   אלשכיבה] [illegible] × GC
٩١ في (الساير P] الى S_1 שכבת זרע] [illegible] G   [illegible] D   فهو] [illegible] × G
٩٢ [illegible] G

[Samaritan] وهو الزمان الذي يلزم بعدها ونفيها فيه عن الاطهار لان الزمان وتفردها فيه عن الاطهار وتنجس الداني بها وحرامة وطيها هو حكم [Samaritan]. والشارع انما قصد [Samaritan] [Samaritan] وقد اشتهر تسمية الدم [Samaritan]. وهو الدم الاول الذي عنه يلزم الحكم كقوله [Samaritan] [Samaritan] [Samaritan] [Samaritan] هو الدم الاول [Samaritan] هو ما يجبها بعده.

ومن كمال خطاه انه جعل الشريعتين واحده وجمع بين ما فرق الكتاب لان الفصل المشتمل على حكم [Samaritan] [Samaritan] هو قوله تعالى [Samaritan] (اح ٢٠ : ١٨). فاوجب الحكم بنصوص جليه وحكم للقتل لا يثبت بمحتمل ولا بقياس بل بنص قاطع. فلهذا تكلف فيه الزياده والزياده على مقتضى ظاهر الخطاب مجاز ولا يقبل المستحق القتل بمجاز

---

٩٣ [Samaritan]] ندته PS_1 ؛ [Samaritan] G   يلزم] > × L   بعدها S_1] بعدتها (الساير) PN   ونفيها] ونظيفها × U   عن (الساير) P] [Samaritan] G   الاطهار] ∩ S_1*   ولان × L ؛ والان × B_2 الزمان] انهان × B_2

٩٤ وتنجس UJ] وينجس × $GLB_2DS_2S_1$ ؛ ونجس CB_1 [Samaritan]] [Samaritan] G

٩٥ تسمية S_1] كيفية × (الساير) N   الدم] > × D   [Samaritan]] [Samaritan] G   عنه يلزم $LB_2NDS_2B_1S_1$] يلزم عنه GCUJ

٩٦ لقوله × S_1 [Samaritan] [Samaritan] [Samaritan] (صح) [Samaritan] G   [Samaritan]] + [Samaritan] HC   [Samaritan] CLB_2] و [Samaritan] J ؛ [Samaritan] × B_1 ؛ فالندوت × S_1 ؛ [Samaritan] US_2 ؛ [Samaritan] × H ؛ [Samaritan] × G   [Samaritan] J] ودوته S_1 ؛ [Samaritan] [Samaritan] × $HUCLB_2DS_2B_1$ ؛ [Samaritan] [Samaritan] × G   وهوا B_1

٩٧ يجبها] + من L   بعد C

٩٨ ومن (الساير) P] من C   انه LB_1S_1] ان $PGCUJB_2DS_2$ جعل S_1] يجعل $GCUJLB_2DS_2B_1$ واحد C   ما] > × J   الكتاب S_1] الله (الساير) P   الفصل S_1] القصد × (الساير) P

٩٩ المشتمل] المحتمل × U   حكم S_1] > (الساير) P   [Samaritan] S_1] [Samaritan] (الساير) ؛ [Samaritan] B_2 هو قوله تعالى S_1] وهو من قوله B_2 ؛ من قوله $GCUJLB_1$ ؛ > DS_2

٩٩-١٠١ [Samaritan] G

٩٩ [Samaritan] $L_2B_1S_1$] [Samaritan] $HCUJDS_2$

١٠٠ [Samaritan] $HLB_2DS_2B_1$] [Samaritan] S_1 ؛ [Samaritan] CUJ   [Samaritan] [Samaritan]] > S_1

١٠١ [Samaritan]] > S_1

١٠٢ بنصوصها × U   بمحتمل] بما يحتمل D ؛ لمحتمل B_2 بل] > × S_2D بنص $PLB_2DS_2B_1S_1$] + صريح GCUJ   فلهذا B_2DS_2] فهذا $PGCULB_1$ ؛ فهذه × J ؛ وهذا S_1

١٠٣ تكلف $GUJB_1S_1$] تكليف × $PCLB_2DS_2$ والزياده] > × S_2D مجاز] محاور × B_1

١٠٢-١٠٣ المستحق القتل بمجاز ولا $PLB_2DS_2B_1S_1$] > × GCUJ

ولا بمحتمل ولا بقياس وكذلك جعل المحتمل وهو قوله تعالى [Samaritan script] ولم يذكر [Samaritan script] جعله صريحا وهو مفتقر في البيان الى قرينه.

والشارع قد جعل هذا النايم او الواطى مع الاحتمال مع جملة اطميا طايهم حاصله بطريق الجواز والعرض لا بطريق الممتنع والخطر لقوله تعالى [Samaritan script] (اح ١٥ : ٣٣). فهذه [Samaritan script] لقوله [Samaritan script] (ايات ٣٢ - ٣٣). فهذه شريعه تعم ساير هذه الاقسام. والذي [Samaritan script] (اح ٢٠ : ١٨) له [Samaritan script] اخرى وهو القتل بجنايه قصديه يحدثها على مقدمه محظوره ممتنعه واستحق حكم القتل بنصوص جليه لا محتمله. وحاصل جميع ذلك ان مقصود الشارع فهمناه من خطابه تعالى وجهله الفيومي وشيعته. فمن ذلك علمنا ان الدم الاول يلزم عنه سبعة ايام.

وما يحدث في اليوم الثاني يلزم عنه حال واحد ان حصل على ثوب او انسان فلا يلزم

---

١٠٤ ولذلك × S_1 جعل] > × GDS_2 وهو S_1] من (الساير) P تعالى S_1] > (الساير)
١٠٥-١٠ [Samaritan script] G
١٠٥ [Samaritan script] > × S_1 [Samaritan script] ؛ G [Samaritan script] S_1
١٠٧ النايم] > × B_2 او الواطى S_1] والواطي × $PGCUJB_1$ ؛ الواطى × LB_2NDS_2 مع] ∩ S_2
اطميا] الطميا × U حاصله (الساير) P] [Samaritan script] G
١٠٩-١٠ [Samaritan script] G
١١٠ [Samaritan script] S_1] [Samaritan script] ؛ B_2 ؛ [Samaritan script] × HL ؛ [Samaritan script] × $CUJB_1$ ؛ [Samaritan script] × DS_2 ؛ [Samaritan script] × G
١١١-١١ [Samaritan script] G
١١٠ [Samaritan script] × J
١١١ [Samaritan script] B_1 [Samaritan script] G
١١٢ تعم] نعم × UJ ساير] [Samaritan script] G
١١٣-١ [Samaritan script] G
١١٣ [Samaritan script] $CUJLB_2DS_2$] تورت S_1 ؛ [Samaritan script] × B_1 ؛ [Samaritan script] × PG يحدثها] تحدها × S_1 ؛ يحدثها B_1
١١٤ واستحق S_1] استحق (الساير) حكم $PLB_2DS_2B_1S_1$] حكمها × GCUJ ان] الى × J
١١٥ يلزم عنه] [Samaritan script] G
١١٧ اليوم] > S_1* الثاني] > × C حال] حاله B_2DS_2 واحده DS_2 حاصل D وانسان B_2 يلزم] > × U

عنه الا حال واحد ولو تكرر حدوث الطمث ثلاثه ايام او اربعه لم يزد الاسبوع. فرق بين [Samaritan] [Samaritan] (انظر اح ١٥ : ١٩، ٢٣، ٣٣، ٣٤) [Samaritan] [Samaritan] (انظر اح ١٢ : ٢). وبهذا بطل قولهم انه يلزم عن كل دم سبعة ايام وانما يلزم عن الدم الاول فقط حسب.

واما دعواهم في اختلاف الدما وان الاصفر لا يلزم عنه حكم وقولهم بالوان مطميه والوان غير مطميه فان الشارع علق الحكم بجنس الدم واطلق القول فيه وعول في البيان على عادات النسوان. وعاداتهن تختلف في الوان ما يجيهن من الدما والمعتبر فيه هو جاري عاداتهن بحسب اختلاف امزجتهن. وقد سلف منا القول بان جنس الدم لا يلزم عنه الحكم لذاته وعينه وجوبا بل يعود الامر في حكمه وحكم نظايره الى تحكم الشارع. ولما كان قصده ومراده خفي عنا نص لنا على معرفة قصده من بعد حجة العقل ادلة الشرع من نحو نطقه ومفهومه وفحواه ومعقوله والقياس وجاري العادات وجاري العاده من النسوان اصل يعول عليه في البيان.

والدليل عليه ما نعلمه من حال [Samaritan] لانها تلتزم بكل لون ولو جاها دم مخالط ليله

---

١١٨ ولو] وان × B_1 الطمث $CUJB_1S_1$] الطما GLB_2DS_2 ثلاثه (ثلاث C) ايام او اربعه] ثلاثة او اربعة ايام U لم $JLB_2S_2DB_1S_1$] ولم GCU يزد JLB_2D] يرد S_1؛ يرد × $GCUB_1$ فرق فوق × LB_2

١١٩ [Samaritan] [Samaritan] B_2؛ [Samaritan] D [Samaritan] وبين] [Samaritan] B_1 [Samaritan] S_1] [Samaritan] $HGCDS_2$؛ [Samaritan] $UJLB_2$؛ [Samaritan] B_1

١٢٠ بطل LB_2] يبطل $GCJDS_2B_1S_1$؛ انبطل U عن (اول)] على LB_2DS_2 عن (ثاني)] على B_2B_1

١٢٢-١٢١ فقط حسب واما $CJLB_2S_1^2$] فقط واما* DS_2S_1؛ حسب واما B_1؛ فقط واما حسب × U؛ فقط حسب × G

١٢٢ دعواهم] عوايدهم × B_1؛ [Samaritan] G عنه] < J حكم $PGCUJB_1S_1$] الحكم LB_2DS_2

١٢٣ الشارع S_1] + تعالى (الساير) P علق S_1] اجرى (الساير) P بجنس S_1] بتنجس × $LB_2DS_2B_1$؛ بتنجيس × PGCUJ في (الساير) P] على B_1

١٢٤ عادات (عاداة S_2) (الساير) P] عادة LB_2 وعاداتهن $PGCUJB_1S_1$] وعادتهن LB_2DS_2 الدما $PGCUJB_1S_1$] الدم LB_2DS_2

١٢٥ عادتهن S_1] عادة التي يجيها (تجيها × $PGCS_2DB_1$) $PGCUJLB_2DS_2B_1$ امزجتهن] + من جهتين S_2؛ امر من جهتين × D منا القول $GCUJB_1S_1$] القول منا PLB_2D؛ القول S_2

١٢٦ تحكم الشارع S_1] تحكمه تعالى $GCUJLB_2DS_2B_1$

١٢٧ معرفة] معرفته × D^2S_2 حجة العقل $GCUJB_1S_1$] الحجه العقليه PLB_2DS_2

١٢٨ وجاري العاده] < × D اصل $PLB_2DS_2B_1S_1$] < GCUJ يعول] يقول × B_2

١٣٠ عليه S_1] على هذا GCU^2JB_1؛ على هذه LB_2DS_2؛ على ذلك *PU ما $GCUJB_1S_1$] على ما LB_2DS_2 [Samaritan] GCUJ] [Samaritan] $LB_2DS_2B_1S_1$ لانها S_1] فانها (الساير) تلتزم B_1S_1] ملتزم × $GCUJLB_2DS_2$ دم] + في × *L مخالط $LB_2DS_2B_1S_1$] + في GCUJ

اخرى وباي لون لو جاها في ࠉࠌࠉ ࠆࠅࠁࠄ بله متغيره عن البياض الى صفره وشقره افسدت ࠆࠅࠁࠄ وعاقها عن الصحه والكمال.

والشارع علق الحكم بجنس الدم ولم يعين بالصرف منه ولا بالمختلط الممازج لغيره بل اطلق القول فيه ورتب الاطلاق على ما يعلم من البيان من العادات الجاريه للنسوان السانفه قبل ظهور شرايع [illegible]. ومن ادعى زياده فعليه البيان واقامة الدليل والبرهان بحيث يثبته من نفس كلام الرسول عن الله تعالى لا بما ابتدعته الحاخاميم كما يزعمون.

وهذا يجري مجرى الزياده في الاصول وهو شريعه ثانيه.

واستدلالهم بقول الكتاب ࠊࠉ ࠉࠐࠋࠀ ࠌࠌࠊ ࠃࠁࠓ ࠋࠌࠔࠐࠈ ࠁࠉࠍ ࠃࠌ ࠋࠃࠌ (تث ١٧ : ٨) فانه استدلال بمحتمل ولان الاظهر من معنايه انما هو الفرق بين من قتل بقصد او بسهو. وما تمسكوا هم به من احد تاويليه ومحتمليه بعيد في العرف وجاري العاده بان يكون المراه اذا جاها دم طمث حملته الى [illegible] (انظر تث ١٧ : ٨) ليمتحنوه الحكام هل هو دم طاهر او دم نجس.

---

١٣١ ولو × S_1 جاها] + دم L^* ࠉࠌࠉ ࠆࠅࠁࠄ [$HCJLB_2DS_2B_1$ + اي ايام عددها U؛ [illegible] G؛ ࠉࠌࠉ ࠆࠅࠁࠄ اى في ايام عدتها S_1 بله [$JB_1S_2^2S_1$ بل × $GCULB_2DS_2^*$ البياض] البيان × L؛ > × B_2 وشقره] او شقره U

١٣٢ ࠆࠅࠁࠄ [DS_1 [illegible] $CJLB_2S_2B_1$؛ العدد GU عن] من B_2

١٣٣ والشارع] + تعالى GC بجنس] بنجس × DS_2 لا D بغيره B_2 للنسوان] بين النسوان B_1؛ [illegible] G ظهور] > D

١٣٥ [illegible] [S_1 [illegible] $GCUJS_2B_1$؛ [illegible] (B_2 [illegible]) [illegible] × LB_2؛ [illegible] × D زياده] > × C^* البيان] > × C

١٣٦ بحيث يثبته [S_1 واثباته × $GCJLS_2B_1$؛ واثبات (واثباه U) × UB_2D ابتدعته [$S_2B_1S_1$ ابتدعت GCUJ؛ ابتدعوه LB_2D الحاخاميم [$GCDS_2B_1S_1$ الحاخامين $UJLB_2$

١٣٩ الكتاب] + بقوله B_1

١٤٠-١ (حروف عربيه) S_1؛ [illegible] G [illegible] ࠁࠉࠍ ࠃࠌ ࠋࠃࠌ] ࠁࠉࠍ ࠃࠉࠍ ࠋࠃࠉࠍ ࠅࠁࠉࠍ ࠃࠌ ࠋࠃࠌ B_1

١٤٠ فانه] + تعالى × S_2^* بمحتمل [S_1 لمحتمل (لمحتملا DS_2) $PUJLDS_2B_1$؛ المحتمل × GCB_2 ولان الاظهر] والاظهر B_1 ولان] [illegible] G؛ والان × S_2؛ لان D من] > × B_1 معنايه (معنيه S_1) [$PCJLB_1S_1$ [illegible] G؛ معناها B_2؛ [illegible] × H؛ معانيه × S_2؛ معاينه × U بين] > × LDS_2

١٤١ بسهو (السابر P)] + او غير ذلك B_1 من [$DS_2B_1S_1$ في $PGCUJLB_2$ احد [S_1 اخذ × (السابر) P؛ [illegible] × G تاويليه [S_1 تاويله × (السابر) P ومحتمله × DS_2 في [S_1 من (السابر) P

١٤٢ بان] ان × B_2 يكون (يكون S_1) [$JLB_2DS_2B_1S_1$ تكون PGCU دم] [illegible] × G طمث] طا × DS_2 حماته [S_1 تحمله (السابر) P الى] > × U [illegible]]

فظاهر الشرع يعلم منه ان كل دم يخرج من الفرج نجس ويتفاوت نجاسته واحكامها باختلاف اوصافه. فاما اعتقاد هولاي ان في الدما البارزه من العضو المعلوم فيها ما له لون الطهر وفيها ما له لون النجس فبعيد.

وقد حكى بعض القراين عن الفيومي انه يزعم ان نسوتنا ونسوتهم اذا جاهم دم هو في نفسه طاهر والتزموا منه النجس قد يجيهم الدم النجس الذي هو احق بان يلزم عنه שבעת ימים اولى لا يلتزموا منه سبعا واذا انتهوا في الاسبوع عن الدم الاول يكون الدم الحقيقي قد بقى من اسبوعه ايام فتطهر وهي בנדתה كما هي ويتطيها الزوج ويجي ولدها בן נדתה. فمع جهله فقد بالغ في الادبار وهذه المسله تنعكس عليهم لان المراه منهم يجيهم دم يكون ما هو عند الله تعالى نجس حسب تحكمه المقبول فلا يجعل به فتبقى على الطهر وهي בנדתה ويتطيها الزوج فيجي ولدها בן נדתה. ونحن تمسكنا بظاهر الكتاب ومع سكوت الشارع في الاطلاق عن البيان بالقراين اللفظيه مع شدة الحاجه اليه وذلك يدل على عدمه. لان كل بيان يسكت الشارع عنه مع الحاجه اليه ضرورة

مقوم مبحر S_1 ؛ [Samaritan] G يمتحنوه الحكام [B_1S_1 يمتحنوه الحكام GCUJ ؛ يمتحنه الحاكم DS_2 ؛ يمتحنه الحاكم PLB_2

١٤٣ او دم [S_1 او طمى (وطمى × B_2) $CUJLB_2B_1$ ؛ ام طمى DS_2 ؛ [Samaritan] G

١٤٤ الشرع] الشارع × C* ويتفاوت [$CUJB_1S_1$ وتتفاوة (G [Samaritan]) $PGLB_2DS_2$

١٤٥ اوصافه [$LB_2DS_2B_1S_1$ اوصافها × GCUJ ان في [S_1 في PLB_2DS_2 ؛ ان $GCUJB_1$ البارزه [$CUJB_1S_1$ البارز $PCLB_2DS_2$

١٤٦ وفيها] ومنها D ما] > × B_2

١٤٧ جاهم] جاها × S_1

١٤٨ [Samaritan] G طاهر] دم طاهر U منه] فيه S_2 الدم النجس [$LB_2DS_2B_1S_1$ > GCUJ عنه] منه DB_2

١٤٩ שבעת ימים [S_1 سبعة ايام (الساير) ولا LB_2DB_1

١٥٠ من] في LB_2DS_2

١٥٠-١٥٣ وهي בנדתה] ∩ S_2

١٥٠ كما هي [S_1 > (الساير) ويتطيها [UJB_1S_1 ويطيها $GCLDB_2$ [Samaritan] G

١٥١ בן נדתה [$HCUJDB_1$ بن ندوت B_2S_1 ؛ ولد [Samaritan] L ؛ [Samaritan] G فمع [$JLB_2DB_1S_1$ مع C ؛ G فنع × U جهله] + [Samaritan] G [Samaritan] G الادبار] (خالي) D وهذه (وهذا S_1*) المسله [S_1 في هذه وهي (الساير)

١٥٢ ما هو] ليسه × C الله تعالى] الله US_1* ؛ تعالى × L* تحكمه] حكمه J

١٥٣ فتبقى] (خالي) D الطهر] الطهور B_2 ويتطيها [$LB_2B_1S_2S_1$ ويطيها GCUJ ؛ فيطيها D الزوج] الزواج × L فيجي [$LB_2DS_2B_1S_1$ ويجي GCUJ ولدها] [Samaritan] G ؛ الولد C בן [Samaritan] [$B_2DS_2B_1$ بن [Samaritan] S_1 ؛ [Samaritan] HCUJ ؛ ولد [Samaritan] L ؛ [Samaritan] G

١٥٤ [Samaritan] G ؛ بالقراين × D يسكت] يسكن × S_2 عنه] [Samaritan] G ؛ فيه S_1*

١٥٥ فسكوته] > GC

فسكوته مع حكمته دليل على نفي ما يدعى. والبيان هاهنا هو عوايد النسوان فلا يفتقر معه الى قرينه لفظيه ولا حاليه.

ثم قال الفيومي فلما عدم العارفون باختلاف الدما اوجبنا عن كل دم سبعة ايام احتياطا ويلزم عن هذا ان يحدث من الدم في خامس الاسبوع وسادسه يلزم عنه سبعة ايام. وهذا يخالف ظاهر الشرع وحقيقته لان الشارع تعالى جعل ࠄࠍࠃࠄ لا تبرز عن الاسبوع ورتب ذلك اصلا وقاعده للقياس لقوله تعالى ࠊࠉࠌࠉ ࠍࠃࠕ ࠃࠅࠕࠄ ࠕࠈࠌࠀ (اح ١٢ : ٢). وقد قلنا ان ࠍࠃࠕ هو اسم شرعي يخص الدم الاول ࠄࠃࠅࠕࠄ يخص ما يجيها في باقي الاسبوع لقوله تعالى ࠅࠕࠄࠉࠄ ࠍࠃࠕࠄ ࠏࠋࠉࠅ (اح ١٥ : ٢٤). فسمى الدم الذي هو علة الحكم باسم الحكم هو الابعاد والنفي من الاطهار اسبوع.

وان حدث في اول الاسبوع الثاني لزم عنه سبعة ايام لانه اول دم يحدث في ابتدى ذلك الزمان وكذلك اسبوع ثالث ورابع. ونهاية ࠃࠌ ࠍࠃࠄ سبع اسابيع لانها عدد كامل وبها يقع التميز والفرق الصحيح بين شريعة ࠄࠍࠃࠄ وشريعة ࠄࠆࠁࠄ. وقد يحدث الدم على وجه الاتصال لا يفرق بايام طهر وقد يكون الامر فيه بخلاف ذلك اذ يحدث تاره ويفرق في حدوثه ذلك بحيث تطهر المراه يومين او ثلاثة ايام ثم تطما فتغير عادتها في زمان الطهر وهو ࠏࠕ ࠍࠃࠕࠄ. ويتكرر ذلك سبع نوب من نوب الطهر فيحكم عليها

١٥٦ على] + ما × GC ؛ > D   ما] وما × LB_2 يدعى] يدعي صاحب الشك B_1 عوايد] عايد LB_2D للنسوان × D   يفتقر] (خالي) D
١٥٧ ولا] والا × B_2
١٥٨-١ ولا حاليه [S_1] ولا جاليه × $GCUJLDB_1$ ؛ ولا جالبه × S_2 ؛ والاجليه × B_2
١٥٨ الدما] الدم B_2 عن [S_1] على (الساير)
١٥٩ من] > B_1 يلزم [$ULB_2DS_2B_1S_1$] فيلرم CJ ؛ ࠅࠉࠋࠆࠌ G
١٦٠ جعل [ULB_2D] + شريعة $GCJS_2B_1S_1$ ࠄࠍࠃࠄ] هنده S_1 ؛ ࠀࠋࠍࠃࠄ G   تبرز] تزيد D   اسبوع DS_2
١٦١ ࠊࠀࠉࠀࠌ ࠍࠃࠀࠄࠄ ࠁࠏࠃࠕࠄࠀ ࠕࠍࠋࠃࠄ G   ࠃࠅࠕࠄ [$HCJDS_1$] ࠃࠄࠅࠕ $ULB_2S_2B_1$
١٦٢ ࠄࠃࠅࠕࠄ] ࠅࠁࠏࠃࠕࠄࠀ G ؛ ࠉࠈࠌࠀ × B_2*
١٦٣ باقي] + ايام S_1 ࠅࠕࠊࠅࠍ ࠍࠃࠀࠕࠄࠀ ࠏࠋࠉࠄ G   ࠀࠋࠕࠉ ࠄࠉ G
١٦٤ الحكم] + الذي D   هو] وهو S_1 ؛ هي × C   من] عن LB_2
١٦٥ وان] فان × U   اسبوع U   لانه] لان × GC
١٦٦ ࠃࠌ] دم L   ࠀࠋࠍࠃࠄ G   سبع] سبعة GC   والفرق (مكتوب والفرق) [S_1] والصرف × B_2 ؛ والعرف × $GCUJLDS_2B_1$
١٦٧ هنده B_2
١٦٨ وجه] + من B_1S_1 بايام .... ويفرق] > ∩ C
١٦٩ ويفرق] + تاره B_2 بحدوثه LB_2D وذلك S_2 ثلاثة [$GCLB_2DB_1$] ثلث UJS_2S_1 ايام] > S_1 ࠕࠈࠌࠀ × B_1
١٧٠ الطهر] ࠀࠈࠄࠓࠄ G   ࠏࠕ ࠍࠃࠕࠄ] ࠅࠒࠕ ࠁࠏࠃࠕࠄࠀ G   ويتكرر [$UJS_2B_1S_1$] فيتكرر GC ؛ وتكرر LB_2D ࠎࠁࠏࠄ G   ࠅࠉࠕࠊࠓࠓ G

بالزبوت وهي النزف وهي عله مشهوره مثل علة ࠄࠆࠁ كل عله منها مرض طويل بالعاده ويكون حدوثه عن اسباب قد ذكرها حذاق الاطبا وذكرناها نحن في عده من كتبنا.

وهذه شريعه بذاتها غير شريعة ࠈࠄࠓࠄ ويلزم عنها ࠎࠐࠉࠓࠄ وقربان لانها مما يكون شاذا نادرا ووقوعها قليل ولهذا رتب الشارع على الابرا منها وعنايته تعالى باصراف هذا المرض قرابين معلومه كالذي شرح على ࠄࠆࠁ.

واما عانان ومن تبعه في اعتقاده ان هذه الشريعه على صعوبتها وصعوبة ما رتب عليها من الاحكام تثبت بيوم واحد تزيد على السبعة الايام. فانه جهله فيها واضح لان هذا خارج عن طاقة المكلف ولا يليق بالحكيم لان المراه يكون عمرها ذاهب في ࠎࠐࠉࠓࠄ اعني عدد قربان. وقد تجد من النسوان من يكون لها عاده بتكرار الطمث وهذه الشريعه انما شرعت لمن خرج امرها عن جاري العاده وباينت المعتاد تباينا عظيما. ثم ان الشارع شرط التكرار وحدد زمانه ࠁࠉࠌࠉࠌ ࠓࠁࠉࠌ (ايه ٢٥) ࠄࠉࠌࠉࠌ ࠓࠁࠉࠌ ما به يفرق بين المعتاد وبين ما هو مرض خارج عن العاده وان كان مبهما مجملا لا يعلم معناه من ظاهره على وجه من الاحكام ومنع الاحتمال فان ظاهره يفيدنا ان الشارع قصد من الزمان المعبر عنه ࠁࠉࠌࠉࠌ ࠓࠁࠉࠌ ما به يفرق بين المعتاد وبين ما هو مرض خارج عن العاده مباين لعوايد النسوان في استفراغ الدم الفضلي حسب المعتاد.

---

١٧١ بالزبوت (بالزبوث S_1 ؛ بالزبوة B_2) LB_2S_1] بالربوث × J ؛ بالربوت × C ؛ بالريوت × U ؛ ࠁࠀࠋࠓࠁࠅࠕ × G ؛ ࠁࠀࠓࠅࠕࠅࠀ × B_1 ؛ ࠁࠀࠋࠆࠁࠅࠀ DS_2 وهي (ثاني)] وهو UJ النزف] الندف × B_1 ࠄࠆࠁ] ࠀࠋࠆࠀࠉࠁ G منها] + عله مشهوره ويورث منها B_1 منها مرض] مرض منها U

١٧٢ قد $LB_2DS_2B_1S_1$] < GCUJ حذاق] احداق B_2

١٧٣ ࠈࠄࠓࠄ] ࠀࠋࠈࠄࠓࠄ G ؛ ࠈࠄࠓࠀࠄ B_2 ࠎࠐࠉࠓࠄ] سفيره S_1 ؛ ࠎࠐࠓࠉࠄ B_2

١٧٤ الابرا (الابره DS_2) $GCUDS_2B_1$] الابرو × B_2S_1 ؛ الايراء × J ؛ الامرو × L باصراف $ULB_2DS_2B_1S_1$] باطراف × GC ؛ بالصرف × J

١٧٥ هده J ࠄࠆࠁ] ࠀࠋࠆࠀࠉࠁ G

١٧٦ وصعوبة] وشعوبة × C

١٧٧ تثبت (ست S_1) $JLB_2DS_2B_1S_1$] ثبت GC ؛ تنبث × U تزيد ULB_2] نريد S_1 ؛ يزيد $GCJS_2B_1$ الايام S_2S_1] ايام (الساير) فانه] ࠐࠀࠍ G ࠁࠄࠀ G ولان D

١٧٨ طاقة] ࠈࠀࠒࠄ G ࠎࠐࠉࠓࠄ] ࠎࠐࠓࠉࠄ B_2 ؛ ࠃࠓࠓࠄࠀ G

١٧٩ قربان $GCUJLB_2$] وقربان $DS_2B_1S_1$ تجد LB_2D] نحد S_1 ؛ نجد $GCUJS_2B_1$ النسا GB_1 الطمث] الطما DS_2

١٨٠ اخرج U الشارع $ULB_2DS_2B_1S_1$] + تعالى GCJ

١٨١ وحدد DS_2B_1] وحد (الساير) ࠁࠉࠌࠉࠌ ࠓࠁࠉࠌ] ࠁࠀࠉࠀࠌ ࠌࠀࠉࠓࠄ G ࠄࠉࠌࠉࠌ ࠓࠁࠉࠌ] ࠄࠀࠉࠀࠌ ࠌࠀࠉࠓࠄ G ؛ < × US_2

١٨١-١٨٢ ما .... كان] < × S_2 ما .... العاده] < × D

١٨٢ وان] لان GC مبهما S_1] منهما × $GCULB_2DS_2$ ؛ متهما × B_1 ؛ مهما × J

١٨٤ عنها J ࠁࠀࠉࠀࠌ ࠌࠀࠉࠓࠄ G ما (ثاني)] < × J

١٨٥ استفراغ $ULB_2DS_2B_1S_1$] استفراق × C ؛ استفراق ايام × J ؛ ࠀࠎࠕࠐࠓࠀࠏ × G

واليهود الربانيين يذهبون في ࠏࠕ ࠍࠃࠕࠄ وهو ما بين نوب درور الطمث انه احدى عشر يوما بين ࠍࠃࠄ ࠋࠍࠃࠄ وهو زمان طهرها فيما بين نوبتي الحادث عنها. قالوا فاذا نقص عن ذلك ولو يوم واحد او يومين وثلث فهي ࠆࠁࠄ. وهذا بعيد لان الشارع شرط ࠉࠌࠉࠌ ࠓࠁࠉࠌ ويوم واحد او يومين وثلث يزيد عن ࠏࠕ ࠍࠃࠕࠄ لا يصح به حكم ࠄࠆࠁࠄ ولان ࠏࠕ ࠍࠃࠕࠄ يختلف في النسوان لانه يكون في بعضهم بعد عشرين يوم او ما يزيد على ذلك وينقص. الادرار المتصل الذي لا يفرق فيه بيوم واحد ظهر ما ذكروه. وانما قالوا احدى عشر يوما بين ࠍࠃࠄ ࠋࠍࠃࠄ فان نقص يوم او يومين او ثلث فهي ࠆࠁࠄ.

وما ذهب اليه سلفنا اصح قول قيل فيه وهو ما حدوه من كمية الزمان في اعتبار التكرار اما متصل او متحلل. اعتبار به يعلم الفرق بين ࠄࠆࠁࠄ ࠅࠄࠍࠃࠄ لان حدوث مثل هذا يكون نادرا شاذا.

واذا تحقق هذا المرض ثبت بكل جاذب دم احمر او اصفر او اسود او متغير عن

١٨٦ الربانيين (الربانين DS₂ ؛ الربانيون C)] ࠅࠀࠋࠓࠁࠀࠍࠉࠉࠍ × G وهو] > × U نوب درور] GCB₂DS₂B₁S₁ نوب دور × L ؛ نوم ورور × J ؛ دروس × U الطمث] ࠀࠋࠈࠌࠕ G
١٨٧-١٨٨ احد عشر LS₁
١٨٧ ࠍࠃࠄ] ࠍࠃࠕ × B₂ نوبتي DS₂] بوتى S₁ ؛ ثبوتي (تبوتي B₂) × CUB₂B₁ ؛ نبوتي × L ؛ تبوتا × J ؛ ࠍࠁࠅࠕ × G فاذا S₁] اذا (الساير)
١٨٨ نقص] انقص L ؛ ࠀࠍࠒࠑࠀ × G وثلث S₁] او ثلاث B₁ ؛ او ثلاثه (الساير) ࠆࠁࠄ] ࠆࠀࠉࠁࠄ G الشارع LB₂DS₂B₁S₁] + تعالى GCUJ
١٨٩ واحد S₁] > (الساير) وثلث S₁] او ثلاث B₁ ؛ او ثلاثه (الساير) ࠏࠕ] ࠍࠃࠕ × L ؛ > × S₁* لا يصح] ويصح × LB₂
١٩٠ لان LB₂DS₂] ولان × GCUJB₁S₁ ࠏࠕ] ࠏࠃ × B₂ لانه] ࠋࠀࠍ G بعضها C
١٩١ على] > U ذلك] > × B₁ الادرار ULB₂D] والادرار GCJS₂B₁S₁ يفرق] يعرف × L واحد] > S₁
١٩٢ ظهر GCUJDB₁] اظهر LS₂ ؛ طهر (طُهر S₁) × B₂S₁ ذكروه] ذكرنوه × L احد عشر GS₂ يوما] + ما L
١٩٣ ثلث (ثلاث B₁) B₁S₁] ثلاثه (الساير)
١٩٤ ذهب S₁] ذهبوا B₁ ؛ ذهب × (الساير) اصح] صح × UB₁ قيل LB₂DS₂] قل S₁ ؛ قبل × GCUJB₁ حدوه JLB₂DS₂B₁S₁] حددوه GCU كمية] فيه × L
١٩٥ متحلل S₁] متحل × UJB₁ ؛ منحل GCLB₂DS₂ اعتبار به] اعتباره B₁ يعلم] بعلم × U ࠄࠆࠁࠄ ࠅࠄࠍࠃࠄ] ࠀࠋࠆࠀࠉࠁࠄ ࠅࠀࠋࠈࠌࠕࠄ G حدوث] + ࠔࠉ G
١٩٧ واذا] ࠅࠀࠍ G ثبت (مكتوب ىب LB₂] ىب S₁ ؛ نبت × GCUJD²B₁ ؛ > × D*S₂ اسواد × U او متغير] ومقتبر × B₁ ؛ + اللون S₂S₁*

البياض تغيرا ما يعتد به ويعول عليه. ولو جاها كما قلنا في ايام ࠈࠄࠓࠕࠄ اصفر او اسود او ابيض فيه تغير ظاهر وجب افساد السفيره واستيناف عدد غيرها.

وقد تعورف في السفيره (انظر ايه ٢٨) انها ايام كامله ࠌࠏࠓࠁ ࠏࠃ ࠏࠓࠁ (اح ٢٣ : ٣٢) ايام خليقيه لا يجوز فيها ما يجوز في غيرها من جبر بعض اليوم بيوم.

واما ما يتعلق بالوالده من الاحكام فظاهر. وحساب ايامها يكون من حال الولاده ويجبر فيه بعض اليوم بيوم. وان تقدم الولاده دم قبل يومها لا يعتد بحكمه لان الاحكام تتداخل ويحكم الاقوى على الاضعف ومن يوم الولاده يقع العدد. والدم الاول الذي يجي مع نفس الولاد يلزم عنه لكل داني به سبعة ايام ان كان عن ذكر وان كان عن انثى فيلزمه عن ذلك الدم بعينه المقارن للولاده اسبوعين لقوله تعالى ࠅࠈࠌࠀࠄ ࠔࠁࠏࠕ ࠉࠌࠉࠌ ࠊࠉࠌࠉ ࠍࠃࠕ ࠃࠅࠕࠄ ࠕࠈࠌࠀ (اح ١٢ : ٢) في حق الذكر وفي حق الانثى قال ࠅࠀࠌ ࠍࠒࠁࠄ ࠕࠋࠃ ࠅࠈࠌࠀࠄ ࠔࠁࠏࠉࠌ ࠊࠍࠃࠕࠄ (ايه ٥).

وما يجي بعد الولاده وانفصال الولد عن الوالده انما يلزم حال واحد كما يلزم عن ࠃࠌ ࠈࠄࠓࠄ (انظر ايات ٤ ، ٥ ، ٦). ومن العلما من يرى ان كل دم يحدث عنها في جملة

---

١٩٨ به] فيه J ࠈࠄࠓࠕࠄ [$S_2B_1S_1$ ࠈࠄࠓࠕࠄ ؛ LD ࠈࠄࠓࠕࠄ ؛ B_2 ࠈࠄࠓࠕࠄ ؛ G ࠈࠄࠓࠕࠄ ؛ HCUJ ࠈࠄࠓࠕࠄ

١٩٩ او ابيض D تغير [$LB_2DS_2S_1$ تغيير × $GCUJB_1$ السفيره [S_1 ࠈࠄࠓࠕࠄ ؛ $GCUJLDS_2B_1$ ࠈࠄࠓࠕࠄ ؛ B_2 ࠈࠄࠓࠕࠄ

٢٠٠ تعورف [S_1 يعرف D ؛ تصودف × U ؛ تصدف (ࠌࠏࠓࠁ H) × HC ؛ تعود × B_2 ؛ نعود × $GJLS_2B_1$ في] الى × L^2B_2 ؛ > L* السفيره [S_1 ࠈࠄࠓࠕࠄ ؛ LB_2 ࠈࠄࠓࠕࠄ (السابر) ࠏࠃ ࠏࠓࠁ G

٢٠١ خلقيه L بيوم] > × S_2

٢٠٢ ما] > × J فظاهر] فظار × C من] في JB_1 الولاده] الوالده × L

٢٠٤ تتداخل (مكتوب سداخل) [S_1 تداخل × (الساير)

٢٠٥ مع] في J نفس] دم *U الولاد [$LB_2S_2B_1S_1$ الولاده GCUJD ان كان عن ذكر] > ∩ B_1 عن (اول)] > LB_2 وان كان] او GC عن (ثاني)] > D فيلزم LB_2D

٢٠٦ عن] > D ذلك] +كل داني L ؛ كل داني B_2D بعينه] بذاته D المقارنه LB_2 تعالي] > CB_2

٢٠٦–٢٠٧ ࠅࠈࠌࠀࠄ ࠔࠁࠏࠕ ࠉࠌࠉࠌ ࠊࠉࠌࠉ ࠍࠃࠕ ࠃࠅࠕࠄ ࠕࠈࠌࠀ G

٢٠٧ ࠍࠃࠕ [ࠍࠃࠕ × LB_2 ࠕࠈࠌࠀ S_2

٢٠٧–٢٠٨ في حق الذكر .... وفوا [LB_2 ࠍࠃࠕ × S_1

٢٠٧ في حق الذكر [LB_2 > ∩ $GCUJDS_2B_1$ وفي] في × B_1

٢٠٨ الانثى] الاثنين × S_2 ࠅࠀࠌ ࠍࠒࠁࠄ ࠕࠋࠃ ࠅࠈࠌࠀࠄ ࠔࠁࠏࠉࠌ ࠊࠍࠃࠕࠄ G ࠔࠁࠏࠉࠌ [ࠔࠁࠏࠉࠌ × B_2

٢٠٩ يلزم] ∩ U عن [$GB_2DS_2B_1S_1$ > CUJL

السبعة الايام حكمه حكم الاول يلزم عنه سبعه وما حدث منه في الثامن او في الخاش عشر انما يلزم عنه حال لان حكمه يغير عن حكم ها يجي في السبعة الايام وفي الاربعة عشر. وقد نجد عادات النسوان ان جاريه باحتراز من كل دم يحدث في السبعه والاربعه عشره لثقل حكمه ومباينته ࠋࠃࠌ ࠈࠄࠓࠄ.

٢١ وما بعد هذه الايام المحدوده تبقى في عقلة ࠃࠌ ࠈࠄࠓࠄ وهو دم النفاس ونقاها منه. واليهود يزعموا ان ࠃࠌ ࠈࠄࠓࠄ طهرها وهو عندهم دم طاهر وغلطهم في هذا ظاهر اذ ليس من الدما الخارجه من الفرج طاهر بل جميعها يحكم عليها بالنجاسه. ولاجل ذلك يبيحون مخالطتها للاطهار و يبيحون للزوج وطيها. وهذا منهم فتوى بحكم فاسد يخالف شريعة الرسول.

٢٢ اولا لان دم ࠈࠄࠓࠄ يحتمل طهورها ويحتمل نقاها من قوله ࠅࠀࠌ ࠈࠄࠓࠄ ࠌࠆࠅࠁࠄ (اح ١٥ : ٢٨). ويريد به نقاها وقوله تعالى ࠅࠊࠐࠓ ࠏࠋࠉࠄ ࠄࠊࠄࠍ ࠅࠈࠄࠓࠄ ࠌࠌࠒࠓ ࠃࠌࠉࠄ (اح ١٢ : ٧). ويناسب هذا قوله تعالى [illegible]

٢١١ السبعة الايام] UCS$_2$S$_1$ السبعة ايام GLB$_2$DB$_1$؛ سبعة الايام J حكم] + ࠀࠋࠃࠌ G لزم B$_1$ سبعه] سبعة ايام GC او في] [illegible] G
٢١٢ انما .... عشره] ∩ U عنه] > J يغيير × C الايام JB$_2$S$_2$B$_1$S$_1$] ايام GCLD عشره US$_1$] عشر (الساير)
٢١٣ نجد] + في LB$_2$ عادة B$_2$D ان LB$_2$S$_1$] > GCUJDS$_2$B$_1$ جاريه] جازيه × L السبعه S$_1$] السبعة ايام (الساير) والاربعه LB$_2$DS$_2$B$_1$S$_1$] وفي الاربعه GCUJ عشره S$_1$
٢١٤ لثقل] لنقل × DS$_2$ ࠋࠃࠌ ࠈࠄࠓࠄ] لدم طهره S$_1$؛ ࠋࠃࠌ ࠈࠄࠓࠄࠀ G
٢١٥ ࠃࠌ ࠈࠄࠓࠄ CUJS$_2$B$_1$] دم ࠈࠄࠓࠄ LB$_2$D؛ دم طهره S$_1$؛ ࠃࠌ ࠈࠄࠓࠄࠀ G منه] + [illegible] G
٢١٦ ࠃࠌ ࠈࠄࠓࠄ] دم طهره U طهرها] [illegible] ࠃࠌ ࠈࠄࠓࠄࠀ G دم S$_2$S$_1$] > (الساير)
٢١٧ اذ (الساير) P] ان B$_1$ طاهره B$_2$D حمعها × B$_2$ بالنجاسه (الساير) P] + عدا دم [illegible] المتقدم عنه الذكر J
٢١٨ الزوج U وهذه PLB$_2$D
٢٢٠ دم S$_1$] ࠃࠌ (الساير) ࠈࠄࠓࠄ] ࠈࠄࠓࠄࠀ G يحتمل] ويحتمل × B$_2$ ويحتمل] وتحتمل × S$_2$ نقاها] بقاها × US$_2$*B$_1$ من قوله PGUJDS$_2$S$_1$] لقوله B$_1$؛ وقوله تعالى B$_2$؛ من قول × C
٢٢١-٢ [illegible] G
٢٢٢-٢ وقوله .... ࠃࠌࠉࠄ] > ∩ GC
٢٢١ تعالى (الساير) P > B$_2$
٢٢٢ تعالى] > D
٢٢٣-٢ [illegible] G
٢٢٢ [illegible] ULB$_2$S$_2$B$_1$S$_1$] [illegible] HCJD
٢٢٣ [illegible] [illegible] B$_2$

דמיה (اح ٢٠ : ١٨). فما صرنا اليه من التاويل وما تمسكنا به من احد محتملي اللفظ وهو اظهرهما اولى. ولو كان هذا الدم المذكور طاهرا لم يكن لقوله וכפר עליה הכהן וטהרה معنى. والمعنى فيه انه يدعوا لها بالطهر من مجمع دمها ومنبع دمها وهذا في غاية المناسبه لقوله והיא גלתה את מקור דמיה فالترجع بما رجعنا نحن اليه اولى واشبه بطريق الاجتهاد ووجوب الاحتياط. وهذا من احد الاصول المقصوده في الاجتهاد في الفقهيات اذا احتمل واحتمل وكان احد المحتملين يقتضي اثبات حكم شرعي والاخر يقتضي الجواز والبقا على ما في العقل فان التمسك بما افاد حكما شرعيا اولى واذا كان اظهر محتملي اللفظ هو متمسكا كان اجرى.

ومن باب القياس ايضا يعلم ان [Samaritan script] وان كان لا يجيها في تلك الايام دم فانها تمتنع من مخالطة الاطهار ومن الاجرى امتناعها من مخالطة الاقداس ولا يحل الانضجاع معها ولا جماعها. والوالده في ايام نقاها لا يامن حدوث الدم فتحريم مخالطتها الاطهار والمنع منه اولى.

وهذا هو حمل الشي في الحكم على ما هو في معنايه لا بل ان الحكم يلزم فيه من طريق الاجرى.

---

٢٢٤ من] < B_2 × احد $[PLB_2S_1$ اخذ × $GCUJDS_2B_1$

٢٢٥ اظهرهما $[LB_2S_2B_1S_1$ اظهرها × PUJ ؛ طهرهما × GC ؛ اطهارها × D

٢٢٥-٢٢٦ [Samaritan script] G

٢٢٦ فيه (الساير P] [Samaritan script] G لها] له × PGS_1^2 بالطهر $[S_1$ + والنقا (والنق P) (الساير P) ؛ [Samaritan script] G مجمع دمها ومنبع $[S_1$ منبع (منع × DS_2) (الساير P)

٢٢٧ [Samaritan script] G [Samaritan script] × C فالترجع $[JLS_1$ فالترجيع × $PGCUB_2B_1$ ؛ فالترجيح × DS_2

٢٢٨ نحن] < U اولى واشبه] < × LD من طريق D

٢٢٩ المقصوده $[UJS_1$ المقصود $PGCLB_2DS_2B_1$ في (ثاني) $[S_1$ ووجوب (الساير) اذا] اذ × U احتمل] (خالي) D

٢٣٠ الجواز] الزواج × B_1 في] < × J

٢٣١ اظهر] الطهر × DS_2 متمسكا (متمسك LB_2)] متى × U اجرى $[PUJLB_2S_2B_1$ احرى S_1 ؛ احرى × GC

٢٣٢ ايضا (الساير P] < B_1 [Samaritan script] G [Samaritan script] [Samaritan script] J*LB_2 ؛ [Samaritan script] D

٢٣٣ مخالطة] ∩ B_2 الاجرى $[PUJLS_2B_1$ الاحرى S_1 ؛ الاحرى × GCD امتناعها (الساير P] منعها C من] عن LDS_2 مخالطة الاقداس] المخالطه (مخالطة × B_2) للاقداس PLB_2D

٢٣٤ الانضجاع (الساير P] الاجتماع C لا يامن] الا يام نان × B_2 لا] الا × J فتحريم] فتحرم × C

٢٣٦ هو] < D معنايه (الساير P] [Samaritan script] G ؛ معنا × B_2 لا (الساير P] < B_2 ان] < DS_2

٢٣٧ الاجرى $[PCUJLDB_2B_1$ الاحرى S_1 ؛ الاحرى × GS_2

وهي في ايام نقاها تدخل تحت عموم النفي والنهي في قوله ࠅࠀࠉࠔ ࠀࠔࠓ ࠉࠔࠊࠁ ࠀࠕ ࠀࠔࠄ ࠃࠅࠄ (اح ٢٠ : ١٨) لان هذا الاسم يعم كل من كانت في ان وزمان يتوقع فيه حدوث الدم وفي عقلة دم متقدم باي وصف وباي حكم فلا يصح جماعها ولا مخالطتها للاطهار.

واما تمسكهم بقوله ࠁࠊࠋ ࠒࠃࠔ ࠋࠀ ࠕࠂࠏ ࠅࠀࠋ ࠄࠌࠒࠃࠔ ࠋࠀ ࠕࠁࠅࠀ (اح ١٢ : ٤) وان الشارع انما منعها بذلك عن مخالطة الاقداس لا مخالطة الاطهار. والجواب انه لا يفهم من هذا اباحة مخالطة الاطهار بل الشارع يذكر في كل اصل من الاحكام ما لا يذكره في غيره ويعول على القياس وعلى طرد الحكم في النظاير ما لا ينبه عن القياس عليه. ولنا ان نقول من طريق الحكم في الدم الحادث في زمان نقا النفاس ان هذا الدم ينجس من يدنو به وتلوث برطوبته.

او يقولو انه اذا يلثق به ثوب وتلوث به او اله من الالات لا ينجس. فان قلتم بنجاسته فقد صرتم الى راينا ضرورة وان قلتم لا ينجس ما يدنو به ذلك الدم ويحصل عليه فقد خالفتم قوله تعالى ࠅࠊࠐࠓ ࠏࠋࠉࠄ ࠄࠊࠄࠍ ࠅࠈࠄࠓࠄ (ايه ٧). وقد نجد ايضا ان قربانها وقربان ࠄࠆࠁࠄ † متاخر الى كمال طهر كل واحده منهما فالمجانسه واقعه

---

٢٣٨ قوله] S_1 + تعالى (الساير) P

٢٣٩-٢٣ [illegible] G

٢٣٩ بعم × S_1

٢٢٣-٢٧ [illegible] G

٢٤٣ وان] [illegible] × G الشارع] الله تعالى B_1 ؛ + تعالى P الاقداس] الاطهار × GC الاطهار] الاقداس × GC

٢٤٤-٢٤ مخالطة الاطهار] ∩ B_2*

٢٤٤ والجواب] S_1 الجواب (الساير) P

٢٤٥ طرد] [illegible] × G

٢٤٦ ينبه] ينه × S_1* عن] على × US_1^2 هذا < S_1*

٢٤٧ وتلوث] S_1^2 ويتلوث (الساير) P^{PL} ؛ ويتلون × $P^{OBJ}S_2$ ؛ ويتلثق × S_1*

٢٤٨ يلثق به ثوب وتلوث به] S_1 حصل على ثوب (الثوب D) (الساير) P اله] $S_2B_1S_1$ + ما $PGCUJLDB_2$ ينجس] $PUJLB_2DS_2B_1S_1$ يتنجس GC بنجاسته] نجاسه × B_1

٢٤٩ صرتم] حريم × B_2 يدنو به (الساير) P] يدنوه B_1

٢٥٠ [illegible] G وطهرها] S_1 + ממקור דמיה (الساير) ان] $UJS_2B_1S_1$ < PLB_2D ؛ في GC

٢٥١ הזבה] + והזב × $CUJLB_2DS_2B_1S_1$ ؛ [illegible] × G ؛ الذايب والذايبه × P^{JPL} ؛ الذايب × P^{OB} واحده] S_1 واحد × (الساير) P منهما] $P^{PLOB}UJLB_2S_2B_1S_1$ منها × $P^{J}GCD$ فالمجانسه] S_1 والمجانسه (الساير) P

٢٥٢ والمماثله (الساير) P] [illegible] G كانت (الساير) P] كان S_1* كذلك] < × B_2

والمماثله حاصله واذا كانت كذلك فالحكم واحد ولا يصح اختلاف الاحكام مع مماثلة الاسباب.

فهذه شرايع [Samaritan] [Samaritan] [Samaritan].

وجملة الخلاف بيننا وبينهم فيها في الدم الاول وذلك في وجهين. احدهما انه نجس بكل لون وليس فيه نوع يوصف بالطهر. الثاني انه وحده هو الذي يلزم منه سبعة ايام بخلاف الحادث في اليوم الثاني. واي شي حصل عليه هذا الدم من انسان الى اله يلزمه سبعة ايام وما يحدث في اليوم الثاني يلزم عنه حال واحد.

[[وايضا وجه ثالث وهو ان شريعة [Samaritan] تدوم سبعة اسابيع ومن بعد ذلك مع اتصال الحادث يكون [Samaritan]. وشريعة [Samaritan] تعرف باتصال حدوث الدم عنها بكل لون من اصفر وغيره.

[[واي شي حصل عليه هذا الدم من انسان الى اله يلزمه سبعة ايام. وما يحدث في اليوم الثاني يلزم عنه حال واحد.]]

[[واما ان يتصل الدم وحدوثه او يتحلل في الايام يعتد ولا بتخلله من بعد الاسابيع المعلومه ويلزمها ما يلزم [Samaritan]. واذا نقيت وطهرت بعد سبعة ايام كمل. وحكمها في [Samaritan] [Samaritan] ان لا تختلط بالاطهار ولا ينضجع معها الزوج كما تقدم ذكره. وان

---

٢٥٤ [Samaritan] [Samaritan] [$P^{B}S_1$ [Samaritan] G [Samaritan] [Samaritan] (الساير) P^{OJPL}

٢٥٥ الخلاف [$LB_2DS_2B_1S_1$ + الواقع GCUJ بالدم GC في (اول)] < × B_2 في (ثاني) [$UJS_2B_1S_1$ من $GCLB_2D$ [Samaritan] G

٢٥٦ انه [S_1 < (الساير)

٢٥٧ هذا الدم] < C الى] + [Samaritan] G

٢٥٨ يلزمه [$GLS_2B_1S_1$ يلزم $CUJB_2$ يلزم] يلزمه LB_2

٢٥٩ [Samaritan] G

٢٦٠ الحادث] الحاصل D [Samaritan] [Samaritan] G [Samaritan] [Samaritan] G حدوث] حصول C

٢٦١ او غيره LB_2D

٢٦٢–٢٦٣ يلزمه .... الثاني] < ∩ D

٢٦٣ حال واحد [S_1 + (واحد < L) يعني يطهر لوقته (الساير)

٢٦٤ ويتحلل GLB_2 ايام S_2 يعتد [LB_2 < × (الساير) ولا [LB_2 + يعتد $GCUJS_2B_1S_1$؛ + يقيد × D

٢٦٤–٢٦٥ بتخلله .... نقيت] < × J

٢٦٤ يتحلله × LB_2 من [S_1 < (الساير)

٢٦٥ نقيت [GC نقيت S_1؛ بقيت (بقية L) $ULB_2DS_2B_1$ كمل] [Samaritan] G في] < × B_2

٢٦٦ [Samaritan] [Samaritan] [$H^2CS_2B_1S_1$ [Samaritan] [Samaritan] L؛ [Samaritan] [Samaritan] H*UJ؛ [Samaritan]

انضجع على سبيل المعصيه ففيه وجهان. احدهما ان يقاس على وطي ࠄࠃࠅࠄ والثاني لا يلزمه والاول اولى لانها في عقلة دم قد تقدم كالدوه. وكذلك ࠄࠉࠋࠃࠄ في ايام نقاها او عقلتها لاجل النقا من دم النفاس.]]

[فصل من كتاب الخلاف]

وقد تكلمت مع بعضهم في بعض معلولات ࠄࠆࠁ في قول الكتاب الشريف ࠅࠊࠋ ࠄࠍࠂࠏ ࠁࠊࠋ ࠀࠔࠓ ࠉࠄࠉࠄ ࠕࠇࠕࠉࠅ ࠉࠈࠌࠀ ࠏࠃ ࠄࠏࠓࠁ (اح ١٥ : ١٠). فقلت له ما قولك فيما يعلوه من غطا وغيره ما حكمه. فقال البقا على حاله لا يلزمه نجس ولا يلزم عنه نجس. قلت فما العله القاصره التي الزمت عندك الاصل ولم يتعداه. فقال نقله واعتماده والاعتماد والنقل انما يكون على ما تحته لا على ما فوقه. قلت له فعلتك هذه مخالفه للاصول وكل عله عارضها اصل فهي فاسده. الا ترى ان الشارع نجس فراشه بقوله ࠅࠊࠋ ࠄࠌࠔࠊࠁ ࠀࠔࠓ ࠉࠔࠊࠁ ࠏࠋࠉࠅ ࠉࠈࠌࠀ (ايه ٤) فهل هذا مقصور على ما يكون تحته او يعم غطاه ايضا او يخص ما تحته من الفراش فان خصصته فقد ادعيت خلاف العاده والمشهور في العرف فان ࠄࠌࠔࠊࠁ اسم يعم كلما يستعمله من وطا وغطا. الا ترى كيف تقول في قوله تعالى ࠅࠀࠉࠔ ࠀࠔࠓ ࠉࠂࠏ ࠁࠌࠔࠊࠁࠅ ࠉࠊࠁࠎ ࠁࠂࠃࠉࠅ ࠅࠓࠇࠑ ࠁࠌࠉࠌ ࠅࠈࠌࠀ ࠏࠃ ࠄࠏࠓࠁ (ايه ٥) وايضا قوله تعالى ࠅࠊࠋ ࠄࠍࠂࠏ ࠁࠊࠋ ࠀࠔࠓ ࠉࠄࠉࠄ ࠕࠇࠕࠉࠅ

ࠈࠑࠃࠉࠄ B₂ ؛ ࠉࠔࠉ ࠈࠑࠉࠃ؛ D ؛ ࠀࠉࠀࠔ ࠏࠃࠃࠄࠀ G لا] < × J تختلط] تخلط S₂

٢٦٧-٢٦ معها .... انضجع] < ∩ U

٢٦٧ انضجع] + معها D ࠄࠃࠅࠄ] ࠀࠋࠇࠉࠑࠄ G

٢٦٨ يلزمه] يلزم LB₂ اولى S₁] + واصح CUJLB₂DS₂B₁ ؛ + ࠅࠀࠇࠄ ࠅࠀࠀࠄࠈࠒ G قد] فقد × J كالدوه S₁] ࠊࠋࠃࠅࠄ × B₂S₂B₁ ؛ ࠊࠋ ࠃࠅࠄ × JL ؛ ࠅࠋࠃࠅࠄ × U ؛ ࠀࠋࠈࠃࠄ × C ؛ ࠊࠋࠈࠃࠄ × D ؛ ࠊࠀࠋࠇࠉࠑࠄ G ࠄࠉࠋࠃࠄ S₁] ࠄࠉࠋࠉࠃࠄ CUJLB₂DS₂B₁ ؛ ࠀࠋࠅࠀࠋࠃࠄ G في] < × B₂

١ قولكم B₁ وما D

٤ نجس] < S₁ فما] فيما × J الذي D عندك] < D

٥ انما] < B₁ لا ما على فوقه D فقلت S₂

٦ فعلتك] فتعليل × DB₁

٧ ࠕࠇࠕࠉࠅ] + ࠄࠆࠁ D

٨ مقصور] مقصود الثارع × DS₂ تحته] + من الفراش DB₁

٩ المشهور × D همشكب S₁

١٠-١٢ الا ترى .... عن B₁] < × GCUJLB₂DS₂S₁

ࠉࠈࠌࠀ ࠏࠃ ࠄࠏࠓࠁ (ايه ١٠) فهذه النصوص تدل بالدليل القطعي ان كل دنا في فراش ࠄࠆࠁ الذي ينام عليه ࠉࠈࠌࠀ. فاذا كان ذات الفراش ينقل الطما الى من دنا به فاولى طما الغطا الذي هو متصل في الفراش وفي نفس ࠄࠆࠁ الذي طما الفراش. هذا ما تقول فيه † فما † اتا بها عن † السلف †.

---

١٦ فما] فما × B_1 السلف] (خالي)] × B_1

TEXT 4

[كتاب الفرايض]

< الفريضه الرابعه والخمسون >

] . . . .
. . . .] وْهٰذْهْ هي
عقيب طهر وهذه ࠄࠆࠁࠄ هي ࠍࠃࠄ.

وهذا الدم يختلف في قوامه في 〈 الرقه 〉 والغلظ. فقد يكون تارة غليظا وقد يكون تارة رقيقا. ويختلف في لونه بان يكون حمرته تارة صافيه ومشيعه وقد يميل الى السواد اكثر من ميله الى الحمره وقد يكون منه ما ميله الى الصفره.

فطهر المراه هو وجود رطوبه بيضا صافيه نقيه فمتى تغيرت هذه الرطوبه عن الصفا والنقا والبياض الى اقل قليلا لزم الطما. لان مثله مثل الما الصافي اذا خالطه يسيرا من ذواب الالوان كالزعفران وغيره فيتغير لونه بمقدار ما يمازجه في باب 〈 〉 الالوان ويكون قوة اللون وضعفه بمقدار ما يمازجه. فان الوجه اعتزال الامراه متى رات ما يخرج عن البياض لجواز كون دم ࠍࠃࠉࠄ يسيرا فلا يغير حاله كثيرا كل ممازجه اثرت فيه. ولم يحصل خلف من احد في ان قليل الدم ككثرته في باب النجاسات. ولمثل ذلك اوجب العلما اعتبارة نفسها بالقطن [او] الصوف النقيين فاذا مال الخارج الى 〈 الغبره 〉 او الى الزرقه او الخضره او الصفره كانت علامه للطما.

فاذا افتقدت المراه نفسها ولم تري علامة النجاسه ثم اعتبرت حالها بعد وقت فراتها فنجاستها المقطوع بها منذ الاعتبار الثاني. الا ان يكون لها عاده قد عرفتها لنفسها عند مجرى الدم من عرض يعرض لها مثل تثاوب او فواق او سمط او وجع راس وما يجري هذا المجرى وعليها ان [. . . . .] ولا [. . . .] بها بقطن كما ذكرناه. وان كانت لم تعتبر نفسها الا من بعده فوجد[ها] علامة النجاسه. لان الدم قد لا يتدارك انبعاثه فكان لا يخفى عنها الامر فيه. بل قد يكون اوله يسيرا ثم يحصل قوته بعد وقت فلا يظهر فيه ما يتباين للنجس بل يظهر بتلك العلامات المذكوره وقد خفي على قلته لا يكثر.

قال الكتاب الشريف ࠁࠁࠔࠓࠄ (اح ١٥ : ١٩) فاقتضى ذلك انه متى حصل في المكان المخصوص منها حصلت النجاسه.

وانه لا يراعي ⟨طهورها⟩ منه كما هذا مراعا في الذكر. قوله ࠔࠁࠏࠕ ࠉࠌࠉࠌ ࠕࠄࠉࠄ ࠁࠍࠃࠕࠄ (ايه ١٩) هي سبعة ايام متصله وقد يكون كامله وقد يكون ناقصه من جهة ابتداها بحيث يحصل الدم وقد مر في اليوم بعضه. فلو قلنا انها قد تحسب تقديرا الطهر من يوم ولزمها ان تراعي سبعة ايام كامله ولا يمكن ان تخرج الى طهر في الطُهُر الذي يكمل لها به سبعة ايام ⟨نجاسه⟩ كون مدة نجاستها ازيد من سبعة ايام ولما لم يلزم ذلك ساغ ان تكون هذه السبعه ⟨ناقصه⟩ من حيث ابتداها لا من حيث انتهاها.

واللغه تقتضي ان ࠍࠃࠕࠄ (ايه ١٩) تقتضي الابعاد وغير منكر ان سمي المنبعث من هذه ࠍࠃࠕࠄ لما تقتضيه من ابعادها عن الاطهار ومعناه تبقى معتزله بسبب ࠍࠃࠕࠄ. وان قلنا [انها] ࠈࠌࠀࠄ لاجل ࠍࠃࠕࠄ جاز لانها قد سميت ࠈࠌࠀࠄ لقوله ࠅࠋࠀࠉࠔ ࠀࠔࠓ ࠉࠔࠊࠁ ࠏࠌ ࠈࠌࠀࠄ والمُعني متقارب.

وانما يبقى النظر على اطلاق هذا الاسم اعني ࠍࠃࠕࠄ هل هو واقع على كل دم يظهر من الامراه في هذه السبعة الايام ⟨او انما⟩ هو مخصوص بالاول منه. والاصح اختصاصه بالاول لان الظاهر كون الكلام في امراه لا نجاسه عليها من دم وتجدد حدوث دم اوجب لها حكما لم يكن من قبل وحدث عقيب حدوثه. ذِكر الاسم بعد قوله ࠔࠁࠏࠕ ࠉࠌࠉࠌ (ايه ١٩) فاذا هو الذي اوجب عليها الاعتزال سبعة ايام. بل لو رات دمًا بالقرب من اخر السابع بحيث تخلص منه بالقرب من وقت الطهر لصح ان تصير طاهرا. وكل هذا مما يوجب اختصاص التسميه بالدم الاول وتعليق الحكم به.

قال ࠅࠊࠋ ࠀࠔࠓ ࠕࠔࠊࠁ ࠏࠋࠉࠅ ࠁࠍࠃࠕࠄ ࠉࠈࠌࠀ وتمامه (ايه ٢٠). ذكر في ࠄࠆࠁࠄ مثل ما ذكر في ࠄࠆࠁ فهو ࠄࠌࠔࠊࠁ ࠅࠄࠌࠅࠔࠁ ࠅࠄࠍࠂࠏ ⟨وفي ࠄࠍࠃࠄ ايضا ذكر⟩ ࠄࠌࠔࠊࠁ ࠅࠄࠍࠂࠏ ⟨بقوله هاهنا ࠅࠊࠋ ࠄࠍࠂࠏ⟩ ࠁࠊࠋ ࠄࠊࠋࠉ ࠀࠔࠓ ࠕࠔࠊࠁ ࠏࠋࠉࠅ (ايــــه ٢٢). وبالجمله كلما ورد في ⟨ࠄࠆࠁ⟩ مثله هاهنا. وان كان الكتاب الشريف اختصر البعض قال هاهنا ࠅࠀࠌ ࠏࠋ ࠄࠌࠔࠊࠁࠄ ࠄࠉࠀ ࠀࠅ ࠏࠋ ࠄࠊࠋࠉ (ايه ٢٣) فاعلم به لان لا فرق بين نجاسة ࠌࠔࠊࠁ ࠍࠃࠄ وهي جالسه عليه او لم تكن جالسه عليه.

قول الكتاب الشريف ࠅࠀࠌ ࠔࠊࠁ ࠉࠔࠊࠁ ࠀࠉࠔ ࠀࠕࠄ ⟨ ⟩ ࠅࠕࠄࠉࠄ ࠍࠃࠕࠄ ࠏࠋࠉࠅ ࠉࠈࠌࠀ ࠔࠁࠏࠕ ࠉࠌࠉࠌ (ايه ٢٤) والوجه فيه انه تكلم الكتاب على رجل يضاجع امراه طاهره فيحدث عليها النجاسه في حال الجماع. فيكون حكم هذا الرجل حكم المراه التي نجس لاجلها في كون نجاسته سبعة ايام. فان نام معها في فراش بغير مجامعه وتلوث بدم ينبعث منها ما حكمه قلنا النجاسه سبعة ايام. وبُعِد بهذا قول من قال ان نجاسة الرجل سبعة ايام فيها شرطان احدهما ࠅࠄࠌࠔࠊࠁ والاخر تلوثه بدمها لان الدم اذا كان قد نجس الامراه سبعة ايام لتلوثها به فالرجل ينجس لذلك

فالسبب الموجب [لطماء] الرجل هو الدم وسبب انبعاث الدم هو ࠄࠔࠊࠉࠁࠄ. وهذا هو ⟨حكم⟩ الدم الاول وهو ࠃࠌ ࠍࠃࠄ كما قلنا في رجل يضاجع امراه طاهره فتحدث عليها نجاسه فى حال الجماع ⟨او مجرد⟩ النوم.

وزعم الفيومي ان هذا الحكم مقول في حق من ⟨اتطا⟩ زوجته في زمان ࠍࠃࠕࠄ وهو عالم بانها ࠍࠃࠄ. وهو لا يعلم ان الذي يُقَصَد ويُعتمد اوجب عليه القتل لقوله ࠅࠀࠉࠔ ࠀࠔࠓ ࠉࠔࠊࠁ ࠀࠕ ࠀࠔࠄ ࠃࠅࠄ ࠅࠂࠋࠄ ࠀࠕ ࠏࠓࠅࠕࠄ ࠀࠕ ࠌࠒࠅࠓࠄ ࠄࠏࠓࠄ ࠅࠄࠉࠀ ࠂࠋࠕࠄ ࠀࠕ ࠌࠒࠅࠓ ࠃࠌࠉࠄ ࠅࠍࠊࠓࠕࠅ ࠔࠍࠉࠄࠌ ࠌࠒࠓࠁ ࠏࠌࠌ (اح ٢٠ : ١٨) لان ࠃࠌ ࠃࠅࠄ ما كان خارجا عن الدم الاول وهو موجودا في باقي الايام ولو انه وطى من علم انها طاهره لما بقى عنه حكم القتل واوجب عليه لزوم الطماء سبعة ايام. فلا يجوز جماع المراه في السبعه.

ويلزم مثله ࠄࠉࠋࠉࠃࠄ في الاربعين يوما في الذكور والثمانين في الاناثي لقوله ࠅࠈࠄࠓࠄ ࠌࠌࠒࠅࠓ ࠃࠌࠉࠄ (اح ١٢ : ٧) فان القياس مطرد كما قال هاهنا ࠅࠄࠉࠀ ࠂࠋࠕࠄ ࠀࠕ ࠌࠒࠅࠓ ࠃࠌࠉࠄ (اح ٢٠ : ١٨).

ويطرد القياس في ࠄࠆࠁࠄ في ايام ࠃࠅࠕࠄ لقوله ࠊࠋ ࠉࠌࠉ ࠆࠅࠁ ࠈࠌࠀࠕࠄ ࠊࠉࠌࠉ ࠍࠃࠕࠄ ࠕࠄࠉࠄ ࠈࠌࠀࠄ ࠄࠉࠀ (اح ١٥ : ٢٥). واما في ايام نقاها وهي ࠅࠋࠎࠐࠉࠓࠄ فمن قوله ⟨ࠅࠊࠐࠓ ࠏࠋࠉࠄ ࠄࠊࠄࠍ ࠌࠆࠅࠁ ࠈࠌࠀࠕࠄ⟩ (ايه ٣٠).

⟨واما حكم هذا الرجل فمن قوله⟩ ࠅࠋࠀࠉࠔ ࠀࠔࠓ ࠉࠔࠊࠁ ࠏࠌ ࠈࠌࠀࠄ (ايه ٣٣).

واعلم ان لفظة ࠆࠁࠄ يعم ويخص.

اما عمومها فلانها تطلق على الاول المسمى ࠃࠌ ࠍࠃࠄ وقد عرفت حكمه. وقد يطلق على ما يسيل باقي الاسبوع ويسمى ࠃࠅࠄ. وان كان مخالفونا يسمونه ࠃࠌࠆࠁࠄ ولا ⟨تمشا حجه⟩ في الاسماء. ⟨وحكمه⟩ تخلص الانسان منه في يوم دنوه به فان الامراه اذا نقيت منه في اليوم السابع قبل غيبة الشمس طهرت الامه مجمعه على ذلك.

وقد يطلق على الدم الخارج عن المعتاد المباين لعوايد النسوان فبعض النسوان يندفع منهن هذا الفصل في الشهر دفعه وبعضهن في اقل وبعضهن في اكثر هذا على الامر الطبيعي. واما الخارج عن الامر الطبيعي فصله بقوله ⟨ࠉࠌࠉࠌ⟩ ࠓࠁࠉࠌ (ايه ٢٥) وهو المخصوص باسم ࠆࠁࠄ.

ࠄࠉࠌࠉࠌ ࠄࠓࠁࠉࠌ يحتمل ان يكون سنينا لقوله ࠁࠉࠌࠉࠌ ࠄࠓࠁࠉࠌ (خر ٢ : ٢٣) ويحتمل ان يكون شهرا او اقل من شهر فلهذا جعل بعض اصحابنا حده المتوسط وهو حدود الشهر فاذا كانت اربعة اسابيع متتاليه لزمها ࠄࠎࠐࠉࠓࠄ. وهذا هو الحق.

وقوله ࠅࠊࠉ ࠕࠆࠅࠁ ࠏࠋ ࠍࠃࠕࠄ ࠁࠋࠀ ࠏࠕ ࠍࠃࠕࠄ (ايه ٢٥) اي مخالف للمعتاد خارج عن لجاري المالوف. ومخالفونا ذهبوا الى 〈ان〉 ࠃࠌ ࠍࠃࠕࠄ اشاره الى مدة سبعة ايام فاذا اتصل واستمر سيلانه في اليوم الثامن وما يليه فذلك يندرج تحت قوله ࠉࠌࠉࠌ ࠓࠁࠉࠌ ࠁࠋࠀ ࠏࠕ ࠍࠃࠕࠄ. وهذا باطل بقوله ࠅࠈࠌࠀࠄ ࠔࠁࠏࠉࠌ ࠊࠍࠃࠕࠄ (اح ١٢ : ٥) فانه سمى هذه المده 〈 〉 ࠍࠃࠕࠄ ولم يسمها 〈 〉 ࠆࠅࠁࠄ فدل على ان 〈 〉 ࠆࠅࠁࠄ اكثر من هذه. اذ من النسا من عادتها يجيها الدم اسبوعين ولو لم يكن على ما قلنا والا لزم عدم الطهر في الاكثر. لان كثيرا من النسا يحصل لهن الطما 〈اربعة عشر يوما〉 〈ويطهرن〉 〈سبعة ايام〉 فاذا تطمين اسبوعين وعملن ࠎࠐࠉࠓࠄ في الثالث قل زمان طهرهن وعاد الدم من الراس. فان اراد بان ابتدا ࠉࠌࠉࠌ ࠓࠁࠉࠌ اليوم الثامن وما [يتـ]ـلاه الى اُنْتُهْى اُلْمْده التي حددناها 〈جار〉 قوله والا فلا 〈يتسوغ〉 . وبعض اصحابنا ذهب ان الامراه ان نظفت من الدم 〈في〉 اخر السابع ثم رات في اي وقت كان من الثامن وهي ࠍࠃࠄ لا ࠆࠁࠄ لكونها فصلت الدمين بزمان هو في حكم الثامن وان لم تفصل سميت ࠆࠁࠄ لان حرف ࠏࠋ من قوله ࠕࠆࠅࠁ ࠏࠋ ࠍࠃࠕࠄ يفيد التالي والتعاقب. والاول اقرب وهو اذا انقض سابعها ورات في ثامنه دم طمث ثم في الاسبوع الثالث كذلك والرابع ايضا اسميت ࠆࠁࠄ لخروجه عن المعتاد.

قال بعض اصحابنا رحمهم الله 〈ان〉 الفرق بين ࠄࠍࠃࠄ ࠅࠄࠆࠁࠄ هو ان ࠄࠆࠁࠄ يكون بعد طما ࠅࠄࠍࠃࠄ بعد طهر. اعترض على ذلك ࠁࠉࠅࠋࠃࠄ التي 〈ترى〉 دم 〈في〉 اخر نهار يوم الاربعين او الثمانين لولادتها وهي ࠍࠃࠄ لا عن طهر بل بعد طما [كـ]ـقوله ࠌࠌࠒࠅࠓ ࠃࠌࠉࠄ (اح ١٢ : ٧). وهذا الاعتراض فيه نظر.

قال ࠅࠊࠋ ࠄࠌࠔࠊࠁ ࠀࠔࠓ 〈ࠕࠔࠊࠁ〉 ࠏࠋࠉࠅ (اح ١٥ : ٢٦). عام لذلك ولغيره كما ذكر في فصل ࠄࠍࠃࠄ ليلزم فيها ما ذكره هناك وقوله ࠅࠊࠋ ࠄࠊࠋࠉ ࠀࠔࠓ ࠕࠔࠁ ࠏࠋࠉࠅ ࠈࠌࠀ ࠉࠄࠉࠄ ࠊࠈࠌࠀࠕ ࠍࠃࠕࠄ (ايه ٢٦) [يفـ]ـيد ان هذه الالات تطما سبعة ايام.

قوله ࠅࠀࠌ ࠈࠄࠓࠄ ࠌࠆࠅࠁࠄ ࠅࠎࠐࠓࠄ ࠋࠄ ࠔࠁࠏࠕ ࠉࠌࠉࠌ وتمامه (ايه ٢٨) يقتضى ظاهره عدا بالقول ويقرب ان الغرض ضبط الايام فسوى. فاْ[وجب] ذلك بالطهر بالعدد او لحفظه او حصول ما يقوم مقام العمد تميزا.

ثم تطهر باستعمال الما في الوقت.

ثم قال ࠅࠁࠉࠅࠌ ࠄࠔࠌࠉࠍࠉ ࠕࠒࠇ الى قوله ࠅࠊࠐࠓ ࠏࠋࠉࠄ ࠄࠊࠄࠍ (ايات ١٩ – ٢٠) هو بفعل القربان. ويلحق بذلك الدعا لها بان يعافيها الله تعالى من هذا المرض لان ࠄࠆࠁࠄ تجرى مجرى ࠄࠍࠃࠄ في كونه ليس مرضا بل تقتضى ࠄࠍࠃࠄ

ضنكـ[ـا] للجسم واعلى ࠄࠆࠁࠄ بانقطاعها واعتزالها عما هو من الاطـ[ـهار] ضرر وكذلك قال ࠌࠆࠅࠁ ࠈࠌࠀࠕࠄ (ايه ٣٠).

١٢ قوله ࠅࠄࠆࠄࠓࠕࠌ ࠀࠕ ࠁࠍࠉ ࠉࠔࠓࠀࠋ (ايه ٣١) هذا امر للرسولين عليهما السلام بان ‹يحيا› بني اسراييل بالقول هذا ادا الرساله بكلما ‹سمعاه› منه تعالى في باب الطما وبغير ذلك على ممر الوقت من قول وفعل. اذا توجه ما يقتضيهما وجب الناشي بفعلهما على ما يلزم فيه من الشروط لكي يستقيم الامه ولا يتوجه منه سبحانه سخط اذا حصل التفريط في النجا [سات] كما قال فيها يناسب هذا ࠅࠀࠕࠍࠄ ࠀࠕ ࠄࠋࠅࠉࠌ
١٢ ࠍࠕࠍࠉࠌ ࠋࠀࠄࠓࠍ ࠅࠋࠁࠍࠉࠅ الى قوله ࠅࠋࠀ ࠉࠄࠉࠄ ࠁࠁࠍࠉ ࠉࠔࠓࠀࠋ ࠍࠂࠐ وتمامه (تع ٨: ١٩).

وقوله ࠌࠈࠌࠀࠕࠌ (ايه ٣١) ويصلح ظـ[ـاهره] للثقيل من النجاسه وللخفيف لا سيما وقد ورد عقيب القسمين والغـ[ـرض] [. . . . .
. . . .

١٣ . . . .].

TEXT 5

[كتاب كاشف الغياهب]

[على الباب الخامس عشر من كتاب الاحبار]

فصل في شرح ذكر شريعة ࠅࠉࠒࠓࠀ

قال تعالى جل شانه وتعالى سلطانه ويدبر يهوه آل مشه وال اهرن لامر دبر ال بني يشرال وامرتم اليهم (اح ١٥ : ١) اي وخاطب الله الى موسى والى هارون قولا خاطبو الى بني اسراييل وتقولون لهم. فقد جعل الخطاب سبحانه وتعالى للرسول ثم للامام بالامر لهم ان يرشدوا لهم بهذا الحكم. وهذه الشريعه وهي قوله ايش ايش كي يهيه زب مبسرو زوبو طما هو (ايه ٢). وهو معنى عن دم او ماده تخرج عن القبل كطريقة الحيض من النسا اما عن مرض او عرض. فمتى حصل ذلك لرجل يحكم نجاسته. وهذا يكون اما عن قروح سيله تحدث في المثانه او انفتاق عرق من عروق الات التناسل او من قروح في القضبه او جرح او من زيادة الدم فى البدن.

وقوله كي يهيه زب مبسرو زوبو (ايه ٢) اي ان يكون ذايبا من بشرته ذوبه. والذوبان بمعنى السيلان ولفظة الحيض ايضا بمعنى السيل والعرب يقولو للوادي اذا سال حاض الوادي. وفي النسا سيل الفرج بما يقدفه الرحم من الدم الزايد وفي الرجل بما يسيل من الذكر.

وعند الحكما ان النسا تحيض بعد ثلاث عشر سنه ويمكن طوقه في السن العاشر وينقطع ما بين الخمسين والستين. والحيض المعتدل الذي يلزم دوره ولا يعديه ومتى اختلف كان من اختلاف المزاج واكثر اقامته في الاعتدال ثلاثة ايام ومنه يستمر الى الخامس وان كانت المراه دموية المزاج امتد الى العاشر.

---

١ ࠅࠉࠒࠓࠀ SU

٢ وتعالى سلطانه] < SU

٣-٤ اي ... لهم] < SU

٤ فقد جعل] فجعل SU   لهم] القوم SU

٦ القبل SU] الفيل × B

١٠ بشرته] بشره SU   اي] + يعني SU

١٢ سيل] سبيل × U

وقال بعض الحكما متى قصر عن اربعه وعشرين ساعه فليس بحيض. وفي الشرع متى سال دم من الرحم يحكم بالعزل سبعة ايام ولو انقطع في وقته. وياتي تفصيل ذلك انشا الله تعالى في محله.

ونحن في قوله ايش ايش كي يهيه زب مبسرو زوبو طما هو (ايه ٢) اي كل رجل ان يكون ذايبا من بشره ذوبةٍ نجسه هي. والذوبه بمعنى السيل وهذا عن الخارج من الذكر لا غير. ومتى حصل ذلك لاي رجل كان فيحكم عليه بالنجاسه ما دامه سايلا ان دام سايلا او انقطع وعاد ما دامه يسيل وينقطع فيقيم نجسا لقوله وزات تهيه طماتو ببسرو رر بسرو ات زوبو او حتوم بسرو مزوبو طما هو لتمامه (ايه ٣).

قوله كل همشكب اشر يشكب عليو هزب يطما (ايه ٤) اي كل الفراش الذي ينضجع عليه ينجس وذلك انه يعتزل كاعتزال الامراه اذا حاضة وكل ما ينضجع من الفراش ينجس وكل شي يجلس عليه ينجس لقوله وكل هكلي اشر يشب عليو يطما (ايه ٤). وكل الداني به وبما يجلس عليه ينجس ويلزمه غسل ثيابه وطبلهم بالما وغسل بشره جميعا واقامته ذلك اليوم الذي ينجس فيه تحت عقلة النجاسه الى الغروب ويطهر لقوله وايشى اشر يجع بمشكبو يكبس بجديو ورحص بميم وطما عد هعرب (ايه ٥). وكذلك الجالس على كل اله ان كان فراشا او غيره يجلس عليه الذايب. وكذلك الداني ببشره لقوله وهيشب عل هكلي وتمامه لقوله وهنجع ببشر هزب (ايتين ٦–٧). وكذلك ان † تفل † على طاهر. ان كان انسانا يطبل ثيابه ويغسل وينجس الى الغروب. وكل مركب يركب عليه الذايب ينجس ان كان سرج او رحل او كل ما يكون مركب. ويلحق بذلك كل شي يدوس عليه وكل شي يدوس عليه ينجس. والرافع لفراشه كذلك لقوله تعالى وكل هنجع بكل اشر يهيه تحتيو يطما (ايه ١٠) اي وكل الداني بكل الذي تحته ينجس. وايضا الحامل بهم.

---

١٩ الدم SU

٢١ ونحن] + هنا SU   ان] < SU

٢٢ ذوبةٍ] ذوبته S   نجسه هي] نجس هو × SU

٢٥ لتمامه] لتمام × SU

٢٦ هزب] < × B

٢٦–٢٧ اي .... ينجس] < SU

٣٢ اله] [Samaritan script] SU   الذايب] [Samaritan script] SU   كذلك S

٣٣ تفل] اتفل × B ؛ تفل [Samaritan script] SU

٣٤ الغروب] + لقوله [Samaritan script] لتمامه SU

٣٦ وكل .... عليه] لقوله [Samaritan script] وكل شي يجلس عليه [Samaritan script] SU   تعالى] < SU   يهيه] < × B

٣٧ اي .... ينجس] < SU   وايضا الحامل بهم] لقوله [Samaritan script] لتمامه SU

واما قوله وكل آشر يجع بو هزب ويدو لا شطف بميم يكبس بجديو ورحص بميم وطما عد هعرب (ايه ٧) اي وكل الذي يدنو فيه الذايب ويده ما شطف بالما يغسل ثيابه ويحم بالما وينجس الى الغروب يدل ذلك ان اذا كان † في ذيابه † ولمس انسان من غير ان يغسل يده بالما قبل طهره فينجس الملموس ويلزمه طبل ثيابه وغسل جسده بالما وتبقى عليه عقلة النجاسه الى الغروب. وذلك مناقضه لقوله وهنجع ببشر هزب يكبس بجديو ورحص بميم وطما عد هعرب (ايه ٧) اي والداني في لحم الذايب يغسل ثيابه ويحم بالما وينجس الى الغروب. ذلك في الظاهر مناقضة تاكيد فالاول امر ماكد والثاني مصروف على الشطف. والاعتماد على الثاني. لان نجاسة الذايب لا تصل مرتبة نجاسة الحيض لانه مرض حادث عن سبب لكون الذكر ليس له عاده بالحيض كالنسا. بل الواجب على من صابه هذا الداء انه لا يلمس شيا الا بعد ان يشطف يده بالما ليكون عمل بالامرتين. ويتوقي لمس ما لا يلزمه لان التشديد في هذه النجاسه ظاهر. اما ترى قوله وكلي حرس اشر يجع بو هزب يشبر وكل كلي عص يشطف بميم (ايه ١٢) اي وانا فخار الذي يدني به الذايب يكسر وكل انا خشب يشطف بالما وذلك كما تقدم في نجاسة البلاء.

وفي الظاهر انه لا يخرج من ذكر الانسان دما او ماده الا عن مرض داخلي اما عن قروح في المثانه او صدق عرق فيها او من قروح في الكلي او صدق عرق فيهما. وانواع ذلك كثيره والعلاج يطلب من كتب الاطبا وقد الفت كتابا في الطب وسميته (بالجوهره المضيه) لايضاح معناه وفيه شرح هذه العلل والمجرب من علاجتها.

ومما اتفق لي في سنة الف ومايه وستين كنت في خدمة ملتزم اسكلة يافا وكان اسمه علي اغا من دار البديري بمدينة صيدا فاعتراه بول الدم فكان عنده حكيم ارمنيا عنده حاسه † نباهه في † الطب فعالجه فلم يشفى فشاركته في علاجه بما هو محرر في كتب المعالجات

٣٨ بو] ببشر × B

٣٩-٤٠ اي ... الى الغروب] > SU

٤٠ ذلك] > SU ان] + [Samaritan] SU في ذيابه] ذايبه × B ؛ فى [Samaritan] SU

٤٣-٤٤ اي .... الى الغروب] > SU

٤٤ مناقضة] مناقضته × SU

٤٥ الذايب] [Samaritan] SU الحيض] [Samaritan] SU

٤٦ على] + كل SU

٤٧ الداء] الامر SU

٤٩-٥٠ اي .... بالما] > SU

٥٠ البلاء] [Samaritan] SU

٥٢ قروح] قروج × S

٥٣ كتب] كبت × B

٥٥-٥٦ في .... صيدا SU] ان دخل ذو ذكر وشيخ على حاموله B

٥٥ يافا S] > × U

٥٧ نباهه في] في نباهة × B ؛ نباهه في × SU يشنى] يبقى × U

والتداوى (كالمنهاج) (وكتاب الحاوي) فلم يشفني. فسالة (الزايرجه) فظهر لي فيها جوابا للعلاج بيتا وهو هذا

وفي الباء من عين الهلوف عنايتاً
بها النصح مطويا ولا يتحولا

فقد طالعت كتبا كثيره فما اجد الى الهلوف اسما بل كنت اعرف عشبة يقال لها لوفاً فكشفت عليها كتاب اولى الالباب فرايته ذاكر لها خاصية في شفا هذه العله فقلت لعلها تكون هذه ولعل ان الها حذفة منها خفة الى لفظها فاخذة من الباء البيص وطبخته مع اللوف واطمعته للمريض المذكور مرتين فشني بعول الله تعالى ولم احوجني الى علاج غيره. فتبارك مودع الاسرار في مخلوقاته بحكمته البالغه.

ونرجع الى ما نحن فيه. واما الحكم في طهارة الذايب فطهارة الذايب حكمها في قوله تعالى وكيّ يطّهر هزّب مزوّبو وسّفر لوّ شبعّت يمّيم لطهّرتو (ايه ١٣) اي وان يطهر الذايب من ذيابه فيعد له سبعة ايام لطهرته يعني متى شني صاحب هذا البلا وانقطع الدم والماده سبعة ايام وهو معزول عن الطهر وهوا صحيح بحيث لم ينزل منه دمًا ولا مادةٍ في مدة السبعة ايام. وفي اليوم الاول يطبل ثيابه ويغسل جسده بالما وينعزل بقية السبعة ايام طاهرا.

وفي اليوم الثامن يقرب قربانه بالحكم المذكور وهو ان ياخذ شنفين والشنف اما ان يكون من انواع العصافير او انه ديكا دجاج والاصح ان الشنف اسما لذكر الدجاج وهو صغير ويقال صوصًا لان العصفور يقال صّفورّ وهذا يقال تّر لقوله هنا وبّيوم هّشميّني يقّح لّو شّتي ترّيم آو شنّى بنّي يونّه (ايه ١٤) اي وفي اليوم الثامن ياخذ له عصفورين او † فرخي † حمام اذ لم يكون شنفين يكون فرخي حمام. ويأتي بهم لباب خبا المحضر ويعطيهم

٥٧ الحاوي] + وغيره SU فسالة (فسالت U)] فاسالت S لي] < SU
٦١ النصح] القصح × U ولا] ولم SU
٦٢ فطالعة SU كتابا كثيره U فما] فلم SU
٦٣ العله] العليه SU
٦٤ الها] لها × U
٦٥ للمريض المذكور] له SU بعول الله تعالى] < SU
٦٧ الذايب (اول)] ࠄࠆࠁ SU فطهارة] فطاهرت × SU الذايب (ثاني)] ࠄࠆࠁ SU
٦٨-٦٩ اي .... لطهرته] < SU
٦٩ هذا البلا] هذه العله U ؛ هذه الداله العله S وانقطع] + نزول SU
٧٤ دجاج] < SU
٧٥ ࠁࠉࠅࠌ SU ࠉࠌ SU
٧٦-٧٧ اي .... حمام] اي SU
٧٧ فرخي] افراخ × SUB

للامام ويقربهم الامام واحد كفاره وواحد صعيده ويكفر عنه الامام ويخلص من نجاسة هذه العله وذلك لقوله وبا فني يهوه الـ فتح اهل موعد ونتنم الـ هكهن (ايه ١٤) اي ويحضر الى بين يدين الله الى باب خبا المحضر ويعطيهم الى الامام لتمام قوله وكفر عليو هكهن لفني يهوه مزوبو (ايه ١٥) اي ويكفر عليه الامام في حضرة الله عن ذيابه.

وقد اتبع الشارع تعالى بهده الشريعه شريعة خروج المنى من الذكر في قوله وايش كي تصا ممنو شكبت زرع ورحص بميم ات كل بشرو وطما عد هعرب (ايه ١٦) اي واي رجل ان تخرج منه سكابة نسل فيرش بالما كل بشره وينجس الى الغروب. فخروج المنى من الانسان يكون اما احتلاما ويسمى قري ليله او يقظتا لزيادة الشبق ومتى خرج المنى بشهوه وتدفق فهذا المعبر عنه سكابة نسل وهو المعول. ومتى خرج المنى بشهوه وتدفق لزمه منه الغسل لساير البدن جميعا لقوله ورحص بميم ات كل بشرو (ايه ١٦) اي ويرش بالما جميع بدنه. ولا يلزم فيه كما يلزم في حكم الذايب بل هنا لا يلزم الا غسل البدن فقط واما الثياب الذي عليه ويدني منهم لا يلزم غسله الا اذ وقع من المنى عليها شيا لقوله وكل بجد وكل عور اشر يهيه عليو شكبت زرع وكبس بميم وطما عد هعرب (ايه ١٧) اي وكل ثوب وكل جلد يكون عليه سكابة نسل فيغسل بالما وينجس الى الغروب.

ومتى وقع من رجل جماع الى امراته فيلزمها الغسل ايضا كرجلها لقوله تعالى واشه اشر يشكب ايشه اته شكبت زرع ورحصو بميم وطما عد هعرب (ايه ١٨) اي وامراه الذي

---

٧٨ نجاسته × S

٧٩ العله] + وذلك كفاره وواحد صعيده ويكفر عنه الامام ويخلص من نجاسته هذه × S   ࠄࠊࠄࠍ S

٧٩-٨٠ اي .... الامام] < SU

٨١ اي .... ذيابه] < SU   عليه] عليها × B

٨٣-٨٤ اي .... الى الغروب] < SU

٨٤ فخروج] فخرج S

٨٥ ࠒࠓࠉ ࠋࠉࠋࠄ SU

٨٦ سكابة نسل] ࠔࠊࠁࠕ ࠆࠓࠏ SU   وتدفق] ويدفق S   لزمه] لزم SU

٨٧-٨٨ اي .... بدنه] < SU

٨٨ الذايب] [illegible] بقوله [illegible] SU

٨٨-٨٩ واما .... منهم] [illegible] SU   غسله] غسلهم SU

٨٩ اذ] ان SU[2]   من المنى عليها] عليه من المنى SU   عليها] عليهما × B

٩٠ وكبس] ورحصو × B   وطما] وطماو × B

٩٠-٩١ اي .... الى الغروب] < SU

٩٢ فيلزمها .... كرجلها] فيلزمها الغسل الاثنين SU   تعالى] < SU

ينضجع الرجل معها سكابة نسل فتغسل بالما وتنجس الى الغروب يعني يضالوا تحت عقلة النجاسه الى الغروب بناءً ان لا يدخلوا معبدا ولا يصنعوا فريضه في ذلك اليوم.

واما ما يخرج من الذكر من غير شهوه وتدفق فينظر فيه فان قارب الى المنى في شكله وكان مدبقا ماثرا فيما ينزل عليه فحكمه كحكم المنى وان كان غير ذلك لا يلزم الغسل منه بل يفسد الوضوء ويلزم غسله وغسل ما يقع عليه.

وفي كتاب الكافي الذي هو تاليف المرحوم الشيخ ابو الحسن الصوري رضى عنه مصرح ذلك ابوابا مرشد للطالبين والله اعلم.

واما حكم النسا في الحيض في قوله وآشه كّي تهّيه زبّه دّم يهّيه زوّبه (ايه ١٩) اي واي امراه ان تكون ذايبه دم يكون ذيابها فقد قدمنا شرح ذلك وانواعه في مبتدا الفصل. وهنا قد بين الشارع تعالى جل شانه في قوله دّم يهيّه زوّبه يعني متى كان السايل دما يلزمها العزله سبعة ايام لا تدنو بطاهر ولا يدنو بها طاهر. وكل من دنا بها ينجس ويلزمه الغسل كسوته وحم جسده بالما والعقله الى الغروب لقوله شبّعتّ يمّيم تهّيه بندّته كّل هنجّع بّه يطّما عّد هعّرب (ايه ١٩) اي سبعة ايام تكون في حيضها كل الداني بها ينجس الى الغروب.

فمن كانت في حيضها فهي وما تدنو به وما تجلس عليه وما تستعمله من انا وغيرها فجميعا محكوما بنجاستهم. ومن دنا بهم يلزمه طبل ثيابه وغسل جسده ويقيم بعد الاغتسال من الوقت الذي يغسل فيه الى الغروب تحت عقلة النجاسه لقوله وكّل آشر تّشكبّ علّيو بندّته يّطما (ايه ٢٠) اي وكل الذي تنضجع عليه في حيضها ينجس لتمام قوله آو عّل هكّلّي آشرّ هّيا يشّبتّ علّيو بنّجعو بوّ يّطما عّد هعّربّ (ايه ٢٣) اي او على الانا الذي هي جالسه عليه بدناه فيه ينجس الى الغروب.

واذا واقع وقت الجماع خروج حيض بحيث ان دم الحيض يصيب الذكر وان ذلك كالواقع في هوده كما يقولون فلان وقع في الجوره وهذا يساوي الحرمه في العزله الى سبعة

٩٣-٩٤ اي .... الى الغروب] < SU

٩٤ يعني] وقوله ࠅࠈࠌࠀࠅ ࠏࠃ ࠄࠏࠓࠁ يعني SU   تحت] + نجاسة × B

٩٥ يصنعوا] + في × B

٩٩-١٠٠ وفي .... ذلك] والكافي رحمه الله صرح ذلك SU

١٠١-١٠٢ اي .... ذيابها] < SU

١٠٣ تعالى] < SU

١٠٤ الغسل] طبل SU

١١٠ اي .... ينجس] < SU   لتمام] لتمامه لتمام SU

١١١-١١٢ اي .... الى الغروب] < SU

١١٢ بدناه] بداينه × B

١١٣ حيض] ࠃࠅࠄ SU   الحيض] ࠄࠃࠅࠄ U ؛ هنده S

١١٤ الهوده SU

ايام. وان وقع عليها الرجوع لا يلزمه وهو يطهر وهي تبقى لقوله تعالى وآم شكب يشكب ايشه اته وتهيه ندته عليو يطما شبعت يميم (ايه ٢٤) اي وان انضجع رجل مع زوجته وتكون حايضه فعليه النجاسه سبعت ايام. وحتى كل شي يجلس عليه ينجس وفي سابع يوم يطهر لقوله وكل همشكب اشر يشكب عليو يطما (ايه ٢٤) اي وكل المنضجع الذي ينضجع عليه ينجس. ولربما ان يكون ذلك عن الفراش الذي حكم الجماع عليه وهو حكم جامع المعنى عن الاثنين الاول قياسا الى الحيض في حيضها والثاني لقوله هاهنا وهمشكب اشر يشكب عليو يطما (ايه ٢٤) اسنادا لمبتدا الامر في قوله وآم شكب يشكب ايشه اته (ايه ٢٤) فهذا امر جايز الحكم به على الاثنين من غير شبهه.

ولا يتجاوز السبعة ايام. وفي الاول يغتسل وفى السابع.

واما الحرم اذا انها في اليوم السابع بعد الزوال نزل عليها ايضا كالحيض فيلزمها عيادة سبعة ايام اخر. وان لم تطهر في السبوع الثاني وترى ايضا في ختامه كالحيض فتعد سبعه اخر. وان لم تطهر في الواحد وعشرين فتكون دخلة في كثر الايام لقوله واشه كي يزوب زوب دمه يميم ربيم بلا عت ندته (ايه ٢٥) اي وامراه ان يذوب ذياب دمها ايام كثيره بغير وقت حيضها وذلك اذا جاوزت السبوع الثالث. فبعده لا تعد الايام الذي يكون بهم نزول النجس بل اذا رات الطهر تعد بعده سبعة ايام طاهره نقيه ومتى رات النجس يبطل ما عدته من ايام الطهر ومتى رات الطهر تعد الى ان تتم لها سبعة ايام طاهره نقيه لا ينزل عليها فيهم نجس ولا ترى ذلك في مدة السبعة ايام فهناك تطهر.

واما قوله آو كي تزوب عل ندته كل يمي زوب طماته كيمي ندته تهيه طماه هيا

١١٤-١١٥ فى .... يلزمه] > S ×

١١٦-١١٧ اي .... ايام] > SU

١١٧ ينجس] نجس S سابع يوم] السابع SU

١١٨-١١٩ اي .... ينجس] > SU

١٢٠ عن] من S الحيض في حيضها] ࠄࠍࠃࠄ ࠁࠍࠃࠕࠄ SU هنا SU

١٢١ يطما] > SU

١٢٣ السابع] + ايضا SU

١٢٤ واما .... ايضا] (مكتوب مرتين) × S فيلزمها] فيلزم S

١٢٥-١٢٦ اخر وان لم تطهر] ∩ B

١٢٧-١٢٨ اي .... حيضها] > SU

١٢٨ فبعده] فبعد U

١٢٩ النجس] النجاسه SU النجس] ∩ U

١٢٩-١٣٠ ومتى رات] ∩ S

١٣١ نجس] نجاسه SU

١٣٢ تزوب] يزوب × B

(ايه ٢٥) وذلك لتعريف الحكم انها ما دامة ذايبه فهي نجسه كحكم الحيض. كل ما تدنو به ينجس ان كان فراشها او ما تستعمله من الاواني وغيره.

واما الحكم في انها اذا طهرة وراة الطهر تعد لها سبعة ايام طاهره نقيه كما قدمنا فهو لقوله تعالى وآم طهره مزوبه وسفره له شبعة يميم واحر تطهر (ايه ٢٨) اي وان طهرة من ذوابها فتعد لها سبعة ايام وبعد تطهر. وبعد طهرها في اليوم الثامن تاخذ لها شنفين او فرخي حمام وتقدمهم للامام والامام يقربهم في حضرة القدس بين يدين الله تعالى واحد كفاره وواحد صعيده وذلك لقوله تعالى وبيوم هشميني تقح له شتي تريم آو شني بني يونه (ايه ٢٩) اي وفي اليوم الثامن تاخذ لها شنفين او فرخي حمام لتمام قوله وكفر عليه هكهن لفني يهوه مزوب طماته (ايه ٣٠) اي ويكفر عنها الامام في حضرة الله عن ذياب نجاستها.

ثم ان الشارع تعالى جل شانه وتعالى سلطانه حذر وانذر ونبه هذه الامه من النجاسه وانهم جميعا يكونو على حذر منها لانه تعالى اراد لهم التقرب اليه وانهم يكونوا دايما طاهرين مطهرين من كل نجاسه وقد صرح ذلك جميعا ونبه عليه في جميع ما تقدم ذكره. وذلك كله ليكونو مقدسين ويستمدو الانعام والخيرات والبركات من الموطن الاقدس وتخدمهم الاقداس وذلك لقوله تعالى وهزهرتم ات بني يشرال مطماتم ولا يموتو بطماتم (ايه ٣١) اي وتحذرو بني اسرايل من نجاستهم كيلا يهلكو بنجاستهم.

وذلك ان اذا ما تحذرو من النجاسه يهلكو لانهم اوقعهم الله في رتبة التقديس وجعل لهم في جملتهم مقدس وهيكلا كالموطن الاقدس ومن عطي هذه الرتبه يجب عليه ان يكون دايما طاهرا من كل نجاسه احتفاظا من سخط الاله الواحد القديم الذي خصهم بهذه الرتبه

---

١٣٣ ذايبه] [illegible] SU   الحيض] [illegible] SU
١٣٤ وغيره] + لقوله [illegible] لتمام قوله [illegible] SU
١٣٥ طهرة] + [illegible] SU
١٣٦ تعالى] > SU   مزوبه] مزوبو × B
١٣٧-١ اي .... تطهر] > SU
١٣٩ تعالى] > SU
١٤٠ اي .... حمام] > SU
١٤١ اي .... نجاستها] > SU
١٤٢ تعالى] > SU   ونبه] وبنه × B
١٤٦ الاقداس] الارواح القدسيه   تعالى] > SU
١٤٧ اي .... بنجاستهم] > SU
١٤٨ ان] انهم SU
١٥٠ طاهرا] + مطهرا S   وخصهم] وجملهم SU

العظيمه التي ما نالها احدا قبلهم من الامم السالفه وايضا لا بعدهم من الامم الاتيه. وتامل في قوله تعالى وَلا يموتو بطماتم بطمام اتَ مشكني اشر بتوكم (ايه ٣١) اي ولا يهلكون بنجاستهم في تنجيس مسكني الذي في جملتهم. وقد ختم هذه الشرايع بهذا الخطاب لزيادة التحذير من نجاسة كل منهما.

والله اعلم بمراده واحكم.

[كتاب كاشف الغياهب]

[على الباب الثاني عشر من كتاب الاحبار]

فصل فى شرح ذكر شريعة الامراه التي تلد ولدها وكيف تكون نجاستها وتطهيرها

وذلك في قوله اشه كي تزرع ويلده زكر (احبار ١٢ : ٢) اي وامراه ان تلد ولد ذكر. وقد قدم ذكر ولادة الذكر لشرفه عن الانثى ولكونه في الابتدا خلق قبلها. فامر سبحانه وتعالى بان الامراه اذا ولدة ذكرا تنجس سبعة ايام كما تنجس في ايام حيضها المعلوم لقوله وطماه شبعت يميم كيمي ندة دبته تطما (ايه ٢) اي وتنجس سبعة ايام كايام حيضها تنجس.

واقول انه ظهر لنا من ذلك ان هذه الشريعه يعني الحرمه اذا نزل عليها حيضها المعلوم كانت متقدمه عند القوم وفاعليها لقوله كايام حيضها تنجس.

ثم في اليوم الثامن يختنو قلفة الولد المولود كما كانت هذه الشريعه متسلسه من ابراهيم

---

١٥٢ تعالى] > SU

١٥٢-١٥٣ اي .... جملتهم] > SU

١٥٣-١٥٤ الخطاب .... منهما] بقوله ࠆࠀࠕ ࠕࠅࠓࠕ ࠄࠆࠁ ࠅࠀࠔࠓ ࠕࠑࠀ ࠌࠌࠍࠅ ࠔࠊࠁࠕ ࠆࠓࠏ لتمامه SU

١٥٥ بمراده واحكم] > SU

١ ويلده زكر] > SU اي .... ذكر] > SU

٣ قبلها] + لقوله [illegible] SU

٥ ࠃࠅࠕࠄ SU اي .... تنجس] > SU

٦ واقول] ثم واقول S

٧ تقدمه متقدمه S كايام حيضها تنجس] ࠊࠉࠌࠉ ࠍࠃࠕ ࠃࠅࠕࠄ ࠕࠈࠌࠀ SU

عليه السلام لانها من شرايعه بقوله وبيوم هشميني يمول ات بشر عرلتو (ايه ٣) اي وفي اليوم الثامن يختن بشرة قلفته.

ثم امر سبحانه وتعالى ان الوالده بعد ذلك تقيم † ثلاثه وثلاثين † يوم متجنبه في دم طهرها لا تدنو بشي طاهر ولا تدخل محل طاهر كالمعبد ونحوه لقوله تعالى بكل قدش لا تجع (ايه ٤) اي في كل قدس لا تدني والى المعبد لا تدخل حتى كمال ايام طهرها.

واما اذا ولدة انثى تقيم سبوعين كايام حيضها وتغتسل وبعده تقيم سته وستين يوم متجنبه كل شي طاهر ولا تدخل معبد كما تقدم في الذكر عن الولد الذكر لقوله تعالى وام نقبه تلد وطماه شبوعيم كندته وششيم يوم وششة يميم تشب عل دمي طهره (ايه ٥) اي وان امراه تلد انثى ونجاستها سبوعين كحيضها وسته وستين يوم تسكن في دم حيضها.

وبعد تمام طهرها ان كان للذكر او للانثى تحضر كبسا ابن سنه للصعيده وفرخ حمام او عصفور للكفاره تاتي بهم الى باب خبا المحضر وياخذهم الامام منها ويقربهم ويكفر عنها وتطهر وذلك لقوله تعالى وبملات يمي طهره لبن او لبت تبيا كبش بن شنتو لعله وبن يونه او تر لحطات (ايه ٦) اي وعند كمال ايام طهرها ان كان ولد او انثى تحضر كبس ابن سنته للصعيده وفرخ حمام او عصفور للكفاره. ومن حلم الله ورافته على خلقه اتبع القول بقوله وام لا تمصا يده دي شه ولقحه شتى تريم او شني بني يونه احد لحطات واحد لعله (ايه ٨) اي وان لا تقدر يدها على ثني فلتاخذ جوز عصافير او فرخين حمام واحد للكفاره وواحد للصعيده لتمامه لانه سبحانه وتعالى لا يريد العسر على خلقه بل يريد اليسر ولا يحمل الله نفس الا وسعها.

٩ بقوله] لقوله SU
٩-١٠ اي .... قلفته] < SU
١١ ثلاثه وثلاثين] ثلاثين × SUB
١٢ تجع] + [illegible] SU
١٣ اي .... طهرها] < SU
١٤ وبعد U
١٥ عن الولد الذكر] < ∩ SU   تعالى] < SU
١٦ طهره] طهرها × B
١٩ الى باب] لباب SU
٢٠ لقوله] قوله SU
٢١ لحطات] + لتمامه SU
٢١-٢٢ اي .... للكفاره] < SU
٢٣ لعله] + لتمامه SU
٢٤-٢٥ اي .... لتمامه] < SU
٢٥ لانه] لان الله SU   يريد] + يد × S   الله] < U

فاقول ان شريعتنا ما عقبت كلمة † القايل † وهي اس كل كتاب كان. وجميع الاقوام استمدو منها فمنهم من اهتدا وسبقة له العنايه ومنهم من ضل لان كل من اخذ له منها مشروب واختلفوا في الدروب. والله يهدي الحق لمن يشا من عباده وهو المتصرف كيف يشا ويختار تبارك وتعالى.

---

٢٧ فاقول] فوالله SU القايل] لقايل × SUB
٢٩ المتصرف] + في خلقه SU
٣٠ ويختار] < SU

TEXT 6

[كتاب الاعتقادات]

الباب السادس

في احكام النجاسات وانواعها وطريقة الطهر منها الجاري عليه الحال عندهم وعاملين به من قديم الزمان والى الان.

اولا نبتدي بذكر الدم. وهو عندهم ينقسم الى سبعة اقسام دم يسما باللغه العبرانيه ندهٓ ودم دوهٓ ودم زبهٓ ودم يليدهٓ وهوا ينقسم قسمان قسم يختص بالذكر وقسم يختص بالانثى ودم نى ودم الاشتباه وكل دم من هولاي له حكم مخالف الاخر.

وبيان ذلك

اما الدم المسمى بالندهٓ وهو الدم المنحدر للامراه عقيب الطهر بادرة النجس ووجوب الحكم. وحكمه ان الامراه منهم متى رات قد انبعث منها رطوبه وبها علامه منجسه من علامات النجس وهي اما علامه من الدم ما قل او كثر او رطوبه مخالطه صفار او غبره او حمار او اي لون خالي من البياض الناقي حالا تنعزل على حيزتها.

ولكل امراه منهم يجيها الحيض لها فراش لحدتها من وطا وغطا وغير ذلك من الات النوم

---

٢ عليها J　　الحال [LPO > BJ

٤ باللغه العبرانيه يسمى P　　نده [LPO نده ࠍࠃࠄ B ؛ ࠍࠃࠄ J

٥ دم ودم دوه × B　　دوه [BLP دوى O ؛ ࠃࠅࠄ J　　ودم زبه] > × P　　زبه [LPO ࠆࠁࠄ زابا B ؛ ࠆࠁࠄ J　　ودم يليده [LP ودم الولاده ࠉࠋࠉࠃࠄ B ؛ ودم الولاده J ؛ > × O　　ينقسم [BJO + الى LP　　قسم] > × P

٦ ࠍࠃࠉ × J

٧ بيان L

٨ بالنده [O بنده P ؛ ࠍࠃࠄ L ؛ بالندى J ؛ ࠁࠄࠋࠍࠃࠔࠄ B　　للامراه] من الانثى J　　عقيب] بعد J

٩ وحكمه [BJO فيه هو LP　　متى [BJO اذا رات] نظرت J　　قد انبعث] انبعاث J　　الرطوبه منها J

١٠ او رطوبه [LPJ ورطوبه BO　　مخالطه [LPJ مخالطها BO

١١ من] عن J　　حيزتها] حيازتها J

١٢ وكل J　　يجيها] يأتيها J　　فراش] + معد LP

١٢-١٣ من .... والشرب] من الات النوم والرقاد وما تحتاج اليه من اواني الطعام J

١٢ الات [BJO لوازم LP

واواني الاكل والشرب. ففي مدة نجاستها على انواع احكام النجاسات تكون على حدتها مع فراشها المعد لذلك. ويعملوا لها حايز بجانب بيتها ولم تقرب شي ما الا ما اعد لها. ولا احدا من اهل ملتها يدنوا بها ولا شي من الالات المعده لها ما عدا من كان بعقلة النجاسه مثلها. واذا كان دنا بها احدا من اهل ملتها كبيرا او صغيرا لزمه النجس ووجب عليه الطهر وحكمه الغسل له ولكسوته والدخول بالما. او دنت باي اله نجستها ووجب عليها الطهر.

ومن خصوص الامراه الذي عليها الحكم متى رات علامة النجس من الانواع المقدم ذكرها وجب عليها نجس سبعة ايام ولو ما رات سوى نقطه واحده.

فهذا حكم الدم الاول المسمى دَم ندّه الموجب الانعزال وحكم النجس سبعة ايام. وكلمن دنا بهذا الدم الاول لزمه كذلك نجس سبعة ايام كالمراه المنبعث منها.

واما الدم الثاني المسمى بدَم دوّه هوا الذي يجي للامراه في مدة السبعة ايام. فهذا حكم نجسه لاحق بالدم الاول فقط الداني به ينجس ويطهر ليومه.

مهما نظرة الامراه من هذا الحكم في مدة سبعة ايام نجاستها لا يزيد حكم نجاستها ولا مدته سوى اذا رات الامراه ليلة الثامن اي في غروب يوم السابع من نجسها اي علامه منجسه لزم عليها حكم سبعة ايام اخره تنجس على الحكم الذي هي عليه وحكم الداني به كحكم الدم الاول. وكذلك اذا رات دم في السبعة ايام الاخره حكمه كحكم الدم الثاني.

---

١٣ للاكل L   على .... تكون] > ∩ J   حدتها مع] > × J
١٤ ويعملوا .... اعد لها] > ∩ L   يعملوا J   ولم] ولا J
١٥ ملتها] قومها J   يدنوا بها] اي ديانها التي تدين لها J   الالات] الاتها L   لها ما] الا ما *J ؛ ما J² عدا] اعد لها × *J ؛ اعد × J²   من] > × LO
١٦ كان BJO] > LP   دنا] ادنى P   بها] منها J   كبيرا او صغيرا] > J   الطهر] ∩ L
١٧ له ولكسوته] > J   بالما] في الما هو وثيابه J   او .... نجستها] واي اله دنت بها نجست J   اله LO] + كانت BP
١٨ ومن خصوص BO] اما بخصوص J ؛ واما LP   الامراه] الانثى J   عليها الحكم] يحكم بنجاستها J   متى] اذا ما J   رات] + اي J   علامة LPO] علامات B ؛ العلامات J   النجس] > J
١٩ نجس] ان تبقى J   ما] > × P   ايام] + نجاستها J   ولو] + انها J   ما رات] لم ترا J   سوى] الا J
٢٠ فهذه P   نده LPO] ܢܕܗ BJ   الانعزال] العزل P
٢١ كلمن P   بهذه P   النجس J   كالمراه] كنفس الامراه J
٢٢ دوه O] دوه ܕܘܗ P ؛ دوه ܕܘܗ L ؛ ܕܘܗ BJ   يجي] يحدث J
٢٤ مهما JO] ومهما LPB   الحكم BJO] الدم LP   لا JBO] فلا LP
٢٥ مدته] مده × L   سوى] الا J   الامراه BO] > LPJ   ليلة] في ليلة J   يوم BO] اليوم LPJ
٢٦ لزم عليها حكم] التزمت ان تعد J
٢٦-٢٧ تنجس .... الاول] > J
٢٧ دم] ∩ LP   الاخره LPO] الاخيره BJ   حكمه كحكم الدم الثاني] يبقى سبعة ايام اخرى J

كذلك اذا رات دم بعد السبوعين اعني الاربعة عشر يوم عند الغروب علامة نجس بقية على نجاستها سبوع ثالث وحكمه كالسبوعين الاولين.

هذه حكم دم الندّه الذي عند طايفة السامره الناقلين اليه والعاملين به وما تبعه ايضا بالدم الثاني وهوا دم دوّه.

واما الدم الثالث وهو دم زبّه. وحكمه وبيانه ان الامراه اذا لم طهرة في الثلاثة اسابيع ودخلت في الرابع تغير دم الندّه وصار دّم زبّه وحكمه انه متى وصلت الاسبوع الرابع والدم نازل عليها لا يعود يحل لها الخلاص من حكم النجس سوى ان تعد سبعة ايام نقى لم ترى فيهم علامات نجس. ولو استقامت يومين او ثلاثه او اربعه لحد اليوم السابع قبل الغروب وهي طاهره من نزول الدم الا انه في اليوم السابع رات علامت نجس فسد عليها الحال ويسقط العدد الذي تقدم ولزمها عدد سبعة ايام اخر نقى. وعند كمالتها عدد السبعة ايام النقى تماما يجوز لها الطهر في غروب اليوم السابع. وصفة الطهر هوا الاغتسال بالما الطاهر ثم الدخول في الما ليعم عليها.

وهكذا حكم طهارة كلمن كانت في عقلة هذه النجاسه.

واما حكم الولاده عندهم ان الامراه اذا ولدت ولد ذكر فمن وقت ميلادها لمضى سبعة ايام منه كل دم يبعث منها يلزم الداني به ينجس سبعة ايام وحكمه حكم النجسه في

٢٨ بعد] في × O* السبوعين (الاسبوعين J)] + المتقدمان J اعني .... الغروب] > J علامة] اي علامة J نجس] > J بقيه] تبقى J

٢٩ على نجاستها] > J ثالث] اخر J كالسبوعين الاولين] كاحكام سابقه J

٣٠ هذه] وهلمجرا هذا هو J النده PO] النده ال ࠍࠃࠄ J ؛ النده ࠀࠋࠍࠃࠄ L ؛ ࠀࠋࠍࠃࠄ B طايفة السامره] هذه الطايفه J الناقلين .... به] > J ايضا] ولحقه J

٣١ دوه O] ࠃࠅࠄ دوه LP ؛ ࠃࠅࠄ BJ

٣٢ الدم] > J زبه O] ࠆࠁࠄ (ࠆࠅࠄ L) زابه LP ؛ ࠆࠁࠄ BJ اذا] اذ P

٣٣ الرابع] + فقد P النده O] نده P ؛ ࠀࠋࠍࠃࠄ LB ؛ ࠄࠍࠃࠄ J زبه O] ࠆࠁࠄ BJ ؛ ࠆࠁࠄ زابه P ؛ ࠆࠅࠄ L متى] + ما J

٣٤ النازل × J عليها JO] اليها × B ؛ منها LP سوى] الا J

٣٥ فيهم] فيها J ؛ + شي من P نجس JBO] النجس LP لحد] حتى J قبل PBO] عند LJ

٣٥-٣٦ السابع] ∩ P

٣٦ علامت (علامة L) LO] علامات PJB

٣٧ اخر PBO] اخرى LJ كمالها J

٣٧-٣٨ عدد .... تماما] > J

٣٨ هوا] > P

٣٩ في .... عليها BJO] بها ليعم عليها الما LP

٤٠ حكم] > J هذا B

٤١ حكم BJO] + دم LP عندهم] + فهي J

٤٢ به] منه P

الحيض. اما هوا كلمن دنا به ينجس ويطهر ليومه. ويدعون الدم المنحدر في مدة السبعة ايام المذكوره دَم اوتَر اي دم التحرز لثقل حكمه.

ثم في اليوم الثامن تغتسل الولاده وتنقى من هذا الدم وتغسل كلما لها. ويغسلوا ايضا الولد ويختنوه في اليوم الثامن حسب الحكم الذي قدمنا بيانه.

وتستديم ايضا في عقلة نجاستها ثلاثه وثلاثين يوما فلا تدنوا بكل طاهر وكلمن دنا بها كذلك لزمه النجس.

فتكون جملة ايام نجسها واحد واربعين يوما وعند انتهاهم يجوز لها الطهر على الحكم المتقدم.

ما عدا اذا رات علامت نجس بعد تمام الواحد واربعين يوما اي ليلة الاثنين واربعين مساءً يلزمها عدد سبعة ايام نقا لم ترى فيهم علايم نجس.

واما اذا كان الولد انثى فالحكم الواجب لذلك عندهم انه من حين ولادتها تعد اربعة عشر يوما اي سبوعين كاملين الطاق مضاعف لولادة الذكر فالدم المنحدر منها حكمه كالحكم الاول فمن دنا به يلزمه النجس اربعة عشر يوما. ويبقى هذا الحكم وثقله الاربعة عشر يوما.

وعند تمامها يجب على الوالده الغسل لها ولكل الاتها اللازمه بها وينفصل هذا الحكم.

وتبقى في حيازتها وحكم النجس مدة سته وستين يوم اخر لا تدنوا بكل طاهر.

ويكون جملة ايام نجاستها ثمانين يوما الى ليلة الواحد وثمانين.

اذا لم تنظر علامة نجس طهرة واذا نظرة ادنا علامة نجس لزمها العدد سبعة ايام نقى لم ترى فيهم شي من علايم النجس وبعد ذلك يجوز لها الطهر.

---

٤٣ فكل من J دنا به ينجس ويطهر] تنجس به يطهر L ويدعون O] ويسمون LPBJ مدة السبعة] سبعة L

٤٥ تغتسل .... الدم] من تغسل الولاده والتنقي J الولاده BO] الوالده LP تغسل J ايضا BJO] < LP

٤٦ في اليوم الثامن] اذا كان ذكرا J قدمنا بيانه O] قدمناه LPBJ

٤٧ ايضا] < L نجاستها JO] النجاسه LPB فلا PBO] لا LJ

٤٨ كذلك لزمه] < J

٤٩ وتكون J نجاستها J على BJO] + حسب LP

٥١ علامت (علامة LP) LPO] علامات BJ والاربعين J

٥٢ فيهم] + شي من L نجس JBO] النجس LP

٥٣ اذا كان الولد انثى BO] اذا كانت انثى J؛ ام الولد الانثى LP لذلك JBO] لها LP

٥٤ ذكر J حكمه] فحكمه J

٥٥ من L

٥٧ تمامهم L الولاده J وكل J الاتها] < P لها J تنفصل L

٥٨ حوزتها P النجس JBO] + عليها LP اخر JBO] ايضا LP بكل طاهر] بشياءً طاهرا J

٦٠ نقى] تنقى J

واما الدم المنحدر في مدة الثلاثه وثلاثين يوما وفي مدة السته والستين يوما ايضا حكمه كحكم دم دوّه الداني به يطهر ليومه. وليس دّم طهرّه باللغه العبرانيه اي دم نقئ او دم البراء لا كما تاوله اليهود انه دما طاهرا وياتي الرد عليهم.

واما معنى دم الاشتباه عند طايفة السامره هو علايم الذي قدمنا الذكر عنها غير الدم الطاهر اي ما كان مخالط من الرطوبه الذي يسمونها الحريم طاهر وهو البياض الناقي فما كدره من اي لون كان وجب منه النجس.

ولقد ذكرنا انواع الدما البارزه من النساء من الحيض وانواعه واحكامه مثلما هوا عند طايفة السامره ومتشرعين به وجارين عليه وعاملين به وتجدهم في غاية من المحافظه والتحرز على هذه الاحكام وناقلين اليها خلف عن سلف. والنساء منهم ينحرزون من وقوع ادنا شبهه مواطيين على ظبط قوانين واحكام انواع الدما عارفين شروطها وعلايمها ناقلين عنمن سبقهم وترى محافظتهم ومعارفتهم في ذلك طبق الامر الوارد الشرعي على يد الرسول سلام الله عليه. وقابلين لهذا التكليف وحاملين الى ثقل هذا الحكم معما هم فيه الان من الضيق والاسر واضمحلال الحال بهم من قصر اليد. ولا يخفي اهل الذكا والمعارف ان هذا التكليف يحتاج الى كد وشغل وزياده عنا حيث يلزم لثقل هذه التكاليف زيادة مصاريف. ولكن مع

---

٦٢ واما LJB] واذا O × ؛ وان P   في LJO < PB   وثلاثين] والثلاثون J   يوما (اول) JBO] + لام الذكر LP   والستين] وستين B   يوما (ثاني) JBO] + لام الانثى LP   ايضا] < B   حكمه] < J

٦٣ دم (اول) PO] ࠃࠌ LJB   دوه] ࠃࠅࠄ دوه P ؛ ࠃࠅࠄ LJB   دم (ثاني) BO] ࠃࠌ LPJ   طهره O] ࠈࠄࠓࠄ LPJB   باللغه العبرانيه (العبراني B) JBO] < LP   العبرانيه] + وفي J   النقى LP

٦٤ انه] < B   عليهم] + على ذلك انشا الله تعالى L

٦٥ معنى JBO] < LP   علايم BO] العلايم LPJ   قدمنا الذكر عنها BO] له قدمنا الذكر L*P ؛ له كما قدمنا الذكر L[2] ؛ قدمناها J   الدم] اليوم × B

٦٧ كدره JBO] عكره LP   من] < P   اى] اي نوع اي L

٦٨ من النساء JBO] < LP

٦٩ به (ثاني) O] فيه LPJB   فتحدهم J

٧٠ على] من P   هذا J   ينحرزون LJO] متحرزين (متحرزون B) PB   شبهه] + عليهم P

٧١ عارفين شروطها BO] وشروطها LP ؛ وشروطها واحكامها J   ناقلين JBO] ونافلين P ؛ < L   عنمن] عن ما J   سبقهم JBO] سلفهم LP

٧٢ الشرعي] < J   الرسول] رسوله P

٧٣ قابلين B   الى ثقل JBO] لثقل LP

٧٣ الى ثقل JBO] لثقل LP

٧٤ الحال] الامر J   من] في P

٧٥ لثقل هذه التكاليف O] لهذا التكليف LJB   مصاريف] + وكد وشغل وزادة عنا × P   ولكن مع] ومع J

هذا جميعه فلا يتركوا بفريضه واحده مما هو ممكن ان يفعلوها ولا يمكن ان يقبلوا التوسيع في الاحكام لتخفيف التكاليف ويحوطوا في كل امر على الاثقل.

ليس كما يفعلوا الغير الذي تركوا ساير تكاليف النجاسات الكليات والجزيات وصاروا ياولون تاويلات في معاني كلامه تعالى الخارجه عن مقاصده. ويقولو ان الدم المنبعث من عضو الامراه المعلوم منه ما هو طاهر ومنه ما هو نجس وان انواع الدما لا تعرفها افراد الناس بل فلا تعرفها سوى العلما فقط اي اصحاب المعارف الكليه وان الامراه اذا جاها دم الحيض حالا تحمله وتذهب فيه الى عند الخاخام الكبير ليعرفها فيه هل هو دم نجس او طاهر. والحال هذا من اكبر جهلتهم بحيث من المعلوم الغني عن البيان ان النساء اعرف من غيرهم في حكم الدم حيث ذلك من ممارستهم له. والدم حكم نجاسته ليس بالالوان ولا الحكم عايد الى جنس الدم وما له من الاوصاف. ولا كما يزعموا ان له الوان يجب عن بعضها النجس وعن بعضها الطهر. وان معرفت الدم الطاهر من الدم المنبعث من الفرج والدم النجس لا يعرفه كاين من كان كما قدمنا بل له علما يعرفونه باختلاف اوصافه وما منه نجس منجس وما منه طاهر. يرجعون في صحة ذلك الى قوله اذا خفي عنك امرا من الاحكام بين دم ودم الخ (تث ١٧ : ٨) وهذا منهم غلط عظيم لان الشارع تعالى انما كلف شعبه اسرايل بالالتزام في احكام الدم المنبعث عن الفرج وتغاير احكامه لتغاير اوصاف

٧٦ فلا] لا P ؛ فانهم لا J فريضه J ممكن] في حد الامكان J ان يفعلوها O] فعله LPB ؛ > J يمكن] يمكنهم J ان JO] انهم LPB

٧٧ لتخفيف O] لاجل تخفيف LPJB ويحوطوا] حتى يحوطوا J في كل] بكل J على الاثقل O] على الاشد والاثقل LPB ؛ شديدا كان وثقيلا J

٧٨ ليس] لا J الغير] الاخرين J تركوا] نبذو وتركوا J تكاليف النجاسات] التكاليف من النحاسات الكليه والجزئيه J

٧٩ تاويلات] تاويلا J تعالى] > J

٨١ بل BO] انما LPJ لا J اي اصحاب] واصحاب J الكليه] > J

٨٢ فيه] به J عند] > L فيه] > L هل هو] اهو J

٨٣ طاهر] طهر J والحال O] والحاله LPJB هذا O] هذه B ؛ هذه فهذا LPJ من BO] انه من J ؛ ان LP

٨٥ الى] على L ولا] > × J ان] انه J الوان] لون L عن] على L

٨٦ من الدم O] > LPJB الفروج J

٨٧ بل O] + انما LPJB علما BO] عرفا LPJ منجس PBO] ومنجس J ؛ > L وما منه PJB] ومنه × O ؛ وما منهم L

٨٨ يرجعون LJO] ويرجعو PB قوله LPO] + ࠊࠉ ࠉࠐࠋࠀ ࠌࠌࠊ ࠃࠁࠓ (+ ࠋࠌ × J*) ࠁࠉࠍ ࠃࠌ ࠋࠃࠌ (ࠌࠃࠌ ࠋࠃࠌ J) وتمامه اي JB عنك] عليك J

٩٠ شعب B عن BO] من LP ؛ > J احكامه لتغاير] > ∩ P

حدوثه وحيث الخارج عنه من هذا العضو يلزم عنه نجس مطلقا وباختلاف اوصاف حدوثه يلزم عنه احكام متغايره.

واول ما حكم بذلك كما صرح بسفر الاحبار اص ١٢ المتضمن احكام الوالده للذكر وللانثى ثم صرح في هذا السفر في ص ١٥ وعين فيه احكام اوصاف دم الذوبان ودم الحيض والدم المزمن وبين حكمه ولم فرق بين الوانه بل عدد احكامه وازمانه ومراتبه.

وجعل للدم الاول الذايب من الامراه مرتبه اوله. وسماه ندّه باللغه العبرانيه المستنبط عن الوحده والابعاد ومشتق هذا الاسم من ندّ ووردة هذه اللفظه دفعتين الاوله قوله تعالى بقايين نّع ونّد تهّي بارّص (تك ٤ : ١٢) بمعنى سريدا وفريدا تكون في الارض والثانيه عن ادم وهو قوله تعالى عنه ويّشبّ بارّص نّد قدّمت عدّن (تك ٤ : ١٦) اي وسكن في الارض سريدا شرقي من النعيم كما صرح في سفر التكوين في اص ٤ وهذا التاويل على حسب ما عند طايفة السامره.

ثم جعل تعالى هذا الدم الذي ترى الامراه باول بروزه قاعده للحكم بمدته وحكمه وهو كما صرح به في حكم من تلد ذكرا او انثى وهو قوله تعالى تكون نجسه سبعة ايام كما في ايام ندّته عليها (اح ١٢ : ٢) ولوالدة الانثى قال وتكون نجسه سبوعين كما في ندّته (ايه ٥).

---

٩٢ ويلزم J عنه] + اي LPJ

٩٣ بسفر الاحبار اصٓ ١٢ O] في سفر الاحبار اصٓ ١٢ LPJ ؛ في صٓ ١٢ سفر الاحبار B

٩٣-٩٤ اص] > ∩ P

٩٣ الولاده J والانثى J

٩٤ والانثى J في هذا السفر] > J فيه] به J دم] > O*

٩٥ والدم] ودم J

٩٦ الذايب LPO] الزايغ J ؛ الزال B نده O] ࠍࠃࠄ نده LP ؛ ࠍࠃࠄ JB عن] من L

٩٧ الاسم (اول)] الاسماء J الواحده × P والابعاد > J ند O] ࠍࠃ ند L ؛ ࠍࠃ JB ؛ ࠍࠃࠄ نده × P ووردة] وفد وردة J² هذا J دفعتين] مرتين J

٩٨ نع .... بارص O] ࠍࠏ (ࠕࠍ J) ࠅࠍࠃ (ࠅࠍࠃ ند L ؛ ࠍࠃ ند P) ࠕࠄࠉࠄ ࠁࠀࠓࠑ LPJB بمعنى JBO] اي LP

٩٩ وهو .... عنه JBO] وهو قوله عن اذم L ؛ > P (حروف عبرانيه) LPJB ويشب] ࠅࠉࠔࠁ × J عدن] ࠒࠃࠌࠕ × J*

٩٩-١٠٠ اي .... النعيم] > J

١٠٠ تكوين J في PBO] > LJ هذا P

١٠٢ الامراه] > J قاعدة الحكم J

١٠٣ في] > P تعالى JBO] > LP

١٠٣-١٠٤ تكون .... عليها LPO] → ࠅࠕࠄࠉࠄ ࠔࠁࠏࠕ ࠉࠌࠉࠌ ࠊࠌࠉ ࠍࠃࠕࠄ اي B ؛ ࠅࠕࠄࠉࠄ ࠔࠁ࠽ ࠉࠌ࠽ ࠊࠉ࠽ ࠍࠃࠕࠄ J

١٠٣ وتكون L

١٠٤ ندته BO] ندته ࠍࠃࠕࠄ LP عليها O] > LPB وتكون .... ندته LPO] ࠅࠕࠄࠉࠄ ࠔࠁࠏࠉࠌ ࠊࠍࠃࠕࠄ JB تكون L

وذلك كما مصرح فيه في ص ١٢ من سفر لاوين من العدد الأول الى ع ٥. وجعل حكم الدم الاول من دنا به ينجس سبعة ايام وكذلك الدما المنحدر لام الولد واضعاف ذلك لام البنت من دنا بهم للذكر سبعة ايام وللانثى اربعة عشر يوما كما قدمنا. ثم جعل زيادة بيان لهذا الدم بحكمه وهوا اذا كان رجل انضجع مع حرمته ونزل عليه من امراته من هذا الدم لزمه نجس سبعة ايام تابعا لحكم هذا الدم لانه ابدا يلزم عنه سبعة ايام. وشاهد ذلك قوله تعالى وان انضجع رجلها معها وطاله من ندتها نجس سبعة ايام (اح ١٥ : ٢٤) وهوا الدم المسمى ندّه وندّته بعرف الشرع كما قدمنا وذلك مصرح في الاصحاح المتقدم ذكره . . . .

. . . .

فهذه شرايع هندّه وهزبه وهيليدّه وذكر الخلاف الذي فما بين السامره واليهود وذكر الاحوال الجاريين عليها الطرفين.

اما طايفة السامره في هذه السنه ان كل من كانت في عقلة النجاسه من ندّه ودّوه ويليدّه يحرموا مخالطتها. واذا حصل خطا من انسان وجامع حريمه وهي في عقلة النجاسه ولا يجوزوا مخالطته البتا. هذا ما هو جاري عليه الحال في ايامنا واما في ايام الرضوان كانوا يقتلوه بحسب الامر الشرعي.

والله اعلم.

---

١٠٥ كما] > P صرح J فيه] به J من] > J من .... ع] ع لحدود عد من سفر لاوين L لاوين O] اللاوين J؛ لاويين B من العدد الاول] عد P الي] في × J

١٠٦ تنجس L الدم J

١٠٧ بهم [JBO به ينجس LP للذكر .... وللانثى] > × L

١٠٨ بحكمه] حكمه × J حرمته [LBO زوجته P؛ امراته J

١٠٩ هذا الدم] منه J

١١٠ تعالى [JBO > LP تعالى] + [Samaritan script] اي JB وان O] وان انضجاعا LP؛ امرئ اذ J؛ امراه اذا B وطاله [LPJ وطالة × B؛ وطالها × O ندتها [JBO ندته LP نجس [LBO ينجس

١١١ وهوا] وهذا B نده وندته O] نده [Samaritan script] وندته LP؛ [Samaritan script] B؛ ندى [Samaritan script] J وذلك مصرح [JBO كما مصرح LP المتقدم [JBO] المقدم LP

١١٤ هنده وهزبه وهيليده O] [Samaritan script] (B [Samaritan script] ؛ LPB [Samaritan script] النده والذاينه والوالده J فما بين السامره واليهود] ما بينهم وبين اليهود J

١١٦-١١٧ نده ودوه ويليده O] [Samaritan script] (P > [Samaritan script] LPJB

١١٧ مخالطتها [JBO] + وجماعها L؛ + او جماعها P حريمه [JBO زوجته LP في [JBO > × LP النجاسه O] + يحرموه LPJB

١١٨ هذا] لهذا J ما .... عليه [JBO > LP ايام [JBO زمان LP

TEXT 7

[شرح سورة ࠅࠉࠒࠓࠀ]

. . . . وكذلك في احكام الندّه احكام ما لم يذكرها في احكام غيرها مع وجوب العموم. ايضا في احكام ࠄࠆࠁ مثل قوله ࠅࠊࠉ ࠉࠓࠒ ࠄࠆࠁ ࠁࠈࠄࠅࠓ ࠅࠊࠁࠎ ࠁࠂࠃࠉࠅ وتمام (اح ١٥ : ٨) مع وجوب العموم لمثل هذا بكل النجاسات.

TEXT 8

[الحواشي]

١ [الحاشيه الاولى في كتاب الطباخ]

الذي معتمده عليه الامه الان ان لا يلزم سبعة ايام نقا الا ان بقى الدم مع الامراه مدة الاسبوع الاول واتصل بالاسبوع الثاني وايضا اتصل بالاسبوع الثالث الى انتهايه ولم تخلص ولو انه في بعض الايام تجد وفي البعض لم تجد. والذي عليه الاعتماد هو اليوم الذي يسمونه النسا يوم المسك فاذا حضر اليها اقل قليل من الدم في ذلك اليوم الذي هو يوم سابع الاسبوع الثالث لزمها ان تمسك بعد ذلك سبعة ايام نقا وهذا الذي يسمونه عدد. ودليل ذلك قوله تعالى ࠉࠌࠉࠌ ࠓࠁࠉࠌ ࠁࠋࠀ ࠏࠕ ࠍࠃࠕࠄ (اح ١٥ : ٣٥).

والله علم. وانا استغفر الله من التردد والنقص.

وكتبه مسلم ابن مرجان الدنني غفي الله عنه يمتد وجوده امين.

---

١ الذي] → ووجد كاتبه مكتوب على حاشية النسخ الذي نقله عنها بخط المرحوم الشيخ مسلم ابن مرجان الدنني هكذا L ؛ → صح وجد على حرز الكتاب M_2^{txt} ؛ → حاشيه منقوله عن الشيخ مسلم M_2^{mg} → ووجد مكتوب على حواشي الكتاب بخط المرحوم الشيخ مسلم الدنني D   الان الامه P_3 ان] > P_3M_2 نقا] + الحايض P_3M_2

٣ البعض] بعض الايام DP_3M_2L وهو D

٣-٤ اليوم .... النسا] > P_3M_2

٤ يوم] > P_3*   اليها] فيه P_3M_2 هو] + يوم المسك P_3M_2

٥ الثالث] الرابع M_2*   لزمها ان تمسك] لزم المسك P_3M_2 نقى] + لا ترى فيهم شي من علامات الدم DL   عدد] + قولاً فلانه دخلت في العدد L ؛ + معلوم بين النسا العبريات P_3M_2

٥-٦ ودليل ذلك] + مستفاد من DL ؛ وقد استدل من P_3M_2

٧ والله اعلم] > P_3M_2

٧-٨ وانا .... امين] > DP_3M_2L

٢ [الحاشيه الثانيه في كتاب الطباخ]

حاشيه لسيدي الشيخ خضر ابن الشيخ اسحاق الامام دام شريف وجوده.

قد وجد اختلاف بين السلف في حكم ࠃࠌ ࠆࠁࠄ. منها هذا الفاصل بقوله ان ࠃࠌ ࠆࠁࠄ يلزم حكمه بعد الاسبوع الاول ان تعد الامراه اذا حضر منها دم من بعده عد سبعة ايام نقا. واما الشيخ منجا ابو الفرج يقول في كتابه مسايل الخلاف انه لا يلزم عد سبعة ايام نقى الذي هو حكم ࠃࠌ ࠆࠁࠄ الا بعد سبعة اسابيع ومستمد من قوله عن ذلك ࠀࠅ ࠊࠉ ࠕࠆࠅࠁ ࠏࠋ ࠍࠃࠕࠄ ࠉࠌࠉࠌ ࠓࠁࠉࠌ (اح ١٥ : ٢٥) ࠄࠉࠌࠉࠌ ࠄࠓࠁࠉࠌ تحتمل هذه المده وهي سبعه في سبعه فيكون معناه حكم ࠄࠍࠃࠄ سبعة ايام وفرقه ࠋࠋࠆࠁ ومضروبه في مثلها. واما الشيخ مسلم ناقل عن السلف الذي قبله. والمعتمد عليه في الزمان الذي نقله من دون مخالفه ولا مشاحنه بذلك ان حكم ࠃࠌ ࠆࠁࠄ لا يلزم سوى بعد ثلاثة اسابيع والمعتمد عليه لحد هذه المده بين النسا العبريات. فقد ثبت هذا الاستعمال وصار ذلك نقل ثابت لعدم الاختلاف فيه لاستعماله وعدم معاكسته من الشرح والتواطي عليه.

والله اعلم بكل الاحوال.

٣ [الحاشيه الاولى في كتاب الكافي]

قوله تعالى ࠅࠊࠋ ࠀࠔࠓ ࠉࠂࠏ ࠁࠅ ࠄࠆࠁ ࠅࠉࠃࠅ ࠋࠀ ࠔࠈࠐ ࠁࠌࠉࠌ وتمامه (اح ١٥ : ١١) يعني ان ࠄࠆࠁ ࠉࠈࠌࠉ ولو ࠉࠃࠅ ناشفه وليس هناك بكل حكم ࠄࠍࠃࠄ.

هذا ظهر للحقير عمران بعد سعي السودان ووسواس ࠁࠓࠅࠊ ࠉࠄࠅࠄ. وقد اختص الشيخ في ذلك لان ࠄࠆࠁ اذا كان † دام † حكمه حكم ࠄࠍࠃࠄ اذا دام خلاف ࠄࠍࠃࠄ لان اقل دم منها يلزم العزله ࠔࠁࠏࠕ ࠉࠌࠉࠌ.

---

١ وجوده] + امين M_2

٢ بقوله ان] بقول انه M_2

٨ مضروبه M_2

١٣ بكل الاحوال] < M_2

٥ دام] ࠃࠌ × في المخطوطه

٤ [الحاشيه الثانيه في كتاب الكافي]

قوله ࠅࠊࠋ ࠀࠔࠓ ࠉࠂࠏ ࠁࠅ ࠄࠆࠁ ࠅࠉࠃࠅ ࠋࠀ ࠔࠈࠐ ࠁࠌࠉࠌ (اح ١٥ : ١١) يعني اذا دنا ࠀࠋࠄࠆࠁ بشي ولو يده بها من ذات عين ࠀࠋࠆࠁ لا يلزم المدنو بها سوى الغسل ويطهر بيومه. وهذا فرق ما بين عين ࠃࠌ ࠄࠍࠃࠄ ࠅࠃࠌ ࠄࠆࠁ لان الداني بعين ࠃࠌ ࠄࠍࠃࠄ؛ يلزمه ࠔࠁࠏࠕ يمم واما الداني بعين هزب لا يلزمه سوا حال واحد. صح.

ناجي بن خضر كهن. م.

٥ [الحاشيه الثالثه في كتاب الكافي]

حاشيه للحقير كاتبه في قوله تعالى ࠅࠊࠋ ࠀࠔࠓ ࠉࠂࠏ ࠁࠅ ࠄࠆࠁ ࠅࠉࠃࠅ ࠋࠀ ࠔࠈࠐ ࠁࠌࠉࠌ وتمامه (اح ١٥ : ١١). معناه في ذلك ان الداني في عين ࠄࠆࠁ لا يلزمه عدد اسبوع كما يجب على البارز منه ࠄࠆࠁ بل يطهر بيوم دنوه به حسب قوله ࠅࠓࠇࠑ ࠁࠌࠉࠌ ࠅࠈࠌࠀ ࠏࠃ ࠄࠏࠓࠁ (ايه ١١). اذ لو لم بين ذلك بهذا الفصل لوجب من طريق القياس على ࠄࠍࠃࠄ ان يطها من خالط عين ࠄࠆࠁ سبعة ايام هذا هو المراد بذكره ࠄࠆࠁ لان جسمه اذا دنا بشي من الاله الطاهره غير لثق لزمه

١ قوله] هذا لابن عمنا خضر في معنى قوله تعالى P
٢ اذا] ان P ࠋࠀ × S_1
٣ الغسل] + اي الصبوغ P
٤ سبعة ايام P ࠄࠆࠁ P
٥ حال واحد] كما ذكرنا P
٦ ناجي بن خضر كهن . م .] صح P
١ حاشيه] مطلب F_1 للحقير كاتبه C] + عفه عنه امين B ؛ للحقير يعقوب عفى عنه W ؛ لسيدي الوالد N ؛ > F_1A
٢ وتمامه] > F_1AW
٣ فلا B يلزمه] يلزم × A به] منه F_1 ؛ > A
٤ ࠅࠈࠌࠀ ࠏࠃ ࠄࠏࠓࠁ] ࠅࠈࠄࠓ ࠁࠏࠓࠁ × W لم [F_1N > × AWCB
٥ من] منه × B من طريق] بطريق F_1
٦ هو] > W بذكر B غير .... الطاهره B] > ∩ F_1AWCN
٦-٧ غير .... الطاهره B] > ∩ F_1AWCN

الطما واذا عرض له ان يلمس شي من الاله الطاهره كذلك لزمه الطما ويطهر ليومه. والله اعلم.

معنى الكلام ان كل داني في صاحب ࠆࠁࠄ والداني في عين ࠆࠁࠄ حكمه واحد ومعنى قوله تخفيف في حق الداني في ࠆࠁࠄ عن الدانى في [Samaritan script] [Samaritan script]. وهذا الفرق ما بين الرجال والنسا والله اعلم.

وهذه الحاشيه اسنادا على قول الشيخ ابو الحسن رضى الله عنه في كتابه الطباخ في باب ࠆࠁࠄ وهذا هو الصحيح حيث هذا الشيخ لم شرح في هذا المعنى كافي. والله تعالى اعلم.

صح. يعقوب هرون هكهن غفه عنه. امين.

٦ [الحاشيه الرابعه فى كتاب الكافى]

مطلب في الامراه بانها تغسل اول نقطه الذي تنزل منها اول دفعه بيدها اليسرى دون بقية اعضائها وتبقى يدها تحت حكم العدد.

---

٧ كذلك] لذلك × F_1A ليومه] لوقته B ؛ بيومه AN

٩-١٠ ࠆࠁࠄ] ∩ W

١٠ عن] من F_1A في (ثالث)] + عين N دم A [Samaritan script] [Samaritan script] F_1A

١٠-١١ وهذا .... والنسا] > BN

١١ والنسا] والمراه F_1

١٢-١٥ وهذه .... امين > A ابو .... امين > F_1

١٢ رضى الله عنه [WC > BN كتابه] كتاب N

١٣ حيث C] بحيث BN ؛ واما W هذا الشيخ [WC] صاحب هذا الكتاب N ؛ هذا الكتاب B لم شرح [WC] لم يشرح BN كافي C] شرح كافي W ؛ جواب يفيد بل سهي عليه هذا الكلام BN تعالى C] > WBN

١٥ > WBN

١ اول دفعه] > A دون] دونه × F_1

٧ [الحاشيه الاولى في كتاب الخلاف]

حاشيه لسيدي الوالد رحمه الله.

ما جا به هذا الفاصل ليس هوا جاري عليه الحال بين جماعتنا في الفرق بين ࠄࠍࠃࠄ ࠅࠄࠆࠁࠄ. فالشيخ هنا لا يلزم حكم ࠄࠆࠁࠄ الا من بعد سبعة اسابيع كامله واما الجاري عليه الحال الان هوا من بعد ثلاثة اسابيع فاستغفر الله قبل ان اقول ان كلام هذا الشيخ في هذه العبره لا سنه له ولا منقول بين الامه. والله اعلم.

٨ [الحاشيه الثانيه في كتاب الخلاف]

حاشيه لسيدي المرحوم والدي هكهن فينحس اسكنه الجنان.

رد على اليهود فيما ابدعوا بقولهم ان ما يعلو ࠀࠌࠄࠆࠁ من غطا لا ينجس من قوله عن فراش ࠄࠆࠁ بالطما ࠏࠋࠉࠅ ࠅࠀࠇࠓࠉࠅ فعللو ذلك بالوطا فقط. والحال اورد نص ينجس كل فراش ࠄࠆࠁ من غطا ووطا وهو قوله ࠅࠀࠉࠔ ࠀࠔࠓ ࠉࠂࠏ ࠁࠌࠔࠊࠁࠅ ࠉࠊࠁࠎ ࠁࠂࠃࠉࠅ ࠅࠓࠇࠑ ࠁࠌࠉࠌ الخ (اح ١٥ : ٥) فهذه الايه بلا شك تفيد نحاسته غطاه ووطاه كونه لا يوجد فيها تعليل ࠋࠀ ࠏࠋࠉࠅ ࠅࠋࠀ ࠀࠇࠓࠉࠅ. فانظرهم دايما يرغبو الترجيس والتوسيع في نسخ فرايض الله في مثل ذلك كثير وسلفنا دايما يقصدوا التحرز والتحويط.

صح.

---

١ الوالد] + فينحس هكهن قدس الله سره امين B_2

٢ هوا] + بما B_2

٥ العبره] > B_2 الامه] + البت B_2

١ المرحوم والدي هكهن] الوالد B_2 اسكنه الجنان] قدس الله روحه الشريفه B_2

٢ رد] قال انني ارد B_2 ابدعوه B_2

٣ ࠀࠇࠓࠉࠅ × B_2 والحال] + الله تعالى B_2

٥ الخ] فتمامه B_2

٧ فانظرهم] ࠍࠄࠁࠄࠌࠌ ࠀࠋࠋࠄ B_2

٩ صح] + والله اعلم B_2

TRANSLATION
AND
COMMENTARY

ABBREVIATIONS IN THIS SECTION

T	Kitâb aṭ-Ṭubâkh
Kf	Kitâb al-Kâfi
Kh	Kitâb al-Khilâf
Far	Kitâb al-Farâ'iḍ
Kâsh	Kâshif al-Ghayâhib
I'tiq	Kitâb al-I'tiqâdât
M.N.	Marginal notes (in the mss.)
N	note
TN	text and note
G.E.	Gan 'Eden
A.E.	Adderet Eliyahu
ch.	chapter

CONVENTIONS

The notes on a longer section of text will come before the notes on shorter sections within that section; and so on.

TRANSLATION

TEXT 1

[THE BOOK OF INSIGHT]

The Kinds of Bleeding that Cause Uncleanness and the Details of their Legal Consequences

(2) Bleeding is divided into seven categories: bleeding of separation [ࠍࠃࠄ *niddå*], bleeding of a menstruating woman [ࠃࠁࠄ *dåbå*], bleeding of a woman with a discharge [ࠆࠁࠄ *zåbå*], bleeding of childbirth [ࠉࠋࠉࠃࠄ *yēlīda*], (3) which is two categories, one in the case of a boy and one in the case of a girl, bleeding of her cleansing [ࠈࠄࠓࠄ *ṭårå*], and bleeding of plausibility. Each (4) of these has its own legal consequences, different to the others.

(5) *The Details*

(6) The first of these is bleeding of separation [*niddå*]. This is the one that appears immediately after cleanness, marking the start of the uncleanness. Its consequences last for seven days, (7) as it says: 'A woman that has a discharge, whose discharge is blood, (8) in her flesh, stays for seven days in her separation [*niddå*] etc.' (Lv XV:19). The evidence (9) for it being what appears immediately after cleanness is the verse 'A woman whose husband (10) lies down with her, and whose [blood of] separation [*niddå*] gets on him, he is unclean for seven days' (11) (v. 24). Any artefact or person that comes in contact with it is affected for seven days.

(12) The second category is bleeding of a menstruating woman [*dåbå*], which appears after the separation [*niddå*] and during the week. Its consequences (13) last for a moment: a person can get over its effect on the day they touch it. The evidence for this is the principle followed by the nation that a woman who has immersed herself — provided (14) she is completely finished bleeding — on the seventh day of the first week becomes clean. (15) This is in the nation's tradition: they agree on it and none of them will be found to say otherwise.

(16) The third category is what is known as 'bleeding of a woman with a discharge' [*dam zåbå*]. It is like this: If the woman's bleeding keeps up and she does not stop bleeding (17) by the sunset of the night of the eighth day, and stops on the eighth or ninth or tenth day, (18) any days after the seventh on

which bleeding occurs are to be disregarded, and she is to count, from the day after the end of the bleeding, seven whole days (19) free of bleeding, without any sign of it, and she becomes clean on that day. As well as this, any woman whose bleeding continues for four days, or any more (20) days than that, then from the day she gets over it, she has to count, from the day after the end of the bleeding, seven days free of it, during which she does not see any blood at all. (21) The evidence for this is the passage 'A woman whose discharge of blood lasts many days, (22) outside the time of her separation [*niddå*], or who has a discharge past her separation [*niddå*], all the days of the discharge (23) of her uncleanness are like the days of her separation [*niddå*] for her ... she is to count (24) seven days, and then she becomes clean' (vv. 25, 28). The text treats the situation (25) of going past the first week as equal to many days when it says, after the phrase 'many days', 'or (26) who has a discharge past her separation [*niddå*]'. With this collapses the argument of those that say that the expression 'days' means (27) forty-nine days, that the expression 'days' on its own does not cover more than this, on the basis of the verse 'in (28) those many days' (Ex II:23), which refers to the period from the time of Joseph to the (29) commission of Moses, and that it implies forty-nine days. (30) These two cases, and anything lasting longer, are both treated as the situation of exceeding the first week, the 'time of her separation [*niddå*]'.

(31) This contradicts the community of the Karaite Jews as well. They take the separation [*niddå*] to be the first blood (32) and what comes straight after to be 'discharge' [ࠆࠁ *zåb*]. This can be contradicted in two ways. First, from the phrase 'outside the time (33) of her separation [*niddå*]', which refers to any continuation past the time of 'her separation [*niddå*]' by any amount, and the 'time of her separation [*niddå*]' is seven days, (34) as it says 'she stays for seven days in her separation [*niddå*]' (v. 19). This establishes that the uncleanness (35) of the first week is a consequence of the 'separation' [*niddå*], not the discharge [*zā̊bå*], and that the 'menstruation' [*dā̊bå*] has no consequences in the first week (36) and there is no ban due to it then. The second is that the word 'time' [ࠏࠕ *at*] in Hebrew (37) has several possible meanings, each of which expresses the idea of an amount of time having length or extent. For instance, there is the story of Rebecca, and the servant's report (38) about her, where it says 'at the time [*at*] of evening, at the time [*at*] the women go out to draw water' (Gn XXIV:11); or the story (39) of Jacob and what the Lord did for him, where it says 'at the mating-time [*at*] (40) of the sheep and goats etc.' (Gn XXXI:10); or Moses's mention of a special position being given to the Tribe (41) of Levi at the time referred to in the verse 'At that time [*at*] the Lord separated (42) the Tribe of Levi' (Dt X:8). Each of these different cases expresses the idea of an amount of time having extent, whereas the amount of time in which the first bleeding, known as the separation [*niddå*], (43) comes, is a tiny instant, much shorter than a unit of time, an indivisible (44) particle like the indivisible particles of simple substances.

(45) The fourth category is bleeding of childbrith, and is divided into two categories. There is the blood that appears on giving birth to a boy, the legal consequences of which last (46) for seven days, as it says 'A woman that conceives and gives birth to a boy is unclean (47) for seven days' (Lv XII:2). The blood is the same as the blood in the days of her *niddå*, known as menstrual [*dåbå*] blood, (48) as it says 'She is unclean as with the days of the separation [*niddå*] of her menstruation [*dåbå*]' (v. 2). The fifth category is the bleeding that (49) comes when giving birth to a girl, the consequences of which last for a fortnight, as it says, 'If she has a girl (50) she is unclean for a fortnight as with her separation [*niddå*]' (v. 5). The blood that comes during the fortnight, (51) following on from the blood of childbirth, has the same legal consequences as the 'separation' [*niddå*]: anyone that touches it or gets it on them is affected for seven days, as it says (52) 'as with her separation [*niddå*]'.

(53) The sixth category is what is known as 'bleeding of her cleansing [*dam ṭårå*]', and it is divided into two categories. The first category is the bleeding that the woman (54) experiences during the thirty-three day period of cleansing, as it says 'For thirty-three (55) days she stays in the bleeding of her cleansing [*ṭårå*]' (v. 4). Its treatment is that any person (56) or artefact that is touched or contacted by it can have it washed off the next instant. The proof is that if the woman completely finishes bleeding on the last day of the thirty-three (57) she becomes clean. Bleeding occuring during the sixty-six days following on from the fortnight, in the case of a girl baby, (58) has the same rules applying to it as the bleeding occurring during the thirty-three days: any person or artefact that touches it can recover (59) the next instant after coming in contact with it, the proof being that if the woman gets over it during the sixty-six days she becomes clean.

(60) If, however, she experiences any bleeding after this period she does not become clean, as it says 'She is not to touch any holy thing (61) or go into the Temple till the completion of the days of her cleansing' (v. 4). (62) The legal consequences of the woman seeing any blood after the completion of the period specified are the same as for the discharge [ࠆࠁ *zåb*]: it requires seven days without bleeding. The reason is that (63) the consequences of going past these two periods are the same as for going past the separation [*niddå*] and its days. The text compares (64) these two periods with the separation [*niddå*] when it says, in reference to a boy 'like the days of her separation [*niddå*]' (v. 2), and in reference to (65) a girl, 'like her separation [*niddå*]' (v. 5), and any bleeding extending past the separation [*niddå*] and the days of her separation [*niddå*] has the consequence of needing seven days (66) without bleeding.

(67) The seventh is plausibility, and it brings on the days of plausibility. The counting is from the day the bleeding occurs. She waits (68) for a week

and then becomes clean provided she stops bleeding by the seventh day before sunset. This is because the outward sign of cleanness is clarity and the visible absence (69) of contaminating matter, and if the stuff turns less clear by the slightest amount it is definitely unclean. It is like when clear water gets a little bit (70) of some pigment such as saffron in it and its colour is affected by it in proportion to the amount of whatever pigment is mixed in with it, with the depth and degree of colour being (71) in proportion to the amount of stuff mixed in. In the same way, if the outward appearance of clearness turns a bit maroon or blue or green (72) or yellow or beige it is a sign of uncleanness, since the outward sign of absence of contaminating matter in questions of cleanness is clearness and the absence of foreign matter, unaffected by anything at all.

(73) These are the colours applying in plausibility, and their treatment is now clear to you.

(74) The legal position if any man lies down with any woman that is in the legal position of any of these categories mentioned, to which (75) the rules for the various kinds of uncleanness apply, and copulates with her, is that both are to be killed, as it says: 'Any man (76) that lies down with a woman with a flow [ࠃࠅࠄ *dåbå*] and uncovers her genitals, the spring (77) of her genitals, and she uncovers the spring of her bleeding both of them are to be cut off (78) from out of their people' (Lv XX:18).

(79) *The Discharge* [ࠆࠅࠁ *zåb*], *the Details of its Categories, and an Analysis of the Rules for the Grades of Uncleanness in it* (80) *as Applying to Males*

(81) (*Note*:

(82) There can occur to males something of the nature of the discharge [*zåb*] that is not discharge [*zåb*], such as an emission of semen (83) while asleep [ࠒࠓࠉ ࠋࠉࠋࠄ *qēri līla*] or during copulation [ࠔࠊࠁࠕ ࠆࠓࠏ *shūkəb zēra*); or the occurrence of certain phenomena on urinating, whether before or after, such as viscosity, (84) or a change in the urine similar to soap solution or soapsuds, stretching out like a thread; or such as the effect on some men (85) of imagining or sexual arousal or hot-bloodedness, or the effect of strenuous exercise or carrying heavy loads or eating blood-thickening food such as (86) chickling or taro or lentils or beef or mutton or goat's meat or milk products or fish. Anything (87) of the nature of the discharge [*zåb*] in any of these categories is treated the same as emission of semen during intercourse [ࠆࠓࠏ (88) ࠔࠊࠁࠕ *ashkåbåt zēra*] or while asleep [ࠒࠓࠉ ࠋࠉࠋࠄ *qēri līla*]: the treatment applying is to bathe in water, thus recovering from it the day it happens.)

(89) The phenomenon demanding a count of seven days free of any issue can be of two kinds. There can be a sticky fluid running out of (90) the end of the penis, not due to any of the causes just mentioned: this is what the text refers to by saying (91) 'his flesh runs with his discharge [ࠆࠅࠁ *zob*]' (Lv XV:3). The second kind is the emergence from the end of the penis of thick stuff (92) with a tendency to congeal which turns into a sort of scale over the end of the penis, sealing it off: this is what the text refers to by saying 'or his flesh (93) is sealed by his discharge [ࠆࠅࠁ *zob*]' (v. 3). Should either of these two kinds occur to a man one day and continue for a second (94) day he is to withdraw himself as long as this lasts, till the flow is ended. Once it is, (95) he is to count, from the day after the end of the issue, seven days without any issue, during which he does not see the slightest sign of it, as it says (96) in the passage 'Any man with a discharge [ࠆࠁ *zåb*] from his flesh, he is unclean (97) because of his discharge [ࠆࠅࠁ *zob*] ... his flesh runs with his discharge [*zob*] or his flesh is sealed with his discharge [*zob*], (98) he is unclean' (v. 3).

(99) As long as he is unclean he is to keep away from where clean people live, outside the town somewhere out of the way (100) and completely uninhabited, in agreement with the verse 'and get them to send anyone (101) suffering from depigmentation and any man with a discharge [*zåb*] and anyone unclean, any person, whether male or female, out of the camp' (102) (Nu V:2-3).

(103) Any clean person that touches his bed or any artefact he has been sitting on or the place he has been standing or (104) an animal he has ridden on becomes unclean and recovers from his uncleanness by washing (105) and bathing, as it says 'Anyone that touches any artefact the man with the discharge [*zåb*] has sat (106) on is unclean' (see v. 5, and vv. 4-6, 9-10).

(107) If he spits on a clean place or clean artefact it has to be rinsed [*ghasl*] and washed [*ḥamīm*] in water, as it says: (108) 'If the man with the discharge [*zåb*] spits on anyone or anything clean [ࠁࠈࠀࠅࠓ *baṭṭå̊'or*] that person is to wash his clothes and wash himself in water (109) and is unclean till sunset' (v. 8).

(110) If the man with the discharge [*zåb*] touches any artefact with his hand while it is damp the treatment for the uncleanness is that the artefact is washed with water and is unclean (111) till the sunset. The reason the text mentions the damp hand is to explain the difference between the treatment in the case of a man with a discharge [*zåb*] and the treatment in the case of the blood of separation [ࠍࠃࠀ *niddå*]: (112) any person or artefact that the *niddå* [blood] gets on is made unclean for seven days, and the discharge of a man [*zåb*] being (113) less unclean than the [blood of] separation [*niddå*], the text specifically states the treatment for anyone that gets it on him, which is for him to wash himself, and to free himself from the uncleanness by means of

water (114) the same day at the time of sunset. Had this not been specifically stated in this passage it would have followed by induction from (115) the separation [*niddå*] that anyone that got it on him — i.e. the actual substance of the discharge [*zåb*] — would be unclean for seven days. This is because the text says that the person from whom it issues counts (116) seven days without issue, and does not become clean till he has completed the seven days. This is what the text intends by the note about the discharge [*zåb*], since if his body (117) touches any clean artefact it is made unclean damp or no.

(118) If this first occurs to him one day, and his issue stops the same day, he does not have to go into withdrawal. He only (119) has to do this if it continues to the next day. This is because its continuation is the sign of a disease needing treatment having arisen (120) in the urethra.

(121) The most effective treatment is seclusion so that he can repent on his own. He needs to keep warm and avoid (122) harmful foods, and concentrate his thoughts on God and try to cure his ailment. Then the man will recover from it, and when he does, (123) he will appreciate the extent of the grace given to him.

(124) *The End*

TEXT 2

[KITÂB AL-KÂFÎ]

[Chapter XI]

The Varieties of Intrinsic Uncleanness Occurring to Men and Women

(2) *Occurring to Men*

(3) There is a category of this called discharge' [ࠆࠁ *zåb*], which is the occurrence of certain phenomena on urinating, whether before or after, such as viscosity, (4) or something similar to soapsuds, or soap, or something that looks like cow's dribble, stretched out like a thread. There is (5) a category of this that can sometimes happen as an after-effect of copulation; there is the kind emitted from the penis due to an ague; there is the kind caused by (6) eating blood-thickening food, which can have this effect; there is one that occurs due to overwhelming sexual arousal. Any instance of a phenomenon (7) belonging to any of these categories is to be treated in the same way as an emission of semen while asleep [ࠒࠓࠉ ࠋࠉࠋࠄ *qēri līla*] or during copulation [ࠔࠅࠊࠁ *shūkəb*], that is, by the person bathing (8) in water and remaining under a ban till sunset.

---

(9) *The Shaykh says*:

(10) If a man experiences a division of the stream or stinging at the end of the penis on urinating, (11) and he had a look at the time of starting without finding anything that could cause this, he does not become contaminated, and the same applies at the end (12) of the urination. Rather, there can be some cause other than the categories mentioned, since stinging or a division of the stream can (13) both occur as a result of hurrying or an obstruction present beforehand. If, however, viscosity appears before or after or during (14) urination, this does cause uncleanness. (15) If the urination is followed by dripping, and there is none of the signs of uncleanness, he does not become unclean; all the same, when he prays, he is to refrain from wearing any clothes on which it has fallen.

(16) Emission of semen while asleep [ࠒࠓࠉ ࠋࠉࠋࠄ *qēri līla*] or during intercourse [ࠔࠅࠊࠁ *shūkəb*] are a single grade of uncleanness. They require (17) washing of the person [ࠓࠇࠉࠑࠄ *rīṣṣa*].

(18) *What is Serious in its Consequences and Requires Counting and Needs Seven Days without Issue*

(19) This is a viscous moisture recurring at each urination, leaving behind a residue of moisture (20) that dries up leaving a thin scale closing the end of the penis off, so that the urine is blocked the next time. The man affected by this (21) is to withdraw himself for as long as it lasts. This is termed 'his flesh is sealed' (Lv XV:3). The alternative, (22) which occurs at the end of the urination, is what is referred to as 'his flesh runs' (same verse). Once this has happened to (23) any man he is supposed to withdraw himself and keep away from anywhere where there are clean people, in agreement with the verse 'and get them to send out of (24) the camp anyone suffering from depigmentation and any man with a discharge etc.' (Nu V:2-3), referring to the different kinds of uncleanness.

(25) Anyone that touches him or any of his belongings or his clothes or his bed needs washing and immersion to remove the effect, in agreement with the verse (26) 'Anyone that touches any artefact the man with the discharge [*zab*] has sat on is unclean' (see (27) Lv XV:5, and also vv. 4-6).

(28) If the man with the discharge [*zåb*] spits on a clean place or a clean artefact it becomes unclean, as it says: 'If the man with the discharge [*zåb*] (29) spits on anyone clean [ࠁࠈࠄࠅࠓ *baṭṭå̊'or*] he is to wash his clothes and wash himself in water and is unclean till (30) sunset' (v. 8). The letter *bâ* [ࠁ *bit*] in the word ࠁࠈࠄࠅࠓ *baṭṭå̊'or* ['on anyone clean'] conveys the meaning of it being on any clean artefact, which gets wetted by it. (31) A new item of clothing, or clothing, is contaminated and has to be cleansed with water in the way commanded, universally (32) practised, and handed down as the law.

(33) *A Question*

(34) If it is asked what the point of the verse 'Anything the man with the discharge [*zåb*] touches without having rinsed (35) his hand etc.' (v. 11) is, the answer is that this stands for the organ out of which issues the contaminating (36) stuff. As well as this, if the man with the discharge [*zåb*] touches his unclean 'flesh' (v. 1 and v. 2), out of which comes (37) the stuff that brings on uncleanness, anything he touches before rinsing his hand in water is contaminated. This is (38) the difference between him and a man in the situation of having had an emission of semen while asleep [*qēri līla*]. Besides, from this can be derived an understanding of the difference between it (39) and the blood of 'separation' [ࠍࠃࠄ *niddå*], since anyone touched by the first can recover from it by bathing and the arrival of sunset, whereas a person touched by (40) the 'separation' [*niddå*] does not recover from it till seven days later.

(41) Any man suffering from any of these complaints should get away on his own and pray for recovery so he can be relieved of his (42) condition.

(43) *The Varieties of Intrinsic Uncleanness Occurring to Women*

(44) There are seven categories of this.

(45) The first in the 'separation' [ࠍࠃࠄ *niddå*], which is the first one to occur to the woman, and it is this and not what follows, (46) that causes seven days of uncleanness.

(47) *The Shaykh says*:

(48) There are seven categories of bleeding.

(49) The first is the 'separation' [ࠍࠃࠄ *niddå*]. The evidence for this is the verse 'A woman whose husband lies down with her, (50) so that her separation [*niddå*] gets on him, he is unclean for seven days' (Lv XV:24). (51) The man would not have copulated with the woman unless she had been clean, since copulation with a woman in the situation of being under a ban due to contamination (52) has been forbidden to Israel by God in the verse 'A man that lies down with a woman (53) with a flow of blood [ࠃࠅࠄ *då̊bå*] ... both of them are to be cut off' (Lv XX:18). He only approached her because she was (54) clean, but she was at the end of the period of cleanness, and the copulation coincided with the onset of the menstrual flow. The text calls this (55) 'separation' [*niddå*], and refers to it in the verse 'so that her separation [*niddå*] gets on him', just quoted.

(56) The second category of bleeding is 'bleeding of a menstruating woman' [ࠃࠅࠄ ࠃࠌ *dam då̊bå*]. It consists of any bleeding occurring after the 'separation' [*niddå*] and at any time (57) during the week. This is proven by the fact that some women see it and some do not, and with some it stops (58) the same day and with some it reappears on the second or third day, up to the end of the week. Some women (59) have profuse bleeding, so that it lasts till the day after the end of the week. In such a case, she has to stay in a state of uncleanness for another week. After that her cycle goes (60) from the starting-point of the period that she has worked out for herself.

(61) The third category is 'bleeding of a woman with a discharge' [ࠆࠁࠄ ࠃࠌ *dam zå̊bå*]. This is when the woman's defilement arrives after the fortnight. (62) As long as it is present she is to suspend the counting. The rule for recovery from it is that the bleeding is to end completely, after which she is to count seven days from then without any bleeding. (63) This is what is described in the text as 'outside the time of her separation [*niddå*]' (64) (v. 25) and defined as 'for many days' (same verse). Each day when she is not counting she is in a condition of 'separation' [*niddå*], but the text calls this 'discharge' [ࠆࠁ *zåb*] (65) because the characteristic quality of the separation

[*niddå*] is the speed of its disappearance and the requirement of a week because of the speed of its disappearance. If it (66) continues it will not be separation [*niddå*], but nevertheless it will be discharge [*zåbå*] rather than menstruation [*dåbå*], which a person contacted by it can wash off (67) straightaway, with the resulting restriction lasting just till sunset.

(68) The fourth category is 'bleeding of childbirth' [ࠃࠌ ࠉࠋࠉࠃࠄ *dam yēlīda*], which is divided into two categories each with their own halachic requirements. One is the bleeding at (69) the birth of a boy and the other is the bleeding at the birth of a girl. The requirement in the case of a boy is seven days, and in the case of a girl the period is doubled.

(70) The reason for the doubling is that the blood is thicker and darker and there is more of it than in the case of a boy. It can be characterized by the example of a garment being dipped (71) in the dyer's vat and not attaining the required colouring till it is re-dipped in the vat and the depth of colour (72) is doubled. The integrated explanation is along other lines: the female is the party concerned with the injunction and its halachic requirements in this matter.

(73) The sixth category is what is termed 'bleeding of her cleansing' [ࠃࠌ ࠈࠄࠓࠄ *dam ṭårå*]. This is something that can be a symptom of women during their period of impurity after (74) childbirth. In the case of a boy, if it occurs on the thirty-third day, she can simply immerse herself straightaway, (75) without any new defilement, and the same applies on the sixty-sixth day, in the case of a girl. If it happens before then it does not (76) have any effect, but if afterwards, then it does.

(77) Some women never see it, as in the case of the separation [*niddå*]: it comes on them at the start, then cuts out straightaway, and they do not (78) see any other bleeding and remain completely free of it.

(79) The seventh category is blood of plausibility. This is an alteration of the colour to maroon or blue or (80) yellow, resulting in 'plausibility'. The woman is to be avoided as long as this lasts, because there can only be cleanness (81) when there is clearness, and whatever is not clear is not clean. It is like when clear water gets something it it (82) and the effect of it shows.

(83) *The Legal Consequences of Touching the Actual Substances of the Various Kinds of Uncleanness*

(84) Anyone that touches the actual substance of the blood of separation [*niddå*] is made unclean 'for seven days' (Lv XV:24). Anyone that touches the actual substance (85) of the menstrual blood [*dåbå*] can wash it off straightaway. The proof of this is that if a woman who normally becomes clean in seven days (86) finishes with the bleeding known as 'menstruation' [*dåbå*] before sunset by the slightest amount she becomes clean and can mix with

clean people (87) and is unaffected: so it follows that anyone that touches the actual substance of the 'menstruation' [*då̊bå̊*] is not affected for a week.

(88) Each one of these kinds mentioned has a certain period, and anyone that touches the actual substance of it has to make a count that is the same as the count that applies (89) to the person from whom it issues.

(90) Copulation with women in any of these categories is very strictly forbidden.

[KITÂB AL-KÂFI]

[Extract From Chapter III]

[*Excursus on the Types and Grades of Contamination*]

(2) *Cleansing with Water from the Various Kinds of Uncleanness*

(3) This falls into two types: one from inside the person concerned, and deriving from them: and one due to the person coming in contact with something else. The type deriving from the person consists of (4) uncleanness that is intrinsic in its nature, and contact with other things includes touching [ࠄࠍࠅࠂࠏ *annūga*], and eating [ࠄࠀࠊࠋ *å:kəl*], (5) and lifting [ࠄࠍࠅࠔࠀ *annūsha*], and actions of the same sort, and actions that fall into one of these general categories as exemplified.

(6) *The Grades of Cleansing*

(7) There are three categories: washing of the person [ࠓࠇࠉࠑࠄ *rīṣṣa*], washing of clothes [ࠊࠁࠉࠎࠄ *kēbīsa*], and immersion [ࠈࠁࠉࠋࠄ *ṭēbīla*]. Some grades of uncleanness demand (8) all three of the person affected; some demand two; and some only demand one. This last is the case of man that has had an emission of semen (9) while asleep [ࠒࠓࠉ ࠋࠉࠋࠄ *qēri līla*] (Dt XXIII:11) or during intercourse [ࠔࠅࠊࠁ *shūkəb*] (see Lv XV:16) to whom only the duty of washing himself [*rīṣṣa*] applies, out of all these. This is shown by (10) the verse about a man that has had an emission of semen while asleep [*qēri līla*]: 'If there is a man among you that is unclean (11) due to an emission during the night [*qēri līla*] ... till he has washed [ࠓࠇࠑ *rå̊s*] his body with water (12) and the sun has set and he becomes clean' (Dt XXIII:11-12). In the case of a man that has had an emission of semen during intercourse [*shūkəb*] the text says (13) 'A woman whose husband lies down with her with an emission of semen [ࠔࠊࠁࠕ ࠆࠓࠏ *ashkå̊båt zēra*], they are to wash themselves [ࠅࠓࠇࠑࠅ *wrå̊ṣu*] (14) with water' (Lv XV:16). It is this person of whom washing of the person [*rīṣṣa*] is required.

(15) There are various traditional practices carried out as standard practice

that are not mentioned explicitly by the text of Scripture, but some of which are alluded to (16) by the wording of the passage. For instance, if the man emits a weak stream of urine, and a division of the stream occurs at the start of the urination, then if (17) he had previously checked the end of the penis without seeing anything before the urination that could have caused this, he has to (18) check when the urination is over, and if he detects viscosity or something stretched out like cow's dribble, he only has to cleanse himself (19) by washing himself [*rīṣṣa*]. If he does not detect anything, either before or after, in spite of the stream being divided, no (20) halachic requirements due to his situation become applicable to him, since a division of the stream can easily occur due to turbulence in the stream as it emerges, and similarly, stinging does not (21) necessitate any cleansing unless some evidence of the kind mentioned is present.

(22) *He says*:

(23) If he is in the position of having had an emission of semen, which is known as *janâbah*, because such a person has to (24) avoid [*yatajannib*] associating with clean people.

(25) *He says*:

(26) If he touches anyone, that person is thereby contaminated, and if that person then touches other people, they are thereby contaminated, ending with the third person, (27) and if any fourth person is touched by the third person, this fourth person is unaffected.

(28) *He says*:

(29) The reason for this is that there are two types of uncleanness, as we have said, intrinsic and not intrinsic, and if the intrinsic one touches anything at all, it is made (30) unclean, but we have said that the interruption is at the third item, since as there is no intrinsic uncleanness in it, no transmission occurs. If anyone says (31) that the second is the same as the third, so why should the end be at the third item, the answer is that the third is a basis for the end (32) of one state of things and their passage into another state, by the text of Scripture and by tradition as normative pratice and revealed law. For instance, when God created the world covered in water, (33) the text mentions it being covered in water, and mentions the third day along with its separation from the original state; and whereas it mentions the firmament at (34) the primal differentiation, the lighting up of it was completed on the third day, with the end of the great dark. People use this (35) as a basis for acting and calculating, as did Simeon and Levi with Shechem, in the passage (36) 'On the third day, when they were sore' (Gn XXXIV:25); and the third is mentioned (37) in the same way in the place where it says: 'On the third day, Pharaoh's birthday' (38) (Gn XL:20); and there are plenty of other instances.

(39) *The Second Grade*

(40) This is the washing of clothes [*kēbīsa*]. If a man that has had an emission of semen while asleep [*qēri līla*] (41) or during intercourse [*shūkeb*] happens to get a bit of stuff of the nature of his uncleanness on his clothes he has to wash himself [*rīṣṣa*] and his clothes [ࠊࠁࠎ *kēbås*]. (42) The same applies to a person becoming clean from depigmentation [ࠑࠓࠏࠕ *ṣårrēt*] or a discharge from the penis [ࠆࠁ *zåb*].

(43) A person unclean due to a corpse, who is termed *nāṭir*, has all three categories applying to him. The same applies for the woman in her separation [ࠍࠃࠄ *niddå*] (44) and other items of the same class; this will be explained, according to its grades, in the chapter on the various kinds of uncleanness.

[KITÂB AL-KÂFI]

[Extract From Chapter XIII]

[*Section on the Contaminating Effect of Bleeding of Childbirth*]

The Shaykh says:

(2) If something happens to the baby, either something to do with the baby itself or some outside circumstance, that prevents it from being washed and cleansed before circumcision, (3) does the person that touches it while circumcising it have to count a week or not?

(4) *The Answer*:

(5) Two opinions have been expressed about this.

(6) One is that he does not have to count a week. This is shown by the practice in some towns of circumcising (7) the baby when it is clean, and as the baby is able to become clean immediately on being washed, a week is not required of the person that touches it before (8) the washing, not the circumciser or anyone else.

(9) The other opinion is that a week is required of the circumciser. The holder of this view says that it is only possible to make the baby clean (10) after a week's counting after the washing, because of its arrival along with the blood, and the counting can only change it to another state after the washing, (11) no matter how much time has passed. It is the same as with a person made unclean by contact with a corpse [*nāṭir*], and who is cleansed to the first stage, and then goes for whatever time it might be without (12) the water of purification [ࠌࠉ ࠍࠃࠄ]: any day on which it touches him is the third day the first time and the seventh day the second time, and the reason for the days

not being counted is that (13) the water of purification had not touched him. In the practice of the Israelite women, if ever (14) the separation [ࠍࠃࠄ *niddå*] comes at the end of the daytime and the woman does not perform the washing before sunset and then washes herself afterwards, (15) that day is lost and is not counted. If she had done this before sunset and had moved out of the first (16) stage by means of water, that day would have been included in the count. The same with the baby as long as it has not been washed with water, seeing that it was (17) in the situation of being surrounded by blood, and after that it came out along with it. There is no cleansing for it without this, and wiping it with rags will not produce cleanness. (18) The first stage can only be ended by means of water.

(19) After being washed, it stays in the legal position of being under the count due to the first discharge. This is confirmed by the principle observed by the women (20) in regard to their left hand with which they wash the place of the bleeding, that after washing with water it stays under (21) the count independently of the other parts of the body.

(22) *He says*:

(23) If the baby had previously been washed, on the second or third day, is the cleansing effective or no?

(24) *The Answer*:

(25) Washing of the baby, on whatever day it occurs, is effective, and it stays under the count from that time. It sometimes (26) happens, however, that a woman has her delivery at the baths, and in that case the effect is accomplished on the removal of the foreign matter.

(27) *He says*:

(28) If the baby is washed with water from above the hips down to the ankles, and the penis, and the circumciser then (29) touches it, he does not require a week's count. But it is known by tradition that a midwife who delivers a baby belonging to the community waits for a period (30) of days known as the 'extra seriousness' [ࠉࠅࠕࠓ *ūtar*] without eating with her hand and without touching anyone's food with it.

[KITÂB AL-KÂFI]

[CHAPTER XII]

A Chapter on the Kinds of Uncleanness and their Details and Treatment

(2) *The Shaykh says*:

(3) They are divided into four categories for the purpose of cleansing: (4) some can be cleansed by water and some can be cleansed by fire, and some can acquire cleanness either way, by water or fire, and some can not (5) be

cleansed by water or fire. The Lawgiver has informed us about this in the passage 'Anything that (6) will go in the fire you can put through the fire ... and anything that will not go (7) in the fire you can put through water' (Nu XXXI:23).

(8) An example of something that acquires cleanness in water rather than fire is a wooden artefact of any sort, which is capable of becoming clean after (9) having undergone rinsing [ࠔࠈࠉࠐࠄ *shēṭīfa*] according to the verse 'Any wooden artefact can be rinsed [ࠉࠔࠈࠐ *yishshåṭåf*] with water' (10) (Lv XV:12). This consists of clearing it out till as much as possible of the stuff absorbed by it during use has been removed. (11) After that it can undergo immersion [ࠈࠁࠉࠋࠄ *ṭēbīla*] if it is in a serious classification, or washing [ࠓࠇࠑ *rå:ṣ*] if it is in a less serious classification on (12) the contamination grading. This is on the authority of normative practice and tradition. The same applies to any kind of lead or copper utensil, (13) which, if it were to go in the fire, would be ruined. (This way its cleansing with water is more correctly performed, so it is preferable for it to be after the process of rinsing [*shēṭīfa*]). (14) The same applies to any kind of gold personal adornments, which would have their shaping spoilt if they came in contact with fire. This is why it says 'Just (15) the gold and silver ... Anything that will go in the fire (16) you can put through the fire so it will be cleansed, and anything that will not go in the fire you can put (17) through water' (Nu XXXI:22-23). If there is anything which, if touched by fire, will not be ruined by it, that someone wants to cleanse (18) with fire, there is nothing to stop them from doing so. Water is the most satisfactory means of cleansing the general range of classes of objects; anyway, some kinds of wrought-metal articles get spoilt if touched (19) by fire, and God has not commanded this, as is conclusively shown by the words 'Anything that will go' (20) meaning any kind of article that will stand up to it during cleansing.

(21) Common sense will settle things in such cases and takes the place of legislation.

(22) *What Acquires Cleanness by Fire*

(23) This includes ground contaminated by a corpse or 'separation' [ࠍࠃࠄ *niddå*] or absorption of moisture from a person under the ban (24) of contamination, either by means of water or a scrap of food which is dropped on the ground and oozes. The cleansing of the place (25) is done by fire. If it is a place of *niddå*, then according to the rule for it known by tradition and derivable from the text of Scripture, it is done once. If affected by a corpse, (26) there is a first step on the first day, when it is done once, then on the third day, once, before the purifying water [ࠍࠃࠄ ࠌࠉ] is sprinkled on it, and once afterwards, with the fire being passed over the place a second (28) time.

This is a law that can be derived from the text of Scripture from the implications of the divisions of the practical legislation [ࠇࠒࠄ *åqqå*], and should be intelligible to anyone that applies himself and anyone that studies the matter.

(29) Any ground where the person under the ban sits that has not absorbed any moisture is unaffected: only if (30) it absorbs some of the unclean substance of the person sitting there, of the same nature as his contamination.

(31) The cleansing of a place that is unclean due to a corpse is by its stages, with fire. A place where a woman gives birth is cleansed by fire (32) and is immediately unaffected, provided the requirements of a corpse do not apply.

(33) If some of the blood of childbirth drips, and is dug up and completely removed, the place becomes clean; but if cleansing (34) with fire is carried out afterwards, this is better.

(35) The same with anything that is too heavy to carry or is too bulky for a place to be found to immerse it. (36) The cleansing of it is by means of fire. We use this as a basis and the treatment of other items of the same nature is derived from it. There is some freedom in this matter and common sense (37) settles things and determines the decision.

(38) *What is Not Cleansed by Water or Fire*

(39) This includes the foreskin of the heart, about which the text says 'Circumcise the foreskin of your heart' (40) (Dt X:16), and this, that is to say, depravity in a person's character, is not cleansed by water or fire. The same applies to the study (41) of what should not be looked at, which the text forbids in the verse 'Do not look round according to (42) your tendencies and desires' (Nu XV:39). The text treats this as equivalent to the action, and even if there is no (43) copulation, it still says 'in your unlawful sexual activities' (same verse). The study that gives rise to the effect is treated as if it were the action. (44) The same applies to marriage with women with whom copulation is forbidden: there can be no cleansing by water or fire. The situation is the same for the presence of the foreskin on a person who has not (45) had it removed: he is never cleansed, as Aba ʿIwaḍ says in *A Beautiful City*: 'The ocean will not (46) purify him'. The same applies to nasty talk. The same with fur and leather from the hides of forbidden animals, or from permitted (47) animals killed outside the community, or killed by members of the community but affected by contamination while still green, before the tanning process (48) is completed; they are never cleansed. The situation is the same for linsey-woolsey [ࠔࠏࠈࠍࠆ *shåṭnəz*], which is formed by combining (49) wool and linen: it is never cleansed. These are representative examples of categories to which other instances of the same class can be assimilated. (50) An instance would be the food belonging to a non-Samaritan: if a Samaritan

eats it he is not cleansed from it by water or fire. These (51) categories are forbidden to Israel.

[*The Text of Mss. JD*]

(52) Certain trades, of which representative examples will be given to be applied to other instances of the same class, are forbidden to them. Examples are tanning (53) and dyeing and so on.

(54) As well as this, they are forbidden to live in defiled areas lacking the means of cleansing and short of water, or to live where there are sinners (55) and drunks, or in places of vice.

(56) All these come under the category of 'unclean' and there can never be any cleansing from them and not one of them can be purified (57) at all at all.

(58) As well as this, if anyone copulates with a woman under the ban of contamination and they bathe themselves afterwards, neither of them can possibly be cleansed by doing this.

[*The Text of Most of the Mss.*]

(59) There are some representative examples of trades forbidden to any Israelite which we will give so that other instances of (60) trades of the same class can be assimilated to them: these are tanning and dyeing and so on.

(61) They are forbidden to live in areas barred to them because of defiled remains, lacking the means of cleansing and short of water. (62) Or such as living in places where there are sinners and drunks, or in places of vice.

(63) All these come under the legal category of uncleanness, and there is no way (64) anyone wanting to be cleansed and claiming to be a member of the Israelite community (63) can remove their effect by bathing, or be cleansed from their effect, except by getting rid of anything (64) out of the categories mentioned, getting rid of anything affecting him that is not (65) cleansed by water or fire.

(66) If anyone copulates with a woman under the ban of contamination, neither of them can ever be cleansed with water.

TEXT 3

[THE BOOK OF DIFFERENCES]

[CHAPTER SIX]

(2) We now treat the subject of the laws of the 'separation' [ࠍࠃࠄ *niddå*], 'woman with a discharge' [ࠆࠁࠄ *zåbå*], and childbirth [ࠉࠋࠉࠃࠄ *yēlīda*]; (3) the various consequences of the kinds of bleeding depending on their various circumstances; the question of whether its nature is uniform, and how an (4) issue from one organ and an issue from another are distinct in having their own legal consequences; how bleeding issuing (5) normally is called 'separation' [*niddå*] bleeding in legal terminology, and bleeding happening repeatedly, in ways to be described, (6) which is abnormal and exceeds its limits, goes into a different category as blood of a 'woman with a discharge' [*zåbå*] (as with the 'man with a discharge' [ࠆࠁ *zåb*], when (7) his discharge is repeated and is exceptional in its amount and quality: in its quality, by being 'running' [ࠓࠓ *rår*] (Lv XV:3) or (8) 'blocked' [ࠄࠇࠕࠌ *ʿā:tom*] (v. 3), viscous or dried-up and dried-out; and he can be distinguished in these respects from a man that (9) has emitted semen while asleep [ࠒࠓࠉ *qēri*]); but how the forms of the bleeding of the new mother are classified according to the nature of the baby, whether male or female, (10) with the difference in the treatment of the bleeding depending on the differences in the baby, i.e. what sex it is; bleeding before, during, and after (11) delivery, with various different consequences depending on the stages of its appearance and the time at which it occurs; an explanation (12) of 'blood of her cleansing' [ࠈࠄࠓࠄ ࠃࠌ *dam ṭårå*] and its meaning according to us and the legal position (13) applying to it, and its meaning according to the others and the legal position applying to it according to their belief as to the interpretation and meaning of this term.

(14) We start first with the 'blood of separation' [ࠍࠃࠄ ࠃࠌ *dam niddå*] and its basic meaning.

(15) (We should say at this point that the Lawgiver has made a decree, and his decree on these kinds of blood is given with a set of rules (16) that demand careful attention. Among the ordinances he has made in his wisdom there is one point that is hard to grasp, and this hard point is the injunction that (17) these requirements are not the inevitable consequences of the varieties of this blood, as if it were impossible for the injunction to be otherwise, (18) so that you could go further with them but not do any less with them, the way you can with the commandments about personal character where the requirements apply because of the actions and (19)

qualities themselves, as with truthfulness and lying, fairness and unfairness, prudence and recklessness, the obligation of self-examination and proper conduct, (20) or frivolousness and drunkenness and irreligiousness. The requirement is the inevitable consequence of these actions being good or bad and it would be (21) inconceivable for the injunction to have been otherwise. The same with such examples as the camel or pig or hare and (22) all the others referred to by the text as 'unclean' [ࠈࠌࠀ *ṭēmi*] or 'not to be eaten' [ࠔࠒࠑ *ashqəṣ*]. No injunction about them other than the one made could be made because they are (23) unclean in their substance and nature and will only take a single legal status. It would be impossible to claim that they, or other things like them, could ever have their legal status revoked (24) or that changes or substitutions in their requirements could ever happen, so that they were unclean in substance one day and the next day were clean in substance (25) and allowable for sacrifice. The law about them is that their properties never leave them and are not changed over or altered at some other (26) time.

(27) The laws about the kinds of bleeding mentioned above are not like that: it is not by virtue of their actual nature or substance that (28) these legal consequences apply to them, and actual blood has no quality in it to make it contaminated. You can plainly see that it is emitted (29) in diarrhoea and vein-opening and virginal bleeding and nosebleeds and medicinal lancing without having any legal status (30) of contamination; so you have to go by the rules, which depend on the changes in the circumstances of it: the fact is simply that the Lawgiver has decreed as he willed. With the confirmation (31) gained from these and others of the same type, the mistaken idea that the legal status can be nullified, and that it can become legally neutral, collapses, since we have been told that (32) the content of the Torah is permanent for principle and practice.

(33) The reason I have put in this preface is that the Jews take the legal consequences of the different kinds of bleeding to depend on the kind of blood and (34) its quality. They define various colours of it, some of which indicate contamination and some cleanness, and say that (35) not everyone has got the skill to tell the clean and contaminated kinds of blood discharged from the vagina and not everyone can recognise contaminated blood. Instead there are experts in it that can tell (36) the different states of it and know what is contaminated and causes contamination and what is clean. They use the verse (37) 'If a decision in a blood case is too hard for you' (Dt XVII:8) to try to justify this. They (38) are mistaken over this. The point is that the Lawgiver has charged his creatures with the observance of the laws of the blood discharged from the vagina and the differences (39) in the laws depend on the differences in the circumstances, so that any emission from this organ causes contamination unconditionally, and as (40) the circumstances of its occurence change, changes are caused in the laws.

(41) The start of this is the verse saying ࠅࠀࠔࠄ ࠊࠉ ࠕࠄࠉࠄ ࠆࠁࠄ ࠃࠌ ࠉࠄࠉࠄ ࠆࠅࠁࠄ ࠁࠁࠔࠓࠄ ['A woman that has a discharge [ࠆࠁࠄ *zåbå*], (42) whose discharge [ࠆࠅࠁ *zob*] is blood, in her flesh'] (Lv XV:19), which means 'A woman who develops a discharge, and whose discharge is blood, emitted (43) from her vagina, stays for seven days under the ban of the separation [ࠍࠃࠄ *niddå*] blood'. This is a reference to a woman whose bleeding (44) comes on at the usual time for its release. The meaning of the word ࠍࠃࠕࠄ *niddåtå* [her separation, her *niddå*] on the basis of its etymology is exclusion and removal and separation (45) and isolation, as in the phrase ࠍࠏ ࠅࠍࠃ *nā wnad* (Gn IV:12, 14), i.e. 'disturbed and separate'; in law it means removal from clean people, (46) and the blood itself is referred to by the same term because it is the cause of the woman being 'in a state of separation' [ࠍࠏࠃࠄ *nå'ēda*]. In legal usage the term comes to be understood as referring exclusively to the first (47) bleeding, which is the cause of the woman being 'in a state of separation' [ࠍࠏࠃࠄ *nå'ēda*].

(48) The set period during which it is emitted from her during the rest of the week is called 'bleeding of a menstruating woman' [ࠃࠌ ࠃࠅࠄ *dam dåbå*].

(49) The basic meaning of ࠃࠅࠄ *dåbå* etymologically is sickness, and it is derived from 'depression' [*dhawabân*] as well, as in the phrase ࠌࠃࠉࠁࠅࠕ ࠍࠐࠔ *mådībot nåfəsh* (50) (Lv XXVI:16) ['making the feelings depressed'], except that ࠌࠃࠉࠁࠅࠕ ࠍࠐࠔ *mådībot nåfəsh* is derived from ࠃࠅࠁࠉࠁ *dūbəb*, maning 'depression' [*dhawabân*] and has no (51) *wâw* [ࠅ *bā*] in its root, but has *bā* [ࠁ *bit*] instead. In legal usage, however, it is a term applied to a woman that has an emission of blood from her vagina, as it says (52) 'A man that lies down with a woman with a flow [*dåbå*]' (Lv XX:18). This covers any woman (53) in such a situation, and is not restricted to the woman in her 'separation' [*niddå*] alone, to the exclusion of the woman with a discharge [*zåbå*] or after childbirth [*yēlīda*]. Certainly (54) the use of it in connection with the 'separation' [*niddå*] is well-known, as in the verse 'as with the days of the separation [*niddå*] of her discharge [*dåbåtå*] (55) is she unclean' (Lv XII:2), and the verse 'she is unclean for a fortnight as with her separation [*niddå*]' (v. 5). (56) The 'days of the separation [*niddå*] of her menstruation [*dåbå*]' are the seven days prescribed by the Torah for the 'separation [*niddå*] (57) of her menstruation [*dåbå*]'; and the 'separation [*niddå*] of her menstruation [*dåbå*]' reduces itself to the first bleeding, since nothing anywhere in the 'blood of her menstruation [*dåbå*]' (58) requires seven days, just the first discharge, which is the 'separation [*niddå*] of her menstruation [*dåbå*]'. The reason is that it is this that demands (59) the romoval and exclusion from which the term 'separation' [*niddå*] is taken. In technical usage this term is the term for the first bleeding of the 'blood (60) of her menstruation [*dåbå*]'.

(61) (The phrase 'a fortnight as with her separation [*niddå*]' is meant to indicate a doubling, and means two exact weeks, neither (62) of which is to be more than seven days.).

(63) (If her separation [*niddå*] recurs, coming on the first day and the eighth day, it still does not become anything more than (64) her separation [*niddå*]' (Lv XV:25), and it does not count as a state of 'discharge' [ࠄࠆࠁࠅࠕ *zībot*] when it recurs, since the emission is normal, not abnormal, (65) contrary to Anan's opinion.).

(66) The first bleeding requires seven days of separation and exclusion from clean people, and this term is used technically to refer to (67) the first bleeding, which is the originating cause, as opposed to what happens to her on the second or third day. If it was the bleeding (68) happening during the week, stopping on one day or another, that had an effect of seven days, the standard set by (69) the Lawgiver as a reference in other situations would be invalidated and inadmissible, and the first bleeding would never require seven days unless no bleeding at all was to happen (70) the whole week aside from the first bleeding, and the standard would not be applicable as a constant. But in fact we do find this standard to be applicable as a constant, since (71) the Lawgiver has stipulated its use as a reference base in other situations, as it says 'For seven days she is unclean; she is unclean as with the days of the separation [*niddå*] (72) of her menstruation [*dåbå*]' (Lv XII:2), and similarly 'She is unclean for a fortnight as with her separation [*niddå*]' (73) (v. 5). Therefore the first bleeding always has an effect for seven days. This is supported by the verse 'If (74) her husband lies down with her at all, and her separation [*niddå*] gets on him, he is unclean for seven (75) days' (Lv XV:24). This is the bleeding known as 'separation' [*niddå*] and 'her separation' [*niddåtå*] (vv. 19, 24, 24) in legal terminology, as we have said.

(76) Al-Fayyûmi disagrees with this and labours to justify his fancies about the legal position — weak arguments more like (77) fallacious sophistry than arguments and evidence. He makes out this passage is meant to refer to a man that (78) copulates with a woman in the time of her separation [*niddå*] when he knew she was in her separation [*niddå*]. What we reckon is that it refers to a man that (79) has lain down with his wife (either literally, to sleep, or to copulate, since this is within the range of meaning of 'sleeping'; but the literal interpretation is preferable) knowing she was (80) clean to start off with, and next thing along comes the onset of bleeding. He is spared the death penalty, (81) and is made unclean for seven days the same as the woman the blood originated from. So the action was forbidden in the first place according to (82) Al-Fayyûmi, and according to us it was allowable, since he went to sleep with her and lay down on the strength of her being clean, and then the bleeding starts (83) straight after and they both become unclean together. The Lawgiver has given this the same legal consequences as

equivalent cases, and the point of agreement in their contamination is that they are all allowed, (84) none of them are forbidden, as it says 'and applying to a man that lies down with an unclean woman' (Lv XV:33). (85) Therefore the contamination of such a man came from an act that was permitted in the first place, not forbidden. The wording (86) of the passage can be taken to refer to literal sleeping or can be taken to refer to copulation: the act was allowable in the first place either way.

(87) Al-Fayyûmi's claim is invalidated in two respects.

(88) One is that he treats an expression with a possible connotation as explicit. If it is explicit why should it depend on another expression to show the sense in which it is being used? (89) Take, for instance, the verse 'A woman whose husband lies down with her with an emission (90) of semen, they are to wash themselves with water' (Lv XV:18). If the expression 'lying down' on its own explicitly means (91) copulation, why should it need another expression, 'with an emission of semen', to show the sense in which it is being used? In his ignorance he has treated a possible connotation as explicit.

(92) Besides this, he misinterprets the phrase 'and her separation [*niddå*] gets on him' (v. 24). The legal consequences of (93) 'her separation [*niddå*]' are the period of time during which she has to stay on her own away from clean people: the period of time and her separation from (94) clean people during this period and the contamination of anyone that touches her and the unlawfulness of copulating with her are the consequences of 'her separation [*niddå*]'. But what the Lawgiver is referring to is the 'blood (95) of her separation [*niddå*]', and it is well known that the blood can be called 'her separation [*niddå*]'. This is the first bleeding, the one that is the cause of the legal consequences, (96) as shown by the verse 'as with the days of the separation [*niddå*] of her menstruation [*då̄bå*]' (Lv XII:2), where the 'separation [*niddå*]' is the first bleeding, and 'her menstruation [*då̄bå*]' is what (97) comes after.

(98) The culmination of his error is that he treats the two laws as one and lumps together what the text of Scripture separates. The passage (99) covering a man that copulates with a woman in her separation [*niddå*] is the verse 'A man that lies down (100) with a woman with a flow [*då̄bå*] and uncovers her genitals, the spring of her genitals, (101) and she uncovers the spring of her bleeding, they are to be cut off' (Lv XX:18). Here the (102) penalty is expressed in unambiguous terms, and the death penalty is never shown to apply by a possible connotation or by induction but by an unequivocal statement. This, however, (103) is a forced interpretation involving an addition [to the sense of the verse], and an addition beyond what is indicated by the natural meaning of a passage is figurative usage, and a person deserving execution is not punished on the basis of a figurative usage (104) or a possible

connotation or an induction. But this is what he does, the way he treats the possible connotation of the verse 'If her husband (105) lies down with her at all', where 'emission of semen' is not mentioned: he treats it as explicit when it needs (106) another expression to show the sense in which it is being used.

(107) The Lawgiver has put this man that was sleeping, or by a possible connotation copulating, in with a whole lot of people whose uncleanness has happened (108) in a way that was allowed and unforeseen, not in a way that was forbidden and pre-meditated, as it says 'and a person with a discharge [ࠅࠄࠆࠁ ࠀࠕ ࠆࠅࠁࠅ *wazzåb at zūbu*] (109) whether male or female, and a man that lies down with an unclean woman' (110) (Lv XV:33). It follows that this is the theoretical instruction [ࠕࠅࠓࠄ *tūra*] applying to him, as it says 'This is the theoretical instruction [*tūra*] of a man with a discharge [ࠆࠁ *zåb*], or who has an emission of (111) semen, becoming unclean by it, and the menstruating woman [*dåbå*] in her separation [*niddå*]' (vv. 32-33). (112) This means that this is legislation covering all these categories. The man that 'lies down with a woman with a flow from her vagina [*dåbå*]' (113) (Lv XX:18) has a different theoretical instruction [*tūra*] applying to him: the death penalty for a deliberate transgression committed as part of an action that was forbidden and not allowed in the first place, (114) and for which the death penalty is laid down in unambiguous terms, not as a possible connotation.

The short of all this is that we have made out (115) the Lawgiver's intended meaning on the basis of the wording of the text, and Al-Fayyûmi and those that agree with him have misunderstood it. From this we learn that the first bleeding has an effect of (116) seven days.

(117) Anything that appears on the second day has the effect of a single instant. If it gets on a garment or a person it only has (118) a single instant's effect, even if the discharge continues for three or four days, provided it does not extend past the end of the week. The text distinguishes between (119) the 'blood of her separation [*niddå*]' (see Lv XV:19, 23, 24, 33) and the 'blood of her menstruation [*dåbå*]' (120) (see Lv XII:2). In the light of this their assertion that all bleeding requires seven days falls through: it is only and exclusively required for the first bleeding, (121) and that's it.

(122) As for their claims about variations in the blood and yellow blood not having any legal consequences and their talk about colours that cause uncleanness (123) and ones that do not: the Lawgiver has made the legal consequences derive from the whole class of blood and has made an unqualified statement about it, relying (124) on the normal phenomena occurring to women for clarification. These normal phenomena show variation in the colour of the bleeding that occurs, and the consideration in this matter is what is normal for (125) women, taking account of the differences in their make-up. We have mentioned that the legal consequences of the whole class of blood are not the inevitable result (126) of its nature or substance, but that

the consequences in this and related matters derive from the decree of God. When his intention (127) and purpose are obscure to us he has provided, aside from deductive reasoning, the methods of inference used in law, such as the wording of the passage (128) and the natural meaning and the overall purpose and what makes sense and induction from other cases and what are normal phenomena; so the phenomena normally occuring to women can be used (129) for clarification.

(130) There is evidence for this in what we know about the situation of discharge [ࠆࠁ *zåb*]: it can be due to any colour, and if it occurs to the woman just before the last (131) night, of any colour, provided she experiences, during the 'days of counting' moisture deviating from whiteness towards yellow or auburn, (132) it invalidates the count and stops her from being in a position to finish it.

(133) The Lawgiver has made the legal consequences derive from the whole class of blood. He has not specified whether it is to be pure or mixed up or mixed in with something else, but (134) has made an unqualified statement about it, and has made the application of it follow from clarificatory information about what normally occurs to women that was available (135) before the revelation of the laws of the state of separation [ࠍࠃࠅࠕ *niddot*] and discharge [ࠆࠉࠁࠅࠕ *zībot*]. Anyone advocating an addition has the burden of giving proof and providing (136) an inductive and deductive demonstration, so as to support it from the actual words of Moses by the authority of God, not from the inventions of the Rabbis, (137) as they do with their claims.

(138) This view is the equivalent of making an addition to the Scriptural commandments, and is a second Torah.

(139) As for their derivation of it from the verse 'If a blood case is too unprecedented for you' (140) (Dt XVII:8): This is a derivation based on a possible connotation, whereas in reality the most natural out of the two meanings is the distinction between someone that (141) kills on purpose or by accident. Their choice of which of the two interpretations and possible meanings to follow is impossible in natural or normal (142) behaviour, as if whenever the woman has any menstrual bleeding she was supposed to take it to the 'Chosen Place' [ࠌࠒࠅࠌ ࠌࠁࠅࠓ *må̊qom mūbār*] (143) (see Dt XVII:8) so experts could tell whether it was clean blood or unclean and contaminated blood.

(144) You can tell from the natural meaning of the law that all blood emitted from the vagina is contaminated, with its contamination and the woman's legal requirements varying (145) according to the changes in its circumstances. The belief of these people that bleeding discharged from the organ in question can be a clean (146) colour or an unclean colour is therefore impossible.

(147) One of the Karaites reports of Al-Fayyûmi that he reckons that when our women or theirs have some bleeding that is clean by (148) nature, they count it as causing contamination, and then they might have some contaminated bleeding that really ought to require (149) seven days, which they do not count as requiring seven days, and when the week from the first bleeding is up a few days out of the week due to (150) the real bleeding are left over, and she is treated as clean when she is still in her separation [*niddå*]; then her husband copulates with her and (151) her child turns out as a 'child of menstrual uncleanness' [ࠁࠍ ࠍࠃࠅࠕ *ban niddot*]; and not satisfied with being wrong, he wants to be ignorant as well. This can all be turned back on them. (152) A woman of theirs can have bleeding which according to the Torah is contaminated, following the decree as known by unimpeachable tradition, but no notice is taken of it (153) and she is still considered clean, even though she is in her 'separation' [*niddå*], and her husband copulates with her and her child turns out as a 'child of menstrual uncleanness [*ban niddot*]'.

We, however, follow (154) the natural meaning of Scripture. As the Lawgiver is silent and dispenses with any clarification by means of other expressions, in spite of the urgent need (155) for it, this is evidence that it is not relevant. If ever the Lawgiver is silent about any clarification in spite of the imperative need of it, (156) then his silence in spite of his wisdom is evidence for rejection of what is proposed. In this case the clarification is from what is normal for menstruating women, which means there is no need for any (157) explanatory expressions or information from the context.

(158) Then Al-Fayyûmi says that for lack of experts in the varieties of blood we impose seven days for any bleeding to be on the safe side, (159) which means that if any bleeding happens on the fifth or sixth day of the week it requires seven days. This (160) disagrees with the natural and basic meaning of the law. The Lawgiver has set the separation [*niddå*] at not more than a week, and has set (161) this up as a standard of reference or model for use in other situations, as it says 'She is unclean as with the days of the separation [*niddå*] of her menstruation [*dåbå*] (162) (Lv XII:2). We have said that separation [*niddå*] is a legal term applying specifically to the first bleeding and that 'her menstruation [*dåbåtå*]' applies specifically to (163) what she experiences during the rest of the week, as it says 'and her separation [*niddå*] gets on him' (Lv XV:24). (164) The bleeding that is the reason for the legal consequences is called after the legal consequences, which are removal and exclusion for a week.

(165) If it happens on the first day of the next week it requires seven days, because it is the first bleeding and happens at the start (166) of this time-period. Similarly for a third and fourth week. The end of separation [*niddå*] bleeding is at seven weeks, because this is a perfect number. (167) It marks the difference and correct distinction between the apllication of the law of the

separation [*niddå*] and the law of the discharge [*zåbå*]. Sometimes the bleeding (168) happens continuously, unbroken by days of cleanness and sometimes, on the other hand, it happens (169) once and cuts out the instant it starts, so that the woman is clean for two or three days, then becomes unclean, so that her cycle alters during (170) the time of cleanness, which is the 'time of her separation [*niddå*]' (see v. 25). This repeats itself in seven of the periods of cleanness and she is judged to be (171) in the state of discharge [ࠆࠁࠅࠕ *zåbot*], or haemorrhoea, a well-known complaint similar to that of the man with a discharge [ࠆࠁ *zåb*], any attack of which will be an illness that needs prolonged (172) medical treatment. The causes of its occurrence have been described by the most expert physicians and have been described by us in some of our books.

(173) This is a law on its own, separate to the law of the separation [*niddå*], and it requires counting and a sacrifice because it is (174) so uncommon and rare and hardly ever happens. This is why the Lawgiver is so insistent on the purification from it. His prescription for its (175) dismissal is certain sacrifices as laid down for the man with the discharge [*zåb*].

(176) Anan and his followers, however, are of the opinion that this law with all its inconvenience and the inconvenience (177) of the associated legal requirements applies if she exceeds the week by a single day. His ignorance here is obvious. This would be (178) beyond the power of the person charged with keeping the commandment and would not agree with the wisdom of God, since the woman would be spending her whole life in ࠎࠐࠉࠓࠄ *sēfīra*, (179) i.e. the counting leading to the sacrifice. You commonly find that there are women that regularly have recurrences of menstrual discharge, whereas (180) this law is intended for a woman whose condition has become abnormal and who is very far from being normal. Besides, the Lawgiver, in specifying (181) recurrence, has set its period at 'many days' (v. 25), 'many days' being the point at which a break is made (182) between what is normal and what is a sickness and abnormal, and although this is cryptic and over-laconic, and the intention can not be worked out from the literal meaning (183) by any analytical technique, the literal meaning does tell us that for the time described (184) as 'many days' the Lawgiver intended the point at which a break is made between what is normal and what is a sickness and abnormal, departing from (185) the usual pattern for women's discharge of menstrual blood.

(186) The Rabbanite Jews reckon that the 'time of her separation [*niddå*]' (v. 25), which is the period between instances of menstrual discharge, is (187) eleven days from separation [*niddå*] to separation [*niddå*]; this is the time of her cleanness between the instances of her menstrual flow. They then say that if (188) it is just one or two days and three days less she is in her discharge [*zåbå*]. This is impossible, because the Lawgiver has specified (189) 'many

days' and one or two days, or three days, exceeding the 'time of her separation [*niddå*]' would not justify the application (190) of the law of the discharge [*zå̄bå*], because the 'time of her separation [*niddå*]' varies in different women, and it can be after twenty (191) days or more or less. The case of a continuous flow uninterrupted by a single day of cleanness (192) is the test of their assertion, but nevertheless, they still say there are eleven days from *niddå* to *niddå*, and if [bleeding occurs] one or two days (193) or three days short of that she is *zå̄bå*.

(194) The view of our ancestors is the most correct statement to have been made about it: it is the length of time they worked out by observation of the recurrence, (195) both continuous and interrupted. Observation teaches the distinction between the woman in her discharge [*zå̄bå*] and in her separation [*niddå*], since an occurence like (196) this is rare and abnormal.

(197) Once this illness is determined as present, it is shown as present by every emission of blood, red or yellow or black or deviating in any way from (198) white, and this is counted and taken as evidence. If she experiences anything similar to what we have described during the days of her count [*sēfīra*], yellow or (199) black or white, with a visible deviation, the count is thereby invalidated and a new count has to be started.

(200) The term 'counting' [*sēfīra*] (see v. 28) is used in technical language to refer to whole days, 'from sunset to sunset' (201) (Lv XXIII:32), natural days: it is not possible to do here what can be done elsewhere, to treat part of a day as a day.

(202) We now come to the legal requirements relating to the new mother, which are quite straightforward. The calculation of her days is from the time of delivery, (203) and here part of a day is treated as a day. If there is any bleeding before the day of giving birth there is no counting because of it, since the legal categories (204) overlap and the strongest takes precedence over the weakest, and the count starts from the day of giving birth. The first bleeding, coming (205) right at the time of delivery, causes anyone coming in contact with it seven days' uncleanness in the case of a boy, and in the case of a girl (206) the actual substance of the blood coming simultaneously with delivery causes a fortnight's uncleanness, as it says: 'She is unclean for seven (207) days, she is unclean as with the days of the separation [*niddå*] of her menstruation [*då̄bå*] (Lv XII:2), and in reference to (208) a girl 'If she has a girl she is unclean for a fortnight as with her separation [*niddå*]' (v. 5).

(209) Blood that appears after delivery and the separation of the child from the mother has a single instant's effect, like the 'blood (210) of her cleansing [ࠃࠌ ࠈࠄࠓࠄ *dam ṭå̄rå*]' (see vv. 4, 5, 6). Some experts are of the opinion that any blood emitted from her any time during (211) the seven-day period has the same legal consequences as the first bleeding, having an effect of seven days, and bleeding on the eighth or fifteenth day (212) has an instant's effect,

because its legal position is different to the position of bleeding that occurs during the seven or fourteen days. We commonly (213) find that women are very careful about any bleeding during the seven or fourteen days because of the seriousness (214) of its legal position, and its differentiation from the 'blood of her cleansing [*dam ṭårå*]'.

(215) Any bleeding after this set number of days falls under the ban of 'blood of her cleansing [*dam ṭårå*]', i.e. the bleeding of delivery, and her recovery from it.

(216) The Jews reckon that ࠈࠄࠓࠄ ࠃࠌ *dam ṭårå* (vv. 4 and 5 and see v. 6) is 'her cleanness' and treat it as clean blood. Their error in this is obvious: (217) there is no kind of blood coming out of the vagina that is clean: all of it is classed as contaminated. Because of this (218) they let her associate with clean people and let her husband copulate with her. This is a fallacious ruling and contradicts the law (219) of Moses.

(220) First, because blood of ࠈࠄࠓࠄ *ṭårå* [her cleansing] can mean 'her becoming clean' or can mean 'her absence of bleeding', as shown by the verse 'If she becomes clean [ࠈࠄࠓࠄ *ṭå'ēra*] (221) from her discharge [ࠆࠅࠁ *zob*]' (Lv XV:28), where it means her absence of bleeding, or as in the verse 'and the priest atones for her, (222) and she becomes clean [ࠅࠈࠄࠓࠄ *wṭå'ēra*] from the spring of her bleeding' (Lv XII:7), where the usage is the same as in the verse 'and uncovers (223) her genitals, the spring of her genitals, and she uncovers the spring of her (224) bleeding' (Lv XX:18). Our decision on the interpretation and our choice out of the two possible meanings of the word — which is the most natural one — (225) is better. If this blood was clean, there would be no point to the verse 'and the priest (226) atones for her and she becomes clean'. The point is that he prays for her to become cleansed of any issue from the pool of her bleeding or spring of her bleeding. (227) This is the exact same usage as in the verse 'and she uncovers the spring of her bleeding'. (228) Our way is better and agrees better with the procedure for reaching legal decisions and the obligation of taking the more rigorous interpretation. This is one of the standard (229) principles for reaching legal decisions in the case of the laws derived by argument: if a passage has two possible meanings, one of which would establish the applicability (230) of an item of law and the other of which would establish that the matter was legally neutral and was up to rational choice, then it is better to follow the one that expresses an item of law, (231) and if the most natural of the possible meanings happens to be commonly accepted, this is better integrated.

(232) Besides, from the point of view of induction, it is known that if a woman with a discharge [*zåbå*] in the 'days of her counting' [*sēfīra*] does not have any (233) bleeding during those days, she still avoids associating with clean things or people (and even more so has to avoid associating with people or things in a state of holiness), (234) and it is not allowed to lie down with

her or copulate with her. In the case of the new mother during the days of recovery from bleeding no notice is taken of the occurence of bleeding, which means the correct thing is to forbid her (235) to associate with clean people and stop her from doing so.

(236) This is how the legal position is, taking the two meanings into account, and in fact this legal position is demanded by (237) the principle of integration.

(238) During the days of recovery from the bleeding she comes under the general declaration of exclusion and prohibition in the verse 'A man that (239) lies down with a woman with a flow [*då̄bå*]' (Lv XX:18), because this term covers any woman during any (240) period when bleeding is expected and who is under the ban of previous bleeding of any kind and of any legal category, and no-one is allowed to copulate with her (241) and she is not allowed to associate with clean people.

(242) As for their interpretation of the verse 'She is not to touch anything holy or go into the Temple' (243) (Lv XII:4), as if the Lawgiver had meant to stop her from having anything to do with things and people in a state of holiness but not ones in a state of cleanness: (244) The answer is that this is not to be understood as letting her associate with things or people in a state of cleanness. The point is rather that the Lawgiver mentions in each law stated in Scripture (245) things he does not mention in others, and induction can be used, or, for anything not demonstrable by induction, a consistent carry-over from the legal position in other cases can be applied; (246) and we conclude, in the matter of the legal position of bleeding happening during the time of recovery from the bleeding of delivery, that anyone that touches this (247) blood and gets its moisture on them is contaminated.

(248) They say, too, that if any garment is wetted by it and gets it over it, or if any artefact does, it does not get contaminated. If you say it gets contaminated, (249) then you agree with us, and if you say that anything that this blood touches and that the blood gets on is not contaminated you thereby (250) contradict the verse 'and the priest atones for her and she becomes clean' (v. 7). Besides, we find that (251) her sacrifice and the sacrifice of the woman with a discharge [*zå̄bå*] are both delayed till the end of the cleansing, so they can be assimilated to each other (252) and are exactly equivalent. If this is the case with her the legal position must be the same; it is impossible for the legal positions to be different if the causes (253) are exactly equivalent.

(254) These, then, are the laws of the woman in her separation [*niddå*] and the woman with a discharge [*zå̄bå*] and the woman who has given birth [ࠉࠋࠃࠄ *yå̄lēda*].

(255) The essential difference between us and them is over the first bleeding, over two points. One is that it is contaminated whatever (256)

colour it is, and there is no variety of it that can be classed as clean. The second is that it is only this that has an effect for seven days, as opposed to (257) any bleeding that happens on the second day. Any person or artefact this blood gets on is affected for seven days, (258) and anything that appears on the second day has a single instant's effect.

(259) [[There is a third point as well, which is that the legal situation of the woman in her separation [*niddå*] lasts for seven weeks, and after that, if (260) the issue continues, there is discharge [*zåbå*]. The legal situation of the woman with a discharge [*zåbå*] is established by her continuous issue of bleeding (261) of any colour, yellow or otherwise]].

(262) [[Any person or artefact this blood gets on is affected for seven days, and anything that appears on the second (263) day has a single instant's effect]].

(264) [[Whether the bleeding is continuous or interrupted some days it is counted. It is not counted if it is interrupted after (265) the set number of weeks, and she has the legal requirements of a woman in her separation [*niddå*]. Once she stops bleeding she becomes clean at the end of seven complete days. (266) Her legal position during her days of counting [*sēfīra*] (see Lv XV:28) is that she is not to associate with clean people and her husband is not to lie down with her, as (267) previously mentioned. If he does, as a deliberate transgression, there are two different opinions. One is that the case is to be treated as equivalent to copulating with (268) a menstruating woman [*dåbå*] and the other is that this is not necessary. The first is better, since she is under a ban due to earlier bleeding, like the menstruating woman [*dåbå*]. The same applies to (269) the new mother [*yålēda*] during the days of her recovery from bleeding or ban for the purpose of recovery from the bleeding of delivery]].

[THE BOOK OF DIFFERENCES]

[ADDITIONAL PASSAGE]

I once spoke with one of them about some of the things contaminated by a man with a discharge [*zåb*], in the verse (2) 'Anyone that touches anything that is under him is unclean till sunset' (3) (Lv XV:10). I asked him: 'What do you say about any bedclothes, or anything else, that are on top of him; what is the legal position? He said: 'They stay as they were. (4) They are not contaminated and do not contaminate'. I asked: 'What exactly is the point that makes you accept the statement of the verse, but deny any (5) extension beyond it?' He said: 'The tradition and normative practice in regard to it. The tradition says it applies to what is under him, not what is on top of him'.

I said: (6) 'This argument of yours contradicts a statement of Scripture, and any argument opposed by a Scriptural statement is invalid. You can plainly see that the Lawgiver has declared (7) his bed contaminated in the verse 'Any bed the man with a discharge [*zåb*] lies on is unclean' (v. 4). (8) Is this limited to whatever is under him, or does it include his bedclothes as well? And is it restricted to the bedclothes that are under him? Because if you (9) do restrict it, you are advocating a contradiction to the normal and accepted way of using the word, since 'bed' [ࠌࠔࠊࠁ *mashkåb*] is a term that includes any (10) bedding or bedclothes he might use. There is the obvious example of the usage in the verse 'Anyone that touches (11) his bed is to wash his clothes and wash himself with water, and is unclean till sunset' (12) (v. 5); or the verse 'Anyone that touches anything that is under him (13) is unclean till sunset' (v. 10). These passages demonstrate conclusively that any contact with (14) the *zåb's* bed, on which he has slept, causes uncleanness [[illegible]]. If the bed by itself can cause uncleanness to someone that touches (15) it, the same must apply to the bedclothes, which come in direct contact with the bed and the *zåb* himself, who was the one that contaminated the bed. This is (16) the usage of the term as transmitted from [our ancestors].

TEXT 4

[THE BOOK OF COMMANDMENTS]

[Commandment No. 54]

. . . .

(2) . . . . and this one is (3) after cleanness, and this discharge [ࠆࠁࠄ *zåbå*] is separation [ࠍࠃࠄ *niddå*].

(4) This blood varies in how watery or thick it is. Sometimes it is thick and other times (5) watery. It varies in its colour as well: sometimes its redness is clear and unsullied; sometimes it is more black than (6) red; sometimes there is a yellowish variety.

(7) The woman's cleanness depends on the presence of a pure clear white moisture, and if this moisture stops being clear, pure, (8) and white by the slightest amount she becomes unclean. It is like when clear water gets a little bit of some soluble (9) pigment such as saffron in it, and its colour is affected in proportion to the amount of pigment mixed in, with (10) the depth or paleness of colour being in proportion to the amount of stuff mixed in. The correct procedure is for the woman to withdraw herself whenever she sees anything that is not completely white, (11) since it is possible for the blood of her separation [*niddå*] to be a very little amount. Its condition would not be any different if it were a lot: any admixture affects it. No-one will be found to deny (12) that a little bit of blood is the same as a lot as far as the varieties of uncleanness are concerned. For reasons such as this the experts require her to test (13) herself with a bit of clean cotton or wool and if the issue has gone slightly maroon or blue or green (14) or yellow, this is a sign of uncleanness.

(15) If the woman checks herself without seeing any sign of contamination, then tests herself later on and does see it, (16) her contamination is counted from the second check onwards. If, however, there is some symptom known to her, which occurs as the blood (17) flows, such as yawning or hiccups or hot flushes or a headache or anything like that, (18) she is supposed to test herself with cotton the way we have described (19) as soon as it happens. If she does not check herself till later on, the feeling she experiences is the sign of contamination. The reason for this is that the flow of blood does not always (20) continue steadily, but she could still tell what was happening. The point is that sometimes the bleeding is slight at first, and then the full flow comes on (21) later, so that there is no obvious sign of it, but it is still apparent from the symptoms mentioned even when (22) so slight as to be invisible.

(23) The text says 'in her flesh' (Lv XV:19), giving the stipulation that whenever it appears in (24) that particular place, contamination arises.

(25) Her cleansing from it is not observed as is done in the case of a male. When it says 'She is in her separation [*niddå*] (26) for seven days' (v. 19), these are seven days in a row, which can be whole or can have a bit missing (27) at the start, if the bleeding appears after part of the day has passed. If we were to say she could count (28) the cleanness as practically equivalent to a day, and that she has to observe seven whole days, she would not be able to reach cleanness in the clean days (29) in which she completes seven days' contamination, because the length of her contamination would be more than seven days; and as this is not required, it must be (30) possible for the seven days to have a bit missing at the start, but not at the end.

(31) The etymological meaning of the term 'her *niddå*' [ࠍࠃࠕࠄ *niddātå*] (v. 19) is 'separation', and it is generally accepted that her issue is called (32) 'her *niddå*' because of the term's implication of her separation from clean people, and the meaning of it is that she stays withdrawn as a consequence of her *niddå*. (33) If we were to say she is unclean due to her *niddå*, this would be acceptable, since she has been called unclean, as it says (34) 'and a man that lies down with an unclean woman' (v. 33), and the meaning intended is practically the same.

(35) It remains to consider the referent of this term 'her separation' [*niddå*]: whether it applies to any bleeding appearing (36) from the woman during the seven days or whether it applies specifically to the start of it. The right answer is that it is specifically (37) the start of the bleeding, since the natural sense is that the verse refers to a woman not contaminated by any bleeding, only to have new bleeding start up, putting her (38) in a situation she had not been in before, and which starts immediately the bleeding does. The term occurs after the words 'for seven days' (39) (v. 19), so it follows that it is this that demands her withdrawal for seven days. In fact, even if she saw some bleeding close to the end (40) of the seventh day, so that she finished bleeding close to the time for becoming clean, it would still be possible for her to become clean. All this is part of the reason for (41) applying the term specifically to the first bleeding and making the legal consequences depend on it.

(42) It says 'Everything she lies on during her separation [*niddå*] becomes unclean etc.' (v. 20). (43) In the case of a woman with a discharge [ࠆࠁࠄ *zābå*] the text mentions the equivalent of what it mentions in the case of a man with a discharge [ࠆࠁ *zåb*] i.e. the bed, the seat, (44) and the person that touches them, and in the case of the woman in her separation [ࠍࠃࠄ *niddå*] as well, the text mentions the seat and the person that touches them, as it says here (45) 'Anyone that touches any artefact she sits on' (v. 22): in short, (46) every detail prescribed for the man with a discharge [*zåb*] has an equivalent here; and although the text abbreviated to some extent the first time, here it says (47) 'If she is on the seat or the artefact' (v. 23). Register this, because it makes no (48) difference to the contaminating [effect] of the seat of a woman in her separation [*niddå*] whether she is sitting on it or no.

(49) The point of the verse 'If her husband lies down with her at all (50) and her separation [*niddå*] gets on him, he is unclean for seven days' (v. 24) (51) is that the text is talking about a man that copulates with a clean woman only to have her contamination come on her during copulation. (52) This man's legal position is the same as the legal position of the woman because of whom he was contaminated, with seven days' contamination applying to him. If he was sleeping (53) with her in the bed but not copulating and he gets the blood discharged from her over him, what is his legal position? We say: contamination for seven days. (54) In the light of this, the opinion expressed by some, that there are two conditions for the man's contamination for seven days, one copulation [ࠔࠊࠉࠁࠄ *shēkība*] and the other (55) getting the blood over him, is shown to be impossible, since the woman got contaminated for seven days from getting the blood over her, and the man gets contaminated by the same thing, (56) so the cause of the man's uncleanness is the blood and the cause of the blood being discharged is the copulation [*shēkība*] (v. 24). This is (57) the treatment of the first bleeding (which is separation [*niddå*] bleeding, as we have said) in the case of a man that copulates with a clean woman only to have (58) contamination come on her during the copulation, or while simply sleeping.

(59) Al-Fayyûmi reckons that this law is meant to refer to the case of a man that copulates with his wife when he (60) knows she is in her separation [*niddå*]. He does not realise that the explicit statement of Scripture and normative practice would require him to be killed, as it says (61) 'A man that lies down with a woman with a flow [*dåbå*] and uncovers her genitals, (62) the spring of her genitals, and she uncovers the spring of her bleeding, both of them are to be cut off (63) from out of their people' (Lv XX:18). The 'flow' [*dåbå*] is anything past the first (64) blood, and occurs over the days that remain. Unless he copulated with her on the strength of her being clean why should he be spared the penalty of being killed (65) and have the legal requirement of seven days' uncleanness apply to him? Copulation with a woman during the seven days can not, therefore, be allowable.

(66) The same applies in the case of the new mother [ࠉࠋࠃࠄ *yålēda*] during the forty days in the case of boys and the eighty days in the case of girls. It says (67) 'and she becomes clean from the spring of her bleeding' (Lv XII:7) where an induction on the basis of equivalent expressions can be made, as it says here (68) 'and she uncovers the spring of her bleeding' (Lv XX:18).

(69) An induction on the basis of equivalent expressions can be made in the case of a woman with a discharge [*zåbå*] in the days of 'her flow' [*dåbåtå*], as it says 'All the days of the discharge [ࠆࠅࠁ *zob*] (70) of her uncleanness she is as in the days of her separation [*niddå*], she is unclean' (Lv XV:25). (71) For the days of her purification or 'counting' [ࠎࠐࠉࠓࠄ *sēfīra*] (see v. 28) it is

derived from the verse 'and the priest atones for her ... from the discharge [*zob*] (72) of her uncleanness' (v. 30).

(73) The legal position of this man, on the other hand, is derived from the verse 'and a man that lies down with an unclean woman' (74) (v. 33).

(75) Notice that the term 'discharge' [*zā̊bå*] has a general and a specific meaning.

(76) It has a general meaning because it is used to refer to the first bleeding, known as 'blood of separation' [*niddå*], the legal position of which you already know, and it can also be used to refer (77) to the issue during the rest of the week, known as the menstruation [or flow] [ࠃࠁࠄ *dā̊bå*]. (Our opponents call this blood of discharge [*zā̊bå*], but there is no (78) valid argument to justify the use of the name. The situation is that the man gets over its effect the day he touches it, and if (79) the woman stops bleeding on the seventh day before sunset she becomes clean — the whole nation agrees on this).

(80) It is also used to refer to abnormal bleeding, deviating from what is usual for women. Some women have (81) an issue of this type once a month, others less often, and others oftener, and this is (82) normal; what is not normal is referred to by the text with the words 'many days' (v. 25) and it is this (83) that is specifically meant by the term 'discharge' [*zā̊bå*].

(84) 'Many days' can have the meaning of years, as it says 'In those many days' (85) (Ex II:23), or a month, or less than a month, so some of our people have settled on its normal extent, (86) which is the length of a month. When four consecutive weeks have passed the 'count' [*sēfīra*] applies to her. This is the correct view.

(87) The text says 'If she discharges past her separation [*niddå*], outside the time of her separation [*niddå*]' (v. 25), i.e. (88) in a way different to the normal, departing from the accustomed course of things. Those that disagree with us take the term 'blood of her separation [*niddå*]' to refer (89) to a period of seven days, and maintain that if the flow keeps up, and still appears on the eighth day or later, this can be counted (90) as 'many days, outside the time of her separation [*niddå*]'. This is refuted by the verse 'she is unclean (91) for a fortnight as with her separation [*niddå*]' (Lv XII:5), where this period is called 'her separation' [*niddå*], not (92) 'her discharge' [*zob*], which proves that her discharge [*zob*] is something more than this. In fact, there are women (93) that normally experience bleeding for a fortnight, and if the position was not as we have said they would have to be unclean most of the time. (94) Many women are unclean for fourteen days and clean for seven days, and if they were unclean (95) for a fortnight and made a count [*sēfīra*] in the third week their time of cleanness would be very short and them the bleeding would be back straightaway. So if he [i.e. Al-Fayyûmi] takes (96) the start of the 'many days' to be the eighth day, and then the time following this up to

the end of the period we have defined, (91) what he says is mistaken and quite unjustifiable.

Some of our people are of the opinion that if the woman finishes with the bleeding (98) near the end of the seventh day then sees blood at any time at all during the eighth day she is in her separation [*niddå*], not discharge [*zåbå*], because she (99) made the break between the two periods of bleeding at a time within the jurisdiction of the eighth day; and if she does not make the break she is declared to be in her discharge [*zåbå*], because the preposition 'past' (100) in the phrase 'she discharges past her separation [*niddå*]' expresses the idea of uninterruptedness and immediate sequence. The first view is more plausible; i.e. if the seventh day (101) is over and she sees menstrual blood on the eighth day, then similarly in the third week and the fourth as well, she is declared to be (102) in her discharge [*zåbå*] because of the deviation of this from what is normal.

(103) Some of our people, may they be favoured, say the difference between the separation [*niddå*] and the discharge [*zåbå*] is that (104) the discharge [*zåbå*] comes after uncleanness and the separation [*niddå*] after cleanness. An objection has been made from the case of the new mother [*yålēda*] who (105) sees blood near the end of the daytime of the fortieth or eightieth day after giving birth and is in her separation [*niddå*] not following cleanness but (106) after uncleanness, as it says 'from the spring of her bleeding' (Lv XII:7). This objection needs further consideration.

(107) It says 'Any bed she lies on' (Lv XV:26). This refers at once to both this (108) and other cases, as mentioned in the section on the woman in her separation [*niddå*], so that whatever was mentioned in that passage applies to her; and the words 'Any artefact (109) she sits on becomes unclean as for the uncleanness of her separation [*niddå*]' (v. 26) (110) indicate that these artefacts are unclean for seven days.

(111) The literal meaning of the verse 'When she becomes clean from her discharge [*zob*] she is to count seven days to herself etc.' (112) (v. 28) would indicate counting aloud. Probably the meaning intended is an exact counting of the days, which amounts to the same thing. So (113) the verse gives the requirement of becoming clean by a count, either by registering it consciously or by the occurence of something that will do instead of attention as a way of telling.

(114) Then she becomes clean using water at the appropriate time.

(115) Then it says 'On the eighth day she is to get ... and the priest atones for her' (116) (vv. 29-30): this is by the performance of the sacrifice. This goes with a prayer on her behalf for God to relieve her of this (117) sickness. (The discharge [*zåbå*] resembles the separation [*niddå*] in not being a sickness, but the separation [*niddå*] (118) does cause physical discomfort, and the discharge [*zåbå*], with her segregation and withdrawal from everything to do with clean

people, causes hardships, (119) and this is why it says 'from the discharge [*zob*] of her uncleanness' (v. 30).

(120) The verse 'Warn the Children of Israel' (v. 31) is a command to the two apostles (121) to save the lives of the Children of Israel by speaking (which is the function of apostlehood) about everything they heard from God regarding (122) uncleanness and other matters over the course of time, by speech and action. When the Creator purposed what he would require of them he obliged the two of them to carry out (123) the steps necessary for the nation's survival. He does not want to become displeased when (124) any kind of contamination is treated negligently, as Scripture tells us, as, for example, in the verse 'I have given the Levites, (125) as attendants to Aaron and his sons ... so that there is no outbreak on the Children of Israel (126) etc.' (Nu VIII:19).

(127) The natural meaning of the phrase 'from their uncleanness' (v. 31) can refer just as well to major or minor contamination, (128) and the verse is put after the two sections, the purpose being . . . .
(129) . . . .
(130) . . . .

TEXT 5

[THE KÂSHIF AL-GHAYÂHIB ON LEVITICUS XV]

The Commentary on the Passage about the Law of the Man with a Discharge [ࠆࠁ *zåb*]

(2) It says: ࠅࠉࠃࠁࠓ ࠉࠄࠅࠄ ࠀࠋ ࠌࠔࠄ ࠅࠀࠋ ࠀࠄࠓࠍ ࠋࠀࠌࠓ ࠃࠁࠓࠅ ࠀࠋ ࠁࠍࠉ (3) ࠉࠔࠓࠀࠋ ࠅࠀࠌࠓࠕࠌ ࠀࠋࠉࠄࠌ i.e. 'The Lord said to Moses and Aaron 'Speak to (4) the children of Israel and say to them' (Lv XV:1-2). The speech is addressed to the Apostle then to the Priest, commanding them to (5) guide them in this commandment. This law is the passage ࠀࠉࠔ ࠀࠉࠔ ࠊࠉ ࠉࠄࠉࠄ ࠆࠁ ࠌࠁࠔࠓࠅ ࠆࠅࠁࠅ (6) ࠈࠌࠀ ࠄࠅࠀ (v. 2), which refers to blood or matter issuing from the genitals the way menstrual bleeding issues from women, whether due to (7) sickness or an accident. When this happens to a man he is classed as contaminated. It can be due to running ulcers (8) that have formed in the bladder, or the rupture of one of the veins in the genital system, or ulcers in the urethra, or a lesion, or (9) an excess of blood in the body.

(10) The phrase ࠊࠉ ࠉࠄࠉࠄ ࠆࠁ ࠌࠁࠔࠓࠅ ࠆࠅࠁࠅ (v. 2) means 'that has a discharge, whose discharge is from his flesh'.

(11) The term 'discharge' [*dhawabân*] is used in the sense of 'running', and the term 'menstruation' [*ḥayḍ*] is also used in the sense of 'running', and the Beduins say of a creek when it is running, (12) *ḥâḍ al-wâdi* [the creek is running]. In women the running of the vagina consists of excess blood discharged by the womb, and in men it consists of an issue (13) from the penis.

(14) According to the physicians women menstruate when they have reached thirteen, and it can set in at the age of ten. It ends (15) some time between fifty and sixty. The typical menstruation causes a period but does not exceed it. Any difference is due to (16) a difference in constitution. It typically last for three days, but can keep up till the fifth day, and if the woman has (17) a sanguine constitution it can continue till the tenth day.

(18) One of the physicians says if it lasts less than fourteen hours it is not menstruation, but according to the law, if ever (19) blood runs out from the womb a period of withdrawal is imposed, even if it cuts out immediately. The details of this will be given (20) at the appropriate place.

(21) We now come to the passage ࠀࠉࠔ ࠀࠉࠔ ࠊࠉ ࠉࠄࠉࠄ ࠆࠁ ࠌࠁࠔࠓࠅ ࠆࠅࠁࠅ ࠈࠌࠀ ࠄࠅࠀ (v. 2), which means 'Any man that (22) has a discharge from his flesh, in the form of a discharge, it is his uncleanness etc.'. The word 'discharge' [*dhawbah*] is used in the sense of running,

and refers exclusively to the issue from a male. (23) If this happens to any man he is classed as contaminated as long as the running continues, and whether the running is continuous, (24) or stops and starts, as long as it keeps on flowing and stopping, he stays contaminated, as it says ࠅࠆࠀࠕ ࠕࠄࠉࠄ ࠈࠌࠀࠕࠅ ࠁࠆࠅࠁࠅ ࠓࠓ ࠁࠔࠓࠅ (25) ࠀࠕ ࠆࠅࠁࠅ ࠀࠅ ࠄࠇࠕࠉࠌ ࠁࠔࠓࠅ ࠌࠆࠅࠁࠅ ࠈࠌࠀ ࠄࠅࠀ (v. 3).

(26) The passage ࠊࠋ ࠄࠌࠔࠊࠁ ࠀࠔࠓ ࠉࠔࠊࠁ ࠏࠋࠉࠅ ࠄࠆࠁ ࠉࠈࠌࠀ (v. 4), meaning 'Any bed the man with a discharge lies (27) on is unclean', indicates that he is to stay out of the way the way a menstruating woman does, and any bed he lies on (28) gets contaminated. Anything he sits on gets contaminated, as it says ࠅࠊࠋ ࠄࠊࠋࠉ ࠀࠔࠓ ࠉࠔࠊࠁ ࠏࠋࠉࠅ ࠉࠈࠌࠀ (v. 4). Anyone (29) that touches him or anything he has sat on gets contaminated and has to wash their clothes thoroughly, and wash themselves as well, (30) and then stays under the ban of contamination for the day on which they become contaminated till sunset, when they become clean, as it says ࠅࠀࠉࠔ (31) ࠀࠔࠓ ࠉࠂࠏ ࠁࠌࠔࠊࠁࠅ ࠉࠊࠁࠎ ࠁࠂࠃࠉࠅ ࠁࠌࠉࠌ ࠅࠈࠌࠀ ࠏࠃ ࠄࠏࠓࠁ (v. 5). The same applies to anyone that sits on (32) any artefact, whether a bed or anything else, that the man with the discharge sits on. The same for anyone that touches him directly, as it says ࠅࠄࠉࠔࠁ ࠏࠋ ࠄࠊࠋࠉ ... ࠅࠄࠍࠂࠏ ࠁࠁࠔࠓ ࠄࠆࠁ (33) (vv. 6-7). The same it he spits on anything clean. If (34) it was a person, that person has to wash their clothes and wash themself and stays contaminated till sunset. Any riding-seat the man with the discharge sits on while riding, (35) such as a horse-saddle or a camel-saddle or anything that can be a riding-seat, gets contaminated. This includes anything he puts his weight on: (36) anything he puts his weight on gets contaminated. The same for anyone that lifts his bed, as it says ࠅࠊࠋ ࠄࠍࠂࠏ ࠁࠊࠋ ࠀࠔࠓ ࠉࠄࠉࠄ (37) ࠕࠇࠕࠉࠅ ࠉࠈࠌࠀ (v. 10), meaning 'Anyone that touches anything under him gets contaminated'. This applies to anyone that carries them as well.

(38) The verse ࠅࠊࠋ ࠀࠔࠓ ࠉࠂࠏ ࠁࠅ ࠄࠆࠁ ࠅࠉࠃࠉࠅ ࠋࠀ ࠔࠈࠐ ࠁࠌࠉࠌ ࠅࠈࠌࠀ ࠏࠃ (39) ࠄࠏࠓࠁ (v. 11), meaning 'Anyone the man with the discharge touches without having rinsed his hand with water is to wash his clothes and bathe in water, (40) and is contaminated till sunset', shows that if he has a discharge and touches someone without having washed (41) his hand in water before becoming clean, the one touched is contaminated and has to wash their clothes and wash themself in water, and the ban (42) of contamination stays on that person till sunset. This contradicts the verse ࠅࠄࠍࠂࠏ ࠁࠁࠔࠓ ࠄࠆࠁ ࠉࠊࠁࠎ ࠁࠂࠃࠉࠅ ࠅࠓࠇࠑ ࠁࠌࠉࠌ ࠅࠈࠌࠀ ࠏࠃ ࠄࠏࠓࠁ (43) (v. 7), meaning 'Anyone that touches the man with the discharge directly is to wash their clothes and bathe in water, and is unclean till (44) sunset'. This is obviously the [apparent] contradiction that proves the rule. The first [verse] is confirmed [by another verse] and the

second [verse] is concerned specifically with the rinsing. (45) The [details] of the second [verse] are to be followed. The reason is that the contamination of a man with a discharge does not reach the level of the contamination of a menstruating woman, since it is an illness (46) with a specific cause, males not being subject to regular menstruation as women are. Anyway, a man with this symptom is not supposed to (47) touch anything till he has rinsed his hand with water, so both commands are applicable. He is to avoid touching anything he does not have to, (48) since the seriousness of this contamination is obvious. You can see this plainly from the verse ࠅࠊࠋࠉ ࠇࠓࠔ ࠀࠔࠓ ࠉࠂࠏ ࠁࠅ (49) ࠄࠆࠁ ࠉࠔࠁࠓ ࠅࠊࠋ ࠊࠋࠉ ࠏࠑ ࠉࠔࠈࠐ ࠁࠌࠉࠌ (v. 12), meaning 'A ceramic artefact touched by the man with a flow is to be broken, and any wooden artefact (50) can be rinsed in water', which is the same as mentioned earlier in regard to the contamination of depigmentation.

(51) It is obvious that no male is going to have a discharge of blood or matter except due to an internal complaint such as (52) ulcers in the bladder or a ruptured blood-vessel in it or ulcers in the kidney or a ruptured blood-vessel in one of them. The possibilities are (53) numerous, and the treatment is to be sought in the works of the physicians. I have written a book on medicine called the *Shining Jewel* [*Al-Jawharah al-Muḍî'ah*] (54) because of the clarity of its expression, which gives a survey of these diseases and the proven remedies.

(55) It happened in 1160 [1747 of the Christian era] that I was working for the Concessionnaire of Customs and Tolls of the Port of Jaffa, called Commissioner Ali, (56) from the Revenue Office of the City of Sidon, who had an attack of bloody urine. He had an Armenian physician attending him who had a penetrating (57) feeling for medicine, and who treated him without success. I was collaborating with him in the treatment as far as the information set out in the textbooks of (58) clinical therapy went, such as the Minhâj and the Kitâb al-Ḥâwi, but unsuccessfully. I consulted the Zâyirjah and there I came across a line that gave the solution (59) to the treatment, as follows:

(60) 'In … from the essence of the *hulûf* is a treatment (61) in which success is contained, and does not leave'.

(62) I went through a lot of books without finding any mention of the hulûf, but I did know a plant called lûf [snakeroot], (63) so I looked it up in the Kitâb Awla 'l-Albâb, and there I found it recommended specifically as a cure for this ailment. I thought this might (64) be it, and the *hâ'* could have been elided for ease of pronunciation, so I got some egg … and cooked it with (65) the snakeroot and gave the patient two doses, and he was cured, with the help of God, without any need for me to use any other treatment. (66) Blessed is he who lays down secrets in his creation in his far-reaching wisdom.

(67) To return to the subject: The legal requirement for the cleansing of the

man with the discharge is contained in the (68) verse ࠅࠊࠉ ࠉࠈࠄࠓ ࠄࠆࠁ ࠌࠆࠅࠁࠅ ࠅࠎࠐࠓ ࠋࠅ ࠔࠁࠏࠕ ࠉࠌࠉࠌ ࠋࠈࠄࠓࠕࠅ (v. 13), meaning 'If the man with a discharge becomes clean (69) from his discharge he is to count to himself seven days for his cleansing', i.e. when the man with this complaint is cured and the flow of blood and matter (70) has been stopped for seven days (while he kept away from anything clean) he is all right because he has not had any issue of blood or matter during (71) the seven days. On the first day he is to wash his clothes and wash himself in water, and he then stays out of the way for the rest of the seven days (72) without any discharge.

(73) On the eighth day he is to offer a sacrifice according to the requirement mentioned. He is to get two *shanfs*. A *shanf* is either (74) a kind of small bird or a rooster. The best explanation is that *shanf* is the name for a male chook when it is (75) young enough to be called a chicken, because a small bird is called ࠑࠐࠅࠓ *ṣibbor* in Hebrew, and this bird is called a ࠕࠅࠓ *tår* in Hebrew, as it says ࠅࠁࠉࠅࠌ ࠄࠔࠌࠉࠍࠉ ࠉࠒࠇ (76) ࠋࠅ ࠔࠕࠉ ࠕࠓࠉࠌ ࠀࠅ ࠔࠍࠉ ࠁࠍࠉ ࠉࠅࠍࠄ (v. 14), meaning 'On the eighth day he is to get two small birds or (77) young pigeons', i.e. if there are no shanfs young pigeons will do. He is to take them to the opening of the Tent of the Presence and give them (78) to the priest, who then sacrifices them, one as an atonement offering and one as a peace offering. The priest atones for him and he recovers from the contamination (79) of this complaint. This is from the passage ࠅࠁࠀ ࠋࠐࠍࠉ ࠉࠄࠅࠄ ࠀࠋ ࠐࠕࠇ ࠀࠄࠋ ࠌࠅࠏࠃ ࠅࠍࠕࠍࠌ ࠀࠋ ࠄࠊࠄࠍ (v. 14) meaning (80) 'He is to go in, into the presence of the Lord, to the opening of the Tent of the Presence, and give them to the priest ... ࠅࠊࠐࠓ ࠏࠋࠉࠅ (81) ࠄࠊࠄࠍ ࠋࠐࠍࠉ ࠉࠄࠅࠄ ࠌࠆࠅࠁࠅ meaning 'And the priest atones for him from his sin in the presence of the Lord' (v. 15).

(82) After this law, the Lawgiver mentions the law of the emission of semen from the male, as it says ࠅࠀࠉࠔ ࠊࠉ (83) ࠕࠑࠀ ࠌࠌࠍࠅ ࠔࠊࠁࠕ ࠆࠓࠏ ࠅࠓࠇࠑ ࠁࠌࠉࠌ ࠀࠕ ࠊࠋ ࠁࠔࠓࠅ (v. 16), meaning 'Any man (84) that has an emission of semen is to rinse his whole body with water, and is contaminated till sunset'. The emission of semen (85) from a man can be either when he is asleep, when it is called ࠒࠓࠉ ࠋࠉࠋࠄ *qēri līla*, or when he is awake, due to strong sexual arousal, and when the semen is emitted with strong sexual desire (86) with a squirt, this is what is termed 'an emission of semen' and belongs with what we are concerned with here. When the semen is emitted with sexual desire, with a squirt, (87) washing of the whole body all over is required, as it says ࠅࠓࠇࠑ ࠁࠌࠉࠌ ࠀࠕ ࠊࠋ ࠁࠔࠓࠅ (v. 16), meaning 'He is to rinse his whole body (88) with water'. The requirement in the case of a man with a discharge does not apply here: in this case it is just the person that has to wash himself, and (89) the clothes on him or that he touches do not have to be washed unless a bit of semen

has got on them, as it says ࠅࠊࠋ ࠁࠂࠃ (90) ࠅࠊࠋ ࠏࠅࠓ ࠀࠔࠓ ࠉࠄࠉࠄ ࠏࠋࠉࠅ ࠔࠊࠁࠕ ࠆࠓࠏ ࠅࠊࠁࠎ ࠁࠌࠉࠌ ࠅࠈࠌࠀ ࠏࠃ ࠄࠏࠓࠁ (v. 17), meaning (91) 'Any piece of clothing and any leather that has the emission of semen on is to be washed with water and is contaminated till sunset'.

(92) If the man copulates with a woman she has to wash herself too, the same as her husband, as it says ࠅࠀࠔࠄ ࠀࠔࠓ (93) ࠉࠔࠊࠁ ࠀࠉࠔࠄ ࠀࠕࠄ ࠔࠊࠁࠕ ࠆࠓࠏ ࠅࠓࠇࠑࠅ ࠁࠌࠉࠌ ࠅࠈࠌࠀ ࠏࠃ ࠄࠏࠓࠁ (v. 18), meaning 'A woman (94) whose husband les down with her with an emission of semen is to wash herself with water and is unclean till sunset'; i.e. they both come under the ban (95) of contamination till sunset, the effect of which is that they are not to go into any place of worship or perform any religious duty that day.

(96) If, however, there is any emission from a male without sexual desire or squirting, he is to examine it, and if it looks and seems like semen, (97) and sticks to anything it falls on and marks it, it is to be treated as semen. Otherwise no washing is required, (98) but it does invalidate the lesser washing [*wuḍû*], and it demands washing of the person and washing of whatever it gets on. (99) In the Kitâb al-Kâfi, by the Shaykh Abu 'l-Ḥasan of Tyre, this is set out (100) category by category for the instruction of the inquirer.

(101) The legal requirements for women when menstruating are in the verse ࠅࠀࠔࠄ ࠊࠉ ࠕࠄࠉࠄ ࠆࠁࠄ ࠃࠌ ࠉࠄࠉࠄ ࠆࠅࠁࠄ (v. 19), meaning 'Any (102) woman that has a discharge, whose discharge is blood', and we have already explained this and the various possibilities of it at the start of the chapter. Here (103) the Lawgiver explains with the words ࠃࠌ ࠉࠄࠉࠄ ࠆࠅࠁࠄ that when the flow consists of blood she has to stay out of the way (104) for seven days and she is not to touch any clean person and no clean person is to touch her. Anyone that does gets contaminated and has to wash their clothes (105) and bathe themself in water, and stays under the ban till sunset, as it says ࠔࠁࠏࠕ ࠉࠌࠉࠌ ࠕࠄࠉࠄ ࠁࠍࠃࠕࠄ ࠊࠋ ࠄࠍࠂࠏ ࠁࠄ ࠉࠈࠌࠀ (106) ࠏࠃ ࠄࠏࠓࠁ (v. 19), meaning 'For seven days she is in her menstruation. Anyone that touches her is contaminated till sunset'.

(107) A woman in her menstruation, as well as anything she touches or sits on or uses, such as crockery or anything else, (108) are all classed as contaminated. Anyone that touches them has to wash (ṭabl) their clothes and wash (ghasl) their body, and once (109) this is done, they then stay under the ban of contamination, from then till sunset, as it says ࠅࠊࠋ ࠀࠔࠓ ࠕࠔࠊࠁ ࠏࠋࠉࠅ (110) ࠁࠍࠃࠕࠄ ࠉࠈࠌࠀ (v. 20) meaning 'Anything she lies down on during her contamination gets contaminated', and as far as the passage ࠅࠀࠌ ࠏࠋ ࠄࠊࠋࠉ (111) ࠀࠔࠓ ࠄࠉࠀ ࠉࠔࠁࠕ ࠏࠋࠉࠅ ࠁࠍࠂࠏࠅ ࠁࠅ ࠉࠈࠌࠀ ࠏࠃ ࠄࠏࠓࠁ (v. 23), meaning 'or on any artefact she is sitting (112) on, when he touches it he gets contaminated till sunset'.

(113) If the menstrual discharge occurs at the same time as copulation, so that the menstrual blood gets on the man, this is (114) like falling into a dip, as when they say 'So-and-so fell in a hole', and the man is in the same position as the woman as far as keeping out of the way for seven (115) days is concerned. If she starts up again he is not affected and is still clean, and she keeps on, as it says ࠅࠀࠌ ࠔࠊࠁ ࠉࠔࠊࠁ (116) ࠀࠉࠔࠄ ࠀࠕࠄ ࠅࠕࠄࠉࠄ ࠍࠃࠕࠄ ࠏࠋࠉࠅ ࠉࠈࠌࠀ ࠏࠃ ࠄࠏࠓࠁ (v. 24), meaning 'If a man lies down with his wife (117) and she starts to menstruate it makes him contaminated for seven days', because the consequences are limited to seven days. Anything at all that he sits on gets contaminated and becomes clean (118) on the seventh day, as it says ࠅࠊࠋ ࠄࠌࠔࠊࠁ ࠀࠔࠓ ࠉࠔࠊࠁ ࠏࠋࠉࠅ ࠉࠈࠌࠀ (v. 24) meaning 'Any couch (119) he lies on gets contaminated'.

Quite often this happens to the bed to which the consequences of the copulation apply, so that the consequences (120) become applicable both ways, first by the application of the principle of the 'menstruating woman during her menstruation' (see v. 20), and second from the phrase here ࠅࠄࠌࠔࠊࠁ (121) ࠀࠔࠓ ࠉࠔࠊࠁ ࠏࠋࠉࠅ ࠉࠈࠌࠀ (v. 24), where the antecedent of the pronoun is the subject of the clause ࠅࠀࠌ ࠔࠊࠁ ࠉࠔࠊࠁ ࠀࠉࠔࠄ ࠀࠕࠄ (v. 24), (122) so this is a case where the consequences apply either way, with no uncertainty.

(123) He does not exceed the seven days. He is to wash himself on the first day and the seventh day.

(124) In the woman's case though, if, on the afternoon of the seventh day, she once again experiences something like menstruation, she is to repeat (125) another seven days. If she does not become clean in the second week and something like menstruation appears at the end of that too she counts another (126) seven days. If she does not become clean on the twenty-first, she then enters into 'many days' (v. 25), as it says ࠅࠀࠔࠄ ࠊࠉ ࠉࠆࠅࠁ ࠆࠅࠁ ࠃࠌࠄ ࠉࠌࠉࠌ ࠓࠁࠉࠌ ࠁࠋࠀ ࠏࠕ ࠍࠃࠕࠄ (127) (v. 25), meaning 'A woman whose discharge of blood lasts for many days, outside (128) the time of her menstruation'. This is when she goes past the third week. After that she does not count the days when contamination (129) appears; but when she sees herself to be clean, she then counts seven clean days without any discharge; and if contamination re-appears, the days of cleanness counted up till then (130) are disregarded; and when she sees herself to be clean she counts till she has completed seven clean days without any issue, during (131) which no contamination appears, and without seeing any sign of it during the seven days, and then she becomes clean.

(132) The passage ࠀࠅ ࠊࠉ ࠕࠆࠅࠁ ࠏࠋ ࠍࠃࠕࠄ ࠊࠋ ࠉࠌࠉ ࠆࠅࠁ ࠈࠌࠀࠕࠄ ࠊࠉࠌࠉ ࠍࠃࠕࠄ ࠕࠄࠉࠄ ࠈࠌࠀࠄ ࠄࠉࠀ (v. 25) (133) is to teach the rule that as long as she still has a discharge she is unclean, as in the

situation of the menstruation, and everything she touches, (134) such as her bed or any crockery she might use or anything else, gets contaminated.

(135) The requirement is that when she has become clean and sees that she is clean she is to count seven clean days to herself without discharge, as we have said, in (136) agreement with the verse ࠅࠀࠌ ࠈࠄࠓࠄ ࠌࠆࠅࠁࠄ ࠅࠎࠐࠓࠄ ࠋࠄ ࠔࠁࠏࠕ ࠉࠌࠉࠌ ࠅࠀࠇࠓ ࠕࠈࠄࠓ (v. 28), meaning 'When she becomes clean from (137) her discharge she is to count seven days to herself, and then she becomes clean'. When she has become clean, on the eighth day she is to get herself two *shanfs* or two young (138) pigeons and take them to the priest, who sacrifices them in the holy presence before God, one as an atonement offering (139) and one as a peace offering, and he atones for her, as it says ࠅࠁࠉࠅࠌ ࠄࠔࠌࠉࠍࠉ ࠕࠒࠇ ࠋࠄ ࠔࠕࠉ ࠕࠓࠉࠌ ࠀࠅ ࠔࠍࠉ ࠁࠍࠉ ࠉࠅࠍࠄ (v. 29), (140) meaning 'On the eighth day she is to get herself two *shanfs* or two young pigeons', and as far as the passage ࠅࠊࠐࠓ ࠏࠋࠉࠄ ࠄࠊࠄࠍ (141) ࠋࠐࠍࠉ ࠉࠄࠅࠄ ࠌࠆࠅࠁ ࠈࠌࠀࠕࠄ (v. 30), meaning 'and the priest atones for her in the presence of God from the discharge of her contamination'.

(142) After this the Lawgiver tells this nation to be careful and warns them and alerts them about keeping away from contamination. (143) All of them are to be careful about it, because he wants them to be close to him and to always be clean, (144) cleansed from all contamination, and he has set all this out and alerted them to it in all that is said before this. All (145) this is so they will be made holy and the benefits and advantages and blessings of the most holy country will continue and the angels (146) will serve them, as it says ࠅࠄࠆࠄࠓࠕࠌ ࠀࠕ ࠁࠍࠉ ࠉࠔࠓࠀࠋ ࠌࠈࠌࠀࠕࠌ ࠅࠋࠀ ࠉࠌࠕࠅ ࠁࠈࠌࠀࠕࠌ. (v. 31), meaning (147) 'Tell the nation of Israel to be careful about their contamination, so they do not die because of their uncleanness'.

(148) This is because if they ever do not be careful about contamination they will perish, because God has appointed them to a state of holiness, and has given (149) them all a Sanctuary and Temple like the most holy country, and anyone granted this state must (150) always be clean of any contamination for fear of the displeasure of the one pre-existent God who set them in this special (151) state, which he has not given to any nation that has existed before them or any of the nations that will arise in the future. Think (152) about this verse, ࠅࠋࠀ ࠉࠌࠕࠅ ࠁࠈࠌࠀࠕࠌ ࠁࠈࠌࠀࠌ ࠀࠕ ࠌࠔࠊࠍࠉ ࠀࠔࠓ ࠁࠕࠅࠊࠌ (v. 31), meaning 'so they do not perish because of their contamination, (153) when they contaminate my dwellingplace which in amongst them'. He has ended these laws with these words so as to re-inforce the warning for them to be careful (154) about the contamination of any flow.

(155) God is all-knowing in his purpose and completely wise.

[THE KÂSHIF AL-GHAYÂHIB ON LEVITICUS XII]

The Explanation of the Text of the Law of the Woman that has had a Baby and the Form of her Contamination and Cleansing

(2) This is in the passage starting ࠀࠔࠄ ࠊࠉ ࠕࠆࠓࠉࠏ ࠅࠉࠋࠃࠄ ࠆࠊࠓ (Lv XII:2), meaning 'A woman that gives birth to a boy'.

(3) The birth of a boy is mentioned first because of his higher status than the girl and because men were created before women. It is decreed (4) that when the woman has a boy she is contaminated as in the days of her menstruation, a contamination already understood, as it (5) says ࠅࠈࠌࠀࠄ ࠔࠁࠏࠕ ࠉࠌࠉࠌ ࠊࠉࠌࠉ ࠍࠃࠕ ࠃࠅࠕࠄ ࠕࠈࠌࠀ (v. 2), meaning 'She is contaminated for seven days; she is contaminated as for the days of her menstruation'.

(6) It seems to me that this passage shows us that this law, of the woman whose already defined menstruation has started, (7) must have been known to the people and their two leaders beforehand, as it says 'she is contaminated as for the days of her menstruation'.

(8) Then on the eighth day they circumcise the baby's foreskin, according to the law handed down from Abraham (9) (this being one of the laws known to him) as it says ࠅࠁࠉࠅࠌ ࠄࠔࠌࠉࠍࠉ ࠉࠌࠅࠋ ࠁࠔࠓ ࠏࠓࠋࠕࠅ (v. 3), meaning 'on (10) the eighth day the flesh of his foreskin is circumcised'.

(11) Then it is decreed that after this the mother spends thirty-three days segregated because of the blood (12) of her cleansing, not touching anything clean and not going into any holy place, such as a place of worship or any similar place, as it says ࠁࠊࠋ ࠒࠃࠔ ࠋࠀ ࠕࠂࠏ (v. 4), (13) meaning 'She is not to touch any holy thing or enter a place of worship till she has completed the seven days of her cleansing'.

(14) If she has a girl she is to spend a fortnight like the days of her menstruation, and is to bathe herself, and after that she spends sixty-six days (15) segregated from anything clean, and is not to go into any place of worship, as previously said in reference to a boy, as it says ࠅࠀࠌ (16) ࠍࠒࠁࠄ ࠕࠋࠃ ࠅࠈࠌࠀࠄ ࠔࠁࠅࠏࠉࠌ ࠊࠍࠃࠕࠄ ࠅࠔࠔࠉࠌ ࠉࠅࠌ ࠅࠔࠔࠕ ࠉࠌࠉࠌ ࠕࠔࠁ ࠏࠋ ࠃࠌࠉ ࠈࠄࠓࠄ (v. 5), meaning 'if (17) a woman has a girl her contamination is for a fortnight as for her menstruation and for sixty-six days she stays in the blood of her menstruation'.

(18) When her cleansing from after a boy or a girl is finished she is to get a one year old lamb as a peace offering and a young pigeon or (19) a small bird as an atonement offering and take them to the opening of the Tent of the Presence, where the priest gets them off her and sacrifices them and atones for her (20) and she becomes clean, as in the passage ࠅࠁࠌࠋࠀࠕ ࠉࠌࠉ

ࠈࠄࠓࠄ ࠋࠁࠍ ࠀࠅ ࠋࠁࠕ ࠕࠁࠉࠀ ࠊࠁࠔ ࠁࠍ ࠔࠍࠕࠅ ࠋࠏࠅࠋࠄ ࠅࠁࠍ ࠉࠅࠍࠄ ࠀࠅ (21) ࠕࠓ ࠋࠇࠈࠀࠕ (v. 7), meaning 'When the days of her cleansing are completed, whether from after a boy or a girl, she is to get a one year old lamb (22) as a peace offering and a young pigeon or a small bird as an atonement offering'. In his compassion and kindness for his creatures God has followed this verse with the verse ࠅࠀࠌ (23) ࠋࠀ ࠕࠌࠑࠀ ࠉࠃࠄ ࠃࠉ ࠔࠄ ࠅࠋࠒࠇࠄ ࠔࠕࠉ ࠕࠓࠉࠌ ࠀࠅ ࠔࠍࠉ ࠁࠍࠉ ࠉࠅࠍࠄ ࠀࠇࠃ ࠋࠇࠈࠀࠕ ࠅࠀࠇࠃ ࠋࠏࠋࠄ (v. 8), meaning (24) 'If she can not afford a sheep in its second year she is to get a pair of small birds or young pigeons, one for an atonement offering and one (25) for a peace offering etc.'. He does not want his creatures to be in difficult circumstances, he wants prosperity, and God does not burden (26) people but eases their condition.

(27) Let me say here that it was our Torah that followed right after the word of the one who spoke, and it is the basis of every book there has ever been. All (28) the nations have borrowed from it; some have succeeded and have got somewhere with their efforts, and some have missed the meaning. They have each had (29) a drink from it and have gone up different tracks. God shows the truth to whoever he wants to out of his servants; he has complete mastery, (30) however he wants, blessed and exalted is he.

TEXT 6

[THE BOOK OF PRINCIPLES]

Chapter Six

(2) *The Laws of Contamination, and its Varieties, and the Method of Cleansing from it as Current among Them at the Present Time and as Practised by Them* (3) *from Time Immemorial up till the Present*

(4) We will start first by discussing bleeding. They divide it into seven categories, called in Hebrew ࠍࠃࠄ *niddå* [separation], (5) ࠃࠅࠄ *dåbå* [menstrual] blood, ࠆࠁࠄ *zåbå* [discharge] blood, blood of childbirth, which is divided into two categories, one in the case of a boy baby and one in the case of a girl, blood (6) of purification, and blood of plausibility. Each of these has its own legal consequences, different to the others.

(7) *The Details*

(8) The bleeding called ࠍࠃࠄ *niddå* is the kind that the woman experiences immediately after the period of cleanness, marking the start of the contamination and the application (9) of the legal consequences. The position is that if any woman of theirs sees that she has had a discharge of moisture showing evidence of (10) contamination, which is evidence of a smaller or greater amount of blood, or moisture tinged with yellow or maroon or (11) red or any colour aside from pure white, she is to immediately withdraw herself.

(12) Every woman of theirs has a bed of her own with pillows and bedclothes and whatever else is needed for sleeping, (13) and crockery and cutlery of her own for when she menstruates. For the period of her contamination, according to whichever kind of contamination applies, she stays by herself and uses (14) her own bed, reserved specially for the purpose. They make her a flat inside her house and she does not go near anything at all except what has been set aside exclusively for her. None out (15) of her nation touch her or any of the things set aside for her, except for someone under the ban of contamination like her. (16) If any person of her nation, adult or child, does touch her, they get contaminated and have to be cleansed, and the treatment applying to them (17) is for them and their clothes to be washed, and to get into water. If she touches any artefact she contaminates it and it has to be cleansed.

(18) As for the woman this applies to, when she sees evidence of contam-

ination of any of the kinds previously (19) mentioned she is contaminated for seven days, even if she only saw one drop.

(20) This is the treatment of the first bleeding, called *niddå* blood, which requires withdrawal and causes a state of contamination for seven days. (21) Anyone that touches this first blood gets contaminated for seven days just like the woman from whom it issues.

(22) The second bleeding, called ࠃࠁࠄ *dā̊bå* blood, is the bleeding occurring to the woman over the next seven days. (23) The consequences of this contamination derive entirely from the first bleeding, and anyone that touches it gets contaminated and becomes clean at the end of that day.

(24) If the woman notices anything of this category during the seven days of her contamination, the length of her state of contamination is not extended; (25) but if, on the night of the eighth day, i.e. at sunset of the seventh day of her contamination, the woman sees any (26) evidence of contamination she has to spend another seven days in the same state of contamination as before, and anyone that touches her is affected (27) as if by the original bleeding. In the same way, if she sees any bleeding during the second lot of seven days the consequences of it are the same as for the second bleeding. (28) In the same way, if she sees any bleeding after the fortnight, i.e. the fourteen days, at sunset, any evidence of contamination, she keeps on (29) being contaminated for a third week, and the treatment of it is the same as for the first two weeks.

(30) This is the law of the *niddå* blood among the Samaritans, who know it by tradition and practise it; and the law of the second bleeding, which follows it, (31) the *dā̊bå* blood, as well.

(32) The third bleeding is ࠆࠁࠄ *zā̊bå* bleeding. The details of its rules are that if the woman does not become clean during the three weeks, (33) and the condition of *niddå* bleeding continues into the fourth week, it turns into *zā̊ba* bleeding. The rule is that once she has passed into the fourth week (34) and is still bleeding she can not be released from the state of contamination till she has counted seven days without bleeding, during which time she does not see (35) any sign of contamination. Even if she keeps on being clean from the flow of blood for two or three or four days, up till the seventh day before sunset, (36) and then sees a sign of contamination on the seventh day, her situation still changes (37) and the count up to that point is invalidated, and she has to count another seven days without bleeding. When she has finished the count of seven days (38) without any bleeding she can become clean at sunset on the seventh day. The procedure for her cleansing is for her to wash herself with clean water and then (39) get in the water so that it covers her.

(40) This is the law for the cleansing of any woman that is under the ban of this contamination.

(41) Their treatment in the case of childbirth is that if the woman gives

birth to a boy baby, then for seven days from the time of delivery (42) any blood that issues from her has the effect of contaminating anyone that touches it for seven days, and the law in this case is the same as for the contaminated woman during (43) menstruation. If, however, anyone touches this person, he gets contaminated and becomes clean at the end of that day. The blood that issues during the seven (44) days is called ࠃࠌ ࠏࠅࠕࠓ *dam ūtar*, i.e. blood of carefulness, because of the seriousness of its effect.

(45) Then on the eighth day the mother washes herself and gets the blood off her, and all her things are washed. The baby is washed too, (46) and is circumcised on the eighth day according to the law as previously set out by us.

(47) She stops under the ban of her contamination for thirty-three days without touching any clean person, and anyone that touches her (48) gets contaminated as well.

(49) The total amount of days of her contamination is forty-one days. When this is over she can become clean following the procedure (50) given above.

(51) If, however, she sees evidence of contamination after the end of the forty-first day, i.e. early on the night of the forty-second day, (52) she has to count seven days without any bleeding, without seeing any sign of contamination during this time.

(53) If the baby is a girl the treatment required by them is for her to count, from the time of delivery, fourteen (54) days, two whole weeks, double the amount for the delivery of a boy, and the blood that issues from her has the same status (55) as the first has, and anyone that touches it gets contaminated for fourteen days. This situation, with its full consequences, lasts for fourteen (56) days.

(57) When this time is up the mother has to wash herself and all the things she has been using, and the situation is over.

(58) She stays on her own and in a state of contamination for another sixty-six days, without touching any clean person.

(59) The total amount of days of her contamination is eighty days, up to the night of the eighty-first.

(60) If she does not notice any evidence of contamination she becomes clean. If she does see the slightest bit, she has to count seven days without any bleeding, without (61) seeing any sign of contamination at all during this time; then she can become clean.

(62) Bleeding that happens during either the thirty-three days or the sixty-six days has the same (63) consequences as *då̄bå* blood: anyone that touches it becomes clean at the end of the same day. The term ࠃࠌ ࠈࠄࠓࠄ *dam ṭå̄rå* does not mean 'pure blood' or 'neutral (64) blood' as the Jews interpret it. A refutation of them is given later on.

(65) The meaning of 'blood of plausibility' among the Samaritans is any sign of the kinds we have mentioned, as opposed to 'clean (66) blood', i.e. stuff tinged with the moisture the women call 'clean', which is pure white; anything (67) darker than this, of any colour, causes contamination.

(68) We have now listed the various kinds of menstrual bleeding that can issue from women, and the varieties of it and their consequences, according to (69) the Samaritans, who treat it as in force and follow the requirements and carry them out, and you will find them as careful and watchful as can be imagined (70) over these laws, which they have had handed down to them generation by generation. The Samaritan women guard against the occurrence of the slightest mistake, (71) and they agree on the precise application of the principles and laws of the various kinds of bleeding, and understand their conditions and characteristic signs, and have had this handed down to them from previous generations. (72) You can see their carefulness and their extensive knowledge of all this conforming to the command of Scripture revealed through Moses. (73) They take this charge on themselves and bear the full burden of this decree in spite of their present circumstances of misery (74) and captivity and deteriorating conditions beyond their control. The intelligent and knowledgeable people do not hide the fact that this charge (75) takes hard work and attention and a lot of trouble, so that the severe requirements of these charges mean a lot of expense. In spite of (76) this they do not neglect a single commandment out of the ones that can possibly be carried out, and they would never agree to a relaxation (77) of any of the laws for the sake of making the burden of the commandments easier: in every aspect they keep to the practice that is most rigorous.

(78) Not like the others, who have abandoned the whole of the general and specific commandments concerning the varieties of contamination and have come up with (79) interpretations of the meaning of Scriptural passages that do not agree with the meaning intended. They say that some of the blood discharged from (80) this organ of the woman's can be clean and some can be contaminated, and that ordinary people do not understand about the varieties of blood, (81) no-one does except the experts, i.e. people with theoretical knowledge, and if a woman experiences any menstrual (82) bleeding she is supposed to get some of it and take it to the Chief Rabbi straightaway so he can tell her whether it is contaminated or clean (83) blood. This is really one of the silliest things they have ever said, since it is self-evident that women know more about the legal position of blood than (84) anyone else because of their experience with it. The status of blood does not depend on the different colours or (85) the kind of blood or its qualities. It is not the way they make out, that there are some colours (86) to be treated as causing contamination and others as not having any effect on cleanness, and that not everyone can

tell clean blood (87) or contaminated blood discharged from the vagina, and that there are experts that can tell the different qualities and what is (88) contaminated and causes contamination, and what is clean. They justify this from the verse 'If a blood case is too unprecendented (89) for you etc.' (Dt. XVII:8). They are completely wrong about this. The truth is that the Lawgiver has charged (90) his people Israel with the observance of the laws of the blood discharged from the vagina, and the variations in the laws depend on the variations in the circumstances, (91) so that any emission from this organ causes contamination unconditionally, and as the circumstances of its occurrence change, (92) changes are caused in the laws.

(93) The start of this legislation is as set out in Leviticus XII, which contains the laws for the new mother after having a boy or a girl; (94) then in chapter XV of the same book are set out and defined the laws for the characteristics of discharge bleeding and menstrual bleeding and chronic (95) bleeding, and the law of it is set out without any distinction between the colours, just the cataloguing of its laws and times and grades.

(96) The first grade is assigned to the first bleeding. The text calls this *niddå* in Hebrew, the implication (97) of this term being isolation and separation. This term is from the same root as ࠍࠃ *nad*, a form that occurs twice, once in reference to Cain, where it says ࠍࠏ ࠅࠍࠃ ࠕࠄࠉࠄ (98) ࠁࠀࠓࠑ (Gn IV:12), meaning 'You will be banished and isolated in the world', and the second time in reference to Adam, where it (99) says ࠅࠉࠔࠁ ࠁࠀࠓࠑ ࠍࠃ ࠒࠃࠌࠕ ࠏࠃࠍ (Gn IV:16), meaning 'He lived in the world in banishment [*nad*], east of Paradise', (100) which is in chapter IV of Genesis. This is the standard Samaritan exegesis.

(101) This blood seen by the woman at the start of the discharge of the blood, with its duration and legal consequences, is the standard (102) of reference for the legal consequences for a woman that has had a boy or a girl in the verse 'She is contaminated for seven days as in the days (103) of her *niddå*' (Lv XII:2), and in reference to the mother of a girl, 'She is contaminated for a fortnight as in her *niddå*' (v. 5). (104) This is set out in Leviticus XII:1-5. It says there that the consequences of the first (105) bleeding are that anyone that touches it is contaminated for seven days, and the same for the bleeding that happens to the mother of the baby, and double that in the case of the mother (106) of a girl: anyone that touches them gets contaminated for seven days in the case of a boy and fourteen days in the case of a girl, as we have said.

Then a further clarification (107) of this bleeding is given in the decree that if a man lies down with his wife and some of this blood gets on him from off his wife (108) he gets contaminated for seven days in a row, as the effect of this blood, which always has an effect of seven days. The evidence for this is the verse (109) 'If her husband lies down with her and gets some of her *niddå* over him, he is contaminated for seven days' (Lv XV:24), where this is the blood (110) called '*niddå*' and 'her *niddå*' [ࠍࠃࠕࠄ *niddå̄tå*] in legal terminology, as we have said. This is proven in the prooftext previously quoted. . . . .

(111) . . . .

(112) These are the laws of the *niddå* and the *zå̄bå* and the *yå̄lēda*; and the differences (113) between the Samaritans and the Jews, and the practice followed by the communities, have been given.

(114) The Samaritans, as part of their normative practice, prohibit association with any woman under the ban of contamination, whether *niddå*, *då̄bå*, (115) or *yå̄lēda*. If any man sins and copulates with his wife while she is under the ban of contamination, (116) they do not let anyone associate with him at all. This is the practice followed (117) at the moment, but in the Time of Favour they would be after killing such a man, in agreement with the command of Scripture.

(118) God knows everything.

TEXT 7

[EXTRACT FROM THE SHARḤ SÛRAT AL-IRBOT]

. . . . Similarly, in the rules for a woman in her separation [ࠍࠃࠄ *niddå*] there are some rules that are not mentioned amongst the rules of other cases, in spite of their general (2) applicability. In the case of the rules for a man with a discharge [ࠆࠁ *zåb*] it says 'If the man with a discharge [*zåb*] spits on any clean person (3) he is to wash his clothes etc.' (Lv XV:8); but this applies to all other kinds of contamination as well.

TEXT 8

[MARGINAL NOTES]

[I]

[NOTE I ON THE BOOK OF INSIGHT]

The principle followed by the nation at the present time is that the woman only requires seven days without bleeding if her bleeding keeps up for the length (2) of the first week and continues into the second week and then continues into the third week, up to the end of it, without it stopping, (3) even if it is present on some days and on others is not present. The criterion is the day called by (4) the women 'the critical day' [*yawm al-mask*]: if the slightest amount of bleeding happens to her on that day, which is the seventh day (5) of the third week, she has to keep [*tumsik*] seven days after that without bleeding, and this is what they call a 'count' [*ʿadad*]. The evidence (6) for this is the passage 'for many days, outside the time of her separation [*niddå*] (Lv XV:25).

(7) God knows best. I ask God's forgiveness for uncertainty and deficiency.

(8) Written by Musallam bin Marjân ad-Danafi, may God, whose existence is unending, forgive him. Amen.

[II]

[NOTE II ON THE BOOK OF INSIGHT]

A note by my Lord the Shaykh Khiḍr son of the Shaykh Isḥâq the High Priest, long may he live.

(2) A divergence of opinion exists among our predecessors over the law of the blood of a woman with a discharge [ࠃࠌ ࠆࠁࠄ *dam zåbå*]. Among them is this authority, who says that (3) the legal situation of the blood of a woman with a discharge [*dam zåbå*] applies after the first week, and that if any bleeding happens to her after this time, (4) she has to count seven days without bleeding. The Shaykh Munajja Abu 'l-Faraj, however, says, in his book *Masâʾil al-Khilâf*, that there is no need to count (5) seven days without bleeding (the requirement for the bleeding of a woman with a discharge [*dam zåbå*]) till after seven weeks, basing himself on (6) the passage to do with this 'or who has a discharge past her separation [*niddå*] ... for many days' (Lv XV:25), (7) and the term "many days" refers to such a period, which is seven squared, so the meaning of it comes out as the legal requirement (8) of the

separation [*niddå*] (which is seven days and a factor of the number of the discharge [ࠆࠁ *zåb*]) multiplied by itself. The Shaykh Musallam, on the other hand, follows a tradition (9) from his predecessors. The principle followed at present, without any disagreement or dispute over the matter, is that (10) the legal position of the blood of a woman with a discharge [*dam zåbå*] does not apply till after three weeks, and the Hebrew (11) women follow the same principle in defining the period. This practice has become standard, and therefore has the status of an established tradition, since there is no disagreement over its practice, (12) and it is not contradicted by the text of Scripture, and is generally agreed on.

(13) God knows best about everything.

[III]

[Note I on the Kâfi]

The verse 'Anything the man with the discharge [ࠆࠁ *zåb*] touches without having rinsed his hand with water (2) etc.' (Lv XV:11) means that the man with a discharge [*zåb*] causes uncleanness even if his hand is dry, and there is none of this anywhere in (13) the law of the woman in her separation [ࠍࠃࠄ *niddå*].

(4) This came to the insignificant ʿImrân after suffering from worry and disquiet, praised be the Lord. The Shaykh (5) mentions this specifically because in some respects his position is the same as the legal position of the woman in her separation [*niddå*] and in some respects is different, (6) since the slightest amount of bleeding from her requires withdrawal for seven days.

[IV]

[Note II on the Kâfi]

The verse 'Anything the man with the discharge [ࠆࠁ *zåb*] touches without having rinsed his hand with water' (2) (Lv XV:11) means that if the man with the discharge [*zåb*] touches anything, then even if his hand has got a bit of the actual substance of the discharge [*zåb*] on, the person touched (3) only needs washing, and becomes clean the same day. This is the difference between the substance of the blood of separation [ࠃࠌ ࠄࠍࠃࠄ *dam anniddå*] and the blood (4) of a man with a discharge [ࠃࠌ ࠄࠆࠁ *dam azzåb*], since anyone that touches the blood of separation [*dam anniddå*] is affected for seven days, whereas anyone that touches the substance of the man with a discharge [*zåb*] is only (5) affected for a single instant.

(6) End of note.

(7) Nâji bin Khiḍr the Priest. Amen.

[V]

[Note III on the Kâfi]

A note, by the insignificant one that writes it, on the verse 'Anything the man with the discharge [ࠆࠁ *zåb*] touches (2) without having rinsed his hand with water etc.' (Lv XV:11). What is meant is that anyone that touches the actual substance of the discharge [*zåb*] (3) does not require the week's count that applies to the man from whom the discharge [*zåb*] issues, but becomes clean the day he touches it, as it says (4) 'he is to wash himself with water and is unclean till sunset'. (v. 11). Had this not been specifically stated in this (5) passage it would have followed by induction from the separation [ࠍࠃࠄ *niddå*] that anyone that got the actual substance of the discharge [*zåb*] on him would be unclean for seven (6) days. This is what the text intends by the note about the discharge, since if his body touches any clean artefact while not damp the artefact is made (7) unclean, and if he happens to touch any clean artefact it is made unclean as well and becomes clean at the end of the day. God (8) knows best.

(9) The meaning of the passage is that anyone that touches the man from whom the discharge [*zåb*] issues and the person that touches the actual substance of the discharge [*zåb*] are both in the same legal position, (10) and the point of the verse is to make the case of someone that touches the discharge [*zåb*] less serious than the case of someone that touches the blood of separation [ࠃࠌ ࠄࠍࠃࠄ *dam anniddå*]. This (11) distinction is the difference between the rules for men and women. God knows best.

(12) This note depends on what the Shaykh Abu 'l-Ḥasan, may God favour him, says in his book the *Ṭubâkh* in (13) the chapter on the man with a discharge [*zåb*], and this is the right answer, the situation being that this Shaykh here has not explained this point properly. God (14) knows best.

(15) End of note. Yaʿqûb Hârûn the Priest, may he be forgiven. Amen.

[VI]

[Note IV on the Kâfi]

A discussion of the point that the woman washes away the first drop to flow from her the first time with her left hand but not (2) with any other part of her, and that her hand stays under the requirement of the count.

[VII]

[Note I on the Book of Differences]

A note by my late father:

(2) What this authority says is not the standard practice in our community for telling the difference between the separation [ࠍࠃࠄ *niddå*] (3) and the discharge [ࠆࠁࠄ *zåbå*]. The Shaykh says here that the situation of discharge [*zåbå*] only applies after seven whole weeks, whereas (4) the standard practice at the present time is that it is after three weeks, and I ask God for forgiveness before saying that what this (5) Shaykh says on this matter has no support from normative practice or tradition among the nation. God knows best.

[VIII]

[Note II on the Book of Differences]

A note by my late father, the Priest Fīnās:

(2) He refutes the Jews over their invention, on the basis of the Scriptural expressions (3) ࠏࠋࠉࠅ (Lv XV:4, 5, 6, 9) and ࠕࠇࠕࠉࠅ (v. 10), that any bedclothes that are on the man with a discharge [*zåb*] do not get contaminated, and bedding alone is affected. The fact is that there is (4) a Scriptural passage that shows the bed used by the *zåb* to be contaminated, both bedclothes and bedding, the passage 'Any person that touches (5) his bed is to wash his clothes and wash himself etc.' (v. 5). This passage (6) unequivocally says that his bedclothes and bedding are contaminated, since there is no qualifying expression ࠏࠋࠉࠅ or (7) ࠕࠇࠕࠉࠅ to be found there. See how they are always wanting to make things forbidden for use or permitted by abrogating the commandments of the Torah in this way (8) all the time, when our ancestors would always be trying to be scrupulous and rigorous.

(9) End of note.

COMMENTARY

TEXT 1

The Book of Insight

1-78 Compare Kf ch. XI, 43-90, and Iʿtiq 4-67, which use the same organisation. Parallels to other texts on individual points are given in the appropriate places.

The division of the content is as follows: list of seven kinds of bleeding 2-4; *niddå* 5-11; *dåbå* 12-15; *zåbå* 16-44; bleeding of childbirth 45-52; bleeding of cleansing 53-59; bleeding after the forty or eighty days 60-65; bleeding of plausibility 66-73; copulating with a woman known to be unclean 74-78.

2-4 Compare Kf 44 and 48; Iʿtiq 4-6, where the same classification is used.

2 The term ࠍࠃࠄ *niddå* is translated as 'separation' because this is the standard Samaritan interpretation and etymology. See Kh 44-47; 58-59; Kâsh ch. XV, 103-106; Iʿtiq 96-100.

2 It is hard to find an English equivalent for *dåba*. The most exact would have been 'woman with a vaginal discharge', but the term 'discharge' takes the attention away from the circumstances of the woman to the nature of the flow, and the term was needed to render *zåbå*, which does refer more to the flow than to the woman.

In Lv XX:18 the word refers to a woman with any discharge, whether due to menstruation or childbirth or anything else. (See Kh ch. XV, 51-53). In this context, however, it refers to a woman who is menstruating, and the translation is appropriate.

2 The term *zåbå* refers specifically to a chronic discharge.

2 The letters ࠉࠋࠃࠄ could equally be read as *yålēda*, meaning 'a woman who has given birth', but the term is translated as ولاده 'childbirth' in Ms. G of the Ṭubâkh, Mss. GH of the Kâfi, and Ms. G of the Khilâf whenever it occurs, and at 45 all mss. of the Ṭubâkh have the Arabic equivalent term ولاده.

3 It is divided into two sub-categories, both of which have to be counted to make up the number of seven.

See the note on Kf ch. XI, 73.

3 This grammatical analysis is assumed in Kh 216, Ms. G of the Ṭubâkh, Mss. GH of the Kâfi and Ms. G of the Khilâf (where the term is translated), the Arabic translation of Leviticus XII, the Targum of Lv XII, and Ben-Ḥayyim's transcription of Lv XII. This analysis is required if the blood is to be counted as unclean, since only in this way can the word be taken to refer to becoming clean rather than being clean.

3 On the term دم الاشتباه 'blood of plausibility' see the note on line 67, where the reasons for choosing this translation are given.

4 The term حكم has no neat equivalent in English. Sometimes it means legal consequences, sometimes the treatment required due to the legal status of a thing, sometimes the legal status, and these meanings shade into each other. The plural has the same range of meaning and in addition means a set of laws or rules or halachot in a certain area. The reader is to understand that the English equivalents 'consequences', 'treatment', 'status' and 'laws' all refer back to the same Arabic word, and one or the other is used according to whichever is most natural in the context and best brings out the author's argument.

6-11 On *niddå* bleeding in general, compare Kf ch. XI, 45-55; Kh 43-116; 255-258; 262-263; Far 2-65; Kâsh ch. XV, 101-123; Iʿtiq 8-21; 96-110; Sharḥ Sûrat al-Irbot.

6 This is the start of the menstrual bleeding, after a period during which the woman was not bleeding and was not in a state of contamination due to any previous bleeding.

8-11 According to the Kâfi, anyone that the blood touches is made unclean for seven days but anyone that the woman touches but who does not come in contact with the blood is only made unclean for one day. The agreement between the Ṭubâkh and Kâfi in other details in this matter indicates that they probably agreed on this point. See the note on Kf 88-89. The Kâshif (ch. XV, 103-106) agrees with the Kâfi.

8-10 The argument based on this verse is not given, so the text is a bit cryptic, but compare Kf ch. XI, 49-55; Kh 107-114; Far 49-65; Kâsh ch. XV, 113-117. The point is that the onset of bleeding is unpredictable.

For the interpretation of the phrase ࠅࠕࠄࠉࠄ ࠍࠃࠕࠄ ࠏࠋࠉࠄ see the passages listed above, and in particular, as well as these, see Kh ch. XV, 92-97, where it is made clear that the word *niddå* here means the substance of the blood, not the legal state of a woman in *niddå*. It follows that we have to translate 'gets on' rather than 'is on' or 'applies to'.

Compare Kf ch. XI, 84.

Notice that it makes no difference whatever whether the blood gets on the man during copulation or not: see Kh 107-110 and Far 49-58.

9 This is a criterion used by some Karaites for telling the difference between *niddå* bleeding and *zåbå* bleeding, and in particular for telling whether bleeding starting after the first week of menstruation marks a second period of *niddå* or is to be counted as *zåbå*. The distinction depends on whether the bleeding finishes before sunset of the seventh day of the first week and whether the woman has undergone immersion on the seventh day, and also on whether there is a period without bleeding on the eighth day, i.e. on whether the woman has broken the continuity of contamination. The details vary slightly from author to author, and the principle is not always used in Karaite practice: for the details see Gan ʿEden 113a middle, the context of the whole of chapter VII, and then p. 113d middle (starting at the words אך חלוקת חכמים) to the end of the chapter; and compare Adderet Eliyahu, ch. XI, and in particular p. 123a top.

The same criterion is put forward for consideration by the author of the Farâ'iḍ (103-110), who gives the same objection to it as is made by the Karaites that do not accept it (see Gan ʿEden 113a middle, the whole of the sentence starting ועוד הקשו).

9-10 The quotation does not agree with the received text of the Torah, and is almost certainly a misquotation caused by conflation with v. 18. Nevertheless, it is clear from the distribution of readings that the misquotation is more original to the text of the Ṭubâkh than the form that agrees with the received text, which is due to secondary emendation.

It remains to consider whether the misquotation goes back to the author of the Ṭubâkh or is an ancient corruption, old enough to be found in all extant witnesses except those that have been emended.

The same misquotation is found in Kf 49-50, where it is supported by all witnesses and is probably original, and is used as part of the same argument as here. This agreement means that the two texts must depend on a literary source containing the misquotation. Direct dependance of the Kâfi on the Ṭubâkh is unlikely, and the situation seems to be that the Ṭubâkh, Kâfi, Khilâf, and Fara'iḍ consistently show signs of the influence of a common literary tradition. It is almost certain, then, that the misquotation was in the source of the Ṭubâkh, and that it was present in the Ṭubâkh from the time of its composition.

The addition of the words ࠔࠁࠏࠕ ࠈࠌࠀࠄ in $P_1{}^2$L*KS is due to the influence of v. 18. It is not well enough supported in the mss. to be certainly the original reading of the Ṭubâkh, although it deserves serious consideration. Mss. OP_1*M_1 can be counted as a single witness, and the addition is only contradicted by the less reliable mss. and a correction in Ms. L, which probably does not depend on the source of Ms. L. Note that the corrected text of Ms. P_1 adds these words, which means they were found in some of the sources of this ms., and that the word ࠔࠁࠏࠕ (an error for ࠔࠁࠏࠕ ࠈࠌࠀࠄ or a partial correction of it) is found in the quotation of this verse in the Farâ'iḍ, 49-50.

11-13 The distinction between contamination due to contact with a woman in a state of uncleanness due to *niddå* blood and *då̊bå* blood might be the cause of the practice of some Dositheans of allowing contact with women during their uncleanness. The relevant passage is Abu 'l-Fatḥ 161:14-15, which reads as follows, speaking of Sakta:

وجعل الطموات قسمين واحد يدعى مبدأ والاخر متعدل وكان يبيح الزواج من الامم ومس الامراه في الطماوات.

Vilmar's text is correct here, except that the reading متعدل has better ms. support than Vilmar's reading معتدل, even in the mss. used by him, and I have altered the word accordingly.

The passage can be translated as follows:

'He put the various kinds of uncleanness into two categories, one called the 'start' [*mabda'*] and the other 'derived' [*muta'addil* or *mu'tadil*]. He allowed marriage with non-Israelites, and the touching of women in the various states of uncleanness'.

The two technical terms used here have baffled the translators and commentators.

Bowman (p. 171) translates them as 'primary' and 'intermediate'. The first term can in fact mean primary, but the second does not mean intermediate in any sense that can fit here, although a superficial reading of Hava's dictionary might have given this impression. Neither does he explain what the two terms are supposed to mean. (Bowman translates الطموات in the first case as 'unclean practices' and in the second case as 'menses'. This is against possible usage).

Scanlon (p. 81) translates the terms as 'primary' and 'secondary'. As elsewhere, Scanlon's translation shows his sound knowledge of Arabic technical terminology. It might be as well to explain here how the term *muta'addil* or *mu'tadil* can mean secondary. The root in the first stem can be used to mean to turn off a path, and by extension to be derived by grammar or etymology. The fifth and eighth stems are to be understood in the same sense. In this case the derivation of the secondary item is not a matter of grammar or etymology, but one of contamination. There is an original source of uncleanness, and then contamination deriving from this.

It now remains to consider precisely how the primary uncleanness and the secondary or derived one differ. Isser does not offer any suggestion, as in the case of so many other halachic matters. (On the desultoriness and lack of thoroughness of Isser's work, see pp. 12-14). Nemoy has two suggestions. One is that the 'primary' uncleanness is what in Mishnaic terminoloy would be called אבות. He does not explain whether he is referring to the use of this term to mean 'major categories' (as in אבות נזיקין) or sources of contamination (i.e. אבות טומאה). His second suggestion indicates that he is thinking of the first meaning of the term אבות, when he offers the comparison with the Moslem division of 'roots' and 'branches'. But this will not do, because the Moslem division of laws as *aṣl* and *far'* has a different function: it has nothing to do with the degree of severity of any matter, but only with the source of authority for the law.

Suppose we let the terms speak for themselves, without giving them any meaning that is not attested in usage. The word *mabda'* means a start, and metaphorically a base point, an axiom etc. The word *muta'addil* or *mu'tadil* means 'something derived'. In what way can uncleanness be divided into two categories, one being the start or first stage or starting point, and the other something derived from that? Two answers spring to mind immediately: The 'start' or 'starting point' is the person unclean because of some emission, the אב טומאה in Jewish terminology, and the derived uncleanness is the uncleanness of a person that has touched the first person, the uncleanness of the וולד טומאה in Jewish terminology. Or, the 'start' is e.g. the instant of *niddå* bleeding, which makes the woman unclean for a week, and what is derived is the uncleanness for the rest of the week.

On face value the two explanations are equally possible, but in fact the second one must be preferred because only then can it be explained how Sakta was able to find theoretical justification for touching women in a state of uncleanness. If the woman is made unclean for a week by the instant of *niddå* bleeding right at the start, then whether or not there is any bleeding after that makes no difference to her uncleanness, i.e. *dåbå* bleeding does not add to the woman's uncleanness. This is a point agreed on by the Samaritans (see T 34-36 TN, and the context). Besides which, it is known that the start of the count of seven days depends on washing the *niddå* blood off (see T 55-57 N and the context), which means that the *niddå* blood continues to re-contaminate the woman till it is washed off, but after that her uncleanness is only due to the blood having been on her. The logical conclusion is that a woman who has been made unclean for a week by *niddå* bleeding, but who has washed off the *niddå* blood, is only unclean because of her earlier condition, not her present condition, and if anyone touches her during the week of her uncleanness, then whether or no she is undergoing *dåbå* bleeding the person that touches her is unaffected because there is nothing in her present condition that can affect herself or any other person. (See below, 13-14 N, for a discussion of the various Samaritan opinions on this matter).

The same argument can be applied in the case of a woman recovering from uncleanness due to *zåbå* bleeding, i.e. during the count of seven days. It is actually known that some Samaritans did hold the opinion that any person that touched such a woman was unaffected: see Kf ch. XI, 64-67 N; Kh 267-269 N.

The same argument can be applied in the case of a woman who has given birth. As it is the very first bleeding, at the time of delivery, that makes her unclean for forty or eighty days, and as the bleeding of the first week or fortnight can be assimilated to the instant of *niddå* bleeding, and the period of thirty-three or sixty-six days that follows corresponds to the period of seven days that follows the *niddå* bleeding, then by the same argument as above a person that touched the woman during the period of thirty-three days or sixty-six days should be unaffected. This is actually known to have been the opinion of some Samaritans: see Kf ch. XIII, 6-8 TN. Of course, if it is only the bleeding at the instant of delivery, and not the bleeding during the whole of the first week or fortnight, that is assimilated to the *niddå* bleeding (which is an attested viewpoint of some Samaritans: see Kh 204-214 TN), then any person that touches the woman at any time at all after delivery will be unaffected, provided the blood of delivery has been washed off.

We see that Sakta was only being logical, but logical or no, his conclusions would have been unacceptable to his opponents.

One interesting point is that Sakta would have agreed with the Rabbanites to some extent over the 'bleeding of cleansing' during the thirty-three or sixty-six days: see Kh 267-269.

11 A person contaminated by this blood obviously has to wash it off before the count of seven days can start, since his contamination is equivalent to the woman's, both of them having been contaminated by the same blood (Kf 88-89 N) and we know that the blood has to be removed before the woman from whom it issues can start counting (T 55-57 N and the cross-references there). Presumably the person contaminated by this blood has to wash or immerse on the seventh day, and this requirement is specifically stated in Kâsh ch. XV, 123 (Compare the note on Kf ch. III, 7-8 N).

On the other hand, a person who touches the woman at the time of *niddå* without getting any of the blood on him is only made unclean for one day, provided he immerses himself before sunset, because he has not come in touch with the *niddå* blood, and the woman herself is only unclean because of her contact with the blood, so that anyone who contacts her is at a lower level of contamination (Kf ch. XI, 88-89 N).

Compare Far 49-58.

12-15 On *då̄bå* bleeding in general compare Kf 56-60; Kh 258; 262-263; Iʿtiq 22-23.

12 After the first instant of bleeding, any bleeding that follows either immediately after or at any time during the next seven days falls into a new category, *då̄bå*.

13-14 Some of the steps in the argument have been left out.

If a woman experiences *då̄bå* bleeding (i.e. any menstrual bleeding other than the very first instant's bleeding at the start of the week) on the last day of the week of menstruation, she can still become clean at sunset the same day provided there is no bleeding between the time of immersion and sunset. This means that whatever contamination the woman is caused by *då̄bå* bleeding does not last beyond sunset of the same day. This means that the contamination of any person who touches this blood can not last past sunset of the same day, since it would not be possible for this person's contamination to be more serious than the woman's.

The same statement about the effect of *då̄bå* blood is made in Kh 117-121; 258; 262-263; and about the effect of *dam ṭårå* in T 53-59; Kh 209-214. We have seen (T 11-13 N) that some Dositheans held a similar opinion.

The standard modern halachah is that *då̄bå* blood and *dam ṭårå* cause one day's uncleanness, and that the person affected can only become clean at sunset. Contact with the woman without contact with the blood will have the same effect (Iʿtiq 22-23; 16-17; 47-48; 62-63; Kâsh ch. XV, 28-33). It is clear, from Kf ch. XI, 66-67, that this is the opinion of the Kâfi as well, and although there is some ambiguity in Kf ch. XI, 84-87, the author's opinion can be left in no doubt in view of the explicit statement of the first passage. It will be seen from Mishnah Niddah VII:4 that some Samaritans must have held this opinion in the time of the Tanna'im.

Comparing this passage and T 34-36, the implication seems to be that the *då̄bå* only contaminates the woman till it is washed off (though this is only a theoretical question since she is still unclean due to *niddå*), and that the same must therefore apply to anyone that touches the blood.

It is to be noticed that all the sources treat *dam då̄bå* and *dam ṭårå* identically in regard to their contaminating effect; and that all of them treat contact with the blood or contact with the woman without contact with the blood as causing uncleanness for the same length of time. In such cases, the Kâshif requires washing all over and the Iʿtiqâdât requires immersion. The Kâfi requires neither, though obviously the blood will have to be removed by washing that spot.

Compare T 34-36 N.

13-14 Compare the note on 16-26.

Notice that the immersion is carried out in the daytime of the seventh day and the woman becomes clean at sunset at the end of the seventh day. This agrees with Karaite practice. The Rabbanite halachah is that the immersion has to be carried out after the sunset at the end of the seventh day and the start of the eighth day, and if it is carried out before the sunrise halfway through the eighth day, she becomes clean at sunsrise. If the immersion is carried out at the wrong time, before the sunset at the end of the seventh day, it is still valid, and she still becomes clean at sunsrise halfway through the eighth day. (See Mikva'ot I:6 for the Rabbanite opinion. The Karaite opinion is specifically stated in A.E. 121d bottom, and is assumed throughout the discussion of the distinction between נדה and זבה in A.E. ch. IX and G.E. ch. IV.)

All the Samaritan sources agree that the woman's immersion is in the daytime on the seventh day of the week (provided the bleeding has stopped) and that she becomes clean at sunset at the end of the seventh day.

This disagreement between the Rabbanites and Samaritans over whether the woman becomes clean at sunset at the end of the seventh day or at sunrise during the eighth day has far-reaching consequences, since it means that according to the Samaritans the woman's bleeding has to finish not only by sunset, but long enough before for the woman to be able to immerse herself before sunset. This is probably related to the question of whether bleeding up till the time of sunset, or past a certain time on the last day of the week, is enough to put the woman in the state of *zåbå*, or whether the bleeding has to continue into the first day of the following week.

Compare T 16-17; Kf 58-61; Kh 63-65; 165-171; Far 89-90 and 97-110; Kâsh 124-128; I'tiq 24-34; M.N. I:3-6; II:2-12. The situation is that the authors of the Ṭubâkh, Kâfi, Khilâf, Farâ'iḍ, I'tiqâdât, and the second marginal note on the Ṭubâkh, do not count the woman as being in the state of *zåbå* unless bleeding occurs on the first day of the following week; an opinion known in two different forms to the author of the Farâ'iḍ is that the bleeding has to occur right from the start of the first day of the following week; the author of the Kâshif counts her as being in the state of *zåbå* if bleeding occurs on the afternoon of the last day of the week; and the author of the first marginal note on the Tubâkh counts her as being in the state of *zåbå* if any bleeding occurs at any time at all on the last day of the week. A similar kind of disagreement, over whether the bleeding has to continue till sunset of the last day of the week or not, is found in Karaism. In Karaism, the question is whether bleeding right at the start of the first day of the next week is required to put the woman in the state of *zåbå*, or whether bleeding at any time on that day is enough, which relates to the question of whether she can possibly become *zåbå* after having immersed herself and become clean at the end of the week before. (See the references in T 9 N). The disagreement in Samaritanism probably has the same origin: i.e. if it is illogical for a woman to be declared *zåbå* on the first day of the next week after she has become clean at the sunset at the end of the week before and the start of this week, and this first day, it follows that the criterion must be bleeding on the last day of the first week, in agreement with some of the Karaites.

There is considerable disagreement in the Samaritan sources over whether a woman can have two periods of *niddå* in two consecutive weeks, and if she can, how many times this can be done before she must be put in the state of *zåbå*. This disagreement probably has the same origin as it has in Karaism: once you maintain, as some Karaites do (G.E. 113b bottom; A.E. 123d middle-124a top; for a Samaritan use of the same argument see Far 97-110), that the state of *zåbå* can logically only occur directly after the state of *niddå* without a period of cleanness in between, then it follows that it must be possible for the bleeding of the next week to be *niddå*; but once you admit that, there is no obvious upper limit to the number of consecutive weeks when the woman can pass into another state of *niddå*, and there must be variation over the maximum number of repetitions that still be regarded as not being enough to put the woman in the state of *zåbå*, since different arguments will produce different answers to the question of what is excessive and what is not. For the various limits that the Samaritans have set, see Kf 58-61 N.

13 The alteration of the words 'the principle followed by the nation' to 'what the women do and the principle followed by the nation' in Mss. GHF is in agreement with the tendency to let the transmission of the halachot of all discharges from the vagina rest with the women, and to rely on the consensus of their practice in matters of doubt, or to verify or establish the details of the halachah.

Compare Kf ch. XIII, 13-15; 19-21; Kh 212-214; I'tiq 66-67; 83-84; M.N. I:3-5; II:9-11.

15 Notice how the point is insisted on. This probably means the author was aware of the existence of a divergent opinion. He might have been thinking of the Rabbanites, who do not distinguish between the first or subsequent bleeding, and count both as causing seven days' uncleanness to anyone who touches them; or he might have been thinking of the Karaites mentioned in the note on 31-32; but the words 'the evidence for this is the principle followed by the nation', in their context, seem to imply pretty clearly that the dispute he has in mind is over the question of whether *dåbå* bleeding causes the woman one day's uncleanness or seven days', i.e. whether the period of purification ends seven days after the first bleeding or seven days after the end of the bleeding, in which case he could have been thinking of the post-Talmudic innovation of the Rabbanite Jews of counting seven days' purification after any bleeding whatever, not counting the day on which the bleeding occurs. The possibility remains, however, that he had in mind a Samaritan group who departed from the standard Samaritan tradition in this matter and agreed in their practice with the later practice of the Rabbanite Jews. We know this to have been a Samaritan practice in the time of the Tanna'im: see Mishnah Niddah IV:1. (This is not the usual interpretation of the Mishnah, but it is supported by the reading of the most reliable mss. and the structure of the Mishnah. See the Sirâj). We know that this was the practice of at least one group of Dositheans, from a statement by Abu 'l-Fatḥ (82:6-8). Saadya knew of this as a Samaritan practice and considers it (or his source considers it) to be the standard Samaritan one (see Kh 159-159 TN). Compare also Kh 200-201 and Kf 45-46, which might be allusions to the existence of this opinion.

The practice of counting seven days' purification after the end of any bleeding, i.e. after the last day on which bleeding occurs, is rejected in the Khilâf 200-201 and Farâ'iḍ 25-30. There the context is different. The argument is over whether, if the woman experiences one day of menstrual bleeding, that day is to be counted in the seven days of purification or not, but the practice rejected there still must be the same as the one rejected here. Such repeated emphasis, without any mention of the Jews specifically, indicates that the authors have a Samaritan group in mind.

Compare the note on 31-32 and Kâsh ch. XV, 115-117.

The opinion rejected here is that the *dåbå* is to be treated like the *zåbå*, by counting seven whole days of purification. The oppposite opinion, that the *zåbå* can be treated like the *niddå*, by counting the day on which the bleeding finishes as one of the seven days, is rejected in Kh 200-201 and Far 25-30. If the authors of the Khilâf and Farâ'iḍ found it necessary to say this, it is quite likely that they knew of it as the opinion of some Samaritans; and apparently it is described as the standard Samaritan opinion in a baraita in Bavli Niddah 33a, commenting on Mishnah Niddah IV:1, and Tosefta Niddah V:1.

16-44 On *zåbå* bleeding in general compare Kf ch. XI, 61-67; Kh 165-201; 259-261; 264-266; Far 80-119; Kâsh ch. XV, 124-141; I'tiq 32-40; Sharḥ Sûrat al-Irbot; M.N. I and II.

16-26 Compare the notes on T 13-14 and Kf 61.

The author gives two criteria according to which the woman passes into the state of *zåbå*: either the bleeding continues till the day after the end of the week of menstruation, i.e. till the eighth day from the start of bleeding, or the bleeding finishes on the last day of the week of menstruation, i.e. the seventh day from the start of bleeding, but re-appears on four days in a row some time in the week that follows. Either of these occurrences puts the woman into the state of *zåbå*.

There is some agreement here with the Rabbanite halachah. The Rabbanite position is that one or two days' bleeding after the end of the week of menstruation puts the woman in a minor state of זבה (זבה קטנה or שומרת יום כנגר יום), requiring one full day's purification, and three days' bleeding in a row puts her in a major state of זבה (זבה גדולה) requiring seven full days' purification. No distinction is made between bleeding on the eighth day and bleeding on any other day (provided it does not extend beyond the eighteenth day).

This author agrees with the Karaites in having one day's bleeding on the eighth day put the woman in a state of *zåbå* (see the note on 13-14). His reference to continuous bleeding could be taken to mean that he recognises the possibility of a second period of *niddå* if there is a break in the continuity of the bleeding between the seventh and eighth days, with some Karaites. It is more likely, however, that he does not make the distinction between the case of a break in the continuity and the case of continuity, since if he did, he would have mentioned it, and it would be hard to reconcile this with the rule that a woman can go into the state of *zåbå* after four days of bleeding in the second week starting *after* the eighth day. We may conclude that when he refers to the bleeding continuing up till the eighth day, this is not to be taken to mean that bleeding has to occur on the seventh day.

16-17 See the note on 13-14 and the cross-references there.

19-20 We are not told what is to be done about bleeding that starts after the eighth day and does not occur on four days in a row. It would be impossible to count such bleeding as *niddå*, and it does satisfy the requirements for *zåbå*. Logically, it would have to be counted as a lesser degree of *zåbå*. Comparison with the Rabbanite halachah, which is the only other system to make the distinction between bleeding on one or two days and over a longer period (but see note 187 in the Conclusions, on the Falashas), confirms this solution. We can assume that the author of the Tubâkh, like the Rabbanites, would put the woman in a lesser degree of *zåbå* requiring a count of only one complete day from sunset to sunset without any bleeding, then immersion on the day after, with complete cleanness being reached at sunset on the day of immersion.

20 There is an apparent inconsistency here between the requirement for the counting to start from the day on which the bleeding finishes and the requirement for it to start from the day after, but the contradiction is not real. When once the woman sees that she has stopped bleeding, she knows she is ready to start the count, and as the count consists of seven complete whole days, it has to start at the next sunset, and finish exactly seven sunsets later.

The repetitiveness of the original has been kept in the translation.

26 The reference is to the fact that the text equates the term 'many days' with bleeding on the eighth day from the start of menstruation.

26-29 The author is quoting an argument only for the purpose of refuting it, and has compressed it in the process, making it a bit obscure.

The argument is as follows: We have to establish what is meant by the term 'many days'. This can be done by first establishing what is the longest period that can be called 'days' without the word 'many' being needed, or in other words, what is the most number of days that could be counted as less than 'many days'; then, when this has been established, it follows that any excess beyond this number of days, even by one day, must be counted as 'many days'. It will be shown that the term 'days' without the word 'many' being needed can refer to a maximum of forty-nine days: anything more than this would have to be called 'many days'.

An instance of the use of the term 'many days' is the passage 'in those many days' in Ex II:23. In this passage the term 'in those many days' rather than the expected and normal 'in those days' is used, the reason being either that the period or stage during which this happened was felt by the Israelites to be interminable because of their misery or was really very long. (It says 'in those many days', not 'after those many days'). As the expression 'in those days' can refer to a very long period, it follows that the term 'in those many days' must refer to a period really exceptional in its length, either absolutely or subjectively. If this is the case with the difference between the expressions 'in those days' and 'in those many days', a similar difference must exist between 'days' and 'many days'. We already know that the term 'those days' refers to a much longer period than the term 'days', so there is no direct way of deriving the maximum length of the term 'days' from 'those days'. But we have established that the term 'many' refers not only to a number that is quite big, but more exactly to a number that is quite out of the ordinary. The number of days expressed by the term 'those days' can be a very big number in absolute terms, so the difference made by adding the word 'many' is not so much that the absolute number is increased as that the number is lifted out of the ordinary, to a new stage or level. This is why the term 'those many days' is so rare: the term 'those days' by itself is quite adequate for expressing a normal length of time, no matter how long absolutely.

Now that we have established that the addition of the word 'many' to an expression raises it from a normal length of time (which may be long or short in absolute terms) to a length of time that is not only long, but also abnormal in its length, so that it falls into another category, and is not just an extension of time, we have to determine at what point a woman's repeated menstruation passes from a normal (even though unusual) condition to an abnormal condition (which need not be any more unusual). The answer is that seven successive weeks during which bleeding occurs on the first day of each week (not necessarily on every day of each week) is within the possibility of a healthy physiology, although quite rare, but any continuation of bleeding beyond the last day of the seventh week is abnormal, and can be classed as lasting for 'many days'. The reason that the figure of seven weeks or forty-nine days is taken as the criterion is that the critical factor is the changeover from one state or level to another, as we have seen, and at the number forty-nine one set of numbers is completed and a new set starts. Fifty is not only one more than forty-nine, it is the first number of a new set of numbers; so bleeding for fifty days is not just bleeding for one day more than forty-nine days, it is a new category of bleeding, and has passed from the level of normality to the level of abnormality.

The figure of forty-nine days, rejected by the author of the Ṭubâkh, is accepted by the author of the Khilâf (165-175), who supplies some parts of the argument not given by the author of the Ṭubâkh, namely the criterion of the changeover from normality to abnormality and the linkage of this with the completion of a set of numbers at forty-nine, but does not give any of the parts of the argument given by the author of the Ṭubâkh. He adds the argument that any bleeding beyond forty-nine days must be pathological, and this is another reason for putting the changeover from one state to another at this point.

It looks as if both the author of the Khilâf and the author of the Ṭubâkh assumed that the argument would be known to the reader and need not be given in full, that a summary of it or an allusion to it would be perfectly adequate. We must conclude that the argument must have been a standard and well-known one in its time, both to those that accepted it and those that rejected it.

A quotation of Ex II:23 is used in a completely different and much less sophisticated way by the author of the Farâ'iḍ, 84-86.

27 It seems that in the major part of the textual tradition of the Ṭubâkh the words لا ياخذ هيمم have been dropped out and then re-inserted after, instead of before, the word فقط. The only text-witnesses to preserve the correct text are OGHF. Ms. O preserves it because it is older than the corruption, or more likely belongs to a different sub-group to P_1M_1 and their relatives, which is where the corruption seems to have arisen. Mss. GHF show evidence of the critical and intelligent editorial work by the Samaritans in modern times that so often brings the reading of the Hebrew translations or the modern mss. into line with an almost lost original reading.

30 The addition of the words هو الدم in some mss. is to be taken as a gloss explaining that the word *niddå* refers to the first instant of bleeding and that the rest of the week is 'the time of her *niddå*'. The Rabbanite interpretation of the phrase 'the time of her *niddå*' is that it refers to a time during which any new bleeding will be counted as *niddå*, not *z̊åbå*. The interpretation of the phrase in Kh 170 is the same as the Rabbanite one, though its application in practice is different because of the different system of calculation being used.

31-32 This is not the standard Karaite opinion, but it is attested, In one version, the very first bleeding is *niddå*, and anything after that hour is *z̊åbå*; in the other version the first bleeding and any other bleeding on the first day are *niddå*, and any bleeding on the second day or later is *z̊åbå* (G.E. 112d middle). Obviously the consequence of this will, unless the woman's period of bleeding lasts less than an hour in one case or less than a day in the other case, be that such Karaites will agree with the post-Talmudic Rabbanite practice of treating all bleeding as *z̊åbå* and requiring a count of seven whole days without bleeding before the woman can become clean. See the note on 15.

32-36 Same refutation in G.E. 112b bottom-113a top.

32 On the use of the masculine form *zåb* compare Kh 130 N and compare T 62. In this passage the use of this form might be due to imitation of Karaite terminology, and the same might perhaps apply in the Khilâf, which depends on a Karaite source, but the use of the masculine form is not well enough attested in the available Karaite texts to make this certain.

33 Compare Kh 167-171 and the note there.

34-36 The rather surprising statement that the *d̊åbå* bleeding has no effect in the first week has caused difficulty to the scribes of the mss. (See the apparatus). In the context, however, it is quite correct. The point is that the verse quoted shows that the contamination of the week of menstruation is due to the first bleeding, the *niddå* bleeding, not the *z̊åbå* bleeding, which was the point to be proven, and in the process it shows that the week's contamination is not due to *d̊åbå* bleeding either, and this is added for the sake of completeness. It is true that it might be argued (as this author himself does; see 12-14 and the notes) that the *dåbå* bleeding does cause contamination for one day, but in the context this is irrelevant, since the question is the cause of the contamination of the whole of the menstrual week, which is independent of any bleeding during the week; and besides, even if the *dåbå* bleeding does cause contamination, the effect is removed at the same time as the contamination due to the *niddå* bleeding is removed.

Admittedly, the reading ࠋࠋࠆࠁࠄ or ࠋࠆࠁࠄ (as in H) is attractive, and has the merit of making a statement that follows on from what was said before, rather than being tacked on as an afterthought. If the source of this statement is a Karaite text in Arabic, as is likely, it is possible that the reading ࠋࠋࠃࠁࠄ is due to a corruption in the Arabic, with للذابيه being written by mistake for للزابيه . Nevertheless, the ms. evidence seems to show that the original reading in the Ṭubâkh was ࠋࠋࠃࠁࠄ, and this is shown not only by the attestation of the reading ࠋࠋࠃࠁࠄ, but also by the attestation of the secondary reading ࠋࠋࠍࠃࠄ, an emendation due to puzzlement over what the point of the reading ࠋࠋࠃࠁࠄ could be. It is possible that the reading of H is a correct emendation, but that it is an emendation that the author of the Ṭubâkh should have made in his source. On the other hand, the textual base of the Ṭubâkh is narrow, and an original reading could easily be corrupted in all the extant mss., and the reading of H could be original.

I do not think it will be possible to solve this question till the Karaite texts on the same subject have been edited.

Compare T 13-14 N.

36 In Moslem legal terminology, the term *ʿuqlah* means sequestration either of goods or of a person, i.e. prohibition of use of goods or association with a person till the legal situation has been resolved or decided or has altered. Its commonest use is the prohibition of intercourse with a woman during contamination or during the period of waiting after divorce to see if she turns out to be pregnant. I have translated the term as 'ban' rather than 'sequestration' because of its very specific use in Samaritan terminology to refer to the prohibition of intercourse with any woman who is unclean due to a vaginal discharge or childbirth.

36-44 This proof depends on accepting the distinction made by the Samaritans and Karaites, but not by the Rabbanites, between the bleeding of the very first instant, called *niddå*, and the bleeding of the rest of the week, called *dåbå*. It is likely that this proof will turn up in a Karaite Arabic source.

45-52 On the question of whether the bleeding during the seven or fourteen days is at the same level of uncleanness as the bleeding at the instant of childbirth or the same level as the bleeding during the thirty-three or sixty-six days, see Kh 204-214 N.

The author of the Ṭubâkh follows the first opinion, as is clear from the context and in particular 50-52.

See Kf ch. XI, 88-89 N.

Compare Kf ch. XI, 68-72; the whole of the extract from ch. XIII of the Kâfi; Kh 202-214; Kâsh ch. XII, 2-7; 14-17; Iʿtiq 41-46; 53-56 for information on the bleeding of childbirth in general.

47-52 Lines 47-48 seem to say that anyone that comes in contact with any of the blood discharged by the woman during the seven days after childbirth is made unclean for one day, just as anyone that comes in contact with any blood discharged by the woman during the week of menstruation is made unclean for one day. It is likely that the author puts the blood that appears at the instant of delivery in the same class with the first instant of menstrual bleeding (*niddå*). It would then make the woman unclean for seven days and make anyone that touches it unclean for seven days. This seems to be implied by the position and use of the quotation.

On the other hand, any bleeding that occurs during the fortnight after giving birth to a girl is put in the same class as *niddå* blood, not *då̄bå* blood, so that anyone that touches it is made unclean for seven days. It may reasonably be asked what effect the blood discharged at the exact time of delivery of a girl would have on anyone that touched it. In the context the conclusion seems inevitable that such a person would be contaminated for a fortnight, and this supposition about the intention of the author of the Ṭubâkh is supported by the fact that we find precisely this to be the modern practice: see Iʿtiq 55 and 105-106.

The Kâfi probably agrees with this: see the note on Kf ch. XI, 88-89. The Khilâf (205-208) is inconclusive. The Kâshif does not mention the question of contamination of other people by contact with the mother. The relevant section of the Farâ'iḍ is not available.

The Scriptural basis for the distinction between the effect of the bleeding during the seven days after giving birth to a boy and the fourteen days after giving birth to a girl is that in the first case the text says 'kå̄yå̄mi niddåt då̄bå̄tå' where *niddå* need not have the specialised meaning of first menstrual bleeding, but may simply mean contamination, and anyway the important word is *dăbătå*, and in the second case it says plainly 'kå̄niddå̄tå'.

There is disagreement between the sources over the classification of the various kinds of bleeding after childbirth. See the note on Kh 204-214.

53-59 On bleeding of cleansing in general, compare Kf 73-78; Kh 215-253; Kâsh ch. XII, 11-17; Iʿtiq 47-50; 58-64.

53-55 The Tubâkh, Kâfi (73-76) and Khilâf (215) agree that the count of thirty-three days starts after the seventh day, so that the total is forty days. The Iʿtiqâdât (47-52) and Kâshif (ch. XII, 8-13) add one day in between the seventh and the start of the count of thirty-three, i.e. the counting of thirty-three days starts the day after the baby is circumcised.

53 On the explanation of the mistake in Ms. M_1* see Kf 73 N.

53 The Jews take the word ࠈࠄࠓࠄ in the first instance in Lv XII:4, and in verse 5, to be a single morpheme, meaning 'cleanness', but in the second instance in v. 4 to be two morphemes, meaning 'her cleanness' according to the Rabbanites, or 'her cleansing' according to the Karaites. The Rabbanites maintain that the woman is clean for all purposes during this period except that she defiles holy things, whereas the Samaritans, like the Karaites, maintain that the woman is unclean during this period. See the Khilâf and the notes there.

I do not believe it has been remarked that the Syro-Palestinian Version reflects the same halachah as the Samaritan and Karaite one in translating טהרה as 'her defilement' in v. 4 in the first instance, and in v. 5, and in translating טהרה in the second instance in v. 4 as 'her cleansing'.

54-55 These days are the thirty-three that follow the seven days that follow delivery of a boy.

55-57 Before explaining this passage, we first have to determine the meaning of the word *yuḥaṣṣil* in line 56. This could be done by examination of all the parallel passages where it occurs, but it is simpler to take the definition from a passage in the Kâfi where it is explained in passing.

The passage occurs in ch. XIII, Ms. J p. 92, Ms. D p. 56, Ms. L_1 p. 134b, Ms. W p. 105. It would have been on p. 82 of Noja's translation except that he leaves it out. It is outside the part of ch. XIII edited here. The context is that the author is trying to show the need for a person made unclean by contact with a corpse to undergo an immersion on the first day before counting to the third day and seventh day, even though this first immersion is not mentioned in Scripture. He says that the third day and the seventh day are calculated from the day of the first immersion, not necessarily from the day of contamination, which means that if the first immersion is delayed the third and seventh days are counted from a later time than the day of contamination. He then supports this statement by showing that the principle involved is one already known to apply to the calculation of the period of seven days required for a woman to become clean after menstruating. Her period of cleansing starts from a first washing (not mentioned in Scripture) which would normally be on the day of contamination, and if the washing is delayed a few days the calculation of the seven days is delayed by the same amount. The essential section reads as follows in ms. J:

... كما ان دم ࠄࠍࠃࠄ الاول متى لم يحصل منه فى نهاره والا سقط ذلك النهار ولم يكن معدودا من الاسبوع.

All mss. except J add غسل after لم يحصل.

The meaning of the words *lam yuḥaṣṣil* here is adequately shown by the addition of the word *ghasl* after, and although the word *ghasl* is probably a gloss, it is a correct gloss. It may be assumed that the verb *ḥaṣṣal* (which means to perform, attain, carry out) has the technical sense of carrying out the step needed next to carry out the purification. In the case of the woman who has started to menstruate, this step is to wash off the *niddå* blood, from which seven days' purification is needed, so that the *niddå* blood not keep on re-contaminating her and the count of seven days can start. We find exactly the same principles and the same terminology in Kf ch. XIII, 13-18. It says there that the day on which the *niddå* bleeding occurs can only be counted in the seven days of the menstrual week, i.e. the count can only start from that day, if the *niddå* blood is washed off before sunset, and the expression used is *idh lam yuḥaṣṣal al-ghasl* 'if the washing is not performed'.

The same principle is used by the Karaites: see A.E. 122b lines 12 to 18.

This requirement follows naturally from the distinction between *niddå* and *dåbå* blood: *niddå* blood contaminates anyone that touches it for seven days, and if it can still have this effect on a second person that touches it some after it is emitted, it must still be able to have this effect on the woman herself.

In the case of a person that has touched *dåbå* blood, or blood of cleansing, which is of the same class as *dåbå* blood, the washing removes the blood, so that it does not keep on re-contaminating them and they can become clean. The Hebrew translation renders the word *yuḥaṣṣal* as ࠉࠔࠈࠐ, which conclusively confirms this interpretation. Compare the parallel passages T 58-59; Kf 66-67; 84-87. Notice that it is not said that the *niddå* blood or the *dåbå* blood has to be removed by immersion: washing is enough because the purpose is only to remove the source of contamination. The implication of saying that the washing can be carried out immediately is that its effect is immediate, that is to say, the 'blood of cleansing' causes uncleanness that lasts only as long as the blood is present. A comparison of the parallel passages will show that the Ṭubâkh and Khilâf hold this opinion in regard to both *dåbå* blood and blood of cleansing, and some Dositheans agreed, but that the opinion of the Kâfi, and the modern halachah, is that the person affected is unclean till sunset. The relevant passages are listed in T 13-14 N and T 11-13 N.

I have translated the verb *ḥaṣṣal* here and in the parallel passages as 'wash it off'. The verb does not mean this on its own but in this context this is what is meant. A translation such as 'perform the washing' would have been clumsy and unnatural.

Compare the notes on 107 and 11, and the note on Kf 85.

We learn from this passage that the Samaritans agree with the Jews that blood still keeps on being a source of contamination after it has dried up, since it is obvious that it will dry up long before the end of the first day.

56 The washing would be effective if carried out at any time before sunset. The person affected becomes clean immediately: see T 13-14 N and Kf 88-89 TN, and see also the previous note for other Samaritan opinions on this matter.

56-57 The point of the proof has been explained above, on 13-14.

The emendation is certain, not only because of the parallel with 56 but also because the argument demands it. For the explanation of the point of the argument see the notes on 13-14. The interchange of لأن and لكن is very easy.

Compare Kf ch. XI, 85 and the note there.

60-65 The Kâfi (75-76) and I'tiqâdât (60-61) agree that bleeding after the thirty-three or sixty-six days puts the woman in the state of *zåbå*, but the Farâ'iḍ (103-106) counts it as *niddå*.

See the note on the Farâ'iḍ for the implications. The Ṭubâkh, Kâfi, and I'tiqâdât agree with the Rabbanites; the Farâ'iḍ agrees with the Karaites. (See A.E. 123d bottom-124a top; G.E. 114b top).

60 This means, after the period of seven plus thirty-three days after giving birth to a boy or fourteen plus sixty-six days after giving birth to a girl.

60-61 The point of the quotation is that this state of contamination lasts 'till the completion of the days of her cleansing', and provided the bleeding has finished by then she becomes clean automatically, but if the bleeding lasts beyond this time, which the first part of the verse, not quoted here, has set at sixty-six days, she can no longer be in the state of bleeding of cleansing and any bleeding must be treated as being in a different category, and it would not be possible for its effect to disappear automatically, as the effect of the blood of cleansing does.

The same applies to any bleeding past the thirty-three days in the case of a boy.

62-65 It is clear from the analogy with the state of *zāba* following the state of *niddå* that the reference is to bleeding that occurs on the day immediately after the sixty-six days or thirty-three days.

This is what we would have expected, anyway, since if there were no bleeding on the sixty-seventh or thirty-fourth there is no reason why bleeding on the sixty-eighty day or the thirty-firth day should not be counted as the start of a new period of *niddå*, not *zåbå*. This is the Jewish position, and it is clear from the implications of this passage that it is the Samaritan position as well. Note that the essential criterion for entry to the state of *zåbå* after *niddå* or *dåbå* in the Samaritan system is continuity, i.e. bleeding on the very next day after the last day of *niddå* or *dåbå*, and the same criterion applies for entry to the state of *zåbå* after bleeding of cleansing in both the Jewish and the Samaritan system.

62 In spite of the use of the masculine gender, the reference is to the female issue usually known as *zåbå*: compare 32 and Kh 130.

67-73 Compare Kf 79-82; I'tiq 65-67 on bleeding of plausibility.

67 In 3 the term *ishtibâh* is used instead of *shubhah*. The form in the other texts (Kf 79; I'tiq 6 and 65) is consistantly *ishtibâh*.

Unlike the Kâfi in the parallel passage 79 the Ṭabâkh adds the phrase *fa-yulzim ayyâm ash-shubhah* 'and it brings on the days of plausibility'. The 'days of plausibility' probably corresponds to the Jewish concept of ספק טומאה 'the possibility of uncleanness', which causes a period when a person has to act as if uncleanness were present to be on the safe side. This is the only explanation that explains the existence of the category of 'days of plausibility'. If this is the case, however, it follows that the 'blood of plausibility' should be discharge that is not certainly unclean, i.e. that does not certainly contain blood. But this not only contradicts the other sources (Kf 79-82; Kh 122-133; Far 7-14; I'tiq 9-11; 65-67; 78-88) which count any coloured substance as definitely containing blood, it contradicts the Ṭubâkh itself (68-73) which says precisely the same thing. The existence of a category of 'days of plausibility' is therefore inexplicable and anomalous and the other sources, including the Kâfi and Farâ'iḍ, which draw on a common literarary tradition with the Ṭubâkh in this matter, do not mention it. Notice that Mss. $P_1M_1M_2N$ of the Ṭubâkh have dropped the word *ayyâm* 'days', so that the 'days of plausibility' are no longer a problem. This reading is obviously secondary, since the words *fa-yulzim ash-shubhah* 'and it requires (a state of) plausibility' are unnecessary. The scribes of the ancestors of these mss. must have found the term 'days of plausibility' unintelligible. It looks as if the category of 'days of plausibility' has been taken over mechanically by the author of the Ṭubâkh from a source that recognised the concept of possibility of uncleanness in this matter without certainty, as does the Karaite halachah, and it is very likely that the term *shubhah* is an Arabic translation of the Hebrew ספק, which has later been re-interpreted to mean plausibility rather than doubt or possibility, as we will see. The Ṭubâkh is the only source to use the form *shubhah* (here, but not in 3), whereas all the rest (and the Ṭubâkh itself in 3) use the form *ishtibâh*, which carries more of the connotation of plausibility than *shubhah* does, which can easily be used to mean possibility or even doubt in the right context. The form *shubhah* might then be older. A noun of the form *shubhah* would be a more natural translation of ספק than the infinitive *ishtibâh*. (In modern usage the word *shubhah* can mean 'suspicion').

The treatment of discolouration as possibly being evidence of the presence of blood, in the case of a woman recovering from the state of *zå̊bå*, is known to the author of the Khilâf, who uses it for his own purposes (see Kh 130-132 N). It looks as if the source of the Ṭubâkh agreed with the Karaites in extending the treatment to other kinds of bleeding as well. Compare Kh 260-261.

The authors of the Ṭubâkh and Kâfi themselves regard any discolouration as certain evidence of the presence of blood, and maintain that it has to be treated as blood in that case, unlike the Rabbanites. The authors make a comparison between water that must have some dye in, because of the discolouration of the water, even though the dye can not be seen, and vaginal fluid that must have some blood in, even though the blood can't be seen, because of the discolouration. This is why the terms *shubhah* and *ishtibâh* in these two texts have to be taken to mean 'plausibility', and why the authors are able to count 'blood of plausibility' as a separate category. It is true that it is treated the same as any other blood, but it differs from other blood in not being visible, only determined as present by other evidence. (The I'tiqâdât only has it as a separate category because of mechanical copying of the Ṭubâkh and Kâfi, as we will see).

The author of the Farâ'iḍ agrees with the Ṭubâkh and the Kâfi that any discolouration is certain evidence of the presence of blood, and is to be treated as blood. This comes through not only from his use of the same comparison with water with dye in, but from his distinction between the colours of blood itself, and the discolouration of the vaginal fluid that is evidence of the presence of blood in lines 7-14, taken together with his insistence that what is visibly blood and what can be deduced to have blood in are to be treated the same.

The terms *shubhah* and *ishtibâh* are quite suitable, since they have a range of meaning extending from 'plausibility' or 'plausible deduction' to 'uncertainty'. In

Moslem law they correspond pretty closely to what in English law is called prima-facie evidence: they refer to evidence that is not conclusive but is adequate to indicate that a certain legal situation *might* exist, and that steps or precautions have to be taken or certain procedures have to be carried out so that the truth can be found, one way or the other. I suggest that the original use of *shubhah* and *ishtibâh* in the Samaritan terminology is similar, although not identical: they refer to *a reasonable deduction*, either certain or highly probable. In other words, they correspond in practice to the term ספק in Rabbanite and Karaite halachah, but indicate a stronger degree of possibility. In origin, if the arguments of this note are correct, they would have referred to a deduction that was highly probable, a usage similar to, though slightly stronger than, its usage in Moslem law, but in full agreement with the non-specialised meanings of these terms and the verb *ishtabah*. Later, the term would have been used in the slightly different signification of a certain deduction, a usage which would derive naturally from the earlier one and is still in agreement with the un-specialised meanings of the words *ishtibâh* and *ishtabah*.

The Khilâf and I'tiqâdât give a much simplified version of the position of the Ṭubâkh and the Kâfi: they say that any discolouration is actually blood itself. I suspect that this is a popular misunderstanding and over-simplification.

We can now set out the various Samaritan and Jewish positions systematically.

(a) The Rabbanites agree with the Ṭubâkh, Kâfi, and Farâ'iḍ that any discolouration is certain evidence of the presence of blood, but do not count it as blood because it is not visibly blood (Issure Bi'ah V:6; and see the context).

(b) The source referred to in the Khilâf (see the note on the Khilâf 130-132) agrees with the Karaites and the source of the Ṭubâkh and Kâfi that deduction from discolouration only shows the possibility of the presence of blood, not the certainty, and applies it in the case of a woman during her recovery from the state of *zåbå*, but not in other cases.

(c) The source of the Ṭubâkh and Kâfi agrees with the Karaites that deduction from discolouration only shows a possibility, not a certainty, and agrees with the Karaites in applying it in all circumstances, whether *niddå* or anything else. (On the Karaite position see the Gan 'Eden 110d bottom and the Adderet Eliyahu 122a middle and the context in both cases).

(d) The Ṭubâkh, Kâfi, and Farâ'iḍ agree with the Rabbanites that any discolouration is certain evidence of the presence of blood, and unlike the Rabbanites, they count it as blood.

(e) The Khilâf and I'tiqâdât say that any discolouration actually is blood.

The question naturally arises, what colours did the people holding opinions (b) (c) (d) count as being the colours of blood itself? Only one of the sources gives that information, and that is the Fara'iḍ, 5-6, where the colours given agree pretty closely with the ones accepted by the Karaites. To the next question, what kinds of discolouration count as evidence of the presence of blood, the answer is, any colour except pure white. (See the note on Kh 179-199).

67-68 This means that she falls into the category of *niddå*, exactly the same as if the discharge had been normal blood. In other words, blood of plausibility is not a category of bleeding in the same way that *niddå* or *dåbå* or *zåbå* bleeding or bleeding of childbirth or bleeding of cleansing are: it is a criterion for judging whether any given discharge is unclean, and if it is, it will then be assigned to one or other of the other six categories. The figure of seven for the various kinds of bleeding belongs to the sources of the Ṭubâkh, but does not fit the Ṭubâkh.

The same classification in the Kâfi has been altered in the secondary text to resolve the same difficulty, although unsuccessfully: see the note on Kf ch. XI, 73.

68-72 Compare Far 7-14 and Kf 78-82, where the same analogy is given. The most original form of the passage is the one in the Farâ'iḍ.

71-72 See Kh 197-199 N on the colours. There are similar lists in Far 4-6 and 13-14; Kf ch. XI, 79-80; I'tiq 10-11.

74-78 On copulation with a woman known to be unclean due to bleeding, see the Kf ch. XI, 45-55; 90; ch. XII, 58; 66; Kh 51-55; 98-110; 112-114; 238-241; Far 59-72; I'tiq 115-117; and compare T 8-10 N.

75-78 The term *dåbå* here means a woman known to have any discharge from the vagina, whether *dåbå* in the narrow sense in which it is used in this chapter, i.e. any menstrual bleeding except for the very start of the bleeding, or whether bleeding of childbirth, or bleeding of cleansing. In fact, it covers any discharge except the *niddå*, which comes without warning: see T 8-10 and the notes and cross-references there. The term 'cut off' in Samaritan interpretation refers to judicial execution, not, as in the majority Jewish opinion, premature natural death. See Kh 98-106; 112-114; Far 59-63; and the Kâshif al-Ghayâhib on Lv XX:18.

79-124 Compare Kf ch. XI, 2-42; ch. III, 8-27; 39-42; Kh 6-9; the Additional Passage from the Khilâf; Kâsh ch. XV, 5-9; 82-100; M.N. III, IV, V, VIII for general information on the discharge [*zåb*] and emission of semen.

81 The word *faṣl* means a sub-section or a self-contained part of a chapter. It refers here to the sub-section 82-88 which lists the circumstances in which any emission can be explained away as not being due to illness or injury. It does not include the sub-section 89-98 or 89-93. The author of the Ṭubâkh, unlike the author of the Kâfi, is very sparing in the use of this heading, and does not use it to mark off sub-sections that can be integrated into the exposition of the chapter: it is reserved for self-contained sub-sections, or for digressions. As there is no reason why the whole section 82-98 should not be an integral part of the line of argument of the chapter, it follows that some part of this passage must be being marked off from the rest of the chapter or from the rest of the passage. The only place to put the dividing line is after 88. As we will see in the next note, the two parts 82-88 and 89-93 do not sit well together in their present form. It would be reasonable to take 82-88 as a preliminary consideration to be disposed of before the text gets on to the essential point. This could fit the normal usage of the term *faṣl* in the Ṭubâkh, and the setting-out of the exposition, with its contrast (clearly indicated in line 89) between what counts and what does not.

This is why the word *faṣl* has been translated as '*note*' here. A clearer translation would have been 'preliminary remark' but this would have been an interpretation rather than a translation.

The analysis assumred here is very adequately confirmed by the corresponding passage in Kf ch. XI, 3-24 (or 3-21), where the division between the two sub-sections is clearly marked at line 18.

81-93 There are three cases in which a discharge from the penis does not count as the discharge of a ࠆࠀࠁ [*zåb*] (man with a discharge): First, if the emission consists of semen and is emitted under normal circumstances. In this case it is treated as an emission of seman and nothing more. Second, if the substance appears along with the urine. In this case it can be assumed that it is simply either semen or seminal fluid from the prostate gland that has been left in the urethra. Third, if the emission can be explained as semen emitted due to exceptional circumstances as listed. In all these cases the emission consists of normal semen or seminal fluid, whether or not it is emitted during intercourse, and comes under a category of its own.

Any discharge occurring under other circumstances can not be explained away as semen and therefore must be the *zåb* [discharge].

The Rabbanite position is similar, but not identical. They are in complete agreement with the Samaritans that an emission of semen is a separate category, and they agree that in the same circumstances as listed here in the Ṭubâkh the emission must be counted as semen. The difference is that they have a second criterion for distinguishing semen from discharge, and this is that the discharge is pathological, due to disease, injury, or debilitation, and unlike semen, which holds together and is bright, the discharge is ropy or waxy and dull. In practice, though, this criterion can be overridden by the circumstances of the emission, so that an inexplicable emission of normal semen counts as discharge, and an emission of an abnormal substance that can be explained away as due to unusual circumstances, the same circumstances as listed in the text here, 85-86, counts as semen and no more. This means that, theory aside, the Samaritans and Rabbanites agree on what emission is semen and what is discharge. (There are refinements and qualifications to the use of exceptional circumstances to explain an emission away as an abnormal emission of semen, but these are only details, and do not affect the essential agreement).

The Karaites agree with the Samaritans and the Rabbanites that normal emission of normal semen is in a separate category. They disagree with the Rabbanites and Samaritans in refusing to recognise the exceptional circumstances listed here (85-86) which the others use to explain the emission away. To them, the circumstances are irrelevant. On the other hand, the criterion of the difference in appearance and consistency of the emission is decisive: the discharge does not hold together and is waxy and tends to dry into a crust, and oozes out rather than being squirted, and is not the result of sexual arousal. They do not use the criterion of brightness or dullness.

The Samaritans agree with the Karaites and Rabbanites on the consistency of the discharge as opposed to semen (T 89-93; Kf 18-22; Kh 6-9), agree with the Karaites in not using the criterion of brightness or dullness, and agree with the Karaites on using squirting and sexual excitement as a mark of an emission of semen (Kâsh 85-86). On the other hand, as we have said, they agree with the Rabbanites in allowing the circumstances of the emission to put it into the category of semen rather than discharge, and they agree, too, in letting this criterion override the others in practice.

In the light of all this, it is remarkable that the Ṭubâkh (89-93) and the Kâfi (18-22) give as much attention as they do to an analysis with some words to the effect that this description gives the criteria for telling a real discharge, as opposed to semen. It is entirely possible that the form of the exposition here is based on a combination of a paraphrase of a Rabbanite treatise (Ṭubâkh 82 onwards; Kâfi 3 onwards) and a Karaite treatise (Ṭubâkh 89 onwards; Kâfi 18 onwards) and that the implication of the words in T 89 and Kf 18 that what follows is an exposition of the real criterion is due to inadequate adjustment of the source. In support of this hypothesis, we can point out that the list of exceptional circumstances in which any discharge counts as semen given by both the Ṭubâkh and the Kâfi is essentially the same as the Rabbanite one (see for example Meḥussere Kapparah II:2) and that the analysis of the description of the discharge in Lv XV:3 is essentially the same as the Karaite one (see, for example, Adderet Eliyahu 120a top; Gan ʿEden 108b top; and see the context in both places).

A more decisive indication that diverse literarary sources have been used is the structure of this section of the Ṭubâkh and the Kâfi. In the Ṭubâkh, the sub-section listing the special circumstances in which an emission is explained away and only counted as an emission of semen is headed as *faṣl* [sub-section; a self-contained part of a chapter], is marked off as a preliminary consideration, and is not well integrated with the next sub-section, describing the appearance of the discharge, as the text stands (see the note on 81, and the remarks in the present note (above) on the unimportance of 89-93 and the corresponding passage in the Kâfi in the Samaritan system). In the Kâfi, the linkage has been done more skilfully by marking off the sub-section 19-22 (on the description of the discharge) and not giving a special heading to the first sub-section 3-8 (on abnormal emission that can be explained away as an emission of semen, and on normal emission of semen), but the two sub-sections are still not really properly integrated. The second sub-section is still unnecessary, or at least irrelevant, and logically the second sub-section should deal with the circumstances in which it is not possible to explain away an emission as being an emission of semen. Besides, the first sub-section in the Kâfi seems to have been drawn from a passage on emission of semen and its rules: see Kf ch. XI, 9-15, the note on Kf 12, and Kf ch. XI, 16-17. (See also Kf ch. XI, 9 N on the sources used).

This does not necessarily mean that the Samaritans have borrowed any of their halachah from the Rabbanites or Karaites: it probably only means that they have found it convenient to use a Rabbanite exposition of a point on which they agree with them, and a Karaite exposition of another point on which they agree with them. The Samaritans could not have borrowed from either, because they do not fully agree with either, and their system is too self-consistent to be eclectic.

The Kâshif (ch. XV, 6-9 and 51-54) differs completely from the other sources in counting an emission of blood as *zâb*. See also the second marginal note on the Khilâf. In 23-25 the Kâshif gives very vague information, possibly wrong, on how often the bleeding has to occur.

83-84 These qualities are characteristic of normal semen or seminal fluid, as opposed to discharge in the technical sense.

84-85 These situations are unlikely to result in an emission of semen, but they will easily cause a leakage of thin seminal fluid at the end of the penis, specially if kept up for a long while.

85-86 All these foods, if consumed in excess by a person suffering from severe hypertension, will aggravate the condition for a short period afterwards. This is particularly true in the case of roast meat. The symptoms are reddening of the face to an unhealthy dark red or brick-red, a rise in temperature, and sweating of the face and forehead.

In the terminology of the author's time, a rise in blood pressure could only be described as a thickening of the blood, and actually the term is fairly accurate, since an abnormal viscosity of the blood can lead to abnormal blood pressure.

86 The emendation is certain. People do not usually eat pomegranate flowers, and even if they did, they would not show these symptoms.

The original error is the reading الجلنان. The other readings are corruptions from this. The original error lies behind all the extant text-witnesses, which means either that the error is very old or that the extant witnesses only represent a small part of the textual tradition. The second is more likely.

The same comment on the textual history applies to the corruption in 59.

86-88 If the emission can be explained away as due to one of these causes, it only counts as an emission of semen.

87 The words 'of the nature of the discharge' show that the criterion of the appearance of the emission is over-ruled by the criterion of the circumstances of the omission: even an emission of abnormal appearance can be counted as just an emission of semen if the circumstances allow it to be explained away. This is in agreement with the Rabbanite halachah (see above, on 81-93).

88 Note that immersion is not required.

88 Recovery is at sunset.

88 This is the end of the sub-section starting at 81. The line in the translation separating the two sub-sections has been put in for clarity. Compare the explicit division in the Kâfi, ch. XI, 18.

90 These are the causes listed in 81-88.

93-94 Compare T 118-120; Kf 19-20; Kh 7; Kâsh ch. XV, 23-25.

We are not told why the emission has to occur on two consecutive days to be counted as discharge, but the answer can probably be found in the Jewish halachah.

The Rabbanite position in outline is that one emission is counted as an emission of semen regardless of its circumstances, but a second emission, on the same day or the next day, if it can not be explained away by special circumstances, is counted as the second discharge, not the first; and a third emission on the same day as the second or the day after, unless it can be explained away by special and abnormal circumstances, is counted as the third discharge, not the second, and requires the man affected to offer a sacrifice at the end of his cleansing. If the flow is continuous, if it lasts for a period long enough for a person to immerse themself, and then dry themself, it is counted as two occurrences, and if it lasts long enough for this to be done twice, it counts as three occurrences. (For the details, see Meḥussere Kapparah II).

The Karaite position is that any emission of an abnormal substance without sexual excitement and without squirting (see the note on 81-93) is enough to put a man in the state of having a discharge, and any man in this state has to offer a sacrifice at the end of his cleansing. (For the details, see Adderet Eliyahu 102b; Gan ʿEden 108c).

We can assume that the Ṭubâkh agrees with the Rabbanites that the first emission is counted as just an emission of semen no matter what, and that a second emission not classifiable as semen is needed to put the man in the state of having a discharge. The Ṭubâkh disagrees with the Rabbanite halachah in not counting a recurrence on the same day as a second emission, disagrees with it in not counting a continuous flow on one day as the equivalent of a recurrence of the emission, but partly agrees with it that a continuous flow can be the equivalent of a recurrence, under the right conditions.

The Kâfi (19-23) and the Kâshif (23-25) could agree with the Karaites that a single emission is enough to put the man in the state of having a discharge, but the Khilâf (6-7) agrees with the Ṭubâkh, at least in principle.

100-101 The translation of Nu V:2-3 given here depends on the philological analysis of these verses in the Kâshif al-Ghayâhib. The Jews take ࠅࠊࠋ ࠈࠌࠀ ࠋࠍࠐࠔ to be another item on the list, of the same order as ࠊࠋ ࠑࠓࠅࠏ or ࠊࠋ ࠆࠁ, take it to be a single phrase, and take it to mean 'and anyone unclean due to contact with a corpse' (see the standard commentators). The Kâshif al-Ghayâhib takes ࠅࠊࠋ ࠈࠌࠀ to be an inclusive generalisation, meaning 'and any unclean person', and takes ࠋࠍࠐࠔ to be a separate expression in apposition, meaning 'any individual'. See the Kâshif al-Ghayâhib on this verse, pp. 244b-245a. It follows that the word ࠋࠍࠐࠔ naturally belongs with ࠌࠆࠊࠓ ࠏࠃ ࠍࠒࠁࠄ at the start of the next verse, and this is precisely what we find in the Kâshif al-Ghayâhib on these verses: when they are quoted, the words ࠋࠍࠐࠔ ࠌࠆࠊࠓ ࠏࠃ ࠍࠒࠁࠄ are treated as a unit, and the next verse is treated as starting at the word ࠋࠍࠐࠔ.

On the other hand, the Samaritans do know the other interpretation. This is shown by the received Samaritan verse-division here, which is the same as the Jewish one; by the translation of the expression ࠅࠊࠋ ࠈࠌࠀ ࠋࠍࠐࠔ as *wa-kull mutanajjis li-mayyit* in the later Arabic version (the earlier Arabic version and the Targum are too literal to be conclusive); and by the use of the term ࠔࠊࠁࠕ ࠆࠓࠏ as a unit, which is known at least to the author of the Khilâf (see the short quotation in the note on the Additional Passage from the Khilâf, line 1).

My reason for translating the verse in agreement with the interpretation of the Kâshif al-Ghayâhib is that the Ṭubâkh and Kâfi do not use the term ࠔࠊࠁࠕ ࠆࠓࠏ (on their terminology see the note on Kf ch. XIII, 11-13), which probably means that their authors separated these two words in their interpretation of the syntax of these two verses. Notice that in the parallel passage, in Kf ch. XI, 23-24, although Mss. JD do not take the quotation far enough to show the syntactic analysis, most of the mss. do, and end the quotation on the word ࠔࠊࠁࠕ, showing the same division and interpretation as I have assumed for the translation here.

101 'Depigmentation' is a literal translation of the Greek *lepra*, which renders ࠑࠓࠏࠕ. Unfortunately the word 'leprosy' is no longer available for use because of its application in modern times to a disease of the nerve endings, completely unrelated to this. The ࠑࠓࠏࠕ no longer occurs.

As the belief in the greater reality of words over facts is still strong enough to make some people, including scholars, imagine that a phenomenon that is called 'leprosy' in translations of the Torah must therefore be identical with a completely separate disease called 'leprosy' in common modern usage, I have felt obliged to find another term. On the nature of this depigmentation and its associated symptoms, see the Mishneh Torah in the relevant chapters, or Mishnah Tosefta and Gemara Nega'im, or the Sifra, or the relevant chapters of the Kâfi or Khilâf, or any Jewish commentary on Leviticus, or the Samaritan commentary on Leviticus, or any other traditional source. The traditional sources are transparently clear, and speculation is pointless.

103-106 We see from this passage that the Samaritans, like the Karaites, treat the ࠌࠅࠔࠁ, the ࠌࠔࠊࠁ, and the ࠌࠓࠊࠁ identically, unlike the Rabbanites, who treat the ࠌࠅࠔࠁ and ࠌࠔࠊࠁ identically but make some minor differentiations for the ࠌࠓࠊࠁ. Compare Kf 25-27; Far 42-48; 107-110; Kâsh ch. XV, 26-27; 107-112; Sharḥ Sûrat al-Irbot; and the second marginal note on the Khilâf.

103 How can a place become unclean and a source of contamination? There are two possible explanations. The first is that the author of the Ṭubâkh agrees with the author of the Kâfi (Kf ch. XII, 23-24 and the notes there) that ground can be contaminated by a corpse having passed over it or by childbirth or *niddå* having occurred there, and extends this idea to cover ground where the man in the state of *zåb* has been. This explanation is very unlikely, because the Ṭubâkh does not mention anything about this in regard to a corpse or the event of childbirth or event of *niddå*; besides which, even the Kâfi, which does mention these, by implication excludes the *zåb*, when it considers the case of ground made unclean by stuff having soaked into it, without mentioning the case of the man having walked over it. The second answer is that the author of the Ṭubâkh is thinking of the possibility of some of the stuff having dripped into the ground, so that anyone that treads there will be contaminated. This second explanation is much more likely to be the right one. Compare the next note. Notice the variant reading, which might be original.

104 This is a major disagreement between the author of the Ṭubâkh, on the one hand, and the Rabbanites and Karaites, on the other hand. According to both the Rabbanites and the Karaites, only people, food, and artefacts can be contaminated by a *zåb* or any other unclean person, no animal can both receive and transmit contamination, and no live animal can transmit uncleanness. The other Samaritan sources omit the mention of the animal in the same context and probably agree with the Jews on this matter (Kâfi 25-27; Kâshif 34-35). A plausible explanation would be that the author of the Ṭubâkh considers the animal to be unclean because it might have got some of the *zåb* stuff on, and to be a source of contamination because some of this stuff could then be touched by another person. I am inclined to think that this is the real explanation. Compare the previous note.

107 On the details of contamination of ground by spit, compare Kf ch. XII, 23-24 and 29-30; and compare Kf ch. XI, 28-30.

108-109 For the explanation of how this verse can be taken to refer to artefacts and not just people, see Kf 28-30. It will then become clear why the word *baṭṭå'or* has been quoted in the translation, and why it has been translated as 'on anyone or anything clean'.

107 Both غسل and حميم are washing in this context. The غسل is to remove the contaminating substance: the حميم is to restore the state of cleanness. See the note on T 55-57, and see Kf ch. XII, 8-12.

110-117 This interpretation of Lv XV:11 is quite different to the Jewish interpretation. The Karaites take 'his hands' to refer to the whole body, and the Rabbanites take it to refer to the whole body aside from the parts not normally visible. The Rabbanites take the words 'everything the man with the discharge touches' to refer to היסט rather than direct touching, and say that this means that the היסט done by the *zåb* only causes contamination if done by holding the instrument of the היסט externally, not in the בית הקמטים or בית הסתרים (as opposed to the related sources of contamination *niddå* etc.) and take the words 'without having rinsed his hands with water' to mean that the immersion after which he no longer causes contamination does not have to include בית הקמטים, as opposed to the *niddå* etc. (The בית הסתרים does not come into the question for any of these, *zåb* or *niddå*). The Karaites take the first half of the sentence to refer to ordinary touching, since like the Samaritans, they do not distinguish between היסט and carrying, and take the verse to mean that the *zåb* does not cause uncleanness after he had washed himself. The Rabbanites would agree with the Karaites that the *zåb* does not cause uncleanness after immersing himself, and that the verse has this meaning. See Issure Bi'ah VIII:5 and Mikva'ot I:10; Adderet Eliyahu 120d top; Gan 'Eden 108d top.

The Ṭubâkh takes the expression 'his hands' literally, and says that the verse means that as long as the contaminating substance is on the man's hands, anything he touches will be contaminated for a day due to contact with it. It was necessary for this to be stated, not to show that the man causes contamination in this way, which would be obvious anyway, but to explain that the substance of the discharge, which causes the person from whom it issues seven days' uncleanness (really seven plus one) only causes anyone else that it touches one day's uncleanness, which would not have been expected (see Kf 88-89 and the comments there), and therefore had to be specifically stated.

The same interpretation is given in the Marginal Notes, III, IV, V; Kâsh 38-46. In the Marginal Notes, IV and V, the Ṭubâkh is quoted directly. Two alternative explanations, along with this one, are given in Kf ch. XI, 33-40.

If the substance of the discharge only causes one day's uncleanness to artefacts or other people, it follows that contact with the man with the discharge himself while he is still discharging only causes one day's uncleanness. See the notes on Kf ch. XI, 88-89 and ch. III, 41-42. Nevertheless, the level of contamination is the same as for touching a *niddå* and the requirements for cleansing are the same.

112 Ms. O stands against all the rest of the mss., but is correct, as can be seen from the context.

114-117 Quoted in the Marginal Notes, V:4-7, and expanded. The readings of the quotation are given in the apparatus to the Ṭubâkh.

115-116 This passage is an excellent example of the need to use as many mss. as possible to remove errors. In 115-116 mss. LP_2C_1SGF have the correct text, the quotation in the marginal note has an omission by homoioteleuton, and $OP_1M_1M_2P_3$ have the same omission by homoioteleuton, which they unsuccessfully compensate for by inserting ان يطها ويعد. Mss. C_2KD adjust this secondary reading by deleting ويعد. Ms. N adjusts the reading of Mss. $OP_1M_1M_2P_3$ against the reading of Mss. LP_2C_1SGF by conflating as ان يطها لانه قال عنها ان صاحبها يعد. In 116 mss. P_2C_1G have an omission by homoioteleuton. The only mss. correct for the whole passage are LSF.

115 The reading of mss. C_2KD is a corruption of *aʿni ʿayn.*

118-120 Compare T 93-94; Kf 19-20; Kh 7; Kâsh ch. XV, 23-25.

124 There is no obvious reason why the chapter should be ended off this way: some other chapters end this way, but most don't. Perhaps this marks the end of a long section, corresponding to all or part of this chapter, borrowed from another work.

TEXT 2

Kitâb al-Kâfî

Chapter XI

1 The term جوهري "intrinsic" refers to uncleanness caused by some phenomenon in the person affected, as opposed to uncleanness caused by contamination from some unclean person or thing. See Kf ch. III and ch. XIII, 2-3 TN, and compare T III:11-13 N and Kf ch. XI, 88-89 in particular.

2-42 For general information on the *zåb* and emission of semen compare Kf ch. III, 8-27; 39-42; T 79-124; Kh 6-9; the Additional Passage from the Khilâf; Kâsh ch. XV, 5-9; 82-100; M.N. III, IV, V, VIII.

On the structure of this section, see T 81 N and 81-93 N.

3-17 This is a description and classification of all the phenomena that can be classed as an emission of semen, as opposed to the *zåb* in the strict sense and as opposed to phenomena that have no halachic consequences at all.

The antecedent of the word منه 'of this' in 3 is to be understood as 'phenomena that count as an emission of semen'. It is therefore quite possible that the place of this section in its source was in a chapter on the emission of semen. The logical division of the chapter is accordingly: Part I: Emission of Semen (up to 17); Part II: Discharge [*zåb*] (18 onwards). The section on the emission of semen stands here in its own right and is not just an explanation of which phenomena are not to be counted as *zåb.*

The Ṭubâkh, on the other hand, treats the corresponding section (T 81-88) as only an introduction to the section on the *zåb* (T 89 onwards). This is done by the use of the heading *faṣl* in 81 (see the note on this) and by the re-wording of 82 as compared to Kf 3 so that the term *zåb* is no longer applied to a category of seminal discharge, but exclusively to the *zåb* in the technical or specialised sense.

The Kâfi has partly turned the section on the emission of semen into an introduction to the section on the *zab* in the strict sense by not giving any special heading to the section on the emission of semen, but it has not taken the process as far as the Ṭubâkh has.

As the Ṭubâkh is known to be earlier than the Kâfi, the two of them must depend on a common source here.

3 The context here and in the Ṭubâkh shows that although this emission is called *zåb* it is not *zåb* in the strict sense of an abnormal discharge, but is an emission of semen in special circumstances. The Ṭubâkh (82) is correct (but not necessarily original: see Kf 3-17 N) in wording this as 'of the nature of *zåb* that is not *zåb*'. The context here and in the Ṭubâkh shows that these phenomena on urinating count as an emission of semen, not discharge in the strict sense.

The reading *ism* [category known by a certain technical name] is probably correct. What we have here is the name of a certain type of discharge of semen, called *zåb*, but having nothing to do with the *zåb* in the strict sense described in 18 onwards. The reading *qism* [category] of Mss. JDB is probably secondary, due to the influence of the same word in Kf 5 and 7. The *zåb* is the only category of emission of semen given a name of its own here, so the reading *ism* is appropriate in this case but not in 5 and 7. The change of reading here in Kf 3 in the mss., and the more extensive change in T 82 indicates that the use of the term *zåb* for this category of emission of semen died out, probably due to the possibility of confusion. As the change in the Kâfi occurs in the oldest witnesses, JD, and as the Ṭubâkh, which has the reading *qism*, was compiled before the Kâfi, the term must have become obsolete very early.

The opposite change, the replacement of *aqsâm* by *asâmi*, occurs in a sub-group of mss. in ch. III, 7.

4 The phrase او الصابون 'or soap' is not in the corresponding passage, T 84. Nevertheless, it is well attested in the mss. of the Kâfi and is probably original in the Kâfi. It is attested in J and S_1, which represent different early branches of the textual tradition. It has probably been omitted in $DN_1L_1S_2F_1GF_2$ because of its clumsiness; the addition of the word نفسه in $S_1^3W^2L_2L_3A$ (which represent a late branch of the tradition) could be due to a need felt to smooth out the reading.

The clumsiness of the phrase او الصابون and its absence in the Ṭubâkh might mean it is an addition made by the author of the Kâfi, and was not present in his source. There are other instances of clumsy expression in the Kâfi, some of which are listed in Kf 31 N.

4 The reading ريال of the majority of the mss., as against the reading of JD, is confirmed by ch. III, 18.

5 The form *ḥalâl* or *ḥilâl* is not found in the dictionaries, but the forms *iḥlîl*, *iḥlâl*, and *ḥalîl* are. Although the basic meaning of *iḥlîl* is an orifice of any kind, it is used in Arabic of this period to refer specifically to the orifice of the penis and then to the penis itself (see Dozy, and Saadya's translation of Lv XII:3 and XV:3) and *ḥalâl* or *ḥilâl* is used in the same transferred meaning here.

The readings *al-khalâl* (the interval, rupture, fissure) and *inḥilâl* (disintegration) are impossible, and are probably due to failure to recognize the form *ḥalâl*, instead of the more usual *iḥlîl* or *iḥlâl*. It is easy to see how الحلال can become الخلال or انحلال.

6-8 Although the discharge is abnormal and occurs in abnormal circumstances, if it can be explained away as an emission of semen caused by some physical strain or temporary physiological disturbance, it can be treated as such. Compare T 86-88.

9 The dividing line after 8 in the translation is meant to mark the division indicated by the heading *faṣl* here. As remarked in T 81 N, the Kâfi uses the heading *faṣl* [subsection] to mark a sub-section within the chapter, without necessarily implying that a new major section is being introduced.

9-17 This passage seems to have been taken from a section in another work on contamination due to a discharge of semen. For the evidence, see Kf ch. XI, 12 N.

There is a direct reference to this passage in Kâsh ch. XV, 99-100, and the section 82-98 in the Kâshif depends on it.

10-15 This section is duplicated with some slight alterations in wording in Kf ch. III, 16-21.

10 A division of the stream might be caused by the presence of a small amount of semen, or more likely, seminal fluid.

10 Inflammation of the prostate gland causes a peculiar feeling somewhere between burning, aching, and stinging, which, because of the linkage of the nerves, is felt inside the urethra, just behind the point where the underside of the glans joins the shaft. Stinging on urination is often a symptom of an unhealthy prostate gland, and an unhealthy prostate gland — specially one that has not been getting enough exercise and is too full — is likely to discharge seminal fluid at any time, which will then be carried out by the urine. A stinging feeling on urinating could therefore be an indication that some seminal fluid has been emitted, and the man should check to see if this is the case. On the other hand, stinging can be caused by a small lesion, or there can be some other cause such as those mentioned in Kf 13, in which case the man would not be unclean.

11-12 If he did not have a look before starting to urinate, he can do so after he finishes, and if there is no sign of contaminating matter then, he can regard himself as clean. In other words, the checking can equally well be done before or after the urination.

12 These categories are the ones mentioned in Kf 3-4. What is meant is that the stinging or obstruction need not be due to the presence of semen, the signs of which are described in 3-4, and it seems from 12-13 that the primary purpose of the passage 3-17 or its source is to show which phenomena can be identified as an emission of semen. The passage 16-17 is in place in a discussion of the emission of semen, but seems tacked on in a discussion of the discharge and its identification. The same conclusion is indicated by the layout of the corresponding passage Kf ch. III, 16-21.

Compare Kf ch. XI, 3-17 N.

15 Urine does not cause uncleanness, but cleanliness in the physical sense is required when performing the set prayers. Judaism has similar usages. The Samaritan usage in this matter is more detailed, and resembles the corresponding Moslem practice. For the details, see Kâsh ch. XV, 98 N (both notes).

16-17 Compare Kf ch. III, 8-9.

17 This is the washing of the whole body, as in Karaite practice.

18-22 See T 81-93 N.

19 We are not told how many times the issue has to recur to be counted as *zåb*, but the Ṭubâkh (93-94 and 118-120) specifies two consecutive days. The Khilâf (6-7) says that repetition is required but does not say how many times. The Kâshif (ch. XV, 23-25) is very vague.

The necessity of recurrence as a precondition has important consequences in the case of a person who comes in contact with the substance of the discharge: see T 100-117 and Kf 39-40 in the light of Kf ch. XI, 88-89 and ch. III, 41-42 N.

The question arises as to how an emission of substance of the recognisable type of the discharge but occurring for just one day is classified. We may assume that the Samaritans, like the Rabbanites, count it as an emission of semen. (This is explained in Kf ch. XI, 88-89 N. The Rabbanite position is set out in Meḥussere Kapparah II:6 and the context; the question does not arise for the Karaites, since they count an emission of a certain type clearly distinguishable from semen as *zåb* from the first time it appears).

23 Instead of *al-aṭhār* [clean people], Mss. F_1GF_2 read *aṭ-ṭahārah* [cleanness, and by implication things in a state of cleanness]. It is uncertain whether this is only a variant of style or is meant to indicate that exclusion from the settlement is unnecessary.

23-24 One Samaritan interpretation of [Samaritan] [Samaritan] and [Samaritan] in v. 2 makes it possible for these verses to refer to people contaminated in any way whatever: see T 100-101 N.

24 See T 101 N.

25-27 Compare T 103-106.

This passage might be taken to indicate that the Samaritans, unlike the Jews, do not put the couch, seat, and saddle contaminated by the *zåb* in a special category as opposed to other artefacts; and the same would then apply by analogy in the case of contamination by the *niddå* and *zåbå*. This is not quite true. The Samaritans do differentiate, but only to the extent that the Karaites do, which means that in many situations there will be no difference in practice. The details are given in the Additional Passage from the Khilâf, 1-10 N. It will become clear from the information given there that the remark made by the author of the Kâfi, that the bedclothes are contaminated, without any qualification to the statement, is indirect proof that the Samaritans do make the distinction.

28-30 Compare 107-109.

This rather obscure line of argument can be understood by reference to Rashi's commentary, taken with the note in the Sifte Ḥachamim. The word ࠁࠈࠄࠅࠓ can be taken to mean [Samaritan] [Samaritan] [Samaritan], i.e. any artefact that the clean person might be holding is contaminated by contact with the spit, and contaminates the person carrying it or touching it. The verse says clearly that any clean person is contaminated by contact with the spit, and it follows that any artefact will be contaminated by contact with it. The point that Rashi is making is that an artefact contaminated in this way becomes ראשון לטומאה and contaminates people by contact or by being lifted. It will be seen that this interpretation of the word ࠁࠈࠄࠅࠓ as referring to artefacts is not needed for its own sake, but only to show that the artefact then contaminates other things and people. This conclusion is not mentioned in the text and the interpretation becomes a bit pointless. It is possible that the interpretation is borrowed from another work where it appeared in the context of the question of subsequent contamination by the artefact.

28 The contamination of the ground is due to the continuing presence of the contaminating substance. The contamination of an artefact can be due to the presence of the contaminating substance, but even if it does not absorb any of the stuff, or if the stuff is washed out, it is still unclean by having previously come in contact with the stuff, and requires purification just as a person would.

On the contamination of ground, see Kf ch. XII, 22-24 and 29-30; Ṭubâkh 107.

30 The spit only causes contamination to people or artefacts when it is wet, not when it is dry (but of course the person or artefact remains unclean even after the spit has dried up or been washed off). The author is presumably using the standard Jewish argument that as the text says specifically 'if he spits on anyone clean' and not simply 'if his spit touches anyone clean' or 'if anyone clean touches his spit', the spit must have to still be wet. This analysis is confirmed by the addition of the words 'and is wetted by it' in the author's comment. Compare Mishkav Umoshav II:1; G.E. 108d line 14 onwards; A.E. 120d middle. (There is an error due to homoioteleuton in line 14 of the Gan ʿEden: read הזוב מטמא בהיותו לח ויבש והרוק אינו מטמא אלא בהיותו יבש שהרי...).

Both Karaites and Rabbanites maintain that the semen of a man in the state of *zåb*, and the actual substance of his discharge, have the same contaminating effect as his spit, and that all three of these have to be wet to contaminate people or artefacts. It is very likely that the Samaritans agree with this.

The rules for the contamination of ground by these substances are different. The ground is contaminated not by the substance having touched it previously, but by the continuing presence of the substance, which continues to have its effect even after it has dried up. The explanation and details of this are given in the notes on Kâfi ch. XII, lines 23-24.

31-32 Why a new item? The answer is that an artefact that has not become the possession of an Israelite for personal use, and has not been used by an Israelite, can not acquire uncleanness, and these conditions will usually apply if the item is new. This rule is in perfect analogy with the two principles, on which Jews and Samaritans agree, that materials or stuff are not capable of becoming unclean till they have been made into an artefact ready for use, and that only Israelites can contaminate or be contaminated. (With the single exception that the corpse of a non-Israelite causes contamination. It is true that the Jewish halachah treats non-Israelites as unclean, but this is a regulation מדרבנן. The principle is well-known. See Tum'at Met I:12-14). If we put these two principles together the rule explained above logically follows.

For proof of the existence of this rule in the Samaritan halachah, consider the following two passages.

The first is a fatwâ by the High Priest Ya'qûb bin Hârûn in ms. Sam. 8° 6 of the Jewish National Library, pp. 56-57.

ما قولكم في امراه ࠔࠌࠓࠉࠄ في ࠄࠍࠃࠄ وقع منها حاجه مثل هدم او غيره في بيت رجل ࠔࠌࠓࠉ او حاجه عماله تشتغل بها لرجل ࠔࠌࠓࠉ وهي في ࠄࠍࠃࠄ فهل يجوز هذه الحاجه او الهدم بان تباع لاحد براني عن ࠀࠋࠃࠀ لاجل تطهر المحل الواقعه فيه ام لا او يحكم على كانت اواني البيت بالنجس او كيف الحاله والله اعلم.

الجواب

اذا كان الهدم جديد وليسه ملبوس يترك ويباع للغير او يوهب لاحد المستحقين من الغير وانما اذا كان هدم او اي شي منتفع به ووقع من ࠀࠋࠈࠌࠀ على الطاهر ينجس لا محاله حسب النص الشريف وهو قوله ࠊࠋ ࠀࠔࠓ ࠉࠂࠏ ࠁࠅ ࠄࠈࠌࠀ ࠉࠈࠌࠀ يعني الداني والساقط من ࠀࠋࠈࠌࠀ للطاهر ينجس ولا شك وانما الاله الذي لم صار استعمالها ولا صارة معده وجرا ذلك المجرا فلا ࠀࠈࠌࠀ والله املم. كيتها خضر اسحق. امين.

'In regard to your question about a Samaritan woman in *niddå* by whom an article such as a garment, or anything else, in a Samaritan's house is stained, or a commissioned article made by her for a Samaritan man when she is in *niddå*, whether or no it is possible for the item or garment to be sold to some foreigner outside the religion so that the place affected can be made clean, or whether the artefacts in the house are to be declared contaminated, or whatever the position might be. God knows.

The answer:

If the garment is new and has not been worn it can be got rid of and sold to an outsider or given to some needy outsider. If, however, the garment or whatever has been used, and something from the unclean person [ࠈࠌࠀ *ṭēmi*] falls on the clean thing, it definitely becomes unclean, as it says: 'Anything the unclean person touches is contaminated' (Nu XIX:22), i.e. a clean thing touched or overshadowed by the unclean person [ࠈࠌࠀ *ṭēmi*] must be contaminated. On the other hand, an artefact not yet used or assigned to anyone to which this happens does not become unclean. God knows best. Thus Khiḍr Isḥâq, may he be forgiven. Amen.'

The second passage is in ch. XIII of the Kâfi, Ms. J p. 98, Ms. S_1 p. 153, Ms. L_1 p. 140a. It is partly translated by Noja, pp. 84-85. The text is given here according to J, with the variants of S_1. Ms. D is not extant here.

قال الشيخ

اذا سافر انسان من اهل الله بتجارة قماش ثم سلك في طريقه في ارض بها قبور فهل يلزم القماش حكم ناطر ام لا.

الجواب

اما في زماننا هذا فلا يلزم حكم الناطر الا له وقماشه الملبوس وانيته واما قماش التجاره فلا يوجب عليه حكم ناطر وكذلك جميع ما يعمله غير اهل الدين ومما يعملوه اهل الدين ايضا مثل المعمول من الحرير الذي اذا حكم عليه بذلك وعمل فيه حكم الناطر فسد والله ما يكلف ما هذا صفته.

قال

فان اخذ انسان من الامه في البلاد الناطره شقه جديده مما تقدم ذكره وفعلها وخيطها غير ملي وخيطها بخيوط مناسبه لها ثم حضر بها الى البلاد الطاهره فهل يلزم ذلك القماش حكم ناطر ام لا.

الجواب

اذا كان بالصفه المذكوره فلا يلزم حكم ناطر واصحابنا في جميع البلاد معتمدي ذلك وهو انه اذا كان القماش الملبوش لم لبس ولا استعمل بعد فلا يتكلفوا فيه حكم الناطر ومتى استعمل ولو ايام قلايل فيلتزموا منه فان قال قايلا الجميع يلزمه الحكم واستدل بنوبة [Samaritan script] وقوله تعالى [Samaritan script] وتمام القول [Samaritan script] [Samaritan script] (تع ١٣ : ٢٠–٢٣)

معنى ذلك مما حكم عليه بالطما وعبور [Samaritan] عليه ان المقول في ذلك عايد الى ما كان معهم من الاتهم وموجودهم وقماشهم فامرهم بقوله [Samaritan] [Samaritan] وتمامه (ايه ١٩) ولا يعود شي من ذلك الى ما كسبوه من [Samaritan] اذ لا يجوز عبور [Samaritan] على ما لا هو لاسرايل والدليل على صحة ذلك قوله [Samaritan] فان [Samaritan] ولا يجوز لهم اخذه من [Samaritan] ولا استعماله فكيف يعبر عليه [Samaritan] واما ما اخذوه من القماش فليس وجب عليه في ذلك الوقت قبل دخولهم في استعمالهم الذي به دخل تحت [Samaritan] شي من ذلك.

[Samaritan] S_1
يوجب] [Samaritan] S_1
[Samaritan] S_1] > J
١٠- اهل الدين ايضا] [Samaritan] S_1 [Samaritan] S_1] من × J
١ والله] + [Samaritan] S_1 [Samaritan] S_1
١ [Samaritan] S_1
٢ في جميع] [Samaritan] S_1
٢ ذلك] + [Samaritan] S_1*
٢ وهو انه] وهو S_1^2 ؛ > S_1*
٢ الملبوس] [Samaritan] S_1 لم] ثم × J   لبس] [Samaritan] × S_1 استعمل]
[Samaritan] S_1
٢ منه] [Samaritan] S_1
٢-٣٣ [Samaritan] (ثاني) .... [Samaritan]] وتمامه J*
٢ القول] [Samaritan] S_1^2
٣ عليه] > S_1 ان] → [Samaritan] S_1 المقول] [Samaritan] S_1
٤ يعبر] [Samaritan] × S_1 اخذه J
٤ دخولهم] دخوله S_1

Having established this rule, we can now see the point of the mention of a new artefact in 31-32. A new artefact would not be affected by being touched by the man because it can not become unclean itself, but if the *zåb* stuff or some of the man's spit gets on it it is unclean till the stuff or the spit is washed out. If this had not been specifically stated, it might have been thought that a new artefact's immunity to contamination even applied if it had absorbed some contaminating stuff, which is not the case. The artefact can still be the vehicle of the stuff.

We are now in a position to understand why it was that some Dositheans, the followers of Sakta, allowed the acquisition of artefacts made by non-Israelites. The relevant passage is Abu 'l-Fatḥ 162:1-3.

Ms. A reads:

واما جميع الاواني التى يستعملوها والثياب التي يلبسوها وسائر الاقمشه الذي يكون اصله شغل الامم
ليس شغل اسرائل لا يطمي.

(Vilmar puts a hamzah on the last letter of the last word but this is not in the ms., and is against normal usage). 'But any artefacts used by them [i.e. the Gentiles] or clothes worn by them, and any kind of clothing made by Gentiles, not Israel, do not become unclean'.

Scanlon's translation of this passage (p. 81) is similar though not identical. The meaning is not substantially affected. Bowman's translation (p. 171) does not agree with the Arabic, nor does it make sense. It reads:

'As for all the pearls which they used, and the clothing which they wore, and the rest of the fine garments which are the root cause of it, it is the business of the Gentiles, not the business of Israel; it does not make unclean'.

Mss. BCD read as follows (correcting the obviously corrupt readings والراي in BD and والداني in C to والاواني):

... والاواني من الامم مثل القراطيس والورق ....

'... and stuff manufactured by Gentiles, such as parchment or paper ...'

Some mss. not available to Vilmar have والذي as the first word, which could be correct, but is more likely to be a secondary correction. Some of the text has been lost, but if we compare this with the text of Ms. A, the meaning is clear.

To understand why items made by Gentiles or used by Gentiles might be thought to be automatically unclean, we must suppose that the Samaritans at this time maintained that Gentiles are to treated as unclean, even though the halachah of uncleanness strictly only applies to Israel. (In Jewish terminology, they are unclean מדרבנן, but not מדאורייתא).

For evidence of this position in Samaritanism, consider the following passage from ch. XIII of the Kâfi, Ms. J p. 97, Ms. S_1 p. 152, Ms. L_1 p. 139b. The text is quoted here according to Mss. JS_1L_1.

ࠄࠏࠓࠋࠉࠌ من حيث سقوط التكاليف الشرعيه عندهم يجب الاحتراز منهم مع عدم امكان الحكم
عليهم فاجريوا الضروره مجرى ࠄࠔࠒࠑ او ࠄࠁࠄࠌࠄ ࠄࠈࠌࠀࠄ.

(Ms. J adds يخلص after the first word, but this is an error due to the presence of this form just before). 'Gentiles, because the commandments of the Torah do not apply to them, have to be treated with care, in spite of the impossibility of the law ever affecting them, so they are treated the same as an animal not to be eaten [ࠔࠒࠑ *ashqəṣ*] or an unclean animal'.

Noja's translation (p. 84) differs.

The author of the Farâ'iḍ, in the last extant chapter, chapter CV, on the Red Heifer, mentions with hesitation but approval on opinion he has heard that Gentiles are to be treated as corpses. The passage is in Ms. Sassoon 719, p. 135-136; Ms. Samaritan 172 of the John Rylands Library, pp. 135-136, just after the start of the chapter. The passage reads as follows in both mss.:

قال بعضهم كما جاز ان يتنجس من موتي ࠄࠏࠓࠋࠉࠌ جاز ان يتنجس من الاحيا ولعمري هو جايز
من العقول ويفتقر ببيانه الى الشرع ولا يكفي هذا الذي ذكره في الدلاله عليه فيجب الرجوع الى غيره.

'Someone has said that as it is possible to be contaminated by corpses of Gentiles, it must be possible to be contaminated by live ones. This is definitely logical, but it will take demonstration from Scripture. His argument is not conclusive, and needs some support from outside'.

This idea must lie behind the treatment of Gentiles as contaminating ground, since only a corpse can contaminate ground just by passing over it, without any substance being deposited on the ground. See ch. XII, 23-24 TN; 23 N; 29-30. (We may compare the concept in Judaism that a new convert has passed from death into life, and is a new person. Compare Issure Bi'ah XIV:11).

Purification of ground after the passage of non-Israelites over it, and the treatment of them as being permanently contaminated and a source of contamination, is well attested in the Roman and Byzantine period. The Arabic Book of Joshua (ch. 47 end in Juynboll's edition) refers to this practice. Montgomery (p. 319) quotes a report by a Christian pilgrim of the sixth century (about 570 according to Wilkinson) to the same effect. The passage is quoted here in full from Wilkinson's edition, p. 81:

'From there we went up past a number of places belonging to Samaria and Judea to the city of Sebaste, the resting place of the prophet Elisha. There were several Samaritan cities and villages on our way down through the plains, and wherever we passed along the streets they burnt away our footprints with straw whether we were Christians or Jews, they have such a horror of both. This is what they tell Christians: "Don't touch what you want to buy until you have paid the money. If you touch anything without buying it there will soon be trouble". Outside each village there is a guard to give the warning. You must put your money into water since they will not take it from your hand. When you arrive they curse you. Nor must you spit. If you do, you start trouble, and later they have to purify themselves with water before entering the village or city'.

The Samaritan opinion that contact with a non-Israelite causes contamination is well-documented in Moslem sources. The matter is discussed, and references given, by Goldziher, *Lā Misāsa*; Heller, *Al-Sāmirī*; Geiger, *Was hat Mohammed aus dem Judenthume aufgenommen*?, pp. 162-164. Unfortunately, most of the sources do not make it clear whether all Samaritans hold this opinion, or only one group do. The Koran, in an impossibly anachronistic legend, makes a Samaritan the instigator of the making of the Golden Calf (Mohammed probably confused the Golden Calf with Jeroboam's two calves, but even then, the story is impossible), and says that his punishment for this was that forever after he had to avoid contact with other people by calling out 'Lâ misâsa' [No touching!] (Koran XX:85-97). The commentators Aṭ-Ṭabarî and Az-Zamakhsharî explain that this is the reason for the avoidance by the Samaritans of social contact with all non-Israelites. The assumption seems to be that the practice is universal, but as they do not distinguish between social and physical contact, and do not mention the question of contamination, this is not very helpful. Ath-Thaʿlabî gives much the same information. Al-Makrîzî (died 1442) says that he has heard it reported that the Samaritans are the same people as those who say *lâ misâsa*, but this information does not add to what is said by the commentators on the Koran. (Silvestre de Sacy, *Chrestomathie*, vol. I, p. 113 Arabic and p. 305 French). He then reports in the name of Al-Bîrûnî (5th c. H) that the Samaritans (apparently all Samaritans) are known by the collective name of 'Al-Lâ-Misâsîyah' [the no-touchings], but no explanation of the name is given. Later, (p. 114 Arabic, p. 305 French), in a list of Samaritan practices, he says that they do not touch other people, and if it ever happens that they do, they wash themselves [ightasalû], but does not connect this information with what he has said previously.

More accurate information is available from a Karaite source. Dâwûd bin Marwân ar-Raqqî, known as Al-Muqammiṣ (9th c. of the Christian era), quoted in the *Eshkol*

Hakkofer, alphabet 97, p. 41c top, says that Samaritans wash themselves as they would after contact with a source of minor uncleanness if they are touched by a non-Samaritan: אף הודיע בספריו כי השומרונים ירחצו מטמאה קלה: אם יגע אחד באחד מי שאינו מדתם:

Al-Qirqisânî (Nemoy's translation p. 36) says that Al-Muqammiṣ, although temporarily a Christian, was originally a Jew, so this information should be accurate. The term טמאה קלה 'minor uncleanness' in Karaite usage means uncleanness due to an emission of semen or contact with semen. The essential characteristic of this type of uncleanness is that the person affected has to wash all over, and then becomes clean at sunset, and that he does not make his couch, seat, or saddle [משכב, מושב, מרכב] unclean by putting his weight on it (see the relevant sections of the Gan ʿEden and Adderet Eliyahu). We may conclude that these Samaritans known to the author applied the same rules to a person who had touched a non-Samaritan. Whether they equated this contact with contact with semen is another matter. It is far more likely that they equated it with contact with a *zåb* or *zåbå*, similarly to the Rabbanites. It is, however, possible that these Samaritans equated contact with a non-Israelite with contact with a [Samaritan script] or [Samaritan script], as the author of the Kâfi does. We are not told if this applies to all Samaritans. It will become clear later that it is highly probable that the followers of Sakta put the contamination at a more serious level.

We conclude with a reference which demonstrates that at least at an early period, the Dositheans agreed with all other Samaritan groups in considering non-Israelites unclean. The source is Epiphanius, *Panarion*, no. 13 (G.C.S., Leipzig 1915, ed. K. Holl. The passage is reproduced by Isser, p. 187. Also Migne, PG, vol. 41, cols. 237-238). The passage was written in the late 4th century. The author is talking about the peculiarities of the Dositheans as compared to the Samaritan Essenes, the Sebuaeans, and the Gorothenians. He makes the point that the Dositheans agree with all other Samaritan groups in the matters of circumcision, the Sabbath, considering outsiders unclean, and the observance of the festivals. (I follow Migne's translation, which seems to be accurate. Isser's (pp. 40-41) goes against the syntax). The relevant sentence reads as follows:

'hōsaútous te peritomḕn kai sábbaton kai tò mḕ thingánein tinòs dià tò bdelýttesthai pánta ánthrōpon homoíōs échousi'

Unfortunately we are not told to what extent non-Samaritans are unclean, or whether all Samaritans put non-Samaritans at the same level of impurity. Nevertheless, the information given here is very valuable in that we are reliably told that all Samaritans, Dositheans or not, treated non-Samaritans as unclean in some way or to some extent. This information confirms our interpretation of the passage in Abu 'l-Fatḥ, as will be seen.

From all this, we conclude that the most likely Samaritan opinion at the time of the Dositheans mentioned by Abu 'l-Fatḥ is that Gentiles are permanently unclean, either as corpses or as *zåb* and *zåbå*. The Dositheans would have maintained that this is true but does not matter, since any artefacts made by them are incapable of being made unclean till they have passed into the possession of an Israelite.

The modern Samaritans agree with the Dositheans that an artefact made by a non-Israelite can not be made unclean till it has passed into the possession of an Israelite. It is true that they require the artefact to be washed or heated before use, but this is just to remove contaminating stuff absorbed into the artefact, not to cleanse the artefact itself. See Kf ch. XII, 10. The reason that Sakta, as quoted by Abu 'l-Fatḥ, does not mention this is probably that he is thinking of the case of contact of the artefact with a Gentile, who is assimilated to a corpse, and the question of the absorption of stuff does not arise. This does not mean he would not have agreed that unclean stuff had to be removed. Probably his main concern was to prove that since the artefact was not contaminated by a corpse it could be washed out and made usable immediately, and would not need sprinkling with the ashes of the red heifer or take seven days to be made clean. The modern Samaritans, who do not assimilate Gentiles to corpses, are naturally more concerned with the more minor matter of the presence of contaminating stuff.

It follows from all this that Abu 'l-Fatḥ or his source disagreed with the modern halachah, and either did not allow the acquisition of artefacts from non-Israelites or at least assumed that they were contaminated and needed purification. This means that he, or his source treated non-Israelites as permanent sources of contamination, probably as *zåb* or *zåbå*.

All Samaritans, including the author of the Kâfi, would agree that artefacts that are irrevocably unclean because of the nature of the materials from which they are made must not be acquired by Israelites, so that certain classes of articles, such as anything made out of leather, must not be bought from Gentiles. See Kf ch. XII, 46-49; 52-53; 59-60.

31 The emendation in the Hebrew translation is brilliant, but unnecessary. See the notes on 31-32, and the next note.

31 The repetition of the words *aw malbûs* is too well attested in the reliable mss. to be deleted. The omission in the less reliable mss. is probably secondary, to remove a difficulty. The clothing referred to here is probably clothing that has become the property of an Israelite and has been worn by an Israelite, so that it is liable to contamination as an artefact. This is why it is referred to as just 'clothing' without any qualification. We may suppose that clothing that can be counted as clothing of an Israelite requires not only washing to remove the contaminating substance, but as well as this, immersion for purification.

The author of the Kâfi has not expressed himself well here. Exactly the same kind of obscure wording is used in line 4, and exactly the same mixture of categories is made in Kf ch. XI, 28 and ch. III, 40-42 and 43-44.

31-32 'Commanded' means stated in the text of the Torah. This includes information derived by exegesis. 'Handed down' means known by tradition. These three principles, Scripture, consensus, and tradition, are of course the three major principles used in Judaism, although this particular formulation is more Karaite than Rabbanite.

The consensus of all three marks a practice as being certainly correct. Compare Kf ch. III, 32.

33-40 There are three interpretations here. The last agrees with the Ṭubâkh (110-117). The first two are not found in the other texts edited here and are specifically rejected in the Marginal Notes, V:12-14.

Compare T 110-117 N and the cross-references there.

35-40 The first two explanations of v. 11 given here are not quite compatible with each other. The first explanation depends on taking the 'hand' to be the penis, so that the verse means that if the stuff is still on the man's penis he causes one day's uncleanness to anyone or anything he touches, but presumably if the stuff has been washed off he does not transmit uncleanness, or at least, the person or thing affected is only unclean till washing is carried out. The second explanation depends on taking the mention of the hand literally, so that the verse means that if the man gets the stuff on his hand then he causes one day's uncleanness to anyone or anything he touches, but presumably if there is none of the stuff on his hand, even if it is still on his penis, he does not contaminate anything he touches, because the uncleanness of the man is only due to the stuff, and so anything that touches some part of his body without touching the stuff is unaffected, or is only affected till washing can be carried out. The first explanation assumes a more stringent rule than the second, since according to the second one it would be possible for the stuff to still be on the man's penis without him affecting anything he touched provided his hands were clean. Both explanations assume that if the man has stopped discharging and has washed the stuff off, he does not cause a day's uncleanness to anyone or anything he touches.

The point of the comparison with the case of a man who has had an emission of semen is that in this case anything he touches before having washed himself is only contaminated till washing can be carried out and does not have to wait till sunset to become clean.

38-40 See T 110-117 N and Kf 88-89 N.

39-40 For an explanation of the apparent anomaly, see Kf 88-89 N.

39-40 The word *niddå* here refers to the blood, not the woman herself, as can be seen from the use of the masculine verb in line 39. It follows that the pronoun of *baynuh* in line 4 refers to the *zåb* stuff, not the man himself.

39 The Arabic والغروب is a bit terse, but is still clear in the context. The reading والعقله للغروب is smoother, but wrong: it is not the sequestration till sunset that makes the man clean, it is the arrival of sunset itself.

43-90 Compare T 1-78 and I'tiq 4-67, which use a similar classification. Parallels to other texts on individual points are given in the appropriate places.

The division of the content is as follows: classification and *niddå* 44-55; *dåbå* 56-60; *zåbå* 61-67; bleeding of childbirth 68-72; bleeding of cleansing 73-78; bleeding of plausibility 79-82; touching the actual stuff of the discharge 83-89; copulation with a woman known to be unclean 90.

44 and **48** For the classification, compare T 2-4 and I'tiq 4-6.

45-55 On *niddå* bleeding in general, compare T 6-11; Kh 43-116; 255-258; 262-263; Far 2-65; Kâsh ch. XV, 101-123; I'tiq 8-21; 96-110; Sharḥ Sûrat al-Irbot.

48 See 73 N.

49-55 On copulation with a woman known to be unclean see the references in T 74-78 N and T 8-10 TN. The reason for translating the verse in this way will then become clear.

49-50 See T 9-10 N; and compare Far 49-50.

56-60 On *dåba* bleeding in general compare T 12-15; Kh 117-121; 258; 262-263; I'tiq 22-23.

56-68 The connection between 56-57 and 57-58 is not explained very well, some of the steps in the proof having been left out. What is meant is this:

We know, on the one hand, that the woman is unclean for a week, which means that some of the bleeding must make her unclean for this period, and we know, on the other hand, that it does not make any difference to the degree or length of her uncleanness whether or not there is any bleeding after the initial bleeding, or however long the bleeding lasts, or whether or not it is continuous provided it is finished by the end of the seventh day. It must follow that it is only the initial bleeding that can contaminate the woman for seven days and that any bleeding after that must only be capable of contaminating her for the rest of the same day, which means in practice that its effect can be ignored, since she would already be unclean due to the first bleeding anyway. This means that the bleeding after the initial bleeding must be a separate category to the initial bleeding, and that the category of bleeding after the initial bleeding must cover any other bleeding any time right up the end of the week.

The same proof seen from a different angle is given in Kh 69-70.

56 See 73 N.

58-61 See T 13-14 N and the cross-references there.

The prescriptions for the repetition of the period of menstruation vary widely in the different sources.

As we have seen, the Ṭubâkh agrees with the Rabbanites in only allowing one period of menstruation, after which the bleeding is to be counted as *zăbå*, although the Ṭubâkh does not agree with the Rabbanites in all details. See T 16-26 N. The opinion of the Ṭubâkh is specifically rejected in Kh 63-65 and 176-177 (where it is ascribed to Anan).

The author of the Kâfi allows a second week of menstruation if bleeding occurs on the eighth day, i.e. the first day of the second week. He does not seem to allow a third period of menstruation if bleeding occurs on the fifteenth day, i.e. the first day of the third week, and in this he agrees with most Karaites. (For the details of the various Karaite positions, see A.E. 123d middle-124a bottom; G.E. all of ch. 7).

The Khilâf (165-171) allows seven periods of menstruation. This opinion is specifically rejected by the author of the Ṭubâkh (26-29) but it seems that he knows it as a Samaritan, not a Jewish, opinion.

The author of the Farâ'iḍ (84-86) allows four periods of menstruation. He knows the opinion of the author of the Ṭubâkh but rejects it (87-97).

In the Kâshif (124-128), the I'tiqâdât (32-34), and the Marginal Notes (I and II), three periods of menstruation are allowed. Other opinions are specifically rejected in the Marginal Notes. Notice that the Hebrew translation of the Kâfi alters the reading in 61 to agree with the modern halachah.

All these passages confine themselves to the case of a woman who bleeds on the first day of the week after the last possible repetition of the menstrual week.

61-67 On *zăbå* bleeding in general, compare T 16-44; Kh 165-201; 259-261; 264-266; Far 80-119; Kâsh ch. XV, 124-141; I'tiq 32-40; Sharḥ Sûrat al-Irbot; M.N. I and II.

61 See 73 N.

61 On the term تعكيس, see 74 N.

64-67 While she is still bleeding, before she starts her count of seven days without any bleeding, her degree of impurity is the same as would be caused by previous *niddå* bleeding, she is segregated in the same way as someone in this condition, and she contaminates a couch or seat in the same way as the *niddå* does. The author is probably thinking of the phrase ࠊࠋ ࠉࠌࠉ ࠆࠅࠁ ࠈࠌࠀࠕࠄ ࠊࠉࠌࠉ ࠍࠃࠕࠄ ࠕࠄࠉࠄ in v. 25. In spite of this, a special term is needed for this bleeding, because the term *niddå* refers to bleeding occurring in different circumstances and for just an instant of time. (The implication of this is that her contaminating effect on other people once she has started the count is the same as in the menstrual week at any time after the first instant of *niddå* bleeding. This is actually the case, as we see from Kh 267-269). Although she is not termed *niddå* while still bleeding, her contamination is the same as that of a woman at the instant of *niddå* and is not at the lower level of a woman undergoing *dăbå* bleeding.

We know that a person who touches a woman at the instand of *niddå*, but who does not come in contact with the blood, is only contaminated for one day, and we know that the same applies to anyone that touches a woman during the *dăbå* period. What then does the difference in level of contamination of the *zăbå* before and after she starts her count consist of, if she resembles the *niddå* in one case and the *dăbå* at the other? The natural answer to this would be that the *zăbå* blood contaminates anyone that touches it for seven days, just as the *niddå* blood does, whereas during the count the woman does not emit any blood, and therefore could not possibly contaminate anyone for more than one day. See Kf 88-89 N for the details.

The Dosithean opinion, or to be more specific, the opinion of the followers of Sakta, seems to have been that contact with the *zåbå* woman during the days of her count did not make a person unclean at all; and the corollary of this would be that contact with her while she was bleeding would cause one day's uncleanness. We do not know whether they would have regarded contact with the blood itself as causing one day's uncleanness or seven's, but considering their tendency towards leniency, it is likely that they would have agreed with the Jews that one day's uncleanness is caused (although they would have disagreed with the Jews and the other Samaritans in the matter of the effect of touching the woman during the days of the count). For the evidence, see Kh 266-267 and T 11-13 N.

The question of contamination caused by contact with the blood as opposed to contact with the woman herself is treated in a wider context in Kf 88-89 N.

66-67 A person who comes in contact with *dåbå* blood can wash it off straightaway and is only unclean till sunset: a person who comes in contact with *zåbå* blood is made unclean for seven days. See 88-89 TN.

66 The word *yuḥṣṣil* [can wash it off] is explained in T 55-57 N, where the reasons for choosing this translation are given.

68-72 For information on bleeding of childbirth in general compare the whole of the extract from ch. XIII of the Kâfi; T 45-52; Kh 202-214; Kâsh ch. XII, 2-7; 14-17; I'tiq 41-46.

68-69 See 88-89 and the cross-references there. Compare 73-76. Lv XII:2 is assumed.

68 See 73 N.

70 This reason, like most reasons produced to explain the ritual or non-moral commandments, is very unconvincing. Besides, it does not agree with the fact of the matter which is that there is no difference in the amount or quality of the blood whether the baby is a boy or a girl. The second explanation is better.

70-72 The comparison is not very enlightening. I suspect that this is an adaptation of a passage similar to Far 8-10, used here in another context and for another purpose, and that the reference to 'doubling' (*fa-yataḍâ'uf*) is ultimately based on a misunderstanding of the word *ḍu'f* (see Farâ'iḍ 10) or some form from the same root, as meaning doubling, a misunderstanding that would be very easy with the word *qūwah* [strength] just next to it.

As the passage stands, the point being made is that the blood that appears at the birth of a girl is twice as dark as the blood that appears at the birth of a boy.

72 All the mss. spell the word اجره with a final *hâ* rather than *yâ*, and it is clear from the mistranslation of it in the Hebrew as 'wages' that the translators had this spelling before them. Nevertheless, the word 'wages' is impossible here, and the word 'integrated' or 'better-integrated' fits exactly. In Arabic of this period the final vowel would have become short, as in modern Arabic, so that the spelling with *hâ*, although historically and etymologically incorrect, would still have represented the pronunciation accurately. The change of spelling is easy to make, not only because of the identity of pronunciation, but because the meaning of *ajra* does not derive very obviously from its verb *jara* or even from the absolute adjective *jâri*, and the connection would not be very strongly felt, unlike, for example, the very obvious and evident relation between the words *af'al* and *fâ'il*. The same substitution in reverse can be seen in the very frequent spelling of البته as البتا.

Whether the author spelt this word with *hâ* is not certain, but as all the mss. agree on this spelling I have taken the balance of probability to be that he did, and have not changed it. Other texts spell it with *yâ*.

The word *ajra* is not found in the dictionaries. This is surprising, but perhaps not completely unexpected, since the dictionaries are generally deficient in terms relating to logic, rhetoric, and jurisprudence. I am able to give the following other passages where the word occurs, and doubtless more will turn up:

1. In the chapter of the Khilâf edited here, 231 and 237.
2. In the Khilâf, 233, in the expression *min al-ajra*, which has a slightly different meaning, as we will see.
3. In the Khilâf, in a passage not edited in this work, in the phrase *min al-ajra*, used in a way where it can be taken as having its usual meaning or the specialised meaning of the fixed phrase. The passage is in Ms. S_1 p. 17, Ms. B_1 p. 17, Ms. B_2 p. 11, in the section on evidence, commenting on Nu XXXV:16-18.
4. In the Farâ'iḍ, in a passage not edited in this work, the last chapter of the work in the mss., on the Red Heifer, ch. CV, p. 138 of the Sassoon Ms. and p. 140 of JRUL Ms. Sam. 172, used in the same way as in the third instance listed above.

The basic meaning of the word is 'better-integrated' or 'fitting in better', that is to say, fitting more neatly into a vacant slot in the system or being in better agreement with the other details of the system or the principles seen elsewhere in the system. This meaning can be seen in the two passages from the Khilâf mentioned as the first instance on the list.

By extension, the expression *min al-ajra* comes to mean 'with even more right' (because the system demands it even more in this case) and it could be taken to mean the same as the Hebrew אף כי or the English 'how much more so', but this would be to lose some of the precision of meaning.

We are now in a position to see what *ajra* means here: it means fitting in better with other facts. This does not mean that the first explanation contradicts the facts, it means that the second one fits better into the system and has a natural justification from other facts in the system and can be linked to them.

73-78 On bleeding of cleansing in general, compare T 53-59; Kh 215-253; Kâsh ch. XII, 11-17; I'tiq 47-50 and 58-64.

73-76 See 88-89 N and the cross-references there. Compare 68-69. Lv XII:5 is assumed.

The Ṭubâkh (53-55) and the Khilâf (215) agree with the Kâfi, but the I'tiqâdât (47-52) and the Kâshif (ch. XII, 8-13) add one day.

73 Mss. JD are correct in counting this as the sixth category, not the fifth: compare T 53. The cause of the mistake in the other mss. is probably the obscurity of the text of lines 68-69, where it is not made at all clear that bleeding of childbirth counts as two items on the list. The same mistake has happened in the Ṭubâkh in Ms. M_1* in 53 because of the obscurity of the text of the Ṭubâkh in 45.

This mistake in the mss. of the Kâfi has then led to the forced, unnatural, and artificial counting of the touching of the blood as one of the seven items in the list of kinds of bleeding in line 83. To make the artificiality a bit less glaring the word اقسام has been glossed as منازل in 48 (but the gloss is obviously tacked on), and the word قسم has been replaced by منزله in 56, 61, 68, and the words المنزله السابعه have been inserted in 83, and the heading فصل, which would have marked off 83-90 as a new section, has been removed in all the other mss.

77-78 Bleeding of cleansing is equivalent in grade to *dåbå* bleeding, and if she finishes bleeding on the thirty-third or sixty-sixth day, she is able to immerse herself straightaway to recover from the bleeding of the seven or fourteen days, which counts as equivalent to *niddå* bleeding, and becomes clean at sunset that day, the same as a woman who finishes the *dåbå* bleeding some time on the last day of the week is then able to immerse herself to recover from the effect of the *niddå* bleeding at the start of the week, and becomes clean from her *niddå* at sunset that day, the last day of the week.

See Kf 88-89 N and T 12-15; Kf ch. XI, 56-58 TN.

74 The immersion is necessary to recover from the bleeding of childbirth, and has nothing to do with any bleeding during the thirty-three or sixty-six days.

I take the term تعكيس or تعكس to mean a change of condition for the worse (a meaning supported by Dozy's examples), and in this case to refer specifically to an entry into *niddå* or *zåbå* uncleanness. The same technical term occurs in line 61.

75-76 The implication of a continuity between the bleeding of cleansing and the day after, and the absence of any reference to *niddå* bleeding, which would otherwise have been expected, indicates that a woman who experiences bleeding on the day after the thirty-third or sixty-sixth day is *zåbå*, just like a woman who experiences bleeding on the day after the end of the last allowable menstrual week.

The Ṭubâkh (60-65) and I'tiqâdat (60-61) agree with this; the Farâ'iḍ (103-106) would count her as *niddå*. See the note on the Farâ'id for the implications of this.

77-78 Some women experience the very first menstrual bleeding, the *niddå*, but no *dåbå* bleeding after; and in the same way some women only experience bleeding during the seven or fourteen days after giving birth, which corresponds to the *niddå* bleeding, and do not experience any bleeding of cleansing, which corresponds to *dåbå* bleeding, during the thirty-three or sixty-six days that follow, which correspond to the seven days after the *niddå* bleeding.

See 88-89 N.

79-82 Compare T 67-73 and I'tiq 65-67 on bleeding of plausibility. The term is explained in T 67 N. See Far 7-14 TN.

79-80 See Kh 179-199 N on the colours.

83-89 This section deals with the question of the contamination caused by touching the substance of the issue, and not by touching the person from whom the issue discharges. Mss. JD are perfectly correct in having the word *a'yân* 'actual substances' in line 83.

83 See 73 N.

84 For the interpretation of this verse, see T 8-10 and the cross-references given in the note there.

84-87 The woman's contamination from the *dåbå* bleeding finishes at sunset, and so the contamination of any other person that touches this blood finishes at sunset. Although it is not directly stated here that the reference is to *dåbå* bleeding that occurs on the seventh day, the argument, the context, and the parallel passages demand this assumption. The point is that contamination from *dåbå* bleeding on any earlier day would still end at sunset that day, but it would not be obvious, since the contamination due to the *niddå* bleeding at the start of the week would still apply and someone could argue that the *dåbå* contamination still applied too, but at the end of the seventh day the *niddå* contamination finishes and if the woman is then clean it is obvious that her *dåbå* bleeding on that same day, the seventh, must have ended its effect by sunset that day.

See T 13-14 N.

85 On the technical meaning of the term *yuḥaṣṣil* in this context, see T 55-57 N.

It is certain, from Kf ch. XI, 66-67, that the opinion of the author is that the person affected becomes clean at sunset, even if the blood is washed off before then.

I conclude that the reading *yuḥaṣṣil* of D* is the correct one, and that the reading *yakhluṣ* is a very ancient emendation made by someone who agreed with the authors of the Ṭubâkh and the Khilâf (for the references see T 13-14 N) that the person affected becomes clean immediately the blood is washed off. (Notice that the reading *yakhluṣ* is at least as old as Ms. J). A second argument in favour of the reading of D* is that the change of *yuḥaṣṣil* to the more common word *yakhluṣ* is more likely than the reverse change. The emendation would have been made easier by the presence of the expression *wa-khalaṣat* soon after, in 86.

Admittedly, the possibility must be considered that the verb *yakhluṣ* here simply means 'he can get rid of it' rather than 'he can recover from its effect'. The difficulty with this explanation is that we would then expect to find the word *minhu* added. The explanation of a deliberate alteration is probably to be preferred.

Both forms are found used interchangeably in T 56 and 58-59. For the author of the Ṭubâkh the use of one term or the other makes no difference, because when the blood is removed the person becomes clean immediately. A person holding this opinion would have found it natural or easy to make the interchange here in the Kâfi.

85-87 The reason for the specification of a woman who normally finishes her bleeding within seven days is that if she has finished bleeding before sunset on the seventh day it is very unlikely that she will start bleeding again after sunset, whereas if she normally did keep on bleeding after the seventh day it would have to be assumed that she might well do the same this time, and although she might have stopped bleeding on the seventh day and become clean at sunset that day, she is still likely to start bleeding again on the eighth day and enter a second menstrual week, and if she does she will contaminate anyone or anything she is touching at the time, so she has to stay out of the way till it is quite certain she is not going to start bleeding again.

Notice that the source of contamination to be avoided is the second *niddå* bleeding and the woman herself at that time, but not necessarily the woman after the instant of *niddå* bleeding. This is very important: see the next note for the implications.

88-89 We have here the implicit statement of a basic principle of Samaritan halachah in which it differs fundamentally from the Rabbanite system.

The Rabbanites put the woman from the blood issues and the blood itself at the same level of uncleanness and say that they both cause the same length of uncleanness to anyone that touches them. (Mishkav Umoshav I:8). It follows from this that the woman and the blood are both אבות טומאה, and anyone that touches the woman or the blood is ראשון לטומאה, and that at whatever stage the chain of contamination finishes, it will have the same number of links whether or not the zero point, the אב טומאה, is the woman herself or the blood itself. (See Tum'at Met V:1-10 for the method of naming the links).

The Samaritan principle is quite different. The Samaritans put the person that touches the woman at the time of her *niddå* and the person that touches the *niddå* blood at two quite different levels of uncleanness. The person or thing that touches the blood itself is made unclean for seven days (T 11; Kf ch. XI, 84; 38-40 TN), but the person that touches the woman is only made unclean for one day (see the passage quoted in Kf ch. III, 22-38 N). No explanation is given for this difference, but the answer is implicit in the passage quoted in the note on the Kâfi ch. III just referred to. We are told there that the reason that the woman from whom the blood issues is unclean for seven days, whereas the person that touches her (the implication is that he touches her at the instand of *niddå*) is only made unclean for one day, is that the woman's uncleanness is essential or intrinsic [*jawharî*], whereas the uncleanness of the person that touches her is only accidental [*'araḍî*]. This is reasonable, and happens to agree approximately with the Rabbanite position. But the question arises as to why the person who touches the blood itself should be made unclean for seven days. In the light of what has been said, the answer must be that his uncleanness is intrinsic. But how is this possible? The answer to this can only be that when he is in contact with the blood he is made unclean in exactly the same way as is the woman from whom it issues. The corollary of this, however, is that the intrinsic uncleanness of the woman is due to her contact with her *niddå* blood, not to the event of *niddå*. This is a surprising conclusion, but it can be demonstrated to be correct. We have seen, in T 55-57 N, that the reason that the woman has to wash off the *niddå* blood before the count of seven days can start is that if she does not, it will keep on re-contaminating her.

The same principle applies in the case of *zā̊bå* blood (assumed by all sources; see Kf ch. XI, 64-67 N) and blood of childbirth (Kf ch. XIII, 1-18, and the notes; Kâsh ch. XII, 14 TN; I'tiq 41-46 and the notes; Kh 267-269); and applies as well in the less serious category of *dā̊bå* blood (T 13-14 and 59; Kf ch. 85-86; assumed by all sources; T 55-57 N) and its equivalent, bleeding of cleansing (Kf ch. XI, 73-76 and 84-87 and the notes).

The Karaites agree with the Samaritans on the distinction between the contamination of a person that touches the substance of the blood and the person that touches the woman from whom it issues. See, for example, A.E. 122b.

We are now in a position to understand why it is that the person that touches the discharge of the *zåb* and the person that touches the *zåb* himself are made unclean for the same period. (T 110-117 TN; Kf ch. XI, 34-40). We would expect the person that touches the discharge to be made unclean for the same period as the man from whom the discharge issues: but remember that it took two consecutive days of discharge to put the man in the condition of *zåb*, and the one that touches him does not get that much contact with the substance. The Rabbanites agree with the Samaritans that it takes more than one occurence for the emission to be counted as *zåb*, and it is logically necessary that the Samaritans should agree with the Rabbanites that a single emission, if it is not treated as *zåb*, must be treated as semen (and see Kf 19 N). If this is the case, then the Samaritans are quite consistent in making the person who touches the substance of the discharge unclean for just one day: as a single emission of the substance of the *zåb* only counts as an emission of semen, it follows that the person that touches it, even if it is a later emission that has been classified as *zåb*, is still in the position of a person who has touched semen. Consider it from the other side: It would be illogical for a single contact with the substance, which only puts the person from whom it issues under one day's uncleanness, and in the state of one who has had an emission of semen, to put some other person who only contacts it once in a more serious grade of uncleanness and make him unclean for seven days. It was not this discharge that made the man from whom it issues unclean: it was this one together with the one the day before.

We see, then that the person who touches the discharge is not counted as having touched the discharge, but as having touched the equivalent of semen, and is only unclean for one day (although it is in fact the *zåb* substance that he has touched, not semen).

The Rabbanites agree with the Samaritans in that once the discharge has occurred often enough to be counted as discharge (*zåb*) anyone that touches it is still only made unclean for one day, but in their case this is because they count the person that touches it as only being ראשון לטומאה. As they do not make the distinction that the Samaritans do between contact with the person and contact with the substance, no problem arises. The Samaritans agree with the Rabbanites that the person that touches the man from whom the discharge issues, without touching the discharge itself, is only made unclean for one day, because his uncleanness is only secondary. (This comes through clearly from the context in the Kâfi and Ṭubâkh). In short, the reason that the Samaritans count the person that touches the man from whom the discharge issues and the person that touches the discharge itself in the same degree of uncleanness is probably not that they regard their uncleanness as identical, but more likely that they regard them as being of different nature but of the same level; whereas the reason that the Rabbanites put them at the same degree of uncleanness is that they do consider the uncleanness of each as being identical to the other's.

We will now consider two applications of this principle.

The question of the length of contamination caused by touching *zåbå* blood is treated in 64-67 N. The principle seems to be that as the blood makes the woman unclean for seven days, it makes anyone else who is touched by it unclean for seven days. The bleeding makes the woman unclean for the rest of that day and the seven days after that day, and the same applies to the person that touches the blood.

The application of the principle that the uncleanness of the person from whom the contaminating substance issues is due to contact with the substance leads to the conclusion that after intercourse the man and the woman are equally contaminated by semen. Compare Kf ch. III, 12-14.

90 The proof-text is Lv XX:18. On copulation with a woman known to be unclean see the references in T 74-78 N and 8-10 N.

Chapter III

2 In spite of the title, the main concern is the classification of contamination. The requirements for cleansing are used as indicators of the extent to which each item or category contaminates people and objects.

3-5 What is meant is that uncleanness falls into two classes, one due to some phenomenon in the person concerned, and one due to contact with such a person — in Rabbanite terminology, a person can be אב טומאה or וולד טומאה.

3 The distinction between intrinsic and accidental uncleanness is explained in Kf ch. XI, 88-89. Compare the references in ch. XI, 1 N.

4-5 'Eating' here is to be understood as referring to eating the meat of an animal killed by a non-Israelite, or eating the meat of a non-kosher animal, and so on. By analogy with the Jewish system, we would suppose that touching applies in the case of any kind of uncleanness, and that lifting applies specifically in the case of a corpse, or a *niddå*, and the related categories of *dåbå*, *zåbå* and *yålēda*, and *zåb*. The Samaritans, like the Karaites, do not seem to make the distinction between lifing (נשיאה) and budging (היסט) that the Rabbanites do.

4-5 The forms of the Hebrew are participles and refer to the person who performs the action.

7-8 There are three ways in which clothes can be contaminated: either by coming in contact with the unclean substance or person, or by being touched by an unclean person, or by absorbing some of the unclean substance. The author of the Kâfi has not separated these. In some cases washing of the person is enough and full cleanness comes at sunset; in other cases the washing only marks the start of a count of seven days and immersion still has to be carried out at the end. The author has not separated these clearly either. See 40-44 and the notes there.

Compare T 11 N.

8-9 A man unclean due to an emission of semen does not contaminate articles, including clothing, by touching them, but does contaminate people: see ch. III, 22-27; ch. III, 22-38 N; Kâsh ch. XV, 88-91.

12-14 Notice that the woman's contamination is equal to the man's. For the theoretical explanation, see Kf ch. XI, 88-89 N.

14 It is this person of whom just washing of the person is required and nothing else.

16-21 This corresponds to ch. XI, 10-15.

22-38 There is a parallel to this in a section of ch. XIII, Ms. J p. 95, Ms. S_1 p. 149, Ms. L_1 p. 137b (partly translated by Noja, p. 83). The additional information given in the parallel passage is explained and put in its context in Kf ch. XI, 88-89 N. The passage is quoted here according to Ms. J, with the variants of Ms. S_1.

قال الشيخ

من كان عليه حكم ࠒࠓࠉ ࠋࠉࠋࠄ وهي الجنابه ومعناه انه يتجنب عن الاطهار مما قد عرض عليه فمن لمس بدنه قبل ان يتطهر لزمه ما يلزمه من التطهر وكذلك لامس لامسه والثالث ثم ينقطع والثالث واما هو فلو لمسه ما لمسه ما لزمه التطهر منه واذا قال قايلا ما الدليل ان الثالث يفصل ولا يفصل ما قبله ولا بعده ولم لا يطرد الحكم فيه ويستمر.

الجواب من وجوه احدها ان الطها ذاهب منه وذلك ان لنا من الطها ما هو جوهري وما هو عرضي فالجوهري هو ما حصل من الانسان نفسه فاوجب طاه والغير جوهري هو ما عرض على الانسان من غيره بطريق اللمس ولا يجري العرضي مجرى الجوهري الا ترى ان الامراه الحايض يجب عليها الطها اسبوع ولا يجب على من لمسها الا الصبوغ في وقته ويخلص وقس على ذلك الثاني ان الثالث يفصل النجاسات الخفيفه مثل الجنابه وامثالها وكل ما لا يفصل في الثالث فيفصل في السابع ولذلك امر تعالى بجعل ࠌࠉࠍࠃࠄ في الثالث والسابع ودقايق الكتاب كافيه لمن فهم الثالث ان الله تعالى ذكر في كتابه العزيز اماكن دلت على ان الثالث فصل اولها لما تبدى في الخليقه قال ࠁࠓࠀࠔࠉࠕ ࠁࠓࠀ ࠀࠋࠄࠉࠌ ࠀࠕ ࠄࠔࠌࠉࠌ ࠅࠀࠕ ࠄࠀࠓࠑ (تك ١ : ١) ثم في الثالث ذكرها بصحة الاسم عليها افرادا قال ࠅࠉࠒࠓࠀ ࠀࠋࠄࠉࠌ ࠋࠉࠁࠔࠄ ࠀࠓࠑ (ايه ١٠) ثم لما ذكر ࠀࠋࠀࠓࠒࠉࠏ لم

يذكر استكماله والغرض منه الا في الثالث منه ثم في نوبة [illegible] [illegible] مع بني يعقوب عليه السلام ثم في الاستعداد لموقف [illegible] [illegible] فالثالث هو قباله السابع فكما جعل السابع يفصل المراتب الكبار كذلك جعل الثالث يفصل المراتب التي دونها.

٢ وهي] [illegible] S_1
٣ انه] < S_1
٤ بدنه] [illegible] × S_1 يطهر J   يلزمه] [illegible] S_1
٥ [illegible] × S_1 لامس] لمس J
٦ ما (ثاني)] < × S_1J   [illegible] × S_1
١٤ [illegible] S_1
١٨ يفصل النجاسات] [illegible] S_1 الخفيفه S_1*J] الحقيقيه × S_1^3
١٩ الجنابه] [illegible] × S_1 يفصل] [illegible] S_1
٢٠ [illegible] S_1
٢٢ كافيه] [illegible] S_1
٢٧ [illegible] S_1 [illegible] S_1
٢٨ [illegible] S_1 [illegible] S_1
٣٠ منه] < S_1
٣٢ [illegible] S_1
٣٣ [illegible] S_1 المراتب (ثاني)] [illegible] S_1

26-27 The third person referred to here is the third if counting starts with the person from whom the semen issues, and the first person is the one from whom the semen issues. This becomes clear from the corresponding sentence in the parallel passage quoted in the note on 22-38 and is supported by the examples given in 32-38 as explained in the notes there. The man from whom the semen issues is the base point, and there are two steps on from him. In Rabbanite terminology we would say that we have אב טומאה, and then two steps of וולדי טומאה, namely ראשון לטומאה and שני לטומאה, and there is no שלישי לטומאה. In Samaritan terminology, we have one person whose uncleanness is intrinsic, and two whose uncleanness is accidental.

Notice, though, that there is no end to the chain of transmission as long as contact is unbroken. See Wreschner, introduction, p. XXIV; and see below, Conclusions, note 163.

31 What is meant is that the second and third are both equally accidentally unclean, so why should the second be able to transmit uncleanness and the third not?

31-32 Compare ch. XI, 31-32, on the agreement of Scripture with tradition. The variant readings *naqlan* 'by tradition' in Ms. J and *ʿaqlan* 'logically' in the rest of the mss. are important. Notice that the title given to the Kitâb al-Iʿtiqâdât in the Cornell ms. is Dalîl ash-Sharʿ wa-'n-Naql wa-'l-ʿAql (see p. 41). See also ch. XII, line 12.

32-33 The day on which the water was separated from the land was the third day of creation. It will become clear by comparison with the next note that the base point here is not the first day of creation, but the point at which creation started, so that step two corresponds to the first day and so on. (Of course this means that the author of the Kâfi took Gn I:1-2 to refer to the state before the first day of creation. Compare Rashi on the these verses and the implications of the syntax). The point of the comparison is that there is an initial situation, then two steps from that, and after the third step there is a change of state and the first set of steps cease.

The word *mustabḥirah* [covered in water] in line 32 is the translation of the word ࠁࠄࠅ in Gn I:2 in Saadya's version and the earlier Samaritan version. Saadya's version would suit this exegesis very well in another respect as well, since he translates the word בראשית as אול מא, meaning 'When at first', and as we have seen, this exegesis is assumed by the author of the Kâfi. (Dérenbourg has misinterpreted the expression אול מא in his note on it). Most mss. of the early Samaritan version available to me do not translate this word as in Saadya's version, but have a form that seems to be due to the influence of the later Samaritan version.

33-34 To see the point of the comparison, you have to realise that the day on which the great dark ended, the day the sun and moon and stars started shining, was the fourth day of creation, not the third. The creation of the sky and the firmament on the first day was the base point. After that there were two days, and the second of these was the last on which there could be complete darkness, because the next day the sun and moon and stars started to shine. (The Samaritans assume that the light created on the first day did not shine on the world till the fourth day or that it was supernatural light, so there is no difficulty in reconciling this idea with the statement of Scripture that God created light on or before the first day: see Macdonald, *Theology*, pp. 118-123, 135-136, 165-172).

34 The primal differentiation was the separation of the waters above the firmament from the waters below the firmament. Obviously this depends on the existence of the firmament.

None of the mss. have a completely correct reading here, but Ms. J is so close to the correct reading that emendation is easy and obvious. The spelling الانواع has been mis-interpreted as the plural of نوع instead of a IVth stem infinitive, and the hamzah has been put in the wrong position. After that, the form الاصلي has been changed to الاصلية to make it agree with a plural noun. After that, the text has undergone secondary emendation to try to make sense out of it. On the grammatical form انواع, see above, p. 51.

34-36 Traditionally it was on the third day later on that Shechem and his people changed their minds about joining Israel. So we have once again a base point, their treaty and circumcision, then two days of holding to the treaty and original intention, then the next day the situation changed.

37 The base point is Joseph's interpretation of the dream, after which there are three days of waiting till the predictions come true.

39 The heading belongs to lines 40-42, but not to lines 43-44.

40-42 Contamination of clothes due to their having absorbed some of the contaminating stuff is not the same as contamination of them due to contact with an unclean person. The contamination due to the semen is of the first kind, whereas the contamination of clothes due to contact with a person suffering from ࠑࠓࠏࠕ or contact with a man with a discharge is different; and we might add that if the clothes absorb some of the *substance* of the discharge they are unclean in the same way as if they absorbed some semen. The author of the Kâfi has not organised his thoughts properly here. For a clearer statement of the distinction, see the extract from the Kâfi quoted by Cohn, p. VIII top. (Compare ch. III, 7-8 N). See the next note.

41-42 If he is becoming clean from his discharge the discharge must have stopped and he must be at the stage of counting seven days without any discharge, which means that the clothes are contaminated by contact with him and not by having absorbed any of the unclean substance. The mention of depigmentation confirms this.

From this we learn that the *zåb*, even after he has stopped discharging, still contaminates clothing during the seven days of cleansing, and it follows that he must contaminate people as well. This contamination can only be for one day, since we already know that even before the discharge stops he only contaminates artefacts and people for one day: see T 100-117 N, and Kf ch. XI, 88-89 N.

43 A person who has touched a corpse is called *nâṭir* up till the time of his first washing or immersion, on the first day. Before this, he contaminates artefacts and people for seven days; after it, he contaminates them for one day. See the notes on Kf ch. XII, 26-28; ch. XIII, 11-13.

The contamination of the clothes is of the same kind as if they had come in contact with an unclean person, not of the same kind as if they had absorbed an unclean substance.

43 The woman in a state of *niddå* has to wash herself at the start of the week to remove the *niddå* blood so as to stop being recontaminated by it, and has to immerse herself at the end of the week, and she contaminates clothes for one day if she touches them herself, and the *niddå* blood contaminates clothes (and people) for seven days if it touches them. The same applies to a woman in the state of *zå̄bå*.

See T 55-57 N and Kf ch. XIII, 13-18; ch. XI, 88-89 N.

44 The chapter referred to is ch. XI.

Chapter XIII

1-18 It becomes clear that the author of the Kâfi agrees with the second opinion. So does the author of the Kâshif: see Kâsh ch. XII, 14.

2-3 *It is essential to realise that whatever is found out about the contamination and cleansing of the baby applies to anyone else contaminated by the blood of childbirth, including very often the mother herself.*

The baby is unclean due to having come in contact with the blood of childbirth, which is of the same degree of uncleanness as *niddå* blood. The purification of the baby will therefore be the same as for a person who has come in contact with the *niddă* blood, namely by washing the blood off so as to stop being re-contaminated by it, waiting seven days, and then becoming clean at sunset on the seventh day. (See the section on the *niddå* in the Ṭubâkh and ch. XI of the Kâfi and the cross-references there, and see in particular T 55-57, Kf ch. III, 43-44 and ch. XIII, 13-18 and the notes on these passages). Obviously the first washing has to be carried out on the day of birth if the baby is to be clean for the eighth day.

Note carefully that the situation imagined is not that the baby has not been washed till after the first day, so that the seven days are not up by the start of the eighth day, but rather that the baby has not been washed *at all* before circumcision. This means that the dispute is over the degree of uncleanness caused by touching the blood of childbirth, and has nothing to do with the question of uncleanness caused by touching the baby without touching the blood. Compare 27-30.

6-8 In the towns referred to they regard the baby as being clean once it has been washed on the eighth day, whether or not it has been washed beforehand at some time during the first seven days. If the baby is able to become clean immediately on being washed, any person who comes in contact with some of the blood of childbirth still on a baby that for one reason or another has not been washed must be able to become clean immediately on washing it off as well.

The problem is, how they could have maintained that the baby or the circumciser could become clean immediately, when it is a consistent principle in the texts edited here that cleansing only comes at sunset. The answer is probably that they based their argument on the fact that as the mother could pass from the state of uncleanness due to bleeding of childbirth to the state of uncleanness due to bleeding of cleansing at the end of the first week or fortnight, even if she had been bleeding up till the end of the last day of the week or fornight, then the blood of childbirth must cease to have any effect on the mother after the end of the week or fornight. Other Samaritans, and the Jews as well, would agree with them so far, since all agree that the woman passes from one state to another at this time. Their conclusion from this would have been that the blood must cease to be able to contaminate any one at all after the end of the week or fortnight.

In the note on T 11-13 this argument is shown to be consistent with what is known to have been the opinion of Sakta on the effect of touching women in the various states of uncleanness due to bleeding, and its relation to the opinions expressed or implied in Kh 267-269 is explained.

9-18 The author of the Iʻtiqâdât says in 11-13 that any person who comes in contact with the blood of childbirth at any time during the seven days is made unclean for seven days from then on. This means that any of the blood of childbirth on the baby on the eighth day should still have its full effect on anyone that touches it, and anyone that touches the baby without touching the blood should be made unclean for one day. We see that the modern opinion is the same as the second opinion in the Kâfi. It is obviously not thought illogical for the contamination of the person that touches the blood of childbirth to last longer than the contamination of the mother herself. Compare the note on line 25, in this chapter of the Kâfi.

11-13 The *nâṭir* is someone who has been made unclean by a corpse, and has not yet performed the first immersion, which must be performed before the count of seven days can start. The Arabic term *nâṭir* is Aramaic in origin (and note that the pronunciation will be nearly identical in Aramaic and Arabic) and means one who has to be careful, who has to watch himself, and the term is used because this person causes the same degree of uncleanness to anyone or anything he touches as the corpse does. After the immersion the person is termed *musammad*, an Arabic word which is either a borrowing from an Aramaic *mēshammad*, or more likely a loan-translation from the same word. This term means excluded or banished or unable to take part in something, and is used because such a person is excluded from the synagogue service and the festivals. Forms from this root are well attested in Jewish Aramaic, Mishnaic Hebrew (probably as a borrowing from Aramaic), and Syriac. In all cases the idea is primarily abandonment of an activity, and then as a derived meaning abandonment of religious practices, exclusion from religious practices, or the attempt to abolish the practice of a religion. This fits in well with the Samaritan usage. The stages of cleansing referred to here are set out and explained very clearly in the chapter of the Ṭubâkh on the Red Heifer and the ࠌࠉ ࠍࠃࠄ. A passage elsewhere in this chapter of the Kâfi, partially translated by Noja, pp. 76-77, but unfortunately omitting certain crucial sentences, shows that the author of the Kâfi agrees with the Ṭubâkh in all details on this matter. The chapter on this subject in the Farâ'iḍ, ch. CV, does not mention the initial cleansing on the first day, and neither does the Kâshif on Nu XIX, or ch. X of the Iʻtiqâdât. It seems that the Ṭubâkh and Kâfi agree against the Farâ'iḍ, Kâshif, and Iʻtiqâdât. See also Abu 'l-Fatḥ 163:7 for an opinion of some Dositheans agreeing with the Ṭubâkh and Kâfi.

Compare Kf ch. III, 43 TN; ch. XII, 26-28 N.

12-13 The first time the water of purification is sprinkled on him counts as the third day, even if it is much later than that, and the second time counts as the seventh day, even if it is much later than that. See Nu XIX:19.

13-18 See T 55-57 N, and the cross-references there.

14-15 See T 13 N; and compare Kf ch. XIII, 19-21.

17 Wiping it with rags will not remove every bit of blood, and one spot is enough to cause uncleanness.

19-21 See 27-30. The extra uncleanness of the hand can only be either that the hand is more unclean than the rest of the body, or is unclean for a longer period. We are told here that in this case the difference is one of time. This can only mean that although the woman's body becomes clean from the effect of the blood of childbirth at the end of the seventh day, her left hand stays unclean for seven days past the time when it last touches the blood of childbirth, and as the final washing would probably be on the seventh day, this probably means her hand is unclean till the fourteenth day. There is probably a difference in the degree of uncleanness as well. Her body would cause one day's uncleanness to anyone that touched it at any time during the seven days or thirty-three days, so for her hand to be special it must cause seven days' uncleanness. This is confirmed in 29-30, where we are told that the midwife's hand is at a special level of uncleanness which is demonstrated in the note there to consist of making anyone it touches within seven days of coming in contact with the blood of childbirth unclean for seven days. *In both cases, the hand is treated as if it were the blood itself.*

It would be expected by analogy with this that the woman's hand with which she washes off the very first menstrual blood, the *niddå* blood, would be contaminated for seven days independently of the rest of her body, and would contaminate anyone or anything it touched for seven days. See Marginal Note VI.

The author does not intend to say that the baby causes seven days' uncleanness to anyone that touches it even after it is washed. This is proven by the fact that the author is contrasting the state before the baby is washed and after, and also by the explicit statement in 27-30. The reason for making the analogy is only to show that the baby's uncleanness lasts for seven days after the blood is washed off. The reason he is unable to use the normal example of the mother herself is that her uncleanness at this grade ends after the seventh day, even if some bleeding occurs up to that day, so that it is impossible to prove the need for counting seven days from the case of the mother herself. Her left hand, however, is in the special category of not becoming clean till seven days after touching the blood even if that means it is unclean for seven days after the seventh day, and so can be used for comparison.

19-21 This seems to be the author's own statement, which indicates that he agrees with the second opinion. Compare 22-26, which gives the same impression.

On the question of the tendency to let the transmission of the halachah rest with the women, compare 13-16 and see the note on the Ṭubâkh 13.

25 This means that it is definitely possible, according to the author of the Kâfi, for the baby's contamination due to the blood of childbirth to last past the seventh day and the end of the mother's contamination. This would agree with the modern halachah: see the note on 6-8.

28-30 We are not told that all the blood is washed off, only the part that the circumciser would be likely to touch. The point of the contrast between the baby and the midwife's hand is that the midwife's hand is an exceptional case, and has the same contaminating effect as if it were the blood itself. (See the note on 19-21). The baby is treated normally, so that contact with it, even when it is still unclean and still has some of the blood on, will only cause one day's uncleanness. To reconcile this with 19-21 we have to assume that in 19-21 the point of the comparison is the need for a count of seven days after the blood is washed off, for both the baby and the mother's hand, not the level of uncleanness.

28-29 The whole of the lower half of the baby's body is washed, which necessarily includes the penis. As the circumciser will not need to touch the upper half of the baby's body, he will not come in contact with any of the blood of childbirth.

Although the circumciser is not contaminated for a week, since he has not touched the blood of childbirth, he still must be contaminated for a day, since he has touched the baby who can still be unclean, in the opinion of this author, after the seventh day if the initial washing was carried out after the first day. See 19-21 N.

28 For once, the reading of Mss. JD is wrong. If the baby is only washed as high as above the knees this will not stop the circumciser from touching the blood. Besides, if the baby is washed from above the hips down to the ankles, the penis will be included, but not if the washing starts above the knees and goes downwards. The change to فوق ركبته from فوق وركيه is very easy. After this, there would have been a secondary correction of ركبته to ركبه. The reading of Ms. D is apparently older than the reading of Mss. JG.

29-30 We are told that during the period of *ūtar* her hand, which has come in contact with the blood of childbirth, is unclean in some way that does not apply to the rest of her body. Obviously her whole body will be unclean for the seven days after childbirth, and will contaminate anything that touches it for one day. The uncleanness of her hand must either be more serious or must last for a longer period. It is hard to see why it should last for a longer period, so it must be more serious (which is indicated by the term itself) but confined to the first week. This can only mean that her hand contaminates whatever it touches for seven days, and this means that the uncleanness of her hand is put at the same level as the blood itself, even after the blood is washed off. The hand is treated as the equivalent of the blood.

We now see the point of comparison between 28-29 and 29-30. Once the blood of childbirth is washed off the baby, any person that touches the baby is contaminated only by the baby, not by the blood of childbirth, and the same should apply to anyone that touches the midwife, who has touched the blood of childbirth and washed it off, but there is the single exception that the midwife's hands remain at the same degree of uncleanness as the blood itself even after the blood is washed off.

Exactly the same principle is used in 19-21, where we are told that the woman's hand with which she washes off the *niddå* blood contaminates anything she touches with it for seven days, quite separately to the rest of her body, which would only cause one day's contamination. The hand is treated as the equivalent of the blood.

29 The baby must be an Israelite because only Israelites can contaminate or be contaminated.

30 On the meaning of the term *ūtar*, see Iʿtiq 43-44 and the note there.

It might be useful to draw the reader's attention here to a *fatwa* at the end of Ms. P of the Kâfi discussing the practical effect of the *ūtar* (there written اوثر) at the time of celebrating the Passover. I have not edited this *fatwa* here, as it would lead too far away from the purpose of this work, but I will return to it in a future publication.

Chapter XII

6-7 It is clear from the discussion that follows that the Samaritans take this verse to mean that whatever can conveniently or safely be heated can be heated, and if both ways are convenient and safe for a given object, either can be used. This is the Karaite interpretation as well: see the Keter Torah on this verse. Compare the translation of vv. 22-23 in 14-17 and see the context there. The meaning is conclusively shown by the gloss in 20.

10 This sentence is absolutely essential for a proper understanding of the discussion. The cleansing spoken of is the *removal of foreign contaminating matter* from the articles before they are immersed. The Jews do exactly the same thing (see the previous note). We can thus dispose of the myth perpetuated by Wreschner (pp. 37-38) and others, that the Samaritans use immersion in fire as the equivalent of the Jewish immersion in water for the purpose of cleansing in general, under heathen influence. No supposition of heathen influence is needed if the Jewish halachah is known and understood.

Washing in water to remove foreign matter is termed *shēṭīfa*, and only after the *shēṭīfa* can the *ṭēbīla* or *rå:ṣ* be carried out. The use of fire is a substitute for *shēṭīfa*, not *ṭēbīla*.

There are two other cases in which cleansing with fire is used other than to remove foreign contaminating matter, and that is the apparently now obsolete practice of cleansing ground where a woman has given birth, or where a *niddå* woman has been, and the practice of cleansing ground where a corpse has been carried. In both these cases, either water or fire can be used. For the details, see below, 23-24 N and 23 N, and the cross-references given there. In these two cases the contamination is probably of the same nature as the contamination under discussion here, and the practice compatible with the Jewish halachah in its rationale. For the justification of this statement, see notes 234, 235, and 237 in the Conclusions, and their context.

11-12 If the article has contacted *niddå* blood, for example, it needs immersion. If it has contacted *dåbå* blood, it only needs washing. Whichever one of these two is required of the person contaminated by the source of uncleanness is required of the artefact as well.

12 See ch. III, 31-32 N.

13 The process of immersion would remove the contaminating matter, so even if the *shēṭīfa* or the passage through fire were neglected, the object would still be cleansed, but this would be a negligent and frivolous treatment of the commandments. It is for the same reason that the Jews expect a person to remove any contaminating substance on their body by washing before immersion. Compare Iʿtiq 38-39.

This sentence is to be taken to refer to both the *shēṭīfa* and the passage through fire: one or other of them should be performed beforehand so as to perform the *ṭēbīla* in the appropriate way.

14-17 The author is back on the topic of the substitution of *shēṭīfa* for passage through fire.

22 What is meant is that this section deals with what can only be cleansed by fire, never by water.

23-24 The modern halachah recognises the contamination of ground by the presence of a corpse, and prescribes water or fire for its cleansing: see Gaster's questionnaires, Rylands Ms. Sam. 317, question 19, and Ms. 318, question 20. The modern halachic sources do not mention contamination of ground from other types of uncleanness, except if unclean stuff is absorbed. In this case, the cleansing need not be carried out by fire: some dirt can be scuffed over the stuff, or the ground can be sluiced with water, or the stuff can be dug up. This accords with Jewish practice. The change in the modern halachah is clearly demonstrated by the following deliberate alterations in the Hebrew translation of the Kâfi:

22: 'Water' instead of 'fire'.

23: 'Unclean water' instead of 'a corpse'.

23: '*Niddå* blood' instead of simply *niddå*. (But this is the reading of the later mss. of the Arabic as well, and need not be a deliberate change in the Hebrew). There is some paraphrasing that does not alter the meaning just after this.

25: 'Water' instead of 'fire'.

25: 'Seat' instead of 'place' (so the word '*niddå*' now has to refer to the woman, not the event).

25: 'And derivable from the text of Scripture' is omitted.

25: 'Once' is omitted.

26-28: Everything from 'There is a first step' to 'who studies the matter' is omitted, and replaced by 'as handed down to them by their ancestors'.

31: 'According to the law of it' instead of 'by its stages', but still reading 'with fire'.

31-32: 'Is cleansed by fire immediately' instead of 'is cleansed by fire and is immediately unaffected'. (This may simply be an error).

32: 'Provided the requirements of a corpse do not apply' is omitted.

33-34: 'But if cleansing with fire is carried out afterwards, this is better' is omitted.

36: 'The law of it is the same as for ground: it is cleansed by means of fire' instead of 'by means of fire'.

23 It should follow that since the *niddå* blood is at the same level of contamination as blood of childbirth, the place where a woman is standing when menstruation starts, or any ground on which she walks before having washed off the *niddå* blood, is contaminated and has to have fire passed over it. It is clear from the parallel made between the corpse and the *niddå* in that this is the case.

In the Roman and Byzantine period ground was purified by fire after non-Israelites had passed over it, probably because they were regarded as equivalent to corpses. See ch. XI, 31-32.

For the theoretical explanation of the contamination of ground, see notes 234, 235, and 237 in the Conclusions.

23 Ms. D is correct in not inserting the word 'blood'. The ground will become unclean by the presence of the woman, even if no blood drips on it. See the previous note, and compare line 25.

23-24 The reference includes a man in the state of *zåb*, as well as a woman in the state of *dåbå* or *yēlīda* (but after delivery) or *zåbå*. The reference to the *zåb* is made certain by the use of the masculine form in line 23 and by the masculine forms in the parallel passage and by the context in both places.

The moisture can enter the ground in one of two ways: either in the form of water, when the person washes himself and the washing water carrying some of the unclean stuff soaks into the ground, or in the form of a crumb of food, when the person eats something and some crumbs, or a bit that he has bitten off and spat out, which have absorbed some of his spit, land on the ground and some of the spit leaks out and soaks into the ground. Compare Kf ch. XI, 28-32, and T 107-109.

25 See Lv XV:19 for the Scriptural proof.

26-28 Half of line 27 is missing in all mss. by homoioteleuton. Its insertion can be demonstrated to be essential and certainly correct. We are told in 28 that these steps can be taken from Nu XIX (see the note on this line). In Nu XIX there is only one case of contamination mentioned that requires more than one day for purification, and that is the case of a person contaminated by a corpse. Logically, then, the intention of the author of the Kâfi must be to make a parallel between the steps for purifying such a person and the steps for purifying the ground.

The passage of the fire over the ground on the first day corresponds to the immersion of the person on the first day, not mentioned in Scripture but known by tradition, which lets the counting of seven days start. The sprinkling on the third day and the seventh day is the same as for a person (v. 12 and v. 19). The passage of fire over the ground after the sprinkling on the seventh day corresponds to the immersion of the person at that time (v. 19). The passage of fire over the ground before the sprinkling on the third day and the seventh day corresponds to the immersion of the person at these times so as to remove any uncleanness he might have contracted, other than his uncleanness due to the corpse, in the days since the previous immersion, so as to put him in a fit state to receive the water of purification. Compare ch. XIII, 11-13 N; ch. III, 43-44 TN; ch. XII, 22-24, on purification from the contaminating effect of a corpse.

28 See the previous two notes, and the references there. The 'practical legislation' [ࠇࠒࠄ *åqqå*] is either Nu XIX:2-13, which is introduced by the phrase ࠆࠀࠕ ࠇࠒࠕ ࠄࠕࠅࠓࠄ, as opposed to vv. 14-22, which are introduced by the phrase ࠆࠀࠕ ࠄࠕࠅࠓࠄ (ࠕࠅࠓࠄ being theoretical information as opposed to instructions to be carried out, ࠌࠏࠔࠄ), or alternatively is the whole of the chapter.

The reason that the word is quoted as ࠇࠒࠕ in the construct is that this is its form in the verse Nu XIX:2.

29-30 Compare 23-24. The presence of the substance of the *zåb* causes contamination, but the mere presence of the person with the discharge does not, as opposed to the more serious categories of a corpse or *niddå*.

31-34 See on 23-24.

31 For the details of these stages, see the notes on 26-28 and 28.

32 The requirements of a corpse would apply if the baby was stillborn.

35-37 We are back to the question of the removal of contaminating matter from artefacts, as in 8-21, and we are given an example of something that can only be cleared of the stuff by fire, as opposed to the earlier examples when either way was possible or only washing with water was possible. Lines 36-37 are to be seen as parallel to 21.

40-43 The traditional interpretation of Nu XV:39, confirmed by the context, is that it refers to the consideration of copulation with non-Israelites, which can lead to idolatry. See the standard Jewish commentators. I have translated the verse literally, except that it was impossible to render some of the Hebrew terms by simple English equivalents, and the metaphors of the first part of the verse had to be replaced by flat statements to bring out the meaning intended. The verb ࠆࠍࠄ in this context has nothing specifically to do with prostitution. It refers to copulation with a non-Israelite, which is its technical meaning in the halachah (see the commentators on this verse, and compare Issure Bi'ah XVIII:1).

45-46 This hymn is reproduced by Cowley, pp. 68-69 and 870-872. The phrase quoted here is from the second verse on p. 68. Cowley's mss. do not give the name of the author, and this is the first evidence to become available. The name Aba ʿIwaḍ would correspond to ࠀࠁࠀ ࠏࠅࠀࠑ. The use of the old accusative form *Aba* in all positions would be the natural development in Arabic of this period. The use of the form *Abu* in all positions in modern Arabic is an artificial copying of classical Arabic, *Abu* being the citation form.

50 Food prepared by a non-Israelite could contain something the eating of which is forbidden, and the Samaritan might eat it without realising. The Hebrew translation gives the example of meat mixed with milk, or meat from animals sacrificed to heathen gods.

52-62 The text of Mss. JD is original: see, for example, the note on 61-62. The text of the other mss. diverges so much from this that it is not practical to collate the two forms of the text.

52-53 and **59-60** Dyeing will bring the Samaritan in contact with linsey-woolsey (see 48-49) and tanning will bring him in contact with the hides of animals killed by non-Israelites and so on (see 46-48). From these examples we deduce that any trade that brings a person into contact with things that are unclean and can never be cleansed is forbidden to Israel.

54 and **61** The term 'defiled areas' or 'areas barred to them because of defiled remains' could refer to places known to have been used as cemeteries at some time, but this is uncertain.

58 and **66** This refers to deliberate transgression. (Compare the Ṭubâkh 74-78 and the cross-references there). If the matter was accidental, the situation is completely different. See the Ṭubâkh 6-10, and the cross-references there. Presumably, even in the case of a deliberate transgression, repentance and prayer would be effective.

61-62 The reader will notice that at the end of line 61 and the start of line 62 there is a fault in the syntax of the translation. This is because there is a fault in the syntax of the original, which I have not plastered over. The original reading is as in 54. The fault has arisen under the influence of 60.

TEXT 3

The Book of Differences

Chapter Six

2-13 The kinds of bleeding are treated as follows: on the *niddå*, 41-116; on the *då̊bå*, 117-121; on the *zå̊bå*, 165-201; on *yēlīda*, 202-214; on *dam ṭaå̊rå*, 215-254.

3-4 See 122-165.

6-9 For general information on the *zåb*, compare T 93-94 and 118-120; Kf ch. XI, 19-20; the Additional Passage from the Khilâf; Kâsh ch. XV, 5-9; 82-100; M.N. III, IV, V, VIII.

7 See T 93-94 and 118-120, and Kf ch. XI, 19; Kâsh ch. XV, 23-25; and see the note on the Kâfi for the details of how often the emission has to occur.

7-8 See Kf ch. XI, 19-22, and T 81-93 N.

15-193 To avoid repetition as each individual point occurs, let us say here that in the matters treated in this section the Karaites and Samaritans agree, except in the matter of the colours of blood.

All of this section is probably influenced by a Karaite source. My reasons for saying this are: the differences in arrangement between this section and the corresponding sections of the other Samaritan texts edited here; the sophisticated use of linguistic arguments; the references to Saadya, which seem to imply direct knowledge of his writings; the references to Anan, whose views would be completely irrelevant to the Samaritans by this time; the use of the Jewish terms ࠌࠔࠍࠄ or ࠌࠉࠔࠍࠄ and ࠕࠒࠍࠄ; the detailed knowledge of Rabbanite arguments and exegesis, as opposed to just knowing their practice; the arguments from observed phenomena; the appeal to what is seen to be natural and reasonable; the argument in 155-157 based on the silence of the text, where the Samaritans would tend to appeal to tradition to supply the details missing in the text; the specific reference to a Karaite source in 147; and the departure from the traditional Samaritan arguments in 33-34 and 122-138.

This does not mean that the whole section is lifted directly from one source. The style is to a great extent the author's typical style, which means that he has edited his material to some extent. The way in which reference is made to a Karaite author in 147-151 implies that he has moved to a new source, but still a Karaite one.

15-32 The point of the comparison is that it is forbidden to eat pork under any circumstances at any time, and it is forbidden to be immoral at any time, whereas blood in its substance is neither clean nor unclean, and only derives its cleanness or uncleanness from the circumstances of its appearance. The circumstance that makes it unclean is its emission from the vagina, and any blood emitted from the vagina is unclean, with the exception of virginal blood.

As the Rabbanites do not maintain that some colours of blood are clean, as the author maintains, but rather that blood can only be certain colours, and other discolourations are not visibly blood, all this is irrelevant. See the notes on 130-132 and 36-40.

18 I have given preference to the reading كالاحكام في العقليه 'the commandments about personal character' in the majority of the mss., as against the reading كالاحكام العقليه 'the commandments that can be justified rationally' in Ms. S_1, as the change from the first to the second reading would be easier than the reverse. It is to be noticed, however, that this change could only happen if the Samaritans formally distinguish, as do the Jews, between rational and non-rational commandments. The distinction would presumably be a philosophical one, as with Jews, with no effect on the degree of observance of one kind of commandment as opposed to the other kind.

20 As a marginal note in Ms. U points out, what is meant is the obligation to avoid frivolousness and drunkenness and irreligiousness.

29 On the grammatical form افواه, see above, p. 51.

27-32 The Jews would agree with all this.

33-37 This is directed against the Rabbanites: see Issure Bi'ah V:6-12.

33-34 For the explanation, see the note on 130-132.

36-40 Compare 139-143.

It is, however, admitted that this is not the literal intention of the verse and that for this purpose the verse is only an אסמכתא: see the commentators.

41-116 On *niddå* bleeding in general, compare Kf. ch. XI, 45-55; T 6-11; Kh 43-116; 255-258; 262-263; Far 2-65; Kâsh ch. XV, 101-123; Iʿtiq 8-21; 96-110; Sharḥ Sûrat al-Irbot.

43-44 The point of saying that its appearance is at the normal time is that it is not *zåbå* blood in that case.

44-47 Compare Far 33-34; Iʿtiq 96-110. This etymology depends on the existence of some such practice as is described in Iʿtiq 12-17; and compare Kâsh ch. XV, 107-112.

45 Notice that the less reliable mss. give an alternative translation of *nā*, equally correct but not the one intended by the author.

46-47 The term ࠍࠏࠃࠄ *nå'ēda* is an Aramaic or Hebrew participle. It is very useful, as it allows the use of separate terms for the *niddå* blood and the *niddå* woman. Its use is confined to the Khilâf as far as I know. (The Sharḥ Sûrat al-Irbot, on pp. 57b and 58b of the ms. used here, uses the term *nå'ēda*, spelt ࠍࠀࠃࠄ, but this is in a reminiscence of the Khilâf, as the context shows). Compare the notes on 64, 130, and 135.

46 The term reffered to is the term *niddå*.

51-55 On copulation with a woman known to be unclean, see the references in T 74-78 N and 8-10 N.

51-53 It applies to a woman with any emission of blood from the vagina. Compare Kh 101-114; Far 59-65; and see T 74-78 and 8-10 N.

57-58 The same information is given in expanded form in 66-67. Compare T 34-36 and 13-14 and the notes there.

61-62 The point of this is that the seven days of the *zåbå*, on the other hand, are not an exact week since you have to count seven whole days after the last day of bleeding, so the minimum period of uncleanness is eight days.

63-65 Bleeding on the eighth day does not mark the start of a period of *zåbå*, according to this author, but the start of a second week of *niddå*. Compare 165-167.

64 The term *zībot* is a Karaite one, formed so as to provide separate terms for the stuff of the issue and the woman from whom it issues. It occurs again in 135 (where the mss. vary between *zībot* and *zåbot*) and 171 (in the form *zåbot*). See 135 N.

65 For Anan's opinion, see 132-177.

66 On the way the separation is carried out see Iʿtiq 12-17 and 114-115.

67-73 The period of uncleanness due to the *niddå* blood is used in Lv XII:2 and 5 as a unit of measurement. Compare 54-58.

69-70 The same proof of the distinction betwean the effects of *niddå* bleeding and *dåbå* bleeding is given as seen from a different angle in Kf ch. XI, 56-58.

73-75 In 92-97 the argument is given in detail.

76 The reproduction of part of this chapter in the Iʿtiqâdât starts here.

76-110 The point that it does not make the slightest differance how the blood gets on the man, which the author makes over and over here, is made by the author of the Farâ'iḍ in 49-58. There is enough similarity in the argument to suggest a common source, and we do find a common source in Kh 73-78 and 98-101 and Far 59-65.

76-78 This is not only Saadya's opinion, but the standard Rabbanite position. See Mishkav Umoshav VI:1-3.

77-110 The analysis and exposition of the argument of this passage by Halkin (*The Relation of the Samaritans to Saadia Gaon*, pp. 293-294) is not very satisfactory, being both excessively abbreviated and unclear, and to some extent confused, or badly expressed.

I take the opportunity to give the text of the ms. borrowed by Halkin the existence of which seems to have been forgotten by the Jewish Theological Seminary Library (see above, Introduction, pp. 40-41), as quoted by Halkin. All the extracts are given in Hebrew letters by Halkin, but it seems that this was only done for convenience, and that the ms. is written in Arabic letters, since the transliteration system is not the one used by the Samaritans. Signs of inconsistency in the transliteration confirm this supposition. I have accordingly re-transliterated the extracts back into Arabic letters.

Corresponding to 77-79 and 87-90 in my edition:

فزعم ان هذا الخطاب مقول في حق من اتطا زوجته فى زمان ࠍࠃࠕࠄ وهو عالم بانها ࠍࠃࠄ وهو على مذهبنا مقول في حق من انضجع مع زوجته اما بمجرد نوم او وطى ... مع علمه اناها طاهره في مبدا الامر ... فان ما اعتمده الفيومي باطل من وجهين احدهما انه محل المحتمل صريحا ولو كان صريحا لما افتقر التعين الى قرينه ونظير ذلك ࠅࠀࠔࠄ ࠀࠔࠓ ࠉࠔࠊࠁ ࠀࠉࠔ ࠀࠕࠄ ࠔࠊࠁࠕ ࠆࠓࠏ.

Corresponding to 92-95 in my edition:

وغلط ايضا في قوله ... حكم ࠍࠃࠕࠄ وهو الزمان الذي يلزم بعدتها ... والشارع انما قصد ࠃࠌ ࠍࠃࠕࠄ وقد اشتهر كيفية الدم ࠁࠍࠃࠕࠄ وهو الدم الاول الذي عنه يلزم الحكم.

Corresponding to 107-108 in my edition:

والشارع قد جعل هذا النايم الواطي مع الاحتمال مع جملة اطميا طمايهم حاصله بطريق الجواز والعرض لا بطريق الممتنع والخطر

Corresponding to 114-115 in my edition:

وحاصل جميع ذلك ان مقصود الشارع فهمناه من خطابه تعالى وجهله الفيومي وشيعته.

In the quotation of Lv XV:18 at the end of the first extract, Halkin has [Samaritan] instead of the correct reading [Samaritan]. As it is far more likely that Halkin was influenced by the variant reading of the MT than that the scribe misquoted a commonly-used verse, I have corrected the error in the quotation. It is to be presumed that the quotation extended to the end of the verse, as in the other mss., but Halkin has followed the word [Samaritan] by an abbreviation symbol, which I take to be his own insertion, as it is one used by Jews and never by Samaritans.

78-81 This is the standard Samaritan exegesis: see T 8-10, and the note and cross-references there. The Rabbanites take the phrase 'and her *niddå* gets on him' to mean that the contamination which is the consequence of the *niddå* applies to him: see Mishkav Umoshav VI:2.

Compare Kh 92-97.

84 The point of the quotation is that this verse occurs at the end of a section giving the details of purification from contamination that has been acquired in an inevitable way and where the procedure is given without any mention of any penalty. The verse quoted and the verse before it class the man who has been contaminated due to copulation with a *niddå* woman along with a woman or man who have been made unclean by a discharge of some kind, to which no blame can attach. See 107-114.

88-91 See Dozy and Fagnan on the term قرينه. There is no simple English equivalent.

92-97 See 78-81 and the note there.

96 Mss. B_2LJC are right in using the word [Samaritan] in the construct state, as this is the form of it in the verse quoted. Compare 113 for another instance of the same phenomenon.

98 The two laws are Lv XV:24 and XX:18.

98-101 On the question of copulation with a woman known to be unclean, see the references in T 74-87 N and T 8-10 N.

101-102 This requirement of an explicit statement of the dealth penalty by Scripture is of course a basic principle in Rabbanite and Karaite halachah. We must remember, however, that the Rabbanites do not find any death penalty mentioned in Lv XX:18, since they take [Samaritan] to be a prediction, not a command, and take it to refer to premature natural death. Therefore, even if the author is correct in accusing them of taking the verse in a figurative sense, they are still innocent of the change of deriving a death penalty from a figurative interpretation of a verse.

Compare Kh 51-53; 102-106; 112-114; T 75-78; Far 59-65; T 8-10 N.

102-106 Compare 139-140 on the inadmissibility of arguments based on a possible connotation.

103 I am not sure that I have fully understood the terminology and have the feeling that the words تكلف and زياده have both got a more technical sense here than the ones I have given in the translation. Nevertheless, the gist is clear: the Rabbanites are being accused of *reading something into the text*, instead of interpreting what is intended. Probably تكلف is forcing a meaning into the text that is not present in the natural meaning of the verse, and زياده is a detail of halachah not mentioned by the verse but added on to the rest of the halachah by finding an אסמכתא in the verse. Compare 135-138.

103-104 See T 75-78 N and T 8-10 N.

104 By a 'possible connotation' [محتمل] is meant an אסמכתא, i.e. a meaning that can be read into the verse but that was not the intention of the author or is not the natural meaning of the verse. Compare 140, and the context.

The translation 'possible connotation' rather than just 'connotation' has been used because the term 'connotation' by itself in English means an impression or implication or addition to the meaning or extra information that the word or phrase bears in itself, so that the connotation is normally received or registered along with the basic meaning, whereas the محتمل is a way in which the expression can be taken, but need not be, and usually would not, unless there was some reason for it.

107-114 See the note on 84. Compare T 8-10; Kf ch. XI, 49-55; Far 49-53.

112-114 See the references in T 74-78 N and T 8-10 N.

113 Mss. $S_1S_2DB_2LJUC$ are right in using the construct form ࠈࠄࠓࠕ, as this is the form in the verse quoted. Compare 96.

115-121 The I'tiqâdât omits everything from 'and Al-Fayyûmi' in 115 to the end of 121.

117-121 On *dåbå* bleeding in general, compare T 12-15; Kf ch. XI, 56-60; Kh 117-121; 258; 262-263; I'tiq 22-23.

117-118 The author of the Ṭubâkh and the author of the Kâfi maintain that the person who touches the *dåbå* blood becomes clean at sunset the same day, provided the blood is washed off before then (T 55-57 N and T 13-14 N; Kf ch. XI, 84-87 N; 85 N), and this is the modern position as well (Kâshif ch. XV, 101-112; I'tiq 23). Sakta the Dosithean seems to have maintained that contact with the woman herself, or with the blood, had no effect (T 11-13 N). This author seems to take an intermediate position, and seems to maintain that the person who touches the woman is unclean as long as they are in contact with her, but when that person lets go of her, there is no more uncleanness. If they come in contact with the blood, they will only be unclean till it is washed off. It will be seen that the result will be the same in practice as it would for Sakta, i.e. there would be no practical effect from contact with a woman in the state of *dåbå*, or *dåbå* blood. The author of the Khilâf has the same opinion in regard to ࠃࠌ ࠈࠄࠓࠄ as well (Kh 209-214 TN), and by analogy would probably have had the same opinion in regard to contact with a *zåbå* woman during the days of her count (for the connection see T 11-13 N). Compare Kh 257-258 and 262-263.

The author of the interpolation in the Khilâf, in 266-269, shows that he knows two opinions on this matter, one the opinion that has become standard, and one an opinion that could be Sakta's or could be the same as the opinion of the author of the Khilâf. The author of the interpolation, in 268-269, gives preference to the first opinion. The author of a gloss inside this same interpolation, at 262-263, agrees with the second opinion, whether in the form that Sakta held it or in the form that the author of the Khilâf held it.

122-138 See the note on 197-199.

122 It is strange that the author should have picked on yellow as an example of a colour that the Rabbanites do not count as blood, since one shade of yellow, saffron, is in fact one of the five colours counted by them as being colours due to the presence of blood. (See Issure Bi'ah V:6-10). Probably the author is thinking of a more definite yellow, or yellow in general, which the Rabbanites would definitely not count as causing uncleanness.

127-129 Compare 156-157.

130-138 Everything after the words ما نعلمه 'what we know' to the end of 138 is omitted in the I'tiqâdât and replaced by the following:

وناقلين اليه لان حكم الدما ونجاسته عاملين بها جارين على حفظها جيلا بعد جيل غير اليهود الذي
عدمت من عندهم حفظ هذه الشريعه حتى صاروا جاهلين افعالها

'And have received by tradition about this, carrying out the requirements of the varieties of blood and their uncleanness and keeping up their observance generation after generation, unlike the Jews, who have abandoned the observance of this law and because of this have lost the knowledge of how to practise it'.

This complaint is a common one of the Samaritans against the Jews. Compare I'tiq 68-79. The complaint is fully justified: see, for example, Issure Bi'ah ch. XI.

130-132 It is hard to see why the knowledge that any colour of discharge is counted as blood in the case of recovery from the condition of *zåbå* should be more certain than the knowledge that the same applies in the case of *niddå*, so that the first could be used as proof for the second by analogy, unless this argument goes back to a time when the Samaritans agreed with the Rabbanites on only counting an issue that was visibly blood-coloured as being blood or evidence of bleeding, except in the case of *zåbå*, which is the most serious of the issues from a woman, and even in this case, only for the purpose of breaking the seven days of counting, not for the purpose of putting the woman in the state of *zåbå* in the first place. Notice carefully the author's choice of wording: he does not say that an issue like this can put the woman in the state of *zåbå*, he says it can keep her there, and it is clear that this distinction is intended from the choice of the case of bleeding just before the end of the seventh day. This interpretation is very nicely confirmed by 197-199, where we are told that an issue of any colour whatever other than white counts as bleeding or evidence of bleeding only after the woman has entered the state of *zåbå*. This interpretation is confirmed as well by the way in which the other Samaritan sources, some more clearly than others, make the point that an issue of one of these colours is evidence of bleeding even though not blood itself. (See the notes on the terms *ishtibâh* and *shubhah* [plausibility] on the Ṭubâkh 66 and the cross-references there). This means that the disagreement between the Samaritans and the Rabbanites was not originally over the colour or kind of blood, but over whether the blood had to be visible or whether its presence could be deduced. The disagreement over whether the woman's menstruation is counted from the time that she experiences some symptom or feeling that tells her she must be menstruating, or from the time that she actually sees some blood, which is treated in the note on the Farâ'iḍ probably has the same origin.

There is a variant opinion in the interpolation in the Khilâf, at 260-261, where we are told that a discharge of any colour at all can put the woman in the state of *zåbå* at the appropriate time.

The situation is, then, that the Rabbanites will only accept what is visibly blood as blood, and do not allow the category of ספק דם (Issure Bi'ah V:6); the Karaites agree that only what is visibly blood is certainly blood, but allow the category of ספק דם, the possibility of blood (Gan 'Eden 110d middle; Adderet Eliyahu 122a middle); and the sources of the Khilâf (but not the author himself) are willing to treat some issue that might be blood as blood in the case of a woman recovering from the condition of *zåbå* (which is the one case in which the distinction between what is possibly and what is certainly blood is the least clear and is perhaps irrelevant), in agreement with the Karaites, but are not willing to do this in other cases, in agreement with the Rabbanites. The position of the author of the Khilâf himself is that any discolouration is not just evidence of the presence of blood, but actually is blood. The evidence he uses would support the proposition that the category of ספק דם should be extended to cover *niddå* bleeding as well, but it does not support the proposition that any discolouration of the vaginal fluid is really and truly blood. Nevertheless, we should be grateful for the author's fuzzy thinking in this case, as it leads him to give information about a divergent opinion that would not otherwise have been well attested.

This information is put in the context of the whole range of variation of opinion on this matter in the note on the Ṭubâkh 66.

130 Mss. $S_1B_1S_2DB_2L$ read *zå̄bå*; Mss. JUCG read *zåb*. The use of the masculine from *zåb* to refer to the female discharge is attested in T 32 and T 62, and the reading of JUCG is probably to be preferred as the harder reading.

131 On the colours, see the note on 197-199.

133-134 See the note on 130-132.

134-135 Compare Kâsh ch. XII, 6-7, for a similar statement in another context.

135 The term *niddot* is a Karaite one, formed so as to provide separate terms for the stuff of the issue and the woman from whom it issues. It occurs again in another context in 151 and 153.

On the term *zībot* or *zå̄bot* see 64 N.

135 What is meant by an addition here is a detail of halachah not given in the text of Scripture. Compare 103 and 138.

138 I take the *uṣûl* to be the Scriptural commandments and the *ziyâdah* to be an extra detail of halachah to be observed in the carrying out of one of these commandments, but not mentioned by Scripture. The meaning of the word *aṣl* assumed is close to its meaning in Moslem law, where it means a law stated by the Koran, as opposed to one known by tradition (*sunnah*) or derived by means of argument (*far*ʿ).

138 This is the standard complaint of the Karaites against the Rabbanites. In the present context the phrase *sharîʿah thâniyah* 'a second Torah' is obscure, but in a Karaite work it would be understood immediately.

139-143 Compare 36-40.

139-141 For the inadmissibility of arguments based on a possible connotation or אסמכתא in a different context, compare 103-106.

140 The *muḥtamal* is an אסמכתא. What is *aẓhar* is the פשט. The Rabbanites agree with the Samaritans on the literal meaning of the verse.

141 The readings احد and تاو يليه are confirmed in 224.

144 Lv XV: 19 and 23 mention blood without any qualification as to substance, only time.

147-215 This is omitted in the Iʿtiqâdât.

147-151 See Mishnah Nidda IV: 1 and the corresponding Tosefta and Gemara, which are the source of this accusation against the Samaritans. (The author of the Khilâf knows the complaint at second-hand, through a Karaite source, not from the original sources or even from Saadya's own works).

156-157 Compare 127-129.

158-159 The Samaritans do not do this at all. As a matter of fact, this is the post-Talmudic Rabbanite practice: see Issure Biʾah ch. XI. It is possible, of course, that Saadya knew of a Samaritan group that did follow this practice: see T 15 N.

Notice that it would only have been reasonable for the Rabbanites to count this practice as an error of the Samaritans before the time when they themselves started doing the same thing, which means that Saadya is quoting an older source uncritically when he says this.

165-201 On *zå̄bå* bleeding in general, compare T 16-44; Kf ch. XI, 61-67; Kh 259-261; 264-266; Far 80-119; Kâsh ch. XV, 124-141; Iʿtiq 32-40; Sharḥ Sûrat al-Irbot; M.N. I and II.

165-171 There is considerable variation in the sources on the question of the number of times in a row that the week of uncleanness due to *niddå* can occur. See the note on the Kâfi, ch. XI, 58-61, and the cross-references there.

The argument assumed and partly quoted by the author here is set out in full in the note on the Ṭubâkh 26-29.

The reason for the author's insistence that bleeding can only put the woman in the state of *zåbå* if it occurs on the first day of the next week is that he is taking the expression *al niddåtå* to mean either "immediately past her *niddå*" or "as a multiple of her *niddå*", and whichever meaning is correct, the result is the same. Compare M.N. II:4-8.

167-171 Compare T 30 N. See also Kh 186-193 N.

This interpretation of the term ࠏࠋ ࠍࠃࠕࠄ in Lv XV:25 is one of the many Karaite ones. See Gan ʿEden p. 112b bottom. There is a different interpretation of the term in T 33.

If the woman starts *niddå* bleeding seven days or less after the end of the previous *niddå* week and does this seven times in a row, she becomes *zåbå*.

Compare Kh 186-193; 264-265.

171 On the term *zåbot*, see 64 N.

176-177 This is a correct statement of Anan's position, See Harkavy's edition, p. 42. It is also the opinion of some Samaritans: see Kf ch. XI, 58-61.

179-185 Compare Far 80-83 and 87-88.

186-193 The Rabbanites take the term ࠏࠋ ࠍࠃࠕࠄ to be the time during which any bleeding that occurs can be counted as *niddå* rather than *zåbå*. This author agrees with them that this is what the term means, but refers the term to the time after the start of the second week of menstruation, when any new onset of bleeding will, according to him, be *niddå*, whereas the Rabbanites refer the term to the seven day period at the start of each eighteen day cycle. Compare 167-171 and the note there.

In the Rabbanite system, there is a cycle made up of seven days, during which any bleeding that occurs counts as *niddå*, and eleven days, during which any bleeding that occurs counts as *zåbå*. When the total of eighteen days are over, a new cycle starts. It will be obvious, as the author of the Khilâf points out, that very few women's real menstrual cycle will match this, so that it must often happen that normal menstrual bleeding is counted as *zåbå*. For instance, if the woman has a twenty-eight day cycle, then the twenty-ninth day, the first day of the second round, will be the eleventh day of the second round of the calculating system, and the bleeding on that day will count as *zåbå*, and the bleeding of the next day, which is still menstrual bleeding, will count as *niddå*. It will take two hundred and fifty-two days, or nine real menstrual cycles or fourteen theoretical ones, before the first day of *niddå* in both cycles coincide with each other.

For the details of the Rabbanite system, see Issure Bi'ah ch. VI.

186-188 Compare Kh 167-171; 264-265; and T 33.

187 When the author calls the period between the instances or periods of menstrual flow the time of her cleanness, he means that the woman normally would be clean at the time, since the week of menstruation is finished. If any bleeding does occur, then the woman becomes unclean, by *niddå* in this author's system and *zåbå* in the Rabbanite system.

187-188 If the start of the next menstruation occurs one or two or three days short of the total of eighteen days it counts as *zåbå* in the Rabbanite system.

191-192 The author does not explain how this proves his point, but what he probably meant was this: If a woman bleeds for, say, nineteen days in a row, with some bleeding on each day, then in the system of this author she is counted as having had three weeks under the contamination of *niddå*, one from the first to the seventh day, one from the eighth to the fourteenth day, and one starting on the fifteenth day which will end on the twenty-first day. In the Rabbanite system she will be counted as having had a week of *niddå* from the first to the seventh day, then eleven days as *zåbå* from the eighth to the eighteenth day, then a week of *niddå* starting on the nineteenth day and which will end on the twenty-fifth and during which she is still unclean as *zåbå* as well because she has not had a chance to count seven days without bleeding. In the system of the author of the Khilâf, the bleeding is treated the same for the whole period, but in the Rabbanite system, the woman is first *niddå*, then *zåbå*, without any corresponding change in her physical condition, and this could be regarded as illogical.

194-196 The distinction between the uncleanness of *niddå* and *zăbå* in this author's system is supposed to match the real distinction between prolonged menstrual bleeding and bleeding due to a longstanding injury or illness, as determined by observation of actual cases.

197-199 We are told here that emissions of these various colours count as bleeding or evidence of bleeding *after* the state of *zåbå* has been determined. Compare the note on 130-132 for the implications of this.

It might be wondered why it is that in the list of colours of the issue that prove that the issue is blood or that blood is present in it, the colour white is included, when it says just before this, and in 131-132, that it is any deviation from white that is evidence of uncleanness, and in the parallel passages T 71-72 and Kf 79-80 the colour white is not mentioned in the list of colours of an unclean issue. The answer is that the term white can refer to two different colours: it can refer to a sort of dirty white or off-white, which is evidence of the presence of blood, or it can refer to a pure white which is evidence that no blood is present. This is why the Farâ'iḍ (7-14) and I'tiqâdât (8-11 and 65-67) say that the characteristic colour of a clean emission from the vagina is not just white, but pure clear white, as the Farâ'iḍ says, or pure white, as the I'tiqâdât says. This explanation is confirmed by the Karaite halachah, which makes exactly this distinction: see G.E. 110d middle and A.E. 122a middle. Compare Far 5-6 N. See also the baraita in Bavli Niddah 33a, explaining Mishnah Niddah IV:1.

200-201 The point is that the *zåbå* is unclean for seven whole days after the day on which the *zåbå* bleeding finishes, so that the minimum number of days is one part day and seven whole days, whereas the woman unclean due to *niddå* is unclean for seven days including the day the bleeding starts, so that the first day out of the seven is only part of a day, not a whole one. It is not to be imagined that the author of the Khilâf means to imply that the terms ࠎࠐࠉࠓࠄ and ࠌࠏࠓࠁ ࠏࠃ ࠏࠓࠁ both occur in the same verse. The verse that proves that the term ࠎࠐࠉࠓࠄ refers to whole days is Lv XXIII:18. The reader is expected to know that this is what the term ࠎࠐࠉࠓࠄ implies, and the reason for quoting the phrase ࠌࠏࠓࠁ ࠏࠃ ࠏࠓࠁ is to specify whole days or natural days with more emphasis. The phrase ࠌࠏࠓࠁ ࠏࠃ ࠏࠓࠁ in Lv XXIII:32 means that the Day of Atonement is to be not less than twenty-four hours, from sunset at the end of the ninth and start of the tenth to sunset at the end of the tenth, and in the Khilâf here it is used as an allusion to this verse to explain what is meant by whole days or natural days. Once it is established that the term ࠎࠐࠉࠓࠄ or the verb ࠎࠐࠓ imply the counting of whole days wherever they are used in the halachic sections of the Torah, this information can be applied to Lv XV:28.

Compare T 15 N and Far 25-30.

203-204 The author allows the uncleanness of childbirth to over-ride the uncleanness of *niddå* or *zåbå*. This means that once the forty or eighty days are up no notice need be taken of bleeding that occurred before delivery. Compare Far 103-110 and the note there for the application of the same principle to bleeding on the forty-first or eighty-first day.

202-214 For information on bleeding of childbirth in general, compare T 45-52; Kf ch. XI, 68-72; the whole of the extract from ch. XIII of the Kâfi; Kâsh ch. XII, 2-7; 14-17; I'tiq 41-46; 53-56.

202 These requirements are said to be straightforward in contrast to what is said about the requirements of the *niddå* in 15-26.

202-214 There is disagreement among the sources on whether any distinction is to be made between the blood that appears exactly at delivery and the blood that appears during the rest of the week or fortnight. This author makes the distinction, but then says that the women normally treat the later bleeding as more serious than ࠃࠌ ࠈࠄࠓࠄ, which means they do not make the distinction. The author of the Ṭubâkh has the strange opinion that the distinction is made in the case of a boy but not in the case of a girl (T 47-52 N). The I'tiqâdât (41-43 and 55-56) specifically says the distinction is not made, the Kâfi (ch. XI, 68-69) implies the same by its silence, and the wording of the Kâfi in ch. XIII, 19-21, the interpolation in the Khilâf in 269, and the Kâshif, ch. XII, 14, can only mean the distinction is not made. All sources assimilate the first category of bleeding in giving birth to the *niddå* blood. The difference lies in whether the first category only covers the bleeding at the instant of delivery or whether it covers the bleeding for the rest of the week or fortnight as well. If it only covers the bleeding at delivery, then logically the bleeding for the rest of the week or fortnight has to be assimilated to *dåbå* blood, as is done by the author of the Khilâf.

There is another disagreement among the sources over whether the blood that appears at the birth of a girl causes a week's uncleanness or a fortnight's to anyone that it touches. It could be argued that if it is equivalent to *niddå* blood, it can only cause a week's contamination, but it could equally well be argued that if it contaminates the mother for a fortnight it ought to do the same to anyone else it touches. The Khilâf, and the I'tiqâdât in 53-56 and 104-106 count it as causing a fortnight's contamination. The Ṭubâkh (47-52) definitely says, and the Kâfi (ch. XI, 68-69) implies by its silence, that it still only causes a week's contamination.

Sakta the Dosithean seems to have maintained that the blood emitted at the birth of a girl caused a fortnight's contamination to anyone that touched it, as we see from the following statement (Abu 'l-Fatḥ 162:5): وقال ان المولود يلزمه ما يلزم والدته من الطماء. 'He said that the same uncleanness applied to the baby as to the mother'. He seems to have agreed with the Falashas that the baby is unclean for the full period of a week plus thirty-three days or a fortnight plus sixty-six days. The requirements of symmetry would then demand a fortnight's contamination of anyone that touched the blood. (All of this requires further study).

The author of the Khilâf maintains that the blood that appears during the rest of the week or fortnight, which to him is a category separate to the bleeding at the instant of delivery, but not to the other sources, is to be assimilated to the *dåbå* bleeding and causes uncleanness for one day to anyone that touches it.

209-214 On the terminology and argument compare 257-258; and see T 11-13 N and T 13-14 N.

212-214 See T 13 N.

215-253 On bleeding of cleansing in general, compare T 53-59; Kf ch. XI, 73-78; Kâsh ch. XII, 11-17; I'tiq 47-50 and 58-64.

215 What is said here about the bleeding of cleansing starting after the seventh day after delivery of a boy is in agreement with T 53-55 and Kf 73-76, but the Iʿtiqâdât and Kâshif start the count after the eighth day. See Iʿtiq 47-52 N and Kâsh ch. XII, 8-13.

215-219 What is said here about the Jews only applies to the Rabbanites, not the Karaites.

220-227 Same proof in Far 66-68, which depends on the same source as this passage, and in shorter form in Kh 249-250.

221 The Iʿtiqâdât omits ويريد به نقاها 'where it means her absence of bleeding', and has instead وقوله عن الذهب الذي امر به بعمل بعض الات الهيكل ذهب طاهر اي ذهب نقي 'and the verse about the gold about which there was a command to make some of the Temple equipment, "clean gold" (Ex XXV:29), i.e. pure gold'.

225 After اولى 'better' the Iʿtiqâdât adds ونقلهم اليه اثبت بجريانهم بعمله والمحافظه اليه 'and their tradition about it is more reliable because they make sure to practise it and they observe it'.

228 I have taken the term *iḥtiyâṭ* to refer to the process of taking the more rigorous interpretation of a verse, the one that leads to an extra detail of halachah or a more exacting way of carrying out an item of halachah, in a case where the verse can be interpreted in two different ways. The term *iḥtiyâṭ* is not a translation of החמרה, but it does express one aspect of the concept. This interpretation has the merit of fitting well into the context, and in particular, of making the sentence in which the word occurs lead naturally into the next sentence.

231 On the meaning of the word *ajra* (better-integrated) here and in 233 and 237, see Kf 72 N. If the interpretation chosen by the application of the principle of choosing the more rigorous interpretation happens to be the normally-accepted interpretation of the verse, the two criteria of right exegesis and general acceptance re-inforce each other and the agreement between the results of the two criteria is the integration spoken of, which agreement or integration is a sign that the interpretation is correct.

234-235 It does not make any difference whether bleeding occurs or not: she is still unclean, just like the *zå̄bå* during her seven days of cleansing, who is unclean even though not bleeding.

238-241 Compare T 74-78 TN and T 8-10 TN.

242-243 This is the Rabbanite interpretation, not the Karaite one. See A.E. 123c, the commentators, and Meḥussere Kapparah I:1.

243 On the meaning of the term *aṣl*, see 138 N.

249-250 Same proof in Kh 200-224 and Far 66-68 in a more detailed form.

The Rabbanite interpretation of this verse is that up till this time the woman is unclean, but only to the extent of making holy things common and being forbidden to enter the Temple, not to the extent of making common things unclean. Compare 242-243.

251-253 There is no exact English name for the argument used here. It is a היקש. If the *zå̄bå* is fully unclean, so must the woman during the thirty-three days or sixty-six days be, since they are treated identically in other respects.

251 The insertion of the word ࠅࠄࠆࠁࠄ in the text can be shown to be an interpolation by two arguments: first, the case of the *zåb* is irrelevant here; second, the words كل واحده 'each one (fem.)' and منهما 'of the pair of them' in line 2 show that the author was not thinking of the *zåb*. Notice that the author or authors of the Iʿtiqâdât have felt the difficulty, and have made various attempts at smoothing the text out.

On the question of interpolations now present in all or most of the mss., compare the notes on 263 and 259-269.

254 After this the Iʿtiqâdât goes its own way: see Iʿtiq 112-118.

257-258 On the terminology and argument, compare 117-118; 209-214; and T 13-14 N.

259-269 This section is an interpolation, or perhaps a series of interpolations:

259-261 does not fit in after the statement that there are two points of difference between the Samaritans and the Jews.

262-263 is a repetition of 257-258, and does not fit in with 260-261.

264-269 is concerned with the *zåbå*, and does not belong for the same reason that 259-261 does not belong. It does not fit in after 262-263, but it does fit after 260-261, which could mean that 262-263 is an interpolation inside an interpolation. Compare the note on 263.

266-267 refers back to a passage in another treatise, not this one.

In 269 the terminology is not the author's.

260-261 contradicts 130-132 (see the next note).

263 There are three separate readings here: حال واحد 'a single instant' in Ms. S_1; حال واحد يعني يطهر لوقته 'a single instant i.e. he can be cleansed immediately' in most of the mss.; and the majority reading with the omission of the word واحد 'single' in Ms. L. The reading chosen is simply 'an instant' as in 212, as this is the only one that accounts for all three of the other readings. The addition of the word واحد 'single' I take to be an accomodation to the more usual phrasing, as in 117; 118; 209. The phrase يعني يطهر لوقته 'i.e. he becomes clean immediately' I take to be a correct gloss. (We have here two different interpolations inside an interpolation. Compare what is said about 262-263 in the note on 259-269. See 117-118 TN and 209-214 TN.

264-265 To put the woman in a state of *zåbå*, the bleeding does not have to be continuous for fifty days. All that is needed is one day's bleeding to put the woman in the state of *niddå*, then another onset of bleeding starting not later than the seventh day after the end of the first week of *niddå*, so that the woman starts a second week of *niddå*, then another onset of bleeding not more than thirteen days after this i.e. not more than seven days after the end of the second nidda week, then five more *niddå* weeks calculated the same way, then more bleeding starting not more than seven days after the end of the seventh menstrual week. It will be seen from this that although it is possible for the woman to become *zåbå* in fifty days [$7 \times 7 + 1$], it can take as long as ninety-two days [$7(7+6)+1$]. If, on the other hand, the sequence is interrupted by one onset of bleeding occurring more than fourteen days [$7+7$] after the one before, i.e. more than seven days after the end of the previous *niddå* week, the new onset of bleeding is counted as *niddå* by itself, and this can happen time after time without the woman becoming *zåbå*; even if she has had seven periods of *niddå* that have been close enough together to be counted together, and only needs one more onset of bleeding to make her *zåbå*, if it happens more than seven days after the end of the seventh *niddå* week it does not count as *zåbå* but as *niddå*. Compare Kh 167-171; 186-193; and T 33. The weeks referred to in line 265 are the weeks after the end of the previous menstrual week when the bleeding has to start again if the uncleanness caused by it is to be counted in the sequence. Compare on all this Kf 59-60.

266-267 We are told that this has already been said, but it has not. The reference is probably to a passage in the treatise this passage is taken from.

267-269 The author is discussing the degree of contamination, not the penalty. The first opinion is the standard Samaritan one. The second opinion could be either a Dosithean one (see 117-118 N) or the author's, or both. We can assume, from the bringing in of bleeding of cleansing in the same context, that these people did not think that a woman caused any contamination during this period either.

It seems to be implied that the people with whom the author of the interpolation disagrees over the question of contamination still agreed that copulation with a woman in these situations was forbidden. By analogy, the same would apply to copulation with a *dåbå* woman.

269 The period referred to is the period of bleeding of cleansing, during the thirty-three days or sixty-six days after the first week or fortnight. The author of the Khilâf would have used the term ولاده instead of نفاس and طهور instead of نقا. Both terms, نفاس and نقا, are borrowed from Moslem terminology.

Additional Passage

1 The meaning of the word معلولات can be demonstrated from the following passage, which occurs shortly before the one edited here (Ms. S_1 p. 108), the subject being contamination from a corpse:

ويلتزموا في المدنو به طما حال فقط لقوله تعالى ࠅࠄࠍࠐࠔ ࠄࠍࠂࠏࠕ ࠕࠈࠌࠀ ࠏࠃ ࠄࠏࠓࠁ
(تع ١٩ : ٢٢) ويقتصرون على نفس الداني بالميت انه يطما ࠔࠁࠏࠕ ࠉࠌࠉࠌ واما من يدني به
ࠈࠌࠀ ࠍࠐࠔ فانما يلزمه حال واحد فلا يلزمون المعلول الثاني سبعة ايام ولا ترشيش ࠁࠌࠉ
ࠍࠃࠄ.

1-10 Both the Rabbanites and the Karaites agree that a couch or seat or a saddle can be contaminated by a *zåb*, *niddå*, *zåbå*, or *yålēda* putting their weight on it, even if there is no direct contact, and that anyone else can then be contaminated by putting their weight on the same couch, even without direct contact, and that the contamination of that person is equal to what would be caused by direct contact with the *zåb*, *niddå*, *zåbå*, or *yålēda* themselves, not to what would normally be caused by contact with something contaminated by these people. Both of them would add, on the basis of v. 10, that anything that is over the *zåb*, *niddå*, *zåbå*, or *yålēda* becomes contaminated, though the Rabbanites admit that this verse is only an אסמכתא and that this contamination is only a תקנה, and the Karaites admit that the verse has another meaning as well. Most Karaites take verse 10 to mean that any person or thing that touches the couch, seat or saddle of the *zåb* is contaminated. The Rabbanites take it to mean that anyone or anything that touches his saddle is contaminated, but not to the extent that would be caused by touching the couch or seat. Both the Rabbanites and the Karaites would agree that the bedclothes on top of the *zåb* and the rest are contaminated, first by contact with him and second by being over him. For the details, see Gan ʿEden 109b top-109c middle; Keter Torah on v. 10; Mishkav Umoshav VI: 1-2, 5-6.

The reader will have noticed an obvious problem: if all Jews agree that the bedclothes on top of the man get contaminated, how can the author of the Khilâf say that any of them say otherwise? The question is best answered by looking at the other half of the statement, where he says that the Jews maintain that the clothes that have been on top of the man do not cause contamination of anyone or anything that touches them, although the clothes that have been under him do. This is the Rabbanite position. The clothes that have been contaminated by contact with the *zåb* or by being over him are ראשון לטומאה, and therefore can not contaminate people or artefacts, but the clothes that have been under him and have been used by him as part of the bed or couch and have had his weight on them are אב טומאה like the *zåb* himself and do contaminate any people or artefacts they touch. This explains the second half of the statement, and the first half can now be explained in the light of all this. The Rabbanites count the couch as אב טומאה, and we see that in fact the author of the Khilâf is objecting to their refusal to count the clothes on top of the man and the pillows or bolster as part of the bed. If they counted them as part of the bed they would count them as אב טומאה and capable of causing contamination to people or artefacts. In the context, the statement by the author of the Khilâf that according to the Jews the clothes on top are not contaminated can be taken to mean they are not at the same level of contamination as the clothes underneath. Either the author is speaking loosely or he has slightly misunderstood his source. Probably he is only speaking loosely, but on purpose: there is no way he could have spoken precisely without adding a disquisition on the Rabbanite principle of אבות טומאה and וולדי טומאה.

We see from all this that the real point of disagreement is whether the clothes on top count as part of the bed or not, or in other words, whether the bed contaminated by having had the weight of the *zåb* on only includes the bedstead and bedding and the clothes underneath, or whether it includes the clothes on top as well. The Rabbanites will only accept as part of the bed something that is a fixture, such as the knobs or the wheels, or something that has been used as a bed by supporting the weight of the *zåb*. This means that the question of whether the clothes underneath, or the mattress for that matter, are part of the bed or not does not arise, since they are treated as a bed by being lain on, and whether they are a unit with the bedstead or with each other does not matter, since any number of beds one under the other can be contaminated at once by having the weight of the *zåb* on top of the lot. In the case of the clothes on top, the Rabbanites are unable to count them as a bed or treat them as a bed in their own right because they have not been lain on, and they are unable to treat them as part of the whole bed because it is a principle in the Rabbanite halachah that two artefacts can only become one for the purpose of contamination if they are attached by nails or screws or glue and are not meant to come apart (even if it might be possible to separate them).

The Samaritans have to count the clothes on top as part of the bed because their criterion for whether two artefacts become one is whether they go together to perform a function that the part on its own would not be able to do, and whether they are treated as a unit. The argument over the extent of the term 'couch' is not really over how the word should be defined, but over the question of whether a set of objects becomes a single object for the purpose of contamination by being used as a single object, and the usage of the word 'couch' is appealed to as evidence that the various part of the couch are treated and used as a single object.

In spite of the difference in practice, there is very little disagreement in theory here between the Samaritans and the Rabbanites. The Rabbanites (and the Karaites as well) maintain that to be contaminated as a couch, by the weight of the *zåb*, an object must be either specifically built as a couch or must be of such a form that a person might normally lie down it, as for instance a cloak, and must not be an object intended for some other purpose and obviously unsuitable as a couch for normal use. It has to actually be a couch, and whether someone uses it to lie down on or no is not the point. It is obvious from the Samaritans' insistence on treating the bed with all the clothes and pillows as a unit that they must follow the same principle. Both agree that only something intended as a couch can be contaminated in this way: the disagreement is over what a couch consists of. Compare Kf ch. XI, 25-27 N.

For another example of agreement in theory but divergence in the application of the theory leading to major differences in practice, see Kf ch. XI, 31-32 N.

4 and **6** On the meaning of the term *aṣl*, see Kh 138 N.

10-16 This section, from 'There is the obvious example' in line 3 to the end of line 12, is missing in all mss. except B_1.

16 The last word of the sentence has been omitted in the ms., though a blank space has been left for it.

TEXT 4

The Book of Commandments

The Heading

After this chapter comes the chapter on commandment no. 55. This one could be no. 54 or could be an earlier one, but it would be unlikely that more than one leaf would have been lost after the start of the part of the ms. preserved, and one leaf would not be enough to finish off this commandment and treat another one, so it seems fairly safe to assume that no other commandment came in between and that this is no. 54. Nevertheless, the matter will not be certain till the number of sheets to quire in the manuscript has been counted and it is worked out how many sheets are missing.

The material in this chapter is set out according to the order of Lv XV:19-33.

2-3 This phrase is taken from a comment on v. 19, where the author points out that the term *zåbå* has two different uses, one as a term for menstrual bleeding in general or the first bleeding, as in v. 19, and one as a technical specialised term for the abnormal bleeding referred to in v. 25, and explains the difference, then says that one way of defining it is that the abnormal bleeding comes after a period of uncleanness, and that the normal menstrual bleeding comes after a period of cleanness, and that the bleeding referred to here is the second, the one that comes after a period of cleanness, known as *niddå*. Compare 75-83, and Al-Qirqisâni, X:50:1.

As v. 19 is the start of the section on the uncleanness that affects women, and this comment is a general one and deals with the first phrase of the verse, it is very likely that only a few lines of the start of the chapter are missing. Compare the note on 127-128.

2 The first word is very hard to make out. It looks like either فهذه or وهذه. The second has been chosen because it fits the context better.

4 The form الرفه of the ms. has been emended to الرقه.

5-6 The range of colours mentioned here is the same as what the Karaites accept, if the yellowish colour corresponds to the one described as nearly white by the Karaites. Compare G.E. 110d middle; A.E. 122a middle.

These are the colours of blood itself; in the passage that follows the author explains which colours are evidence of the presence of blood.

7-14 This is a fuller and clearer version of the related passages T 66-73 and Kf 79-82. All three have a common source. The author agrees with the usual Samaritan opinion that any deviation from pure white is blood or evidence of blood (see Kh 197-199 N). Here it seems to be said that the discoloured moisture is not blood itself, but that the discolouration is evidence that it contains blood. (There is some disagreement on this point in the sources: see T 66 N). On the list of colours in 13-14, compare also Iʿtiq 8-11.

9 After في باب the ms. has the word من, which I have omitted as a duplicate reading.

12-22 This is the only mention in the Samaritan sources, as far as I know, of the practice of the woman testing herself for the presence of blood inside the mouth of the vagina. This practice is found in both the Rabbanite system (see Issure Bi'ah VIII-IX and Mishkav Umoshav III-IV) and the Karaite system (G.E. 111bc).

The details given here do not correspond exactly to either system. In the first case (15-16), the Karaites and Rabbanites would agree with each other against this author in making the contamination retrospective from the time of the previous check (Mishkav Umoshav III:4; G.E. 111bc). In the second case (16-19), the Rabbanites (Mishkav Umoshav III:5) and the Karaites (G.E. 111a bottom and 111b bottom) would agree with this author.

It will be seen that this author allows contamination to be calculated retrospectively to as far back as the appearance of the symptoms, but not as far back as the previous check.

13 The word او is illegible but the restoration is certain from the context.

13 The ms. has الغيره instead of الغبره. The emendation is confirmed by the parallel passages and the context.

18 Although it is not possible to supply the exact wording of the missing bits, the gist is clear, and the missing bits can be inserted in the translation with confidence, as long as it is understood that it is only the meaning of the sentence that is restored, not the actual missing words.

19 The word فوجدها comes at the end of a line. The first four letters are certain. After that there is enough room for two letters. The letters are completely illegible, to the extent that it is impossible to tell if one or two letters should be present. The restoration made here is probably the only one that could fit the context.

23-24 What is meant is that only blood coming from the vagina causes uncleanness.

25-27 The first day of *niddå* contamination can be defective at its start. In the case of the *zåb* (and, we could add, the *zåbå*) the seven days are complete from start to finish because the partial day is before the seven days are counted. Compare Kh 200-201. This is a point insisted on by the Karaites: see G.E. IIIc middle; A.E. 122a bottom.

Compare T 15 N.

25 The form ظهورها of the ms. has been emended to طهورها.

25-30 This is an argument against the opinion that to be cleansed from *niddå* contamination the woman has to count seven whole days without bleeding, starting the day after the last day of bleeding, and can immerse herself on the seventh of the days that bleeding does not occur, becoming clean at the time of immersion, (provided of course no bleeding occurs afterwards), so that the last day is actually incomplete at the end. The objection to this opinion is that she would not become clean on whichever day out of the days without bleeding it was that marked the seventh of her contamination, since even if the bleeding only lasts one day, she still has to count seven days after this day, so that the seventh day of contamination is only the sixth of the days without bleeding, and she can not become clean that day according to this system. This means that according to this system the absolute minimum number of days the woman can be unclean is eight, made up of one incomplete day then seven days complete at the start and defective at the end. This is impossible, because the text of Scripture says, in Lv XV:19, that the uncleanness is only to last for seven days. As this system is contradicted by Scripture, it follows that the usual system, according to which the woman is unclean for seven days, with the first day of uncleanness defective at the start, till bleeding occurs, but with the last day complete till the end, since full cleansing does not come on immersion, but at sunset, must be the right one. See the Ṭubâkh 15 and the note and cross-references there.

29 The form نخا منهُ of the ms. has been emended to نجاسه.

30 The form الناقصه has been emended to ناقصه.

32 The word [Samaritan] occurs at the end of a line and is abbreviated as [Samaritan].

33-34 Compare Kh 44-47; Iʿtiq 96-100. Although the basic meaning of the word *niddå* is the segregation of the woman from people in a state of cleanness, it can be used as the name for this particular category of bleeding. We know she is unclean, and this is an appropriate name for her uncleanness due to this bleeding. In fact the term is used to refer to the particular category of uncleanness, and as well as this, to refer to the woman herself. This etymology depends on the existence of some such practice as is described in Iʿtiq 12-17.

33 The word انها is completely illegible but the restoration is certain from the context.

33 The word [Samaritan] occurs at the end of a line and is abbreviated as [Samaritan] in the ms.

33-34 Compare 73-74.

34 For the proof that the verse refers to the *niddå* and not to any other kind of uncleanness due to an issue of blood, see T 8-10 N and the cross-references there.

35-41 On the effect of the *niddå* bleeding, compare Iʿtiq and Kâsh ch. XV, 18-20 and 101-123. On the effect of the *dåbå* bleeding, compare T 13-14 N and 34-36 N. All the sources agree on the distinction, implicitly or explicitly.

36 The form وانما of the ms. has been emended to او انما.

35-41 See Kh 204-214 N.

42-48 The quotation of v. 20 is to be understood as referring to the whole of the verse and vv. 21-23 as well. We are told in these verses that the woman's couch and seat are made unclean, that anyone that touches them is made unclean for one day, and then that even if the woman is still on them the person that touches them is still only made unclean for one day. The author then says that the elements of the situation are the same for the *zåb* and *zåbå*, since the laws of the uncleanness of the couch and seat and the person that touches them are the same for both, and these elements are found as well in the laws of the *niddå*, so that the laws of the *zåb* and *zåbå*, which we can see ought to be identical with each other, ought to be identical with the laws of the *niddå* as well. (We might add here that although the author does not mention the point, an identification of the laws of *zåbå* and *niddå* is specifically stated in v. 26). There is one point that the text did not mention the first time round, in relation to the *zåb*, that it does mention in relation to the *niddå*, and that is that even if the woman is on the couch or seat at the time, anyone that touches it is only made unclean for one day, and not seven as might have been expected. If there is no difference in the level of contamination of the couch or seat whether or no the *niddå* is still on them, then there must be no difference in the level of contamination of the couch or seat affected by a *zåb* or *zåbå* whether or no the person that is the source of the contamination is still sitting on them.

Compare Far 107-110; T 103-106; Kf ch. XI, 25-26; Kâsh ch. XV, 26-37; 107-112; the Additional Passage from the Khilâf and the second marginal note on the Khilâf; Sharḥ Sûrat al-Irbot.

43 [Samaritan] has been corrected to [Samaritan] in the ms., probably by the original scribe.

43-45 The ms. has [Samaritan] فهو (فهو originally وهو) at the end of a line; then in the margin in the handwriting of the original scribe [Samaritan] [Samaritan]; then at the start of the next line enough room for one or two letters now obliterated but with traces remaining; then very clearly the last two letters of a word, ࠋࠁ; then ࠀࠀࠋࠓࠃ ࠁ. ࠀ. ࠌ. ࠍ. with the abbreviations expanded in minuscule script (all other Hebrew words in this chapter are in majuscule), probably in the handwriting of the original scribe so that it now reads ࠁ. ࠀࠋࠄࠉ ࠌࠔࠄ ࠍࠔࠋࠁ ࠃࠄࠉࠀ. It looks as if the word ࠀࠀࠋࠔࠋࠁ has been written at the end of the line and then partially repeated at the start of the next line. The scribe has then copied the words that should have come after the second occurence of this word, leaving out all the words between the two occurrences of it. The restoration in the margin is correct, but does not go far enough. The restoration given here is the only one that can fit the argument and makes sence of the second occurrence of ࠀࠀࠋࠓࠃ. Some textual error must have occurred at the word ࠀࠀࠋࠓࠃ at the end of line 44, since this does not fit onto the following quotation, and it is impossible to join it to the verse without something in between because the word ࠀࠀࠋࠓࠃ is needed as an accompaniment to ࠀࠋࠔࠋࠁ and can not be part of the verse quoted. The restoration must therefore include the addition of the words ࠀࠋࠄ ࠀࠋࠓࠃ, leaving the word ࠀࠀࠋࠓࠃ after ࠀࠋࠔࠋࠁ. This means we have remedied a case of homoioteleuton, and the words in between can now be supplied in what is probably their original form. There must be an introductory expression before the quotation, and in this text that would be بقوله in this context. The word هاهنا has been supplied on the model of its occurrence in line 46, where it is an important word, and it is really needed in line 19 for the same reason as in line 46.

The expression *wa-bi-'l-jumlah*, meaning 'in short' or 'to sum up' at the start of line 46 clearly indicates that the words that follow are not an additional piece of information but a comment on something already said, which means that the content of the restoration in line 18 is cetain. The wording is very likely to be correct, on the analogy of the rest of the passage.

46 Instead of the word ࠀࠌࠁ there is a blank space of exactly the right size for this word, where the microfilm shows no trace of any writing.

49-58 The point that it does not make any difference how the blood gets on the man is made in the Khilâf over and over in the section 76-110.

49-53 See T 8-10; Kf ch. XI, 49-54; Kh 107-114.

49 After the word ࠌࠍࠀ the ms. adds ࠔࠋࠁࠍ, the result of an incorrect reminiscence of v. 18. Compare T 9-10 N.

54-56 On the identification of the cause of the woman's uncleanness and the man's, see Kf 88-89 N.

The opinion refuted here about the difference between the level of contamination due to contact with the woman and due to copulating with her is the Rabbanite one that copulation with a *niddå* woman causes seven days uncleanness but touching her or touching the blood only causes one day's: see Kh 78-81 and 92-97, which have the same source as this text.

The two conditions mentioned in 54-55 are not really both necessary according to the Rabbanites, who would make the man unclean for seven days after copulation with a menstruating woman whether she was bleeding at the time or not, but it must be remembered that the author is thinking in terms of the Samaritan system, in which *niddå* blood is the very first menstrual blood, so that if the woman is *niddå* at the time, then by definition some blood must be present.

56 Of the word لطماء only the first letter and the hamzah are legible, but the restoration is certain from the context.

57 The word حكم is not in the ms. but is demanded by the context.

57 The original reading of the ms. is ࠃࠅࠄ instead of ࠍࠃࠄ. The word ࠍࠃࠄ is added above the line in minuscule letters. I am unable to say if the handwriting is the original scribe's or not.

58 The form ومجرد of the ms. has been emended to او مجرد.

59-65 On copulation with a woman known to be unclean see the references in the notes on T 74-78 and 8-10.

This passage has the same source as Kh 76-78 and 98-101.

59 The ms. has انطا for اتطا.

60-63 Compare T 75-78; Kh 101-104; 112-114; and compare T 8-10 N.

66-72 The argument referred to here by saying يطرد القياس, which I have translated as 'an induction on the basis of equivalent expressions' is the same as the בנין אב.

66-68 This is intended as proof that copulation with a woman who has given birth is forbidden during the forty or eighty days. Compare Kh 220-227, which has the same source as this text. The same proof is used in Kh 249-250.

69-72 This is intended as proof that copulation with the *zåbå* is forbidden, whether during the time when she is still bleeding, or during the seven days without bleeding when she is waiting to become clean.

71-73 The restoration of the quotation of v. 30 in is required by the argument, and once that is done, it is obvious that homoioteleuton has occurred and that some words similar to those inserted in 73 are needed.

73-74 This follows on from 65, and refers to the case mentioned in 57-58. The verse quoted refers specifically to this situation: see 33-34.

75-83 See 2-3 and the note there.

76 The word ࠃࠅࠄ is corrected to ࠍࠃࠄ in the ms., apparently in another hand.

77 It is uncertain whether the author is referring to another Samaritan group or some Karaites. The opinion is attested as a Karaite one: see T 31-32 N.

77 ࠃࠌࠈࠓࠄ is written as one word in the ms.

78 The form مساحجه of the ms. has been emended to تمشا حجه.

78-79 The same passage in different wording is found in T 12-15.

78 The form وحكم of the ms. has been emended to وحكمه.

80-88 See Kh 179-185 and the cross-references there.

84-106 For the place of all these opinions in the Samaritan system, see Kf ch. XI, 58-61 N.

82 The word ࠉࠌࠉࠌ is missing in the ms.

84-86 This verse is used in a more sophisticated way in T 26-29.

88 The original form, للمتعاد, has been corrected to للمعتاد, apparently by the original scribe.

88 The word ان is missing in the ms.

88-97 This is directed against the Rabbanites, but compare below, 97-110, where a similar Samaritan opinion is discussed.

91-92 Before the word ࠍࠃࠕࠄ in 91 the ms. inserts ايام, and before the word ࠈࠅࠓࠄ in 92, in both places, the ms. inserts ࠉࠌࠉ. The word must be omitted in both places, since there is a clear allusion to Lv XII:5 here, and the word ࠉࠌࠉ does not occur in this verse. It has probably crept in through failure to recognise the direct allusion ar as a reminiscence of Lv XII:2. The word ايام in 91 could perhaps be left.

94 The form ويطهر ان of the ms. has been emended to ويطهرن, and the figures seven and fourteen interchanged, as the context requires.

96 The first two letters of يتلاه are obliterated.

96 The word انتهي is only partly legible. The spelling with *yâ* is certain. Of the word الله the article is almost completely obliterated.

97 The form جاز of the ms. has been emended to جار.

97 The form بنسوغ of the ms. has been emended to يتسوغ.

98 The word في is missing in the ms.

97-110 Compare 88-90 and see T 13-14 N.

97-99 The point is that there was no bleeding at the start of the eighth day, so there was no connection between the original seven-day period of uncleanness and the next period starting part-way through the eighth day. See Kf ch. XI, 58-61 N.

103-106 This is not just a matter of definition of *niddå* and *zå̊bå*, but a criterion for determining whether bleeding on the day after the menstrual week is to be counted as *zå̊bå* or a new onset of *niddå*, the distinction depending on whether the bleeding was continuous from the end of the last day of the menstrual week to the next day, or whether there was a break before the end of the day and the woman had time to immerse herself and become clean at sunset. Compare 97-102 and Kf ch. XI, 58-61 N. This is why the example of bleeding near the end of the fortieth or eightieth day after giving birth can be used to refute this opinion. If the bleeding occurs near the end of the day, the woman will not have time to immerse herself, and will not become clean at sunset, so that the next day, if bleeding occurs, she becomes unclean due to *niddå* on a day when she is still unclean due to childbirth. This proves that the state of *niddå* can start when the woman is unclean and by analogy with this the criterion given above fails.

Notice that this author counts bleeding on the day after the end of the uncleanness due to childbirth as *niddå*. This is not the opinion of the author of the Ṭubâkh (60-65), or the Kâfi (ch. XI, 74-76), or the Iʿtiqâdât (60-61), who count it as *zå̊bå*.

This author allows the *niddå* to over-ride the minor uncleanness due to childbirth after the fortieth or eightieth day, just as the author of the Khilâf (203-204) allows the major uncleanness of childbirth to over-ride the uncleanness of *niddå* or *zå̊bå*, on the principle that a major contamination over-rides a minor one. The two authors seem to be working on the same principle. The matter is not brought up in the other texts edited here.

103 The word ان is not present in the ms.

105 The form يرى of the ms. has been emended to ترى.

105 The ms. omits the word في, but compare 98 and 77. This might not be an error.

106 The first letter of كقوله is obliterated.

107-110 What is meant is that the laws of Lv XV:26-27, given in reference to the *zå̊bå*, apply well to the *zåb* and *niddå*, so that the extra detail of v. 23, which is not mentioned in the versions of the same set of laws given for the *zåb* and *zå̊bå*, can be applied to them. Compare 42-48 and the Sharḥ Sûrat al-Irbot.

107 The ms. has ࠌࠔࠊࠁ instead of ࠕࠔࠊࠁ. The word ࠉࠈࠌࠀ is abbreviated to its first letter.

110 The word يفيد occurs at the start of a line and the first two letters are missing or obliterated.

111-112 The comment relates to the word ࠈࠀ.

112 Of the word فاوجب only the *alif* is legible, and the *fâ*, though probable, is uncertain, so the restoration made might not be the right one. Nevertheless the meaning of the sentence is clear.

118 The word ضنكا is at the end of a line and is obliterated starting part-way through the third letter, so it is impossible to tell if the final *alif* was written or not.

118 The word واعلى is to be read as *wa-iʿlâʾ*.

118 The word الاطهار occurs at the end of a line and only the first four letters remain.

120-122 The reference to saving the lives of the children of Israel depends on the phrase ࠅࠋࠀ ࠉࠌࠅࠕࠅ ࠁࠈࠌࠀࠕࠌ in the same verse.

121 The form نحينا of the ms. has been emended to يحييا.

121 The form سمعناه of the ms. has been emended to سمعاه.

124 The word النجاسات occurs at the end of a line and the last three letters are obliterated.

127-128 The two sections mentioned here are Lv XV:2-15, with the appendix vv. 16-18, which treats the uncleanness of males, and vv. 19-30, which treats the uncleanness of females. Major contamination is the contamination of the *zåb* or *niddå* or *zåbå*, minor contamination is the contamination of semen and perhaps the *dåbå* as well. The content of the missing section immediately following would have to be something to the effect that the command of v. 31 and warning against uncleanness apply to all the kinds of uncleanness mentioned in ch. XV, both those that occur to males and those that occur to females, so as not to defile the Sanctuary by any kind of uncleanness, whether the ones that occur to males or the ones that occur to females. Presumably this would have been followed by the observation that the Sanctuary is not to be defiled by any of the kinds of uncleanness that can apply equally to either sex, such as depigmentation (ࠑࠓࠏࠕ) or contamination from a corpse, and is not to be defiled by moral impurities in the people of Israel either.

As this comment deals with the third-last verse of the chapter, and the last two verses are only summary and will not need much comment, it is very likely that only a few lines are missing from the end of the chapter. Compare the note on 2-3.

127 The word ظاهره occurs at the end of a line and all except the first four letters are obliterated.

128 The word والغرض occurs at the end of a line, and all except the first letter are obliterated.

TEXT 5

The Kâshif al-Ghayâhib on Leviticus XV

1-100 For general information on the discharge [*zåb*] and emission of semen compare T 79-124; Kf ch. XI, 2-42; ch. III, 8-27; 39-42; Kh 6-9; Kâsh ch. XV, 18-20; M.N. III, IV, V, VIII.

5-9 This statement is flatly contradicted by the other treatises, which agree with the Jews, both Rabbanite and Karaite, that the *zåb* of a male is not blood but a substance resembling semen but of a pathological nature, or an oozing of semen under abnormal circumstances. See T 89-93; Kf 19-20; Kh 6-9, and the notes on those passages. It is hard to see how a statement like this could be made unless by the time this commentary was written the practice of the halachot of the *zåb* had been abandoned by the group of Samaritans the author belonged to. Compare the note on 23-25, and see 51-54.

The author says the same thing in his comment on Nu V:2-3.

Nevertheless, the second marginal note on the Khilâf shows that the laws of the *zåb* are still practised in the modern halachah, so we might perhaps regarded the Kâshif as only representing some of the Samaritans of its time, or as simply being in error. Strangely enough, however, the same opinion is given in the second marginal note on the Kâfi.

10 The analysis of the syntax and interpretation assumed by ending the quotation at the word ࠆࠅࠁࠅ is quite different to the analysis assumed in 21-22.

11-13 Notice that the author gives the etymology of the Arabic term, not the Hebrew one, in line with his tendency to use the Arabic terminology without reference to the Hebrew. Compare the note on 22.

14-15 The range of ages for the start and end of menstruation given here does not agree with the situation at the present time.

15 The typical or normal menstrual discharge causes a period of seven days' uncleanness but the bleeding does not last any longer than seven days and in fact does not even last that long usually.

18-19 This is in agreement with the halachah that it is the very first bleeding that causes seven days' uncleanness. Compare Iʿtiq 18-19 and Kh 51-60; 66-75, where the same information is given in different words. All the sources assume this fact.

For the other side of this, in relation to the *då̊bå* bleeding, see the notes on T 13-14 and 34-36. The passages from the Khilâf just referred to give both sides.

19-20 The reference is to 101-123.

21-22 See the note on 10.

22 Notice that this author treats the Arabic term ذوبه as the standard, not the Hebrew. The statement that the term ذوبه is only used to refer to a discharge from a male is inexplicable unless we assume that what the author means is that the text of Scripture only uses the term ࠆࠅࠁࠄ in reference to the discharge of a male, but in reference to a female, in vv. 25 and 28, the masculine form ࠆࠅࠁ is used. This can only mean that the misunderstanding of the form ذوبه in v. 2 as a feminine noun is due to this author himself and not a later copyist.

For other examples of misunderstanding due to the use of the Arabic without reference to the Hebrew, see the next two notes, and see 67-77; 137-141.

22 The case-ending of the word ذوبةٍ is given in the mss. The reading of the received text of the Arabic translation of this verse is ذوبه *dhawbuh* 'his discharge' in agreement with the Hebrew. The form ذوبةٍ is attested by Mss. BU, i.e. by witnesses from both branches of the textual tradition, and so any explanation of the development of the reading has to assume that this reading is old, and is probably older than the reading of Ms. S. I suggest that an original ذوبه (masculine noun with suffix) has been re-interpreted as a feminine noun under the influence of the following word wrongly read as a feminine adjective instead of a masculine noun with a suffix. (See the next note). The reading of Ms. S would then be a secondary correction.

Although the reading ذوبةٍ is a mistake, the mistake was probably made by the author himself, since he uses the feminine form in the discussion that follows, and his comment that the feminine form is only used to refer to a discharge from a male, not a female, leads to the same conclusion, as is explained in the previous note. Because of this I have not corrected the form of the quotation.

This is further evidence for this author's tendency to use the Arabic translation of the Torah without reference to the Hebrew, since a glance at the Hebrew would have shown how to interpret the Arabic. Compare the next note.

22 The words نجسه هي in the Arabic translation of v. 2 are probably to be read as *najasuh hîya*, depending on a reading ࠈࠌࠀࠕࠅ ࠄࠉࠀ under the influence of v. 3. (See 25). The reading of Mss. US is probably a secondary correction made after reference to the Hebrew.

23-25 This is very vague. We are not told how often the flow has to occur to count as discharge, and anyway, the verse quoted has nothing to do with the question of the criteria for the man's entry into the state of *zåb*, but is a description of the discharge.

On the other hand, it is entirely possible that the author takes verse 3 to mean 'These are the conditions for his uncleanness in his discharge: whether his flesh runs continuously with his discharge, or whether his flesh has stopped running with his discharge, he is unclean', which would explain the comment and the use of this verse as a proof-text, but would be an interpretation based on the author's own exegesis, without any knowledge of the standard interpretation of this verse. If this is the case, we have here another piece of evidence that the laws of the *zåb* were not practised in the time of this author.

For the standard interpretation of this verse, see T 89-98 and Kf ch. XI, 19-22; and see T 93-94 N.

26-37 On the couch, seat, and saddle, compare Kâsh ch. XV, 26-33; T 103-106; Kf ch. XI, 25-27; the Additional Passage from the Khilâf and the second marginal note on the Khilâf; Far 42-48; 107-110; Sharḥ Sûrat al-Irbot.

28-31 On the contamination of the person touched by the *zåb*, see 38-50 and the notes there.

31-32 This depends on v. 6.

32-34 This depends on v. 8, which is quoted in Mss. US.

34-35 This depends on v. 9.

The author takes ࠌࠓࠊࠁ to mean a saddle or saddle-cloth, as the Jews do, and not a steed, as the author of the Ṭubâkh does. See the Ṭubâkh 104 and the note there.

35-36 The words كل شي يدوس عليه would normally mean 'anything he treads on' but in this context the meaning is rather 'anything he puts his weight on', i.e. any couch, seat, or saddle that he puts his weight on. The words 'this applies to anything' are probably to be understood as limited to the couch, seat, and saddle in this context. The text mentions the saddle specifically here, and the author is saying that v. 10 shows that the same rules apply to the couch and seat as to the saddle. This is the standard Karaite interpretation of the verse. See the Additional Passage from the Khilâf and the notes there. The Jewish term for this mechanism of contamination is מדרס. The Arabic verb داس is used here as the equivalent of the Hebrew verb דרס, in its technical halachic sense.

38-47 The apparent contradiction with v. 7 referred to is that whereas v. 11 could be taken to mean that the man only causes one day's contamination if the stuff is on his hand, v. 7 implies that contact with him is enough, even if there is no contact with the stuff. The answer given is that the inconsistency can be explained by assuming that v. 7 is mainly concerned with giving the requirements for cleansing, and there is no need to be specific about whether contact with the man has to include contact with the stuff, whereas v. 11 is mainly concerned with giving the distinction between contact with the man that does include contact with the stuff and contact that does not. The comment on v. 11 in 45-47 depends on the same interpretation as the third one in the Kâfi, that this verse is meant to show that the contamination due to the *zåb* stuff is less than the contamination due to the *niddå* stuff.

See the cross-references in T 110-117.

50 The Arabic بلاء means ࠑࠓࠏࠕ here.

51-54 The author says once again that the *zåb* stuff in a male can consist of blood. Compare 5-9.

60 and **64** The word الباء is not in the dictionaries, and none of the native speakers of Arabic consulted by me knew the word. The hamzah is in the mss.

67-77 This is an example of the use of the Arabic for exegesis with negligible understanding of the Hebrew. For a start, the form شفنين about which there is so much speculation, is a corruption of شفنينين, which means 'two doves' and is the word used in this verse in the received text of the Samaritan Arabic version. Besides which, the word ࠏࠅࠐ in Hebrew is a perfectly common one and it is hard to see how its meaning can be in doubt. When the author says in 73-74 that one opinion is that what is meant is a small bird, he is quoting a correct opinion, but has failed to understand that a *particular kind* of small bird is meant, and seems to have taken this statement to mean that ࠏࠅࠐ means any kind of small bird, and it is on the strength of this misunderstanding that he makes the objection that the general word for a small bird in Hebrew is ࠑࠐࠅࠓ. I do not think we need to take this passage as evidence that the Samaritans or some Samaritan group took ࠏࠐࠉࠌ to be fowls, but only as evidence that some people were unable to make an obvious emendation in the text of the Arabic translation and did not know much Hebrew. Compare the notes on 22 TN and 137-140.

79 The received text has [Samaritan word] in v. 14.

82-98 See the note on 99-100.

82-91 Compare Kf ch. XI, 6-8; 16-17; ch. III, 8-14.

86 The phrase 'an emission of semen' is an allusion to v. 16.

89-91 Compare Kf ch. III, 8-9, and the note there.

92-95 This section is not in the corresponding section of the Kâfi and this information is not given in any of the other sources, though it has to be assumed that they would have agreed with it.

98 See Kf ch. XI, 15. The Kâfi does not give the detail that this invalidates the lesser washing, but it is obvious from what the Kâfi says that this must be the case, since the Kâfi tells us that an emission of this type is to be treated as urine, and any emission of urine invalidates the lesser washing, and besides, the Kâfi tells us that any garment this stuff gets on can not be worn while praying, and if this renders a garment unfit for use when praying it must invalidate the lesser washing, which is the preparation for prayer.

98 The wuḍû is fully treated in ch. III of the Kâfi, p. 34 bottom to the end of p. 36 in Noja's translation (immediately after the extract from ch. III edited here). Note that in Noja's translation the word *abluzione* renders *wuḍû*, but in the section immediately before the word *ablutio* renders [Samaritan word], which is something different.

The wuḍû is performed after urination and defecation and before prayer. The details of how to perform it and when to perform it are given in the Catechism, pp. 74-81 of the Arabic text.

The procedure for the wuḍû as practised by the Samaritans is nearly the same as in Moslem practice. As the Samaritans are able to back up every detail from Scripture, and found the institution on the Priests' preparation for offering sacrifices, the borrowing must have been from the Samaritans or a Jewish group with the same practice over to the Moslems.

99-100 This comment refers to all of 82-98. The passage in the Kâfi referred to is ch. XI, 9-17. The Kâfi does not give all the information given here, but it is the categorisation in the Kâfi that the author of the Kâshif is referring to.

101-123 On *niddå* bleeding in general, compare T 6-11; Kf ch. XI, 45-55; Kh 43-116; 255-258; 262-263; Far 2-65; Iʿtiq 8-21; 96-110; Sharḥ Sûrat al-Irbot.

101-102 The reference is to 14-17.

103-106 Compare T 8-11 and the cross-references there.

107-112 The author does not seem to make any distinction between the couch, seat, and saddle and any other artefact, but see the cross-references in the note on 26-37, and in particular the Additional Passage from the Khilâf and the notes there. It will be seen from the information given there that the distinction between the couch, seat, and saddle on one hand, and other artefacts, on the other hand, is not as important in Samaritan halachah as in Rabbanite halachah, and in most situations would not make any difference.

113-117 What is meant is that his contamination is unforeseen and accidental. Compare T 8-11 and the cross-references there.

115-117 It would not have been expected that the author would need to say this, but it is a point that is insisted on in the other texts. See T 15 and the cross-references there.

119-122 Both the man and the woman contaminate the bed, the man by an emission of semen and the woman by *niddå*.

123 The washing on the first day is to get rid of the *niddå* blood so he can start counting and not be re-contaminated. Compare the notes on T 11; 55-57. Notice that on the seventh day he does not need to immerse, just wash himself. The other texts edited here do not say whether this person requires washing or immersion, but we can assume that there is no disagreement.

124-141 On *zåbå* bleeding in general, compare T 16-44; Kf ch. XI, 61-67; Kh 165-201; 259-261; 264-266; Far 80-119; Iʿtiq 32-40; Sharḥ Sûrat al-Irbot; M.N. I and II.

124-128 See T 13-14 N on the disagreements on this matter.

128-131 What is meant by saying the days of cleanness are disregarded is that the days without any discharge counted up till then are disregarded if the discharge starts again, and she has to wait till the discharge stops and then start a new count and count seven days in a row without any discharge. The same information is given in the Iʿtiqâdât 35-37. All the sources assume this. For example, it is assumed in an argument in another connection in the Khilâf 130-132.

137-140 On the non-existent *shanfs* see the note on 67-77.

THE KÂSHIF AL-GHAYÂHIB ON LEVITICUS XII

2-7 and **14** For information on bleeding of childbirth in general, compare T 45-52; Kf ch. XI, 68-72; the whole of the extract from ch. XIII of the Kâfi; Kh 202-214; Iʿtiq 41-46; 53-56.

6-7 Compare Kh 134-135 for a similar statement in another context.

11-13 and **14-17** On bleeding of cleansing in general, compare T 53-59; Kf ch. 73-78; Kh 215-253; Iʿtiq 47-50 and 58-64.

14 If the mother has to wash herself a fortnight after the birth of a girl, it follows that she has to wash herself a week after the birth of a boy. The purpose of the washing is to remove the blood of childbirth so it will not keep on re-contaminating her. It follows from this that this author counts the blood of childbirth as being any bleeding during the week or fortnight, not just the bleeding at the instant of delivery, and that he considers that the blood of childbirth does not lose its contaminating effect after the end of the week or fortnight. For the significance of these three points see the notes on Kh 204-214 and Kf ch. XIII 5-18.

22 and **24** The translation of ࠍࠑ as عصفور is very vague. The correct equivalent would be شفنين. See the note on ch. XV, 67-77.

27-30 When God spoke, it was the Torah that was created as the results of his speaking, not Jesus and not the Koran. This is a flat contradiction of the Moslem claim that the Koran is as original as the Torah, in spite of its late date, because it is the manifestation of the Heavenly Book in the material world, and is directed against the Moslem belief that lets them call the Koran الكلام القديم and similar names. It is equally a flat contradiction to the claims of John's Gospel.

27 The form لقايل of the mss. is impossible. The emendation القايل has been chosen as the minimum alteration of the form as it stands, but perhaps we should read القبيل instead.

27-29 The Christians and the Moslems have taken over bits and pieces of the Torah and sometimes they have understood it and sometimes they have misunderstood it. The Moslems have taken over a lot of halachah. (This might be the appropriate place to say that whatever there is in the original Moslem law that can not be explained from the Jewish halachah can be explained from the Samaritan halachah, as I hope to show in a projected monograph). One of the scattered bits of halachah that the Christians have taken over is the Churching of Women. This ceremony is practised by all the denominations that would have been known directly to this author. This is about the only remnant of the laws of uncleanness that the Christians have taken over. The Moslems of course have a full apparatus of laws of uncleanness, including uncleanness due to childbirth. So we see that this comment is put in a very appropriate place, since it is one of the few places where both the Christians and the Moslems have a practice recognisably the same as the one given to Israel.

28-30 The ones to whom the truth has been shown are Israel. Some bits of the truth have been shown to the Christians and Moslems.

TEXT 6

The Book of Principles

Chapter Six

4 This sentence might depend on Kh 14. Direct dependence on the Khilâf starts at 87.

4-6 This depends for its structure and some of its content on T 1-78. A comparison with the corresponding section of the Kâfi, 43-90, shows to the extent that the author borrows at all it is from the Ṭubâkh, not the Kâfi, except for a few possible instances of the influence of the Kâfi.

4-6 The source is T 2-4, but re-worded. The same classification is probably assumed in Kf ch. XI, 44 and 48.

6 The reasons for choosing the translation 'blood of plausibility' are set out in T 67 N.

7-9 The source is T 6, but re-worded.

8-50 On *niddå* bleeding in general, compare Iʿtiq 96-110; T 6-11; Kf ch. XI, 45-55; Kh 43-116; 255-258; 262-263; Far 2-65; Kâsh ch. XV, 101-123.

8-11 Compare 65-67, and see the note and cross-references there. This passage is not in the corresponding section of the Ṭubâkh and is the author's own insertion. It ultimately depends on T 68-72.

12-17 This passage has been composed by the author of the Iʿtiqâdât. Compare 114-115 and Kh 66.

The etymology of the word *niddå* in Iʿtiq 96-100, Kh 44-47, and Far 33-34 assumes the existence of some kind of effective separation. These practices were apparently rejected by one group of Dositheans, the followers of Sakta, as we see from the information in the note on T 11-13. We have seen that these practices are assumed by the authors of the Khilâf and Farâ'iḍ. The Kâfi and Ṭubâkh do not mention them but this could be an accident. Compare Mishnah Niddah VII:4.

13 The reference to different kinds of contamination is to be taken as meaning that the *zå̊bå* and *yå̊lēda* stays separated in the same way as the *niddå*.

14-15 The flat need not be a separate room, but can be a separate section of a room, as we see from Petermann, *Samaria und die Samaritaner*, p. 384:

> 'Die Wöchnerin erhält eine besondere Abtheilung in dem Zimmer, und wird durch eine von Steinen aufgerichtete, niedrige Wand von den Uebrigen geschieden. Sie bekommt ihre eigenen Löffel, Schüsseln u.s.w., und Niemand darf sie berühen'.

(The same passage occurs again with no significant variations in *Reisen im Orient*, I:277).

Petermann is speaking of a woman who has given birth, but the same rules would apply to the *niddå*.

16 The reference seems to be to contamination by contact with a woman after she has washed off the *niddå* blood. In this author's terminology 'getting in the water' means immersion: see 38-39.

18-19 This passage has been composed by the author. The same information in different words is in Kh 57-58; 66-76; Kâsh ch. XV, 15. The other texts assume this.

For the other side of this, in relation to the effect of *då̊bå* bleeding, see the notes on T 13-14, and 34-36. The passages in the Khilâf just referred to give both sides.

20-21 This is an expansion of T 11.

22-23 This depends on T 12, but only indirectly.

23 Compare 62-63, and T 13-14 and 34-36 and the notes and cross-references there. Washing has to be carried out before sunset if this person is to become clean by then.

24-31 This section has been composed by the author.

24-27 See T 13-14 N.

26-27 The original bleeding referred to in line 9 is the *niddå* bleeding at the start of the first week. The second bleeding referred to in line 27 is the *då̊bå* bleeding of the first week.

30-40 This is partly dependent on T 16-17 or the Kâfi 58-61 or both, but with the author's own expansions, and with the necessary alteration because the author allows a sequence of three weeks of menstruation, not two weeks as the Kâfi does and not one week as the Ṭubâkh does.

32-40 On *zå̊bå* bleeding in general, compare T 16-44; Kf ch. XI, 61-67; Kh 165-201; 259-261; 264-266; Far 80-119; Kâsh ch. XV, 124-141; Sharḥ Sûrat al-Irbot; M.N. I and II.

32-33 On the disagreements on how often *niddå* bleeding can occur before it turns into *zå̊bå* bleeding, see Kf ch. XI, 58-61 N.

35-37 The same information is given in Kâsh ch. XV, 128-131. All the sources assume this. For example, it is assumed in an argument in another connection in Kh 130-132.

38-39 The person must be clean in the usual sense before entering the water for the purpose of immersion. The immersion would still be effective even if the person did not wash first, but this would be a frivolous and unseemly way of carrying out the commandment. Compare Kf ch. XIII, 13 TN, where we are told that all contaminating stuff has to be washed off before immersion. The author of the Iʿtiqâdât not only requires any contaminating stuff to be removed, but requires ordinary cleanliness as well. It can be assumed that the other sources would have agreed if the matter had come up. There is a similar usage in the Jewish halachah.

41-46 and **53-56** For information on bleeding of childbirth in general, compare T 45-52; Kf ch. XI, 68-72; the whole of the extract from ch. XIII of the Kâfi; Kh 202-214; Kâsh ch. XII, 2-7; 14-17.

41-59 This section has been composed by the author.

41-43 and **55-56** On the range of variation on this, see the note on Kh 204-214.

If the person that touches the blood at any time during the seven days is unclean for seven days after that, it follows that the mother's contamination due to the blood of childbirth does not end at the end of the seventh day after delivery but at the end of the seventh day after the finish of bleeding of childbirth, and as any bleeding in the first week counts as bleeding of childbirth it follows that the woman might not become clean from it till the end of the second week. (Of course she is still unclean during the following period of bleeding of cleansing).

Note that although anyone that touches the blood is contaminated for seven days, anyone that just touches the woman without touching the blood is only contaminated for one day. See the note on Kf 88-89 for the explanation.

43 The reason that the person that touches the person that touches the woman is only contaminated for one day is that there is no contact with the blood.

43-44 The translation of ࠃࠌ ࠉࠕࠓࠄ as 'blood of carefulness' is not a literal one, but it does give the meaning quite well. The meaning of ࠉࠕࠓࠄ should be 'an increase' or 'an excess' and in this phrase it means an increase in the degree of seriousness. The term ࠉࠕࠓࠄ is used in the Kâfi, ch. XIII, 30, for the period of seven days during which the midwife's hand is treated as having the same effect as the blood itself, and there I have translated it as 'extra seriousness' to agree with the etymology given in the I'tiqâdât. I suggest, however, that the possibility should be considered that ࠉࠕࠓࠄ means 'remainder' and that the blood of childbirth during the rest of the week is called that to distinguish it from the blood at the time of delivery, and that the contamination of the midwife's hand is called that because it lasts for the rest of the week.

45-46 It has been shown in the note on 41-43 that the mother of a boy does not recover from the contamination of the bleeding of childbirth till seven days after the end of the bleeding of childbirth. This means that the purpose of the washing on the eighth day is not to attain cleanness but to remove the blood so that the count of seven days can start. It might then be asked why the washing is not performed as soon as the bleeding stops. One answer would be that most women still have some bleeding after the seventh day after delivery, so that the only time the bleeding of childbirth can be deemed to have stopped is when the first seven days are up and any bleeding still present is counted as bleeding of cleansing. Then if the woman washes herself on the eighth day the blood of childbirth is removed and any blood visible after that is only blood of cleansing, which is at a lower grade of uncleanness. Another answer might be that as the blood of childbirth corresponds to the *niddå* blood, just as the blood of cleansing corresponds to the *dåbå* blood, and as the time of *niddå* bleeding is an instant and the blood is washed off after that instant, and as the time of bleeding of childbirth is seven days, then it should follow that the blood of childbirth should be washed off after the seven days, since the seven days of bleeding of childbirth corresponds to the instant of *niddå* bleeding.

Compare the note on 57-58.

The baby has to be washed on the eighth day for a different reason. Provided the blood of childbirth was washed off on the first day, the baby should be able to become clean at the end of the seventh day. But there would be no point in washing it all over on the seventh day so that it could become clean at sunset that day because it would promptly be re-contaminated after the washing by contact with the mother, who is in the situation of contaminating anyone or anything she touches for one day, like the woman in the state of *niddå*. This would nullify the effect of the washing and the passage of sunset. On the eighth day the woman is still unclean and presumably would still contaminate anyone or anything she touched for one day, like the woman in the state of *dåbå*, but this does not matter, since the baby can be washed and then circumcised before being handed back to the mother. It is true that the baby would still be unclean, but this can not be helped, and at least after having been washed, although still unclean, it will not contaminate anyone that touches it, just as a person that has been contaminated by a *niddå* or *dåbå* woman stops contaminating other people after the washing, even before the passage of sunset.

46 The information is in the chapter on circumcision.

47-50 and **58-64** On bleeding of cleansing in general, compare T 53-59; Kf ch. XI, 73-78; Kh 215-253; Kâsh ch. XII, 11-17.

47-52 It is clear that the eighth day is not included in the thirty-three days, i.e. that the count of thirty-three days starts on the day after the seventh. This contradicts the Ṭubâkh (53-55) Kâfi (73-76) and Khilâf (215). (Although none of these say specifically that the eighth day is included in the thirty-three they all assume that the thirty-three days start after the seventh day). The Kâshif (ch. XII, 8-13) seems to agree with the I'tiqâdât. The Rabbanites and nearly all Karaites calculate the thirty-three from after the seventh day, but there is a minority Karaite opinion, quoted with disapproval in the Keter Torah, in the comment on Lv XII:4, p. 32a top, that agrees with the I'tiqâdât.

The basis of this minority Karaite opinion is probably that the prescription of v. 4 is seen as the sequel to the prescription of v. 3 instead of to the prescription of v. 2.

Notice that according to this opinion the relationship between the calculation of purification after giving birth to a boy or a girl is destroyed. Instead of a week plus thirty-three days, making forty days, which is exactly half of a fortnight plus sixty-six days, making eighty days, we get a week plus a day plus thirty-three days, making forty-one days, which will not divide into eighty. Considering the Karaite love of symmetry in their Biblical exegesis, it is not surprising that this interpretation did not find much favour with them. What is surprising is that the Samaritans, who are equally fond of symmetry, should have ended up accepting it as standard.

49-50 The reference is to the rules for recovery from the states of *niddå* and *dåbå* mentioned earlier. Compare 59 N.

53-56 Compare 104-106 and see Kh 204-214 N.

57-58 The implication is that the washing of the mother and her things is on the day after the end of the fortnight, not on the last day of the fortnight. Compare the note on 45-46 for a possible explanation.

59 She has to immerse herself on the forty-first or eightieth day, as we see from Petermann, *Samaria und die Samaritaner*, p. 384 (continuing on from the passage quoted in the note on 14-15):

> 'So bleibt sie, wenn sie einen Sohn geboren hat (nach 3 Mos. 12.), 33, hat sie aber eine Tochter geboren, 66 Tage, nach deren Verlauf sie in ein Bad gehen muss, und alle ihre kleider gereinigt werden'.

(The same passage occurs with no significant changes in *Reisen im Orient* I:277). Petermann's calculation of the overall timing is clearly wrong, due to ignorance of the halachah.

60-61 This means that bleeding after the forty-one days or eighty days is counted as *zåbå*, not *niddå*. This agrees with the Ṭubâkh (60-65) and the Kâfi (75-76) but disagrees with the Farâ'iḍ (103-106). (The Rabbanites would count it as *zåbå* and the Karaites as *niddå*: see A.E. 123d bottom-124a top; G.E. 114b top).

See the note on the Farâ'iḍ for the implications of this opinion.

62-64 The reference is to the passage in the Iʿtiqâdât corresponding to Kh 216-253.

65-67 This corresponds to T 67-73 and Kf 79-82, but the wording is the author's. Compare 8-11 and 84-88. On the various opinions on this matter, see the note on T 67. On the definition of the shade of white meant as clean see the note on Kh 197-199.

66 On the tendency to make the women the bearers of this information, see the note on T 13; and compare Iʿtiq 83-84.

68-79 This section is original to the author.

Compare Kh 130-138 for another expression of the same complaint.

79-82 This depends on Kh 33-40.

83-84 This is the author's own comment. Compare 66 and see T 13 N.

93-110 This section is the author's own composition. The use of the chapter and verse numbering of the printed editions of the MT shows that it was intended from the start to be read by foreigners.

96-100 Compare Kh 44-47 and Far 31-34. The source is probably the Khilâf, but the passage has been re-written. This etymology depends on the existence of some means of separation similar to what is described in Iʿtiq 12-17.

98-99 Actually this verse refers to Cain too, not Adam.

101-106 There are two interpretations of the expressions ࠊࠉࠌࠉ ࠍࠃࠕࠄ and ࠊࠍࠃࠕࠄ in Lv XII:2 and 5 here. What is meant is that the level of contamination due to childbirth is the same as would be caused by *niddå* blood, and that the seven days of uncleanness due to *niddå* bleeding are used as the unit of measurement in giving the length of the period of uncleanness due to childbirth.

Compare T 47-52; Kh 56-62; 67-72; 160-162; 204-208; Kâsh ch. XII, 3-5; 14-17 for other examples of these two interpretations, and see the cross-references in the note on Kh 204-214 for the various opinions on the extent of contamination due to bleeding of childbirth.

104-106 Compare 53-56.

106 The pronoun is plural because two different cases are imagined, the case of the mother of a boy and the case of the mother of a girl.

106 In the matter of contamination due to contact with the blood emitted after the delivery of a girl this author agrees with the author of the Khilâf against the Ṭubâkh and Kâfi. See the discussion in the note on Kh 204-214.

106-110 See the cross-references and discussion in the note on T 8-10.

110 After this the author quotes almost word for word from Kh 76-253; so there is no need to translate or edit the section that follows. A short section original to the author is edited immediately following.

112-113 See the previous note. At this point the author of the Iʿtiqâdât departs from the Khilâf. 112 corresponds to Kh 254; everything onwards is original. The chapter ends at line 118.

114-115 See the note on 12-17.

115-117 On copulation with a woman known to be unclean compare the references in the notes on T 74-78 and 8-10. The passage of Scripture alluded to is Lv XX:18.

TEXT 7

Extract from the Sharḥ Sûrat al-Irbot

1-3 The context is that the author is making the point that if the same details apply to two or more separate cases, then the text of Scripture gives some of the details in the sections on all of the cases to show that all the details will be the same, and gives some of the rest of the details in the section on one case and some others in the section on another case, and the details not given in one section can be supplied from the other section. In other words, he is explaining the general validity of the principles of the היקש and בנין אב.

1 For the details, see Far 42-48 and 107-110 and the notes there.

2-3 We learn from this that the spit of a *niddå*, *zåbå*, and *yålēda* contaminates to the same extent as the spit of the *zåb*. For the details of contamination due to the *zåb's* spit, see T 107-109; Kf ch. XI, 28-32 and the notes there.

TEXT 8

MARGINAL NOTES

I

Note I on the Book of Insight

1-8 This note refers to T 16-44. It is found in M_1^{mg} L^{mg} D^{mg} M_2^{txt} P_3^{txt}. In Ms. M_1 it is in the handwriting of Musallam bin Murjân himself. Its place of insertion in M_2 P_3 is after the word الجواهر 'simple substances' in 44.

For the place of this statement in relation to the other opinions, see the note on the Kâfi 58-61. It is remarkable that this note disagrees with the Kâshif, which was composed only slightly later than it, and disagrees with modern practice as well.

4 The term يوم المسلك 'the critical day' is only mentioned here.

On the question of the tendency to leave the transmission of the halachah in these matters in the hands of the women, see T 13 N.

5 This is the only place where the term *ʿadad* is specifically stated to be a technical term.

II

Note II on the Book of Insight

1-13 This note refers to the same passage in the Ṭubâkh as the previous one does. It is found in Mss. M_2N in the margin. The author is Nâji bin Khiḍr.

Compare Kf 58-61 N.

10-11 See T 13 N on the tendency to make the women the bearers of the information about the impurity relating to them.

8-9 This refers to the first marginal note on the Ṭubâkh, which disagrees with modern practice. See the note on M.N. I:1-8.

11-12 This principle is one commonly used by the Karaites.

We see from this passage that disagreements are resolved by the arising of a consensus. The author does not say that the other opinions are invalid: they are theoretically equally valid, since they are not contradicted by Scripture either. If it could be demonstrated that the other opinions contradicted Scripture they would be invalidated, but till then, they remain valid in practice for the community to which the author of this note belongs. As by his time practice had become uniform for all Samaritans, he can say that this is now the correct practice and the only correct one, even if it is not the only possible correct interpretation of this passage of Scripture.

Compare M.N. VII:3-4.

III

Note I on the Kâfi

1-6 This note is only in ms. S_1. It refers to Kf 33-40. It is written by ʿImrân bin Salâmah, the restorer of the ms.

1-3 This is obscure. What seems to be meant is that the *zåb* contaminates anything he touches whether or no the *zåb* stuff is on his hand, and that either way the degree of contamination is the same. A *niddå* woman, on the other hand, although she contaminates anything she touches whether or no the *niddå* blood is on her hand, causes seven days' contamination if the stuff is on her hand and only one day's if it is not.

This note agrees with the second and third marginal notes on the Kâfi.

5-6 The details of the law of the *zåb* and *niddå* are partly the same and partly different, and the text has to specify the details separately for each when they are different. One drop of *niddå* blood on one day at one time puts a woman in the state of *niddå*, but it takes at least two emissions of *zåb* stuff two days in a row to put a man in the state of *zåb*. (See T 93-94 N and the cross-references there). Since it takes more than one discharge of *zåb* stuff to put the man in the state of a *zåb*, it is only logical that if another person comes in contact with the *zåb* stuff that person should not be contaminated for the same length of time as the person from whom it discharges. (Compare the note on T 110-117).

Out of the three marginal notes on this passage, this is the only one to explain why it should be that contact with the *zåb* stuff is less serious in its effect than contact with the *niddå* blood. The author does not express himself well but he has a penetrating insight.

IV

Note II on the Kâfi

1-7 This note refers to the same passage of the Kâfi as the one before. It is only found in Mss. S_1P.

It agrees with the previous note and the third explanation in the Kâfi.

3-4 On the mention of blood, see Kâsh ch. XV, 5-9 N.

A gloss in Ms. P explains the term "washing" as actually meaning immersion.

V

Note III on the Kâfi

1-15 This note refers to the same passage as the one before and agrees with it. It is found in Mss. NBCWAF$_1$. The author is Yaʿqûb bin Hârûn.

4-7 This is an expanded quotation of T 114-117. The variants of this quotation are given in the apparatus to the Ṭubâkh.

VI

Note IV on the Kâfi

1-2 This note refers to Kf ch. XIII, 19-21. It is only in Mss. F_1A, and was probably composed by the scribe.

The author of the note has misunderstood this passage as referring to the washing off of the initial bleeding of menstruation, the *niddå* bleeding. This probably means that it is modern practice to count the woman's left hand as being specially contaminated by the *niddå* blood, in the same way as the Kâfi counts the woman's hand as being contaminated for seven days by blood of childbirth.

VII

Note I on the Book of Differences

1-4 This note refers to Kh 165-167. It is only found in Mss. B_2L. The original author of the note is Khidr bin Ishâq, the father of the copyist, Nâji bin Khiḍr. Compare the second marginal note on the Kâfi, which has the same content.

3-4 The opinion of the author of the Khilâf is not contradicted by Scripture but disagrees with traditional practice. Compare M.N. II:11-12 and the note there.

VIII

Note II on the Book of Differences

1-9 This note is by Khidr bin Isḥâq, the father of the copyist, Nâji bin Khiḍr. It is only in Mss. B_2L. It refers to the Additional Passage from the Khilâf. It does not add anything to what is said in the Khilâf but is valuable as confirmation that the modern position is the same as set out in the Khilâf.

CONCLUSIONS

I. SUMMARY OF THE DETAILS AND PRINCIPLES OF THE HALACHOT

1. *Preamble*

Set out below are all the halachot relating to the ࠍࠃࠄ *niddå*, ࠃࠅࠄ *dåbå*, ࠆࠁࠄ *zåbå*, ࠉࠋࠃࠄ *yålēda*, ࠆࠁ *zåb*, and ࠔࠊࠁࠕ ࠆࠓࠏ *shūkəb zēra* that could be derived from the texts edited. There are no doubt refinements and additional details and procedures for rare cases still to be elucidated, but this will have to be done by systematic observation of the practice of the Samaritans and judicious questioning on the spot. Nevertheless, the essentials of the system can now be seen.

In the process of editing the texts and commenting on them, some information on contamination from human corpses was obtained. It is not part of the purpose of this work to go into this matter, which would take a substantial monograph on its own; but so that the information is accessible, the places where it is to be found are listed here:

Kf ch. III, 43 TN; ch. XIII, 11-13 TN; ch. XII, 22-32; ch. XI, 31-32 N; the Additional Passage from the Khilâf, 1 N.

This summary is at the same time a Scriptural index. Scriptural references have been given if the matter is treated in the text of Scripture as interpreted by the Samaritans, which means the summary is at the same time an explanation of the Samaritan interpretation of chapter XV and chapter XII of Leviticus, and verse 18 of chapter XX.[1]

2. *The Intrinsic Uncleanness of Women*

Women are made unclean by an emission of blood from the vagina.[2]

There is a distinction to be made between the very first menstrual bleeding, which marks the start of the menstrual week, and any bleeding after this time, during the rest of the week. The first bleeding, or the start of the bleeding, is called ࠍࠃࠄ *niddå*; the bleeding after this is called ࠃࠅࠄ *dåbå*.[3] The term *niddå* refers properly to a condition, and the term *dåbå* to a woman in a certain condition; but in practice the two terms apply equally well to the woman herself, or her condition, or the blood.[4]

---

[1] On Lv XX:18 see note 7 and note 118.

[2] Kh 3-4; 27-32 and the context; Far 23-24. Assumed by all the sources as self-evident. Lv XV:19.

[3] Far 35-41. Assumed by all the sources. Lv XV:19.

[4] Consistent usage of all sources. The Jewish usage is the same.

The Khilâf has a derived term ࠍࠏࠃࠄ *nå̊'ēda*, an Aramaic or Hebrew participle, to refer specifically to the woman herself as opposed to the blood or the condition, but it is not used consistently.[5] The Khilâf also has a derived term ࠍࠃࠅࠕ *niddot* to refer to the condition of uncleanness, as opposed to the woman or the blood, but this term is not used consistently either.[6]

There are no special terms related to the word *då̊bå*.

There is a more general use of the term *då̊bå* to refer to a woman unclean because of any kind of emission of blood from the vagina, whether as *niddå*, or *då̊bå* in the narrow sense, or *zå̊bå*, or *yå̊lēda*, but this is a separate usage and is clearly distinguished by the sources from the specialised use of the term.[7] In all that follows, the term is used in its specialised meaning.

The Khilâf derives the term *då̊bå* from the verb ࠃࠅࠄ 'to be sick', and relates it to ࠃࠁࠁ 'to be depressed'; and takes it to be an adjective or noun.[8]

The term *niddå* is taken to mean literally 'banishment' or 'exclusion', and the term is said to be used because it is this bleeding that makes the woman unclean and causes her to be segregated for a week. It is accordingly an abstract noun.[9]

As it is the *niddå* bleeding that puts the woman in a state of uncleanness for a week, it makes no difference whatever in practice whether or no any bleeding occurs after the instant of *niddå* bleeding, provided the bleeding finishes early enough on the seventh day for the woman to immerse herself.[10]

Before intercourse, or when the expected time of the start of the menstrual bleeding is approaching, the woman is supposed to check herself for the presence of blood in the vestibule using a bit of rag or cotton-wool. If some sign of blood is seen, she is counted as unclean from that time onwards. If the woman is able to tell when the bleeding has started or is about to start by some symptom that generally appears at that time, then she is to check herself for the presence of blood if the symptom is felt. If she experiences the symptom, but does not check herself at the time, it has to be assumed that she started to bleed and became unclean at that time, even if no blood runs out of the vagina till later on.[11]

The woman is made unclean not only by the event of the emission of *niddå* blood, but also by her contact with it. She must, therefore, wash the blood off herself at some time on the first day if that day is to be counted in the

---

[5] Kh 46-47 TN and the cross-references.
[6] Kh 135 TN.
[7] Kh 51-53 TN and the cross-references.
[8] Kh 49-51. Lv XX:18.
[9] Kh 44-47 TN and the cross-references. Lv XV:19.
[10] Kf ch. XI, 56-58 TN: T 13-14 TN; 34-36 TN: Kh 57-58 and 66-75; Kâsh ch. XV, 18-19; I'tiq 18-29; Lv XV:19.
[11] Far 12-22.

minimum seven days of uncleanness. If she does not wash the *niddå* blood off, it will keep on re-contaminating her. The count of seven days can only start when the *niddå* blood has been removed.[12] Notice, though, that it makes no difference whatever to the count whether there is *dåbå* bleeding or no.[13] One Samaritan opinion is that the reason for this is that she is already unclean because of the *niddå* bleeding, so that the *dåbå* blood, although unclean, is not able to add to her uncleanness. Some Samaritans, however, seem to have maintained that the *dåbå* blood had no contaminating effect at all, or that its effect only lasted for the period of contact. This theory is treated further on.[14]

The week of uncleanness consists of one incomplete day, the day on which the *niddå* blood is washed off, which will usually be the day on which the *niddå* blood was discharged, followed by six complete days, calculated from sunset to sunset. Provided the woman immerses herself before sunset on the seventh day, she becomes clean at sunset; but this immersion is only effective if the *dåbå* bleeding is completely finished, and if any bleeding were to occur later on, the immersion would be invalidated.[15]

There is a variant Samaritan opinion, which was the opinion of some Dositheans but need not have been confined to them, and was apparently one Samaritan opinion in the period of the Tanna'im, that the woman is to count her seven days from the day after the *dåbå* bleeding finishes, counting seven complete days, from sunset to sunset, as in the case of the *zåbå*.[16] This is of course the same as the innovation in Rabbanite practice of post-Talmudic times, but there is no apparent mechanism by which the Samaritans could have borrowed from the Rabbanites, since the Samaritan practice is attested long before the Rabbanites had abandoned the traditional correct practice as too hard for most people to calculate or keep track of.[17]

Any person or artefact that comes in contact with the *niddå* blood is made unclean for seven days, just like the woman herself.[18] If the contact of the second person or the artefact occurs after the day on which the blood is discharged, the person or artefact will be unclean for seven days from that time onwards, and will necessarily still be unclean when the woman has become clean.[19]

---

[12] Kf ch. XI, 88-89 N; ch. XIII, 13-18; T 55-57 N and the cross-references.

[13] See note 10.

[14] See notes 27 and 28.

[15] Kf ch. III, 43 TN: T 12-15; Far 25-30 and 35-41; I'tiq 38-39.

[16] T 15 N. See note 63.

[17] See the Mishneh Torah, Issure Bi'ah XI.

[18] T 8-11 TN; Kf ch. XI, 83-89; 39 and 40 TN; Kh 78-81; Kâsh ch. XV, 101-106; I'tiq 106-110; M.N. 111; M.N. IV; M.N. V. See also Kf ch. XI, 88-89 TN.

[19] I'tiq 41-43 and 53-56. Compare Kf ch. XIII, 9-18 N. Lv XV:24.

A person or artefact contaminated by *niddå* blood is cleansed by having the blood removed,[20] waiting till the seventh day, and then either being immersed, according to the Ṭubâkh, Kâfi, and Iʿtiqâdât, or washed all over, according to the Kâshif, and waiting till sunset.[21]

A person or artefact in contact with the woman at the instant of *niddå* bleeding, but not touched by the blood itself, is only made unclean for one day. Cleansing is by immersion, according to the Kâfi, Ṭubâkh, and Iʿtiqâdât, or washing all over, according to the Kâshif, and the arrival of sunset.[22] We are not told directly whether contact with the woman after the instant of *niddå*, but before the *niddå* blood is washed off, has the same effect, but it is very likely that it does have.[23] It seems best to assume that the woman at the instant of *niddå* bleeding, and after that instant but before having had the blood washed off, are treated the same way in all respects.[24]

According to the Kâfi, Kâshif, and Iʿtiqâdât, a person or artefact that comes in contact with *dåbå* blood is made unclean for one day, and provided the blood is removed before sunset, becomes clean at sunset.[25] The Kâshif requires washing all over,[26] and the Iʿtiqâdât requires immersion. The Kâfi requires neither. The opinion of the authors of the Tubâkh and Khilâf seems to be that the person or artefact becomes clean as soon as the blood is removed,[27] and this was probably the opinion of Sakta the Dosithean and others as well.[28]

According to the Kâfi, Kâshif, and Iʿtiqâdât, a person or artefact that comes in contact with a *dåbå* woman, without any contact with the blood, is made unclean for one day, and becomes clean at sunset. The Kâshif requires washing all over, and the Iʿtiqâdât immersion.[29] The opinion of the authors of the Tubâkh and Khilâf seems to be that the person or artefact is only unclean as long as contact lasts, and becomes clean the instant contact is

---

[20] T 55-57 N; Kf ch. XI, 88-89 N; ch. XI, 74-76 N; ch. XII, 10 TN; ch. XIII, 13-18; Lv XV:24.

[21] See the references in note 20; and add T 8-11; Kf ch. XI, 38-40; Kâsh ch. XV, 117-123, and the context. On the time of immersion or washing all over in this case and all other cases, see note 168.

[22] Kf ch. III, 22-38 N, in the quotation; Kf ch. XI, 88-89 N; T 8-11 TN; Kâsh ch. XV, 103-106; Iʿtiq 16 TN.

[23] Kf ch. XI, 88-89, and the cross references; and the analogy of the case of bleeding of childbirth.

[24] Argument from the silence of the sources to the contrary, and the analogy of the fact that a person on whom there is *niddå* blood originally discharged by a different person has the same contaminating effect as the woman from whom the blood discharges at the instant of *niddå*. (See note 43).

[25] Kf ch. XI, 88-89 N; 84-87; Iʿtiq 16.

[26] As the Kâshif requires washing all over of the person that touches the woman without touching the *dåbå* blood, this is almost certain. See Kâsh ch. XV, 107-112.

[27] T 13-14 TN and the cross-references there. T 34-36 N.

[28] T 11-13 N; Kh 267-269 N; 204-214 N; Kf ch. XIII, 6-8 TN.

[29] See the references in notes 25 and 26.

broken.[30] The Dosithean opinion seems to have been that the person or artefact is completely unaffected.[31]

The woman's hand with which she washes off the *niddå* blood (apparently the left hand is used) is treated as being at the same level of uncleanness as the *niddå* blood itself for the whole of the menstrual week, even if there is no blood on it, and whoever or whatever she touches with it is made unclean for seven days. The hand is treated as if it were the blood itself.[32]

According to the Kâfi, ground is contaminated by the presence of a woman at the instant of *niddå*, or by the presence of the woman before she has washed the *niddå* blood off, even if there is no contact of the blood with the ground. None of the other sources mention this and it is not modern practice. The ground apparently becomes unclean by the absorption of airborne molecules of the unclean substance by the natural moisture in the ground. The ground is cleansed by fire.[33]

A woman at the instant of *niddå* makes any couch, seat, or saddle on which she puts her weight unclean, even if there is no direct contact, and the couch, seat, or saddle contaminates any person or artefact that touches it. The contamination lasts for one day. The person or artefact washes all over or is washed all over, and becomes clean at sunset.[34]

It seems that the woman has the same effect even after the instant of *niddå* bleeding if the *niddå* blood is still on her.[35]

According to the Kâshif, any person made unclean by any artefact at all that has itself been made unclean by contact with a *niddå* woman has to wash all over, and becomes clean at sunset. It is to be assumed that all the other sources would agree with this; and in fact we find that although artefacts contaminated by the person contaminated by the *niddå* woman have to be washed, the term 'immersion' is not used in the context in the sources in treating this situation.[36]

The couch, seat, or saddle is unclean for a week, and becomes clean by washing.[37]

The degree of uncleanness and the contaminating effect is no greater if the woman's weight is still on the couch, seat, or saddle than it is when she has moved off.[38]

---

[30] Kh 117-118 TN; T 13-14 TN. All this paragraph follows necessarily from the previous one.

[31] See note 28.

[32] M.N. VI.

[33] Kf ch. XII, 23-24, and the various notes there.

[34] Far 42-48 TN and the cross-references; 107-110; Kâsh ch. XV, 107-112 and 119-122; Sharḥ Sûrat al-Irbot; Lv XV: 20; and see note 139.

[35] See note 24.

[36] Kâsh ch. XV, 107-112; I'tiq 16. Notice the choice of wording in Lv XV:21-22 for the washing of the clothes.

[37] Argument from silence and the analogy of the Karaite system.

[38] Far 42-48; Lv XV:23.

A couch or bed for this purpose includes the frame, bedding, and clothes, all of which are considered as one artefact.[39]

Any person whose weight is rested on the couch, seat, or saddle becomes unclean, even if there is no direct contact.[40] Any person that carries the couch, seat, or saddle becomes unclean, even if there is no direct contact.[41] Lifting the object partly or wholly without moving it from the spot is treated the same as carrying.[42]

Any person to whom any *niddå* blood attaches has the same effect on a couch, seat, or saddle as the woman from whom the blood originates. The commonest instance of this happening will be if the woman starts to menstruate during intercourse and the blood gets on the man.[43]

According to all the sources except the Ṭubâkh, a woman can enter the states of *niddå* and *dằbå* more than once, in consecutive weeks. The number of consecutive weeks allowed is limited, and one the limit is passed, any new bleeding puts the woman in the state of ࠆࠁࠄ *zằbå*. The maximum number of consecutive weeks allowed is: one by the Ṭubâkh; two by the Kâfi; three by the first marginal note on the Ṭubâkh, the Kâshif, the Iʿtiqâdât, the second marginal note on the Ṭubâkh, the first marginal note on the Khilâf and the Hebrew translation of the Kâfi in ch. XI, XI:1; four by the Farâ'id; and seven by the Khilâf.[44] The opinion of the Khilâf is specifically rejected by the Ṭubâkh.[45]

The Ṭubâkh only allows one week's menstruation at a time, and if any bleeding occurs at any time on the eighth day, the woman enters the state of *zằbå*. If there is no bleeding on the eighth day, but it occurs on some later day in that week, and continues for four consecutive days, the woman becomes *zằbå*.[46] We are not told how bleeding that does not occur on four consecutive days is treated, but logic and the analogy of the Rabbanite system indicates that she is made unclean for the day or days on which bleeding occurs and one complete day after, like the זבה קטנה or שומרת יום כנגד יום in the Rabbanite system. We are not told what happens if the bleeding starts on the fifth day or later in the second week, so that the four days have not been completed by the end of that week, and bleeding then occurs on the first day

---

[39] The Additional Passage from the Khilâf and the notes there.

[40] By analogy with the case of the *zåb*: see Kâsh ch. XV, 31-32, and Lv XV:6.

[41] By analogy with the case of the *zåb*: see Kâsh ch. XV, and see Lv XV:10.

[42] By analogy with the case of the *zåb*: see Kâsh ch. XV, 36-37, and see Kf ch. III, 4-5 TN and Lv XV:10.

[43] T 8-10 TN and the cross-references there. Lv XV:24.

[44] Kf ch. XI, 58-61 N; T 13-14 N; Lv XV:25. Notice the reading of Ms. M_2 in M.N. I:5, made under the influence of the modern halachah.

[45] T 26-29 TN. Although the Khilâf is much later than the Ṭubâkh, we see that some Samaritans held this opinion as early as the time of composition of the Ṭubâkh.

[46] T 16-26 TN; Lv XV:25.

of the third week. Again, logic and the analogy of the Rabbanite system indicates that the days of bleeding in the two weeks are not added together, so that her bleeding on the first day of the third week is counted as the start of a new period of *niddå* and *dåbå*, and the days in the second week just before this when she was bleeding are counted as זבה קטנה, which is superseded by the more serious state of *niddå*.[47]

There is disagreement over how soon the bleeding of the next week has to start for it to be counted as consecutive to the week before.

The Khilâf counts bleeding on any day of the next week as consecutive, both for the purpose of adding to the progressive total of weeks and for the purpose of putting the woman in the state of *zåbå*.[48]

According to the first marginal note on the Ṭubâkh, written by Musallam bin Marjân in the early eighteenth century, bleeding is counted as consecutive for the purpose of making the progressive totals of the menstrual weeks if it occurs on the first day of each successive week, but for the purpose of putting the woman in the state of *zåbå*, the bleeding is counted as continuous if it occurs at any time on the last day of the week before, i.e. the last day of the third week. Presumably if there is any bleeding on the first day of the fourth week, but there had not been any bleeding on the last day of the third week, the bleeding is not counted as consecutive. The last day of the third week is termed *yawm al-mask* 'the critical day'.[49]

The Kâshif agrees with Musallam bin Marjân, except that it only counts the bleeding as consecutive for the purpose of putting the woman in the state of *zåbå* if it occurs on the afternoon of the last day of the third week.[50]

The Ṭubâkh counts bleeding on the first day of the second week as putting the woman in the state of *zåbå*, but does not count bleeding that starts on some later day as being consecutive unless it occurs on four days in a row.[51]

The Kâfi and Farâ'id count bleeding on the first day of the next week as consecutive to the week before, but not bleeding that starts on some later day.[52]

The I'tiqâdât counts bleeding that occurs exactly at sunset at the end of the seventh day of one week and the start of the first day of the next week as consecutive, both for the purpose of the progressive total of menstrual weeks and for the purpose of making the woman *zåbå*.[53]

---

[47] T 16-26 N. Some details of what is assumed here might well have to be modified when more evidence turns up.
[48] See note 44. See also Kh 264-265.
[49] See note 44.
[50] See note 44.
[51] See note 44.
[52] See note 44.
[53] See note 44.

An opinion of some Samaritans, considered by the author of the Farâ'iḍ, is that if the bleeding finishes before the end of the last day of one week, and the woman becomes clean at the end of the day, the continuity is broken, and bleeding on the first day of the next week will not put the woman in the state of *zåbå*. Presumably the only way that the woman could become *zåbå* would be if she had no time to immerse herself between the end of the bleeding and sunset of the seventh day, or if bleeding continued right up till sunset and a few seconds past. This is a very lenient opinion. We are not told how these people defined continuity for the purpose of counting the progressive total of menstrual weeks, but presumably the definition was the same.[54]

An opinion of some Samaritans rejected by the author of the Farâ'iḍ is that if there is no bleeding at the start of the first day of the next week, the continuity is broken, and if bleeding starts partway through the day the woman will not become *zåbå*. Apparently this would be the case even if the woman had not had time to immerse herself before the end of the last day of the week before and was still unclean at the sunset at the end of one week and the start of the next, but the text is not specific on this point. We are not told whether this criterion applies for the purpose of making the total of consecutive weeks leading up to the time when the woman becomes *zåbå*, but it probably does. This opinion is compatible with the other one mentioned by the author of the Farâ'iḍ.[55]

The use of the term *zåbå* as a specialised term for a woman whose bleeding is abnormal is to be distinguished from its use to refer to a woman who is menstruating.[56]

In the specialised sense, the term *zåbå* is used by all the sources to refer to the woman's condition, the blood, and the woman herself, though the last is the etymological meaning.[57] The Khilâf has a special term ࠆࠁࠅࠕ *zåbot* or ࠆࠉࠁࠅࠕ *zībot* to refer specifically to the condition, but it is not used consistently.[58] The authors of the Kâfi and Khilâf know of a usage according to which the condition or the blood are called *zåb*, in the masculine, as opposed to the woman herself, who is referred to as *zåbå*, but they do not make the distinction consistently.[59]

The Khilâf and Farâ'id maintain that as opposed to the state of *niddå* or *dåbå*, which is normal, the state of *zåbå* is abnormal, and this is why it is treated more stringently.[60]

---

[54] See note 44, and Far 103-106. The text is terse, and its implications not entirely clear.

[55] See note 44, and Far 97-102.

[56] Far 2-3 TN and 75-83; Lv XV:19 and 25.

[57] Consistent usage of all the sources. The Jewish usage is the same.

[58] Kh 64 TN.

[59] T 32 TN and 62; Kh 130-132 TN.

[60] Kh 194-196; 165-172; 179-185; Far 80-83 and 87-97.

Once the continuity of bleeding is broken, any bleeding that occurs later on is counted as *niddå* bleeding followed by *dåbå* bleeding.[61] It is possible for the woman to enter the state of *niddå* week after week without limit provided there is no continuity between the bleeding of one week and the next. (The definition of continuity varies from source to source, as previously explained). A corollary of this is that if a woman passes through a certain number of periods of *niddå*, one week after the other, some of which are separated by the requisite amount and some of which are not, only the ones that are joined together are counted for the purpose of reaching the total and putting the woman in the state of *zåbå*.

A woman that has entered the state of *zåbå* is cleansed by counting seven complete days, from sunset to sunset, starting on the day after the bleeding finishes, provided the blood has been washed off the day before, immersing herself on the seventh complete day, and waiting till sunset. If any bleeding occurs on any of the seven days, the count is stopped, and has to start again from scratch the day after the bleeding finishes.[62] There is evidence of a divergent opinion according to which the woman need only count an incomplete day followed by six complete days, as in the case of the *niddå*. This seems to have been the practice of some Samaritans in the time of the Tanna'im.[63]

The *zåbå* before her count has started is treated the same as the *niddå* for the purpose of contamination.[64] It seems that the *zåbå* woman while she is still bleeding, and after she has stopped bleeding but before she has washed the blood off, are treated the same way in all respects.[65]

Contact with *zåbå* blood makes a person or artefact unclean for seven complete days, the remainder of the day on which contact occurred, and then seven complete days from sunset to sunset. The person or artefact becomes clean by the removal of the blood on the first day, immersion or washing all over on the seventh of the complete days, and the arrival of sunset. The count can only start after the blood has been removed.[66] The opinion of the Kâshif is probably that washing all over is required; the opinion of the other sources is probably that immersion is required.[67] One Dosithean opinion was

---

[61] Consistently in all the sources.

[62] T 16-44 TN and cross-references; Kh 200-201; I'tiq 83-89; Lv XV:28.

[63] T 15 TN and cross-references; Bavli Niddah 33a (in a baraita); Tosefta Niddah V:1. Notice that Mishnah Niddah IV:1 and the other sources also say, on the contrary, that the Samaritans "count" (a technical usage meaning a count of seven complete days) after any bleeding. It seems that some Samaritans assimilated the *niddå* to the *zåbå*, and others did the exact opposite.

[64] Kf ch. XI, 64-67 TN; Far 69-72; Lv XV:25.

[65] Kf ch. XI, 88-89 N; and the analogy of the treatment of *niddå* blood (see note 24).

[66] Kf ch. XI, 88-89 TN; T 55-57 N; Kf ch. XI, 66-67; 84; the whole of Kf ch. XIII, and the notes. See note 12.

[67] On the analogy of the case of contamination from *niddå* blood (see notes 25 and 26).

probably that the blood only caused contamination for one day, and that the person or artefact was cleansed by the removal of the blood, immersion, and the arrival of sunset.[68]

As contact with a *zåbå* woman before her count is treated the same as contact with a woman at the time of *niddå* in degree of seriousness, the sources, including the Dositheans, agree that a person or artefact contaminated by her is made unclean for one day, and becomes clean by immersion and the arrival of sunset.[69] The Kâshif requires washing all over rather than immersion.[70]

Contact with a *zåbå* woman during her count seems to be treated the same as contact with a *dåbå* woman. This means that the Kâfi, Kâshif, and I'tiqâdât would maintain that the person or artefact is made unclean for one day and does not need washing, the Ṭubâkh and Khilâf would maintain that they were only unclean during the period of contact, and the Dositheans would maintain that they were completely unaffected.[71]

It is reasonable to assume that contact with the blood of the lesser degree of *zåbå*, in the system of the Ṭubâkh, would have the same effect and be treated the same as contact with *dåbå* blood, and that contact with the woman herself, without any contact with the blood, would be treated the same as contact with a *dåbå* woman.[72]

A woman in a state of *zåbå* before she starts her count of seven days without bleeding contaminates a couch, seat, or saddle in the same way as a *niddå* woman does.[73]

It is reasonable to assume that a woman's hand with which she washes off the *zåbå* blood is at a higher level of uncleanness than the rest of her, on the analogy of a woman who has washed off *niddå* blood or the blood of childbirth.[74]

When a woman gives birth, she is made unclean by the event of delivery and by the blood emitted at the instant of delivery.[75] The Ṭubâkh, Kâfi, Khilâf and Farâ'iḍ set the period of her uncleanness at a week plus thirty-three days, making forty days altogether, if the baby is a boy, and a fortnight plus sixty-six days, making eighty days altogether if the baby is a girl. The Kâshif and I'tiqâdât agree with the other sources in the case of contamination from giving birth to a girl, but set the uncleanness after giving birth to a

[68] T 11-13 N and cross-references; Kf ch. XI, 64-67 N and cross-references.

[69] Kf ch. XI, 88-89 N, and the cross-references.

[70] Kf ch. XI, 88-89 N. Lv XV:25. See also note 68.

[71] See note 68 and note 28. See also Kh 267-269 N.

[72] The requirements of logic and symmetry and the analogy of the Rabbanite system. See note 44.

[73] Far 42-48; 69-72; 107-110; Lv XV:26-27.

[74] See note 32 and note 101.

[75] Kf ch. XI, 88-89 N. *This is a fundamental principle of Samaritan halachah.*

boy at a week plus one day plus thirty-three days, making forty-one days altogether.[76] For this purpose, the day on which delivery occurs is treated as the first day, so that the first day can be incomplete at the start, as in the case of the *niddå*. All the sources agree that any bleeding that happens during the thirty-three or sixty-six days is to be treated as *då̊bå* bleeding would: that is to say that the woman is equally unclean whether or not there is any bleeding, and her level of uncleanness and degree of contaminating effect is the same as for a woman during her menstrual week after the instant of *niddå* is past and the *niddå* blood has been washed off.[77]

The author of the Khilâf treats the bleeding that occurs exactly at delivery as equivalent to *niddå* bleeding in its level of uncleanness and degree of contaminating effect, but treats the bleeding that happens during the week or fortnight as equivalent to *då̊bå* bleeding. The blood discharged on delivery of a boy makes anyone that touches it unclean for a week, and the blood discharged on delivery of a girl makes anyone that touches it unclean for a fortnight. The difference between the woman's uncleanness during the week or fortnight and during the thirty-three or sixty-six days is not explained. It seems likely that the difference is that although any blood emitted during either period, that is during the week or fortnight on one hand, or the thirty-three or sixty-six days on the other hand, will have the same effect on anyone that touches it, there is a distinction to be made in the case of contact with the woman without contact with the blood, so that such contact during the first period would make a person unclean for one day, and in the second period would have no effect.[78]

The Kâfi, the interpolation in the Khilâf, the Kâshif, and the Iʿtiqâdât treat all bleeding during the week or fortnight as equivalent to *niddå* bleeding, as opposed to bleeding that occurs during the thirty-three days (one plus thirty-three days in the case of the Kâshif and Iʿtiqâdât) or sixty-six days. The author of the Khilâf says that the standard opinion and practice of women in his time is to treat all bleeding during the week or fortnight as equivalent to *niddå*. The Kâfi treats the contaminating effect of the blood emitted during the week or the fortnight after delivery of a girl as the same as the effect of *niddå* blood, causing seven days' uncleanness to anyone that touches it. The Iʿtiqâdât says that blood emitted during the week after delivery of a boy makes anyone that touches it unclean for a week, and that blood emitted during the fortnight after delivery of a girl makes anyone that touches it unclean for a fortnight.[79]

---

[76] T 45-49; Kf ch. XI, 68-78; Kh 202-253; Kâsh ch. XII, 2-17; Iʿtiq 41-64; 47-52 N; Lv XII 2-5.

[77] T 47-52 N; 53-59; Kh 200-214 N; Iʿtiq 62-64; 101-106; Lv XII:2-5.

[78] Kh 204-214 N; Lv XII:2 and 5.

[79] See note 78.

Sakta the Dositheanseems to have maintained that the blood discharged at the birth of a boy made anyone that touched it (including of course the baby itself) unclean for a week, and that the blood discharged at the birth of a girl made anyone that touched it (including the baby itself) unclean for a fortnight.[80]

The Ṭubâkh counts bleeding at the instant of delivery of a boy as equivalent to *niddå* blood, and bleeding during the rest of the week as equivalent to *dåbå* blood, but counts all bleeding during the fortnight after delivery of a girl as equivalent to *niddå* blood. The blood discharged at the instant of delivery of a boy, at the instant of delivery of a girl, or during the fortnight after delivery of a girl, makes anyone that touches it unclean for a week. The blood discharged during the week after delivery of a boy makes anyone that touches it unclean for one day. The blood discharged during the thirty-three days or sixty-six days makes anyone that touches it unclean only till the blood is removed.[81]

According to the Kâfi, Kâshif, and Iʿtiqâdât, blood of childbirth keeps on being a cause of contamination even after the end of the week or fortnight, so that the woman has to wash this blood off herself before she can enter the lower degree of uncleanness of the thirty-three or sixty-six days.[82] The other sources are silent on this matter.

A corollary of this opinion that the blood of childbirth still keeps its full contaminating effect after the week or fortnight is that any person or artefact touched by it is made unclean for seven days, and has to be cleansed in the same way as if contact had been made during the week or fortnight.[83] Another corollary is that if the contact happens less than seven days before the end of the week or fortnight, the person or artefact contaminated will still be unclean after the woman has become clean.[84]

Some Samaritans, including some Dositheans, seem to have maintained that the blood of childbirth lost its contaminating power after the end of the week or fortnight, so that any person that touched it after this time became clean as soon as it was washed off, apparently without even having to wait till sunset. The same Dositheans seem to have maintained that anyone that touched blood emitted during the thirty-three or sixty-six days could become clean as soon as the blood was washed off, without having to wait till sunset, and that anyone that touched the woman herself during this period, without

80 See note 78.
81 See note 78 and note 27.
82 Kf ch. XIII, 5-18 TN: 6-8 N; Kâsh ch. XII, 14 TN: Iʿtiq 41-43.
83 See note 82.
84 Kf ch. XIII, 9-18 TN; Iʿtiq 41-43 and 55-56 TN; and the silence of all the sources to the contrary.

coming in contact with the blood was completely unaffected. For this reason, there was no need for her to be segregated.[85]

The sources agree on treating the 'bleeding of cleansing' [ࠈࠄࠓࠄ] during the thirty-three or sixty-six days as equivalent to *dåbå* bleeding in all respect.[86] Logically the two have to be treated as equivalent if the bleeding of childbirth is equivalent to *niddå* bleeding.

The blood emitted at delivery and during the first week or fortnight is called ࠃࠌ ࠉࠋࠉࠃࠄ *dam yēlīda* or *dam al-wilâdah* 'blood of childbirth'.[87] The woman is termed ࠉࠋࠉࠃࠄ (or ࠉࠋࠃࠄ) *yålēda*.[88] The blood emitted during the thirty-three or sixty-six days is called ࠃࠌ ࠈࠄࠓࠄ *dam ṭårå* 'blood of her cleansing'[89] or *dam ṭuhûrhâ* or *dam aṭ-ṭuhûr*.[90] There is another set of terms, *nifâs* for the bleeding of the week or fortnight and the uncleanness of this period, and *naqâ* for the bleeding of the thirty-three or sixty-six days and the uncleanness of this period, used in the interpolation in the Khilâf.[91] The blood that issues during the first week or fortnight, as opposed to the bleeding at delivery, is called ࠃࠌ ࠉࠅࠕࠓ *dam ūtar*, which could mean 'more serious blood' and is so taken in modern times, but is more likely to mean 'the remaining blood' or 'the blood of the remaining period'.[92]

The woman washes herself at the end of the week or fortnight, i.e. on the eighth or fifteenth day, so as to remove the blood of childbirth.[93] It can be assumed that if only the bleeding at the instant of delivery is counted as bleeding of childbirth, that the blood can be washed off on the first day,[94] but the author of the Khilâf does not raise the matter.

A woman who has given birth is still unclean during the thirty-three or sixty-six days of cleansing, whether or not there is any bleeding, and it is forbidden to copulate with her till the end of the forty (or forty-one) or eighty days.[95] This follows logically from the analogy made between *niddå* blood

---

[85] Kf ch. XIII, 6-8 TN, and the context; T 11-13 N; Kh 204-214 N. The Mishnah knows of Samaritan 'houses of uncleanness' (like those of the Falashas) but it seems that by the time of editing the Mishnah they were no longer in use. (See Mishnah Niddah VII:4 and note the wording, and compare Tosefta Niddah VI:15).

[86] See note 77. The Khilâf and Farâ'iḍ do not use the identification in argument (see notes 97 and 98). See also T 13-14 N.

[87] T 2 TN and the cross-references at the end of T 45-52 N; T 45-52.

[88] Far 66 and 104; I'tiq 112; The Arabic terms *wâlidah* or *wallâdah* are better treated as ordinary nouns rather than technical terms.

[89] Lv XII:4-5. All the sources use this term consistently.

[90] These are direct translations of the Hebrew terms.

[91] Kh 269 TN.

[92] I'tiq 43-44 TN.

[93] Kâsh ch. XII, 14; I'tiq 45 and 57; 45-46 N.

[94] See note 78.

[95] Kh 215-253; Far 66-68; Kâsh ch. XII, 11-13; I'tiq 47-48 and 58. This is assumed in T 47-48 in its context and Kf ch. XI, 90 in its context.

and blood of childbirth: if the *niddå* blood makes the woman unclean for seven days, regardless of whether there is any bleeding after the *niddå* bleeding, then the bleeding of childbirth makes the woman unclean for the whole forty (or forty-one) or eighty days, regardless of whether there is any bleeding after the time of delivery.[96] The Khilâf and Farâ'iḍ prove the point by comparison with a woman recovering from the state of *zå̊bå*, during her count, when she is still unclean and a source of contamination even though not bleeding,[97] and by arguments from the text of Scripture.[98] On the last day of the forty (or forty-one) or eighty days she immerses herself, and becomes clean at sunset. All this is analogous to the procedure for cleansing from the states of *niddå* and *då̊bå*.[99]

During the first week or fortnight she contaminates a couch, seat, or saddle in exactly the same way as does a *niddå* woman.[100]

The woman's hand, with which she washes off the blood of childbirth at the end of the first week contaminates any person or artefact that she touches with it for seven days if she has given birth to a boy, so it seems reasonable to assume that if she has given birth to a girl her hand, with which she washes off the blood at the end of the fortnight, contaminates people and artefacts for a fortnight. Presumably the hand loses its contaminating effect after a week or fortnight. The midwife's hands are put in the same state by her delivery of the baby. If she has delivered a boy anyone or anything she touches is contaminated for seven days, so presumably if she has delivered a girl anyone or anything she touches is contaminated for a fortnight. The midwife's hands lose their contaminating effect at the end of the week or fortnight. In all these cases, the hand is treated as if it were the blood itself. The period during which the midwife's hand has this effect is called the ࠀࠅࠕࠓ *ūtar*.[101]

According to the Kâfi, ground is contaminated by the presence of a woman at the time of childbirth, even if there is no contact of the blood with the ground. We are not told whether the presence of the mother during the rest of the week or fortnight has the same effect, but seeing that in the system of the Kâfi the whole of the first week or fortnight is equivalent in degree of uncleanness to the instant of *niddå*, it seems likely that her presence during this time would have such an effect. The other sources do not recognise this

---

[96] Kf ch. XI, 77-78 and see note 86.

[97] Kh 220-231; Far 66-68.

[98] Kh 226-227; Far 66-72.

[99] Kf ch. XI, 74; I'tiq 49-50 TN; 57; 59 N.

[100] This is not stated explicitly, but can be assumed from the principle that the *niddå* and *yå̊lēda* are equivalent for the purpose of contamination, and the analogy of the Karaite and Rabbanite systems.

[101] Kf ch. XIII, 19-21 TN and 29-30 TN.

kind of contamination of ground and it is not modern practice. The ground apparently becomes unclean by the absorption of airborne molecules by the natural moisture in the ground. It is cleansed by fire.[102]

According to the Khilâf, if the woman is already unclean and in a state of *då̊bå* or *zå̊bå* at the time of delivery, there is no need to perform any additional cleansing or to treat the situation as different in any way to the situation of a woman giving birth while in a state of cleanness.[103] The matter is not raised in the other sources.

If bleeding occurs on the day after the thirty-three or sixty-six days of bleeding of cleansing, then whether or not she has been bleeding up till the end of the thirty-three days or sixty-six days, and whether or not any bleeding occurs on the thirty-third day or sixty-sixth day, she becomes *zå̊bå*, according to the Ṭubâkh, Kâfi, and Iʿtiqâdât, or *niddå*, according to the Farâʾiḍ.[104]

Blood itself, as opposed to a discolouration of the vaginal fluid, is recognised as being pure red, blacky-red, or yellowy. The colours are apparently the same as the ones recognised by the Karaites.[105]

Any vaginal fluid that is not either colourless or pure white is termed *dam ash-shubhah* or *dam al-ishtibâh*, meaning 'blood of plausibility' or 'blood of possibility'. Not all the sources use these terms. Those that do are the source of the Ṭubâkh, the Ṭubâkh itself, the Kâfi, and the Iʿtiqâdât.[106]

The treatment is different in the different sources.

A source of the Khilâf maintains that discolouration of the vaginal fluid is to be treated as evidence of the possibility of the presence of blood in the case of a woman who has become *zå̊bå* and is waiting for seven days without bleeding to elapse before becoming clean, but in other cases has no effect whatever.[107]

A source of the Ṭubâkh and Kâfi counts such discolouration as evidence that blood might be present, but need not necessarily be present. Nevertheless, the woman is to behave as if she were unclean, to be on the safe side. We are not told what practical distinction is made between the case of a woman certainly unclean and one possibly unclean, but it can be assumed by analogy with Karaite practice that whereas the woman who is certainly unclean need only avoid people who are clean, and can associate freely with people who are unclean, the woman who is only possibly unclean has to avoid

[102] See note 33.
[103] Kh 203-204 TN.
[104] Far 103-106 TN and cross-references.
[105] Far 5-8 TN.
[106] T 66-73 TN and cross-references; T 66 N.
[107] T 66 N and Kh 130-132 N. The interpolation in the Khilâf, at 260-261, says that any discolouration can actually put the woman in the state of *zå̊bå* at the appropriate time, but with the implication that this would not apply when marking the start of *niddå*.

both people who are clean, in case she is unclean and contaminates them, and people who are unclean, in case she is clean and is contaminated by them.[108]

According to the Ṭubâkh, Kâfi, and Farâ'iḍ, discolouration of the vaginal fluid is certain evidence of the presence of blood, and the woman is to be regarded as certainly unclean by *niddå* or *zåbå* or whatever is appropriate.[109]

The Khilâf and I'tiqâdât maintain that any discolouration of the vaginal fluid is due to the presence of blood and is to be treated as such whatever the circumstances, and that what is seen as the discolouration is the actual blood.[110]

A woman recovering from the states of *niddå* and *dåbå*, or bleeding of cleansing, or *zåbå*, is just as unclean after her immersion as before, and has exactly the same contaminating effect on other people and artefacts. She does not stop being a source of contamination till sunset, when she becomes clean herself.[111]

It is a general principle that a person or artefact is contaminated by blood for the same length of time as the woman from whom it issues. The details of the interpretation of this rule are given in the Commentary, instance by instance.[112]

Blood is equally contaminating whether wet or dried up.[113]

It is to be noticed that nowhere in the sources is any distinction made between a discharge of blood from the womb and bleeding from some place in the vagina, and that all blood emitted from the vagina is unclean.

According to the Kâfi, blood contaminates ground on which it has fallen and is to be removed. It is desirable to pass fire over the ground afterwards. It is not modern practice to use fire, but simply to dig the stuff up, scuff dirt over it, or sluice it with water till it is no longer visible.[114]

As long as a woman is unclean, whether as *dåbå*, *zåbå*, or *yålēda*, she is segregated, according to all or most of the sources.[115] The Dositheans disagreed.[116]

The spit of a woman in a state of uncleanness has the same contaminating effect on people and artefacts as the blood itself would.[117]

---

[108] See note 107.

[109] See note 107.

[110] See note 107.

[111] See notes 169-172.

[112] Kf ch. XI, 88-89 TN.

[113] T 55-57 N.

[114] Kf ch. 23-24 N; 23-24 TN.

[115] Kf ch. XI, 86; Kh 44-47; 58-59; 93-94; Kâsh ch. XV, 27; 103-104; I'tiq 12-17; 14-15 N; 47; 114-115. See note 9.

[116] T 11-13 N. Notice that the Tubâkh does not raise this question.

[117] Sharḥ Sûrat al-Irbot.

Copulation of a man with a woman unclean because of any kind of bleeding from the vagina is forbidden and if done with intention is punishable by death for both parties.[118] Nevertheless, it makes no difference to the degree or length of the man's uncleanness whether he makes contact with the blood during copulation or in some other way, so that if there was no deliberate transgression the question of how the blood got on the man is irrelevant.[119] The most common instance of accidental copulation with an unclean woman will obviously be if the woman is clean beforehand and emits *niddå* blood during intercourse.[120]

3. *The Intrinsic Uncleanness of Men*

A man is put in the state of ࠆࠁ *zåb* by abnormal discharge from the penis on two days in a row.[121] An abnormal discharge that occurs on just one day is counted as an emission of semen.[122]

An abnormal discharge is one that occurs under abnormal circumstances, that is to say, without sexual excitement,[123] and has a distinctive appearance, as explained below. If, however, the discharge can be explained away as the effect of illness or exertion, or if it accompanies urination, it is counted as an emission of semen, no matter how many times it occurs.[124] Any emission accompanied by sexual excitement is counted as an emission of semen, whether during intercourse or not.[125]

The essential criterion is that the emission should occur under abnormal circumstances.[126] The second criterion is that it should be a sticky fluid, or a more glutinous stuff with a tendency to form a scale on drying.[127] It will be observed that this second characteristic will equally well suit a normal emission of semen, so that the circumstances of the emission are the essential criterion.[128]

The Kâshif, and the second marginal note on the Kâfi, count a discharge of blood from the penis as *zåb*.[129]

---

118 T 74-78 TN and cross-references; Lv XX:18.
119 T 8-10 TN and cross-references; Kh 77-110; Far 49-58.
120 T 8-10 TN and cross-references: Lv XV:24.
121 T 93-94 TN and cross-references.
122 T 93-94 N.
123 T 89-93; Kf ch. XI, 19-22; Kâsh ch. XV, 96; Kh 6-9. See the next note.
124 T 81-93; Kf ch. XI, 3-8; Kâsh ch. XV, 82-91.
125 See notes 123 and 124.
126 See note 123.
127 See note 123, and Lv XV:3.
128 See note 122.
129 Kâsh ch. XV, 5-9 TN and cross-references. It is to be noticed that this opinion in the second marginal note on the Kâfi, by Nâji bin Khiḍr, occurs in a context where the Kâfi itself is

The man can start the process of becoming clean once the discharge is finished. He is to wash the stuff off, then count seven complete days, from sunset to sunset, on which no discharge occurs, and is to wash himself all over on the seventh day, and he becomes clean at sunset on the seventh day.[130]

While unclean he is to stay away from people in a state of cleanness and stay away from human habitation.[131]

Any person or artefact that the man touches while he is unclean, whether he is still discharging or not, and whether contact is made with the stuff or not, and whether the man has washed the stuff off or not, is made unclean for one day. This is the opinion of the author of the Ṭubâkh,[132] and is the modern opinion as well.[133] The Kâfi quotes three opinions on this matter, the last one agreeing with the Ṭubâkh. The first opinion quoted is that the man is not a source of uncleanness after he has washed the stuff off himself. The second opinion is that contact with the stuff causes contamination, but that contact with the man himself, without contact with the stuff, does not cause contamination, even if the man has not washed himself yet. The author of the Kâfi does not specifically reject the first two opinions, but does seem to prefer the third one.[134]

The person or artefact is made clean by having the stuff removed, being washed all over, and waiting till sunset. A variant opinion requires immersion.[135]

Contact with *zåb* stuff has exactly the same effect as contact with the man himself.[136]

The *zåb* stuff is only a source of contamination while it is wet, not once it has dried up.[137]

The unclean man's spit has exactly the same effect as the discharge itself has. We are not told whether the man's semen had the same contaminating

---

clearly *not* talking about blood. We may conjecture that this is a specifically modern opinion, if it is not an error.

[130] T 94-98; Kf ch. XI, 40; Kâsh ch. XV, 67-72; 97.

[131] T 99-102; Kf ch. XI, 22-24; Kâsh ch. XV, 26-27; 38-47.

[132] T 110-117 TN; Lv XV:11.

[133] Kâsh ch. XV, 38-47; M.N. III; M.N. IV; M.N. V; Lv XV:11.

[134] Kf ch. XI, 33-40; Lv XV:11.

[135] The usual opinion seems to be that washing all over is required: see T 113-114; Kf ch. III, 41-42; ch. XI, 38-40; 88-89 N; Kâsh ch. XV, 29-30 and the context. But notice Kf ch. XI, 3-6, and the second marginal note on the Kâfi, line 3, according to the reading of Ms. P, where immersion is specified. It is not certain whether the reading of Ms. S_1 is meant to specify washing all over or the washing off of the contaminating stuff, but I would be inclined to take the second meaning as the one intended. Both mss. agree in making the person affected clean immediately afterwards, without having to wait till sunset. See Lv XV, 7 and 8.

[136] See notes 132 and 133; and see Kf ch. XI, 39-40 TN. For the theoretical reason, see Kf ch. XI, 88-89 N.

[137] Kf ch. XI, 30 TN; Lv XV:8.

effect as his spit does, but by analogy with the Jewish halachah it seems reasonable to assume that it has.[138]

The man in the state of *zåb*, like the woman in the state of *niddå*, contaminates any couch, seat, or saddle on which he has put his weight, and the couch, seat, or saddle then becomes a source of contamination. The details are as for the *niddå* in all respects.[139]

Ground can be contaminated by some of the *zåb* stuff, or some of the man's spit, falling on it. The *zåb* stuff, and the man's spit, keep on being a source of contamination in ground even after they have dried up or soaked in. According to the Kâfi, the ground is to be cleansed by passing fire over it so as to remove the contaminating stuff, but the Ṭubâkh allows washing with water and does not mention fire.[140] Modern practice agrees with the Ṭubâkh.[141] Analogy with the case of ground contaminated by blood of childbirth would indicate that the ground could be cleansed by digging out the unclean stuff, but that even if this were done, it would still be desirable to pass fire over the ground or sluice it with water, according to whichever method is to be followed.[142]

Although we are not told this, it is practically certain by comparison with the Jewish system and by the analogy of the prohibition of intercourse of a man with an unclean woman that it must be forbidden for a woman to have intercourse with a man in the state of *zåb*.[143]

4. *Sexual Intercourse and Emission of Semen*

Any emission of semen or seminal fluid, whether during intercourse or not, makes a man unclean.[144]

An emission of some semen or seminal fluid on urinating, due to its presence in the urethra beforehand, is termed ࠆࠁ *zåb* by the Kâfi, but the term is not used in the other sources. This use of the term is to be clearly and sharply distinguished from its more usual meaning of an abnormal discharge. The use of the term in this special meaning was probably abandoned because of the confusion that could occur.[145] An emission of semen on urination,

---

[138] T 107-109; Kf ch. XI, 28-30; Kâsh ch. XV, 32-34; Lv XV:8.

[139] T 103-106; Kf ch. XI, 25-27 TN; the Additional Passage from the Khilâf; Far 42-48; Kâsh ch. XV, 26-37; and see notes 34-42; Lv XV:4, 5, 6. We are not told how long the contamination lasts, but the analogy of other kinds of contamination by the *zåb* would indicate that it only lasts for one day.

[140] T 107-109 and 103 N; Kf ch. XII, 22-34 and the notes there; Kf ch. XI, 28 TN.

[141] Kf ch. XII, 23-34 N.

[142] See note 114.

[143] See note 118.

[144] T 81-88; Kf ch. XI, 3-17; ch. III, 8-14; 22-24; Kâsh ch. XV, 82-91; Lv XV:16.

[145] Kf ch. XI, 3-17 TN and 3 N.

whether before, after, or during the flow, is counted as a normal emission of semen and no more.[146]

An emission of semen or seminal fluid that occurs as the result of sexual excitement, or because of illness, particularly a fever, or because of high blood pressure, or over-exertion, is treated in exactly the same way as an emission during intercourse,[147] and such an emission can occur an unlimited number of times and still be counted as an emission of semen, not *zåb*.[148]

The emission of semen during intercourse is called ࠔࠊࠁࠕ ࠆࠓࠏ *ashkåbåt zēra* and the man is called ࠔࠅࠊࠁ ࠆࠓࠏ *shūkəb zēra* or ࠔࠅࠊࠁ *shūkəb*. Emission of semen while asleep is called ࠒࠓࠉ ࠋࠉࠋࠄ *qēri līla*.[149]

Once the man has become unclean, he is termed *mutajannib* and his condition is termed *janâbah*.[150] He becomes clean by washing the stuff off, and washing himself all over, and waiting till sunset.[151] After intercourse the woman is just as unclean as the man, and has to wash the stuff off, wash herself all over, and wait till sunset before becoming clean.[152]

Contact with the man after his emission contaminates people[153] but not artefacts.[154] Contact with the semen contaminates people and artefacts.[155] People and artefacts made unclean in either of these ways are cleansed in the same way as the man himself.[156]

People contaminated by contact with the man or his semen contaminate other people in the usual way,[157] but contaminated artefacts do not contaminate other artefacts or people.[158]

The man does not contaminate a couch, seat, or saddle by putting his weight on them, in the way that the *niddå* or *zåb* do.[159]

5. *The Uncleanness of Gentiles*

Gentiles, i.e. non-Israelites, can neither contaminate nor be contaminated according to the Torah, but there is evidence that at times they have been

---

146 T 81-93 TN; Kf ch. XI, 3-15.
147 T 84-88; Kf ch. XI, 4-8. See the previous note.
148 T 81-93 N and 87 TN; Kâsh ch. XV, 96-97.
149 T 82-83 and 87-88; Kf ch. XI, 7; ch. III, 9; Kâsh ch. XV, 85; Lv XX:16 and Dt XXIII:11.
150 Kf ch. III, 23-24.
151 T 88; Kf ch. XI, 7-8 and 16-17; ch. III, 8-14; Kâsh ch. XV, 87-91; Lv XV:18.
152 Kf ch. XI, 88-89 N; Kâsh ch. XV, 92-95; Lv XV:18.
153 Kf ch. III, 22-38 TN.
154 Kf ch. III, 6-14 and 8-9 N; Kâsh ch. XV, 86-91.
155 Kf ch. III, 40-42 TN; Kâsh ch. XV, 89-91; Lv XV:17.
156 See note 152 and note 155.
157 Kf ch. III, 22-27.
158 If the man does not contaminate artefacts by contact, then artefacts contaminated by contact with semen will not contaminate other artefacts or people. This conclusion is confirmed by the silence of the sources to the contrary and the analogy of the Karaite halachah.
159 Argument from silence and the analogy of the Jewish halachah.

treated by custom as unclean, as the equivalent of a corpse or ࠔࠓࠑ, or the equivalent of a *zẘbå* woman or *zåb* man. For this reason, it has at times been prohibited to acquire artefacts from them. The Dosithean practice was to allow the acquisition of artefacts, and to treat them as necessarily clean because they can only be contaminated when they have become the property of an Israelite. The opinion of the author of the Kâfi, and the modern opinion, is the same as the Dosithean one. Nevertheless contaminating stuff has to be removed from the artefact, by water or fire, before it can be used by an Israelite, so the Israelite will not be contaminated by the stuff and so that the artefact will not be contaminated by the stuff after it has passed into the Israelite's possession.

In earlier times, in the Byzantine period, ground was treated as contaminated if foreigners (i.e. non-Israelites) passed over it, and it had to be cleansed by fire, like ground contaminated by a woman in the condition of *niddå* or *yẘlēda*. We do not know if this means they treated female foreigners as *zẘbå* and male ones as *zåb*, or treated them both as equivalent to corpses. If the first alternative is the correct one, it would necessarily follow that ground could be contaminated by the presence of a Samaritan in the state of *zåb* or *zāba*, but as the only source to mention contamination of ground by the mere presence of an unclean person or object only mentions the cases of the *niddå* and *yẘlēda*, or the case of a corpse, it seems best, in the present state of knowledge, to assume that foreigners were treated as the equivalent of corpses.[160]

6. *Susceptibility to Uncleanness*

Of people, only an Israelite can contaminate or be contaminated, with the one single exception that any human corpse causes uncleanness. Of objects, only completed artefacts can be contaminated or contaminate. Of completed artefacts, only those belonging to an Israelite can be contaminated or contaminate, and this does not include artefacts that have not yet been used or that the Israelite has bought only for the purpose of sale.[161]

A single artefact can be made up of separate parts not permanently joined on to each other, provided all the parts make up a whole that is treated or used as a single artefact.[162]

7. *The Transmission of Uncleanness*

The details of this subject have been given in the appropriate places in the

---

[160] Kf ch. XI, 31-32 N.

[161] See the previous note.

[162] The Additional Passage from the Khilâf, 1-10 N.

preceding sections. We will now give some general rules apllicable to all the categories of uncleanness previously treated.

Uncleanness transmitted from an unclean person or the discharge of an unclean person to another person can then be transmitted to another person, who can then transmit it to another, so that there can be three stages of the transmission, the person made unclean by his or her discharge, then two other people. The third person does not contaminate a fourth.[163] Artefacts contaminated by the original unclean person, or by the discharge or spit of that person, can contaminate other artefacts or people.[164]

The Samaritan terms *jawhari*, meaning 'intrinsic', applied to the uncleanness of the person from whom the discharge issues, and *ʿaraḍi*, meaning 'accidental', referring to the uncleanness of the person or artefact contaminated by the person whose uncleanness is intrinsic, express the same ideas as the Jewish terms אבות טומאה and וולדי טומאה. In Jewish terminology, the Samaritans recognise אב טומאה, and ראשון לטומאה, and שני לטומאה, but not שלישי לטומאה.[165] It is to be noticed, however, that there is an important exception to this rule in that a man that has had an emission of semen can only contaminate people, not artefacts: see Kf ch. III, 8-9 N. Compare the differentiation of this uncleanness in the Jewish systems, in not needing immersion. (See note 192 on the Rabbanite תקנה changing this detail).

We see that the Samaritans recognise the same modes of transmission of uncleanness as the Jews do: in Jewish terminology, these are: נגיעה, נשיאה, היסט, מדרס, אהילה.[166] As in the Jewish system, there is no contamination by אהילה from the categories of uncleanness treated here.

It is a consistent principle throughout the sources that becoming unclean by contact with unclean people or things is to be avoided as far as possible. Sakta the Dosithean is a notable exception to this: see the quotation in T 11-13 N.

8. *The Stages of Cleansing*

These have been explained for each category of uncleanness. We give here a few general observations.

---

[163] Kf ch. III, 22-38 TN; 26-27 N. Notice, though, that according to the Khilâf there is no end to the chain of transmission as long as contact from one link to the next is unbroken (Wreschner, introduction, p. xxiv). The other sources do not raise the matter.

[164] Assumed throughout by all sources.

[165] Kf ch. XI, 1 TN; ch. III, 3-8 and 22-38 TN; 26-27 N and 31 N; Kf ch. XI, 88-89 N; T 11-13 N; Kf ch. XIII, 2-3 N.

[166] See notes 34-42. It must be admitted that none of the sources specifically describe a mechanism of contamination corresponding to היסט, and its inclusion in this list is mainly justified by the silence of the sources to the contrary and the analogy of the Jewish system. See Kf ch. III, 4-5 N. (צריך עיון!).

No cleansing can be effective till the contaminating stuff has been removed. It is removed from a person by washing, and from an artefact by either using water or fire, whichever is more convenient and will not damage the artefact. After that washing all over or immersion can be performed at the appropriate time.[167]

In all cases, the immersion or washing all over can be performed in the day-time of the last day of the minimum prescribed number of days of uncleanness.[168]

It seems that a person or artefact after having undergone washing all over (*rīṣṣa, ḥamîm*) or immersion (*ṭēbīla, ṣubûgh*) is just as unclean as before and has just the same contaminating effect as before, and that cleanness and loss of the contaminating effect either comes immediately, or comes at sunset, but always in one step, directly from uncleanness to complete cleanness. There is no equivalent of the טבול יום.[169]

The removal of contaminating blood before immersion can lessen the degree of uncleanness, but this is something different. A woman passes into a lower degree of uncleanness, and has less of a contaminating effect, when she has washed off the *niddå* blood, whether or not there is any *dåbå* blood on her, or when she has washed off the blood of childbirth, whether or not there is any blood of cleansing on her, or when she has washed off the *dåbå* blood. This has nothing to do with the immersion.[170] Similarly, according to one opinion mentioned by the author of the Kâfi, but which is not the standard opinion, and does not seem to be accepted by the author himself, a man in the state of *zåb* stops being a source of contamination once he has washed the stuff off himself, but this has nothing to do with the washing all over that follows for the purpose of cleansing.[171] In all these cases, once the stuff has been removed, the man is in the same state before and after the washing all over, and the woman is in the same state before and after the immersion, and cleanness and loss of contaminating effect comes all at once at sunset. It is of course true that the arrival of sunset is only effective if the immersion or washing all over has been carried out beforehand, and that these can only be carried out after the stuff has been removed.[172]

---

[167] Ch. XII of the Kâfi treats this subject. See in particular 10 TN. See also Kf ch. XI, 88-89 TN; T 55-57 N. Nu XXXI:22-23. For a very clear statement distinguishing washing all over as a separate category from washing the stuff off, and at the same time as a separate category from immersion, see Kâsh ch. XV, 97-98. There is a clear parallel in this to Karaite practice.

[168] T 13-14 N.

[169] Argument from silence. There is, however, an analogy in one tradition in the case of the removal of the condition of *nâṭir*: see Kf ch. XIII, 11-13 N.

[170] See the appropriate sections on these two subjects in the first part of this Summary.

[171] See note 134.

[172] See note 167.

A person who has been unclean in the state of *zåba* or *yålēda* or *zåb* is required to offer certain sacrifices after all the other steps are completed. The information is given in the text of Scripture, in Lv XV:29-30, XII:6-8, and XV:14-15, and is repeated in the Farâ'iḍ and Kâshif in the appropriate places.[173]

II. OBSERVATIONS AND THEORETICAL CONSIDERATIONS

1. *Preamble*

The following observations are based mainly, though not entirely, on the texts edited here. In one way, the material on which they are based is limited, because so much of the Samaritan halachic literature remains to be made available; but in another way, the material is complete, since it includes all the extant Samaritan texts on the subjects under discussion, including even stray comments made in another context. The sources go into the matters with which these observations are concerned whenever it is appropriate or useful to do so, and though they are not always as thorough in their discussions as could be desired in each instance, comparison of the various passages on a given subject will yield very extensive and detailed information not obtainable from any of the passages considered separately.

Some of these observations are concerned with the Samaritan halachic system as a whole, and some specifically with the subject of the kinds of uncleanness with which the texts edited are concerned. The comments on this specific subject are based on all the material available, and should be accurate; the comments on the system as a whole, being based on a study of one subject, are presumably accurate, but research in the future might well show them to be incomplete, or not to apply to all subjects within the halachic system. The main value of these observations is seen as a summary of the present state of knowledge, which others, whether Samaritans or not, can use so as to see which questions have not been fully or satisfactorily answered in these sources, or which questions have not even been considered in the sources. The answers to such questions are to be sought in the treatment of other subjects in the sources, or in the modern traditional practice, which must be a plentiful source of theoretical information if the right questions are asked of those who practice it, or if the Samaritans themselves reflect on the significance of the principles not mentioned in the literature but assumed in practice.

---

[173] Far 115-119; Kâsh ch. XV, 67-81; ch. XII, 18-26.

2. *Variation within the Samaritan Halachic System*

The Samaritan halachic practice is necessarily uniform in modern times, because the small numbers of the nation and their centralisation makes divergence impractical. In earlier times, though, there was considerable divergence, in both theory and practice, sometimes over minor points and sometimes over major ones. The opinion has been expressed that the halachah was once uniform, and that the divergence came later, through ignorance or carelessness.[174]

This assumption does not seem to be supported by the evidence available, and is open to strong counter-arguments.

First of all, the variation within the Samaritan halachah is less than within the Jewish halachah, and even if it is allowed that the extant sources might not record all the Samaritan opinions, it still remains that the variation in the Samaritan opinions is equalled by the variation in the Jewish opinions. It will not do to limit the comparison to the Samaritan halachah, on one hand, and the Rabbanite halachah on the other hand: we have to take notice of the whole range of Jewish opinions on each point of halachah, and this means not only the opinions of the Karaites, but also the opinions of the Sadducees, the Qumran sect, the authors of the Book of Jubilees and other books of the Pseudepigrapha, the translators of the Peshitta, the older Targums, Anan, and the Falashas; and, in some cases, the divergent opinions recorded in the Mishnah and other Tannaitic texts.[175] The diversity of Jewish opinions had been considerably reduced by the time the earliest extant Samaritan halachic texts were written, because of the disappearance of many of the Jewish sects and religious groups, and the achievement of uniformity inside the Rabbanite system: but the divergence was originally there, and remained to a great extent. In this context, the question of whether the divergent opinions of different Karaites go back to separate old traditions, or whether the divergence is the result of individual exegesis of Scripture, does not matter, first because there are numerous points on which all the Karaites agree with each

---

[174] Wreschner insists on this throughout the whole of section I of his introduction, and consistently throughout the second part of the work; he gives a clear statement of this opinion on p. 33.

[175] I have not compared the Samaritan halachah with Anan's for the purely practical reason that it would take a separate monograph to try to disentangle what is the result of exegesis and what is tradition supported by exegesis in his system.

The Pharisaic (= Rabbinic = Rabbanite, depending on the period) halachah was fixed, at least officially, with the completion and acceptance of the Mishnah. Original differences between the sub-traditions were removed before the completion of the Mishnah by voting or by one school agreeing to accept the tradition of another school on a particular matter. The final fixed halachah is no older and no younger than the divergent opinions recorded in the Mishnah, Tosefta, and Baraitot when the disagreement is due to divergencies in the tradition. When disagreement is over the merits of a גזרה or תקנה, the matter is quite different.

other as opposed to the Rabbanites, and are presumably following a tradition, and second because there are numerous points about which there is considerable disagreement amongst the Jews even if the Karaites are left out of consideration.[176] If, then, the Samaritan halachah had originally been uniform, and lost its uniformity later, its history would have been the exact opposite of the Jewish halachah's history, and *a priori* this seems very unlikely.

The second difficulty is that the Samaritans are very careful and exact in their religious practice,[177] and it is hard to see how anything could have been forgotten or become misunderstood, particularly if it is borne in mind that the matters about which there are divergent opinions include ones such as the uncleanness of the *niddå*, *dåbå*, *zåbå*, *yålēda*, *zåb*, and *shūkəb zēra*, which would have been brought to people's attention continually, so that every adult Samaritan would have had to carry out certain precepts relating to these matters and would have had to know all the rules.[178]

The third difficulty is that the points on which the Samaritans disagree are the same as the ones on which the Jews disagree, and so we find that one Samaritan opinion is the same as the Karaite one and another is the same as the Rabbanite one, or one Samaritan opinion is the same as one Karaite one and another Samaritan opinion is the same as another Karaite one.[179] It does not seem likely the same set of divergent opinions should have one origin in Judaism and a different one in Samaritanism.

It seems, then, that there is no evidence for a state of uniformity in the Samaritan halachah before modern times. The question arises, then, as to how old the divergencies might be in absolute terms. As the answer to this depends on the historical relationship between the Samaritan halachic traditions and the Jewish ones, and the relationship of the various Jewish traditions to each other, it is best to put off the treatment of it till after these matters have been treated in the next section, and the question is treated separately in Section 3.

The amount of variation of opinion on specific individual points will now be set out.

It is desirable to divide the disagreements into two categories: ones that are due to divergencies in the tradition of halachah from time immemorial,

---

[176] Some examples are given in Section 3.

[177] This comes through very clearly from their behaviour and their literature, including the texts edited here.

[178] Compare Tosefta Pesaḥim I:15. These matters would be brought to people's attention almost every day, and the practice of the halachot relating to them would not be significantly affected by war or persecution. If any knowledge were lost, these areas would be the last to be affected.

[179] See Section 3.

having no visible origin and theoretically going back to the time of the giving of the Torah; and ones that are due to what in Jewish terminology are called גזרות or תקנות or מנהג. The distinction is not always easy to make, but it has to be made to the extent that it is possible to do so. Otherwise it becomes impossible to make profitable comparisons with Jewish halachah or work out the differences in theory within Samaritanism that have given rise to the differences in practice.[180]

We will start with divergencies of the second kind.

A fairly clear example of a divergence of this kind is the treatment of non-Israelites as either permanently unclean or as incapable of being either clean or unclean. The Jews and Samaritans all agree that the laws of cleanness and uncleanness only apply to Israel, and that a non-Israelite can neither contaminate nor be contaminated, with the single exception that any human corpse is a source of uncleanness by direct contact. Nevertheless, Rabbanites, Karaites, and Falashas treat non-Israelites as if they were unclean, as the result of a גזירה or תקנה,[181] and we have seen that in earlier times most Samaritans did the same. The modern practice is not to treat non-Israelites with the same stringency as in earlier times, but as this treatment of them was an ordinance rather than a tradition, the discontinuing of it is equally well only an adjustment of an earlier ordinance, and there is no difference in theory or tradition lying behind the difference in practice.

There is some evidence that when non-Israelites were treated as if they were unclean, they were treated by some groups or at one time as the equivalent of corpses, and by other groups or at a later time as the equivalent of a זבה and זב. The author of the Kâfi treats them as the equivalent of a שקץ or unclean animal.[182]

There are five different opinions on the number of times in a row a woman can be unclean as *niddå* and *dåbå* before she becomes *zåbå*. Leaving out the Ṭubâkh for the moment, which does not allow any repetition of consecutive weeks of *niddå* at all, there are four different opinions. These are the opinion of the Kâfi, that two are allowed; the modern opinion, that three are allowed; the opinion of the Farâ'id, that four are allowed; and the opinion of the Khilâf, an opinion attested as early as the time of composition of the Ṭubâkh,

---

[180] The most convenient source of information on this is Bloch, שערי תורת התקנות. Maimonides points out individual instances where appropriate in the Mishneh Torah.

[181] Yalon, *Ṭum'at Nochrim*.

For the Falashas, see Leslau, p. 72.

[182] See the Summary of Halachot on all this, and the references given there.

Throughout all the exposition that follows, it is assumed that the reader will look up the sources of the statements in the Summary of Halachot, which is arranged by subject, so there is no need to give separate references for each item. The sources for the examples relating to contamination from corpses are given in the Preamble to the Summary of Halachot.

that seven are allowed. There is some evidence that the disagreements on this point are not due to divergent traditions, but are due to different decisions. The Karaites, who recognise the possibility of consecutive weeks of *niddå* just as the Samaritans do, rest the whole distinction between a repetition of *niddå* and entry into the state of *zåbå* on whether the bleeding of the second week is continuous with the bleeding of the week before, and all the disagreements amongst the Karaites on the requirements for entry into the state of *zåbå* are due to disagreements on the definition of continuity.[183] If there is no continuity, (according to whichever definition is used) the woman enters the state of *niddå* again, and can keep on doing this without limit. What the Samaritans have done is to elaborate the definition of continuity. Bleeding that is continuous (according to whichever definition is used) from the week before is effectively not counted as such for a certain number of weeks in a row (the number varying from source to source) till the limit of the number of times this can be done is reached, and then if the bleeding continues (according to the definition used) into another week, the woman is *zåbå*. At first sight this seems to be a relaxation of the rules, but it could well be the opposite. It might equally well be that the definition of continuity has been altered so that what would not have been counted as continuous before is now counted, but that on the other hand a certain number of instances of what would be continuity under the more severe definition are not counted as making the woman *zåbå*, though they are registered, and when the allowable total of exceptions has been reached, the definition of continuity in its severe form is applied and the woman is *zåbå*. This would explain why it is that the two sources that give the most lenient requirements for counting the bleeding as continuous from one week to the next, for the purpose of finally making the woman *zåbå*, Musallam bin Marjân and the Kâshif, have a more severe definition of continuity for making up the progressive total of weeks beforehand. For the purpose of finally making the woman *zåbå*, the bleeding is only continuous if it occurs on the last day of the last *niddå* week, but for the purpose of making the progressive total the bleeding is continuous if it occurs at any time at all on the first day of the following week, which is a more severe definition. This would explain as well why it is that the source that gives the most rigorous requirements for counting bleeding as continuous, the Khilâf, which counts bleeding at any time on the first day of the following week as continous, is the most lenient in the number of repetitions of *niddå* that are allowed.

It is equally possible that in some cases the opposite has happened, i.e. that the definition of continuity has been made more lenient, so that it is less likely

[183] Both the A.E. and the G.E. devote a whole chapter to this matter. Both authors are concerned throughout the chapter with the definition of continuity.

that a woman will become *niddå*, and that the restriction on the number of repetitions allowed is compensation for this.

This is of course speculation, but the point remains that the limitation of the number of repetitions of *niddå* is linked to the definition of continuity. It is possible that at one time the Samaritans, like the Karaites, knew by tradition that entry into the state of *zåbå* depended on the bleeding being consecutive, but like the Karaites derived the exact definition of continuity by logic, analogy, and exegesis of Scripture. Notice that the figure of seven weeks is arrived at by logical argument,[184] that the figure of four weeks is arrived at by analogy with the length of a month,[185] that three is an attractive number in any such problem of definition,[186] and that two is the lowest possible number of repetitions.

The system of the Ṭubâkh in this matter belongs to a different tradition altogether, one that is very close to the Rabbanite one and the Falasha one.[187]

Probably the Samaritans originally agreed with the Karaites in not setting any upper limit to the number of times in a row a woman could become *niddå*, but eventually had to set a limit, even if that meant contradicting the theory.

Some Dositheans (but not apparently Sakta and his followers), as well as some Samaritans in the time of the Tanna'im, used to count seven complete

---

[184] T 26-29 TN and Kh 165-171. Notice particularly Kh 194-196.

[185] Far 84-86. The author admits that a decision had to be made.

[186] Kf ch. III, 30-38, and the extract from ch. XIII of the Kâfi in Kf ch. III, 22-38 N.

[187] See note 193 on the confusion amongst scholars on this very elementary point in the Rabbanite system.

As the accounts of the Falasha system fail to take account of the difference between נדה and זבה in both the Rabbanite system and the Falasha one, I quote here the explicit statement on the matter by a well-informed Falasha:

> 'Lorsqu'une une femme a ses règles, il faut qu'elle entre dans la hutte de malédiction ... Là elle reste sept jours jusqu'à ce qu'elle se purifie de son sang. Si son sang n'a pas cessé de couler le septième jour, il faut qu'elle reste dans la hutte de malédiction jusqu'à ce que son sang s'arrête. Le septième jour, ou bien le jour où son sang s'arrête en dépassant le septième jour, elle lave ses vêtements et son corps et, au coucher du soleil, elle rentre chez elle.' (Leslau, p. 91).

We see from this that the Falashas distinguish between the נדה and the זבה קטנה, and that they do not require a count of seven complete days without bleeding for a woman to become clean of ordinary menstrual bleeding, as Aešcoly has it (p. 45). Aešcoly put too much faith in the exactness of the wording of his sources, who were not Jews and did not know how to interpret what they saw or were told, or even what to ask.

It is, however, true that the Falashas do count seven complete days without bleeding after the end of זבה bleeding of some particular kind, as the sources quoted by Aešcoly (p. 43) state, and as they are obliged to do by the express command of Scripture. It follows that they distinguish between זבה קטנה and זבה גדולה. Unfortunately, we are not told how many days in a row bleeding has to occur before the woman becomes זבה גדולה. A plausible guess would be either three days, in agreement with the Rabbanites, or four days, in agreement with the Ṭubâkh.

days of cleansing after the last day of bleeding even in the case of *niddå* or *då̊bå* bleeding.[188] We do not know why they did this. It might have been for the same reason as the modern Rabbanite Jews do, that they did not credit people with having enough wit to keep the more complicated correct practice.[189] It might have been because there was a disagreement of some kind over the calculation and this practice satisfied both parties, being more rigorous than either required by theory or tradition. It might have been due to a divergent tradition. The answer will have to wait till more evidence is available. The assimilation of the *zå̊bå* to the *niddå* is attested at the same period.[189]

The divergency in the treatment of menstrual fluid that is not clearly blood-coloured but shows some sign of containing blood is probably due to a divergency of decisions on הלכה למעשה rather than divergent traditions. The Samaritans seem to accept the same colours as being certainly blood as the Karaites do. The divergence is over the degree of certainty as to whether vaginal fluid that is discoloured, but is not one of the colours of blood itself, contains blood, and to what extent a deduction that blood must be present can be treated like an observation of blood itself.[190]

The treatment of the woman's hand with which she washes off the *niddå* blood or blood of childbirth, or the midwife's hand, as equivalent to the *niddå* blood or blood of childbirth itself, seems to be a חומרה that some Samaritans have imposed on themselves.

There is disagreement over whether ground from which unclean substances have been removed is to have its cleansing completed by means of water or fire, and over whether water or fire is to be used to remove or neutralise the stuff if it is not dug out. The Kâfi requires the use of fire, and the Ṭubâkh and modern practice allow the use of water. This is a disagreement on how to remove the stuff, not a theoretical one. The same principle applies in cleansing ground affected by a corpse.

These are all the divergencies that seem at the present state of knowledge not to be due to differences in tradition. We will now list the ones that do seem to represent differences in tradition. It should be borne in mind, however, that some of these could turn out to be due to the self-imposition of a more rigorous practice (החמרה) by some groups when more evidence becomes available.

The items are listed in the order of their appearance in the Summary of Halachot for convenience of reference.[191]

---

[188] See above, p. 287. Sakta's opinion is entirely different: see p. 289.

[189] See note 63; see also p. 317 and note 193.

[190] T 67 N.

[191] The comment made in note 182 applies here as well.

Sakta the Dosithean seems to have maintained that neither *dăbå* blood nor blood of cleansing had any contaminating effect at all. The majority opinion is otherwise.

The Kâshif allows washing all over instead of immersion for the cleansing of a person or artefact contaminated by *niddå* blood or by contact with a woman in the state of *niddå*. The majority opinion is that immersion is required.

The Kâshif does not require the washing all over of a person or artefact contaminated by *dåbå* blood. The I'tiqâdât requires immersion. The Kâfi requires neither. The opinion of the authors of the Ṭubâkh and Khilâf seems to be that contamination only lasts till the blood is removed, and this seems to be the opinion of Sakta as well. It follows from this last opinion that immersion or washing all over are not required.

There are three opinions on the contaminating effect of a *dåbå* woman, a woman during the thirty-three days of bleeding of cleansing, or a *zåbå* woman during her count. The opinion of the Kâfi, Kâshif, and I'tiqâdât is that one day's uncleanness is caused. The Kâshif requires washing all over and the I'tiqâdât requires immersion. The opinion of the Ṭubâkh and Khilâf is that the uncleanness only lasts till contact is broken. The opinion if Sakta is that there is no contamination.

The system of the Ṭubâkh in calculating the arrival of the state of *zăbå* is quite incompatible with the system of the other sources in not allowing a repetition of the *niddå* in consecutive weeks, in distinguishing between *zåbå* bleeding on the first day of the second week and *zåbå* bleeding on the other days of the second week, and in distinguishing two separate grades of *zåbå*.

There seems to have been a minority opinion that for cleansing from the state of *zåbå* one incomplete and six complete days without bleeding have to be counted, so that the day on which the bleeding finished was counted as one of the seven. The majority opinion is the same as the Jewish one.

There are three different opinions on the requirements for cleansing of a person or artefact contaminated by contact with *zåbå* blood. The majority opinion is that seven complete days, calculated from sunset to sunset have to be counted, that immersion is carried out on the seventh day, and the person or artefact becomes clean at sunset. The Kâshif agrees on the calculation of the seven days but allows washing all over instead of immersion. One Dosithean opinion seems to have been that immersion was required, and the person or artefact became clean at sunset the same day.

The majority opinion is that a person or artefact made unclean by contact with a *zåbå* woman before her count has started requires immersion. The Kâshif allows washing all over.

The standard modern opinion is that the thirty-three days of bleeding of cleansing after delivery of a boy do not include the eighth day, so that the total period of uncleanness is seven plus one plus thirty-three days, making forty-one days. The older sources do count the eighth day in the thirty-three and arrive at a total of forty days.

There is disagreement as to whether bleeding that occurs during the week after delivery of a boy or the fortnight after delivery of a girl is to be treated the same as the bleeding at the time of delivery or the same as bleeding of cleansing or *dåbå* bleeding in its contaminating effect. The Khilâf has the second opinion. The Kâfi, the interpolation in the Khilâf, the Kâshif, and the Iʿtiqâdât have the first opinion. The Ṭubâkh has the first opinion in the case of a girl and the second opinion in the case of a boy.

The Khilâf, the Iʿtiqâdât, and Sakta the Dosithean maintain that the bleeding of childbirth in the case of a girl contaminates anyone or anything that it touches for a fortnight. (Note that for the Khilâf the bleeding of childbirth is the bleeding at the instant of delivery, and for the Iʿtiqâdât is any bleeding during the fortnight). The Ṭubâkh and Kâfi maintain that it only causes a week's contamination.

There seems to have been disagreement on whether the blood of childbirth could still keep its full contaminating effect after the week or fortnight were over. The Kâfi, Kâshif, and Iʿtiqâdât maintain that it can. Sakta the Dosithean and his followers, and perhaps other people as well, seem to have maintained the contrary. This difference has important practical consequences for the uncleanness of a baby due to contact with the bleeding of childbirth.

According to the Ṭubâkh, Kâfi, and Iʿtiqâdât, a woman that experiences bleeding on the day after the last day of the bleeding of cleansing enters a state of *niddå*. According to the Farâʾiḍ, she enters a state of *zåbå*.

There are three different opinions on the contaminating effect of a man in the state of *zåb* and the *zåb* stuff. The majority opinion is that contact with the man causes uncleanness whether or not he has washed the stuff off, and contact with the stuff has the same effect. A variant opinion quoted in the Kâfi is that contact with the man does not cause contamination if he has washed the stuff off. Another opinion quoted in the Kâfi is that contact with the man does not cause contamination at all.

There seems to be a disagreement between the Ṭubâkh and Kâfi, and some Dositheans, on one hand, and the Farâʾiḍ, Kâshif, and Iʿtiqâdât, on the other hand, over whether a person contaminated by a corpse has to wash on the first day of the seven-day period of purification.

There seems to be another disagreement between the same sources over whether it is washing or immersion that is required on the seventh day of purification from contact with the corpse, but this question needs further study.

3. *The Relationship between Samaritan and Jewish Halachah*

In considering the relationship between the Samaritan and Jewish halachah, it is essential, to avoid confusion, to distinguish as far as possible between divergencies that are due to an innovation in one system or the other, and divergencies between the traditions going back to time immemorial. Such innovations in the Samaritan system have been listed in as complete a form as possible in Section 2. We will now consider disagreements between Samaritans and Jews caused by innovations in the Rabbanite system and the Karaite system.

The Rabbanite requirement of immersion for a man that has had an emission of semen is a תקנה ascribed to Ezra.[192]

The modern Rabbanite practice of not distinguishing between the conditions of נדה and זבה, and counting seven complete days without bleeding for the purpose of cleansing without regard to whether the woman is נדה or זבה, is a post-Talmudic innovation.[193]

The Karaites agree (with very few exceptions[194]) that the essential criterion for distinguishing between זבה bleeding and a repetition of נדה bleeding is that if there is continuity of bleeding from one week to the next, the bleeding of the second week is זבה, and if there is no continuity, it is נדה. In this they agree with the Samaritans and Falashas,[195] and seem to be following a tradition. The disagreement between different Karaites is over the definition

---

[192] Bavli Berachot 22ab. It is only a statement of common knowledge to add that this practice has been generally abandoned by most modern Rabbanites.

[193] Mishneh Torah, Issure Bi'ah XI.

It is surprising how easily scholars who are Jews can be ignorant of their own halachah, and so fail to see that the Samaritans and Jews follow the same tradition in this case.

For instance, Kirchheim does this (Karme Shomron, p. 26) and is then led to misinterpret a passage on the Samaritan halachah in Bavli Niddah 33a (in a baraita), commenting on Mishnah Niddah IV:1, which accuses Samaritan men of copulating with נדות. Because he does not realise that the Talmudic halachah was different to modern practice, he fails to realise that the Baraita quoted by him does not explain why Samaritan men can be accused of copulating with נדות, but only with זבות. The Baraita reads יום שפסקה בו ספרה למנין שבעה. The Tosefta (Niddah V:1) adds the same explanation with slight rewording. The Baraita says that the Samaritans allow the first of the seven days of cleansing to be incomplete, starting when the bleeding finishes. (See note 63). This might be right, but it is not to the point. (The texts add the information והן יושבות על כל דם ודם. It is quite possible that these words in the Mishnah are not meant as an explanation of why Samaritan men can be accused of copulating with נדות, but as additional information. Notice that the reliable mss. have והן, not שהן. See the commentators, and see T 15 N).

Aešcoly (p. 45) states categorically that the Talmudic halachah is to count seven complete days from the end of any bleeding, and the context, in which he compares the Rabbanite and Falasha halachah with the Samaritan and Karaite halachah, shows that he is not aware that the Talmud agrees with the Samaritans and Karaites on the question of cleansing from a state of נדה. (He is wrong about the Falashas too: see note 187).

[194] A minority of Karaites follow the same principle as the Rabbanites in regarding bleeding as נדה or זבה depending at which stage in the cycle it occurs. See G.E. 112c bottom.

[195] See the Falasha text quoted in note 187, and the comments there.

of continuity, and the numerous solutions to the question seem to be based on logic, analogy, and exegesis rather than tradition. The same conclusion was reached in regard to the various Samaritan solutions.[196] If, then, a particular Karaite opinion on the definition disagrees with a particular Samaritan one, this will not be a disagreement between two traditions, but between two different solutions to a practical question and two different ways of interpreting a verse of Scripture.[197]

The Rabbanites and some Karaites agree on the innovation of the concept of the מדרף.[198]

We will now show the distribution of the agreement and disagreement of the various Samaritan traditions with the various Jewish traditions.[199] Instances of Karaite opinions avowedly based on exegesis of Scripture and not tradition are not mentioned.

(a) *Agreement of the Samaritans with the Karaites against the Rabbanites*

The Samaritans agree with the Karaites on the distinction between the first instant of menstrual bleeding, and the bleeding during the rest of the week.[200]

The Samaritans agree with the Karaites and Falashas in counting a woman who has given birth as unclean in all respects till the end of the whole period of her uncleanness, and in not allowing copulation with her till the end of the forty or eighty days. The Rabbanites allow copulation after the first week or fortnight.[201]

The Samaritans agree with the Karaites against the Rabbanites that a *zåbå* woman does not contaminate a couch, seat, or saddle by pressure without direct contact during her count of seven days without bleeding.[202]

The Samaritans agree with the Karaites in not making any distinction

---

[196] See Section 2, p. 313, and the context of the argument there.

[197] This being the case, it would be expected that changes could readily occur in practice, and that there would be disagreement between different authorities, and the striking degree of variation on the matter in the Samaritan and Karaite traditions becomes fully explicable.

[198] G.E. 109c top; A.E. 120c bottom; Mishneh Torah, Mishkav Umoshav VI:3.

[199] The comments made in note 182 apply here as well.

[200] G.E. ch. IV; A.E. ch. X. It can be expected that the reader will be familiar with the Rabbanite halachah of the subjects treated in this section. The information is readily available from Hirsch's commentary or Hoffman's commentary on Lv XII and XV. The reader is reminded that the original sources are quoted in full in the *Torah Shelemah* on Lv XV and XII, verse by verse.

[201] G.E. ch. IX; A.E. ch. XII; Leslau p. 73 and pp. 91-92.

Some Rabbanite communities used to avoid copulation during the thirty-three or sixty-six days, but this is only a מנהג לחומרה, and does not mean that they considered the woman unclean during this period. See the Mishneh Torah, Issure Bi'ah XI:15.

[202] G.E. p. 114a middle.

between the effect of contact with menstrual blood during intercourse or in some other way.[203]

The Samaritans agree with the Karaites against the Rabbanites that a man that has had an emission of semen does not contaminate artefacts by contact, but agree with the Rabbanites against the Karaites that he does contaminate people.[204]

The Samaritans agree with the Karaites against the Rabbanites that an artefact contaminated by semen does not contaminate other artefacts or people.[205]

The Samaritans agree with the Karaites and the Qumran sect against the Rabbanites in requiring washing, not immersion, for a *zåb*.[206]

The Samaritans agree with the Karaites against the Rabbanites that a person contaminated by contact with an artefact that has itself been contaminated by contact with a *niddå* woman requires washing all over, not immersion.[207]

The Khilâf (the matter is not mentioned in the other sources) seems to agree with the Karaites in practice when it says that it makes no difference whether or not a woman gives birth while in the state of *då̊bå*, but it must be admitted that the theoretical reasoning of the Samaritans might not be the same as for the Karaites. The Rabbanites maintain that it does make a difference. (The Khilâf disagrees with both Karaites and Rabbanites when it

---

203 G.E. 112a; A.E. 122a bottom-b top.

204 G.E. 115c top; A.E. 124a middle.

205 A.E., start of ch. XIII. The word איגם in the third line of the chapter is to be corrected to אינו.

206 See the very important passage A.E. 121 a from the middle of the column to the end, from which it becomes clear that the Karaites require washing all over if the text of Scripture uses the verb רחץ and immersion if the text uses the verb טבל. (Note, however, that the text *never* uses the verb טבל in reference to the immersion of people. In all instances where the verb רחץ is not used, the text is silent as to the means of purification, and although the Karaites and Samaritans agree with the Rabbanites in these cases on the need for immersion, not washing, it is by tradition, not exegesis, that all three groups derive their halachah. On the significance of this, see the discussion below, on pp. 333-336). The Karaite version of washing all over is to pour the water over the whole body from the head downwards. In fact, the Gan ʿEden and Adderet Eliyahu distinguish carefully between washing (showering might be a better term for the Karaite way) and immersion in all cases. When neither verb is used by Scripture, as in the case of the נדה, the זבה, and the יולדת, the Karaites take this to mean that immersion is required for the unclean person and washing for anyone contaminated by that person.

On the Qumran sect, see Yadin, vol. I, 226. On the Falashas, see below, p. 335.

The distinction between the requirements of ࠓࠇࠉࠑࠄ and ࠈࠁࠉࠋࠄ is put into a wider context later on, near the end of this section, pp. 333-336.

There is apparently an alternative Samaritan opinion that immersion is required: see note 135. If this is the case, then this item is to be re-classified under (d). The matter is not, however, entirely certain.

207 See the previous note.

says that it makes no difference if the woman gives birth in a state of *zåbå*).[208]

The Samaritans agree with the Karaites and the Sadducees in not recognising the Rabbanite concept of the טבול יום.[209]

The Samaritans agree with the Karaites against the Rabbanites in not distinguishing between bleeding the source of which is in the vagina and bleeding the source of which is in the womb.[210]

The Samaritans agree with the Karaites against the Rabbanites that a couch, seat, or saddle contaminated by a ࠆࠁࠄ woman having put her weight on it without direct contact is unclean for seven days, not one. (Note, however, that the Samaritans and Karaites limit ࠆࠁࠄ in this context to the very first bleeding, and do not consider the woman as having this effect during the rest of the week).[211]

The Samaritans seem to agree with the Karaites against the Rabbanites in maintaining that a couch, seat, or saddle can be contaminated by the weight of a man on whom there is some *niddå* blood, even without dirẹct contact, in the same way as the woman can contaminate it.[212]

(b) *Agreement of the Samaritans with Some Karaites against Other Karaites and the Rabbanites*

The Kâshif and Iʿtiqâdât agree with a minority Karaite opinion that the uncleanness of a woman after giving birth to a boy lasts for forty-one days; the other sources agree with the majority Karaite opinion and the Rabbanites and the Falashas in making it forty days.[213]

(c) *Agreement of the Samaritans with Some or All Rabbanites against the Karaites*

The Samaritans agree with the Rabbanites against the Karaites that a man that has had an emission of semen contaminates people by contact, but agree with the Karaites against the Rabbanites that he does not contaminate artefacts.[214]

---

208 G.E. ch. VIII: A.E. 123b.

209 I have not seen any specific rejection of the idea for polemical purposes, but the Karaite and Samaritan sources all assume that cleanness comes in one go, at sunset or immediately, as the case may be. See above, p. 307. On the Sadducees, see Le Moyne, pp. 268-280.

210 G.E. 110d-111a; A.E. 122ab.

211 A.E. 122c.

212 Some Karaites maintain that although the man does contaminate a couch, seat, or saddle, he does so to a lesser degree. See G.E. 112c top; A.E. 122c bottom-122d top.

213 Keter Torah p. 32b top. On the Falashas, see Leslau, *Falasha Anthology*, introduction, p. xv.

214 See note 204.

The Samaritans agree with the Rabbanites against the Karaites in requiring a certain number of repetitions of an abnormal discharge over a certain period before a man can enter the state of *zåb* (though the requirements of the repetition are different) and in making this criterion at least as important as the criteria of the appearance of the stuff and the circumstances of its emission.[215]

(d) *Agreement of Some Samaritans with the Karaites and Other Samaritans with the Rabbanites*

The Ṭubâkh and Kâfi prescribe immersion for a person contaminated by contact with *niddå* blood, or the woman at the time of *niddå*, but the Kâshif (and probably the Iʿtiqâdât) agrees with the Karaites in prescribing washing all over. Allowing for the difference in the definition of *niddå*, the Ṭubâkh and Kâfi agree with the Rabbanites.[216]

The author of the Ṭubâkh agrees essentially with the Rabbanites and Falashas in the definition of the conditions for entry into the state of *zå̊bå*. All other Samaritan sources agree essentially with the Karaites.[217]

The Kâshif agrees with the Karaites that a person contaminated by a *zå̊bå* woman or *zå̊bå* blood requires washing all over; the Ṭubâkh and Kâfi and Dositheans probably agree with the Rabbanites in requiring immersion.[218]

The Farâ'id agrees with the Karaites that a woman that has an emission of blood on the day after the forty or eighty days after delivery becomes *niddå*; the Ṭubâkh, Kâfi, and Iʿtiqâdât agree with the Rabbanites that she becomes *zå̊bå*.[219]

The Kâfi and Ṭubâkh and some Dositheans agree with the Rabbanites and the Falashas and one textual tradition of the Book of Tobit against the Karaites and the Qumran sect and one textual tradition of the Book of Tobit in maintaining that a person contaminated by a corpse is cleansed by immersion, not washing. The opinion of the other sources is not certain, but the Farâ'iḍ, Kâshif, and Iʿtiqâdât seem to assume that only washing is required.[220]

See notes 206 and 223 for another possible instance.

---

215 T 81-93 N.

216 See note 206.

217 See G.E. ch. VII; A.E. ch. XI; and the passage quoted in note 187 and the comments there.

218 See note 206. On the Falashas, see below, p. 335.

219 G.E. 114b; A.E. 123d bottom-124a top.

220 See note 233.

It is clear from Tobit II:9 and II:5 that the author requires either washing or immersion on the first of the seven days of purification from contact with a corpse. From II:5 we see that

(e) *Disagreement of Some or All Samaritans with Both Karaites and Rabbanites*

The Kâfi disagrees with both the Karaites and the Rabbanites in not requiring washing all over or immersion of a person or artefact contaminated by contact with a *dåbå* woman, or a woman during the thirty-three days or sixty-six days of bleeding of cleansing, or a *zåbå* woman during her count of seven days without bleeding.[221]

The Ṭubâkh and Khilâf disagree even more by not requiring a day's uncleanness of the person contaminated, but limiting it to the period of contact.[222]

Sakta the Dosithean seems to have disagreed even more by maintaining that such contact did not cause uncleanness at all.

There is an opinion quoted by the author of the Kâfi that once a man in the state of *zåb* has washed the stuff off, he does not contaminate people or artefacts. This is similar to the opinion of the Ṭubâkh and Khilâf just mentioned.[223]

There is another opinion quoted by the author of the Kâfi that a man in the state of *zåb* does not contaminate people or artefacts at all, that only the stuff of his discharge can do so. This is similar to the Dosithean opinion just mentioned.[224]

Tobias was able to come back into the house after performing the initial washing, according to the Greek version. There is a remnant of this in one of the Hebrew texts, where the washing of hands is mentioned. The other textual traditions do not mention either washing or immersion. From II:9 we see again that the Greek version requires washing on the first day, and we see that the Hebrew text (not the same recension as mentioned before) and the Aramaic text require immersion on the first day. The Aramaic says that Tobias had not performed the immersion. The reason must be, from the context, that in the first case he was able to wash or immerse himself because it was before sunset, and in the second case it was after sunset. In both cases the time, whether before or after sunset, is given. We learn from this that the author required the initial washing or immersion to be in the day-time. This is the reason why Tobias had to sleep in the yard. It is for this reason as well why the versions are so vague in v. 4 about where the corpse was put the first time. Notice the reading of the Hebrew in particular. It is very likely that the reading of the Hebrew, that Tobias had performed the immersion, or the reading of the Greek, that he had performed the washing, are secondary corrections of an original statement, as in the Aramaic text, that he had not, a statement which is needed in the context.

It is to be assumed that a halachic tradition that requires washing, not immersion, on the first day will require washing, not immersion, on the seventh; and the other way round.

On the Qumran sect, see Yadin, vol. I, pp. 256-257. On the Karaites, see note 206. On the Falashas, see Leslau, p. 97. The Samaritan sources are listed in Kf ch. XIII, 11-13 N. See also pp. 333-336, and Kf ch. III, 43 TN.

[221] See note 206 and note 29. The Kâshaf requires washing all over, and the I'tiqâdât immersion.

[222] See note 30.

[223] See notes 30, 134, 135. From the information in note 135 it seems that this opinion is part of a set of variants that would add another example to category (d). The situation is not entirely clear, and the original passages should be consulted.

[224] See note 223. Compare note 135.

Most Samaritans seem to disagree with both the Karaites and Rabbanites in maintaining that a person or artefact is contaminated for seven days by *z̊ābå* blood, not one day. The Dositheans seem to have agreed with the Karaites and Rabbanites.[225]

The Samaritans disagree with both the Karaites and the Rabbanites in identifying the first week or fortnight after delivery with the first instant of menstrual bleeding and identifying the next thirty-three or sixty-six days with the rest of the menstrual week. The Khilâf and Ṭubâkh go their own way, and to some extent identify the rest of the week or fortnight as equivalent to the rest of the menstrual week (the Ṭubâkh only does this for the week after delivery of a boy), but they still hold to the other opinion at the same time, by counting the thirty-three or sixty-six days as equivalent to the rest of the menstrual week.[226]

The Khilâf and Iʿtiqâdât, and probably Sakta the Dosithean as well, maintain that the blood emitted in delivery of a girl contaminates anyone that touches it for a fortnight, not a week. (The Iʿtiqâdât, and probably Sakta as well, make this apply to any blood discharged during the fortnight; the Khilâf limits this to the blood discharged at the instant of delivery, and treats the bleeding of the rest of the fortnight as equivalent to *d̊ābå* bleeding). The Kâfi and Ṭubâkh agree with the Jews that the blood only makes a person that touches it unclean for a week. (They differ from the Karaites in making this apply to the bleeding of the whole fortnight).[227]

The Dosithean opinion that the blood of childbirth lost some or all of its contaminating power after the first week or fortnight does not seem to be shared by any Jews. The other Samaritans seem to agree with the Jews.[228]

The Khilâf (the other Samaritan sources do not raise the matter) disagrees with both the Karaites and Rabbanites when it says that it makes no difference if a woman gives birth while in a state of *z̊ābå*. (It agrees with the Karaites against the Rabbanites in the matter of giving birth while in a state of *d̊ābå*).[229]

The Samaritans disagree with the Karaites in limiting the period during which a menstruating woman can contaminate a couch, seat, or saddle by putting her weight on it without direct contact to the instant of *niddå* bleeding. (The Rabbanites do not distinguish between *niddå* and *d̊ābå* and therefore must agree in practice with the Samaritans that the woman has this

[225] A.E. 123b bottom.

[226] On the Karaite opinion, see the start of ch. IX of the Gan ʿEden.

[227] The Karaite sources do not specifically state that the uncleanness in both cases is for a week: they simply assume it. See the Keter Torah on Lv XII:4-5.

[228] I have not come across any clear statement on this matter in the Karaite sources, but their silence is evidence that they agree with the Rabbanites on this.

[229] G.E. ch. VIII; A.E. start and end of ch. XII.

effect for the whole of the menstrual week, but this gives a completely different theoretical justification of their position).[230]

The Samaritans disagree with both the Karaites and the Rabbanites in maintaining that an artefact is only susceptible to uncleanness if owned by an Israelite and intended for personal use, not for sale. This is probably by analogy with the principle, on which Jews and Samaritans agree, that of people, only an Israelite can contaminate or be contaminated.[231]

The Samaritan definition of a single artefact differs from the Jewish one in that the criterion is whether it is used as a unit rather than whether the parts are joined together.[232]

For a possible extra instance, see note 129.

It is to be noticed that in most of the instances listed here, some Samaritans agree with the Jews.

(f) *Some or All Samaritans Disagree with the Karaites and Rabbanites, but Agree with an Alternative Sub-Tradition in the Pharisaic Halachah or Some Other Jewish Tradition*

The Ṭubâkh and Kâfi disagree with the Farâʿiḍ and the modern halachah, and disagree as well with the Karaites, Rabbanites, and Falashas, but agree with the Book of Ezekiel, the Book of Tobit, and the Qumran sect in requiring an initial immersion on the first day before the seven-day process of purification from contact with a corpse can start.[233]

The Samaritans disagree with both the Karaites and Rabbanites in maintaining that ground can be contaminated by a corpse having been carried over it, but this is known as a Jewish opinion.[234]

---

[230] A.E. 122c.

[231] I have not come across an express statement of this rule in any Karaite work, but their agreement with it can be assumed from their silence to the contrary.

[232] See the discussion in the notes on the Additional Passage from the Khilâf. It is to be noticed that there is no disagreement *in principle* in this case between Samaritans and Jews, as I have shown in the notes on this passage.

[233] See note 220. The Rabbanites and the Hebrew and Aramaic texts of the Book of Tobit require immersion. The Qumran sect (Yadin, vol. I, pp. 256-257) and the Greek text of the Book of Tobit require washing. The Book of Ezekiel (XLIV:26) requires one or the other, but it could be either. See Yadin's comments on this halachah. Sakta the Dosithean agreed with the Karaites, Rabbanites etc.; other Dositheans, who held Sakta in esteem, agreed with the Ṭubâkh and Kâfi. See Abu 'l-Fatḥ 162:4-5 and 163:7. Notice, though, that Sakta does not put the uncleanness of the first day in a separate category to the effect of the uncleanness of the remaining days.

[234] I do not believe it has been noticed that the majority reading of the last sentence in the *Baraita Deniddah* II:3 is

א״ר יוחנן אסור לאדם להלך אחר הנדה ולדרוס את עפרה שהוא טמא כמת כך עפרה טמא ואסור ליהנות ממעשה ידיה.

This is the reading of all the witnesses known to the editor except for his basic manuscript, which

The Samaritans disagree with both the Karaites and Rabbanites in maintaining that ground is contaminated by the presence of a *niddå* woman, but this is known within the Rabbanite tradition as a minority opinion.[235]

The Ṭubâkh and Kâfi disagree with both the Karaite halachah and the modern Rabbanite halachah in setting the degree of exclusion of the *zåb* as the same as for the ࠌࠇࠍࠄ, that is, by requiring him to be excluded from the settlement; whereas the Rabbanites and Karaites set his degree of exclusion as the same as for the *niddå*, *z̊ābå*, and *ẙālēda*, that is by allowing him to enter

---

has כמות שהיא טמאה instead of כמת. We see from this that ground over which a corpse has been carried was regarded as unclean by the people responsible for one textual tradition.

A related opinion, that ground, stones, and wood inside a house where a corpse has been become unclean, even though it is normally only artefacts that can become unclean, is given by the Targum Yonatan on Nu XIX:14. The same opinion was held by the Qumran sect. For the details and references, see Ginzberg, pp. 81-82, 115-116, and 351-355, on the Damascus Documents, XII:15-18; and Yadin, I:253-254. Although this is not the usual Karaite opinion, it is attested: see the Eshkol Hakkofer, chapter 290.

Another related opinion, that ground where a corpse has been buried is unclean in itself, is held by some Karaites: see the Eshkol Hakkofer, chapter 291.

A related opinion, that an object attached to the ground can become unclean, was held by the Qumran sect and seems to have existed in the early Pharisaic halachah: see Ginzberg, as above, and in particular pp. 351-353.

Yadin puts forward convincing evidence that the Qumran sect held that the natural moisture in the materials inside the house absorbed contamination. This is precisely the reason given by the *Baraita Deniddah*, II:4, for declaring a stone on which a נדה woman has sat as unclean: אמר להם אסור להניח ידה על הכר [נ״ל שצ״ל הכד] לפנות ממנו מים מפני שהיא טמאה אפילו ישבה על האבן אסור ליגע בו מפני שהוא בולע ואינו פולט ...

Ginzberg (p. 81) expresses surprise at the explanation given, but as Yadin has shown, it is the opinion of the Qumran sect as well, and is explicable as a חומרה based on the standard Rabbinic halachah.

In the light of all this the Samaritan practice of treating ground over which a corpse has been carried or where a *niddå* woman, or woman who has given birth, has been, as unclean, is explained, and we see, too, not only why the purification can be carried out by either water or fire, but also why fire is better. The natural moisture in the stuff absorbs actual molecules from the source of uncleanness, and the moisture and its contaminant have to be got rid of. All the various practices mentioned above now become explicable.

The opinions mentioned above are related to a persistent minority Rabbanite practice of treating all water in unsealed containers in a house where a corpse has been as irrevocably contaminated, presumably because of the absorption by it of molecules carried in the air. For the evidence, see Lehmann, *The Temple Scroll as a Source of Sectarian Halakhah*, 584-585. Lehmann has not fully explained the reason for the practice, which is to be understood in the light of the arguments and instances given above. See also on this practice Roth, *Marranos*, 190.

[235] See the passages from the *Baraita Deniddah* quoted in the previous note, and notice the minority reading in the first passage quoted. This opinion is attested among the Jews of Berber countries in the Middle Ages: see Ginzberg, p. 147.

(The separation of menstruating women from other people by the Falashas, treated by Ginzberg, p. 354, is another matter altogether, in spite of Ginzberg's presentation. Without going into the matter in detail, we will point out that the Falashas separate all people that are unclean, whether intrinsically or by contact, and there is nothing special about the case of a menstruating woman).

See also note 237.

a settlement (specifically, a walled city) but not to enter any part of the Temple. There is, however, excellent evidence that the pre-Mishnaic Pharisaic halachah, and probably the Sadducean halachah as well, agreed to some extent with the Ṭubâkh and Kâfi. Apparently an original divergency of tradition within the Rabbanite tradition has been standardised, and the sub-tradition that has become standard is the one that disagrees with the Samaritan tradition. On the other hand, the other Samaritan sources seem to agree with the Karaite and standardised Rabbanite halachah in this matter.[236]

The Samaritans disagree with both the Karaites and the Rabbanites in maintaining that in some circumstances a *niddå* woman can contaminate all the artefacts within a house, but the Falashas agree with the Samaritans on this.[237]

---

[236] According to the Rabbanite halachah, the מצורע is excluded from the settlement (specifically, from any walled city). The זב, the זבה, the נדה, and the יולדת are excluded from the Temple but not from the city. A person contaminated by a corpse is allowed to enter the outer courts of the Temple. What the Ṭubâkh and Kâfi do is put the ࠑࠓࠅࠏ and ࠆࠁ mentioned in Nu V:2-3 at the same level of uncleanness, by specifying that the degree of exclusion of the ࠆࠁ is the same as for the ࠑࠓࠅࠏ. (See the references in note 131). The Rabbanite interpretation of this verse, and apparently the Karaite one as well, is that the מצורע, the זב, and the טמא לנפש mentioned in the verse are three separate grades, and the זב is representative of the זבה, the נדה and the יולדת as well. (See the standard Rabbanite commentators, and the Keter Torah). Neither the Rabbanites nor the Karaites require the זב to be excluded from the city. It is true that the Mishnah mentions special dwellings for menstruating women, but these are inside the city (Mishnah Niddah VII:4).

There is no point in comparing the halachah of the Qumran sect, because they excluded all unclean people from any city, and there does not seem to be any distinction between them in this respect. (Yadin, vol. I, 235-238).

We see, then, that the Ṭubâkh and Kâfi disagree with the Rabbanites, the Karaites, and the other Samaritan sources in requiring exclusion of the ࠆࠁ from the city, and treating the ࠆࠁ like the ࠑࠓࠅࠏ instead of like the ࠍࠃࠄ, the ࠆࠁࠄ, and the ࠉࠋࠃࠄ. Nevertheless, we find that Josephus says that a זב and a מצורע are equally excluded from entry into the city of Jerusalem and were equally excluded from entry into the Camp in the Wilderness. In other respects he agrees with the standardised Rabbinic halachah (War V:227; Antiquities III:261-264). As Josephus did not have any polemical purpose in the first passage, and reports the rule as fixed, we must assume that in his time the Pharisees and Sadducees agreed on it. Notice, however, that the subject is the city of Jerusalem or the Camp in the Wilderness, and that this rule of excluding the זב need not have applied, in Josephus's opinion or in the opinion of the Pharisees and Sadducees of his time, to other cities.

[237] See the responsum quoted in the note on Kf ch. XI, 31-32. For the Falasha halachah, see Leslau, p. 91 note 3, quoting Flad. The reason for this, in the case of the Samaritans, is probably that the natural moisture in the artefacts absorbs some airborne molecules of the *nidda* blood (see above, notes 234 and 235). This could be the explanation in the other cases as well.

There seems to be a reminiscence of this opinion in the question asked of the High Priest, quoted in Kf ch. XI, 31-32 N, which seems to consider the possibility that the presence of a woman in a state of *niddå*, or perhaps more precisely a woman at the instant of *niddå*, contaminates all the artefacts in the house. Notice, though, that there is no hint of this opinion in the answer given. The discrepancy between the assumptions of the question and the answer could be evidence of a very late standardisation of the halachah on this point.

Sakta the Dosithean disagreed with the other Samaritans and the Rabbanites and Karaites, but agreed with the Falashas, in maintaining that the uncleanness of the baby was the same as the mother's, lasting a total of forty days in the case of a boy and eighty days in the case of a girl.[238]

4. *Summary*

We will now set out the rules of the general tendencies of the relationship between the Samaritan and Jewish halachah.

(a) In the overwhelming majority of cases, the Jews and Samaritans all agree with each other.

(b) When the Samaritans disagree with each other, it nearly always happens that at least some of them agree with the Jews.

(c) The Samaritans tend to agree with the Karaites against the Rabbanites, but the opposite does occur, and not infrequently.

(d) When the Samaritans disagree with each other, it usually happens that the Karaites disagree with each other, or that the Karaites and Rabbanites disagree with each other, or that some Jewish group shows a divergent opinion.

(e) When the Samaritans disagree with each other, it often happens that some of them agree with the Karaites and some of them with the Rabbanites.

(f) In most instances of disagreement with the Jewish opinion, some Samaritans will agree with the Jewish opinion against other Samaritans, so that there are very few cases of disagreement of *all* Samaritans with the Jewish opinion.

(g) There is a very small residue of cases in which all Samaritans disagree with all Jewish opinions *known to us at the moment*. It is to be noticed that there are instances of disagreement of the Samaritans with both the Karaites and the Rabbanites, when some other Jewish halachic tradition agreed with the Samaritans. As the opinion of the other Jewish traditions, or the earlier divergence within the Pharisaic tradition, is usually only known to us by accident, it must be assumed that such agreement with the Samaritans must have occurred in numerous other instances not now known about.

(h) The Dositheans have no clear tendency to agree with either the Rabbanites or Karaites or any other Jewish group or sect any oftener than other Samaritans do, though in any given instance they might well agree with one Jewish group when other Samaritans agree with another Jewish group.

(i) The Samaritan halachah is no more uniform than the Jewish one is;

---

[238] Aešcoly, pp. 43-44.

that is to say, different Samaritan sects and groups disagree with each other just as much as different Jewish sects or groups do or did.

It will be seen that there is very little in the Samaritan traditions that is not in one of the Jewish traditions. When it is borne in mind that hardly anything is known of the Jewish traditions except for the Rabbanite and Karaite ones, that the Sadducee system is almost completely unknown, the Falasha system is only very imperfectly known, only isolated details are known of the Qumran system, and some systems are only known to us by allusions in the Pseudepigrapha or the Versions, so that there must once have been much more variety than is now apparent, it is an inevitable conclusion that much or most or all of what seems to be distinctly Samaritan was once equally part of the Jewish tradition. When it is borne in mind as well that in the numerous instances of disagreement between one Samaritan tradition and another the overwhelming tendency is for at least one Samaritan tradition to agree with one Jewish tradition or another, so that some Samaritans agree with some Jews against other Samaritans, who very often agree with other Jews, the conclusion seems inevitable that there is no uniquely Samaritan tradition of the halachah, unconnected with the Jewish one. This conclusion is reinforced when it is borne in mind that in most instances of disagreement between the Samaritans on one hand and the Jews on the other, the Jews themselves disagree with each other, that is to say, there are variant Jewish traditions, and the difference between the Samaritan tradition and the tradition of one of the Jewish groups is no more than the difference between any two of the Jewish traditions. If we then consider the fact that the agreements between Jews and Samaritans by far outnumber the disagreements, we come to the following conclusions: *There is a halachic tradition common to all Israel, both Jews and Samaritans. There are some points on which there is variation within the tradition. Both in given individual instances and overall the variation is independent of the division between Samaritans and Jews.*

The corollary of this is that the halachic tradition of Israel is older than the division between Samaritans and Jews. As this is in fact an accurate statement, it is confirmation of the conclusions reached.

Another corollary is that the variations within the tradition are older than the division between Samaritans and Jews.

5. *Historical Excursus*

We now have to reconcile this variation within the halachic tradition with the uniformity of the text of the written Torah, which all Jews and Samaritans accept. If there are no variations in the written text, how is it that there are variations in the halachic tradition?

Before showing how this question is to be answered, we have to explain what is meant by saying there are no variations in the written text, a statement that requires careful definition.

It will be agreed that the Karaites and Rabbanites use exactly the same text of the Torah, even though there are divergencies between their traditions. It will equally well be agreed that even though all Karaites use the same written Torah as each other, there are divergencies between their traditions.

Now let us consider whether for the present purpose there are any differences between the Samaritan Torah and the Masoretic Torah.

First of all, it is now known that the Samaritan Torah was originally neither Samaritan nor Jewish, but the common property of both. (The passages commonly considered to be tendentious are discussed below). But aside from this, what concerns us at the moment are the halachic passages in the texts used by the Samaritans and Jews. Now, an examination of the two texts shows that there is very little difference in wording between the Masoretic Torah and the Samaritan one in the halachic passages, that what variants there are do not usually affect the meaning, and that there are very few halachic differences between Samaritans and Jews that can be related to differences in the text. In most cases, when the Samaritans argue that the text of the Torah supports their opinion and refutes the Jewish one, the argument is independent of the question of textual differences, either because there are none, or because they have no bearing on the question at hand. The same argument can be used with either text. In the relatively very few cases where the wording of the Samaritan Torah seems to favour the Samaritan tradition on a point of halachah, it is quite common to find that the Karaites agree with the Samaritans and are able to support the same opinion from the Masoretic Torah.[239] In such cases the Rabbanites are able to produce equally convincing arguments from the same wording of the same verse to refute the Karaites.

We can now rephrase our earlier statement more precisely and definitely by saying that there are no differences in the wording of the halachic passages that will *unequivocally* support one variant opinion on a point of halachah against another. Or at least, if there are any, the differencies of opinion on items of halachah far outnumber them. We can turn this statement round and say that quite often several contradictory traditions (note that it is first a

[239] As in Lv XII:4-5 (if we count the two traditional pronunciations as a textual difference) on the word טהרָה or טהרהּ. In Lv XI:25, the MT omits the words ࠅࠓࠇࠑ ࠁࠌࠉࠌ, but the Karaites still agree with the Samaritans that a person that has touched a ࠍࠁࠋࠕ requires washing, not immersion. On the other hand, the absence of these words in the MT is not required by the Rabbanites to support their opinion that this person, like nearly all other unclean people, requires immersion, since they maintain that the verb רחץ always means immersion, except in the one case of Lv XV:16, as we have seen.

question of differences in tradition, not exegesis) can be supported from the same verse.

To return to the original question. There are variations within the halachic tradition of Israel, and yet where the text of the written Torah treats the matter on which there is variation, it is very nearly the same from one recension to another, and what variations there are have no necessary connection with variations in the halachic tradition. At what period could this situation have come about?

The most obvious solution is that the variations within the tradition arose after the final editing of the written Torah, which in this context means after the halachic passages had been given their present wording, which as we have seen is effectively the same in all the recensions. This solution when examined raises so many difficulties that it is unlikely to be the correct one.

First, it seems unlikely that so much variation in the halachah could have occurred after the final editing, since the outlook of the times would have been against it. It can be conceded that changes in civil law would have occurred, but it is to be noticed that the instances quoted here as evidence are all in the area of ritual purity, and similar technical matters, which, although susceptible to variation in the degree of strictness of observance, are not very susceptible to alteration in fundamental calculation. The second objection is, as we have said, that the verses to which the variant traditions are linked do not compellingly favour one interpretation over another, and there is no reason why they should have been re-interpreted. The third objection is that the phenomenon of the halachah being changed to accord with the apparent meaning of the text of Scripture is either non-existent or very rare. It is true that the Qumran sect and the Karaites maintain that the tradition has been lost in some instances, and that the correct practice can only be recovered by exegesis of Scripture; but this does not apply to most items of halachah, which are still known by tradition and on which the Qumran sect express no doubt and on which the Karaites are in agreement with each other. Besides, when we find several different groups agreeing with each other on a certain practice and exegesis against several other groups, it seems easier to suppose that the ones that agree with each other are each the heir of the same wide-spread ancient tradition on this matter than to suppose that one has taken over another's exegesis of a verse and altered the practice and tradition to match. This becomes even harder to suppose when we consider that the distribution of agreement and disagreement between groups is different in each case.

Let us suppose instead that the variants in the halachic tradition are older than the final editing of the written Torah. How could this have come about? And can the traces of such variation be seen in the text as it now stands?

The Torah, both traditional and written, is the possession of all Israel and was intended as such from the time of its composition. It has been accepted by all Israel, the ancestors of all the known and unknown Samaritan and Jewish groups and sects. When edited in its final form it would have had to be acceptable to the bearers of all the existing halachic traditions. This means that the final editors, whether they touched up an existing book, or put a book together out of existing sections, or however they did their work, were faced with the problem of producing an edition that could be used by people following different traditions of halachah. Perhaps there were already several different versions, in which crucial verses had slightly different wording in agreement with one tradition of halachah or another. How was the problem solved? I suggest that if we look at the qualities of the text of the Torah now in existence the answer will be given to us, and if we re-examine the traditional explanations and justifications of the concept of the halachic tradition we are given the same answer. The text of the halachic sections of the written Torah is normally very precise in its wording, but is cunningly ambiguous or vague on purpose in the verses that lay down a point of halachah about which there is disagreement between different Jewish groups, or different Samaritan groups, or between Jews and Samaritans. The text has been worded very carefully, it is very precisely vague and unequivocally ambiguous so that it will bear a certain number of interpretations and no more, and will agree with all the halachic traditions in mind. This way, each tradition can be supported by the text of Scripture. This explains why the text is so vague or uses wording that does not seem completely appropriate in verses on the interpretation of which there is disagreement: *the disagreement is older than the present form of the verse*. This explains, as well, how it is that the Pharisees (or Rabbanites) can say that the tradition is to be followed in interpreting Scripture even if a verse has to be understood in a way that seems unnatural: *the verse was phrased so as to make their interpretation possible, even if unnatural*. It equally well explains how the Karaites and Samaritans (and apparently the Sadducees) can object to the Rabbanite theory, and maintain that their tradition never contradicts Scripture: *the text of Scripture is formulated with their traditions* (*along with everyone else's*) *in mind*. We see, then, that although the two sides contradict each other over the relationship between written and oral Torah, they are both equally historically correct, and differ only in the expression of their theory.

There is an obvious objection to this theory of the process of editing that has to be considered before proceeding. Why not simply assume that each set of divergent traditions of halachah that are linked to various divergent interpretations of a given verse is the result of various re-interpretations of the verse, with the traditions of practice having been altered to match? We have said that that it would be hard to imagine the mechanism for halachah to change to suit exegesis (whereas the opposite process is quite easily possible). But this assumption is more convincingly refuted by pointing out its incompatibility with two persistent phenomena. The first is, as we have said, that differences in practice are often connected with verses the apparent meaning of which does not strongly favour one reading over another, so that each traditional practice will be seen, to those that accept it, as representing a possible, if not entirely compelling interpretation of the verse with which it is linked, and rival interpretations would not be attractive. The second phenomenon is that the verse to which the different traditions are linked and which is interpreted in one way or another is often so obscure or vague that it is hard to see how it could have got past the editors unless the wording is deliberate. The wording of the written Torah is normally very precise.

Instances of the first phenomenon make up most of the examples of divergence discussed by Revel. We will add a few more.

The Samaritans and Karaites make a distinction between the first drop of menstrual blood and all the bleeding that follows. The Rabbanites do not make the distinction. The Scriptural passages on the subject, Lv XV:19, 20, 24, and 25, will equally well support either opinion, depending on how the word ࠍࠃࠄ is interpreted.[240]

The Samaritans and Karaites maintain that it makes no difference whether a man makes contact with a woman's ࠍࠃࠄ bleeding during intercourse or by some other form of contact. The Rabbanites do make a distinction. The relevant verse, Lv XV:24, will equally well support either position, depending on whether the word ࠍࠃࠕࠄ means 'her ࠍࠃࠄ bleeding' or 'her condition of ࠍࠃࠄ'.[241]

The Samaritans consider any breaking of the prohibition of intercourse between a man and an unclean woman to be punishable theoretically by execution. The Rabbanites and Karaites deny this. The relevant verse, Lv XX:18, will equally well support either position, depending on whether the expression ࠅࠍࠊࠓࠕࠄ ࠄࠍࠐࠔ ࠄࠄࠅࠀ means 'that person is to be removed (by execution)' or 'that person will be removed (by premature natural death)'.

A striking incidence of the second phenomenon, the verse that is inexplicably vague or ambiguous, is Lv XXIII:11 and 15, which give the method of calculating the time of Pentecost each year. As is well known, the expression ࠌࠌࠇࠓࠕ ࠄࠔࠁࠕ has been used to support four different and incompatible ways of calculating the date. The Rabbanites and Dositheans take the word ࠔࠁࠕ to mean the first day of the Passover week; the Falashas, the translators of the Peshitta, and apparently the author of IV Ezra, take it to mean the whole Passover week; the Karaites, Boethusians,

[240] As we have seen, the Samaritans agree with the Karaites in taking the word ࠍࠃࠄ to mean the very first flow of menstrual blood.

[241] See note 191.

and all Samaritans except the Dositheans take it to mean the Sabbath day that falls somewhere in the Passover week; the author of the Book of Jubilees and the Qumran sect take it to mean the first Sabbath day after the Passover week.[242] The verses will support all these opinions. A good case can be made for a use of the word ࠔࠁࠕ to mean a festival, and a good case can be made out for an archaic use of the word to mean the whole festival week.[243] The problem is that if such usages are possible, the meaning of the term ࠔࠁࠕ in this verse is only made less clear, because the usage of the term to mean a festival day or week seems to demand an indication from the context or some qualifying expression that it is not being used in its normal sense of the seventh day of the week. In these verses the use of the term without any qualification to show which seventh day is meant would favour taking it to refer to the first day of the festival or the festival week; but on the other hand there is no clear indication that it is not being used in its normal meaning of the seventh day of the week. The Rabbanites, Karaites, and Samaritans all put up excellent arguments for their opinion, arguments that will each convince the reader that they have really interpreted the term properly, and doubtless the other groups could have supported their position equally well. Perhaps they are all right, even though they contradict each other. Perhaps the verses that seem so obscure and ambiguous have been carefully worded so as to give the four meanings required *and no more.*

The written Torah shows the same apparently inexplicable vagueness or ambiguity in its prescriptions for the cleansing of a person who has become unclean. The Rabbanites maintain that unclean people, of whatever kind, are cleansed by טבילה, immersion, although as we have seen a person contaminated by an emission of semen only requires washing all over מדאורייתא, and the requirement of immersion is a תקנה. They maintain that whenever the text uses the verb רחץ, it is to be taken as the equivalent of the verb טבל. This is very forced and unnatural, as the Karaites take great delight in pointing out.[244] It is particularly unnatural that the verb רחץ in Lv XV:16 must be taken in its obvious meaning of washing, if the immersion of a man who has an emission of semen is only a תקנה. This means that there is not even an illogical rule for the interpretation of the use of this verb: sometimes it means what it says and sometimes it does not.

It is true that the exact expression of the Rabbanite rule is that the verb רחץ means immersion if the text says that the person's clothes have to be washed, and that in Lv XV:16 it does not say this, but although this gives a

[242] Le Moyne, pp. 180-183.
[243] Ibid.
[244] See A.E. 121a, and see note 206 and its context.

rule applicable to all situations, it does not make the use of the verb רחץ any more natural.[245]

The Karaites assume that whenever the text uses the verb רחץ it means exactly what it says, and that whenever it uses neither רחץ nor טבל, but does mention that the person is to wash their clothes, as part of the process of becoming clean, or simply says that the person becomes clean, then immersion is required if the person is the source of uncleanness, as the זב, the נדה, the זבה, the יולדת and the מצורע; but that washing is required if the person has been contaminated by something else, such as a dead animal or an unclean person, and is not the source of the uncleanness. If this is what the text of Scripture means, it could have been put much more clearly. Notice that the Karaites need a halachic tradition and a tradition of the interpretation of Scripture just as much as the Rabbanites do in this matter.[246]

The Samaritans agree with the Karaites, with the following exceptions: some Samaritans requere immersion instead of washing for a person contaminated by a corpse,[247] and some Samaritans require immersion instead of washing for a person contaminated by contact with a woman at the instant of *niddå*, or a *zåbå* woman before her count has started, or a *yålēda* during the first week or fortnight, or with the blood emitted by any of these.[248]

There is no conflict over the principle of exegesis between the Samaritans mentioned and the Karaites and other Samaritans in the case of a person contaminated by a corpse. It is true that the verb ࠓࠇࠑ is used in Nu XIX:19, but it is equally true that in verse 12 the verb ࠈࠄࠓ is used, without the verb ࠓࠇࠑ being used. The Karaites take v. 19 as a supplement to v. 12, and it seems from the lay-out of ch. CV of the Farâ'iḍ, and the section of the Kâshif on Nu XIX, that the Samaritans that agree with the Karaites on the requirement of washing rather than immersion do the same. I suspect the other Samaritans argued that if v. 19 was a supplement to v. 12, then v. 12 was unnecessary, because there was nothing in v. 12 that was not in v. 19, so that if v. 12 refers to the process of cleansing of the person contaminated by a corpse, v. 19 refers to the actions of the person who performs the purification ceremony. Each verse refers to the same event, but in relation to two different people. This means that v. 19 is taken to mean 'The clean person sprinkles the unclean person on the third day and the seventh day, and makes him guiltless on the seventh day, and then he (i.e. *the*

---

245 Mishneh Torah, Mikva'ot I:2. See also Mishneh Torah, She'ar Avot Ṭum'ah V:1, and the commentators.

246 I have not seen this rule stated explicitly in any Karaite text, but it does accurately sum up the Karaite halachah.

247 On contamination from a corpse, see notes 220 and 233.

248 This is set out above, in Section 2.

one that did the sprinkling) washes his clothes, washes himself in water, and becomes clean at sunset'. Compare v. 9, on cleansing from the contaminating effect of the ashes.

It is not entirely clear why some Samaritans maintain that a person that touches *niddå* blood should require immersion rather than washing, but one explanation is given in the note to Kf ch. XI, lines 88-89, where it is shown that as it is the flow of blood that makes the woman unclean, anyone that touches the blood must be unclean to exactly the same degree, and if she requires immersion, so must anyone else that touches the blood. Effectively the person that touches the blood is treated as אב טומאה like the woman herself. This interpretation is made easier by the ambiguity of the phrase ࠅࠕࠄࠉ ࠍࠃࠕࠄ ࠏࠋࠉࠅ in Lv XV:24, which can equally well mean 'so that her condition of *niddå* applies to him' or 'and her *niddå* blood gets on him'. The ambiguity is helped by the unexpected tense of the verb ࠅࠕࠄࠉ instead of ࠅࠄࠉࠕࠄ. The requirement of immersion for a person that touches the woman without touching the blood is probably by analogy.

To sum up: the Karaite principle is that a ראשון לטומאה requires washing, never immersion, and that an אב טומאה requires washing if the text uses the verb רחץ, and immersion if the text is silent about the matter. The Samaritans agree with them on this rule, and any exceptions are only apparent, being due to a disagreement over what is אב טומאה,or over which person the verb רחץ refers to in one case where the wording is ambiguous.

The impression gained from the sources available is that the Falashas do not distinguish between washing and immersion, but use the same procedure for removing all kinds of uncleanness. Aešcoly uses the word טבל throughout, in every instance of cleansing from uncleanness. It does seem, though, that the Falashas use washing in all cases, not immersion, since Leslau's French translation consistently uses the verb *se laver* for every instance of recovery from uncleanness. It seems that the Falashas take the verb רחץ (or its equivalent in the Ethiopic translation of the Torah) literally, as do the Samaritans and Karaites, but that unlike them, and unlike the Rabbanites either, they take the absence of a prescription to mean that the normal procedure is required, i.e. washing all over. This matter needs further investigation.

The text of Scripture is able to agree with all these traditions and support all these interpretations because of its ambiguity in Lv XIX:19 or Lv XV:24; its apparent repetitiveness in Nu XIX:19 and its context as compared to v. 12 and its context; and its vagueness in Lv XV:19, XV:25 and 28, and XII:2 and 5, where the essential piece of information, namely whether immersion or washing is required, is left out. These passages give an impression of being inter-dependent.

We have seen that the Rabbanite principle requires an unnatural interpretation of the meaning of the verb רחץ, but once this is accepted, it is at least natural to take the silence of the text as meaning that immersion is required. On the other hand, the Karaite and Samaritan principle, although allowing the natural interpretation of the verb ࠓࠇࠑ in all instances, demands the unnatural or at least forced interpretation of the silence of the text as meaning that immersion is required.

We must now consider the very strange fact that the verb ࠈࠁࠋ is not used by the Pentateuch in the instances where Rabbanites, Karaites, and Samaritans agree that immersion is required. Instead, the method of cleansing is not mentioned at all. The result is that *the Pentateuch never uses the verb* ࠈࠁࠋ *in reference to the immersion of people.* This is very strange, particularly because in so many passages it would have seemed almost inevitable that the verb would have to be used.

Leaving out the verb ࠈࠁࠋ in some instances would not be needed for the Falasha halachah (if the interpretation of the sources given just before is right), but obviously it would not be possible to use the verb ࠓࠇࠑ, not even in reference to the ࠆࠁࠄ. But even leaving the tradition now represented by the Falashas out of consideration, it seems that the text would still be unable to use the verb ࠈࠁࠋ in the instances in which in post-Biblical times the Karaites, Rabbanites, and Samaritans agree that immersion is required, because only by doing so can the verb be made ambiguous. By not giving the required information in the instances where these traditions agree, the text is able to agree with all of them in the instances where they do disagree.[249] This is the sign of purposeful, systematic, and subtle editing.

When we consider that the text of the written Torah is normally very precise, these instances of vagueness, ambiguity, or omission of the essential are so untypical that they must be deliberate. It is very unlikely that the avoidance of the obvious verb ࠈࠁࠋ can be accidental.

Another objection that could be made to the hypothesis put forward here is that there are disagreements between the MT and the Samaritan Torah that could be regarded as due to tendentious alteration of the text, whether by the Jews or the Samaritans, so as to either remove possible references to Mt. Gerizim as the prescribed site for the Temple, or to insert such references. If there are such tendentious alterations, the hypothesis becomes complicated, because we have to assume that the readings were altered at some time after the composition and editing of the Torah. On the other hand, if it can be shown that the differences between the readings need not be tendentious in origin (however they might have been interpreted later on by Jews and

[249] Let us say once and for all that there is no anachronism in relating differences in tradition in Biblical times to differences in tradition attested in later times. The later traditions are used for comparison because they are attested, but they go back to antiquity.

Samaritans) and that in each instance the reference to Mt. Gerizim or Jerusalem is equally clear or unclear according to the reading of the MT or the Samaritan Torah, then the hypothesis is strengthened. Furthermore, if such turns out to be the case, the hypothesis can be developed and made more detailed, and it can be suggested that the differences between the two readings go back to the original text of the Torah as finally edited, and that the differences were allowed to stand during the process of editing because they did not necessarily affect the meaning, or at least, did not make any difference to the halachah. It can then be suggested that the reason why there are some real differences in meaning between the various recensions of the Torah outside the halachic passages[250] is that these differences go back to the time of final editing, and that they were allowed to stand because they did not affect the halachah, which is the real criterion of agreement or disagreement, relative orthodoxy or relative sectarianism, between the various Samaritan and Jewish religious groups. Besides, although it is possible to make an ambiguous halachic statement, it is very hard to make an ambiguous statement about chronology or historical events, and unification of the text of the Torah in such cases would have needed unification of the tradition by discarding some sub-traditions, which would have spoilt the purpose of the effort. (Nevertheless, there is a good example of an ambiguous chronological statement in Ex XII:40 in the MT).

The implication of all this is that contradictions in statements of historical facts and other differences outside the halachic sections between the various traditions of the Torah are older than the time when uniformity in the halachic sections was achieved. (Uniformity here is to be understood as defined above, that is to say almost complete uniformity of wording, with the few differences not necessarily affecting the meaning). The conclusion would be that *no recension of the Torah is any older than the others, and that all are of equal validity and accuracy*. The only exception to this would be in certain passages where isolated scribal error could have occurred in one recension or several recensions. This is not to deny that modernization of the language and spelling has probably occurred in both the MT and the Samaritan,[251] or that

---

[250] The differences between the MT and Samaritan (and other recensions) in, for example, Gn IV:8 or II:2, do not affect the meaning, but there is a residue, admittedly small, but nevertheless real enough, of differences that do affect the meaning, as in Gn X:4 or XV:21. The most striking examples of such real differences are in the chronological systems. Five different systems are known: the systems of the MT, the Samaritan, the LXX, the source of the Book of Jubilees, and the recension used by Josephus in his *Antiquities* where he departs from the LXX. In addition, there are traces of other systems in the mss. of the LXX and in the Peshitta. There might well have been other systems not now attested.

[251] It is possible that the linguistic differences between the MT and the Samaritan are partly due to incomplete normalisation of dialect in the process of editing the Pentateuch, and that such dialect differences were therefore in existence at all times.

there could have been a certain amount of secondary touching up of the text of each recension. Nor is this to deny that only one text is now authoritative halachically for Jews and only one for Samaritans.[252].

We will now take the three sets of readings that could most plausibly be regarded as the result of tendentious alteration by either Jews or Samaritans, and see if they really are such when considered on their own, without the polemical Jewish and Samaritan arguments that we normally think of when calling them to mind.

The most striking example of all is the Samaritan Tenth Commandment. As is well known, the Samaritans count as nine Commandments what the Jews count as ten, and count as the Tenth Commandment a passage following which is omitted in the MT.[253] All the parts of this passage can be found elsewhere in the Torah. The critical part corresponds to Dt XXVII:4, where the MT has בהר עיבל and the Samaritan has ࠁࠄࠓࠂࠓࠉࠆࠉࠌ. Whether this is the Tenth Commandment or not depends entirely on the system of counting the Commandments, and its presence here does not necessarily make it one of the Ten Commandments. Even with this passage present, the Jewish division of the Commandments, with verse 2 being counted as the First Commandment, is still possible. Bowman and Talmon have demonstrated

---

[252] It must be emphasized that all the arguments put forward and conclusions reached here are about the editing of the Torah in its completed or final form. When we say that all the recensions are equally valid we mean that all of them go back to the same final edition, which still had some divergencies in the historical passages, which it was not possible or not desirable to remove. This is not to deny that the various historical traditions themselves, as they stood before the final editing and compilation, were not necessarily of equal accuracy. We are still justified in preferring the reading of one recension to the reading of another in certain cases of fact. For instance, we can choose between the forms *Rodanim* and *Dodanim* in Gn X:4: both forms go back to the final editing of the Torah, but at some time before that the form was apparently corrupted in one tradition. In some cases of divergence in historical statements, as in Gn X:19, both statements seem to be correct and ancient. So much for historical statements; but when the divergences are in statements outside the realm of history, as for instance in the chronology of the antediluvian Patriarchs, all that can be said is that the divergences are older than the final editing and compilation of the Torah, and nothing can be said about the superiority of one set of readings over another, though in some such such cases it might be possible to show that one reading or set of readings is older than another, which is another matter.

In my thesis *The Text of Isaiah I-XXXV in the Talmudim and Midrashim*, presented at Sydney University for the degree of Master of Arts with Honours in 1972, I demonstrated, developing a suggestion by Chaim Rabin, that the very minor variants within the MT are as old as the MT itself as a recension or separate text-form. These minor variations are to be found in all books of the MT, although it is noticeable that there are apparently considerably less of them in the Pentateuch than in the other books. Within the Pentateuch the frequency of such minor variants within the MT seems to be slightly higher in the historical passages than in the halachic passages, but this judgment needs to be verified by future study. It seems that similarly, on a bigger scale, the differences between the MT and the other recensions existed right from the start, that is to say, from the time of final editing.

[253] The Samaritan Tenth Commandment does not correspond to the whole of the passage missing in the MT, but only to the section starting at ࠅࠄࠉࠄ ࠁࠏࠁࠓࠊࠌ.

that this passage referring to Mt. Gerizim appears quite late in Decalogue inscriptions, and have concluded that the passage was added late to the text of the Samaritan Torah.[254] On the contrary, the evidence can equally well be taken to show that the present Samaritan system of counting the Commandments is late, and that the passage in question was present all the while but was not counted as part of the Ten Commandments. Whether it is or is not counted as one of the Commandments is a matter of traditional exegesis, not text. If it is one of the Commandments, then it is הלכה לדורות and is Scriptural warrant for the siting of the Temple on Mt. Gerizim. If it is not one of the Ten Commandments, then it is הלכה לשעה, something to be carried out once, immediately after crossing the Jordan, and has nothing to do with the site of the Temple. It need not even refer to the same Mt. Gerizim as the one usually understood.[255] Neither need the fact that this passage and the section immediately before, and other sections nearby, correspond to verses or groups of verses elsewhere in the Torah mean that the passage in secondary, because we find exactly the same phenomenon in the MT, where for example a whole chapter, namely ch. XXX of Exodus, corresponding to various groups of verses elsewhere in the Torah, is inserted in the MT and not in the Samaritan; and there are numerous shorter instances, such as Ex XXIX:21.

The second example is the other place where this passage occurs, Dt XXVII:4, which Jews interpret as הלכה לשעה, and the context implies as much. The main disagreement is not over whether to read הר עיבל or ࠄࠓࠂࠓࠉࠆࠉࠌ. *If this was the only disagreement, Jews would have to maintain that the verse was Scriptural warrant for siting the Temple on Mt. ʿEval!* The main disagreement is over whether Dt XXVII:4 is meant to set the location of the Temple or not. The reading הר עיבל would make it impossible for the verse to refer to the site of the Temple. With the reading ࠄࠓࠂࠓࠉࠆࠉࠌ, the verse can be taken to refer to the siting of the Temple, but need not, and if read in its context, would not naturally be taken in this way. In fact, the reading הר גריזים is attested as a Jewish reading: it is the reading of the Old Latin.[256] Whether the Old Latin is translated direct from

---

[254] Bowman and Talmon, *Samaritan Decalogue Inscriptions.*

[255] There is an ancient controversy on whether Gerizim and ʿEval in the context of Dt. XXVII are the same ones as generally known. See Eusebius's *Onomastikon* and the commentators on Dt XXVII. The sources are conveniently assembled in the Midrash Haggadol. It could be suggested that both sides were right in their opinion, and that there is an ancient divergence of tradition on this matter.

[256] It is almost certain that this text of the Old Latin is Jewish, not Samaritan, in origin. It is Samaritan practice to write and pronounce ࠄࠓࠂࠓࠉࠆࠉࠌ as one word in Hebrew, and because of this they transliterate the whole name as a unit and do not translate the first word, whenever they are writing in some other language. This statement can be verified from the Aramaic, Arabic, and Greek translations of the Samaritan Torah, and from the surviving fragments of Samaritan Hellenistic texts. In the fragment of the Old Latin under discussion, the

the Hebrew, or represents the original reading of the LXX, in this passage, does not matter.

The third example is the disagreement between the Samaritan Torah and the MT on whether to read ࠁࠇࠓ or ࠉࠁࠇࠓ in Dt XII:5, 11, 14, 18, 21, 26; XIV:23-25; XV:20; XVI:2, 6, 7, 11, 15, 16; XVII:8-10; XVIII:6; XXVI:2; XXXI:11. The usual Samaritan argument is that Mt. Gerizim had already been sanctified by the Patriarchs, and the usual Jewish argument is that the site was still to be chosen. It will be seen, though, that according to the reading of the MT any site at all can be intended. The argument that it must be a new site, not yet identified, is a fallacy. The point is that the location was not given in the revelation of the Torah through Moses, and that the revelation of the choice is to be made by God at some later time, when it might or might not be a site already sanctified by the Patriarchs that is designated. On the other hand, a little reflection will show that any site at all can be intended by the Samaritan reading. The verb can be regarded as being in the past tense because this is natural if the point of reference assumed is the time in the future when the site has been chosen. See also Segal, pp. 87-88, for an argument that leads to a similar conclusion.

We see, then, that there is nothing in the Samaritan Torah that is necessarily unacceptable to Jews, and nothing in the MT that is necessarily unacceptable to Samaritans. It is true that there are instances where the textual disagreements have been used by Jews and Samaritans as props for their tradition of the location of the Temple, but if the Jews had accepted the Samaritan text, and the Samaritans the MT, by the accident of history, then they would not have found any disagreement between the text and their tradition, and would doubtless have been able to use other instances of textual divergence to support their opinion.

We conclude from all the foregoing that just as the compilation of the Pentateuch brought together and combined whatever forms of the book had been current in different parts of the country or amongst different groups, and produced a book acceptable to the whole nation, the final editors acted in the same spirit and as part of the same movement, and chose a wording in crucial places that would suit the bearers of all the variant sub-traditions of the halachah. The Pentateuch in its completed form had to be a unity in spite of its disparate sources, to fulfil its function as the version that would serve and be acceptable to the whole nation as spiritually (though not politically) united. The compilers did manage to turn the parts into a unity, integrating

word הר is translated, not transliterated. Aside from this, this text of the Old Latin tends to agree with the LXX against the Samaritan. Finally, there is no evidence to suggest that any of the fragments of the Old Latin now surviving are Samaritan (although this last statement might well be modified by future research).

the different outlooks of both kingdoms and all groups or movements or traditions, and people capable of such a compilation would have had the ability to choose the precise details of the wording of the halachic passages needed to satisfy the same disparate groups of people, and would have seen the need to do so.[257] The compilers were the ones that integrated the sources, and were the final editors as well. Although the work probably took several generations, the ones that finished it were working in the same spirit as the ones that started it, and were part of the same organization. The compilers, who brought the source-books together, the redactors, who turned them into a unified work, and the final editors, who attended to the details of the wording, must have all had the same purpose: otherwise they would not have needed to touch up the text or alter the texts as they had stood for generations. This is not to deny that the written Torah goes back to time immemorial, or to Moses, depending on the system of terminology: it is simply to say that various books making up the written Torah in different traditions were deliberately combined into one in a form that every Israelite could accept. Rather than suppress or ignore any tradition, the compilers and editors achieved a near-uniformity of wording in the halachic sections, a wording into which could be read (artificially if necessary) the halachah of each tradition. Where uniformity was not reached, the alternatives of wording were either inconsequential and trivial, or were both equally ambiguous, as in Lv XI:25 (see p. 329), or as in the passages discussed above on pp. 338-340. Because of the impossibility of finding an ambiguous wording of historical or chronological statements, existing differences between the source-books would have had to be allowed to stand, so that the final edited written Torah would have had to have several different recensions, according to the source of the historical sections in each case. This would not have been a serious difficulty, since in later times it has always been halachah and basic theology that have divided Israel into sects or religious factions, not disputes over historical details or the chronology of the Patriarchs, and the outlook would presumably have been the same in earlier times. Given the uniformity of wording of the halachic sections, the use of variant recensions of the Torah need not have been regarded any differently than the use of variant orders of synagogue service by different communities in modern times.

We could re-phrase all of this by saying that the Torah will show no contradictions in the *ʿOlam ha-Yiḥud*, but must necessarily manifest itself in contradictory forms in the *ʿOlam ha-Perud*, and that the function of the editors was to devise a text that would be an accurate reflection of the

---

[257] People who could write a book to be read on four levels (פרד״ס) and still be accurate in all details on all of them, could certainly word a sentence to mean so many different specific things but no more, to be precisely ambiguous.

original revelation and all of its subsequent manifestations as well. Such a view, although quite divergent from the usual assumptions on which discussions of these issues are based, would not ultimately (and after any necessary modification) conflict with Jewish tradition, I hope. More work is needed on all this.

6. *The Halachic Texts*

(a) *The Relationship of the Texts to Each Other*

The I'tiqâdât[258] depends mainly on the Kâfi, Ṭubâkh, and Khilâf. In the chapter edited here the influence of the Ṭubâkh is slight, but it is more prominent in the other chapters.

The Khilâf and Farâ'iḍ have a tendency to agree in their halachah, and even more noticeably, to use similar arguments, as can be seen from a careful reading of the commentary on the Farâ'iḍ.[259] The Ṭubâkh and Kâfi have a tendency to agree in their halachah, and again even more noticeably, to use a similar layout and similar arguments, as can be seen by comparing the chapter of the Ṭubâkh edited here with ch. XI of the Kâfi.[260] There is some use of the same arguments in the Ṭubâkh, Kâfi, and Farâ'iḍ: see, in particular, Far 7-14 and the notes there. There is some use of the knowledge of the same arguments in the Ṭubâkh and the Khilâf: see T 26-29 and the notes there. In all the cases mentioned, the impression given is that the relationship between the texts is the result of the use of common sources rather than direct dependence. This impression is confirmed by the fact that there are so few references to different opinions in the texts, even though they disagree so often, and the fact that the relationship between the halachah of the texts is very complicated, since in spite of the tendency of certain ones to agree with each other, in individual instances every possible combination of agreement and disagreement between them will occur.

It is to be noticed that the modern halachah depends on tradition, not literary sources, as we will see in the next section, and that this tradition does not agree completely with any of the earlier halachic texts known to us. It tends to agree with the Kâfi, but in other instances agrees with the Ṭubâkh, Kâshif, or Farâ'iḍ, and in some instances, as in the number of days of uncleanness of a woman that has had a boy baby, disagrees with all of them. The ancient literary representatives of the tradition that is now standard must have perished, and it is not to be imagined that the collected texts we have necessarily contain more than a small fraction of what once existed as separate short pieces, and so it is not surprising that although there are

[258] Commentary on I'tiq 4-67 and 79-92.
[259] See, for example, the Commentary on Far 49-58; 54-56; 59-65.
[260] The similarity extends through the whole of the chapter in each case.

relationships between the extant texts, they do not depend directly on each other.

It is to be noticed that differences in the halachah continued as late as the middle of the eighteenth century, as we see from the fact that the Kâshif and I'tiqâdât do not entirely agree. The most striking example is the case of the method of determining whether a repetition of menstrual bleeding is to be counted as *niddå* or *zåbå*, where there are three separate modern opinions recorded, one the opinion of Musallam bin Marjân, writing in the early eighteenth century, who clearly states that his opinion is in agreement with current standard practice, one the opinion of the author of the Kâshif, writing in the mid eighteenth century, and one of the opinion of the author of the I'tiqâdât, writing in the late nineteenth century. In the early eighteenth century all three opinions and practices must have existed.

The modern standardisation is the result of a long process, and it is truly remarkable how much variation in the halachah there was in earlier centuries. It seems that a gradual accommodation of views has gone on, perhaps starting with the reconciliation of the Dositheans and Sebuaeans, as the disappearance of distinct sectarian divisions would have had to come before the standardisation of the halachah. There is some direct evidence for this reconciliation. In ch. XIII of the Kâfi, at the start of the section edited here, the author very politely argues against an opinion that seems to be Dosithean, and the same politeness in arguing against what seems to be a Dosithean opinion occurs at the end of the interpolation at the end of the chapter of the Khilâf edited here. In the note on Kf ch. XI, 31-32, it is shown that the opinion that it is permissible to acquire artefacts from Gentiles, and the reasoning behind this opinion, were originally Dosithean, but that the modern halachah agrees almost entirely with the Dositheans on this point. The existence of hymns in the standard order of service that are ascribed to الدستان is well-known.[261]

---

[261] Cowley, pp. 69-72, 209, 869; Ben-Ḥayyim vol. III part 2, pp. 280-287.

There is no reason why the term دستان should not mean what it says.

The word *Dustân* in Abu 'l-Fatḥ is a collective noun meaning Dositheans. The singular would be *Dustâni*, and the plural *Dustâniyîn*, and the collective would be formed from the singular and plural. The singular and plural would be a borrowing from an Aramaic ࠃࠎࠕࠍࠉࠀ. (This is an essential point: the grammar of the word has been adapted to Arabic. This point seems to have been generally missed in discussions of the etymology). The Aramaic itself is simply an adaptation of the Greek *Dositheānoi*, with an Aramaic suffix instead of a Greek one.

There is a theological point in these hymns that does not occur elsewhere, as far as I know, in Samaritan literature, and that is the idea that the Sabbath is to be treated as, or perhaps in some way really is, *a place*. This would give a sound theoretical justification for the extreme Dosithean insistence on purity on the Sabbath: if the Sabbath is in some way or other a place, then it is just as holy a place as the Tent of Meeting, and whatever requirements of purity apply to a person who enters one apply to a person who enters the other.

It is true that the modern Samaritans have no tradition that the word Dustân means

This process of standardisation seems to be the explanation for the otherwise inexplicable phenomenon of texts that disagree with each other in their halachah showing signs of the use of a common literary tradition, not usually for polemical purposes, but naturally, as if the sources were common property. The reconciliation between the sects would naturally lead to the study of each other's literature, and even after the sects and sub-divisions of sects had become united, their literature would survive as common Samaritan property. In the later stages of the process, when there were no sectarian divisions but there were still some variations between different halachic traditions, it would probably not have been possible to tell which sect or division of a sect had produced any given work, and the literary influences would then become independent of halachic agreements and disagreements.

(b) *Authority*

The halachic texts seem to possess authority by virtue of the learning and competence of the author. If they contradict tradition or seem to be wrong on any point, they are to be disregarded, as we see from the third marginal note on the Kâfi. If they contradict each other, then one is right and one is wrong, or one agrees with tradition and one does not, as we see from the first and second marginal notes on the Ṭubâkh. *The texts are not canonical.*

Nevertheless, the texts have value as systematic expositions of certain areas of halachah and sources of arguments to justify particular points of halachah and are studied for these reasons. The Iʿtiqâdât uses the earlier texts for these purposes.

The real authority is tradition, as we see from the marginal notes (specially the ones just mentioned), from the lack of concern over the contradictions between one text and another or between one text and the modern tradition, and the references to custom as the criterion for decisions on halachic points, as in T 13 and the other passage listed in the note there, or Kf ch. XIII, 29-30.

The authors of the texts themselves do not claim any authority except as bearers of tradition or interpreters of the text of Scripture, and are often ready to admit that other Samaritans who disagree with their halachah are not necessarily wrong: see, for example, Kh 209-214 of Far 84-86 or Far 97-106.

Dositheans in the ascriptions of these hymns, but this is not a strong argument against the identification. First, because the Samaritans have no tradition at all on what the word means. Second, because the name ad-Dustân is grammatically collective and has the definte article. Third, because no person called Ad-Dustân is known. Fourth, because the modern Samaritans seem to known the Dositheans only as a reference in the histories. Fifth, because other evidence indicates that the Dositheans and the others amalgamated: otherwise, where did the Dositheans go to? Sixth, the coincidence would be too much otherwise. Seventh, the hymns are unique in their theology in at least one respect, as we have seen.

When the authors do reject the halachah of other Samaritans, they do so not by their own authority, but on the strength of whatever arguments they can produce to support their own tradition: see T 26-29 and Kf ch. XIII, 4-18. Exegesis and logic then work together: see Kh 194-196.

The assertion often made, that the Samaritans interpret the text of Scripture literally and then fix their halachah accordingly, has no support from the facts. The Samaritans rely on a tradition of halachah which, just like the Rabbanite one, includes the traditional interpretation of certain terms or verses (שמועה, in Rabbanite terminology), but it is the meaning of the text that is determined by the tradition, and not the tradition by the text. See Kf ch. III, 15-16 for an explicit acknowledgment of this principle. A conclusive example of this principle is the allowance of consecutive weeks of *niddå*, something that is not derivable even by implication from the text of Leviticus ch. XV, and actually goes against the implication of the wording of the text.

Only if tradition does not give any answer at all can a decision be made on the basis of exegesis: see, for example, Kh 165-171 N, and see above, p. 313. On the other hand, if different sub-traditions disagree on a given point, then obviously each will be supported by exegesis, and arguments will be found to refute each opinion as well; but these arguments have no conclusive power to convince anyone except those that put them forward, and if uniformity is achieved, it is by a natural development in general practice, which is then authoritative: see M.N. II.

There is so much left unsaid in the texts that they could never have been meant to be authorities in their own right: and on this, see below.

There is no evidence that the priests have any more authority than any other learned person to state what is the halachah, or to transmit it.

The bearers of tradition are the nation as a whole, as can be seen from the facts set out here. A corollary of this principle is that the fine points of the halachot of *niddå* and related matters are known by the traditional practice of the women in general. This mechanism of transmission is eminently practical. We now see why Samaritans do not need halachic books as Jews do: the nation is itself its own Mishnah and Code!

(c) *Expected Readership and Purpose of the Texts*

The Iʿtiqâdât, being intended for foreigners, is a unique case in Samaritan literature.[262]

The purpose of the Kâshif is self-evident. It is a commentary on the Torah, and though it necessarily treats the halachic sections, it is not primarily a

[262] Introduction, p. 24.

halachic treatise. It is intended as a source of information on the meaning of the text of Scripture.

The Kitâb al-Farâ'iḍ is a halachic treatise. (The nearest Jewish analogy would be the Sefer Hammitsvot Haggadol). It is set out on the lines of a commentary on the sections of the Torah that treat the various commandments, and has both the strengths and weaknesses of such an arrangement. It does cover every area of halachah, but it leaves out a considerable amount of detail within each area, if the matter is not suggested by the text of the Torah, and is not a complete guide to the practical observance of the commandments. An ordinary person could use it as a guide to practice, but would have to get the details from some form of teaching by authorities or by observation. To an expert, its main value would be as a systematic exposition, not as a source of information.

The Kitâb al-Khilâf is a halachic treatise, but as the title shows, it is not intended to be complete but only to cover the areas of halachah on which the Jews disagree with the Samaritans. It is not meant to be read by Jews, but by Samaritans, to give them necessary information on the Jewish halachah and arguments to be used in discussions with Jews, on the lines of דע מה שתשיב. Nevertheless, the author does spread himself, and for the sake of completeness gives information on each particular area of halachah that is not a matter of dispute between Samaritans and Jews. As a source of arguments, it would be useful to experts more than to laymen.

The Ṭubâkh is not primarily a halachic treatise, but a compendium of necessary information, some halachic, some theological, some exegetical, some polemical. It does not cover all areas of halachah, but mainly those that will most commonly affect the ordinary observant Israelite. The items of theology are all essential ones. The items of polemics are such as would need to be presented to any observant person for the sake of showing that the Samaritan tradition has as much validity as the Jewish one, i.e. for the sake of חיזוק אמונה. The book would be valuable for both laymen and experts.

The Kâfi is a halachic treatise. It does not cover all areas of halachah, but it does cover all that would need to be known to any observant person, and a few that would be more the concern of experts on the halachah. It is to be noticed that the Kâfi gives answers to problems that will arise in practice, and accordingly gives much more detail than does the Ṭubâkh. For example, it really would be possible for an Israelite to know whether or not he was in a state of cleanness or uncleanness in foreign territory in most situations after having read ch. XIII.

It will be seen that the Ṭubâkh, Kâfi, and Khilâf between them give nearly all the information on everyday halachah, basic theology, and exegesis of key passages of Scripture that the layman will need, as well as useful insights and arguments for the learned or for the teachers. If any one of these three is less essential than the others, it is the Khilâf, because much of its halachic information is given by the other two, and the longwinded polemical arguments will not be needed by most people.

This evaluation is supported by the distribution of the numbers of manuscripts of the texts. Manuscripts of the Ṭubâkh and Kâfi are plentiful in about equal numbers. Manuscripts of the Khilâf are not as common, but are certainly not rare either. Manuscripts of the Farâ'iḍ are rare, and incomplete.

It seems that the Samaritans have done what the Yemenite Jews did. Being faced with persecution, poverty, and inadequate numbers, they have studied a few books which between them give all the information required for practice and for a complete theology. It seems that books that were useful in themselves, but did not add anything absolutely essential, reflective works such as the Sharḥ Am Baqqūti, or halachic works such as the Kitâb al-Farâ'iḍ (both by Abu 'l-Faraj ibn al-Kaththâr), were not studied or copied because their content was paralleled by other works, and people were probably not able to study more than the minimum essential. The Kitâb al-Farâ'iḍ was duplicated to a great extent by the Ṭubâkh and Kâfi, and the Sharḥ Am Baqqūti by later reflective works. The earlier commentaries on the Torah are subsumed in the Kâshif al-Ghayâhib, except for short pieces on Deuteronomy, which the Kâshif does not cover. Matters not adequately covered in the books that became standard reading are treated in modern short compositions specifically for the purpose, such as the Sharḥ Sûrat al-Irbot.[263]

[263] This is just what the Yemenite Jews did. Most people learnt their halachah from the Mishnah with Maimonides's commentary, and the Mishneh Torah, not the Talmud itself. They learnt Scripture not from the individual midrashim but from the Midrash Haggadol, which gave them essential passages of the Talmud and midrashim. They composed general *musar* books of their own. They did not lose their knowledge of the Talmud, the midrashim, the various Biblical commentaries, and so on, but most people had all they could do to read and learn the Mishnah, the Mishneh Torah, Alfasi, the Midrash Haggadol, and a few *musar* books, and to keep these books safe. In the same way, most Samaritans would have had all they could manage in learning the order of the synagogue service, the Ṭubâkh and Kâfi, the Khilâf, a few eschatological works, one or two chronicles, and at times the commentaries on Genesis, Exodus, and Deuteronomy XXXII.

BIBLIOGRAPHY

I. MANUSCRIPTS

These are listed in the Introduction, pp. 26-47.

II. PRINTED BOOKS (Including Printed Facsimiles of Manuscripts) AND ARTICLES.

Section 1

אברהם אבן עזרא, פירושי התורה, מה' אשר וייזר, ג' כרכים. מוסד הרב קוק, ירושלים, תשל״ו, 1976.

(אברהם אבן עזרא) ספר אבן עזרא מרבנו אברהם בן מאיר אבן עזרא הספרדי ז״ל לספר שמות ... פירוש הקצר ..., מה' יהודה ליב בן ר' יעקב צבי פליישער. וינה, תרפ״ו. הודפס מחדש ע״י הוצאת ציון, תל אביב, תש״ל.

גדליהו אלון, טומאת נכרים, בתוך: מחקרים בתולדות ישראל בימי בית שני ובתקופת המשנה והתלמוד, ב' כרכים. ההסתדרות הכללית של העובדים העברים בארץ־ישראל, הוצאת הקיבוץ המאוחד, תשכ״ז. כרך ראשון, עמ' 121־147.

(אלוני ולוינגר, עיין מדינת ישראל)

א. ז. אשכלי, ספר הפלשים: יהודי חבש, תרבותם ומסורותיהם. ראובן מס, ירושלים, תשל״ג.

יהושע בלאו, דקדוק הערבית־היהודית של ימי הבינים. הוצאת ספרים ע״ש י״ל מאגנס, האוניברסיטה העברית, תשכ״ב, 1961.

מ. א. בלאָך, ספר שערי תורת התקנות, ג' חלקים ב־5 מחברות. וינה ומקומות אחרים , תרל״ט־תרס״ו.

זאב בן חיים, עברית וארמית נוסח שומרון, 5 כרכים ב־ו' חלקים. האקדמיה ללשון העברית, ירושלים, תשי״ז־תשל״ז.

ברייתא דמסכת נדה, מה' חיים מא״ר הורוויץ הלוי, בתוך: ספרי תוספָתא עתיקָתא, 5 חלקים, מגנצא ופראנקפורט על נהר מיין, תרמ״ט־תר״ן, חלק רביעי. הדפסה חדשה בלי מקום ותאריך.

אליהו בשייצי, ספר המצות של היהודים ·הקראים, אדרת אליהו. אודיסה התרל״א. הודפס מחדש ע״י המועצה הארצית של עדת היהודים הקראים בישראל, (רמלה), התשכ״ו.

משה גושן־גוטשטיין וחנן שירון (עורכים), המקרא בתרגום הסורי־ארצישראלי. חלק ראשון: תורה ונביאים. הוצאת ספרים ע״ש י״ל מאגנס, האוניברסיטה העברית, ירושלים, תשל״ג.

אברהם גייגר, קבוצת מאמרים, נעריכת ש. א. פאזנאנסקי. ורשה תר״ע. הודפס מחדש ע״י ״לסטודנט״, בית ההוצאה של אגודת הסטודנטים במכון האוניברסיטאי של חיפה, תשכ״ז, במהדורת מוגבלת.

אברהם גייגר, המקרא ותרגומיו בזיקתם להתפתחותה הפנימית של היהדות. מוסד הרב קוק, ירושלים, תש״ט. (תירגום מספרו *Urschrift und Übersetzungen der Bibel in ihrer Abhängigkeit von den innern Entwicklung des Judenthums*, 1857, מהדורה שניה, וינה, 1928)

משה גינזבורגר (עורך), תרגום יונתן בן עוזיאל על התורה. ברלין תרס״ג. הודפס מחדש ע״י הוצאת מקור, ירושלים, תשל״ד, 1974.

נפתלי יוסף דירינבורג (עורך), תרגום חמשה חומשי תורה בלשון ערבית לרבינו סעדיה גאון בן יוסף הפיומי. פאריס, תרנ״ג. *Version Arabe du Pentateuque de R. Saadia ben Iosef al-Fayyoûmî, revue, corrigée, et accompagnée de notes hébraïques, avec quelques fragments de traduction française d'après l'arabe*, par J. Dérenbourg. Saadia Ben Josef Al-Fayyoûmî, *Œuvres Complètes publiées sous la direction de J. Dérenbourg*: הדפסה חדשה. 5 Bande in 2 Bänden. I: Band 1 [und] 3. Georg Olms Verlag, הילדסהיים ונין יורק, 1979.

יהודה בן אליהו הדסי, ספר אשכל הכפר. גוזלוו, התרקצ״ו. הדפסה חדשה, בלי מקום ותאריך. (הוצאת מקור, ירושלים).

ד. צ. הופמן, ספר ויקרא מפורש, ב' כרכים. הדפסה רביעית. מוסד הרב קוק, ירושלים, תשל״ב. (ספרית יעקב מיכאל, א').

א. ש. הלקין, תרי״ג מצוות אצל השומרונים, בתוך: ספר זכרון לכבוד פרופ' יצחק יהודה גולדציהר ז״ל, חלק שני. ראובן מס, ירושלים, תשי״ח. עמ' 86־100.

אברהם הרכבי (עורך), זכרון לראשונים, מחברת שמינית: והוא חלק שני מספר לקוטי קדמוניות לקורות דת בני מקרא וספרותם. השריד והפליט מספרי המצוות הראשונים לבני מקרא: לענן הנשיא, בנימין

נהאונדי ודניאל אלקומסי. פעטערבורג, תרס״ג. הודפס מחדש ע״י הוצאת מקור, ירושלים, בלי תאריך.

חומש תורה שלמה, בעריכת מנחם מ. כשר. חלק שלשים: פרשת תזריע ופרשת מצורע. הוצאת בית תורה שלמה, ירושלים, תשל״ט.

חמשה חומשי תורה רב פנינים, 5 כרכים. לוין־אפשטיין, ירושלים, תשכ״ד.

יגאל ידין (עורך), מגילת המקדש, ג׳ כרכים. החברה לחקירת ארץ ישראל ועתיקותיה, והמכון לארכיאולוגיה של האוניברסיטה העברית, והיכל הספר, ירושלים, תשל״ג.

ילקוט שמעוני ... לר׳ שמעון ... מפראנקפורט דמיין, ב׳ כרכים. ווארשא תרל״ו. הודפס מחדש ע״י פרדס, ניו יורק, בלי תאריך.

כתבא קדישא ה: דיתקא עתיקתא. (המקרא בתרגום הפשיטתא). אורמיא 1852. הדפסה חדשה, לונדון, 1954.

מדינת ישראל. משרד החינוך והתרבות. המכון לכתבי־היד העבריים. רשימת תצלומי כתבי־היד העבריים במכון. חלק א: כה״י בספריות אוסטריה וגרמניה, מאת נ. אלוני וד. ש. לוינגר. מוסף לכתב העת בחינוך ובתרבות, ירושלים, תשי״ז.

שלמה מאנדלקרן, קונקורדנציה לתנ״ך, מה׳ שביעית עם... ההוספות של מ. גושן־גוטשטיין ופ. מרגולין. הוצאת שוקן, ירושלים ותל־אביב, תשכ״ז.

מדרש הגדול על חמשה חומשי תורה, חיברו רבי דוד ב״ר עמרם העדני. ספר ויקרא, בעריכת עדין שטיינזלץ, תשל״ו, 1975. ספר דברים, בעריכת שלמה פיש, תשל״ג, 1972. מוסד הרב קוק, ירושלים

ע. צ. מלמד (עורך), ספר האונומאסטיקון לאבסביוס. תרביץ, כרך י״ט, 1948, עמ׳ 65־88; 129־152; כרך כ״א, 1949־1950, עמ׳ 1־24; 65־91. (גם הופיע בהוצאה נפרדת, ע״י ישיבת שערי רחמים, ירושלים, תשכ״ו)

משה בן מימון, משנה תורה הוא היד החזקה, ע״פ דפוס ויניציאה של״ד־של״ו. מנוקד עם השגות הראב״ד פירוש מאת ... דוד בן ... עמרם עראמה. ח׳ כרכים. הוצאת שלימות, ירושלים ותל־אביב, תשכ״ו.

משנה עם פירוש רבינו משה בן מימון, מקור ותרגום, מה׳ יוסף קאפח, ו׳ כרכים. מוסד הרב קוק, ירושלים, תשכ״ט.

משנה עם פירוש ... עובדיה מברטנורה ועם ... עיקר תוספות יום טוב, ב׳ כרכים. הוצאת משניות, תל אביב וירושלים, תשי״ט.

(משנה: עיין גם ששה סדרי משנה)

אהרן בן אליהו ניקומודיאו, ספר המצוות הגדול גן עדן. גוזלווא, התרכ״ד. הודפס מחדש ע״י המועצה העליונה ליהודים הקראים בישראל, (רמלה), התשל״ג, 1972.

אהרן בן אליהו ניקומדיאו, ספר כתר תורה. גוזולווא, התרכ״ז. הדפסה חדשה, רמלה, התשל״ב, 1972.

(סעדיא גאון: עיין דירינבורג)

(ענן בן דוד: עיין הרכבי)

אברהם עפשטיין, כתבים, נקבצו ... ע״י א. מ. הברמן. מוסד ה הרב קוק, ירושלים, הדפסה שניה, תשכ״ה.

פרקי רבי אליעזר מהתנא רבי אליעזר הגדול בן הורקנוס עם ביאור הרד״ל דוד לוריא, ווארשא, תרי״ב. הודפס מחדש ע״י הוצאת אום, ניו יורק, תש״ו.

אברהם ורצון צדקה (עורכים), חמשה חומשי תורה, נוסח יהודי ונוסח שומרוני, עם הדגשה של השינויים בין שתי הנוסחאות, לפי כתב־יד שומרוני מן המאה ה 11. תל־אביב, תשכ״ג 1962־ תשכ״ו 1966, שנת ג׳ אלפים ווק (3600) מנין שומרוני.

משה צוקר, על תרגום רס״ג לתורה: פרשנות הלכה ופולימה בתרגום התורה של ר׳ סעדיה גאון. הוצאת פעלדהיים, ניו יורק, תש״ט.

יוסף קאפח, פירושי רבינו סעדיה גאון על התורה. מוסד הרב קוק, ירושלים, תשכ״ג.

רפאל קירכהיים, כרמי שומרון: פתיחה למסכת כותים. פראנקפורט, תרי״א. הודפס מחדש ע״י הוצאת קדם, ירושלים, תש״ל.

רפאל קירכהיים (עורך), שבע מסכתות קטנות ירושלמיות. פראנקפורט תרי״א. הודפס מחדש ע״י הוצאת קדם, ירושלים, תש״ל.

חסיב שחאדה, התרגום הערבי של השומרונים לתורה. תרביץ, שנה נב, תשמ״ג, עמ׳ 59־82.

ששה סדרי משנה, מפורשים בידי חנוך אלבק, ומנוקדים בידי חנוך ילון, ו׳ כרכים. מוסד ביאליק, ודביר, תל־אביב, תשל״ב.

תוספתא, מה׳ משה שמואל צוקרמאנדל. פאזעוואלק, תר״מ, והוספה, טריר, תרמ״ב. הודפס מחדש ע״י ספרי ואהרמן, ירושלים, תשכ״ם.

ספר התורה: א. המקור, ב. תרגום ערבי, ג. תרגום ארמי (הנוסח השומרוני). תצלום כתב היד של המאה הי״ג [ווטיקן־ Barberini 1] הדפים החסרים הושלמו בצילום מתוך כ״י של המאה הי״ג־הי״ד [בריטיש מוזאון .OR]. חולון, ג׳ תר״ה למושב בני ישראל לארץ כנען, י״ט למדינת ישראל, 1967.

תורה נביאים וכתובים מדויקים היטב על פי הניקוד הטעמים והמסורה של אהרן בן משה בן מאיר בכתב יד לנינגרד, בידי אהדן דותן. הוצאת עדי, תל־אביב, בשיתוף עם בית הספר למדעי היהדות של אוניברסיטת תל־אביב. בלי תאריך.

(תודה: עיין צדקה)
(תורה שלמה: עיין חומש תורה שלמה)
תלמוד בבלי, מנוקד ומבואר ע״י הרב עדין שטיינזלץ. המכון הישראלי לפרסומים תלמודיים, ירושלים, תשכ״ח, 1968, ואילך.
תלמוד בבלי, עם כל המפרשים ... י״ב כרכים. ירושלים, בלי תאריך. (כנראה תצלום של אחת ממהדורות ראָם, בווילנא).
תלמוד ירושלמי, נדפס בבית דניאל בומבירגי ... ויניציאה רפ״ג. הודפס מחדש ע״י הוצאת מעשה רוקח, בלי מקום ותאריך.
תלמוד ירושלמי או תלמוד המערב, ויש קורין לו תלמוד ארץ ישראל, ח׳ כרכים. מכון חתם סופר, ירושלים, בלי תאריך.
(תרגים יונתן על התורה: עיין גינזבורגר)
תרגום שומרוני על התורה, בעריכת אלחנן ברילל. *Das samaritanische Targum zum Pentateuch*, ed. Adolf Brüll פראנקפורט על נהר מיין, התרל״ו. הודפס מחדש ע״י Georg Olms, הילדסהיים וניו יורק, 1971.

Section 2

(Abû Isḥâq Ibrâhîm: see Pohl).
(Abulfatḥ: see Vilmar).
[Adler, E. N.], *Catalogue of Hebrew Manuscripts in the Collection of Elkan Nathan Adler*, Cambridge, 1921.
Adler, E. N. and M. Séligsohn [eds.], "Une nouvelle chronique samaritaine", Revue des études juives 44 (1902), 188-222; 45 (1902), 70-98; 233-254; 46 (1903), 123-146. (Appeared also as a monograph, Paris, 1903).

(Barton, W. E.: see Yḁ:qob bin Ḁrron).
[Ben-Ḥayyim, Ze'ev], *Preliminary Handlist of Samaritan MSS. in the Semitic Museum Collection* [of Harvard University] (*based on rough notes by Professor Z. Ben-Hayyim*). [Unpublished, n.d.].
(Ben Kori, Abdullah: see Yḁ:qob bin Ḁrron).
The Bible in Aramaic, Based on Old Manuscripts and Printed Texts, ed. Alexander Sperber. *Volume I: The Pentateuch according to Targum Onkelos*, E. J. Brill, Leiden, 1959.
Biblia Sacra iuxta Vulgatam Versionem, ed. Robertus Weber et. al., 2 vols., Würtembergische Bibelanstalt, Stuttgart, 1969.
Biblia Sacra juxta Versionem Simplicem quae dicitur Pschitta, 2 vols., Imprimerie Catholique, Beirut, 1951. [Reprint of the Mosul ed. of 1887-1891].
Bloch, Josef, *Die samaritanisch-arabische Pentateuchübersetzung Deuteronomium I-XI mit Einleitung und Noten. Inaugural-Dissertation zur Erlangung der Doktorwürde eingereicht bei der Hohen Philosophischen Facultät der Kaiser-Wilhelms-Universität zu Strassburg*, Berlin, 1901.
[Bodleian Library. Summary of an unpublished list of the Samaritan mss. in the Library that are not mentioned in any printed catalogue. Private communication from the Librarian dated 12/6/1974].
[Bodleian Library. The original of the summary just mentioned. No title (in my copy), n.d.].
Bóid, Ruairidh, *The Text of Isaiah I-XXXV in the Talmudim and Midrashim*. [Thesis for degree of M.A. Hons., Sydney Univ., 1972]. Reprinted Jerusalem 1973.
Bóid, Ruairidh, *Catalogue of the Microfilms of Samaritan Manuscripts and Printed Books Relating to the Samaritans in Melbourne University Library*. 1974. [Catalogue of a substantial collection of microfilms not mentioned or appearing in any way in the Library's general catalogue]. Sydney 1975.
Bowman, John [translator and ed.], *Samaritan Documents Relating to their History, Religion and Life*. The Pickwick Press, Pittsburgh, Pennsylvania, 1977.
Bowman, John, and Shemaryahu Talmon, "Samaritan Decalogue Inscriptions", Bulletin of the John Rylands Library 33 (1951), 211-236.
Brown, F., S. R. Driver, and C. A. Briggs, *A Hebrew and English Lexicon of the Old Testament*, Oxford, 1907. Reprinted 1959.

Büchler, Adolph, *Types of Jewish-Palestinian Piety from 70 B.C.E. to 70 C.E.*, London, 1922. Reprinted 1969 by Gregg International Publishers Limited, Westmead, England.

Cohn, Naphtali, *Die Vorschriften betreffend die Zarâath nach dem Kitâb al-Kâfi. Ein Beitrag zur Pentateuchexegese und Dogmatik der Samaritaner. Inaugural-Dissertation zur Erlangung der Doktorwürde der hohen philosophischen Fakultät der Friedrich-Alexanders-Universität Erlangen*, Kirchhain N.L., 1898.

Cohn, Naphtali, *Die Zarâath-Gesetze der Bibel nach dem Kitâb al-kâfi des Jûsuf ibn Salâmah. Ein Beitrag zur Pentateuchexegese und Dogmatik der Samaritaner. Nach Hdschrn. der Deutschen Morgenländischen Gesellschaft zu Halle und des Brit. Mus. zu London herausgegeben und mit einer Einleitung und Anmerkungen versehen*, Frankfurt on Main, 1899.

[Cornell University Library. Unpublished catalogue of the Oriental mss. No title (in my copy), no author, n.d.].

Cowley, A. E. [ed.], *The Samaritan Liturgy*, 2 vols. Oxford, 1909.

Cureton, William, and Charles Rieu, *Catalogus Codicum Manuscriptorum Orientalium qui in Museo Britannico Asservantur. Pars Secunda, Codices Arabicos Complectens*, London, 1871.

Dozy, R., *Supplément aux dictionnaires arabes*, Leiden, 1881. Reprinted by the Librairie du Liban, Beirut, 1968.

Drabkin, Abrahamus, *Fragmenta Commentarii ad Pentateuchum Samaritano-Arabici Sex*, Leipzig, 1875.

Fagnan, E., *Additions aux dictionnaires arabes*, Librairie du Liban, Beirut, n.d.

Fleischer, H. L., *Studien über Dozy's Supplément aux Dictionnaires arabes*, in his *Kleinere Schriften*, 1885-1888, reprinted by Biblio-Verlag, Osnabrück, 1968, vol. II, part 1, pp. 470-781; vol. III, pp. 1-102. (Appeared also in Berichten über die Verhandlungen der Königlichen Sächsischen Gesellschaft der Wissenschaften, Philologisch-historische Classe, 1863, 93-176; 1882, 1-56; 1884, 1-80; 1885, 346-410; 1886, 28-92; 156-214; 1887, 171-212).

[Fraser, J. G., An unpublished list of the Samaritan mss. in the British Library that are not mentioned in any printed catalogue].

[Fraser, J. G., An unpublished list of the Samaritan mss. in the Bodleian Library at Oxford that are not mentioned in any printed catalogue].

[Fraser, J. G., An unpublished list of the Samaritan mss. in the French National Library in Paris that are not mentioned in any printed catalogue].

Fraser, J. G., "Documents from a Samaritan Genizah in Damascus", Palestine Exploration Quarterly 103 (1971), 85-92.

[Freiherr] von Gall, August [ed.], *Der Hebräische Pentateuch der Samaritaner*, Walter de Gruyter, Giessen 1918, Berlin 1966.

Gaster, Moses, *The Samaritan Law and Oral Traditions: Vol. I* [all published]: *Samaritan Eschatology*, The Search Publishing Company, n.p., 1932.

Gaster, Moses, "The Samaritan Literature", in: *The Encyclopaedia of Islam*, vol. IV, Leyden and London, 1934. [Separately paginated].

Geiger, Abraham, *Was hat Mohammed aus dem Judenthume aufgenommen?*, Baden 1833, Leipzig 1902. Reprinted by Biblio-Verlag, Osnabrück, 1971.

Abraham Geiger's Nachgelassene Schriften, ed. Ludwig Geiger, 5 vols., Berlin, 1875-1878.

Ginzberg, Louis, *An Unknown Jewish Sect, The Jewish Theological Seminary of America*, New York, 5736, 1976. (Translation and expansion of *Eine Unbekannte Jüdische Sekte*, New York, 1922; which also appeared in the Monatsschrift für Geschichte und Wissenschaft des Judentums LV-LVIII (1911-1914).

Goldziher, Ignaz, "Lā Misāsa", Revue Africaine no. 268 (1908), 23-28.

Halkin, A. S., "Samaritan Polemics against the Jews", Proceedings of the American Academy for Jewish Research VII (1935-1936) 13-59.

Halkin, A. S., "The Relation of the Samaritans to Saadia Gaon", in: The American Academy for Jewish Research, *Texts and Studies, Vol. II, Saadia Anniversary Volume*, New York, 1943, 271-325.

Hanover, Siegmund, *Das Fesgesetz der Samaritaner nach Ibrâhîm ibn Ja'ḳûb. Edition und Uebersetzung seiner Kommentare zu Lev. 23 nebst Einleitung und Anmerkungen*, Berlin, 1904.

Hava, J. G., الفرائد الدريه عربي – انكليزي. *Al-Faraid. Arabic-English Dictionary*, 3rd printing, Dar al-Mashriq, Beirut, 1970.

Heller, Bernhard, "Al-Sāmirī", in: *The Encyclopaedia of Islam*, vol. IV, Leyden and London, 1934, 135-136.

Hirsch, S. R., *The Pentateuch, Translated and Explained...... rendered into English by Isaac Levy. 2nd edition (completely revised)*, 5 vols. in 6 parts, Judaica Press Ltd., Gateshead, England, 1973.

Isser, S. J., *The Dositheans: a Samaritan Sect in Late Antiquity*, E. J. Brill, Leiden, 1976. (Studies in Judaism in Late Antiquity, XVII).

Jastrow, Marcus, *A Dictionary of the Targumim, the Talmud Babli and Yerushalmi, and the Midrashic Literature*, 2 vols, Pardes Publishing House, New York, n.d. [1950].

[Jewish National and University Library. An unpublished handlist of the Samaritan manuscripts. No title (in my copy), no author, n.d.].

[Jewish Theological Seminary of America. An unpublished handlist of the manuscripts in the Sulzberger Collection. No title (in my copy), no author, n.d.].

(Josephus: see Thackeray et al.).

Juynboll, T. G. J., *Chronicum Samaritanum, Arabice conscriptum, cui titulus est Liber Josuae*, Leiden, 1848.

Klumel, Meier, *Mischpâtîm. Ein samaritanisch-arabischer Commentar zu Ex. 21-22, 15 von Ibrâhîm Ibn Jakûb. Nach einer Berliner Handschrift herausgegeben und mit einer Einleitung und Anmerkungen versehen. Inaugural-Dissertation zur Erlangung der Doktorwürde der philosophischen Fakultät der Kaiser-Wilhelms-Universität zu Strassburg*, Berlin, 1902.

Kuenen, A. [ed.], *Libri Exodi et Levitici secundum Arabicam Pentateuchi Samaritani Versionem ab Abū-Sa:īdo Conscriptam*, Leiden, 1854.

Lane, E. W. [and S. Lane-Poole], *An Arabic-English Lexicon*, 8 vols, London and Edinburgh, 1863-1893. Reprinted by the Librairie du Liban, Beirut, 1968.

Le Moyne, Jean, *Les Sadducéens*, Librairie Lecoffre, J. Gabalda & Cie, Paris, 1972.

Lehmann, Manfred R., "The Temple Scroll as a Source of Sectarian Halakhah", Revue de Qumran IX (1978), 579-587.

Leslau, Wolf, *Coutumes et Croyances des Falachas (Juifs d'Abyssinie)*, Institut d'Ethnologie, Paris, 1957. (Travaux et Mémoires de l'Institut d'Ethnologie de l'Université de Paris, LXI).

Leslau, Wolf, *Falasha Anthology*. Schocken Books, New York, 1969.

Loewe, Herbert, *Catalogue of the Printed Books and of the Semitic and Jewish MSS in the Mary Frere Hebrew Library at Girton College, Cambridge*, Girton College, Cambridge, 1916.

Lowy, S., *The Principles of Samaritan Bible Exegesis*. E. J. Brill, Leiden, 1977. (Studia Post-Biblica, XXVIII).

Macdonald, John, *The Theology of the Samaritans*, SCM Press, London, 1964.

Margoliouth, George, *Descriptive List of the Hebrew and Samaritan Manuscripts in the British Museum*, London, 1893.

Mendelsohn, *Catalog of Semitic Manuscripts* [in Columbia University Library]. [Unpublished; full name of author not given in my copy; no date in my copy].

Mills, John, *Three Months' Residence at Nablus, and an Account of the Modern Samaritans*, London, 1864.

Montgomery, J. A., *The Samaritans: The Earliest Jewish Sect*, Philadelphia, 1907. Reprinted by Ktav, New York, n.d. [1968].

Nemoy, Leon, "Al-Qirqisānī's Account of the Jewish Sects", Hebrew Union College Annual VII (1930), 317-398.
Nemoy, Leon [ed.], *Kitāb al-Anwār wal-Marāqib. Code of Karaite Law by Ya'qūb al-Qirqisānī*, The Alexander Kohut Memorial Foundation, New York. Vol. I, 1939; vol. II, 1940; vol. III, 1941; vol. IV, 1942; vol. V, 1943.
Nemoy, Leon, [occasional notes on Abu 'l-Fatḥ, quoted by Isser].
Neubauer, M. A. [ed.], "Chronique samaritaine", Journal Asiatique, December 1869, 385-470.
Nicoll, Alexander, *Bibliothecae Bodleianae codicum manuscriptorum orientalium catalogi. Partis secundae volumen primum, Arabicos complectens*, Oxford, 1821.
Noja, Sergio [translator], *Il Kitāb al-Kāfī dei Samaritani*, Istituto Orientale di Napoli, Naples, 1970. (Also appeared in Annali dell'Istituto Orientale di Napoli, new series, XVIII (1968), 253-288; XIX (1969), 17-44; 333-360; XX (1970), 167-207; 447-481).

The Old Testament in Greek. Vol. I, part II: Exodus and Leviticus, ed. A. E. Brooke and N. McLean, Cambridge, 1909.
The Old Testament in Syriac, according to the Peshitta Version. Edited on behalf of the International Organisation for the Study of the Old Testament by the Peshitta Institute, Leiden. Vol. I, fascicle 1: Genesis-Exodus, E. J. Brill, Leiden, 1977.

Payne Smith, J., *A Compendious Syriac Dictionary, Founded upon the Thesaurus Syriacus of R. Payne Smith*, Oxford U.P., 1903. Reprinted 1957.
Pearson, J. D., *Oriental Manuscripts in Europe and North America*, Zug 1971. (Bibliotheca Asiatica, VII).
Petermann, Heinrich, "Samaria und die Samaritaner", in: *Realencyclopädie für protestantischer Theologie und Kirche*, 1st ed., 1860, vol. XIII.
Petermann, Heinrich, *Reisen im Orient*, 2nd ed., 2 vols., Leipzig, 1865. Reprinted in one vol. by Philo Press, Amsterdam, 1976.
Pohl, Heinz, *Kitāb al-Mīrāṯ. Das Buch der Erbschaft des Samaritaners Abū Isḥāq Ibrāhīm. Kritische Edition mit Übersetzung und Kommentar*, Walter de Gruyter, Berlin, 1974. (Studia Samaritana, II).
Purvis, James D., *A Brief Catalogue of the Materials in the William E. Barton Collection, Special Collections Division, Mugar Library, Boston University*. 1969. [Unpublished].

(Qirqisâni: see Nemoy).

Rabin, Chaim, *The Zadokite Documents. I. The Admonition. II. The Laws. Edited with a Translation and Notes. Second revised edition*, Oxford U.P., 1958.
Revel, Bernard, "The Karaite Halakah and its Relation to Sadducean, Samaritan and Philonian Halakah, Part I" [all published], Jewish Quarterly Review, new series, II (1911), 517-544; III (1912-1913), 337-396. (Also appeared as a monograph, Philadelphia, 1913. Reprinted in *Karaite Studies*, ed. Philip Birnbaum, Hermon Press, New York, 1971, unnumbered leaf + pp. 1-88).
Robertson, Edward, *Catalogue of the Samaritan Manuscripts in the John Rylands Library, Manchester*, vol. I, Manchester, 1938; vol. II, 1962.
Robertson, Edward, "Ibrahim Al-ʿAyyah: A Samaritan Scholar of the Eighteenth Century", in: *Essays in Honour of the Very Rev. Dr. J. H. Hertz on the Occasion of his Seventieth Birthday*, ed. I. Epstein, E. Levine, and C. Roth, London, 1944, 341-350.
Roth, Cecil, *A History of the Marranos*, 4th ed., Schocken Books, New York, 1974.

Sassoon, D. S., *Ohel David: A Descriptive Catalogue of the Hebrew and Samaritan Manuscripts in the Sassoon Library*, London, 1932.
Scanlon, Lee, [translations of extracts from Abu 'l-Fatḥ, reproduced by Isser].
Segal, M. Z., *The Composition of the Pentateuch and Other Biblical Essays*. Jerusalem, The Magnes Press, 1972.
Septuaginta. *Vetus Testamentum Graecum. Auctoritate Academiae Scientiarum Gottingensis*

editum, Vandenhoeck & Ruprecht, Göttingen. Vol. I, Genesis, ed. J. W. Wevers, 1974; vol. III: 1, Numbers, ed. J. W. Wevers and U. Quast, 1982; vol. III: 2, Deuteronomy, ed. J. W. Wevers, 1977.

Septuaginta: Id est Vetus Testamentum graece iuxta LXX interpretes, edidit Alfred Rahlfs. Editio Septima, Würtembergische Bibelanstalt, Stuttgart, 1935. Reprinted 1962.

Shehadeh, Haseeb J., *The Arabic Translation of the Samaritan Pentateuch — Prolegomena to a Critical Edition.* [Doctoral thesis at the Hebrew University, approved 1978. See also section I of this Bibliography].

Shunnar, Zuhair, *Katalog Samaritanischer Handschriften I*, Verlag Richard Seitz & Co., West Berlin, 1974.

[Baron] Silvestre de Sacy, [Antoine], *Chrestomathie Arabe, Tome Ier*, 2nd ed., Paris, 1826.

Simpson, D. C. [ed.], *Tobit*, in: *The Apocrypha and Pseudepigrapha of the Old Testament in English ... Edited in Conjunction with many Scholars by R. H. Charles.* Vol. I, Apocrypha, Oxford U.P., 1913. Reprinted 1976.

Thackeray, H. St. J., R. Marcus, and I. H. Feldman [eds.], *Josephus*, [*Works*] *in Nine Volumes.* [The Loeb Classical Library], William Heinemann Ltd., London, and Harvard University Press, 1926-1965 and reprinted.

[Baron] de Slane, Mac Guckin, *Bibliothèque Nationale: Catalogue des manuscrits arabes*, Paris, 1883-1895.

(Tobit: see Simpson).

Vilmar, Eduardus [ed.], *Abulfathi Annales Samaritani*, Gotha, 1865.

Vilsker, L. H., *Manuel d'Araméen samaritain*, Editions du Centre Nationale de la recherche scientifique, Paris, 1981.

Wehr, Hans, *Verzeichnis der Arabischen Handschriften in der Bibliothek der Deutschen Morgenländischen Gesellschaft*, Deutsche Morgenländische Gesellschaft, Leipzig, 1940. Reprinted by Kraus Reprint Ltd., Nendeln, Liechtenstein, 1966. (Abhandlungen für die Kunde des Morgenlandes, XXV: 3).

Wehr, Hans, *A Dictionary of Modern Written Arabic*, ed. J. Milton Cowan, Wiesbaden: Otto Harassowitz, London: George Allen and Unwin Ltd., 1966.

Weis, P. R., "Abū'l-Ḥasan Al-Ṣūrī's Discourse on the Rules of Leprosy in the Kitāb Al-Ṭabbākh, Rylands Samaritan Codex IX", Bulletin of the John Rylands Library 33 (1950), 131-137.

Wilkinson, John, *Jerusalem Pilgrims before the Crusades*, Warminster, 1977.

Wreschner, Leopold, *Samaritanische Traditionen, mitgeteilt und nach ihrer geschichtlichen Entwickelung untersucht. Inaugural-Dissertation zur Erlangung der philosophischen Doctorwürde bei der hochloblichen philosophischen Facultät der Kgl. Preussischen vereinigten Friedrichs-Universität Halle-Wittenberg*, Halle, 1888.

Wright, W., W. Roberton Smith, and M. J. de Goeje, *A Grammar of the Arabic Language*, 2 vols, Cambridge, 1874. Reprinted by Cambridge U.P., 1962.

[Yå:qob bin Årron], "The History and Religion of the Samaritans, [translated by Abdullah Ben Kori], with an Introduction by W. E. Barton", Bibliotheca Sacra 63 (1906), 385-426. (Appeared also as a monograph, Oak Park, Illinois, 1906). [= ch. I of the Kitâb al-Iʿtiqâdât, according to the recension of Yå:qob bin Årron].

[Yå:qob bin Årron], "Mount Gerizim, the One True Sanctuary. Translated from the Arabic by Abdullah Ben Kori. Edited by W. E. Barton", Bibliotheca Sacra 64 (1907), 489-519. (Appeared also as a monograph, Oak Park, Illinois, 1907). [= ch. II of the Kitâb al-Iʿtiqâdât, according to the recension of Yå:qob bin Årron].

[Yå:qob bin Årron], "The Samaritan Sabbath. Translated by Abdullah Ben Kori. Edited by W. E. Barton", Bibliotheca Sacra 65, (1908), 430-444. [= ch. III of the Kitâb al-Iʿtiqâdât, according to the recension of Yå:qob bin Årron].

[Yå:qob bin Årron], "Circumcision among the Samaritans. Translated by Abdullah Ben Kori. Edited by W. E. Barton", Bibliotheca Sacra 65, (1908), 694-710. [= ch. IV of the Kitâb al-Iʿtiqâdât, according to the recension of Yå:qob bin Årron].

[Yå:qob bin Ārron, Ch. X of the Kitâb al-I'tiqâdât, published in translation by Moses Gaster in: *The Samaritan Oral Law and Ancient Traditions: Vol. I: Samaritan Eschatology*, The Search Publishing Company, n.p., 1932, pp. 129-187].
(Ya'qûb bin Hârûn: see Yå:qob bin Ārron).

Zettersteen, K. V., *Die Arabischen, Persischen, und Türkischen Handschriften der Universitätsbibliothek zu Uppsala*, Uppsala, 1930.
Zotenberg, H., *Catalogue des Manuscrits hébreux et samaritains de la Bibliothèque Impériale*, Paris, 1866.

INDEXES

(See also p. 20 and p. 285)

I. The Torah

Gn I:1-2 152, 241
II:2 337
IV:8 337
IV:12 160, 191
IV:14 160
IV:16 191
X:4 337, 338
X:19 338
XV:21 337
XXI:10 142
XXIV:11 142
XXXIV:25 152
XL:20 152
Ex II:23 142, 175, 206-207
XII:40 337
XXV:29 59
XXIX:21 339
XXX 339
Lv XI:5 329
XI:25 341
XII 143-308 *passim*
XII:2-5 335
XII:4-5 329
XV 143-308 *passim*
XV:16 333
XV:19 332, 335
XV:20 332, 335
XV:24 333, 335
XV:25 335
XV:28 335
XX:16 304
XX:18 144, 162, 163, 169, 174, 198, 278, 286, 287, 332
XXIII:11, 15 332-333
XXIII:18 257
XXIII:32 167, 257
XXXVI:16 160
Nu V:2-3 148, 217-218, 223, 326
VIII:19 177
XV:39 156,248
XIX 247-248, 334-335
XIX:12-19 335
XIX:22 224
XXXI:22-23 155
Dt X:8 142
X:16 156
XII:5, 11, 14, 18, 21, 26 340
XV:20 340
XVI:2, 6, 7, 11, 15, 16 340
XVII:8 159, 164, 191, 340
XVII:9-10 340
XVIII:6 340
XXIII:11 151, 304
XXIII:12 151
XXVI:2 340
XXVII:4 338, 339-340
XXXI:11 340

II. Minor Samaritan Sources

Abu 'l-Fatḥ
History
82:6-8 204
161:14-15 200
162:1-3 227-230
162:4-5 324
162:5 258
163:7 243, 324
Arabic Book of Joshua
ch. 47 end 228
Arabic translation of the Torah
Gn I:2 241
Lv XII 198
Nu V:2-3 217-218
Catechism
Paris ms. pp. 74-81 272
Kitab al-Farâ'iḍ
ch. CV 227-228, 243, 334
Fatâwa
Fatwa by Yaʿqûb bin Hârun
in JNUL Ms. Sam. 8 Octavo 6 56-57
Fatwa in Ms. P of the Kafi 245
Gaster's questionnaires 246
Kâshif al-Ghayâhib
on Nu V:2-3 217-218
on Nu XIX 243, 334

Kitâb al-Iʿtiqâdât
ch. X 243
Kitâb al-Kâfi
ch. III 272
ch. X 241
ch. XIII 210, 225-226, 227, 239-240, 243
Marginal Note
in Ms. U of the Khilâf 250
Targum
on Lv XII 138
on Nu V:2-3 217-218
Kitâb aṭ-Ṭubâkh
on the Red Heifer 243

III. Jewish Sources

GENERAL

Ezekiel
XLIV:26 324
IV Ezra 332
Peshitta
Lv XXIII:11, 15 332
Syro-Palestinian Version
Lv XII:4-5 209
Targum Yonatan
Nu XIX:14 325
Tobit
ch. II 321-322, 324

KARAITES

ʿAnan
Book of Commandments ed. Harkavy
p. 42 256
Adderet Eliyahu
102b 217
120c 215
120c 318
120d 219, 223
121a 319, 333
121abcd 319-320
122a 213, 254, 257, 259, 263
122b 210
122c 324
123b 320, 323
123d-124a 203, 211, 277, 321
124a 319
ch. X 200
ch. XI 199, 321
ch. XII 318, 323
ch. XIII 319
Eshkol Hakkofer
ch. 97 228-229
ch. 290 325
ch. 291 325
Dâwûd bin Marwân
228-229
Gan ʿEden
108b 215, 219
108c 217
108d 223
109c 318
110d-111a 320
110d 213, 254, 257, 263
111 264
112a 319
112b 256
112c 317, 320
113 199
113b 203
114a 318
114b 211, 277, 321
115c 319
ch. IV 318
ch. VII 321
ch. VIII 320, 323
ch. IX 318, 323
Keter Torah
on Lv XII:4 277
on Lv XII:4-5 323
on Nu V:2-3 326
on Nu XXXI:23 246
32d 320
Al-Qirqisâni
Kitab al-Anwâr wa-'l-Marâqib
tr Nemoy p. 36 229
X:50:1 263

RABBANITES

Baraita Dennidah
(Baraita Demassechet Niddah)
II:3-4 324-325
Al-Fayyûmi
Arabic translation of the Torah
Gn I:2 241
Ibn Ezra
Commentary on the Torah
Ex XII:22 and Lv XIV:4 13
Josephus
War
V:227 326

Antiquities
III:261-264 326
Mishnah
Niddah IV:1 13, 204, 205, 255, 257, 293, 317
Niddah VII:4 7, 202, 274, 297, 326
Mishneh Torah
Issurei Bi'ah
V:6 213, 254
VIII:5 219
VIII-IX 264
XI 254, 255, 287, 317
XI:15 318
XIV:11 228
XVIII:1 248
Meḥusserei Kapparah
I:1 259
II 217
II:2 215
II:6 222
Mishkav Umoshav
I:8 236
II:1 223
III-IV 264
VI:2 252
VI:3 318
Miḳva'ot
I:2 334
I:10 219
She'ar Avot Ṭum'ah
V:1 334
Ṭum'at Met
I:12-14 224
V:1-10 236
Rashi
Commentary on the Torah
on Gn I:2 241
on Ex XII:22 13
on Lv XV:8 223
Siftei Ḥachamim
on Rashi's commentary to
Lv XV:8 223
Talmud Bavli
Berachot 22ab 317
Nidda 33a (in a baraita) 204-205, 255, 257, 293, 317
Tosefta
Pesaḥim I:15 310
Niddah V:1 13, 205, 255, 293, 317
Niddah VI:15 7, 274, 297

IV. Moslem Sources

Al-Bîrûni
Description of Egypt 228

Koran
XX:85-97 228

Al-Makrîzi
Unidentified work, quoted by Al-Biruni in his Description of Egypt 228

Aṭ-Ṭabari
Commentary on the Koran
XX:85-97 228
Ath-Thaʿlabi
Commentary on the Koran
XX:85-97 228
Az-Zamakhshari
Commentary on the Koran
XX:85-97 228

V. Christian Sources

Anonymous pilgrim
ed. Wilkinson p. 81 228

Eusebius
Onomastikon
article *Gerizim* 339

Epiphanius
Panarion
13 229
Origen
Principles
IV:17 14

VI. Samaritan Authors And Scribes

Aba ʿIwaḍ 156, 248
ʿAbdullâh bin Marjân 27
Ăbīsha bin Fīnās 42
Åbrå̊m bin Yē'ūsha 32
Abu 'l-Faraj ibn al-Kaththâr (see also Kitâb al-Farâ'iḍ) 23
Abu ʿl-Ḥasan aṣ-Ṣûri (see also Kitâb aṭ-Ṭubâkh) 23, 182, 196
Abu 'l-Ḥasan bin Yaʿqûb 28, 29, 33, 34, 35, 36, 40, 43
Abu 's-Surûr bin Yûsuf 33
Barhûm bin Yûsuf 35
Fīnās bin Yūsəf 23
Ghazâl bin Abi-'s-Surûr 23
Ibrâhîm bin Ismâʿīl 27
Ḥilmi bin Yaʿqûb 28
Ibrâhîm bin Marjân 27
Ibrâhîm bin Yaʿqûb (see also Kâshif al-Ghayâhib) 23
ʿImrân bin Isḥâq 43
ʿImrân bin Salâmah 27, 38, 195, 280
Ibrâhim bin Yûsuf 28
ʿIzzat bin Ismâʿīl 29
Jamīl bin Marjân 39
Khiḍr bin Isḥâq (see also Kitâb al-Iʿtiqâdât, Sharḥ Sûrat al-Irbot, and Catechism) 24, 25, 44, 197, 225, 281 (twice)
Marjân bin Ibrâhīm 27
Mufarrij bin Yaʿqûb 26, 38
Munajja bin Ṣadaqah (see also Kitâb al-Khilâf) 22, 194
Munīr bin ʿAbd Allâh 40
Marjân bin Asʿad 27
Musallam bin Marjân 23, 27, 194, 195, 279, 291, 312, 343
Nâji bin Khiḍr 22-25, 32, 35, 39 (twice), 44, 45 (twice), 195, 279, 281 (twice), 301
Nimr bin Salâmah 34
Nuʿmân bin Yûsuf 39
Salâmah bin ʿImrân 29, 35
Shafīq bin Yaʿqûb 44
Yaʿqûb bin Hârûn (see also Kitâb al-Iʿtiqâdât and Fatâwa) 22-25, 27, 28, 35, 39, 40, 44 (twice), 45, 46, 196, 224, 280
Yaʿqûb bin Shafīq 44
Yûsuf bin Abi'l-Ḥasan 30, 35, 36 (twice)
Yûsuf bin Salâmah bin Surûr 34
Yûsuf bin Salâmah bin Yûsuf (see also Kitâb al-Kâfī) 22

VII. Technical Terms

Arabic

ʿadad 196, 279
ajra 50, 233-234, 259
ʿaql 240
ʿaraḍi 237, 306
aṣl 255, 259, 263
aẓhar 255
balâ' 271
dâs 271
dhawb 51
farâ'iḍ 51
ḥayḍ 51
ḥaṣṣal 209-210, 235-236
ḥukm 198
iḥtiyâṭ 259
Imâm 51
ishtibâh 198, 211-213, 254, 299
jawhari 220, 236, 306
Al-Maqdis 51
mask 196, 279, 291
mabda' 200-201
maʿlûlah 50, 261
muḥtamal 253, 255
musammad 51, 243
mutaʿaddil, muʿtadil 200-201
mutajannib, janâbah 51, 152, 304
najâsah 51
naqâ' 261, 297
naql 240
nâṭir (nâẓir) 51, 153, 242, 243, 307
nifâs 261, 297
qarînah 252
sharʿ 240
sharîʿah 51
sharîʿah thâniyah 255
shubhah 211-213, 254, 299
takalluf 252
ṭama, ṭamâwah 10, 50, 51
taʿkîs, taʿakkus 232, 235
ṭubâkh, ṭabâkh 22
ṭuhûr 261, 297
ʿulamâ' 51
ʿuqlah 208
wilâdah 261
ziyâdah 252

Hebrew and Aramaic

nå'ēda 160, 250, 286
nâṭər 51, 153, 242, 243, 307
niddot 164, 165, 249, 255, 286
ūtar 154, 189, 244, 245, 258, 276, 297, 298
zåbot, zībot 161, 164, 166, 249, 251, 255, 256, 292

Greek

diēgēsis 14

VIII. Subjects

Arabic translation of the Torah 22, 25, 27
asmachta 250, 253, 255, 261
Adderet Eliyahu 19, 312
ahilah 3
Amdina Yåyå (A Beautiful city) 156, 248
Anan 161, 166, 232, 249, 251, 256, 309
Baraita Denniddah 7
binyan av 267, 279
Catechism 22, 25, 47
Christians 228, 273, 274
Chronicle Adler XIII
cleansing of ground 7, 155-156, 246-247, 289, 299, 303, 305, 314
Damascus Genizah 26
Dositheans (see also Sakta) 12-14, 22, 46-47, 202, 204, 226, 229, 233, 243, 260, 274, 287, 288, 289, 293-294, 296-297, 300, 305, 313, 315, 316, 321, 322, 323, 324, 327, 332, 343-344
Ad-Dustân 343-344
Eshkol Hakkofer 19
experts (ʿulamâ') 51, 172, 344-345
fatâwa 22, 46, 56-57, 245
Al-Fayyûmi 47, 161-163, 165, 174, 175, 204, 241, 249, 251, 255
Frere collection 28, 29
Gan ʿEden 19, 312
Gaster's questionnaires 22, 25, 47
Gorothenians 229
hekkesh 259, 279
History of Abu 'l-Fatḥ XIII, 12-14, 25, 42, 46-47
houses of uncleanness 297, 313
inheritance 12, 15
Al-Jawharah al-Muḍī'ah 180
Jewish sources 19
Jews
  general 7, 13-14, 18-19, 143-328 *passim*, 200, 211, 214, 254, 287, 292, 294, 303, 304, 309-310, 311, 317, 347
  Boethusians 332
  Falashas 18, 205, 258, 297, 309, 311, 313, 317, 318, 319, 320, 321-322, 325, 326, 327, 328, 332, 335, 336
  Karaites 7, 14, 17, 18-19, 143-328 *passim*, 142, 165, 199, 203, 204, 205, 207, 208, 209, 210, 211, 212, 213, 215, 216, 228-229, 289, 298, 299, 304, 307, 309-310, 311, 312-313, 314, 317-338, 329-336
  Rabbanites (see also Al-Fayyûmi) 7, 13-14, 17, 18-19, 143-328 *passim*, 159, 163-164, 166-167, 168, 169-170, 170-171, 190-191, 192, 201, 203, 204, 205, 207, 208, 209, 211, 212, 213, 215, 216, 287, 290-291, 298, 309-310, 311, 313, 314, 317-328, 329-336, 345
  Qumran sect 18, 309, 319, 321-322, 324-325, 326, 328, 330, 333
  Pharisees 309, 326, 327, 331
  Sadducees 18, 309, 320, 326, 328, 331
  Jubilees 333
Kâshif al-Ghayâhib 5, 8, 21, 23, 43-44, 48-50, 342-347
Keter Torah 19
Kitâb al-Anwâr wa-'l-Marâqib 14, 19, 229
Kitâb Awla 'l-Albâb 180
Kitâb al-Farâ'iḍ 21, 23, 31, 42-43, 48, 49, 342-347
Kitâb al-Kâfi 6, 8-12, 16, 21-22, 27, 30, 32-37, 48, 50, 51, 82, 342-347
Kitâb al-Kâfi (Hebrew translation) 210, 246-247
Kitâb al-Iʿtiqâdât 16, 21, 23-25, 39, 44-45, 48, 51, 342-347
Kitâb al-Khilâf 6-8, 21-23, 27, 37-42, 48, 50, 51, 194, 342-347
Kitâb al-Mîrâth 12
Kitâb aṭ-Ṭubâkh 8-11, 16, 21-22, 26-31, 48, 196, 342-347
lost mss. 30, 26-37, 40-41, 251-252
marginal notes 21, 30, 48, 250
majoram 13-14
Massechet Kutim 5
midras 271
Al-Minhâj 180
minor uncleanness 228-229
Mishneh Torah XIII, 19, 311
Moslems 201-202, 208, 213, 222, 228, 272, 273, 274
Mt. Gerizim 338-340

Al-Murshid 19
non-Israelites 224-230, 238, 247, 248-249, 303-305, 343, 345
Origen 14
Pentateuch 328-341
Pentateuch recensions 336-341
Pentecost 332-333
Sabbath 14, 343
Sakta XIII, 200-202, 227-230, 233, 243, 253, 258, 274, 288, 296, 306, 313, 314, 315, 316, 322, 323, 324, 327
ṣårrēt 3, 5, 8, 15, 218, 334, 269, 271, 325-326
Sebuaeans 229, 343
Sharḥ Am Baqqūti 23, 347
Sharḫ Sūrat al-Irbot 21, 25, 45, 347
shåtnəz 156
shemuʿah 345
Targum 22, 27
Tenth Commandment 338-339
ṭevul yom 307, 320
Torah Shelemah 19, 318
uncleanness from corpses 3, 153, 155-156, 227-230, 242, 243, 245, 246-247, 248, 261, 269, 285, 305, 314, 316, 326, 334-335
Uppsala collection 43
wuḍû 182, 272

IX. Secondary References

ʿAbd al-ʿĀl, D. M. 8-11
Aešcoly, A. Z. 313, 317, 335
Adler, E. N. 29
Alon, G. 311
Ben-Ḥayyim, Z. XIII, 198, 343
Bloch, Y. 311
Bóid, I. R. M. 338
Bowman, J. 8, 9, 200, 227, 338, 339
Büchler, A. 7
Cohn, N. 3, 8, 241
Cowley, A. E. 248, 343
Crown, A. D. 25, 26, 32, 33, 38, 42
Derenbourg, J. 241
Dozy, R. 50, 235, 252
Drabkin, A. 6, 41
Fagnan, E. 252
Flad, J. M. 326
Fraser, J. G. 26, 27, 44
Gaster, M. 22, 23, 24, 25, 47, 246
Geiger, A. 5-6, 228
Ginzberg, L. 325
Goldziher, I. 228
Halkin, A. S. 23, 30, 40-41, 251-252
Hanover, S. 8
Harkavy, A. 256
Hava, J. G. 200
Heller, B. 228
Hirsch, S. R. XIII, 13
Hoffman, D. 318
Holl, K. 229
Huntington, R. 26
Isser, S. J. 12-14, 200, 229
Juynboll, T. G. J. 228
Kahle, P. 29
Kirchheim, R. 5, 317
Klumel, M. 8
Le Moyne, J. 320, 333
Lehmann, 325
Leslau, W. 311, 313, 318, 320, 322, 326, 335
Linder, S. 43
Loewe, H.
Lowy, S. 9, 14-15
Macdonald, J. 241
Migne, J. P. 229
Montgomery, J. A. 26, 228
Noja, S. 12, 209, 225, 227, 243
Petermann, H. 275, 277
Pohl, H. 12, 22, 31, 43
Rabin, C. 338
Revel, B. 332
Robertson, E. 23, 25
Roth, C. 325
Scanlon, L. 13, 200, 227
Shehadeh, H. 25, 47
Shunnar, Z. 28, 31, 37, 41
Talmon, S. 338, 339
Vilmar, E. XIII, 12, 42, 46, 200
Vilsker, L. H. 37
Wehr, H. 33
Weiss, P. R. 3, 8, 22, 34
Wilkinson, J. 228
Wreschner, L. 6-8, 23, 50, 240, 246, 306, 309
Yadin, Y. 319, 322, 324, 326